The Economic Problem

The Economic Problem

ROBERT L.
HEILBRONER

LESTER C.
THUROW

Sixth
Edition

PRENTICE-HALL, INC., Englewood Cliffs, NJ 07632

Library of Congress Cataloging in Publication Data
Heilbroner, Robert L.
The economic problem.

1. Economics. I. Thurow, Lester C., joint author. II. Title.
HB171.5.H39 1981 330 80-16631
ISBN 0-13-233304-X

THE ECONOMIC PROBLEM, 6th edition
Robert L. Heilbroner and Lester C. Thurow

Printed in the United States of America.

10 9 8 7 6 5 4 3 2 1

This is a Special Projects book.
Maurine Lewis, *director*
Susan Adkins, *editor*
Ray Keating, *manufacturing buyer*

Cover design by Olympia Shahbaz.
Cover drawings by Bernarda Bryson.
Front cover drawing from "Economic Psychology" by George Katona,

Illustrations by Don Martinetti.

Prentice-Hall International, Inc., *London*
Prentice-Hall of Australia Pty. Limited, *Sydney*
Prentice-Hall of Canada, Ltd., *Toronto*
Prentice-Hall of India Private Limited, *New Delhi*
Prentice-Hall of Japan, Inc., *Tokyo*
Prentice-Hall of Southeast Asia Pte. Ltd., *Singapore*
Whitehall Books Limited, *Wellington, New Zealand*

TO THE INSTRUCTOR

Here is a considerably rethought and restructured *Economic Problem*—one that we think will prove interesting and useful for students, challenging and practical for instructors. Let us begin by pointing out some of its new features.

PART 1: INTRODUCING THE SUBJECT

The great problem for all instructors is *time,* and the great sacrifice that time exacts is that important problems get crowded out by the need to use class time for exposition of analytic material.

We have tried to help with this problem by presenting a background to economic analysis in Part 1, designed either to be taught in class or to be assigned as supplementary reading. Part 1 has four chapters with clearcut objectives: (1) to give an overview of economic history; (2) to give a brief introduction to three of the worldly philosophers, Smith, Marx, and Keynes; (3) to fly the student over the economy and point out what is there; and (4) to convey a first sense of the economy in motion, in growth. We think that every student ought to read these new chapters, whether or not they are formally taught.

PART 2: BASIC TOOLS

Part 2 will, we think, be used by all instructors. It is an essential introduction to economic reasoning itself and to the tools of the trade. Its three chapters present the ideas of maximizing and constraining; supply and demand; and elementary techniques, such as graphs and equations. The central chapter on supply and demand will certainly be used by everyone. The preceding chapter on maximizing and constraining can be assigned as reading, or taught together with supply and demand. And the third chapter, on the kit of tools, will need more or less attention, depending on the level of preparation of the class.

PART 3: ON TO MACRO

We have put macro before micro largely because a majority of our readers prefer it this way. But we wrote micro before macro to make it possible to go directly to micro first, if so desired.

Macro is organized in three sections. First we examine growth, which takes us in four easy chapter-stages into saving and investment. In the next section we trace the determination of income, sector by sector—a familiar route. And in the third section, we examine money: how it is created and how it "works."

All through the macro section three themes are sounded again and again. One is the inflationary propensity of the system. A second is the problem of unemployment. A third is the trajectory of growth. However, we do not bring these themes to a climax until Part 5, where we have special chapters devoted to each one. But we have made our macro section (and micro too) a self-contained "text within a text," devoted to giving the student what is needed to come to grips with the great issues that we address in later chapters.

PART 4: MICRO NEXT

The great difficulty with micro, it seems to us, is that it tends to go on and on, losing the students' interest. We have tried to cope with this by grouping micro into three separate sections. The first, and to our minds by far the most important section, consists of four chapters devoted to markets with their successes and failures. The second section is about the economics of business—the standard analysis of the firm. We have tried to take the curse off the tedious computations of the conventional approach to the firm by taking the student through the plant twice—the first time on an informative sightseeing tour, the second time with clipboard and pencil. We think this will make for good teaching and easier learning. Thereafter comes a trip through a big business, and we conclude with a chapter on the social problems of large-scale enterprise.

The last of the three micro sections is concerned with income distribution. Important though it is, if time is short, it is probably the section that can most readily be passed over.

PART 5: BIG ISSUES

Part 5 is the reward for hard work. It is a group of five chapters, each devoted to a major problem, and each using the knowledge the student will have gained after going through macro or micro.

Our five major issues are inflation, unemployment, taxing and spending, defending the dollar, and energy. Inflation and unemployment form chapters that are, of course, natural sequels to macro. Taxing and spending and energy follow naturally upon micro—the first of them a microeconomic analysis of government operations, the second, a special study in allocation. But defending the dollar? Doesn't that require previous knowledge of international economics? We think not. It can be tackled right after the macro sequence—and in light of today's concern with the dollar, we hope it will be tackled.

PART 6: THE REST OF THE WORLD

That leaves Part 6, where we take up the gains from trade, the mechanisms of international exchange, the problem of underdevelopment, and a speculative chapter on the drift of market systems. Much of this, too, can be assigned as outside reading if classroom time is too tight to enable it to be taught.

SPECIAL FEATURES

Pedagogy is enormously important in textbooks and we have given a lot of thought to helping the instructor in his task. All chapters in our book are prefaced by "A Look Ahead" which lists for the student the main topics to be covered. The postface, "Looking Back," is designed to help with the review of main points; in its margin are key concepts, a condensed review of the review. A section on vocabulary and a series of questions conclude the lesson.

No less useful, we think, are the captions that now accompany every graph and nearly every table, summing up the points of the graphical or numerical illustration. The student can review a lot of the material by running back over these expository sections which have been planned to make the figures come alive.

You'll also note that the chapters are not long. There is a kind of "chapter illusion" that, like the money illusion, ensnares us all: Two short chapters seem less formidable than one long one. Perhaps they *are* less formidable because there is a sense of completion as each chapter is mastered. At any rate, that is the direction in which we have aimed in this new edition—short, tight chapters.

TEACHING AND PREACHING

Textbooks exist to stimulate students, not just to fill them with knowledge—especially where knowledge is itself in the process of change and development. We have tried to make the text stimulating, which has meant orienting it to the "real world" whereever possible.

This opens the danger, of course, that we will become preachers instead of teachers—worse, that we will preach pretending to teach. We have sought to avoid the pitfall in two ways. First, policy-oriented materials are often presented in "An Extra Word," separate sections where they are identified as being policy ideas, not "facts." Second, like all reputable texts, we try valiantly to make our value judgments explicit and open, not to smuggle them in as something else.

CHAPTER BY CHAPTER ANALYSIS

In the "Guide to Chapters and Extra Words," we have established three categories: Basic, Institutional and Historical, and More Advanced. We hope that this will help organize your own teaching program. But in the end we can only put this book at your disposal to use as you see fit. The crucial ingredient is the instructor's skill and enthusiasm, for which any text can provide only the first underpinnings. We hope these are useful ones.

FINALLY, THE WORKBOOK AND READER

We recognize that not all users of the text will want to use the companion volume, the combined student workbook and guide, but we should like to point out that the second book offers a reexposition of certain points that often present difficulties, a detailed set of "do-it-yourself" exercises, and a battery of true-false and multiple choice questions (and answers), as well as a number of readings. In addition there are major tests for each section of the text, answers for which will be found in the *Instructor's Manual* along with additional test material.

A GUIDE TO CHAPTERS

BASIC

AND EXTRA WORDS

*Extra Word

CONTENTS

Part 1 The Economic Background

Part 2 A Kit of Economic Tools

Part 3 Macroeconomics: The Analysis of Prosperity and Recession

Part 4 Microeconomics: The Anatomy of a Market System

Part 5 The Major Economic Challenges

Part 6 The Rest of the World

Robert L. Heilbroner and Lester C. Thurow are among the most widely known economists in the nation. Robert Heilbroner rose to attention in 1953 with the publication of *The Worldly Philosophers* when he was still a graduate student. Over 25 years later it continues to be a campus favorite. Among his many books since then, an *Inquiry into the Human Prospect* has probably drawn the greatest comment. Lester Thurow early gained national prominence as an expert on income distribution. His most recent book, *The Zero Sum Society,* has received widespread praise. Professor Heilbroner teaches on the graduate faculty of the New School for Social Research in New York; Professor Thurow at the Massachusetts Institute of Technology in Cambridge. Both authors lecture to many university and other groups, appear frequently on television, and write extensively for the general public.

Part 1 The Economic Background

Chapter 1 WHAT THIS BOOK IS ALL ABOUT

A LOOK AHEAD

This is the chapter in which to get your bearings. As you read, keep in mind these objectives:

(1) to get a feel for what is to come;

(2) to learn how the book is organized; and

(3) most important of all, to pick up a few study hints—you really want to pay attention to these.

THE ECONOMIC MYSTIQUE

Most students begin a first course in economics with mixed feelings. On the one hand, everyone knows that economics is terribly important. On the other hand, everyone has the uneasy feeling that it is terribly difficult. It may reassure you to learn that you are not alone in this frame of mind. Every year, national pollsters report that economic problems, such as inflation or unemployment or taxes, rank high on the public's agenda of worries. But every year the pollsters also discover that the economics and business pages of newspapers and magazines are those that are *least* read. It seems that we all worry about economic matters, but we all throw up our hands at the idea of trying to understand what worries us.

Why does economics have this curious mystique? Three reasons suggest themselves. The first is that economics is inextricably involved with money, and money is certainly perplexing.

1. MYSTERY OF MONEY

Why is a piece of paper worth anything at all? What do banks do with the money we put into them? Why isn't there enough money to go around at some times, "too much" money at others—to repeat the baffling opinions we hear?

Money is surely one reason for the economic mystique. But the problem with money is not just its inherent complexity. It is that we all use money, talk about money, worry about money, without ever having been educated about it. One purpose of learning economics is to repair that serious omission in our knowledge.

2. LANGUAGE OF ECONOMICS

A second reason why economics is generally regarded with unease is that it speaks in a tongue we don't quite understand. "Prices are up because of rising demand," says the TV commentator, and we nod our heads. But exactly what is "demand"? What makes it "rise"? What are those other words that the news commentators use with such assurance—gross national product, consumption, investment? What do they really mean? Because we do not "speak" economics, we wonder whether or not we are being bamboozled; and when we ourselves use the words of economics, we often know that we are partly bluffing.

Therefore another purpose of this book is to introduce you to the language of economics. Like all disciplines, it has a fair number of specialized terms, but it is certainly no more difficult to speak or to understand than any of a dozen familiar subjects. By the end of the course you should speak it pretty fluently.

3. THE "DIFFICULTY" OF ECONOMICS

Last, there is the matter of the mystique itself, the reputation for difficulty that economics has acquired. It may come as a surprise to learn that there was a time when economics was reputed to be a rather easy subject, especially suited to the education of proper young ladies (this was in the 1830s). Later—indeed, up to the Great Crash of 1929—economics was still widely regarded as little more than common sense, instantly comprehensible by all right-thinking persons, especially if they thought along Solid Business Principles.

The aura of mystery that clings to economics today is mainly a product of the past generation or so, when economics itself came into national prominence. The aura is undoubtedly mixed up with the increased use of government powers in the economy, especially the use of spending and taxing to affect the level of national well-being. Here *is* something to be learned that is different from Solid Business Principles. But as you will discover, it is still nothing but logical thought, although applied from a national perspective, rather than from that of an individual enterprise.

Thus if there is one overriding aim of our book it is to demystify economics. Of course this does not mean that we can give you answers to all the problems of the economy. We don't know them. But we hope that when you finish the book, you will never again throw up your hands at the idea of thinking about economic problems. Once and for all, that should have lost its terror.

ORGANIZING THE SUBJECT

How are we going to study economics? We have planned this book to be as flexible as possible because the length of courses and the interests of instructors differ. It may help orient you if we explain the basic layout.

Our book is organized into six parts on the economic background, economic reasoning, macro- and microeconomics, major issues, and international problems.

PART 1. ECONOMIC BACKGROUND

Most students would like to jump right into the midst of our current economic problems, and some instructors like to teach their courses that way. In fact, our book is organized so that a direct approach to major issues is possible by starting in "Macroeconomics," Part 3, or "Microeconomics," Part 4.

But ideally we ought to acquire some perspective on our subject before getting embroiled in how things work. We ought, for example, to have a good working idea of economic history—of how our economy got where it is. We should know at least the rudiments of what some great economists of the past have said about how the economic system works. And we should be familiar with the economy in the same sense that we are familiar with the size and shape of the United States and where its great rivers and mountain ranges are.

That is what Part I is about. Its initial chapter will give you a jet-speed voyage through economic history. The next chapter takes you rapidly down the gallery of the world's great economists—the "worldly philosophers." Then, in two successive chapters we fly you over the economic continent. *Try to read these chapters as background, even if your instructor doesn't have time to assign them as classwork.*

PART 2. FROM FACT TO THEORY

In Part 2 we turn to a very different subject—the "kit of tools" that economists use. There is as you will quickly see, a special, *theoretical,* way of considering economic problems. By this, we mean that economists do not examine each problem by itself, contenting themselves with a careful description of what they see. Rather, economists try to examine problems to discover their underlying characteristics, much as a doctor examines a patient to discover "disease."

In Chapter 6 we tell you something about the basis on which economic theory rests. Then we go on to equip you with a good working understanding of the most important single application of economic theory—supply and demand. Thereafter, to complete your kit of tools, we offer a quick run through the main "technical" things you ought to know, such as how to read graphs or how to say some useful mathematical sentences.

PARTS 3 AND 4. FROM THEORY TO PRACTICE: MACRO AND MICRO

Part 2 is a first guide to economic theorizing. But the main purpose of our study lies ahead in Parts 3 and 4, "Macroeconomics" and "Microeconomics." It doesn't matter which part you study first; they are equally important. The purpose of each is to extend your vocabulary and the application of economic reasoning to problems that have been allocated to that particular branch.

What are the two branches? **In Macroeconomics the focus will be mainly on inflation, unemployment, and economic growth.** These are problems that we study from the *"macro" perspective* of the economy as a whole. **In microeconomics we will investigate a set of problems ranging from farm prices to monopolies, and from urban decay to industrial pollution**—problems whose common denominator is that we approach them from the *"micro" perspective* of the decision makers of the economy, mainly households, business enterprises, and individual government agencies.

PART 5. THE BIG ISSUES

Most people want to study economics to learn about the major issues of our time. So Part 5, which deals with these issues, should be the "best" part of the book. In this part you will find chapters that highlight five economic problems you have certainly heard about, and have perhaps already thought hard about: inflation, unemployment, government taxing and spending, defending the dollar, and energy.

In many of these chapters you will learn what economists do *not* know, as well as what they do know. And in all of them, you will find that your macro and micro training stands you in good stead in making sense out of difficult problems. We hope that you enjoy these chapters.

PART 6. THE REST OF THE WORLD

There is a terrible parochialism, or narrowness, that affects most of us in studying an economy as vast and powerful as our own. We think that it stops short at our national borders. It does not. The American economy is closely tied into the world economy, as we discovered with a shock when the Arab oil embargo created long lines at the gas pumps in the fall of 1973 and again in the summer of 1979. In addition, theories and prescriptions of economics apply just as much to international economic dealings as they do to intranational (or internal) relationships.

Therefore in Part 6 we explore the world of international trade, international finance, and international economic trends. Some of these matters you will already have encountered in Part 5. Here we go into them much more systematically. Possibly you may not have time for this section in your course. We hope that you will skim over the chapters when you have time to do so.

HOW SHOULD YOU STUDY ECONOMICS?

VOCABULARY

We have already stressed the importance of acquiring a new economic vocabulary. **To become economists, you will have to learn at least a dozen words and phrases that have meanings somewhat different from those of everyday usage: *capital, investment, demand,* for example.** You will have to master another dozen phrases that come awkwardly to the tongue (and sometimes not at all to the mind): *marginal propensity to consume* is a good example.

In economics, as in French, some people acquire new words and phrases easily, some do not; and in economics, as in French, until you can say things correctly, you are apt to say them very wrongly. So when the text says *gross private domestic investment* those are the words to be learned, not just any combination of three of them because they seem to mean the same thing. Fortunately, the necessary economic vocabulary has far fewer words than French has, and the long and awkward phrases seem shorter and easier after you've said them a few times.

DIAGRAMS

Associated with learning the vocabulary of economics is learning how to draw a few diagrams. **Diagrams are an immensely powerful way of presenting many economic ideas.** Far from complicating things, they simplify them enormously. A supply and demand diagram makes things immediately clear in a way that a dozen pages could not.

So you must learn to draw a few diagrams. There is a great temptation to do so hastily, without thinking about the problem that the diagram is trying to make clear. A little care in labeling your axes (how else can anyone know what the diagram is about?) or in making lines tangent where they are supposed to touch, or cross where they are supposed to intersect, will not only make the difference between a poor grade and a better one, but will demonstrate that you truly understand the matter being illustrated.

You will also note that throughout the book, under each figure and most tables, there is a sentence or a paragraph which highlights the point being made. This should help you in reviewing the material.

KEY IDEAS

Studying a vast subject requires organization. This means putting first things first and keeping details and secondary material in the background.

We've tried to simplify the task of learning by putting a highly abbreviated and goal-oriented "A Look Ahead" and "Looking Back" at the beginning and at the end of each chapter. These sections do not necessarily embrace all the vocabulary or ideas in each chapter; instead they try to give you objectives to bear in mind before starting, and summaries to collect your thoughts when you're done.

At the end of each chapter, first read over the general review. Then look only at "Key Concepts" to see if you can yourself reproduce that review. Lastly, a glance at "Economic Vocabulary" will serve as a final vocabulary test. Page numbers follow each word for easy reference.

QUESTIONS AND EXTRA WORDS

Next, take time to answer all the questions at the ends of chapters. We have tried to make them few and central. If your instructor assigns the Student Guide that accompanies this text, do those problems too. There is no substitute for working out an example or for jotting down three reasons for this, four reasons for that. Learning is a process about which we know very little, but we do know that the physical and intellectual act of writing (or mumbling to yourself) is much more effective than merely thinking. Practice, as they say, makes perfect. You might reflect on the story of the sailor on a sinking ship. When asked if he knew how to swim, he answered, "Well, I understand the theory of it. . . ."

Economics has to be learned by arguing about it. Therefore after many chapters you will find a few additional pages—sometimes to add to your historical, statistical, or analytic knowledge, more often to open for your consideration problems of public policy that are related to the issues we have studied. The policy issues are often controversial. We hope you will worry about them—not just read them. They are there to open debate, not close it.

ANALYSIS AND ABSTRACTION

The idea of arguing brings us to our last word of counsel. Economics, as we have been at pains to say, is really not a hard language to learn. The key words and concepts are not too many or too demanding; the diagrams are no more difficult than those of elementary geometry. It is economic *thinking* that is hard, in a way that may have something to do with the aura of mystery we are out to dispel.

The hardness is not the sheer mental ability that is required. The reason lies, rather, in a **special attribute of economic thought: *its abstract, analytic character.*** Abstractness does not mean an indifference to the problems of the real world. Economics is about things as real as being without work. Nevertheless, as economists we do not study unemployment to learn firsthand about the miseries and sufferings that joblessness inflicts. We study unemployment to understand and analyze the causes of this malfunction of the economic system. Similarly, we do not study monopoly to fulminate against the profiteering of greedy capitalists, or labor unions to deplore the abuse of power by labor leaders, or government spending to declaim against politicians. We study these matters to shed light on their mechanisms, their reasons for being, their consequences.

There is nothing unusual in this abstract, analytic approach. All disciplines necessarily abstract from the immediate realities of their subject matters so that they may make broader generalizations or develop theories. What makes abstraction so difficult in economics is that the problems of the discipline are things that bother and affect us deeply in our lives. It is difficult, even unnatural, to suppress our feelings of approval or anger when we study the operations of the economic system and the main actors in it. The necessary act of analysis thus becomes mixed up with feelings of economic concern or even partisanship. **Yet, unless we make an effort to think analytically and abstractly in a detached way, we can be no more than slaves to our unexamined emotions.** Someone who *knows* that corporations or labor unions or governments are "good" or "bad" does not have to study economics, for the subject has nothing to teach such a person.

You must, therefore, make an effort to put aside your natural partisanship and prejudice while you study the problems of economics from its abstract, analytic, detached perspective. After you are done, your feelings will assuredly come back to you. No one has ever lost a sense of social outrage or social justice by taking a course in economics. But many students have changed or modified their preconceived judgments in one way or another. There is no escape, after all, from living in the world as economic citizens. But there is the option of living in it as intelligent and effective economic citizens. That is the prize we hope you carry away from this course.

Chapter 2 THE EVOLUTION OF THE MARKET SYSTEM

A LOOK AHEAD

There is one central idea that this chapter will present—a very simple but exceedingly important idea. It is that capitalism—our Western economic society—represents a dramatic change in the way that mankind has grappled with its economic problems. In this chapter we will trace three main aspects of this change:

(1) the emergence of a market society;
(2) the development of a powerful industrial technology; and
(3) the assertion of political limits on the economic machinery.

The purpose of this chapter is not only to review these critical elements of economic history, but to make you think about the subject of economics itself in a historical, evolutionary way.

WHERE DID CAPITALISM COME FROM?

The economic system that we are going to study in this book is called **capitalism,** or sometimes the *free enterprise system.* In a way, we all know what capitalism is, because it surrounds us. It is the world we live in. But the question we are going to start with is far removed from our daily experience: Where did capitalism come from? How did the free enterprise system come to be?

People sometimes talk about capitalism as if it were as old as the hills, as ancient as the Bible. Yet, on reflection, this is clearly not the case. Nobody ever called the Egyptian pharaohs "capitalists." The Greeks about whom Homer wrote were not a business society, even though there were merchants and traders in Greece; neither was imperial Rome a capitalist system. Medieval Europe was certainly not capitalist. Nor would anyone use the word *capitalist* to describe the brilliant civilizations of India or China, about which Marco Polo wrote, or the great empires of ancient Africa or the Islamic economies of which we catch glimpses in *The Arabian Nights.*

We will make explicit *why* these were not capitalist economies in a moment. But we must begin by realizing that capitalism is a modern economic system—and furthermore, a geographically limited one. **Most of the people in the world's history have never had any contact with it whatsoever; even today, only a quarter or so of the world's population lives in a system that we would call capitalist.**

STEREOTYPES OF CAPITALISM

Why is capitalism so exceptional? Let us answer the question in a curious way, by first asking people what they think capitalism is. If you asked a random sampling of Americans why they call our economy capitalist, you would be likely to hear answers such as these:

"It recognizes the right of private property."
"It's run by a market system, not by the government."
"It believes in economic freedom."

You might also hear some less flattering characterizations:

"It puts moneymaking over everything else."
"It's capitalist because the rich own most of the wealth."
"It's unstable, constantly producing problems."

There is some truth in all these stereotypes, flattering or otherwise. But we are not yet going to talk about capitalism as such. Instead, let us use these characterizations, which we have all heard many times, to reconstruct what must have come *before* capitalism. That may clear up the mystery of why capitalism is the exception in the world's economic history, not the rule.

BEFORE CAPITALISM

If society before capitalism was very different from society today, it follows that it must have looked something like this:

1. **No general recognition of private property rights.**
2. **No market network.**

3. No importance given to the idea of economic freedom.
4. Moneymaking generally held in low esteem.
5. Most wealth not owned by "the rich."
6. Economic life generally stable, not beset by problems.

Was there ever such a society? There were, indeed many such societies: Egyptian, Greek, Roman, African, and feudal societies throughout Europe.

1. Private property. All of these societies recognized the right of some individuals to own wealth, often vast wealth. **But none of them legally accorded the right of ownership to all persons.** Great lords, priestly orders, patricians, or kings owned the fields; land was not owned by the peasants who worked it. Slavery was common, and slaves *were* property; they themselves did not own property (with a very few exceptions). The idea that a person's property was inviolate—protected by law—was far from generally recognized: Recall how the Tudor monarchs, relatively enlightened as monarchies went, could strip a man or a religious order of possessions as easily as they could award a fortune.

2. Markets. Certainly there were markets in all these societies, often colorful and important, where spices, gold, slaves, cloth, pottery, and foodstuffs were offered for sale. But when we look over the vast expanses of ancient Asia, Africa, or the Egyptian or Roman empires, we can see nothing like a great web of transactions, guiding the efforts of the country as a whole. Most production, and most distribution, took place by following the dictates of tradition or under the orders of a local lord. Only the small leftovers found their way to the market stalls. Even more important, **there was no market at all to buy and sell land or to hire labor or to borrow or lend capital.** Markets were the ornaments of the economy; tradition or command was its iron structure.

3. Economic freedom. Under such conditions, of course, the idea of economic freedom was held in little regard. Why worry about the *idea* of economic freedom when the *fact* did not exist—when peasants were not free to move as they wished, when artisans were bound to trades, when the relation of field workers to their masters was that of serf to lord, not employee to employer? The difference is that **an employee has the legal right to quit a job, to work or not to work, as he or she chooses, whereas a serf is legally bound to a lord's land and to the work a lord assigns him.**

4. Wealth and values. In such a setting, moneymaking was not much esteemed. Ambitious persons from the better walks of life sought fame and fortune in military exploits, in government, in the service of the court, or in the hierarchies of religion. Next time you are in a museum, take a look at some medieval art and notice how men of money are almost invariably painted as twisted, mean, and grasping, whereas soldiers and nobles are portrayed as tall, handsome, and grand. Moneymaking was generally considered beneath a person of noble blood; indeed, in Christendom it was a pursuit that was uncomfortably close to sin. In fact, usury—lending at interest—*was* a sin, and a mortal sin, at that.

The Bettmann Archive, Inc.

OFFICE OF A BANKER — Marinus von Romerswayle

***5. The rich and the powerful.* As a consequence, society's wealth was not owned by "the rich." It was owned by the powerful—the winners in the struggle for armies and territory.** Of course, the winners were also rich, sometimes unimaginably rich; but they were rich largely because they had attained power. Julius Caesar, for example, was made rich by being appointed governor of Spain, a position that was supposed to make its holders wealthy, which it unfailingly did.

***6. Stability.* And finally, economic life was stable.** To be sure, it did not seem stable to peasants or merchants whose lives were constantly disrupted by war, famine, merciless taxation, and pervasive insecurity. But it was very stable compared to the factors that constantly alter economic existence in our time. The basic rhythms and techniques of economic life were steady and repetitive. Men

Peter Adelberg, NYC

RIDER **Cathedral of Bamberg, Germany**

and women sowed and reaped, using the same kinds of plows and scythes; potters and metal workers turned and hammered, using the same kinds of tools; weavers spun and wove on much the same looms for decades, generations, and centuries. While you are in the museum looking at pictures of medieval times, notice how the clothes or utensils, the materials of the buildings, the means of conveyance are similar to those of ancient Rome. Of course there was *some* change—but how little, over a thousand years! That gives one a sense of how vast a change was about to take place in the next act of history, when capitalism would burst upon the scene.

MARKET SOCIETY ERUPTS

Thus we begin to see that the emergence of capitalism was a volcanic event in history, upsetting every aspect of daily life. Yet it is surprisingly easy to identify the principal change that the new system entailed. It was the creation of a **market society** as the means of mobilizing and coordinating the activities by which society reproduced itself.

BREVIARIUM GRIMANI

MARKET SOCIETIES

What is a market society? We have already caught its flavor in casting our glance backward at precapitalist economies. **A market society is one where economic activities are left to men and women freely responding to the opportunities or discouragements of the marketplace, not to the established routines of tradition or the dictates of someone's command.**

Specifically this means that in a market society individuals seek work for wages and salaries, not because they are born to a certain station in life. It means that land can be transferred from one person to another and will be offered for use in exchange for rental payments. A good example of what it means to have a market in land is the way real estate developers are able to buy farm land and turn it into shopping centers; by contrast, there is no market in which the governors of Rhode Island or Nevada can purchase a nice taxable county from neighboring Massachusetts or California.

Finally, a market in capital means that there is a regular flow of wealth into production—a flow of savings and a flow of investment—organized through banks and other financial companies, where borrowers pay interest as the reward for having the use of the wealth of lenders. There was nothing like this before capitalism, except in the very small and disreputable capital markets personified in the hated moneylender.

THE FACTORS OF PRODUCTION

We have a name for the services of labor, land, and capital that are hired or fired in a market society. They are called the *factors of production*, and a great deal of economics is about how the market combines their essential contributions to production. But just because they *are* essential, a question must be answered. How were the factors of production put to use prior to the market system? The answer comes as something of a shock, but it tells us a great deal.

There were no factors of production before capitalism. Of course, human labor, nature's gift of land and natural resources, and the artifacts of society have always existed. But labor, land, and capital were not commodities for sale. Labor was performed as part of the social duties of serfs or slaves, who were not paid for doing their work. Indeed, the serf paid fees to his lord for the use of the lord's equipment, and he never expected to be remunerated when he turned over a portion of his crop as the lord's due. So, too, land was regarded as the basis for military power or civil administration, just as a state is regarded today—not as real estate to be bought and sold. And capital was thought of as "treasure" or as the necessary equipment of an artisan, not as an abstract sum of wealth with a market value. The idea of liquid, fluid capital would have been as strange in medieval life as we would find it strange to think of stocks and bonds as heirlooms never to be sold.

THE ECONOMIC REVOLUTION

How did wageless labor, unrentable land, and private treasures become "factors of production"; that is, homogeneous commodities to be bought and sold like so many yards of cloth or bushels of wheat? The answer is that **a vast revolution undermined the world of tradition and command and brought into being**

the market relationships of the modern world. Beginning roughly in the sixteenth century—although with roots that can be traced much further back—a process of change, sometimes gradual, sometimes violent, broke the bonds and customs of the medieval world of Europe and ushered in the market society we know.

We can only touch on that long, tortuous, and sometimes bloody revolution here. In England the process bore with particular severity on the peasants who were expelled from their lands through the "enclosure" of common grazing lands. This enclosure took place to make private pasturage for the lord's sheep, whose wool had become a profitable commodity. As late as 1820, the Duchess of Sutherland evicted 15,000 tenants from 794,000 acres, replacing them with 131,000 sheep. The tenants, deprived of their traditional access to the fields, drifted into the towns, where they were forced to sell their services as a factor of production: *labor.*

In France, the creation of factors of production bore painfully on land. When prices began to rise in sixteenth-century Europe as gold from the New World flowed in, feudal lords found themselves in a terrible squeeze. Like everything in medieval life, the rents and dues they received from their serfs were fixed and unchangeable. But the prices of merchandise were not fixed. Although more and more of the serfs' obligations were changed from "kind" to cash, and from physical duties to money dues, prices kept rising so fast that the feudal lords found it impossible to meet their bills.

Hence we begin to find a new economic individual, the *impoverished aristocrat.* In the year 1530, in the Gévaudan region of France, the richest manorial lord had an income of 5,000 livres; but in towns, some merchants had incomes of 65,000 livres. Thus the balance of power turned against the landed aristocracy, reducing many to shabby gentility. Meanwhile, the upstart merchants lost no time in acquiring lands that they soon came to regard not as ancestral estates but as potential capital.

This brief glance at economic history brings home an important point. **The factors of production, without which a market society could not exist, are not eternal attributes of a natural order. They are the creations of a process of historic change, a change that divorced labor from social life, that created real estate out of ancestral land, and that made treasure into capital.** Capitalism is the outcome of a revolutionary change—a change in laws, attitudes, and social relationships as deep and far-reaching as any in history.*

FREEDOM AND NECESSITY

The revolutionary aspect of capitalism lies in the fact that an older, feudal way of life had to be dismantled before the market system could come into being. This brings us to think again about the element of economic freedom that plays such an important role in our definition of capitalism. For we can see that eco-

*One of the many fascinating questions that surround the origins of capitalism is why it arose only in Europe, and never in any other part of the world. The probable explanation is that the collapse of the Roman Empire left many towns without an allegiance to anyone. In time, these towns, which were naturally centers of trading and artisan work, grew powerful and managed to bargain for privileges with kings and lords. Capitalism thus grew up in the interstices of the medieval system. A similar opportunity and stimulus did not present itself elsewhere.

nomic freedom did not arise just because men and women directly sought to shake off the bonds of custom and command. It was also thrust upon them, often as a very painful and unwelcome change.

For feudalism, with all its cruelties and injustices, did provide a modicum of economic security. However mean a serf's life, at least he knew that in bad times he was guaranteed a small dole from his lord's granary. However exploited a journeyman, at least he knew that he could not be summarily thrown out of work under the rules of his master's guild. And however squeezed a lord, at least he, too, knew that his rents and dues were secured by law and custom and would be coming in, weather permitting.

The eruption of the market system destroyed all of that. **The creation of the factors of production meant the end of assured livelihoods.** If a landless laborer could not find work, that was not the responsibility of his lord, for he no longer *had* a lord. Nor was it the lookout of any former employer, who had no obligation to pay anyone who was not an employee. So, too, if a worker in the market system was fired, he or she could not complain to the guild, because there *was* no guild. For that matter, neither could his employer protest to the guild about some intruder who was "stealing" his trade. And if a landlord's rents declined in a bad year, that was no one's worry but his own; there were no more "customary" rents to rely on.

Economic freedom therefore meant that each person was thrown on the marketplace to sink or swim. This freedom could be a precious achievement for individuals who had formerly been deprived of the right to enter into legal contracts. For many, it meant the chance to rise out of a station in life from which, in earlier times, there was no exit. But economic freedom had another equally important aspect. This was the necessity to stay afloat by one's own efforts in rough waters where all were struggling to survive, and where no one much cared when a laborer, a landowner, or a capitalist disappeared from view.

The market system was thus the cause of unrest, insecurity, and individual suffering, just as it was also the source of progress, opportunity, and fulfillment. In this contest between the costs and benefits of economic freedom lies a theme that is still a crucial issue for capitalism.

THE UNLEASHING OF TECHNOLOGY

The creation of a market society also paved the way for a change of profound significance in bringing about modern economic life. This was the incorporation of science and technology into the very midst of daily life.

PRECAPITALIST TECHNOLOGY

Technology is not, of course, a modern phenomenon. The gigantic stones that form prehistoric Stonehenge, the precision and delicacy of the monumental Egyptian pyramids, the Incan stone walls fitted so exactly that a knife blade cannot be put between adjoining blocks, the Chinese Great Wall, and the Mayan observatories attest to mankind's long possession of the ability to transport and hoist staggering weights, to cut and shape hard surfaces, and to calculate complex problems. Indeed, many of these works would challenge our present-day engineering capabilities.

THE DIFFERENCE TECHNOLOGY MAKES: THREE FIELDS VS. TWO

Until the Middle Ages, the prevailing system of cultivation was to plant half of a lord's arable land in a winter crop, leaving the other half fallow. The second year, the two fields simply changed functions.

Under the three-field plan, the arable land was divided into thirds. One section was planted with a winter crop, one section with a summer crop, and one was left fallow. The second year, the first section was put into summer crops, the second section left fallow, and the third put into winter grains. In the third year, the first field was left fallow, the second used for winter crops, the third for spring planting.

Therefore, under the three-field system only one-third, not one-half, of the arable land was fallow in any year. Suppose that the field as a whole yielded 600 bushels of output. Under the two-field system, it would give an annual crop of 300 bushels. Under the three-field system the annual crop would be two-thirds of the area, or 400 bushels—an increase of one-third. Further, in those days it was customary to plough fallow land twice, and cultivated land only once. By cutting down the ratio of fallow to cultivated land, plowing time was greatly reduced, and peasant productivity even more significantly improved. For more on this and other fascinating advances in precapitalist technology, see Lynn White, *Medieval Technology and Social Change* (Oxford: Clarendon Press, 1962).

Nonetheless, although precapitalist technology reached great heights, it had a very restricted base. We have already noted that the basic tools of agriculture and artisan crafts remained little changed over millennia. Improvements came very slowly. So "simple" an invention as a horse collar shaped to prevent a straining animal from pressing against its windpipe did not appear during all the glories of Greece and triumphs of Rome. Not until the Middle Ages was there a switch from the ox to the draft horse as a ploughing animal (a change that improved efficiency by an estimated 30 percent), or was the traditional two-field system of crop rotation improved by adopting a three-field system. (See box.)

Thus precapitalist technology was lavished on the needs of rulers, priests, warriors. Its application to common everyday work was virtually ignored.

WHY TECHNOLOGY SLUMBERED

There were, of course, good reasons why the technology of daily life was ignored. The primary effect of technological change in daily activity is to increase output, to enhance the productivity of the working person. But in a society still regulated by tradition and command, where production was mainly carried on by serfs and slaves and custom-bound artisans, there was little incentive to look for increases in output. The bulk of any increase in agricultural yields would only go to the lord in higher rents, not to the serf or the slave who produced them.* Any artisan who altered the techniques of his trade would be expected, as a matter of course, to share these advances with his brethren. And how could his brethren, accustomed over the years to disposing of a certain quantity of pots

*To be sure, a lord would benefit greatly from increases in agricultural output. But how could a great noble be expected to know about, or to concern himself with, the dirty business of sowing and reaping?

or pans or cloth in the village market, expect to find buyers for more output? Would not the extra production simply go begging?

Thus productive technology in precapitalist societies slumbered because there was no incentive to search for change. Indeed, powerful social forces were ranged *against* technological change, which could only introduce an unsettling element into the world. How could a society whose whole way of life rested on the reproduction of established patterns of life even imagine a world where the technology of production was constantly in flux, and where limits were no longer recognized in any endeavor?

THE INCENTIVE OF CAPITALISM

These inhibiting forces were ruthlessly swept away by the currents of the emerging markets for labor, land, and capital. Serfs were uprooted to become workers forced to sell their labor power; aristocratic landlords were rudely shouldered aside by money-minded parvenus; guild masters and artisans watched commercial enterprises take away their accustomed livelihood; a new sense of necessity, of urgency, altered economic life. What had been a more or less dependable round of life became increasingly a scramble for existence. The feeling that one's economic interests were best served by following in the footsteps of one's forebears gave way to the knowledge that economic life was shot through with insecurity, and was at worst a race for survival in which each had to fend for him- or herself.

The growing importance of the market, where many a producer had to win a place for himself every day, radically altered the place of technology, especially in the small workshops and minuscule factories that were the staging areas of the capitalist revolution. Here the free-for-all brought a need to find toeholds in the struggle for a livelihood. And one toehold available to any aspiring capitalist with an inquiring mind and a knowledge of the actual processes of production was technology itself—some invention or improvement that would lower costs or change a product to give it an edge on its competitors.

Thus in the late eighteenth and early nineteenth centuries capitalism raised a crop of technology-minded entrepreneurs, a wholly new phenomenon in economic history. For example, there was John Wilkinson, son of an iron producer, who became a driving force for technical change in his trade. Wilkinson insisted that everything be built of iron—pipes and bridges, bellows and cylinders (one of which powered the new-fangled steam engine of John Watt). He even constructed a much derided iron ship—later much admired! There was Richard Arkwright, barber by trade, who made his fortune by inventing (or perhaps by stealing) the first effective spinning machine, becoming in time a great mill owner. There were Peter Onions, an obscure foreman who originated the puddling process for making wrought iron; Benjamin Huntsman, a clockmaker who improved the method of making steel; and a score more. A few, like Sir Jethro Tull, a pioneer in the technology of agriculture, were great gentlemen, but on the whole the technological leaders in industry were men of humble origin.

THE INDUSTRIAL REVOLUTIONS

The new dynamism revealed itself in a series of technological "revolutions" —periods in which the basic ways of making things suddenly underwent startling

changes, and in which new kinds of goods and services entered, and radically changed, daily life.

The first of these periods is often called *the* Industrial Revolution, although actually it was only the initial rush of a long, multiphase process. Beginning in the late eighteenth century and continuing for over twenty-five years, the first industrial revolution mechanized spinning and weaving, enormously improved and expanded iron production, brought the all-important gift of power in the form of the steam engine, and introduced a crucial change in the application of technology to production—the large, controlled workplace we call the factory.

The second industrial revolution followed in the mid-nineteenth century, bringing railroads and steamships, cheap steel, agricultural machinery, and the first mass-produced chemicals. Then in the early years of the twentieth century, a third burst came with the development of the automobile, electrical power, and consumer durable goods; and in our own day we are witnessing a fourth—the revolution of computers, air transportation, perhaps nuclear power.

THE EFFECTS OF TECHNOLOGY

Many profound changes have followed in the wake of capitalism—no other socioeconomic upheaval has so fundamentally altered life in its every aspect. But of the changes wrought, none was more dramatic than the industrial revolutions. The new technology literally remade life, and we should take a few moments to clarify some of the ways in which it did so.

1. Output increased enormously, raising living standards

First a few figures. Between 1701 and 1802, as the technology of spinning and weaving was gradually perfected, the use of cotton in England expanded by 6,000 percent. Between 1788 and 1839, when the process of iron manufacture passed through its first technological upheaval, the output of pig iron jumped from 68,000 to 1,347,000 tons. In France, in the thirty years after 1815, iron output quintupled, coal output grew sevenfold, and transportation tonnage mounted ten times.

But these figures do not convey a sense of the effect of technology on daily life. *Things* became more common—and more commonplace. As late as the seventeenth century, what we would consider the most ordinary possessions were scarce. A peasant counted his worldly wealth in terms of a few utensils, a table, perhaps one complete change of clothes. Shakespeare left Ann Hathaway his "second best bed." Iron nails were so scarce that pioneers in America burned down their cottages to retrieve them. In the wilder parts of Scotland in Adam Smith's time, nails even served as money.

Technology brought a widening and deepening and ever faster flowing river of things. Shoes, coats, paper, window glass, chairs, buckles—objects of solicitous respect in precapitalist times for all but the privileged few—became everyday articles. **Gradually, capitalism gave rise to what we call a "rising standard of living"—a steady, regular, systematic increase in the number, variety, and quality of material goods enjoyed by the great bulk of society. No such process had ever occurred before.**

THE CORLISS ENGINE

2. The scale of economic organization grew vastly larger

A second change wrought by technology was a striking increase in the size of society's productive apparatus.

The increase began with the enlargement of the equipment used in production—an enlargement that stemmed mostly from advances in the technology of iron and, later, steel. The typical furnace used in extracting iron ore increased from 10 feet in height in the 1770s to over 100 feet a century later; during the same period the crucibles in which steel was made grew from cauldrons hardly larger than an oversized jug to converters literally as big as a house. The looms used by weavers expanded from small machines that fitted into the cottages of artisan-weavers to monstrous mechanisms housed in mills that still impress us by their size. Perhaps the thrust to bigness in machinery was best symbolized in the great Corliss engine (see illustration) that dominated the Philadelphia Exposition of 1876, perfectly illustrating the technological imperative for power and strength.

Equally remarkable was the expansion in the social scale of production. The new technology almost immediately outstripped the administrative capability of the small-sized business establishment. As the apparatus of production increased in size, it also increased in speed. As outputs grew from rivulets to rivers, a much larger organization was needed to manage production—to arrange for the steady arrival of raw materials, to supervise the work process, and not least to find a market for its end product.

Thus we find the size of the typical business enterprise steadily increasing as its technological basis became more complex. In the last quarter of the eighteenth century, a factory of ten persons was worthy of note by Adam Smith, as we shall see in our next chapter. By the first quarter of the nineteenth century, an ordinary textile mill employed several hundred men and women. Fifty years later, many railways employed as many individuals as constituted the armies of respectable monarchs in Adam Smith's time. And in still another fifty years, by the 1920s, many large manufacturing companies had almost as many employees as the populations of eighteenth-century cities. The Ford Motor Company, for example, had 174,000 employees in 1929.

3. The division of labor changed the nature of work

Technology also played a decisive role in changing the nature of that most basic of all human activities, work. **It did so by breaking down the complicated tasks of productive activity into much smaller subtasks, many of which could then be duplicated, or at least greatly assisted, by mechanical contrivances. This process was called the division of labor.** Adam Smith was soon to explain, as we shall see in our next chapter, that the division of labor was mainly responsible for the increase in productivity of the average worker.

The division of labor altered social life in other ways as well. Work became more fragmented, monotonous, tedious, "alienated." And the self-sufficiency of individuals was greatly curtailed. In precapitalist days, most people either directly produced their own subsistence or made some article that could be exchanged for subsistence: peasants grew crops; artisans produced cloth, shoes, implements. But as work became more and more finely divided, the products of work became ever smaller pieces in the total jigsaw puzzle. Individuals did not spin thread or weave cloth but manipulated levers and fed the machinery that did the actual spinning or weaving. A worker in a shoe plant made uppers or lowers or heels, but not shoes. No one of these jobs, performed by itself, would have sustained its performer for a single day; and no one of these products could have been exchanged for another product except through the complicated market network. **Technology freed men and women from much material want, but it bound them to the workings of the market mechanism.**

4. A new form of economic insecurity arose

Not least of the mighty impacts of technology was its exposure of men and women to an unprecedented degree of change. Some of this was welcome, for change literally opened new horizons of material life: travel, for instance, once the prerogative of the wealthy, became a possibility for the masses.

However, the changes introduced by technology had their negative side as well. Already buffeted by market forces that could mysteriously dry up the need for work or just as mysteriously create it, society now discovered that entire occupations, skills acquired over a lifetime, companies laboriously built up over generations, age-old industries could be threatened by the appearance of techno-

For the first time in history, machinery appeared as the enemy, as well as the ally, of humankind. No wonder that the textile weavers, whose cottage industry was gradually destroyed by competition from the mills, banded together as Luddites to burn down the hated buildings.

These aspects of change do not begin to exhaust the ways in which technology, coupled with the market system, altered the very meaning of existence. But in considering them, we begin to see how profound and how wrenching was the revolution that capitalism introduced. Technology was a genie that capitalism let out of the bottle; it has ever since refused to go back in.

THE POLITICAL DIMENSION

The disturbing, upsetting, revolutionary nature of the market and of technology sets the stage for one last aspect of capitalism that we want to note. This is the political currents of change that capitalism brought—political currents that are as much a part of the history of capitalism as the emergence of the market or the dismantling of the barriers against technical change.

POLITICAL FREEDOM

One of these political currents was the rise of democratic, or parliamentary, institutions. Democratic political institutions far predate capitalism, as the history of ancient Athens or the Icelandic medieval parliamentary system shows. Nonetheless, the rise of the mercantile classes was closely tied to the struggle against the privileges and legal institutions of medieval European feudalism. The historic movement that eventually swept aside the precapitalist economic order also swept aside its political order. **Along with the emergence of the market system we find a parallel and supporting emergence of more open, libertarian political ways of life.**

We should be cautious, however, in maintaining that capitalism either guarantees, or is necessary for, political freedom. We have seen some capitalist nations, such as pre-Hitler Germany, descend into nightmarish dictatorship. We have seen other capitalisms, such as Sweden, move toward a kind of socialism without impairing democratic liberties. Moreover, the exercise of political democracy was very limited in early capitalism: Adam Smith, for example, although comfortably off, did not possess enough property to allow him to vote!

Therefore we cannot claim a hard and fast tie between capitalism and political freedom. It is true nonetheless that political liberties do not exist or scarcely exist in communist nations that have deliberately sought to remove the market system. This suggests, although it does not prove, that some vital connection exists between democratic privileges as we know them and an open society of economic contract, whether it be formally capitalist or not.

LAISSEZ-FAIRE VS. POLITICAL INTERVENTION

Because of the economic freedom on which the market system rested, the basic philosophy of capitalism from Adam Smith's day forward has been laissez-faire—a French phrase, difficult to translate exactly, that means "leaving things alone."*

*It is said that a group of merchants called on the great Colbert, French finance minister from 1661 to 1683, who congratulated them on their contribution to the French economy and asked what he could do for them. The answer was *Laissez-nous faire*—"leave us alone." Since Colbert was a strong proponent of the complex regulations and red tape that tied up industry in France at this time—a system we call *mercantilism*—we can imagine how gladly he received this advice.

In our next chapter we will pursue further the rationale behind the idea of laissez-faire. But within a few years of Adam Smith's time, the idea of leaving things alone was already being breached. In England, the Factory Act of 1833 established a system of inspectors to prevent child and female labor from being abused. The Ten Hour Act (1847) set limits to the number of hours that an employer might demand of his work force. In the United States, the Sherman Antitrust Act (1890) made illegal the banding together of large companies to create "trusts." In the 1930s, the Social Security Act established a system of old-age pensions; unemployment insurance assured unemployed workers of incomes; the Securities and Exchange Act imposed restrictions on the issuance of new securities. And in our time, a long roster of legislation has imposed government regulations with respect to the environment, occupational safety, and nuclear power, to mention only a very few instances.

The effects of these interventions into the market process have become central questions for economics itself. As we study micro- and macroeconomics, we will be studying not only how the market system works, but how various efforts to interfere with the market system exert their influence. Needless to say, intervention into the market is one of the most controversial aspects of economics. But we are not interested at this juncture in taking sides, pro and con. Rather, we should understand that from the first Factory Acts, intervention has largely arisen from a desire to impose corrective limits on the way in which the market system worked or on the unwanted effects produced by technology.

Thus, if capitalism has brought a strong impetus for laissez-faire, it has also brought a strong impetus for political intervention. **Indeed, the very democratic liberties that capitalism has encouraged have been a main source of demands for political action to curb or change the manner in which the economic system worked. The political economy of capitalism has always revealed a tension between laissez-faire and intervention—a tension rooted in the tug of war between the equal distribution of voting power and the unequal distribution of buying power.** That tension continues today, a deeply embedded part of the historic momentum of the capitalist system.

KEY CONCEPTS

LOOKING BACK

The purpose of this chapter is to set our economic system into historic perspective. We have highlighted a few central ideas to give structure to this perspective, many of them surprisingly linked to the off-hand, slogan-like ways in which we often think or talk about capitalism.

Private property undergirds capitalism

1. Capitalism is built on the idea that each individual is entitled to own and control his or her property, including the very important property of his or her own labor. Thus, under capitalism, there is no forced labor comparable to that of serf- or slave-based systems. There is also the firmly established right of individuals to own land or capital.

Factors of production testify to a market for land, labor, and capital

2. The services of these owners of property—the workers who own their laboring power, the landlords who own land, and the capitalists who own capital—are called the factors of production. The existence of factors of production tells us that labor, land, and capital have become

commodities offered for hire on a vast market system where their owners are paid wages, salaries, rents, or interest. This way of bringing the services of these forces of production into social use contrasts sharply with the older means of tradition or command. Capitalism relies on economic freedom and its linked aspect, economic necessity.

The market contrasts with tradition and command

Capitalism encourages technology which has come in waves—industrial revolutions

3. Capitalism is closely entwined with technology. The market system encouraged the introduction of technology into everyday productive use by removing the inhibitions of serf- and slave-based modes of production and by thrusting responsibility for economic success or failure on the shoulders of each person. Technological advance has come in a series of great bursts or waves called industrial revolutions, beginning with *the* Industrial Revolution (spinning, iron-making, steam power) of the late eighteenth and early nineteenth centuries.

Technology affects output, scale, and the division of labor

4. Technology profoundly affected economic and social life. It was responsible for the beginning of the rise in standard of living associated with capitalism. It was the main factor in the vast growth in size of business organizations. It was the source of a much greater division of labor and of a highly intensified interdependence of individuals.

The rise of capitalism is associated with political liberty. This has created a tension between laissez-faire and intervention

5. Capitalism is closely connected with political movements. One of these is the association with parliamentary democracy, arising from the struggle to break the hold of feudalism. Another has been the underlying belief in laissez-faire as the main principle of economic policy. A third has been the effort to intervene against the workings of the market and technology, when these powerful forces have disrupted or endangered social life.

ECONOMIC VOCABULARY

Market society 13
Factors of production 15
Industrial revolution 19
Division of labor 22
Laissez-faire 23

QUESTIONS

1. Are there elements of tradition and command still visible in our market system? How important do you think they are? Can you imagine a system in which there was *no* guiding force of tradition and *no* exercise of command (government) at all?
2. What reasons do you think are plausible in explaining why it took so long before capitalism finally burst on the scene; and how do you explain the fact that it emerged only in Europe, not in Africa, Asia, or South America? Note: If you devise a really persuasive answer to this question, you will be well on your way to becoming a world-famous historian. The question is far from settled.
3. Profit-making is certainly as old as man. Why are not the institutions of capitalism equally old?

4. Describe the social, political, and economic repercussions of the following: the typewriter, the jet plane, TV, penicillin. Is the economic impact always greater than the social or political impact? Is the economic impact always favorable?
5. Do you think capitalism is necessary for political freedom? First, frame your answer, and then test it against these facts: (a) There has been no political freedom in any modern nation that has decisively rejected capitalism (that lets out Sweden and England, which do not actively oppose capitalism). (b) The Union of South Africa is certainly capitalist, and is not a politically free nation, especially if you are not white. Note: These facts suggest that there are *no* open-and-shut answers to this question. The issue is a complicated one—more complicated than one would expect.

ADAM SMITH

Chapter 3 THE GREAT ECONOMISTS

A LOOK AHEAD

The rise of the market system brought with it a great puzzle: to explain how such a system "worked"—what kept it together and in what direction it was headed. The name of this puzzle is economics.

In this chapter we shall learn more about the background of economics by looking into the ideas of three great economists whose thoughts still dominate our understanding of capitalism: Adam Smith, Karl Marx, and John Maynard Keynes.

As we study them, a few central questions come to the fore:

(1) What holds the system together and gives it "micro" order?

(2) Where is the system headed, giving it "macro" motion?

(3) What should we do to improve the system's operations, or what policies should we pursue?

THE INVENTION OF ECONOMICS

The emergence of capitalism brought an extraordinary puzzle into being. The puzzle was to explain how a society could hang together when the time-honored mechanisms of tradition and command no longer played their accustomed roles. How could economic life unfold in an orderly and reliable fashion when each actor on the marketplace was out for himself, devil take the hindmost; and when it was already clear that change, not inertia, was to be the order of the day?

MERCANTILISM

Capitalism needed a philosophy—a reasoned explanation of how it worked. But the philosophy was a long time in emerging. All during the seventeenth and eighteenth centuries, for example, the understanding of market society was very imperfect. One group of British pamphleteers, whom we call the Mercantilists, tried to explain its workings in terms of a struggle among nations to gather "treasure"—gold and silver bullion. In this struggle, the Mercantilists saw merchants (hence *Mercant*ilism) playing a central role because they exported goods that were paid for in treasure.

Mercantilist policy was therefore very simple: Let England sell as much and buy as little abroad as possible. In that way, its national wealth would steadily pile up. No mercantilist seems to have been concerned about the impossibility of applying this philosophy to *all* nations. Can you see why it is impossible?

PHYSIOCRACY

In France during the eighteenth century an entirely different and equally inadequate explanation was called Physiocracy. In many ways the French school of ideas was the opposite of the British school. Physiocracy taught that the real wealth of economic life was production, not gold—an important step in the right direction. But the Physiocrats believed that production was essentially a gift of nature (*physiocracy* means the order of nature), and that therefore only labor working with nature was truly productive. Thus, whereas the Mercantilists extolled the merchants as active agents in creating national wealth, the Physiocrats regarded them as a "sterile" class that did no more than handle the wealth produced by the agriculturalist.

Mercantilism and Physiocracy are both indispensable stepping stones on the road to modern economics. Each yielded useful insights into the still unfinished economic revolution. But neither made the crucial breakthrough of seeing that the market was a system. That is, neither the Mercantilists nor the Physiocrats saw that the market network possessed an internal guidance mechanism to keep it on a steady course and that a society powered by the market was headed toward a visible destination.

These crucial insights came with Adam Smith, patron saint of our discipline and a figure of towering intellectual stature.

ADAM SMITH (1723–1790)

Adam Smith's fame resides in his masterpiece, *The Wealth of Nations,* published in 1776, the year of the Declaration of Independence. All things considered, it

PORTRAIT OF AN ABSENT-MINDED PROFESSOR

"I am a beau in nothing but my books" was the way that Adam Smith once described himself. Indeed, the famous medallion profile shows us a homely face. In addition, Smith had a curious stumbling gait that one friend called vermicular and was given to notorious fits of absent-mindedness. On one occasion, absorbed in discussion, he fell into a tanning pit.

Few other adventures befell Smith in the course of his scholarly, rather retiring, life. Perhaps the high point was reached at age four when he was kidnapped by a band of gypsies passing near Kirkaldy, his native hamlet in Scotland. His captors held him only a few hours; they may have sensed what a biographer later wrote: "He would have made, I fear, a poor gypsy."

Marked out early as a student of promise, at 16 Smith won a scholarship that sent him to Oxford. But Oxford was not then the center of learning that it is today. Little or no systematic teaching took place, the students being free to educate themselves, provided they did not read dangerous books. Smith was nearly expelled for owning a copy of David Hume's *Treatise of Human Nature,* a work we now regard as one of the philosophic masterpieces of the eighteenth century.

After Oxford, Smith returned to Scotland, where he obtained an appointment as Professor of Moral Philosophy at the University of Glasgow. Moral philosophy covered a large territory in Smith's time: We have notes of his lectures in which he talked about jurisprudence, military organization, taxation, and "police"—the last word meaning the administration of domestic affairs that we would call economic policy.

In 1759 Smith published *The Theory of Moral Sentiments,* a remarkable inquiry into morality and psychology. The book attracted widespread attention and brought Smith to the notice of Lord Townshend, one day to be the Chancellor of the Exchequer, responsible for the notorious tax on American tea. Townshend engaged Smith to serve as tutor to his stepson, and Smith resigned his professorial post to set off on the Grand Tour with his charge. In France he met Voltaire, Rousseau, and François Quesnay, the brilliant doctor who had originated the ideas of physiocracy. Smith would have dedicated *The Wealth of Nations* to him, had Quesnay not died.

Returning to Scotland in 1766, Smith lived out the remainder of his life largely in scholarly retirement. It was during these years that the *Wealth* was slowly and carefully composed. When it was done, Smith sent a copy to David Hume, by then his dear friend. Hume wrote: "Euge!* Belle! Dear Mr. Smith: I am much pleased with your Performance. . . ." Hume knew, as did virtually everyone who read the book, that Smith had written a work that would permanently change society's understanding of itself.

*Greek for "Well done!"

is not easy to say which document is of greater historic importance. The Declaration sounded a new call for a society dedicated to "Life, Liberty, and the pursuit of Happiness." The *Wealth* explained how such a society worked.

THE ROLE OF COMPETITION

Smith set himself two main problems, one on the micro, and one on the macro level (although you will not find these terms used in his great, rambling, discursive tract). The first problem was to elucidate how a market-run economic system was articulated, how it achieved what we would call micro-order.

Here Smith begins by resolving a perplexing question. The actors in the market, as we know, are all driven by the desire to make money for themselves—to "better their condition," as Smith puts it. The question is obvious: How does a market society prevent self-interested, profit-hungry individuals from holding up their fellow citizens for ransom? How can a socially workable arrangement arise from such a dangerously unsocial motivation as self-betterment?

The answer introduces us to a central mechanism of a market system, **the mechanism of competition. For each person, out for self-betterment, with no thought of others, is faced with a host of similarly motivated persons. As a result, each market actor is forced to meet the prices offered by competitors.**

In the kind of competition that Smith assumes, a manufacturer who tries to charge more than other manufacturers will not be able to find any buyers. A job seeker who asks more than the going wage will not be able to find work. And an employer who tries to pay *less* than competitors pay will not find anyone to fill the jobs.

In this way, the market mechanism imposes a discipline on its participants—buyers must bid against other buyers and therefore cannot gang up against sellers. Sellers must contend against other sellers and therefore cannot impose their will on buyers.

THE INVISIBLE HAND

But the market has a second, equally important function. Smith shows that the market will arrange for the production of the goods that society wants, in the quantities society wants—without anyone ever issuing an order of any kind! Suppose that consumers want more pots and fewer pans than are being turned out. The public will buy up the existing stock of pots, and as a result the price of pots will rise. Contrariwise, the pan business will be dull; as pan-makers try to get rid of their inventories, pan prices will fall.

Now a restorative force comes into play. As pot prices rise, so will profits in the pot business; and as pan prices fall, so will profits in that business. Once again, the drive for self-betterment will go to work. Employers in the favored pot business will seek to expand, hiring more factors of production—more workers, more space, more capital equipment; and employers in the disfavored pan business will reduce their use of the factors of production, letting workers go, giving up leases on space, cutting down on their capital investment.

Hence the output of pots will rise and that of pans will fall. And this is what the public wanted in the first place. **Thus the pressures of the marketplace direct the selfish activities of individuals as if by an Invisible Hand (to use Smith's wonderful phrase) into socially responsible paths. The Invisible Hand transmutes private, self-regarding motives into public, socially oriented behavior. The market becomes a mechanism for the allocation of resources into the channels desired by society.**

THE SELF-REGULATING SYSTEM

Smith's demonstration of how a market performs its social functions has never ceased to be of interest. Much of microeconomics, as we shall see in Part 4, consists of learning again, or of examining more closely, how the Invisible Hand works. Not that it always does work. There are areas of economic life where the

Invisible Hand does not exert its influence at all. In every market system, for instance, tradition continues to play a role in nonmarket methods of remuneration such as tipping. So, too, command is always in evidence *within* organizations or in the exercise of government powers such as taxation. Further, the market system has no way of providing certain public goods—goods that cannot be privately marketed, such as national defense or public law and order. Smith knew about these and recognized that such goods would have to be supplied by the government, not by the market. Then, too, the market does not always meet the ethical or aesthetic criteria of society, or it may produce goods that are profitable to make, but harmful to consume. We shall look into these problems in due course. At this juncture, however, we had better stand in considerable awe of Smith's basic insight, for he showed his generation and all succeeding ones that a market system is a responsive and reliable force for basic social provisioning.

He also showed that it was self-regulating. The beautiful consequence of the market is that it is its own guardian. If anyone's prices, wages, or profits stray from levels that are set for everyone, the force of competition will drive them back. Thus a curious paradox exists. The market, which is the acme of economic freedom, turns out to be the strictest of economic taskmasters.

SMITH'S PHILOSOPHY

Because the market is its own regulator, Smith is vehemently opposed to government intervention that will interfere with the workings of self-interest and competition. Therefore, laissez-faire becomes his fundamental philosophy—not because Smith is opposed to the idea of social responsibility, but because he thinks it will be most effectively provided by the Invisible Hand, not by the efforts of government.

His commitment to laissez-faire does not make Smith a conventional conservative. The *Wealth of Nations* is shot through with biting remarks about the "mean and rapacious" ways of the manufacturing class (Smith does not use the word *capitalist*), and the book is openly sympathetic with, and concerned about, the lot of the workingman, hardly a popular position in Smith's day. If Smith is passionately in favor of the "system of natural liberty"—the system founded on economic freedom—the reason is that he believed it would benefit the general public, not the narrow interests of any single class.

ECONOMIC GROWTH

Smith's discovery of the self-regulating properties of a market system was his great "micro" insight (remember that is our phrase, not his). But his vision of an internally coherent market system was matched in importance by a second, "macro" vision. **Smith saw that the market system, left entirely to its own devices, would grow, that the wealth of a nation under a system of "natural liberty" would steadily increase.**

What brought about this growth? As before, the motive force was the drive for self-betterment, the thirst for profits, the wish to make money. This meant that every employer was constantly seeking to accumulate more capital, to expand the wealth of the enterprise; in turn, this led each employer to seek to increase sales in the hope of gaining a larger profit.

THE DIVISION OF LABOR AGAIN

But how to enlarge sales in a day long before advertising existed as we know it? Smith's answer was to improve productivity: Increase the output of the work force. And the road to increasing productivity was very clear: *Improve the division of labor.*

In Smith's conception of the growing *wealth* (we would say the growing *production*) *of nations,* the division of labor therefore plays a central role, as this famous description of a pin factory makes unforgettably clear:

> One man draws out the wire, another straits it, a third cuts it, a fourth points it, a fifth grinds it at the top for receiving the head; to make the head requires two or three distinct operations; to put it on is a peculiar business; to whiten it another; it is even a trade by itself to put them into paper.
>
> . . . I have seen a small manufactory of this kind where ten men only were employed and where some of them consequently performed two or three distinct operations. But though they were poor, and therefore but indifferently accommodated with the necessary machinery, they could when they exerted themselves make among them about twelve pounds of pins in a day. There are in a pound upwards of four thousand pins of middling size. These ten persons, therefore, could make among them upward of forty-eight thousand pins in a day. . . . But if they had all wrought separately and independently . . . they could certainly not each of them make twenty, perhaps not one pin in a day.[1]

CAPITAL AND GROWTH

But how is the division of labor to be enhanced? Smith places principal importance on the manner already announced in his description of the process of making pins: *Machinery is the key.* The division of labor—and therefore the productivity of labor—is increased when the tasks of production can be taken over, or aided and assisted, by the capacities of machinery. In this way each firm seeking to expand, is naturally led to introduce more machinery as a way of improving the productivity of its workers. **Thereby the market system becomes an immense force for the accumulation of capital, mainly in the form of machinery and equipment.** Moreover, Smith showed something remarkable about the self-regulating properties of the market system as a growth-producing institution. We recall that growth occurred because employers installed machinery that improved the division of labor. But as they thereupon added to their work force, would it not follow that wages would rise as all employers competed to hire labor? And would that not squeeze profits and dry up the funds by which machinery could be bought?

Once again, however, the market was its own regulator. For Smith showed that the increased demand for labor would be matched by an increased supply of labor, so that wages would not rise or would rise only moderately. The reason was plausible. In Smith's day, infant and child mortality rates were horrendous: "It is not uncommon," wrote Smith, ". . . in the Highlands of Scotland for a mother who has borne twenty children not to have two alive." As wages rose and better food was provided for the household, infant and child mortality would decline. Soon there would be a larger work force available for hire: Ten was the working age in Smith's day. The larger work force would hold back the rise in wages—and so the accumulation of capital could go on. Just as the system assured internal micro order, it also provided an overall macro dependability.

[1]Adam Smith, *The Wealth of Nations* (New York: Modern Library, 1937), pp. 4, 5.

SMITH TODAY

Of course, Smith wrote about a world that is long since vanished—a world in which a factory of ten people, although small, was still significant enough to mention; in which remnants of mercantilist, and even feudal, restrictions determined how many apprentices an employer could hire in many trades; in which labor unions were largely illegal; in which almost no social legislation existed; and above all, where the great majority of people were very poor.

Yet Smith saw two essential attributes in the economic system that was not yet fully born in this time.

1. **A society of competitive profit-seeking individuals can assure its orderly material provisioning through the self-regulating market mechanism.**
2. **Such a society tends to accumulate capital, and in so doing enhances its productivity and wealth.**

These insights are not the last word. We have already mentioned that the market mechanism does not always work successfully, and our next two economists will demonstrate that the growth process is not without serious defects. But the insights themselves are still germane. Micro- and macroeconomics are about internal order and growth, even though we may come to different conclusions than those of Smith. What is surprising after two centuries is not how mistaken Smith was, but how deeply he saw. In a real sense, as economists we are still his pupils.

KARL MARX (1818–1883)

Every economist is roughly familiar with the ideas and influence of Adam Smith. Not so many recognize the degree to which economics also owes a debt to Karl Marx—not as the founder of a political movement that has troubled the world ever since, but as an economist whose dissection of capitalism has much to teach us.

CLASS STRUGGLE

Adam Smith was the architect of capitalism's orderliness and progress; Marx the diagnostician of its disorders and eventual demise. Their differences are rooted in the fundamentally opposite way that each saw history. In Smith's view, history was a succession of stages through which humankind traveled, climbing from the "early and rude" society of hunters and fisherfolk to the final stage of commercial society. **Marx saw history as a continuing struggle among social classes, ruling classes contending with ruled classes in every era.**

Moreover, Smith believed that commercial society would bring about a harmonious, mutually acceptable solution to the problem of individual interest in a social setting that would go on forever—or at least for a very long time. Marx saw tension and antagonism as the outcome of the class struggle, and the setting of capitalist society as anything but permanent. Indeed, the class struggle itself, expressed as the contest over wages and profits, would be the main force for changing capitalism and eventually undoing it.

PROFILE OF A REVOLUTIONARY

A great, bearded, dark-skinned man, Karl Marx was the picture of a revolutionary. And he was one—engaged, mind and heart, in the effort to overthrow the system of capitalism that he spent his whole life studying. As a political revolutionary, Marx was not very successful, although with his lifelong friend Friedrich Engels, he formed an international working class "movement" that frightened a good many conservative governments. But as an intellectual revolutionary Marx was probably the most successful disturber of thought who ever lived. The only persons who rival his influence are the great religious leaders, Christ, Mohammed, and Buddha.

Marx led as turbulent and active a life as Smith's was secluded and academic. Born to middle-class parents in Trier, Germany, Marx was early marked as a student of prodigious abilities but not temperamentally cut out to be a professor. Soon after getting his doctoral degree (in philosophy) Marx became editor of a crusading, but not communist, newspaper, which rapidly earned the distrust of the reactionary Prussian government. It closed down the paper. Typically, Marx printed the last edition in red. With his wife Jenny (and Jenny's family maid, Lenchen, who remained with them, unpaid, all her life), Marx thereupon began life as a political exile in Paris, Brussels, and finally in London. There, in 1848, together with Engels, he published the pamphlet that was to become his best known, but certainly not most important work: *The Communist Manifesto.*

The remainder of Marx's life was lived in London. Terribly poor, largely as a consequence of his hopeless inability to manage his own finances, Marx's life was spent in the reading room of the British Museum, laboriously composing the great, never finished opus, *Capital.* No economist has ever read so widely or so deeply as Marx. Before even beginning *Capital,* he wrote a profound three-volume commentary on all the existing economists, eventually published as *Theories of Surplus Value,* and filled 37 notebooks on subjects that would be included in *Capital*—these notes, published as the *Grundrisse* (Foundations) did not appear in print until 1953! *Capital* itself was written backwards, first Volumes II and III, in very rough draft form, then Volume I, the only part of the great opus that appeared in Marx's lifetime, in 1867.

Marx was assuredly a genius, a man who altered every aspect of thinking about society—historical and sociological as well as economic—as decisively as Plato altered the cast of philosophic thought, or Freud that of psychology. Very few economists today work their way through the immense body of Marx's work; but in one way or another his influence affects most of us, even if we are unaware of it. We owe to Marx the basic idea that capitalism is an *evolving* system, deriving from a specific historic past and moving slowly and irregularly toward a dimly discernible, different form of society. That is an idea accepted by many social scientists who may or may not approve of socialism, and who are on the whole vehemently "anti-Marxist"!

1. CAPITALIST GROWTH: USING M

A great deal of interest in Marx's work focuses on that revolutionary perspective and purpose. But Marx the economist interests us for a different reason: Marx also saw the market as a powerful force in the accumulation of capital and wealth. From his conflict-laden point of view, however, he traces out the process —mainly in Volume II of *Capital*—quite differently than Smith does. As we have seen, Smith's conception of the growth process stressed its self-regulatory nature, its steady, hitch-free path. Marx's conception is just the opposite. To him, growth

Courtesy of the Library of Congress

KARL MARX

is a process full of pitfalls, a process in which crisis or malfunction lurks at every turn.

Marx starts with a view of the accumulation process that is much like that of a businessman. The problem is how to make a given sum of capital—money sitting in a bank or invested in a firm—yield a profit. **As Marx puts it, how does *M* (a sum of money) become *M′*, a *larger* sum?**

Marx's answer begins with capitalists using their money to buy commodities and labor power. Thereby they ready the process of production, obtaining needed raw or semi-finished materials, and hiring the working capabilities of a labor force. Here the possibility for crisis lies in the difficulty that capitalists may have in getting their materials or their labor force at the right price. If that should happen—if labor is too expensive, for instance—*M* stays put and the accumulation process never gets started at all.

2. THE LABOR PROCESS

But suppose the first stage of accumulation takes place smoothly. Now money capital, *M*, has been transformed into a hired work force and a stock of physical goods. These have next to be combined in the labor process; that is, actual work must be expended on the materials and the raw or semi-finished goods transformed into their next stage of production.

It is here, on the factory floor, that Marx sees the genesis of profit. **In his view, profit lies in the ability of capitalists to pay less for labor power—for the working abilities of their work force—than the actual value workers will impart to the commodities they help to produce.** This theory of *surplus value* as the source of profit is very important in Marx's analysis of capitalism, but it is not central to our purpose here. Instead, we stop only to note that the labor process is another place where accumulation can be disrupted. If there is a strike, or if production encounters snags, the M that is invested in goods and labor power will not move along toward its objective, M'.

3. COMPLETING THE CIRCUIT

But once again suppose that all goes well and workers transform steel sheets, rubber casings, and bolts of cloth into automobiles. The automobiles are not yet money. They have to be sold—and here, of course, lie the familiar problems of the marketplace: bad guesses as to the public's taste; mismatches between supply and demand; recessions that diminish the spending power of society.

If all goes well, the commodities *will* be sold—and sold for M', which is bigger than M. In that case, the circuit of accumulation is complete, and the capitalists will have a new sum M', which they will want to send on another round, hoping to win M''. But unlike Adam Smith's smooth growth model, we can see that Marx's conception of accumulation is riddled with pitfalls and dangers. **Crisis is possible at every stage. Indeed, in the complex theory that Marx unfolds in *Capital*, the inherent tendency of the system is to generate crisis, not to avoid it.**

We will not trace Marx's theory of capitalism further except to note that at its core lies a complicated analysis of the manner in which surplus value (the unpaid labor that is the source of profit) is squeezed out through mechanization. A student who wants to learn about Marx's analysis must turn to other books, of which there are many.*

INSTABILITY AND BREAKDOWN

Our interest lies in Marx as the first theorist to stress the instability of capitalism. Adam Smith originated the idea that growth is an inherent characteristic of capitalism; but to Marx we owe the idea that that growth is wavering and uncertain, far from the mechanically assured process Smith described. Marx makes it clear that capital accumulation must overcome the uncertainty inherent in the market system and the tension of the opposing demands of labor and capital. The accumulation of wealth, although certainly the objective of business, may not always be within its power to achieve.

In *Capital*, Marx sees instability increasing until finally the system comes tumbling down. His reasoning involves two further, very important prognoses for the system. **The first is that the size of business firms will steadily increase as the consequence of the recurrent crises that wrack the economy.** With each crisis,

*At the risk of appearing self-serving, a good first reader is R. L. Heilbroner, *The Worldly Philosophers* (New York: Simon & Schuster, 6th ed., 1980), Chapter V. The bibliography suggests a number of other books about Marx.

small firms go bankrupt and their assets are bought up by surviving firms. Thus a trend toward big business is an integral part of capitalism.

Second, Marx expects an intensification of the class struggle as the result of the "proletarianization" of the labor force. More and more small businesspeople and independent artisans will be squeezed out in the crisis-ridden process of growth. Thus the social structure will be reduced to two classes—a small group of capitalist magnates and a large mass of proletarianized, embittered workers.

In the end, this situation proves impossible to maintain. In Marx's words:

> Along with the constant decrease in the number of capitalist magnates, who usurp and monopolize all the advantages of this process of transformation, the mass of misery, oppression, slavery, degradation and exploitation grows; but with this there also grows the revolt of the working class, a class constantly increasing in numbers, and trained, united and organized by the very mechanism of the capitalist process of production. The monopoly of capital becomes a fetter upon the mode of production which has flourished alongside and under it. The centralization of the means of production and the socialization of labour reach a point at which they become incompatible with their capitalist integument. This integument is burst asunder. The knell of capitalist private property sounds. The expropriators are expropriated.[2]

WAS MARX RIGHT?

Much of the economic controversy that Marx generated has been focused on the questions: Will capitalism ultimately undo itself? Will its internal tensions, its "contradictions," as Marx calls them, finally become too much for its market mechanism to handle?

There are no simple answers to these questions. Critics of Marx vehemently insist that capitalism has *not* collapsed, that the working class has *not* become more and more "miserable," and that a number of predictions that Marx made, such as that the rate of profit would tend to decline, have not been verified.

Supporters of Marx argue the opposite case. They stress that capitalism almost did collapse in the 1930s. They note that more and more people have been reduced to a "proletarian" status, working for a capitalist firm rather than for themselves; in 1800, for example, 80 percent of Americans were self-employed; today the figure is 10 percent. They stress that the size of businesses has constantly grown, and that Marx did correctly foresee that the capitalist system itself would expand, pushing into noncapitalist areas such as Asia, South America, and Africa.

MARX'S SOCIOANALYSIS

It is doubtful that Marx's contribution as a social analyst will ultimately be determined by this kind of score card. Certainly he made many remarkably penetrating statements, and equally certainly, he said things about the prospects for capitalism that seem to have been wrong. **What Marx's reputation rests on is something else. It rests on his vision of capitalism as a system under tension, and in a process of continuous evolution as a consequence of that tension.** Many economists do not accept Marx's diagnosis of class struggle as the great motor of change in capitalist and precapitalist societies or his prognosis of the inevitable arrival of socialism, but few would deny the validity of that vision.

[2]Karl Marx, *Capital,* Vol. I (New York: Vintage, 1977), p. 929.

There is much more to Marx than the few economic ideas sketched here suggest. Indeed, Marx should not be thought of primarily as an economist, but as a pioneer in a new kind of critical social thought: It is significant that the subtitle of *Capital* is *A Critique of Political Economy.*

In the gallery of the world's great thinkers, where Marx certainly belongs, his proper place is with historians, rather than economists. Most appropriately, his statue would be centrally placed, overlooking many corridors of thought—sociological analysis, philosophic inquiry, and of course, economics.

For Marx's lasting contribution was a penetration of the *appearances* of our social system and of the ways in which we think about that system, in an effort to arrive at buried essences deep below the surface. That most searching aspect of Marx's work is not one that we will pursue here; but bear it in mind, because it accounts for the persisting interest of Marx's thought.*

JOHN MAYNARD KEYNES (1883-1946)

Marx was the intellectual prophet of capitalism as a self-destructive system; John Maynard Keynes (the name should be pronounced "canes," not "keens") was the engineer of capitalism repaired. Today, that is not an uncontested statement. To some people, Keynes's doctrines are as dangerous and subversive as those of Marx—a curious irony, since Keynes himself was totally opposed to Marxist thought and wholly in favor of sustaining and improving the capitalist system.

The reason for the continuing distrust of Keynes is that more than any other economist he is the father of the idea of a "mixed economy" in which the government plays a crucial role. To many people these days, all government activities are suspicious at best and downright injurious at worst. Thus, in some quarters Keynes's name is under a cloud. Nonetheless, he remains one of the great innovators of our discipline, a mind to be ranked with Smith and Marx as one of the most influential our profession has brought forth. As Nobelist Milton Friedman, a famous conservative economist, has declared: "We are all Keynesians now."

THE GREAT DEPRESSION

The great economists were all products of their times: Smith, the voice of optimistic, nascent capitalism; Marx, the spokesman for the victims of its bleakest industrial period; Keynes, the product of a still later time, the Great Depression.

The depression hit America like a typhoon. One half the value of all production simply disappeared. One quarter of the working force lost its jobs. Over a million urban families found their mortgages foreclosed, their houses lost to them. Nine million savings accounts went down the drain when banks closed, never to reopen.

Against this terrible reality of joblessness and loss of income, the economics profession, like the business world or government advisers, had nothing to offer.

*What about the relation of Marx to present-day communism? That is a subject for a book about the politics, not the economics, of Marxism. Marx himself was a fervid democrat—but also a very intolerant man. Perhaps his system of ideas has encouraged intolerance in revolutionary parties that have based their ideas on his thought. Marx himself died long before present-day communism came into being. We cannot know what he would have made of it—probably he would have been horrified at its excesses but still hopeful for its future.

Fundamentally, economists were as perplexed at the behavior of the economy as were the American people themselves. In many ways the situation reminds us of the uncertainty that the public and the economics profession share in the face of inflation today.

THE GENERAL THEORY

It was against this setting of dismay and near-panic that Keynes's great book appeared: *The General Theory of Employment Interest and Money.* A complicated book—much more technical than the *Wealth of Nations* or *Capital*—the *General Theory* nevertheless had a central message that was simple enough to

PORTRAIT OF A MANY-SIDED MAN

Keynes was certainly a man of many talents. Unlike Smith or Marx, he was at home in the world of business affairs, a shrewd dealer and financier. Every morning, abed, he would scan the newspaper and make his commitments for the day on the most treacherous of all markets, foreign exchange. An hour or so a day sufficed to make him a very rich man; only the great English economist David Ricardo (1772–1823) could match him in financial acumen. Like Ricardo, Keynes was a speculator by temperament. During World War I, when he was at the Treasury office running England's foreign currency operations, he reported with glee to his chief that he had got together a fair amount of Spanish pesetas. The chief was relieved that England had a supply of *that* currency for a while. "Oh no," said Keynes. "I've sold them all. I'm going to break the market." And he did. Later during the war, when the Germans were shelling Paris, he went to France to negotiate for the English government; on the side, be bought some marvelous French masterpieces at much reduced prices for the National Gallery—along with a Cezanne for himself!

More than an economist and speculator, he was a brilliant mathematician; a businessman who very successfully ran a great investment trust; a ballet lover who married a famous ballerina; a superb stylist and an editor of consummate skill; a man of huge kindness when he wanted to exert it, and of ferocious wit when (more often) he chose to exert that. On one occasion, banker Sir Harry Goshen criticized Keynes for not "letting things take their natural course." "Is it more appropriate to smile or rage at these artless sentiments?" wrote Keynes. "Best, perhaps, to let Sir Harry take *his* natural course."

Keynes's greatest fame lay in his economic inventiveness. He came by this talent naturally enough as the son of a distinguished economist, John Neville Keynes. As an undergraduate, Keynes had already attracted the attention of Alfred Marshall, the commanding figure at Cambridge University for three decades. After graduation, Keynes soon won notice with a brilliant little book on Indian finance; he then became an adviser to the English government in the negotiations at the end of World War I. Dismayed and disheartened by the vengeful terms of the Versailles Treaty, Keynes wrote a brilliant polemic, *The Economic Consequences of the Peace,* that won him international renown.

Almost thirty years later, Keynes would himself be a chief negotiator for the English government, first in securing the necessary loans during World War II, then as one of the architects of the Bretton Woods agreement that opened a new system of international currency relations after that war. On his return from one trip to Washington, reporters crowded around to ask if England had been sold out and would soon be another American state. Keynes's reply was succinct: "No such luck."

The Bettmann Archive, Inc.

JOHN MAYNARD KEYNES

grasp. The overall level of economic activity in a capitalist system, said Keynes (and Marx and Adam Smith would have agreed with him) was determined by the willingness of its entrepreneurs to make capital investments. From time to time, this willingness was blocked by considerations that made capital accumulation difficult or impossible: In Smith's model we saw the possibility of wages rising too fast, and Marx's theory pointed out difficulties at every stage of the process.

But all the previous economists, even Marx to a certain extent, believed that a failure to accumulate capital would be a temporary, self-curing setback. In Smith's scheme, the rising supply of young workers would keep wages in check. In Marx's conception, each crisis (up to the last) would present the surviving entrepreneurs with fresh opportunities to resume their quest for profits. For Keynes, however, the diagnosis was more severe. **He showed that a market system could reach a position of "underemployment equilibrium"—a kind of steady, stagnant state—despite the presence of unemployed workers and unused industrial equipment. The revolutionary import of Keynes's theory was that there was no self-righting property in the market system to keep capitalism growing.**

THE ROLE OF GOVERNMENT

We will not understand the nature of Keynes's diagnosis until we study macroeconomics, but we can easily see the conclusion to which his diagnosis drove him. If there was nothing that would automatically provide for capital accumulation, a badly depressed economy could remain in the doldrums—unless some substitute were found for business capital spending. And there was only one such possible source of stimulation. This was the government. **The crux of Keynes's message was therefore that government spending might be an essential economic policy for a depressed capitalism trying to recover its vitality.**

Whether or not Keynes's remedy works and what consequences government spending may have for a market system have become major topics for contemporary economics—topics we will deal with later at length. But we can see the significance of Keynes's work in changing the very conception of the economic system in which we live. Adam Smith's view of the market system led to the philosophy of laissez-faire, allowing the system to generate its own natural propensity for growth and internal order. Marx had stressed a very different view in which instability and crisis lurked at every stage, but of course Marx was not interested in policies to maintain capitalism. Keynes propounded a philosophy as far removed from Marx as from Smith. For if Keynes was right, laissez-faire was not the appropriate policy for capitalism—certainly not for capitalism in depression. And if Keynes was right about his remedy, the gloomy prognostications of Marx were also incorrect—or at least could be rendered incorrect.

But was Keynes right? Was Smith right? Was Marx right? To a very large degree these questions frame the subject matter of economics today. That is why, even if their theories are part of our history, the "worldly philosophers" are also contemporary. A young writer once remarked impatiently to T. S. Eliot that it seemed so pointless to study the thinkers of the past, because we knew so much more than they. "Yes," replied Eliot. "They are what we know."

LOOKING BACK

KEY CONCEPTS

This chapter has tried to give us a conception of capitalism as seen by the three greatest economists—conceptions that still powerfully affect our understanding of the system. Let us go over the main ideas that have emerged from this survey:

Mercantilists and physiocrats extolled treasure and land

1. Economics itself is a modern intellectual invention that awaited the advent of market society. Prior to Adam Smith, the main attempts to understand and explain the system were those of the Mercantilists, who stressed the importance of foreign trade as a means of gaining gold or treasure; and those of the French Physiocrats, who extolled the wealth-generating powers of the land and who dismissed the merchant class as sterile.

Adam Smith's Invisible Hand—competition plus self-interest

2. Adam Smith contributed two immensely important ideas to economic understanding. The first was the idea of an Invisible Hand by which the market system converted the selfish drives of individuals to a

coordinated mechanism for social provisioning. Smith showed how this fortunate outcome arose from the workings of competition, which prevented the drive for profits or selfish interest from simply gouging the consumer or the worker.

Capital accumulation and division of labor bring growth

3. Smith was also the first economist to explain how the market provided a powerful mechanism for accumulating capital. Smith's theory of economic growth hinged on the steady improvement in productivity that occurred when machinery was added to production, making possible a finer division of labor.

Class struggle

4. Marx was the great prophet of capitalism's doom. The essential cause of its demise would be the class struggle between workers and capitalists.

The unstable process of production

5. Marx also saw the market mechanism as inherently unstable—as tending toward crisis or disruption in the accumulation of capital. He analyzed this instability by tracing the obstacles faced by a firm as it sought to convert M, a sum of capital, into M', a larger sum. This was done in three stages: first by using M to buy labor power and materials, then by combining labor power with materials, and finally by selling the finished goods. At each stage, the accumulation process was subject to disruption of various sorts.

Growth of monopolies and proletarians lead to revolution

6. In Marx's view the process of capitalist accumulation lead to the growth of big business and an "immiserated" proletariat. As successive crises wracked the system, the working class would eventually revolt, and a transition would be made from capitalism to socialism.

Marxism as a system of thought

7. Marx's system of thought was much larger than an effort to analyze the economic tensions of capitalism. Essentially it embraced a mixture of philosophy, historical analysis, and a critique of economic beliefs and forms.

Keynes's *General Theory* with its idea of underemployment equilibrium, ushered in the mixed economy

8. John Maynard Keynes's *General Theory* (as it is widely called) was an attempt to explain how capitalism could have a *lasting* depression. In technical terms, Keynes's breakthrough was the explanation of underemployment equilibrium.

9. Equally important was Keynes's work in paving the way for the mixed economy in which government plays a crucial role in maintaining the economic growth of capitalism. Mixed economies are found in every capitalist system today; we shall be studying them in depth in the pages to come.

ECONOMIC VOCABULARY

Mercantilism 28
Physiocracy 28
Competition 29
Invisible Hand 30
Self-regulation 30
Growth 31, 32
Marx's circuit of production: *M*-into-*M'* 35
Underemployment equilibrium 40

QUESTIONS

1. Why does Smith's model of the economy require *two* elements—the motivation of self-betterment and the restraining institution of competition? Explain why the system would not work with only one of the two.
2. From your own experience, think of how the division of labor can increase productivity. Choose one example from agriculture, one from manufacturing, and one from a service industry such as hotel management, transportation, or retailing.
3. Is the accumulation of capital needed for the improvement of productivity today? In what ways could additional capital—more machines, buildings, roads, etc.—improve the amount of production that a typical farmer or worker could create.
4. Take any business you know about and see if you think that Marx's description of the circuit M-into-M' describes the way in which that business tries to accumulate capital. Which of Marx's three phases of the accumulation process is most likely to lead to trouble, in your opinion?
5. How do you feel about the idea of a mixed economy? Do you think it means an economy in which the government does a lot of interfering? Could a government simply spend money—for example, for Social Security—and not interfere in the market system at all? Could it interfere extensively, but not spend much money? Which of the two functions—interfering (regulating) or spending—is basic to Keynes's theory? Is it possible, do you think, to have a basically laissez-faire policy with respect to the market, and yet have government spending to cure a depression?

AN EXTRA WORD ABOUT *PARADIGMS*

How does science advance? The prevailing view used to be that it grew by accretion, gradually adding new knowledge and better established hypotheses while shedding error and disproved hypotheses. That view has now been seriously challenged by the influential book, *The Structure of Scientific Revolutions,* by Thomas Kuhn, published in 1962.

Kuhn's view is that the growth of science is not a continuous, seamless extension of knowledge. Rather, science grows in discontinuous leaps, in which one prevailing paradigm is displaced by another. *A paradigm is a set of premises, views, rules, conventions, and beliefs that form the kinds of questions that a science asks.* For example, the Ptolemaic paradigm, with its view of the earth as the center of the universe, was replaced by the Copernican paradigm, which based its questions on the premise that the planets revolve around the sun. In cosmology the Newtonian paradigm was displaced by the Einsteinian, in biology the biblical paradigm by the Darwinian.

Paradigms change, says Kuhn, when the puzzles encountered by scientists become more and more difficult to answer within the existing set of ground rules. Then, usually in a short space of time, a new view of things comes to the fore, explaining the puzzles of the earlier paradigm and reorienting the questions for scientists who will work within the new rules.

PRECLASSICAL AND CLASSICAL ECONOMICS

Kuhn's short, provocative book is worth reading by anyone interested in science or social science. The question it raises for us is whether economics also has paradigms. The answer seems to be both yes and no.

First the yes answer. We can easily separate the history of economic thought into paradigm-like divisions that resemble the bounded inquiries of science. One of the first such paradigms was the economics of the medieval schoolmen, who argued and worried about the moral problems raised by the emerging market process. For example, one of their main concerns was whether lending money at interest (usury) was in fact a sin (remember, in the early Middle Ages it had been considered a *mortal* sin); and they endlessly discussed the criteria for the "just" prices at which commodities should sell.

That view of the economic world was displaced by the Classical economists, whose most brilliant achievements were expressed in the works of Adam Smith and David Ricardo (1772–1823). The Classical economists had no interest whatever in "just" prices or in the sinfulness of usury. For them the great question was *how to understand, not evaluate, economic processes, in particular the accumulation and distribution of national wealth.* Smith, as we have seen, wrote an extraordinary exposition of how the members of society, although engaged in a search for their individual betterment, were nonetheless guided by an Invisible Hand (the market) to expand the wealth of nations. Ricardo wrote with equal force about the course of national economic growth, arguing that a growing population, pressing against limited fertile acreage, would drive up crop prices and divert the wealth of the country into the hands of the landlords.

MARGINALIST ECONOMICS

The Classical paradigm concerned large issues of national growth and dealt boldly with the fate of social classes. The Marxian paradigm, in turn, grew out of the Classical, differing from it in its much more critical approach to society and to thinking about society. Then, around the 1870s, a new angle of vision abruptly displaced the older one. The new view had numerous European originators, preeminent among them W. Stanley Jevons and Leon Walras. As a group they are referred to as the Marginalists, for *they turned the focus of economic inquiry away from growth and class conflict into a study of the interactions of individuals.*

The new paradigm explained many things that the older one did not, above all the finer workings of the price system. But just as the Classical or Marxian paradigms had dropped all interest in the just prices of the medievalists, so the Marginalists paid little attention to the questions of growth and class fortune that had so preoccupied the Classicists and Marxists.

KEYNESIAN ECONOMICS

Inherent in the Marginalist view of the world, with its extreme emphasis on interacting individuals rather than on classes, was a micro approach to economic problems. The next radical shift in view came from the work of John Maynard Keynes, whose perception of the economic system brought into focus a macro perspective on *total* income, *total* employment, *total* output. The most striking result of Keynes's shift from a micro to a macro perspective was his discovery that an economy that worked well at the micro level did not necessarily work well at the macro level. From the perspective of the Marginalists, such an economic state of affairs could hardly be envisioned.

PARADIGMS OR NOT?

Hence we can certainly discern sharp changes in the views and visions of economics. The very definition of the economic problem itself alters as we go from the medieval schoolmen to the Keynesians.

Why, then, should we not call this a series of paradigmatic shifts, similar to those in science? *The main reason is that the new economic paradigms do not explain the questions of the older views they displace. Unlike the new paradigms of natural science, which embrace the problems of their predecessors, the shifts in economics are characterized by the fact that they ignore or dismiss the very questions that disturbed their predecessors.* Classical economists, as we have said, forgot about economic justice; Marginalist economists, about growth or classes; Keynesian economists, about the inner working of the market.

Hence the shifts in economics are not quite like those in science, although the concept of a change of perspectives, bringing new problems into view, is as applicable to one as to the other. We can relate these shifts in perspective to the changing backdrop of social organization. Each paradigm of economic thought reflects to some degree the historical characteristics and problems of its time. This reflection of social issues and problems in economic thought differs, too, from the nature of scientific paradigms. Change in social structures generally plays a small role in causing one scientific perspective to replace another.

What paradigm rules economics today? A mixture of Marginalist and Keynesian thought lies behind most contemporary micro- and macroeconomics. A Marxian view underlies much of the radical critique of our time. Perhaps it is fair to say that no paradigm is firmly ensconced today. We live in a period in which much of the conventional wisdom of the past has been tried and found wanting. Economics is in a state of self-scrutiny, dissatisfied with its established paradigms, not yet ready to formulate a new one. Indeed, perhaps the search for such a new paradigm, a perspective that will highlight new elements of reality and suggest new modes of analysis, is the most pressing economic task of our time.

Chapter 4
A BIRD'S EYE VIEW OF THE ECONOMY

A LOOK AHEAD

Before we begin our study of economics as a subject, we ought to know something about the economy. In this chapter we take a high altitude pass over the terrain.

Things to watch for are:

(1) the general dimensions of the two worlds of business—big business and small business;

(2) the way in which income is divided up among households; and

(3) the size of the various government sectors. Note the plural—there is more than one meaning to "the government."

We can't begin to study economics without knowing something about the economy. But what is "the economy"? When we turn to the economics section of *Time* or *Newsweek* or pick up a business magazine, a jumble of things meets the eye: stock market ups and downs, reports on company fortunes and mishaps, accounts of incomprehensible "fluctuations in the exchange market," columns by business pundits, stories about unemployment or inflation.

How much of this is relevant? How are we to make our way through this barrage of reporting to something that we can identify as the economy?

BUSINESS

Of course we know where to start. Business enterprise is the very heart of an economic system of private property and market relationships. Let us begin, then, with a look at the world in business.

The first thing we notice is the enormous number of business enterprises—about 14 million in all. If we divide them into proprietorships (businesses owned by a single person), partnerships, and corporations, the world of business is classified in Table 4.1.

SMALL BUSINESS

Just looking at Table 4.1 makes one conclusion immediately clear: *There are at least two worlds of business.* One of them is the world of small business. It embraces nearly all proprietorships and partnerships as well as a very large percentage of corporations. Here are the vast bulk of the firms we find in the yellow pages of the phone book, the great preponderance of the country's farms, myriad mom-and-pop stores, restaurants, motels, movie houses, dry cleaners, druggists, retailers—in short, perhaps 95 percent of all the business firms in the nation.

Small business is the part of the business world with which we are all most familiar. We understand how a hardware store operates, whereas we have only vague ideas about how General Motors operates. But the world of small business warrants our attention for two other reasons.

First, small business is the employer of a substantial fraction—about a third—of the nation's labor force. Second, the world of small business is the source of much "middle-class" opinion. Of the 14 million small businesses in the country, three-quarters have sales (not profits) of less than $50,000 a year. These are tiny enterprises, but they certainly give a small business point of view to at least 10 million households—one out of every seven households.

	Total number of firms (000s omitted)	*Total sales* (billions)	*Average sales per firm*
Proprietorships	10,882	$ 339	$ 31,152
Partnerships	1,073	146	136,067
Corporations	2,024	3,199	1,580,533

TABLE 4.1 DIMENSIONS OF BUSINESS, 1975

Note that corporations are overwhelmingly the most important, but by no means the most numerous, form of business organization.

We should know something about what life is like in this world, and indeed, a considerable amount of economics is concerned with the problems of operating a small business. Later, in Chapters 25 and 26, when we reach microeconomics, we will study how small business fits into the economic picture.

BIG BUSINESS

We have already glimpsed another business world, mainly to be found in the corporate enterprises of the nation. Compare the average size of the sales of corporations (Table 4.1) with those of proprietorships and partnerships. But even these figures hide the extraordinary difference between very big business and small business. Within the world of corporations, for example, 90 percent do less than $1 million worth of business a year. But the 10 percent that do more than $1 million worth of sales a year take in 88 percent of the receipts of all corporations.

Thus, counterposed to a world of very numerous small businesses, there is the world of much less numerous big businesses. How large a world is it? Suppose we count as a big business any corporation with assets worth more than $250 million. There are roughly 3,000 such businesses in America. Half of them are in finance, mainly insurance and banking. A quarter are in manufacturing. The rest are to be found in transportation, utilities, communication, trade. Just to get an idea of scale, the largest enterprise in the nation is A.T.&T., with assets of $114 billion and sales of $45 billion in 1979. The largest *industrial* firm was Exxon, with assets of nearly $50 billion and sales of $85 billion. These two firms together probably commanded as much wealth (assets) as all the ten million proprietorships of the nation.

THE INDUSTRIAL SECTOR

Big business is to be found in all sectors; but its special place is the industrial sector, in which manufacturing plays the predominant role.

TABLE 4.2 INDUSTRIAL SECTOR, 1978

	$ billion
Total sales of all 468,000 industrial firms	$1,497
Total sales of the 500 biggest industrial corporations	1,219

The 500 biggest firms—about 0.1% of all industrial firms—account for 80% of all sales.

The figures in Table 4.2 show once again the twofold division of the business world. If we subtract the 500 biggest industrial corporations and their sales from the total of all manufacturing firms and their sales, we see that 467,500 industrial firms sold $278 billion worth of output—about a fifth of the total. The top 500 firms—one-tenth of one percent of the total number—accounted for almost 80 percent of all sales. *Indeed, if we take only the biggest 100 firms, we find that they are the source of almost half the sales of the entire industrial sector.*

SECTORS

Economists are always talking about sectors. Sometimes, as is frequently the case in this book, they mean a part of the economy in which motivations are similar. For example, we talk of the business sector, the household sector, the government sector.

Sometimes, however, economists mean a "functional" division of the economy's activities. Then they typically speak of three sectors: (1) an agricultural sector that grows and harvests natural products, (2) an industrial sector that extracts and alters and assembles raw materials, and (3) a service sector that performs a miscellany of tasks: providing power and transportation, performing the tasks of storage and selling, and furnishing the thousand ministrations of personal service—legal services, maids' services, doctors' services, various governmental services.

There are many problems associated with this functional grouping. But because it is commonly used, we should have a general idea of the way in which employment and output is distributed among the three main functional sectors:

THREE MAIN SECTORS, 1979

	Employment	*GNP*
Agriculture	3%	3%
Goods	28	31
Services	69	66

Notice that roughly two-thirds of all employment and output takes place in the service sector. This does *not* mean that industry and agriculture are therefore less vital. Try to imagine the consequences of a six-months' shutdown in our smallest sector, farming!

BIG EMPLOYERS

Big business obviously dominates many areas of the marketplace. Is big business also a big employer? That varies from one field to another. In manufacturing enterprises, the top 500 firms employ about 75 percent of all persons in manufacturing. In transportation and public utilities, about half the work force is hired by a giant utility or airline or railway (most of the rest work for small trucking firms). In finance, insurance, and real estate, the top 150 companies employ about 30 percent of the persons working in that area. In retail trade, the top 50 companies hire about 20 percent of the total.

In all, about a third of the nation's work force is employed by a firm that we would call a "big business."* To put it differently, 800 leading firms in manufacturing, transportation, utilities, finance, and retailing employ roughly as many persons as the remaining 13 million proprietorships, partnerships and smaller corporations.

HOUSEHOLDS

Business is not the only institutional feature we need to inspect in this introduction to the economy. How could business operate without a work force? Let us look at this work force as a collection of "households" as shown in Table 4.3.

*There is no official designation of a "big" business. We have used the *Fortune* magazine list of the top 500 industrial firms plus their list of the top 50 firms in banking, insurance, finance, transportation, utilities, and retailing.

TABLE 4.3 HOUSEHOLD CHARACTERISTICS, 1979

	Millions
Total population	220
Number of households	77
Families	55
Non-family households	22
Individuals in work force	105

There are more workers than households.

THE WORK FORCE

Our table shows us an interesting fact about the household "sector." There are more individual workers than there are households. This means that a typical household must have more than one member in the labor market.

But what is a typical household? The answer is not easy to give because there are many kinds of households: young or elderly households with only one individual in them; young married households without children; families with young children; families with offspring who are no longer young.

Economists look at the relation between households and work in terms of a **participation rate,** showing the percentage of various groups who are working or looking for work. In the formal language of the statistician, they are "in the labor market." Table 4.4 shows how considerable is the variation of these rates.

TABLE 4.4 PARTICIPATION RATES, 1979

	Percent of group in labor market
Males, 20 years and older	80
Females, 20 years and older	50
Both sexes, 16–19	64
Males, 65 and older	20
Females, 65 and older	8

Participation rates vary greatly.

OCCUPATIONS

The table shows us some unexpected things about our work force. It is still made up mainly of men. Thus sex is still a decisive element in determining the characteristics of the labor force, although we will see in our next chapter that this has changed significantly and will probably change still further in the years to come. Age is also a powerful determinant of participation.

What sort of work does our labor force perform? Table 4.5 tells us.

TABLE 4.5 OCCUPATIONAL DISTRIBUTION OF THE LABOR FORCE, 1979

		Percent	
Professional	white collar	15	50
Managerial		11	
Sales		6	
Clerical		18	
Craftsmen	blue collar	13	
Operatives		15	36
Nonfarm laborers		5	
Farm workers		3	
Service workers	both	14	

About half the work force is white collar.

A PARADE OF BUSINESS FIRMS

We shall have a good deal to investigate in later chapters about the world of big business. But it might be useful to end this initial survey with a dramatization of the problem. Suppose that we lined up our roughly 14 million businesses in order of size, starting with the smallest, along an imaginary road from San Francisco to New York. There will be 4,000 businesses to the mile, or a little less than one per foot. Suppose further that we planted a flag for each business. The height of the flagpole represents the volume of sales: each $10,000 in sales is shown by one foot of pole.

The line of flagpoles is a very interesting sight. From San Francisco to about Reno, Nevada, it is almost unnoticeable, a row of poles about a foot high. From Reno eastward the poles increase in height until, near Columbus, Ohio—about four-fifths of the way across the nation—flags fly about 10 feet in the air, symbolizing $100,000 in sales. Looking backward from Columbus, we can see that 10 million out of 12 million firms have sales of less than that amount.

But as we approach the eastern terminus, the poles suddenly begin to mount.. There are about 300,000 firms in the country with sales over $500,000. These corporations occupy the last 75 miles of the 3,000-mile road. There are 200,000 firms with sales of over $1 million. They occupy the last 50 miles of the road, with poles at least 100 feet high. Then there are 1,000 firms with sales of $50,000,000 or more. They take up the last quartermile before the city limits, flags flying at skyscraper heights, 500 feet up.

But this is still not the climax. At the very gates of New York, on the last 100 feet of the last mile, we find the 100 largest industrial firms. They have sales of at least $1.5 billion, so that their flags are already miles high, in the clouds. Along the last 10 feet of the road, there are the ten largest companies. Their sales are roughly $10 billion and up: their flags fly 120 miles in the air, literally in the stratosphere.

Later we will be looking more carefully into problems of occupations. Here we might note in passing that "white-collar" jobs—professional, managerial, sales, and clerical—include about half the working force. Here is another strong root of the American middle-class mentality.

DISTRIBUTION OF INCOME

Households interest us not only because they are the source of our labor power, but also because they are the focus of our income and our wealth. Much of the buying that powers the economic machine is cycled through the household, where purchasing power is collected as wages, salaries, dividends, interest, and rents, to be pumped out again as a flow of spending for consumers' goods. Consumer buying, as we will see later, is a strong force in the momentum of our economy, although we should emphasize right away that household buying is not the only force. Business and government are also buyers in their own right and strong influences in maintaining the flow of purchasing power.

If we focus on households at this stage of our inquiry, it is because their function as buyers leads us naturally to inquire into the distribution of purchasing power among families. This is a subject about which many people are very sensitive. A persistent stress on *political* equality leads us to ignore or play down the facts of economic inequality. We even lack adequate statistics about wealth,

UNIONS

How many members of the labor force offer their services through labor unions? In 1978 there were 22 million. That was 23 percent of the labor force. The figures do not convey the power of labor unions, because they do not point out the strength of unions in the industrial sector. The table below shows more accurately how labor unions fit into the overall work picture.

LABOR UNIONS IN THE MAIN SECTORS, 1978

Sector	*Employment (millions)*	*Unionized*
Agriculture	3	1%
Industry (mfg. and mining)	27	45
Services and other	48	13
Government	16	18

Like corporations, unions show great disparity of size and strength. In 1978 there were some 53,000 local unions. Many of these small unions had memberships of 50 persons or fewer and were confined to a single enterprise. At the other end of the scale we find 210 large "national" unions, including such giants as the Teamsters (19 million members in 1978) or the United Auto Workers (1.4 million members in the same year). In fact, the 10 biggest unions in the country account for almost 50 percent of all union membership. Thus unions, like corporations, divide into a world of small and large operations, although the contrast in the unions is not quite so dramatic as in the corporations.

largely because of an unwillingness to pay official recognition to this aspect of our economic realities.

There are many ways of describing income distribution. We will use a method that will divide the country into five equal layers, like a great cake. The layers will help us give dollars-and-cents definitions of what we usually have in mind when we speak of the poor, the working class, the middle class, and so on. As we will see, the amounts are not at all what most of us imagine.

THE POOR

We begin with the bottom layer, the poor. By our definition, this will include all the households in the bottom 20 percent of the nation. From data gathered by the Census Bureau, we know that the highest income of a family in this bottom slice of the five-layered cake was $8,700 in 1978. By coincidence, this corresponds almost exactly to the income computed by the Bureau of Labor Statistics as representing a level of "near-poverty" for a family of four persons.

The box headed "Poverty" shows some of the characteristics of poor families, but there are two additional facts about poverty that we should note.

First, not all families who are counted as poor in any given census remain poor in the next census. About one-seventh of all poor households are young people, just starting their careers. Some of these low-income beginners will escape from poverty. In addition, about a third of the members of the poverty class are older people. Many of these were not poor in an earlier, more productive stage of their economic lives. At the same time, this also means that some families that are not poor when a census is taken will fall into poverty at a later stage of their lives. The moral of this is that poverty is not entirely static. At any moment, some families are escaping from poverty, some entering it. What counts, of course, is whether the net movement is in or out.

A second characteristic also deserves to be noted. Sixty percent of the families below the poverty line have at least one wage earner in the labor force. Thus their poverty reflects inadequate earnings. A considerable amount of poverty, in other words, reflects the fact that some jobs do not pay enough to lift a jobholder above the low-income level. In some regions, certain jobs are so low-paying that even two jobholders in a family (especially if one works only seasonally) will not suffice to bring the family out of poverty. This is often the case, for example, with migrant farm workers, or with immigrants who must seek employment in the least desirable jobs.

THE WORKING CLASS

We usually define the working class in terms of certain occupations. We call a factory operative—but not a sales clerk—working class, even though the factory employee may make more than a sales clerk.

For our purposes, however, we will just take the next two layers of the income cake and call them working class. This will include the 40 percent of the population that is above the poor. We choose this method to find out how large an income a family can make and still remain in the working class, as we have defined it. The answer is just under $21,000. To put it differently, 40 percent of the families in the country earn more than $8,700 but less than $21,000 a year.

THE RICH AND THE UPPER CLASS

With the bottom three-fifths of the nation tagged—one-fifth poor, two-fifths working class—we are ready to look into the income levels of upper echelons.

First the rich. Where do riches begin? A realistic answer is probably around $100,000 a year, the magic six-figure income that goes with major corporate responsibility. There are probably fewer than 500,000 such rich families in America. They are literally the icing on the cake.

POVERTY

What characteristics distinguish poor families? Old age is one: almost a third of the low-income group consists of retirees. Curiously, youth is also characteristic. A household (married or single) headed by someone under age 25 is much more likely to be a low-income family than one headed by an older person. Color counts. About 9 percent of the white population is poor; about one third of the black population. Sex enters the picture. Households headed by a female are twice as likely to be poor as one headed by a male. Schooling is an attribute. Almost half of all poor families have only grade school educations. Occupation is another: one fourth of all the nation's farmers are poor.

Many of the characteristics overlap: poor families are often old and black and poorly educated. No one characteristic is decisive in "making" a family poor. The poor are not poor just because they have no education, but often have no education because they have come from poor households themselves.

But under the truly rich is a considerably larger group that we will call the upper class. This is the top 5 percent of the nation, its doctors, airline pilots, managers, lawyers—even some economists. Some 2.9 million families are in this top 5 percent.

How much income does it take to get there? In 1978 a family made it into the upper class with an income of $45,000. These numbers have a certain shock value. It takes more money to be rich, but less to be upper class, than we ordinarily think.

THE MIDDLE CLASS

This leaves us with the middle class—the class to which we all think we belong. By our method of cutting the cake, the middle class includes 35 percent of the nation—everyone above the $21,000 top working-class income and below the $45,000 upper-class income. In 1978 an average white married couple, both working, earned about $21,000—just enough to enter middle class economic territory. No wonder that a middle-class feeling pervades American society, regardless of the occupation or social milieu from which families come.*

WEALTH

It is obvious that there are great extremes of income distribution in the United States. Paul Samuelson, perhaps the nation's most famous economist, has made the observation that if we built an income pyramid out of children's blocks, with each layer representing $1,000 of income, the peak would be far higher than the Eiffel Tower; but most of us would be within a yard of the ground.

Even more striking than the inequality of income, however, is the inequality of wealth.

TABLE 4.6 DISTRIBUTION OF WEALTH 1969 (latest data)

Percent of total population		*Percent of total wealth*
Lowest	25.0	0.0
Next	32.0	6.6
Next	24.0	17.2
Next	18.5	50.4
Top	0.5	25.8

Wealth is distributed more unevenly than income.

As Table 4.6 shows, the bottom quarter of American households—roughly the group we have called the poor—*had no wealth at all.* The group that we have designated the working class had little more, by way of wealth, than the net value of its cars and houses and perhaps a small savings account.†

*Maybe you wonder how an "average white married couple" could enter an income group that we have defined as being not average. The answer is that not every household in our national layer cake is white or married, with both husband and wife working. You may also be curious to know if these figures apply to 1980 (for which statistics were not yet available as we wrote this chapter). You can adjust for 1979 by raising all the numbers 10 percent, and for 1980 by raising 1979 figures by another 10 percent. That's not exactly correct, but it's close enough. It brings the boundaries of the "Middle Class" to $25,410 and $54,450 for 1980.

†Remember that you own only that part of a house or car that you have paid for. Someone else owns the rest.

A PARADE OF INCOMES

Suppose that like our parade of flags across the nation representing the sales of business firms, we lined up the population in order of its income. Assume the height of the middle family to be 6 feet, representing a median income of $18,000 in 1978. This will be our height, as observers. What would our parade look like?*

It would begin with a few families *below* the ground, for there are some households with negative incomes; that is, they report losses for the year. Mainly these are families with business losses, and their negative incomes are not matched by general poverty. Following close on their heels comes a long line of grotesque dwarfs who comprise about one-fifth of all families, people less than 2 feet tall. Some are shorter than 1 foot.

Only after the parade is half over do we reach people whose faces are at our level. Then come the giants. When we reach the last 5 percent of the parade —incomes around $45,000—people are 18 feet tall. At the end of the parade, people tower 600 to 6,000 feet into the air—100 to 1,000 times taller than the middle height. What is the largest income in the country? We do not know: Probably our one or two billionaires have incomes of over $100 million.

*See the brilliant description of an "income parade" by Jan Pen, *Income Distribution,* trans. Trevor S. Preston (New York: Praeger, 1971), pp. 48–59.

MIDDLE-CLASS WEALTH

Recent figures tell us something additional about the distribution of wealth. In 1972 there were just under 13 million households with a net worth of $60,000 or more. This is approximately as many households as we would find in the top fifth of the nation—all the middle class plus the upper class and the rich. Of those 13 million wealth holders, 5 million had estates of less than $100,000—say the value of a house and a modest insurance policy—and another 5 million had estates worth between $100,000 and $200,000, a sum that probably represents savings accounts, life insurance, some real estate, and perhaps a few stocks and bonds. This is certainly affluence, although not on a princely scale.

Next we find approximately 2 million families with estates ranging from $200,000 to $500,000. This number dovetails more or less with the number of families in the top 5 percent. This is certainly a class of the well-to-do. But compared with what is to follow, it is not yet the class of the rich. In 1972 there were an estimated 425,000 families with assets worth half a million to a million, and just under 225,000 households with estates of $1 million or more. These last households are what we call millionaires.

MILLIONAIRES

How much wealth do millionaires own in all? We are not sure. Estimates for the 1960s indicated that millionaire families owned half to three-quarters of the value of all stocks and bonds and private real estate. But these figures may have been changed by inflation. According to a survey made by the U.S. Trust Company in 1979, the number of families owning $1 million or more in assets has grown to 520,000, more than double the figure for 1972. On the other hand, there is ample evidence that large wealth holding families have been severely hit by inflation because stocks and bonds, the main repositories of large wealth, have both failed to keep abreast of rising prices. In real terms a 1972 millionaire with an average portfolio would have lost about half his wealth by 1980!

We ought to know more than we do about the ownership of wealth in the most affluent households because there is no doubt that capital is heavily concentrated. The top 10 percent of all households owns 90 percent of all corporate stock.* The middle and working classes enjoy property incomes in the form of interest on their savings accounts, or as part of their pension plans, but the bulk of the dividends and interest paid to households goes to the families at the top. This is an important area where our knowledge about the economy is inadequate.

GOVERNMENT

We have almost completed our first overview of the economy, but there remains one last institution with which we must gain a first acquaintance: the government.

How shall we size up such a vast and complex institution? Let us begin by thinking about production. We do not ordinarily think of the government as a producer of goods and services, for under capitalism most production is carried out by private business firms. Yet a substantial fraction of our total output is directly produced by government employees, and an even larger fraction of our incomes is received from government agencies, as Table 4.7 shows.

TABLE 4.7 SIZE OF GOVERNMENT SECTOR, 1979

	Percent of total
Output produced by government	10
Personal incomes paid by government	26
Employment by government	16
Output purchased by government	20

Government buys about one-fifth of output

GOVERNMENT AS BUYER AND PRODUCER

The table shows us that the government as a whole employs about one-fifth of our work force and consumes about one-fifth of our output. A large portion of the output purchased by government is actually made by private business and then ultimately bought by government. Armaments are a good example. Built in private factories for the most part, arms count as public output only because government is the final buyer of the missile or plane.

The amount of output *directly* produced by government is much less than that bought by it. But it is a very important *kind* of output as Table 4.8 shows.

Table 4.8 makes two points that we would be wise to remember. The first is that **the word "government" in economics does not mean just the federal government.** As we will see, the federal government plays a crucial role when it comes to efforts to change the course of economic events, but from the point of view of government as a major economic institution—an employer of labor and a source of direct production—state and local governments surpass the federal!

**Federal Reserve Bulletin,* March 1964, p. 265.

	Federal	State	Local
	(number of employees) in thousands		
National defense	3,561	—	—
Postal service	666	—	—
Education	20	1,260	4,367
Highways	5	291	315
Health	217	570	549
Police	34	63	484
Fire protection	—	—	276
Sanitation	—	—	195
Resources and recreation	228	159	209
Financial administration	101	98	153
Other	109	535	1,325
Total	2,795	2,937	7,872

TABLE 4.8 KINDS OF DIRECT PUBLIC OUTPUT, AS SHOWN BY PUBLIC EMPLOYMENT 1972

Most public employees work for states and localities, not for the federal government

Second, **the variety of public outputs reminds us that government is not just a dead weight on the economy, as so many tend to think.** Anyone who has ever gone to a public school, been treated in a public hospital, traveled on a public road, or flown in a plane guided by a public beacon system has been the recipient of government production and knows how vital public output can be. Even those who emphasize the maddening bureaucracy and inefficiency that can come from government activity (although government has no monopoly on either) should reflect that the system of private enterprise itself depends on the invisible output of law enforcement on which this economy, like all economies, rests.

KEY CONCEPTS

LOOKING BACK

The purpose of this chapter is not to load you with facts and figures, but to give you a sense of economic geography—a feeling for the terrain we call the Economy. The central ideas that we ought to have clearly in mind are these:

Business institutions: corporations partnerships proprietorships

1. Business is the most distinctive and important institution in a capitalist system. There are a very large number of private business organizations, but by far the most important of them are corporations, not partnerships or proprietorships. If you are not sure of the difference, read the important "Extra Word" following this.

Big business accounts for the preponderance of sales; small business is a substantial source of employment

2. In the world of corporations there are clearly visible two subworlds of business—big business and little business. There is no official dividing line between the two. But if we take the top five hundred corporations, we find that we account for 80 percent of all industrial sales, 75 percent of all industrial employment, and about 30 percent of all employment. Small business is important because it is a big employer of nonindustrial workers—retail or service workers—and because it is an important source of middle class political sentiment.

Households are the source of labor

3. Households are the source of the nation's labor force. Most households supply more than one worker, but participation rates vary widely among age and sex groups.

Income distribution: about one-fifth poor; about one-third middle class; about 5 percent affluent

4. Household income distribution shows us that roughly one-fifth of all families and individuals can be classified as poor; about two-fifths as working class; about one-third as middle class, and about five percent as upper class. These are arbitrary dividing lines that serve only to give us some idea as to what family incomes are like in the different layers of the national income cake. We should note that the distribution of wealth is much more lopsided than the distribution of income.

The government sector varies in size, depending on what you measure

Federal government is a major spender, but state and local government is a major employer

5. Government is a very important but confusing institution to study. The importance of government in the economy varies, depending on whether we measure its contribution to production (about 10 percent) or to incomes (about 26 percent). Speaking very roughly, government accounts for about 20 percent of all employment, but we should make a point of learning that most employment is at the state and local level. The federal government is big, not so much as an employer, but as a source of national spending. We will learn a lot more about this when we come to macroeconomics.

ECONOMIC VOCABULARY

Sector 49 **Participation rates** 50 **Public output** 57

QUESTIONS

1. How would you explain the fact that big business has made so much headway in industrial production, but not in farming or retailing?
2. Do the facts of income and wealth distribution surprise you? Please you? Shock you? With what arguments would you defend the existing distribution: Fairness and equity? Efficiency? Natural differences among individuals?
3. When we say that the government is "too big" in this country, do we mean as a producer, employer, or payer of incomes? Is it possible to argue that the government is too *small* a producer, employer, or income payer? Suppose that you wanted to increase our defense budget. Would you not be arguing just that?

AN EXTRA WORD ABOUT *BUSINESS ORGANIZATION*

Business is a central institution in our economic system, and all of us ought to know something about how business, especially the corporation, is legally organized. Although corporations are the dominant form of business property, too few people are well informed about them. Here is a brief introduction to the main forms of business organization.

PROPRIETORSHIPS

A proprietorship is the simplest kind of business organization. Usually it can be set up without any legal fuss at all, simply by opening a place of business. Sometimes one has to register or get a license, for instance, to open a liquor store or to set up practice as a physician or lawyer. But proprietorships are the easiest to understand of all forms of business.

They are also, as we have seen, the most widespread form (see Table 4.1). Why are not all businesses proprietorships? The answer lies in certain problems that proprietorships have.

1. *A proprietorship has difficulty growing because its ability to borrow money is limited to the amount of credit that its owner-proprietor can raise.* Only a very rich man can borrow very much.

2. A proprietor is personally liable for all losses that his business may incur (he also gets all its profits). A rich man is not likely to open a proprietary business, because if an unexpected loss is incurred—if his business is sued by an irate customer and it loses the case—*the proprietor must pay from his own funds any obligations that the business cannot pay from its funds.* In fact, there is really no division between the property of the owner and that of the business.

3. *When a proprietor dies, the business comes to an end.* All debts must be paid, and a new business established to take over the old. This is hard on the spouse of the proprietor, the employees, and the creditors.

PARTNERSHIPS

Partnerships remedy many of these difficulties. Basically, a partnership is a combination of proprietors who have agreed, usually by legal formalities, to share a certain proportion of the profits and the losses of their business. The fact that there are now several people associated in the business obviously makes it easier to raise additional capital. Very large businesses have been partnerships, at least until recent days.

Nonetheless, there are still problems for partnerships.

1. *Partners are together responsible for all the losses or debts of the business.* Jointly they have, like proprietors, "unlimited" liability, although some partners may have limited liability.

2. *The death of each partner requires the business to be legally reconstituted.* When a partner of a firm dies, the firm usually has to undergo a reorganization. This is expensive and bothersome and often creates frictions.

CORPORATIONS

The corporation, as we have seen, is the most powerful although not the most prevalent form of business organization. Let us be sure that we understand exactly what a corporation is.

1. *A corporation is a legal entity created by the state.* Unlike a proprietorship or a partnership, all corporations must apply to their states for a charter allowing them to carry on business. The charter specifies in general terms the kinds of business they will carry on and the general financial structures they will have. Charters cost money, which is one reason that all proprietorships are not corporations. Another reason is that corporations pay income taxes on their income, before it goes to stockholders.

2. *Once a corporation is chartered, it exists as a* "person"; that is, the cor-

poration itself—not the individuals who own it or work for it—can bring suit, be sued, or own property. This has an immediate advantage. It is that the liability of an owner of a corporation is limited to the money he has put into the corporation. If the corporation is sued for more funds than the business possesses, the corporation will declare bankruptcy, and there is no recourse to the private funds of the persons who own it.

3. *Because the corporation is a "person" it does not go out of business when its owners die.* The corporation is "immortal." It goes on until it fails as a business organization or voluntarily goes out of business, or until its charter is revoked by the state.

CORPORATE ORGANIZATION

Clearly, the corporation has substantial advantages over proprietorships and partnerships. But how does it run? Who owns it?

A corporation is owned by the individuals who buy shares in it. Suppose that a corporation is granted a charter to carry on a business in retail trade. The charter also specifies how many shares of stock this business enterprise is allowed to issue. For example, a corporation may be formed with the right to issue 100,000 shares. If these shares are sold to individuals at a price of $10 each, the original shareholders (also called stockholders) will have put $1 million into the corporation. In return each will receive stock certificates indicating how many shares that person has bought.

These stock certificates are somewhat like a partnership agreement, although there are noteworthy differences. If you buy 1,000 shares in our imaginary corporation, you will own one percent of the corporation. You will have the right to receive one percent of all income that it pays out as dividends on its stock. You will also be entitled to cast 1,000 votes—one vote per share—at the meetings of shareholders that all corporations must hold. In this way, a shareholder is very much like a junior partner who was given a one percent interest in a business.

ADVANTAGES OF SHARE OWNERSHIP

But here are the critical differences between corporations and partnerships.

1. *As we have already said, a stockholder is not personally liable for any debts that the corporation cannot pay.* If the company goes bankrupt, the shareholder will lose his investment of $10,000 (1,000 shares @ $10) but cannot be sued for any further money. *Liability is thereby limited to the amount the shareholder has invested.*

2. Unlike partnership shares, which are usually very difficult to sell, corporation shares are generally easy to sell if one owns the stock of a company that is listed (bought and sold) on one of the nation's several stock markets. (The shares of a very small corporation are not, of course, so easy to sell, although they are less difficult to dispose of than a partnership.) Moreover, a stockholder may sell shares to anyone, at any price. If our imaginary corporation prospers, its shares may sell for $20 each. A stockholder is perfectly free to sell his or her shares at that price. As we have just mentioned, marketplaces for stocks and bonds have developed along with the corporation, to facilitate such sales of stock. The most important of these markets, the New York Stock Exchange, was organized in 1817. Today over 20 billion shares a year are bought and sold on the stock exchange. Thus, with the corporation comes the advantage of a much greater "liquidity" of personal wealth—that is, greater ease of turning assets into cash.

3. Shares of stock entitle the stockholder to the dividends that the directors of the corporation (see below) may decide to pay out for each share. But a shareholder is not entitled to any fixed amount of profit. If the corporation prospers, the directors may vote to pay a large dividend. But they are under no obligation to do so. They may wish to use the earnings of the corporation for other purposes, such as the purchase of new equipment or land. If the corporation suffers losses, ordinarily the directors will vote to pay no dividend or only a small one to be paid from past earnings. Thus, as an owner of ordinary common stock, the stockholder must take the risk of having his dividends rise or fall.

4. Corporations are also allowed to issue bonds, as well as stock. A bond is different from a share of stock in two ways. First, a bond has a *stated value* printed on its face, whereas a share of stock does not. A $1,000 bond issued by a corporation is a certificate for a debt of $1,000. The bondholder is not a sharer in the profits of the company but a creditor of the corporation—someone to whom the corporation is in debt for $1,000. In case of corporate bankruptcy, the claims of bondholders take precedence over those of shareowners.

Second, a bond also states on its face the *amount of income* it will pay to bondholders. A $1,000 bond may declare that it will pay $80 a year as interest. Unlike dividends, this interest payment will not rise if the corporation makes money, nor will it fall if it does not. Thus there is no element of profit-sharing in bonds, as there is in stocks.

There is a compensation for this, however. The risk of owning a bond is usually less than that of owning a stock. A bond is a legal obligation of the corporation, which *must* pay interest, and which *must* buy back the bond itself when a fixed term of years has expired and the bond becomes "due." If it fails to meet either of these obligations, the courts will declare the firm bankrupt, and all its assets will be turned over to the bondholders to satisfy their debts. If the firm's assets are not enough to repay the bondholders, they will suffer a degree of loss; but the shareholders will lose *all* of their equity, for a share of stock has no such obligations attached to it and never becomes due. No shareholder can sue a corporation if it fails to pay a dividend.

OWNERSHIP AND CONTROL

One last matter is also of significance in discussing the organization of the corporation. The new mode of structuring enterprise has made possible a development of great importance: the separation of ownership and control.

As we have seen, stockholders are the actual owners of a corporation, but it is obviously impossible for large numbers of stockholders to meet regularly and run a company. A.T.&T. has well over 1,000,000 stockholders. Where could they meet? How could they possibly decide what the company should do?

All corporations, small or large, therefore, are run by boards of directors (who may or may not own stock in the company), and who are elected by the stockholders. At regular intervals, all stockholders are asked to elect or reelect members of the board, each casting as many votes as the number of shares that he owns. In turn, the board of directors appoints the "management" —main officials of the corporation; for example, its president and vice-presidents. Management hires the rest of the employees. As the number of shareowners grows, it is not surprising that power drifts into the hands of the management. (The extent to which managers can operate independently of, or even contrary to, the interests of stockholders is one of the hotly debated questions in economics.)

STOCK EXCHANGES

We have mentioned stock exchanges as the organized markets in which shares are traded. An important thing to realize is that buying a share of stock does not put money into a corporation, unless the stock is newly issued by the company.

Most of the shares bought and sold on the stock exchanges are old shares, issued years ago. When you buy a share of General Motors, the money you pay does *not* go to General Motors. It goes to the individual who sold you the shares. If you own shares in a company that produces cigarettes, and you want to get out of this business because you disapprove of smoking, you sell your shares. *But doing so does not take any money out of the cigarette business.* It simply transfers your shares to another person who will pay you for your stock certificates.

Does it then make no difference to a cigarette company whether you buy its shares or not? Not quite. Corporations like to have their shares well regarded by the public, because from time to time they *do* issue new shares, and they want an eager market for these shares. So, too, if their shares are in general disfavor, they will sell for lower prices, and at a lower price a company is easier to "take over" than at a higher price.* Finally, managers usually own shares in their own companies. As the shares go up, they become richer. So companies are far from indifferent to the fate of their shares. Nonetheless, we should clearly understand that we do not put money into businesses when we buy their outstanding shares.

*A "take-over" is a concerted effort, usually by a small group of individuals who own a considerable amount of the company's stock, to round up enough proxies (votes) to oust an incumbent management and to install a management of its own. Take-overs are dramatic when they occur. They are not frequent, but they happen often enough so that corporations keep an eye out for "raiding" interests. If the price of their stock falls, it is often an invitation to be taken over, simply because it is cheaper to buy the votes (shares) when their price is depressed.

Chapter 5 THE TREND OF THINGS

A LOOK AHEAD

The last chapter was an aerial photo of the economy, giving us the lay of the land. Now we want to take a series of pictures over time to give us a sense of change in the economic landscape. This will fit into our first historic conception of capitalism, gained in Chapter 2, and will also give us a chance to test some of the theories about capitalism that we covered in Chapter 3.

In particular we are going to examine four major trends of modern times:

(1) the growth of production measured by GNP—gross national product;
(2) trends in income distribution;
(3) the drift toward big business; and
(4) the rapid rise in government.

Warning before you begin: Don't get bogged down in facts and figures. Keep your eye out for trends and for explanations of trends. The facts are there to illustrate these trends and to test explanations, not to be learned for themselves.

THE PROCESS OF GROWTH

Imagine that we have had a camera trained on the U.S. economy over the last 80 years or so. What would be the most striking changes to meet our eye?

There is no doubt about the first impression: It would be a sense of growth. Everything would be getting larger. Business firms would be growing in size. Labor unions would be bigger. There would be many more households, and each household would be richer. Government would be much larger. And underlying all of this, the extent of the market system itself—the great circular flow of inputs and outputs—would be steadily increasing in size.

Growth is not, of course, the only thing we would notice. Businesses are different as well as bigger when we compare 1980 and 1900: There are far more corporations now than in the old days, far more diversified businesses, fewer family firms. Households are different because more women work outside the home. Labor unions today are no longer mainly craft unions, limited to one occupation. Government is not only bigger but has a different philosophy.

TOTAL OUTPUT

Nonetheless, it is growth that first commands our attention. The camera vision of the economy gives us a picture that keeps widening. It *has* to widen to encompass the increase in the sheer mass of output. Hence the first institution

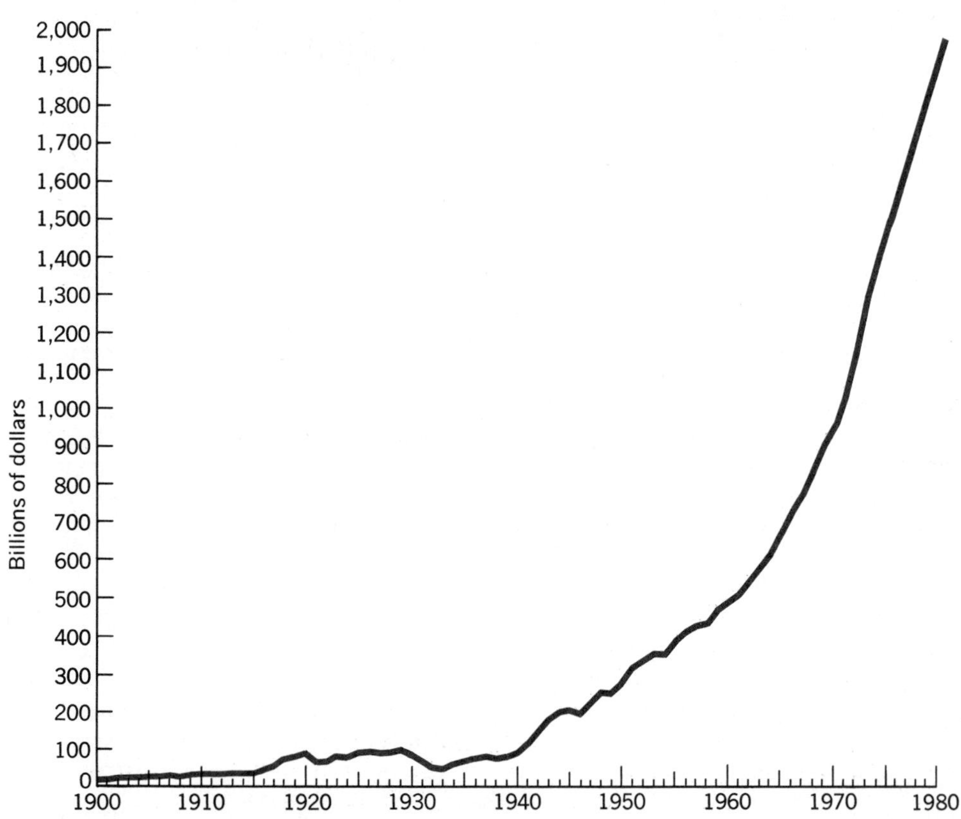

FIGURE 5.1 VALUE OF GNP 1900–1980

Gross National Product (GNP) has increased 100 fold in three quarters of a century, measured in the prices of each year's production.

VOLUME AND VALUE

You should be warned that there is no entirely satisfactory way of wringing price increases out of the hodgepodge of goods and services called GNP, because different items in this collection of goods rise or fall in price in different degrees. There is always a certain element of arbitrariness in correcting GNP for price changes. Different methods, each perfectly defensible, will yield somewhat different measures of "corrected" GNP.

Isn't there some way of getting around the problem of dollar values when we compare GNPs? One way is to measure actual physical volumes. When certain kinds of outputs, such as foodstuffs, bulk very large in GNP as they do in India or China, we sometimes measure growth just by adding up the tonnages of food production. The problem, of course, is that the composition of these tonnages may change—more wheat one year, more rice another—which gets us into another comparison problem. And then such a measure ignores entirely the outputs of nonagricultural goods. (We meet the same problem if we try to measure growth by tonnages of freight, metal production, etc.)

A more defensible way might be to consider GNP as a sum total of labor time, the embodiment of so many million hours of work. Even this does not get us around the measurement and comparison problem, for we use different kinds of labor as time goes on. Therefore, we have to make the difficult assumption that all kinds of labor, skilled and unskilled, trained and untrained, can be "reduced" to multiples of one "basic" kind. That basic labor, in turn, would have to boil down to some constant unit of "effort." But does the unit of "effort"—of human energy—remain constant over time?

In the end, the task of measuring an aggregate of different things can never be solved to our complete satisfaction. Any concept of GNP always has an element of unmeasureableness about it. Growth is a concept that we constantly use, but that remains tantalizingly beyond precise definition.

whose growth we must examine is that of the market system itself.

More specifically, we must trace the tremendous growth in our total output. The technical name for this flow of output is gross national product (GNP), a term we will use many times in the future and which we will later define more carefully. Here we only note that it is the dollar value of our annual flow of final output. Figure 5.1 gives us a graphic representation of this increase in yearly output.

CORRECTING FOR INFLATION

As we can see, the dollar value of all output from 1900 to 1980 has grown by a factor of about 100. But perhaps a cautionary thought will have already struck you. If we measure the growth of output by comparing the dollar value of production over time, what seems to be growth in actual economic activity may be no more than a rise in prices. If the economy in 1980 produced no more actual tons of grain than the economy in 1900, but if grain prices today were double those of 1900, our GNP figures would show growth where there was really nothing but inflation.

To arrive at a measure of real growth, we have to correct for changes in prices. To do so, we take one year as a *base* and use the prices of that year to evaluate output in all succeeding years.

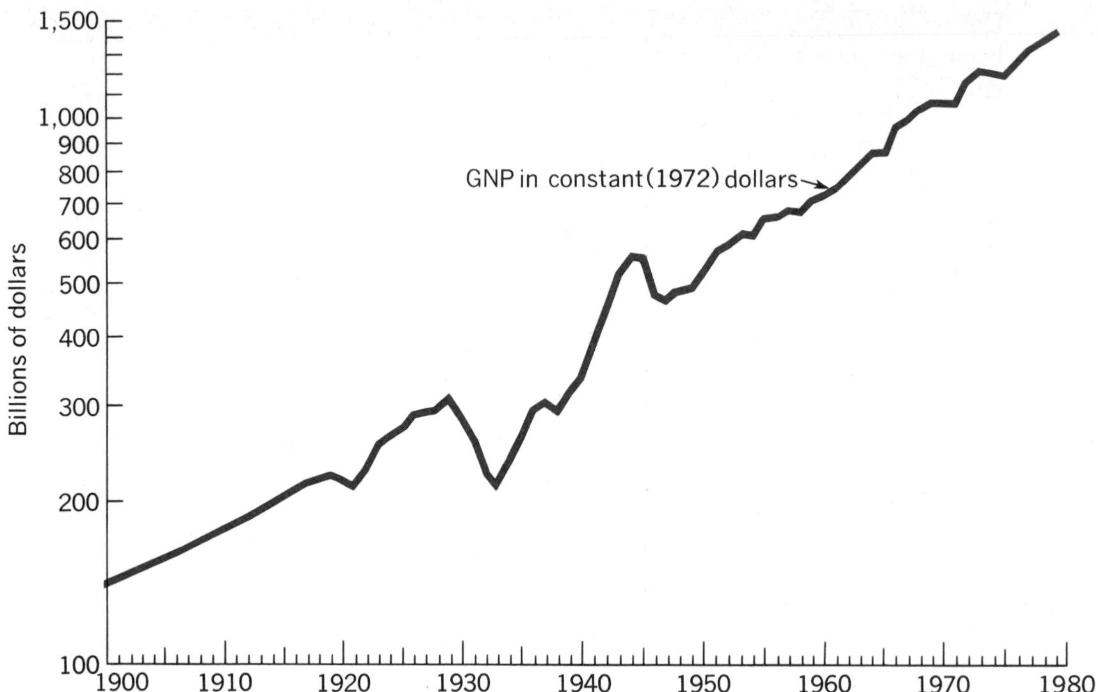

FIGURE 5.2 GNP IN CONSTANT (1972) DOLLARS

Measured in real terms, GNP has increased only 8 times, not 100 times. In this graph we use a semi log scale because it shows more clearly the *rate of growth* rather than the absolute dollar growth of GNP.

Here is an elementary example. Suppose that our grain economy produces 1 million tons in 1900 and 2 million tons in 1980, but wheat sells for $1 in 1900 and $2 in 1980. Our GNP in the current prices of 1900 and 1980 is $1 million for 1900 and $4 million 80 years later. But if we evaluate the GNP using only the 1900 prices (i.e., $1 per bushel), our GNP is reduced to $2 million in 1980. This constant dollar GNP is often referred to as the **real GNP**, while the current dollar GNP is called the **nominal GNP.** We can use the prices of any year as the base. The important thing is that all outputs must be evaluated with only one set of prices.

Figure 5.2 shows us the much reduced growth of output when output is measured in 1972 dollars.

PER CAPITA GROWTH

As we can see, growth in real (or constant dollar) terms is much less dramatic than growth in current dollars that make no allowance for rising prices. Nonetheless, the value of 1980 output, compared to that of 1900, with price changes eliminated as best we can, still shows a growth factor of almost ten.

But there still remains one last adjustment to be made. The growth of output is a massive assemblage of goods and services to be distributed among the nation's households, and the number of those households has increased. In 1900,

United States population was 76 million; in 1980 it was about 222 million. To bring our constant GNP down to life size, we have to divide it by population, to get GNP per person, or per capita.

HISTORICAL RECORD

In Figure 5.3 we see the American experience from the middle of the nineteenth century in terms of real per capita GNP this time in 1929 prices.* Viewed from the long perspective of history, our average rate of growth has been astonishingly consistent. This holds true for an average over the past thirty-odd years since the Great Depression or back to the 1870s (or even 1830s). As the chart shows, the swings are almost all contained within a range of 10 percent above or below the trend. The trend itself comes to about 3.5 percent a year in real terms, or a little over 1.5 percent a year per capita. Although 1.5 percent a year may not sound like much, remember that this figure allows us to double our real per capita living standards every 47 years. This is Adam Smith's growth model come to life!

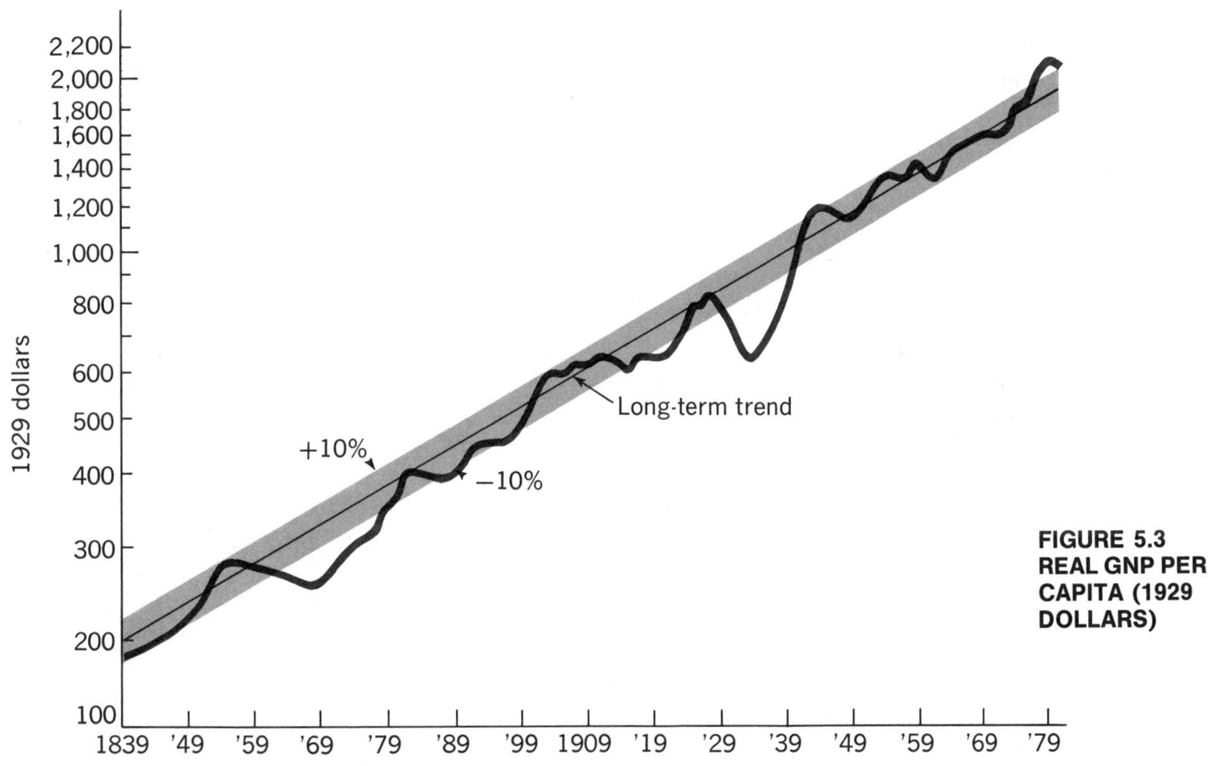

FIGURE 5.3 REAL GNP PER CAPITA (1929 DOLLARS)

Real GNP per capita has shown a long, irregular, but fairly steady upward trend.

*Why do we use 1929 as a base here and 1972 as a base in Figure 5.2? We do it to accustom you to the idea that different years can serve as the basis for comparison.

THE DIFFERENCE THAT GROWTH RATES MAKE

The normal range in growth rates for capitalist economies does not seem to be very great. How much difference does it make, after all, if output grows at 1.7 or 2.7 percent?

The answer is: an amazing difference. This is because growth is an *exponential* phenomenon involving a percentage rate of growth on a steadily rising base. At 1.7 percent, per-capita real income will double in about 40 years. At 2.7 percent, it will double in 26 years.

Professor Kenneth Boulding has pointed out that before World War II no country sustained more than 2.3 percent per-capita growth of GNP. Since World War II, Japan has achieved a per-capita growth rate of 8 percent. Boulding writes: "The difference between 2.3 and 8 percent may be dramatically illustrated by pointing out that [at 2.3 percent] children are twice as rich as their parents—i.e., per capita income approximately doubles every generation—while at 8 percent per annum, children are six times as rich as their parents."

SOURCES OF GROWTH

How do we explain this long upward trend? Here we can give only a brief summary of the causes that we will study more systematically in Part 3, "Macroeconomics." Essentially, we grew for two reasons:

1. The quantity of inputs going into the economic process increased

In 1900 our labor force was 27 million. In 1980 it was almost 110 million. Obviously, larger inputs of labor produce larger outputs of goods and services. (Whether they may even produce *proportionally* larger outputs is another question that we will investigate later.)

Our inputs of capital increased as well. In 1900 the total horsepower energy delivered by "prime movers"—engines of all kinds, work animals, ships, trains, etc.—was 65 million horsepower. In 1980 it was around 30 *billion.*

Land in use also increased. In 1900, there were 839 million acres of land used for cultivation, and over 1,000 million acres for other purposes such as grazing. By 1980, land in cultivation had increased to over 1,000 million acres, and land in grazing use had also increased: We had reclaimed virgin land and made it economically productive.

2. The quality of inputs improved

The population working in 1980 was not only more numerous than in 1900, it was better trained and better schooled. The best overall gauge of this is the amount of education stored up in the work force. In 1900, when only 6.4 percent of the working population had gone beyond grade school, there were 223 million man-years of schooling embodied in the population. In 1980, when over two-thirds of the population had finished high school, the stock of education embodied in the population had grown to over a billion man-years.

The quality of capital has also increased, along with its quantity. As an indication of the importance of the changing quality of capital, consider the contribution made to our output by the availability of surfaced roads. In 1900 there were about 150,000 miles of such roads. In 1980, there were almost 4 million miles. That is an increase in the quantity of roads of over 25 times. But that increase does not begin to measure the difference in the transport capability of the two road systems, one of them gravelled, narrow, built for traffic that averaged 10 to 20 miles per hour; the other, concrete or asphalt, multilane, fast-paced.

PRODUCTIVITY

There are still other sources of growth, such as shifts in occupations and efficiencies of large-scale operation, but the main ones are the increase in the quantity and the quality of inputs. Of the two, **improvements in the quality of inputs—in human skills, in improved designs of capital equipment—have been far more important than mere increases in quantity.** Better skills and technology enable the labor force to increase its productivity, the amount of goods and services it can turn out in a given time.

Figure 5.4 shows the trend in productivity during recent years. As you can see, the growth has been fairly steady up to the early 1970s, despite occasional dips. After 1972 the trend seems to shift downward. We will look into the reasons for this later. Here we want to emphasize the contribution made to long term growth by our normal steady improvement in our ability to grow and extract and handle and shape and transport goods.

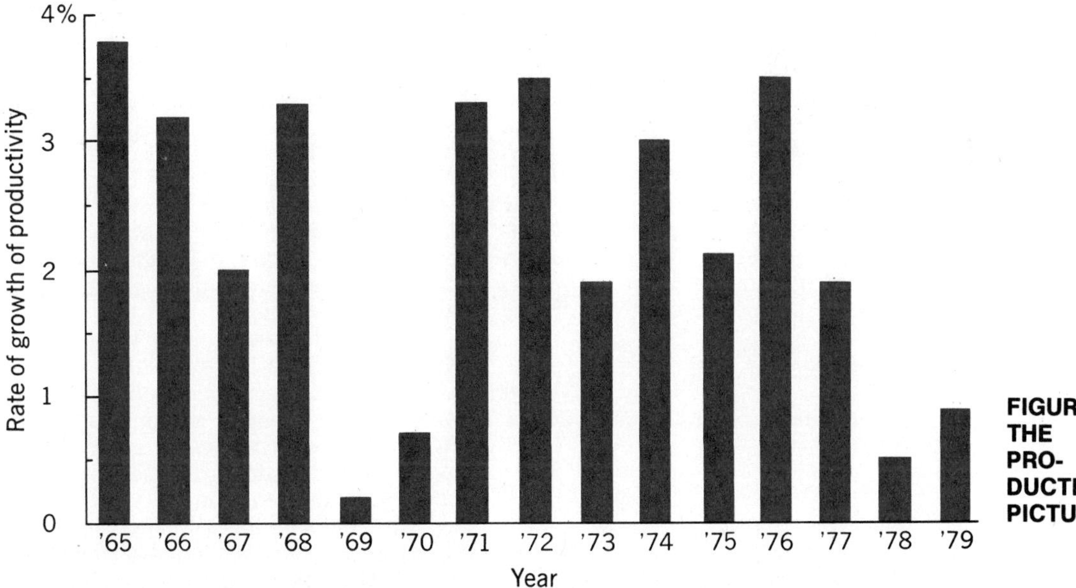

FIGURE 5.4 THE PRODUCTIVITY PICTURE

These data show that our increases in productivity have been steadily falling in recent years. The causes for this productivity decline will interest us later in our book.

CHANGES IN DISTRIBUTION

We have seen how striking was the increase in output in the twentieth century, but what happened to the division of this output among the various classes of society? Have the rich gotten richer and the poor poorer? Has the trend been in the direction of greater equality?

CHANGES IN DOLLAR INCOMES VS. CHANGES IN SHARES

The question is not easy to answer. Remember, we are interested in the changes in shares going to different groups, not just in absolute amounts. There has certainly been a tremendous change in the dollar amounts that we have used to define different social classes, as Figure 5.5 shows.

The figures show that growth has helped boost all income classes, but has the *proportion* of income going to the various classes also changed? That is not what we find. Figure 5.6 shows that sharing-out of incomes among social groups has been remarkably steady.

Thus the distribution of total income among those at the top, in the middle, and on the bottom has not shifted very much. The poor have a little larger share of the income cake; the well-to-do, a little smaller. Only if we go back to the 1920s do we see a marked change. In those days, the share of the top 5 percent

---

POVERTY AGAIN

In a box on page 53 we took a quick look at some of the characteristics of the poor. Here is a second, more systematic glance. It puts all households—families and individuals—into various categories and shows us the chance that someone in a given category will be a member of a low-income (poor) household.

But we must always be very careful before we impute poverty to any single source. One of the authors, sitting in a Ph.D. exam, was questioning a candidate about a dissertation on poverty. It seemed there were many causes for poverty, all impressively substantiated with evidence.

"But if you had to single out one cause as the *most* important," asked the examiner, "which would it be?"

The candidate hemmed and hawed. There was skill. There was health. There was culture. There was native ability. But if he *had* to choose, he would say that education—or rather, the lack of it—was the greatest contributory factor in poverty. Most poor people simply didn't have the knowledge to enable them to get high-paying jobs.

"And why didn't they have the education?" asked the examiner.

That was easy. Education was expensive. Poor people couldn't afford private schools. The need for income was so great that they dropped out of school early to earn money.

"I see," said the examiner. "People are poor because they are uneducated. They are uneducated because they haven't the money to buy education. So *poverty causes poverty*."

CHANCES OF BEING POOR (1978)

All families	11.4
Single persons	22.1
White families	9.1
Black and other nonwhite families	27.5
Families headed by females	
White	23.5
Black, other	50.6

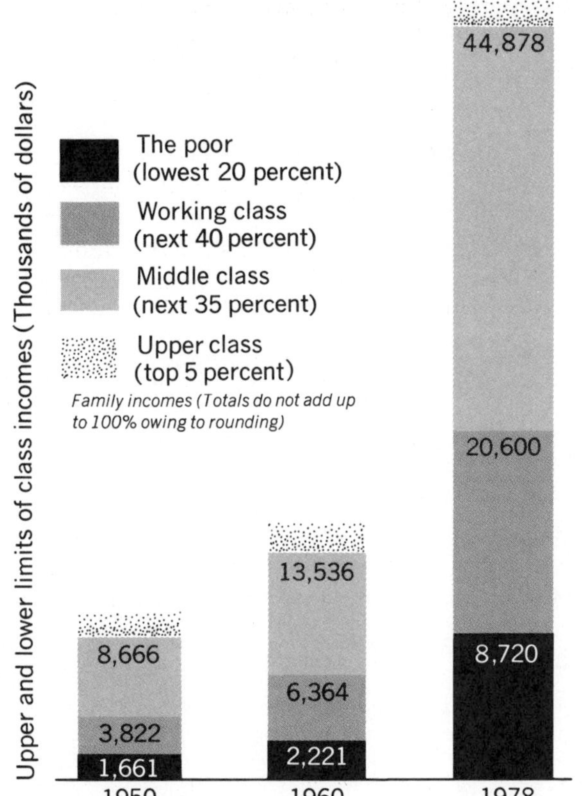

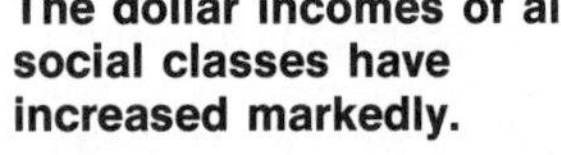

The dollar incomes of all social classes have increased markedly.

FIGURE 5.5 CHANGES IN DOLLAR LIMITS OF SOCIAL CLASSES

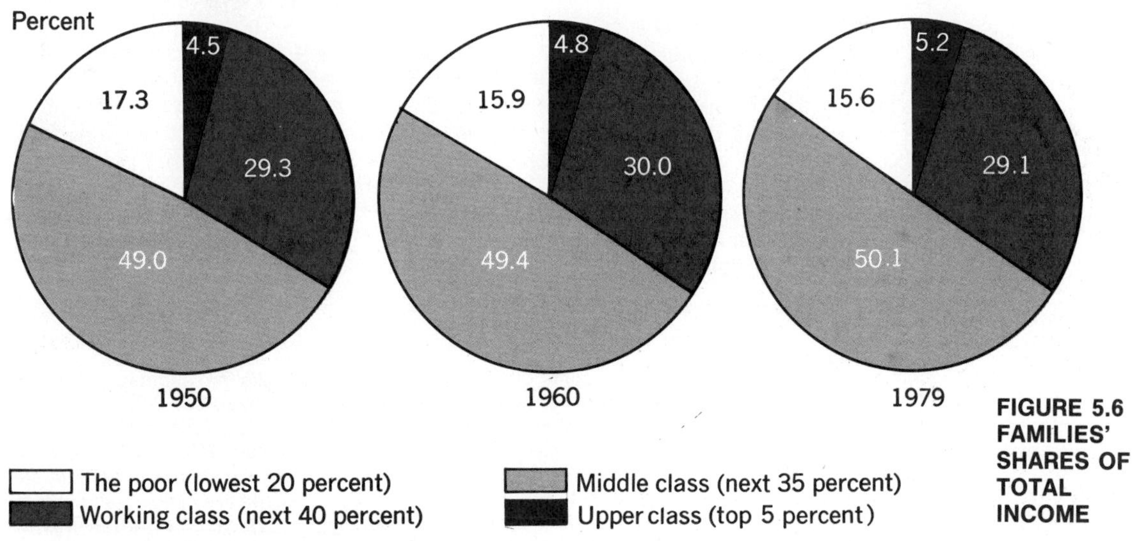

FIGURE 5.6 FAMILIES' SHARES OF TOTAL INCOME

The distribution of income among different social classes has shown very little change.

was perhaps twice as large as it is today. In addition, various social programs, such as Medicare or state-supported higher education, have probably raised the the real income of the poorest 20 percent somewhat more than Figure 5.6 shows.*

THE ELIMINATION OF POVERTY?

Does this mean that poverty is being eliminated from the United States? Without a question the number of persons below the designated low-income level has been dropping, both absolutely and relative to the larger population, even though the threshold of a poverty income has been steadily adjusted upward to allow for inflation. We can see this gradual shrinkage in Table 5.1, where we should note the reversal of the trend in the 1975 recession.

TABLE 5.1 PERSONS BELOW LOW-INCOME LEVEL

	1959	*1965*	*1969*	*1975*	*1979*
All persons (millions)	39.5	33.2	24.1	25.9	24.5
Percent of population	22.4	17.3	12.1	12.3	11.4

There has been a steady fall in measured poverty.

HOW BIG IS BIG?

Just to get an idea of scale, the 100th largest industrial corporation in 1978 ranked by sales was P.P.G. Industries. Its sales that year were $2.8 billion. It was not the 100th largest in terms of assets, which just topped $1 billion. The 100th biggest firm in assets was Pennzoil, with $2.1 billion. Its sales were $1.7 billion.

Thus it makes a difference whether we rank companies in size by sales or assets. At the very top of the heap, 8 of the first 10 firms in sales are also among the top 10 in assets, but this coincidence is no longer true once we get part way down the list. Examples: Esmark was 38th in sales, 98th in assets; Greyhound 55th in sales, 129th in assets; Burroughs 64th in assets, 118th in sales.

Which is more important, sales or assets? Sales measure the dominance of a company within its field; assets measure its overall financial strength. Actually both sales and assets measure size, but what counts in the marketplace is profitability. Here the correct measure is the net rate of return: the rate of profit earned per dollar of capital. The average big business earns twice to three times the return of the average small business, but really spectacular rates of return are usually found in smaller businesses on their way to stardom.

Last rule of thumb: To make it into the top 500 companies, your sales have to be about $250 million; your assets $30 million.

*A more detailed study of changes in income distribution would have to take into account some facts that are not included in the figures above. For technical reasons, the Census Bureau does not include most forms of capital income (such as capital gains on stocks or real estate) in its computation of incomes. If it did, the share of the top 1 percent would be larger. The Census Bureau also does not fully take into account cash and noncash payments to the poor, such as food stamps or welfare aid. This would add to the share of the poor. In other words, the Census figures are mainly derived from earnings, not returns on capital or "transfers" that may benefit high- or low-income groups. It is extremely difficult to net out the effects of all these flows of money. The result is probably more favorable to lower income groups, but it is not possible to say by exactly how much. In all likelihood, the net change is not very great.

These figures do not tell us, however, whether poverty simply melts away as a result of overall growth or whether we eliminate certain kinds of poverty (eg. poverty from low wages), while leaving other kinds relatively untouched. During the past 20 years, the conditions of life in the slums of many big cities have worsened. This makes it difficult to say that we have less of a poverty problem in the nation as a whole. Possibly we have a greater one.

Such considerations make it difficult to pass judgment on Marx's expectations of "increasing misery." Many people have argued that this is the least justified of Marx's expectations about capitalism. Others have claimed that by "misery" Marx did not mean money income, but the quality of life. Perhaps a fair judgment is that misery measured in money has probably decreased much more than Marx ever imagined, but that misery measured in the experience of social life may not have disappeared nearly as much as Marx's critics expected.*

TRENDS IN BUSINESS

We have examined the main trends in personal income. Now let us turn to business. Here one change immediately strikes the eye. There is a marked decline of the independent, small business—with its self-employed worker—as a main form of enterprise.

In 1900 there were about 8 million independent enterprises, including 5.7 million farms. By 1980, as we saw in our last chapter, the number of proprietorships had grown to over 10 million, a figure that included some 2.8 million farms. Meanwhile, the labor force itself more than tripled. Thus as a percentage of all persons working, the proportion of self-employed has fallen from about 30 percent in 1900 to under 10 percent today.

RISE OF BIG BUSINESS

With the decline of the self-employed worker has come the rise of the giant firm. Back in 1900, the giant corporation was just arriving on the scene. In 1901, financier J. P. Morgan created the first billion-dollar company when he formed the United States Steel Corporation out of a dozen smaller enterprises. In that year, the total capitalization of all corporations valued at more than $1 million was $5 billion. By 1904 it was $20 billion. In 1980 it was over about $5 trillion.

It hardly comes as a surprise that the main trend of the past 80 years has been the emergence of big business. More interesting is the question of whether big business is continuing to grow. This is a more difficult question to answer, for it depends on what we mean by "growth."

Certainly the place of the biggest companies within the world of corporations has been rising, at least during the years up to the early 1970s, as Table 5.2 shows. Marx was also indubitably right in predicting this trend. Indeed, as

*It is worth remarking that Adam Smith also expected "misery" to increase, despite a rise in income, because commercial society (as he called it) exposed the working population to the dulling influence of monotonous work. A capitalist society, Smith believed, was rich but its working classes were likely to be made less alert and intelligent, because of the labor they performed. See *Wealth of Nations*, p. 734.

TABLE 5.2 LARGEST MANUFACTURERS SHARE OF ASSETS (%)

	1948	1960	1970	1975
100 largest corporations	40.2	46.4	48.5	46.5
200 largest corporations	48.2	56.3	60.4	58.5

The share of the biggest corporations grew rapidly during the fifties and sixties, but may now have stabilized.

Table 5.2 shows, the top 100 companies in the 1970s held approximately as large a share of total corporate wealth as the top 200 companies in 1948.

SALES VS. ASSETS

This growing concentration of assets in the hands of the mightiest corporations is not the same thing, however, as a growing predominance of those companies in *each marketplace.* The share of the biggest companies in various markets has tended to remain about the same—up in a few industries, down in others. This is a matter we will look into much more carefully in Chapter 20, but it is important to have the general conclusion now. **Over the last quarter-century, concentration of business has continued to increase if we measure assets, not if we measure sales.**

EXPLAINING THE TREND TO BUSINESS SIZE

Can we explain the long-term trend toward the concentration of business assets, as we did the trend toward growth in GNP? By and large, economists would stress three main reasons for the appearance of giant enterprise.

1. **Advances in technology have made possible the mass production of goods or services at falling costs**

For reasons that we explored in Chapter 2, the rise of bigness in business is very much a result of technology. Without the steam engine, the lathe, the railroad, it is difficult to imagine how big business would have emerged.

But technology went on to do more than make large-scale production possible. Typically it also brought an economic effect that we call **economies of scale.** That is, technology not only enlarged, it also cheapened the process of production. Costs per unit fell as output rose. The process is perfectly exemplified in the huge reduction of cost in producing automobiles on an assembly line rather than one car at a time (see box).

Economies of scale provided further powerful impetus toward a growth in size. **The firm that pioneered in the introduction of mass production technology usually secured a competitive selling advantage over its competitors, enabling it to grow in size and thereby to increase its advantage still further.** These cost-reducing advantages were important causes of the initial emergence of giant companies in many industries. Similarly, the absence of such technologies explains why corporate giants did not emerge in all fields.

2. **Concentration is also a result of corporate mergers**

Ever since J. P. Morgan assembled U.S. Steel, mergers have been a major source of corporate growth. At the very end of the nineteenth century there was the first great merger "wave," out of which came the first huge companies, including U.S. Steel. In 1890 most industries were competitive, without a single company dominating the field. By 1904 one or two giant firms, usually created by mergers, had arisen to control at least half the output in 78 different industries.

Again, between 1951 and 1960 one-fifth of the top 1,000 corporations disappeared—not because they failed, but because they were bought up by other corporations. In all, mergers have accounted for about two-fifths of the increase in concentration between 1950 and 1970; internal growth accounts for the rest.

3. **Depressions or recessions plunge many smaller firms into bankruptcy and make it possible for larger, more financially secure firms to buy them up very cheaply**

This is once more as Marx anticipated. Certainly the process of concentration is abetted by economic distress. When industries are threatened, the weak producers go under; the stronger ones emerge relatively stronger than before. Consider, for example, that three once-prominent American automobile producers succumbed to the mild recessions of the 1950s and 1960s, and to the pressure of foreign competition: Studebaker, Packard, Kaiser Motors. And Chrysler is currently threatened with bankruptcy.

FROM PIN FACTORY TO ASSEMBLY LINE

We recall Adam Smith's pin factory (p. 32). Here is a later version of that division of labor, in the early Ford assembly lines:

Just how were the main assembly lines and lines of component production and supply kept in harmony? For the chassis alone, from 1,000 to 4,000 pieces of each component had to be furnished each day at just the right point and right minute: a single failure, and the whole mechanism would come to a jarring standstill. . . . Superintendents had to know every hour just how many components were being produced and how many were in stock. Whenever danger of shortage appeared, the shortage chaser—a familiar figure in all automobile factories—flung himself into the breach. Counters and checkers reported to him. Verifying in person any ominous news, he mobilized the foreman concerned to repair deficiencies. Three times a day he made typed reports in manifold to the factory clearing-house, at the same time chalking on blackboards in the clearing-house office a statement of results in each factory-production department and each assembling department.[1]

Such systematizing in itself resulted in astonishing increases in productivity. With each operation analyzed and subdivided into its simplest components, with a steady stream of work passing before stationary men, with a relentless but manageable pace of work, the total time required to assemble a car dropped astonishingly. Within a single year, the time required to assemble a motor fell from 600 minutes to 226 minutes: to build a chassis, from 12 hours and 28 minutes to 1 hour and 33 minutes. A stopwatch man was told to observe a 3-minute assembly in which men assembled rods and pistons, a simple operation. The job was divided into three jobs, and half the men turned out the same output as before.

As the example of the assembly line illustrates, the technology behind economies of scale often reduced the act of labor to robot-like movements. A brilliant account of this fragmentation of work will be found in Harry Braverman's *Labor and Monopoly Capital* (New York: Monthly Review Press, 1974).

[1]Allan Nevins, *Ford, the Times, the Man, the Company* (New York: Scribner's, 1954), 1,507.

A CONTINUING TREND TO BIGNESS?

Recent statistics suggest that the trend to bigness may have levelled off, as we can see if we compare the figures for 1970 and 1975 in Table 5.2. On the other hand, there is evidence that a new merger wave may have broken out in the late 1970s. We will not have data on this for a few years. It seems doubtful, however, that we have heard the last of the problem of business concentration. This is because the main forces making for concentration—technical advances, mergers, and business cycles—are still very much with us.

LABOR UNIONS

What about labor unions? Have they also shown trends comparable to the big corporation? Their history is parallel in many ways. Over the last 75 years, the percent of the labor force belonging to a union has increased from 3.2 to 22.6. Thus, the twentieth century has seen the emergence of big labor alongside big business. Yet, as Table 5.3 shows, the percent of unionized nonagricultural workers has actually declined in recent years.

This does not mean, of course, that all unions today are diminishing. The last two decades have brought a boom in unions for white-collar workers, such as teachers or office workers; in unions for municipal employees, such as police, firemen, transit workers; in diversified union organization, such as the powerful Teamsters. The declines have come where industries are declining, such as amongst railwaymen or clothing trades workers. Unions are certain to remain a major force in crucial areas of the economy.

TABLE 5.3 LABOR FORCE IN UNIONS

	1940	*1950*	*1960*	*1970*	*1979*
Percent unionized	27.2	31.9	31.4	30.1	22.0

The importance of unions in the labor force has been falling, although unions remain powerful in key sectors.

FROM SMALL TO LARGE GOVERNMENT

We pass now to the last great trend of the economy, a trend whose end result has been the emergence of that large government apparatus we noted in our previous chapter.

RISE OF THE PUBLIC SECTOR

There are three quite different ways of measuring the rise of the public sector. The first is to examine the proportion of GNP that government directly produces or purchases. This might be regarded as a rough indication of the degree to which we have become a "statist" economy.

A second way is to inquire into the extent to which the government reallocates incomes by taxing some persons and giving others "transfer payments" such as Social Security benefits or welfare or unemployment insurance. This might be regarded as an index of the degree to which we have become a welfare state.

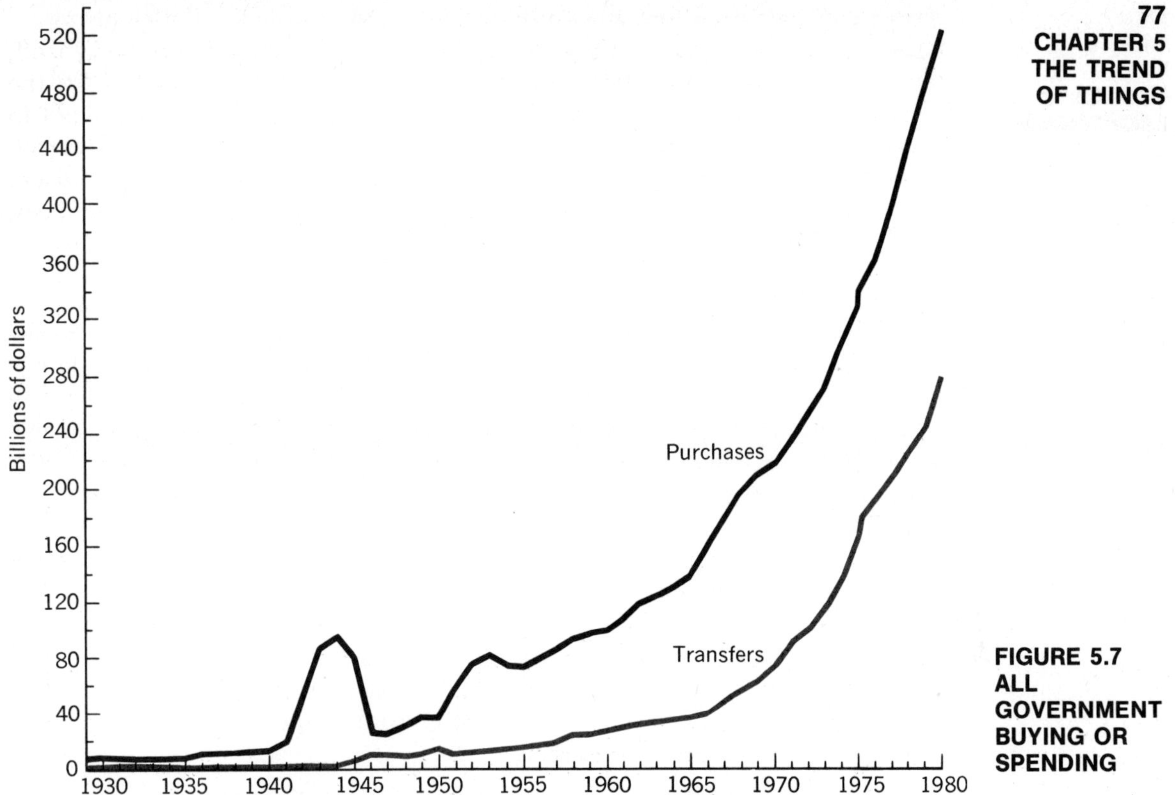

FIGURE 5.7
ALL GOVERNMENT BUYING OR SPENDING

Government trends are sharply up both in purchases and in income payments for transfer purposes. This is traceable mainly to defense buying and to social security and other welfare payments.

Last is the extent to which government interferes in the working of the economy by regulating various aspects of economic life or by exercising its economic powers in other ways. This, by far the most difficult to measure exactly, might be thought of as an indication of the extent to which we have moved in the direction of a guided or controlled capitalism.

1. Purchases Figure 5.7 shows the first two measurements: public purchases and income reallocation. Let us begin by examining the trend of production or purchases. As we can see, a steadily rising fraction of GNP is produced or bought by government. **Today about a fifth of all output is produced to fill government demand. What the graph does not show, however, is that increased state and local buying, even more than federal buying, causes the rise.**

Federal purchases have increased mainly with our growing role in world affairs. In 1900, total U.S. military purchases came to $300 million; in 1980, to over $115 billion. But nonfederal purchasing—for education, roads, police, and similar functions—accounts for the major portion of total government buying. In 1980 the states and localities bought over $325 billion worth of GNP; the federal government (including defense) bought only some $175 billion.

2. *Transfers* **Next, we notice the rapid rise in the amount of GNP reallocated by government. Here is where the expansion of the federal sector has played the leading role.** In 1929, only .9 percent of GNP was redistributed by government. In 1980, transfer payments amounted to 10 percent of GNP, and the great bulk of this originated with the federal government. If we add both the goods produced or purchased by the federal government and the various transfer payments it has made, a total of over $800 billion passed through its hands, or about one-third of GNP.

3. *Intervention* What reasons lay behind this swelling volume of government buying or spending? Let us defer the answer until we examine the last indication of the growing presence of government, the widening role of government as a supervisor or regulator of the economy.

Because of its varied nature, and because the importance of government intervention is not always shown by the amount of money that an agency spends or the number of personnel it employs, this is a trend that defies easy quantification or graphic representation. Much of the spending that we have noted, for example, is carried out through established departments of the executive branch of government, especially Health, Education, and Welfare, from which Social Security checks flow, and the Defense Department, source of military spending.

But we ought to have at least some indication, however impressionistic and incomplete, of the widening reach of government concern within various areas of the economic system. The following list gives us some inkling of the variety and importance of these functions:

Agency	*Function*
Civil Aeronautics Board	Regulates air routes and fares
Environmental Protection Agency	Administers antipollution legislation
Federal Reserve Board	Regulates supply of money
Federal Communications Commission	Assigns airwave frequencies to stations
Federal Trade Commission	Polices business activities in restraint of trade
Interstate Commerce Commission	Regulates rail, canal, and truck industry
National Labor Relations Board	Supervises union elections
National Science Foundation	Supports scientific research
Tariff Commission	Holds hearings on tariff matters
Office of Economic Opportunity	Oversees employment practices

BEHIND THE RISE IN GOVERNMENT

How shall we account for all these trends of government: more buying, more transfer payments, more regulation and intervention? Among the many causes are these developments:

• **The growing size of business has evoked a need for government supervision.** As business firms have increased in size, private decisions have become fraught with social consequences. It is impossible for a big company to make an important decision that does not have widespread repercussions. Building or not building a plant may spell prosperity or decline for a town, even a state. Cutthroat competition can spell ruin for an industry. Polluting a river can ruin a region. Much government effort, at the local and state as well as federal level, represents attempts to prevent big business from creating social or economic problems, or to cope with problems it has created.

•**Technology brings a need for public supervision.** An impressive amount of government effort goes into the regulation of problem-creating technologies. Examples: the network of state and local highway and police authorities that deal with the automobile; the panoply of agencies designed to cope with airplanes, television and radio, atomic energy, new drugs, and weaponry. As long as technology increases its power to affect our social and natural environment, it is likely that public supervision will also increase.

•**Urbanization brings a need for centralized administration.** City life has its appeals, but it also has its perils. Men and women cannot live in crowded quarters without police, public health, traffic, sanitation, and educational facilities far more complex than those needed in a rural setting. Government is, and always has been, concentrated in cities. As a nation urbanizes, it requires more government.

•**Unification of the economy creates additional problems.** Industrialization knits an economy together into a kind of vast, interlocked machinery. An unindustrialized, localized economy is like a pile of sand: if you poke a finger into one side of it, some businesses and individuals will be affected, but those on the other side of the pile will remain undisturbed. The growing scale and specialization of industrial operations unifies the sandpile. You poke one side of it, and the entire pile shakes. Problems can no longer be localized. The difficulties of the economy grow in extent: there is a need for a national, not a local, energy program, for national transportation, urban and educational programs. Government—largely federal government—is the principal means by which such problems are handled.

•**Economic malfunction has brought public intervention.** Fifty or seventy-five years ago, the prevailing attitude toward the economy was a kind of awed respect. People felt that the economy was best left alone, that it was fruitless as well as ill-advised to try to change its normal workings. That attitude changed once and for all with the advent of the Great Depression. In the ensuing collapse, the role of government greatly enlarged, to restore the economy to working order. The trauma of the Depression and the determination to prevent its recurrence were a watershed in the trend of government spending and government intervention. Keynes's thinking played a very important part in this transition to a mixed economy.

•A new philosophy of "entitlement" has replaced the older one of "rugged individualism." Largely, but not wholly as a consequence of the experience of the Depression, a profound change has been registered in public attitudes toward the appropriate role of government. We no longer live in a society in which old-age retirement, medical expenses, and income during periods of unemployment are felt to be properly the responsibility of the individuals concerned. For better or worse, these and similar responsibilities have been gradually assumed by governments in all capitalist nations. In fact, the United States is a laggard in these matters compared with many European capitalist states. Here lie crucial reasons for the swelling volume of state, local, and federal production and purchase that have steadily enlarged the place of government within the economy.

No doubt there are other causes that could be added to this list. Bureaucracies have ways of feeding on themselves. But the overall conclusion is already evident. In modern capitalism, government is a major factor in the economic system. How well it fulfills its functions and to what extent it realizes the hopes that have been thrust upon it are themes that will constantly occupy us as we continue with our studies.

KEY CONCEPTS

LOOKING BACK

This chapter has been concerned with the economy in movement—not in quick, month-to-month fluctuations of the kind that will concern us when we study macroeconomics, but in longer-run, year to year, or decade to decade changes. Here are the most important of them.

Real vs. nominal growth

More inputs and more productive inputs

1. There is a long-term growth pattern to GNP—a pattern that is much more striking in nominal GNP than in real GNP (that is, in figures uncorrected for inflation than in corrected figures), but remarkable even with all adjustments for rising prices. The source of this growth can be attributed mainly to two factors: an increase in the quantity of inputs as our labor force and our stock of wealth grows, and an increase in the quality and effectiveness of inputs as our productivity grows. Here is Adam Smith's growth projection in reality.

Rise in incomes but little change in distribution

2. A second main trend is directly connected with the rise in output. It is the rise in dollar incomes for all levels of households—a rise that is, of course, much greater before we adjust for inflation than after. The distribution of income among classes changes only very slowly, however. Poverty is gradually being eroded, but remains a stubborn problem.

Big business share of assets has grown, but not its share of individual markets

3. The share of total assets belonging to the biggest corporations has shown a startling increase in the decades of the 1950s and 1960s. However, the increase in the share of sales in different markets going to the biggest firms has shown no significant change. Big firms get bigger by absorbing assets of companies in *different* branches of business, so that their degree of monopoly control within markets shows little change. The main sources of business growth have been technology (recall Chapter 2) and mergers. Marx's view of business expansion seems to have been correct.

Growth in government buying is mainly for defense

Increased government spending is mainly transfer payments like Social Security

4. The fourth main trend has been the striking rise in the size of the government sector. Here we have to make careful distinctions between different meanings of the expansion of government. Government buying of goods has increased within the economy mainly because of much greater federal defense expenditure, and swollen state and local spending for education, roads, and the like. Government income payments have increased largely as a result of larger federal transfer payments, like Social Security.

Reasons for growing public regulation are linked to the attributes of evolving capitalism

5. There are many reasons for the rise of regulatory government, some of which we have already noted in our earlier chapters. Here is a list of the most important causes:

the growing size of business,
the disruptive effects of technology,
urbanization,
the unification of the economy,
a Keynesian remedy for economic malfunction,
a new philosophy of entitlement

Thinking about these background elements, what do you believe is likely to be the direction of future change in government's place in the economy? How would you seek to alter things, if you could?

ECONOMIC VOCABULARY

Gross national product 65
Real and nominal GNP 66
Per capita growth 66
Productivity 69
Economies of scale 74

QUESTIONS

1. Here are some raw data:

	(current $billions)	*Price index*	*Population (millions)*
1965	$ 688	100	194
1970	982	123	204
1975	1,498	170	214

What is real GNP per capita in 1970 and 1975 in 1965 dollars? In 1975 dollars? Hint: You will need a new price index with 1975 = 100.

2. If there were no change whatsoever in technology, do you think that a larger quantity of labor might result in GNP growing faster or slower than the sheer increase of man-hour input? Hint: Can people organize their activities better as their numbers change? Does this continue indefinitely?

3. Do you think it might be possible to construct a theory to explain why the pretax, pretransfer shares of income are so fixed? Could there be a kind of pecking order

in society? Could different income groups establish economic distances that satisfy them? Would they then strive only to retain, not to increase, those differences?

4. Can you imagine an invention that would result in rapid concentration in a very unconcentrated industry, say the restaurant business? Or the laundry business? Can you imagine an invention that could radically deconcentrate an industry? How might a watch-sized CB radio affect A.T.&T.? What invention could do the same for Exxon? U.S. Steel?

5. Do you think the rise of government within the economy is "socialistic"? "Capitalistic"? What do you mean by either term?

Part 2
A Kit of Economic Tools

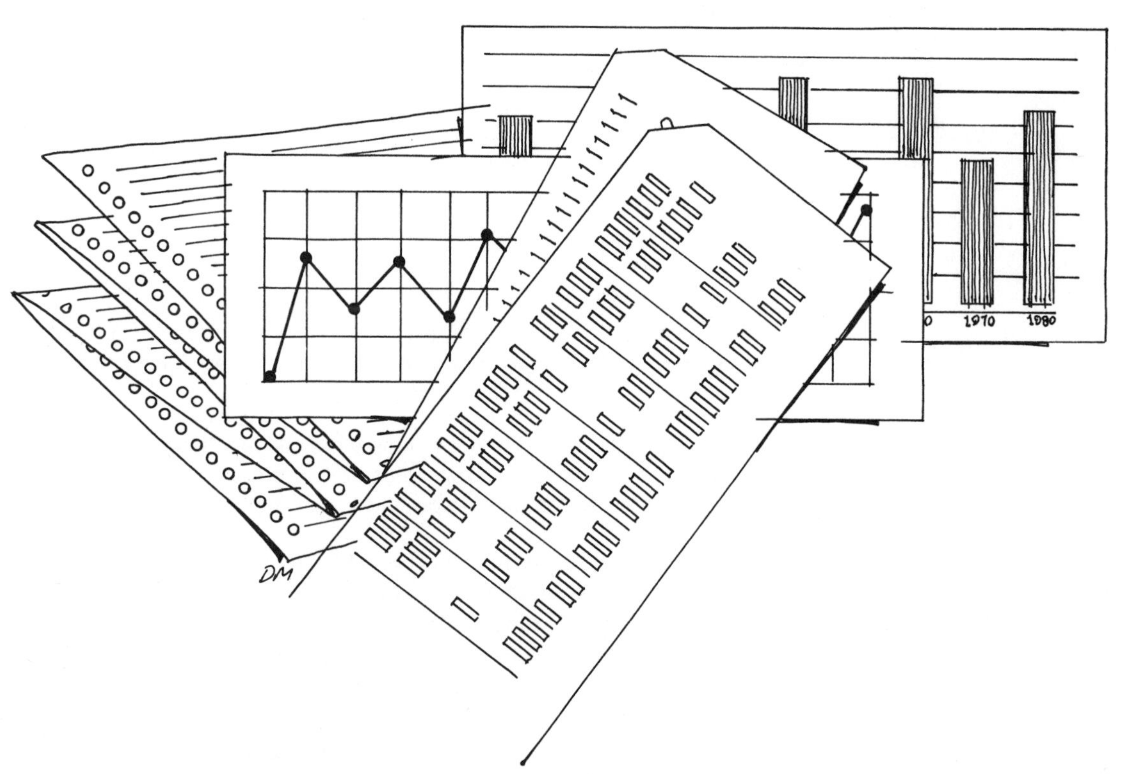

Chapter 6 ECONOMIC SCIENCE

A LOOK AHEAD

Now that we have some background in the field, we are ready to take the next step toward becoming economists by learning something of the ways economists think. Here we are dealing with the abstract and analytic aspects of the field that we mentioned in Chapter 1.

Essentially this short chapter tells you that economic theory is about maximizing behavior that takes place against constraints. Acquisitiveness is a good first approximation of the meaning of "maximizing," and "constraints" implies limits, boundaries, or costs. Economic reasoning consists of puzzling out what happens when rational acquisitors face constraints imposed by nature or society. Keep that in mind and the chapter will unfold step by step.

What it is that we are trying to reason about as economists? Certainly it is not the economic attributes of *all* societies. Our first chapters focus on the United States not merely because we are naturally interested in the economic aspects of our own country, but also because the United States is a kind of society that lends itself to economic analysis. Economic reasoning, we should note at the outset, applies most cogently to societies that are built on the foundations of economic individualism. These are market societies, capitalisms.

Equally to be noted, economic reasoning will not try to come to grips with all of society. Our earlier survey paid no attention to vast areas of social life that we call sociological or political, much less religious or artistic. Economics is concerned with the facts that bear on only one aspect of our social life: our efforts to produce and to distribute wealth. Boom and bust, inflation and depression, poverty and riches, growth or no growth—all can be described in terms of the production of wealth and its distribution.

MAXIMIZING VS. CONSTRAINTS

Our task, then, is to find some way of explaining production and distribution in scientific terms. Therefore, economists observe the *human* universe, just as natural scientists observe the physical universe, in search of data and orderly relationships that may permit them to construct hypotheses.

What do economists see when they scrutinize the world of economic activity? Two attributes of a market society attract their attention:

1. **Individuals in such a society display a particular behavior pattern when they participate in economic activities, as consumers or business people. They behave in acquisitive, money-searching, "maximizing" ways.** (See box, p. 86.)

2. **A series of obstacles or constraints stands between the acquisitive drive of marketers and their realization of economic gain. Some are the constraints of nature; some are the obstacles of social institutions.**

Thus an extraordinary conclusion begins to dawn. A great deal of the activity of a market society can be explained as the outcome of two interacting forces. One is the force of maximizing behavior—a force that we have described in terms of the acquisitive behavior of men and women in a market society. The other is the constraining counterforce of nature or of social institutions—a series of obstacles that holds back or channels or directs the acquisitive drive. This suggests the daring scientific task that economics sets for itself. It is to explain the events of economic reality—even to predict some of the events of future economic reality—by reasoning based on fundamental hypotheses about maximizing behavior and its constraints.

HYPOTHESES ABOUT BEHAVIOR

Obviously we must investigate these hypotheses with a great deal of care. Let us start with the economist's assumption about behavior. We can sum it up in a sentence: *Man is a maximizer.*

MAXIMIZING UTILITIES

What does that hypothesis mean? Essentially, it means that people in market societies seek to gain as much pleasurable wealth from their economic activity as they can. **We call this pleasurable wealth "utility." Thus we hypothesize that men and women are utility-maximizers.**

Note that we define utility as *pleasurable* wealth. Economists do not argue that people try to accumulate the largest amount of wealth possible, regardless of its pleasures. We all know that after a certain point, wealth-producing work brings fatigue or even pain. Therefore we assume that as people work to maximize their wealth, they take into account the pains (or disutilities) of achieving it.

It is impossible to *prove* that people maximize in this fashion. But it seems plausible that most of us do seek wealth both as wage-earners or as businessmen, and that we take account of the nuisances and difficulties of achieving it.

SATIABLE AND INSATIABLE WANTS

Economics not only assumes that men and women are maximizers, but it also has a hypothesis about why they behave so acquisitively. **The hypothesis is that peoples' wants are insatiable; that human desires for utility can never be filled.**

Are our wants, in fact, insatiable? Does human nature keep us on a treadmill of striving that can never bring us to a point of contentment? As with maximizing, there is a prima facie plausibility about the assumption. For if we include among our aims leisure as well as goods, more time to enjoy ourselves as well as more income to be enjoyed, it seems true enough that something very much like insatiability afflicts most people. At least this seems true in societies that encourage striving for status and success and that set high value on consumption and recreation.

For example, surveys regularly show that men and women at all economic levels express a desire for more income (usually about 10 percent more than they actually have), and *this drive for more does not seem to diminish as we move up the economic scale.* If it did, we would be hard put to explain why people who are generally in the upper echelons of the distribution of wealth and income work just as hard as, or even harder than, those on the lower rungs of the economic ladder.

There is, however, a very important qualification to the assumption that wants are insatiable for all wealth, including leisure. **The qualification is that economists assume that human wants for particular kinds of wealth, including**

ACQUISITIVENESS

Remember that we are talking about the kind of behavior that we find in a market society. Perhaps in a different society of the future, another hypothesis about behavior would have to serve as our starting point. People might then be driven by the desire to better the condition of others rather than of themselves.

A story about heaven and hell is to the point. Hell has been described as a place where people sit at tables laden with sumptuous food, unable to eat because they have three-foot long forks and spoons strapped to their hands. Heaven is described as the very same place. There, people feed one another.

leisure, are indeed capable of being satiated. This idea of the satiability of particular wants will play a key role in our next chapter, when we shall see how we can derive the concept of demand and demand "curves" from our hypotheses concerning behavior.

RATIONALITY

Equally important is an assumption about the way that individuals think and act as they go about striving to fulfill their insatiable wants-in-general or their satiable wants-in-particular. **This assumption is that man is a *rational* maximizer.** By this economists mean that people in a market milieu stop to consider the various courses of action open to them and to calculate in some fashion the means that will best suit their maximizing aims. There may be two different ways of producing a good. As rational maximizers, people will choose the method that will yield them the good for the smallest effort or cost.

This concept of rational maximizing does not mean that human beings may not wish, on some occasions, to go to more trouble than necessary. After all, people could worship God in very simple buildings or out-of-doors, but they go to extraordinary lengths to erect magnificent churches and decorate them with sculpture and paintings. It is meaningless to apply the word *rational* to pursuits such as these, which may have vast importance for society.

But when people are engaged in producing the goods and services of ordinary life, seeking to achieve the largest possible incomes or the most satisfaction-yielding patterns of consumption, the economist assumes that they *will* stop to think about the differing ways of attaining a given end and will then choose the way that is least costly.

THE ECONOMIST'S VIEW OF MAN

Of course, economists do not believe that men and women are solely rational, acquisitive creatures. They are fully aware that a hundred motivations impel people: aesthetic, political, religious. If they concentrate on the rational and acquisitive elements in people, it is because they believe these to be decisive for economic behavior; that is, for the explanation of our productive and distributive activities.

Economic theory is therefore a study of the effects of one aspect of human behavior as it motivates people to undertake their worldly activities. Very often, as economists well know, other aspects will override or blunt the acquisitive, maximizing orientation. To the extent that this is so, economic theory loses its clarity or may even suggest outcomes different from those that we find in fact. **But economists think that rational maximizing—the calculated pursuit of pleasurable wealth—is universal and strong enough to serve as a good working hypothesis on which to build their complicated theories.** To put it differently, economists do *not* think that political or religious or other such motives regularly overwhelm maximizing behavior. If that were so, economic theory would be of little avail.

A final point. Economists regard maximizing as a potentially useful mode of behavior. Of course economists understand that there is a lot more to life than making as much money as possible. But economics allows us to see that maximizing can be a beneficial activity. Business schools exist, in part, to teach people to be better maximizers—that is, more efficient, productive, socially useful managers. We will learn more about this in Part 4, "Microeconomics."

HYPOTHESES ABOUT CONSTRAINTS

So far, we have traced the basic assumptions of economic reasoning about behavior. What about constraints? As we have seen, people do not maximize in a vacuum or, to speak in more economic terms, in a world where all goods are free, available effortlessly in infinite amounts. Instead, people exert their maximizing efforts in a world where nature, technical limitations, and social institutions oppose those efforts. Goods and services are not free but must be won by working with the elements of the physical world. Land, resources, man-made artifacts inherited from past generations are not boundlessly abundant. Laws and social organizations constantly impede our maximizing impulses.

Another way of putting it is that maximizing describes what we *want* to do while constraints describe what we *cannot* do. Economics thus studies the problems, and sometimes the impossibility, of achieving what we want. That is why economics is often characterized as maximizing subject to constraints.

CONSTRAINTS OF NATURE

Constraints are obviously very important. But we cannot sum them up as simply as we can sum up the idea of maximizing.

Let us first think about some constraints on our maximizing desires that are imposed by nature. There are three of them. Later we will study these constraints in greater detail, but this is a good time to become generally familiar with them.

1. Diminishing Returns

It's quite apparent that we cannot grow all the world's food requirements in a flowerpot. But why not? Why can't we go on adding seeds and getting more and more output?

The answer has to do with the physical and chemical properties of nature. If you go on adding more and more of any single input to a fixed amount of other inputs, after a time you will run up against obstacles imposed by the structure of things. Add more and more labor to a factory, and after a time it will be so crowded that output will fall. Add more and more ships to the earth's fishing fleet, and after a time the catch will diminish; in fact, as Figure 6.1 shows, that seems to be exactly what is happening today.

Thus nature imposes limits or constraints because we have to expect, and allow for, diminishing returns. **We can't always count on twice as much output just by doubling one input.**

2. Returns to Scale

A second constraint has to do with sheer size, or scale. **It describes the fact that size matters—also a consequence of the physical world.** You can't mass produce automobiles in a garage. Why not? Because mass production requires giant presses and an organized flow of assembly, and those require a big scale of production.

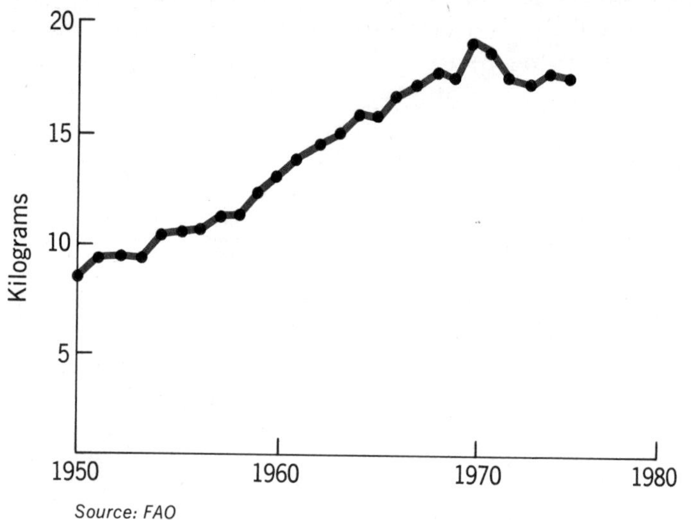

FIGURE 6.1 WORLD FISH CATCH PER CAPITA, 1950–75

Despite steadily increasing inputs of capital (ships), the output of fish has dwindled.

This constraint means that small might be more beautiful, but big is often more economical. It means that we can expect that production will become more efficient, and that each additional unit will become cheaper, as we move from small scale to large scale production—at least up to a point.

3. Increasing Cost

The last constraint is the least familiar. It looks like diminishing returns, but it is different. It has to do with the fact that not all land or labor or resources are alike, so that **as we move from one kind of production to another, we are likely to find it more and more costly to produce more and more of the new output.**

Here a diagram can help us visualize the problem. In Figure 6.2 we see a community that can produce two kinds of output—milk and grain. If it puts all its labor and all its land into milk production, it can produce an amount of milk that we'll represent by the distance *OA* on the milk axis. If it puts all its land and labor into grain, it will produce *OB* of grain, as represented on that axis.

Now suppose that our community is producing nothing but milk and that it decides to balance its output. It cuts its milk production in half (to *OX*), moving land and labor into grain. We can see that it thereby gains *OY* amount of grain. Now notice what happens if the community moves the remaining half of its land and labor into grain. Output rises only a small amount, *YB*. Why is the second half of the community investment in land and labor less productive than the first half? Because we have already plowed the best fields and availed ourselves of the most skilled farmers. The last bushels of grain are much harder to win than the first. And of course the same result would take place in reverse if we started from all grain, at *B*, and switched over into milk. **The constraint means that the more of any one product that we want, the more of some other product we have to give up to get it.**

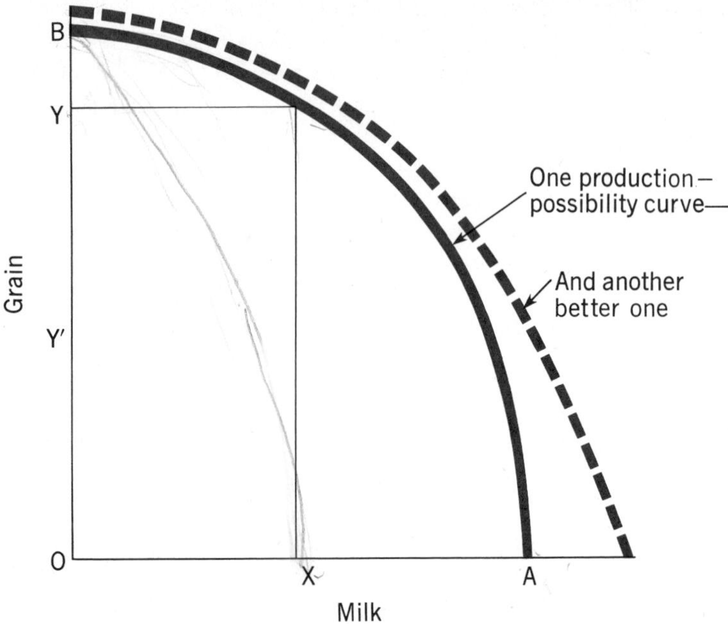

FIGURE 6.2 INCREASING COST

The curve *AB* is called a production possibility curve. The dotted line shows how better technology, for instance, could move such a curve out. What would an earthquake do to it? Draw in such a reduced production possibility curve. The curve bows because of the law of increasing cost—that is, because it becomes less and less efficient to move labor and resources from one use to another. Compare how much grain we get (*OY*) as we cut milk production in half (moving from *OA* to *OX*), with how little we get (*BY*) as we move the remaining half (*OX*). Use a pencil to see if it works the other way round. Start from all grain (*OB*) and zero milk. First chart how much milk you get if you move the economy out of grain (from *OB* to *OY′*). Now eliminate all grain production. How much *additional* milk do you get?

How much of one thing do we have to surrender to get something else? That depends on a host of things—the resources available, the skills we can call on, the energy we can muster. The curve in Figure 6.2 shows us the grain-milk trade-off in our hypothetical community on some imaginary date, but a new invention, a change in climate, even a new economic system could change the efficiency with which we use our wealth. Thus the curve in Figure 6.2, which we call a **production-possibilities curve,** can move—loosening our constraints, as the dotted line shows, or possibly tightening them. We will come back to study this when we take up the subject of economic growth in Chapter 9.

OPPORTUNITY COST

Here is a good place to make a very important point about the constraint of cost. Cost constrains us because it means that we have to give something up to gain wealth: The cost of the grain in Figure 6.2 is the milk we had to give up to get it, and the cost of the milk is the grain we had to forego. That is why economists say "There is no such thing as a free lunch." Even if you did not pay money for it, someone had to produce that lunch, and the labor and materials in it are locked up forever and ever, and can never be retrieved to make something else.

All costs, to economists, are opportunity costs. They are the utilities we must do without because we have chosen to devote our energies and wealth to creating the utilities we have. Later on, we will be talking about costs in dollars and cents, which is the way we usually think of cost. But when we say that something costs $10, what we really mean is that it costs us whatever utilities we might have enjoyed if we had spent the $10 on something else. Have you ever hesitated over whether to buy this *or* that? Then you know what opportunity cost means.

CONSTRAINTS AND COSTS

All these properties of nature set the stage for maximizing behavior. People seek wealth through the production and exchange of goods and services, but they do not maximize in a world where goods can be limitlessly and effortlessly obtained. Nature and our given technology offer us their services easily or reluctantly, depending on whether we are trying to maximize output by adding more and more of one kind of input (when we encounter diminishing returns); whether we are seeking to organize our production in accordance with the technological characteristics of the agencies of production (economies of scale); or whether we are trying to increase the output of one good or service at the expense of others (when the law of increasing cost comes into play).

Thus constraints will play a basic role in establishing costs or supplies. We shall return to these considerations in our next chapter, where we encounter a *supply curve,* the counterpart of the demand curve, about which we first heard a few pages back.

CONSTRAINTS OF SOCIETY

Perhaps we can already see the makings of a powerful analytic device in the interplay of maximizing drives and constraining influences. Before we move on, however, it is necessary to recognize that nature is not the only constraint on the maximizing force of behavior.

Society's constraints on our behavior are just as effective as nature's. The *law* is a major constraining factor on our acquisitive propensities. *Competition* also limits freedom of action, preventing us from charging as much as we would like for goods or services. The banking system, labor unions, the legal underpinnings of private property are all *institutions* that operate like the constraints of nature in curbing the unhampered exercise of our maximizing impulse. So is the constraint of our available resources, our *budget.* Like technology, this is partly a constraint imposed by nature, partly one that is the consequence of man. Different societies enjoy different settings in nature—rich or poor soils, cold or warm climates, easily available or scarce mineral deposits. These gifts of nature help establish the limits of our productive activities, our national budget of annual output. We shall spend a lot of time later investigating how all these various constraints affect individual behavior.

BASIC HYPOTHESES

Let us briefly review the basic propositions in this first look into economic analysis. They can be summed up very simply.

Because economics generalizes about human behavior and the behavior of nature, it can theorize about, and predict, the operations of a market society. If we were not able to make such generalizations, if we could not begin with the plausible hypothesis that people are maximizers and that nature (and social institutions) constrain their behavior in clearly defined ways, we could not hazard the simplest predictive statement about economic society. We could not explain why a store that wants to sell more goods marks its prices down rather than up or why copper costs will probably rise if we try to double copper production in a short period of time.

ECONOMICS AS A SOCIAL SCIENCE

Perhaps these simple generalizations about behavior and nature do not seem to be an impressive foundation for a social science. Ask yourself, though, whether we can match these economic generalizations when we think in political or sociological terms. Are there political or social laws of behavior that we can count on with the same degree of certainty we find in laws of economics? Are there constraints of nature, comparable to the laws of production, discoverable in the political and social areas of life? There are not. That is why we are so much less able to predict political or sociological events than to predict economic events.

Although economic prediction has sharp limitations, its underlying structure of behavioral and natural laws gives it unique strength. Its capabilities we must now explore. The place to begin must be obvious from our look into economic reality and our first acquaintance with supply and demand. It is the market mechanism.

KEY CONCEPTS

LOOKING BACK

This chapter covers quite a few technical ideas, such as diminishing returns or increasing costs. Don't try to master them yet. Instead, be sure that you have the following simple conception of economic reasoning firmly in mind.

Economics is about production and distribution

1. Economic reasoning is about production and distribution of wealth, and only about those things. Economics has nothing to say about politics, religion, or anything other than material wealth.

Economics theorizes from two premises: utility maximizing and constraints

2. Economics erects hypotheses—or, much the same thing, economics theorizes—about the production and distribution of wealth. In doing so, it begins from two premises: (a) Men and women are maximizers of utility, and (b) they maximize in the face of well-defined obstacles or constraints.

Maximizing means insatiable desire for utility in general, not for any one kind of utility

3. Maximizing behavior means that individuals seek as much pleasurable wealth as possible. This pleasurable wealth is called utility. Economists believe that in a market society such as ours, there is an insatiable desire for pleasurable wealth in general, although not for each

particular kind of pleasurable wealth; after a certain point, more food makes us sick, more leisure is a bore.

Maximizing is guided by rational choice

4. Economists also assume that individuals pursue their maximizing goals rationally—not in a haphazard, thoughtless way, but by making the best choices they can. Maximizing can therefore be socially useful.

Nature's constraints:

5. Maximizing behavior has to contend with the obstacles set by nature and by society. Nature and technology together establish three important kinds of constraints:

law of diminishing returns

The law of diminishing returns puts limits on the amount of output we can get from adding any one input—we can't grow all the world's food in a flowerpot.

law of increasing costs

The law of increasing costs limits our attempts to maximize because not all resources can be applied efficiently to any given purpose: We can't raise dairy cattle in Nevada. We can graph this in a production possibility curve.

law of scale

Returns to scale inhibit maximizing, because it is not efficient to produce all kinds of goods on a very small (or a very large) scale. Small may be beautiful, but it is also very expensive if you are thinking about making steel.

Institutional and budget constraints

6. Society also imposes constraints on maximizing—laws, institutional barriers, competition, and the like. Another important limit is imposed by budget considerations.

7. A powerful social science has been derived from the idea of interplay between maximizing and constraining forces. We shall see a demonstration of this power as we enter into a discussion of supply and demand in the next chapter.

Costs are missed opportunities

8. Finally, remember that costs are basically missed opportunities. The phrase "opportunity cost" makes it clear that costs are not just sums of money, but possibilities for making wealth of various kinds that are forever missed because we have chosen to make wealth of one kind.

ECONOMIC VOCABULARY

Maximizing 85	**Constraints** 88	**Increasing cost** 89
Utilities 85	**Diminishing returns** 88	**Production possibility curve** 90
Rationality 87	**Scale** 88	**Opportunity cost** 90

QUESTIONS

1. Do you feel like a maximizer? Are you content with your income? If you are not, do you expect that some day you will be satisfied?
2. Do you act rationally when you spend money? Do you consciously try to weigh the various advantages of buying this instead of that, and to spend your money for the item that will give you the greatest pleasure? Consciously or not, do you generally act as a rational maximizer?

3. How valid do you think the laws of economic behavior are? If they are *not* valid, why does economic society function and not collapse? If they *are* valid, why can't economists predict more accurately?
4. In what way is competition an institution? Are people naturally competitive? Would there be competition in a society that denied spatial or social mobility to labor, as under feudalism?
5. Can you think of any political activities or limits comparable to economic maximizing or constraints? Are there constraints of national size? Might it be possible to devise an economics of politics?
6. Suppose that you had a very large flowerpot and extraordinary chemicals and seeds. Could you conceivably grow all the world's food in it? Why would you still get diminishing returns?
7. Describe the economies of scale that might be anticipated if you were opening a department store. What economies might be expected as the store grew larger? Do you think you would eventually reach a ceiling on these economies?
8. What is the opportunity cost of undertaking a program such as the NASA space exploration? Of mounting a vast slum clearance program? Suppose the two cost the same amount of money? Does that mean the opportunity cost is the same?

Chapter

SUPPLY AND DEMAND

A LOOK AHEAD

Here is your first real encounter with economics. In it you come to grips with the most important and powerful tool that economic reasoning gives us. The tool is an understanding of supply and demand and how they drive the market system.

It will help you to go through this chapter if you keep the following three steps in mind:

(1) You are going to learn exactly what the word "demand" means, and what a "demand curve" represents.

(2) You will learn the same thing about supply—what the word "supply" means and what a "supply curve" represents.

(3) You will put the two together and see how demand and supply give rise to the idea of an equilibrium price.

Our quick look at economic history has given us a general understanding of the market system. The next step in understanding the fundamental concepts of economics is to learn much more about that system.

What impresses us first when we study the market as a solution to the economic problem? The striking fact is that the market uses only one means of persuasion to induce people to engage in production or to undertake the tasks of distribution. It is neither time-honored tradition nor the edict of any authority that tells the members of a market society what to do. *It is price.*

PRICES AND BEHAVIOR

Thus the first attribute of a market system that we must examine is how prices take the place of tradition or command to become the guide to economic behavior.

The key lies in maximization. Through prices, acquisitive individuals learn what course of action will maximize their incomes or minimize their expenditures. This means that in the word *price* we include prices of labor or capital or resources that we call wages, profits, interest, or rent. Of course, within the category of prices we also include those ordinary prices that we pay for the goods and services we consume and the materials we purchase in order to build a home or to operate a store or factory. In each case, the only way that we can tell how to maximize our receipts and minimize our costs is by reading the signals of price that the market gives us.*

Therefore, if we are to understand how the market works as a mechanism—that is, how it acts as a guide to the solution of the economic problem—we must first understand how the market sets prices. When we say "the market," we mean the activity of buying and selling, or in more precise economic language, *demand and supply.* Let us discover how demand and supply interact to establish prices.

DEMAND

TASTE AND INCOME

When you enter the market for goods and services (almost every time you walk along a shopping street), two factors determine whether or not you will actually become a buyer and not just a window-shopper. The first factor is your taste for the good. It is your taste that determines in large degree whether a good offers you pleasure or utility, and if so, how much. The windows of shops are crammed with things you could afford to buy but which you simply do not wish to own, because they do not offer you sufficient utility. Perhaps if some of these were cheaper, you might wish to own them; but some goods you would not want even if they were free. For such goods, for which your tastes are too weak to motivate you, your demand is zero. **Thus taste determines your willingness to buy.**

*In the real world, reading prices can be very complicated, for it involves not only how much we know about the market, but how much we *think* we know about it. Here we simplify matters and assume, to begin with, that we all have perfect knowledge.

On the other hand, taste is by no means the only component of demand. Shop windows are also full of goods that you might very much like to own but cannot afford to buy. Your demand for Rolls Royces is also apt to be zero. **In other words, demand also hinges on your ability to buy—on your possession of sufficient wealth or income as well as on your taste.** If demand did not hinge on ability as well as willingness to buy, the poor, whose wants are always very large, would constitute a great source of demand.

BUDGETS

Note that your demand for goods depends on your willingness and ability to buy goods or services *at their going price*. From this it follows that the amounts of goods you demand will change as their prices change, just as it also follows that the amounts you will demand change as your wealth or income changes. There is no difficulty understanding why changing prices should change our ability to buy: Our wealth simply stretches further or less far. **In economic language, our budget constraint is loosened when prices fall and tightened when they rise.**

DIMINISHING MARGINAL UTILITY

Why should our *willingness* to buy be related to price? The answer lies in the nature of utility. People are maximizing creatures, but they do not want ever more of the *same* commodity. On the contrary, as we saw, economists take as a plausible generalization that additional increments of the same good or service, within some stated period of time, will yield smaller and smaller increments of pleasure. **These increments of pleasure are called marginal utility, and the gen-**

UTILITIES AND DEMAND

UTILITIES AND DEMAND

Does diminishing marginal utility really determine how much we buy? The idea seems far removed from common sense, but is it? Suppose we decide to buy a cake of fancy soap. In commonsense language, we'll do so only "if it's not too expensive." In the language of the economist this means we'll only do so *if the utilities we expect from the soap are greater than the utilities we derive from the money we have to spend to get the soap.*

If we buy one or two cakes, doesn't this demonstrate that the pleasure of the soap is greater than the pleasure of holding onto the money or spending it for something else? In that case, why don't we buy a year's supply of the soap? The commonsense answer is that we don't want *that much* soap. It would be a nuisance. We wouldn't use it all for months and months, etc. *In the language of the economist, the utilities of the cakes of soap after the first few would be less than the utilities of the money they would cost.*

In the accompanying diagram we show these diminishing marginal utilities of successive cakes. The price of soap represents the utility of the money we have to pay. As you can see, if soap costs *OA*, we'll buy three cakes; no more.

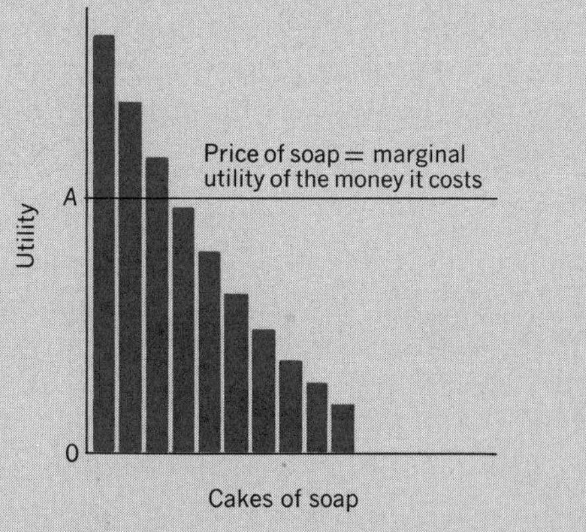

FIGURE 7.1 DIMINISHING MARGINAL UTILITY AND A DEMAND CURVE

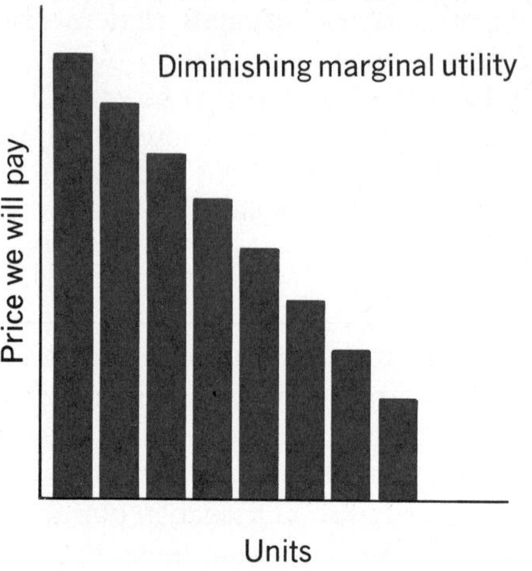

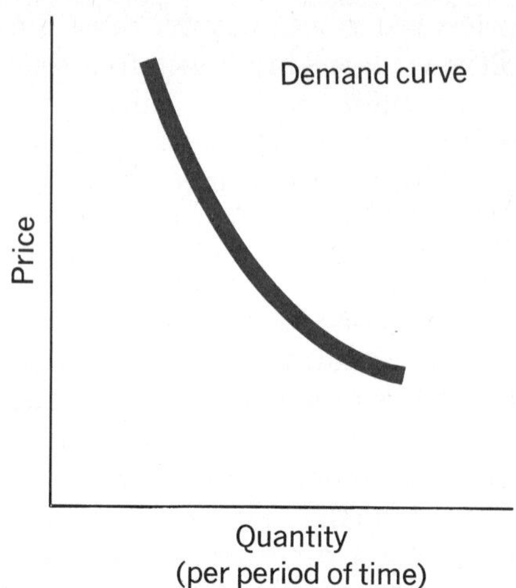

Notice, on the left, how the marginal utility of each additional unit of a good diminishes. The curve on the right simply generalizes the fact that each additional unit yields less pleasure than the one before it, and will therefore command a smaller price.

---

eral tendency of marginal utility to diminish is called the law of *diminishing marginal utility.* Remember: Diminishing marginal utility refers strictly to behavior and not to nature. The units of goods we continue to buy are not smaller —it is the pleasure associated with each additional unit that is smaller.

DEMAND CURVES*

In the bar chart on the left of Figure 7.1, we show the ever smaller amounts of money we are willing to pay for additional units of some good or service, simply because each additional unit gives us less utility than its predecessor. In the graph on the right, we have drawn a *demand curve* to generalize this basic relationship between the quantity of a good we are interested in acquiring and the price we are willing to pay for it.

Figure 7.1 deserves a careful look. Note that each *additional* unit affords us less utility, so we are not willing to pay as much for the next unit as for the one we just bought. This does not mean that the *total utility* we derive from all 3 or 4 units is less than that derived from the first. Far from it. It is the *addition* to our utility from the last unit that is much lower than the *addition* of the first or second.

THE PUZZLE OF BREAD AND DIAMONDS

The notion of diminishing marginal utility also clears up an old puzzle of economic life. This is why we are willing to pay so little for bread, which is a necessity for life, and so much for diamonds, which are not. The answer is that we have so much bread that the marginal utility of any loaf we are thinking of buying is very little, whereas we have so few diamonds that each carat has a very high marginal utility. If we were locked inside Tiffany's over a long holiday, the

*Anyone unfamiliar with graphs should turn right now to page 112 and learn how to read them and use them. Look as well into the Extra Word on graphs at the end of Chapter 8.

prices we would pay for bread and diamonds, after a few days, would be very different from those we would have paid when we entered.

SUPPLY

What about the supply side? Here, too, willingness and ability enter into the seller's actions. As we would expect, they bring about reactions different from those in the case of demand.

At high prices, sellers are much more *willing* to supply goods and services because they will take in more money. They will also be much more easily *able* to offer more goods because higher prices will enable less efficient suppliers to enter the market, or will cover the higher costs of production that may result from increasing their outputs.

Therefore, we depict normal supply curves as rising. These rising curves present a contrast to the falling curves of demanders: sellers eagerly respond to high prices; buyers respond negatively. Figure 7.2 shows such a typical supply curve.

SUPPLY AND DEMAND

The idea that buyers welcome low prices and sellers welcome high prices is hardly apt to come as a surprise. What is surprising is that the meaning of the words *supply* and *demand* differs from the one we ordinarily carry about in our heads. It is very important to understand that when we speak of demand as economists, we do not refer to a single purchase at a given price. **Demand in its proper economic sense refers to the various quantities of goods or services that we are willing and able to buy at different prices at a given time. That relationship is shown by our demand curve.**

The same relationship between price and quantity enters into the word *supply*. When we say *supply*, we do not mean the amount a seller puts on the market at a given price. We mean the various amounts offered at different prices. Thus our supply curves, like our demand curves, portray the relationship between willingness and ability to enter into transactions at different prices.

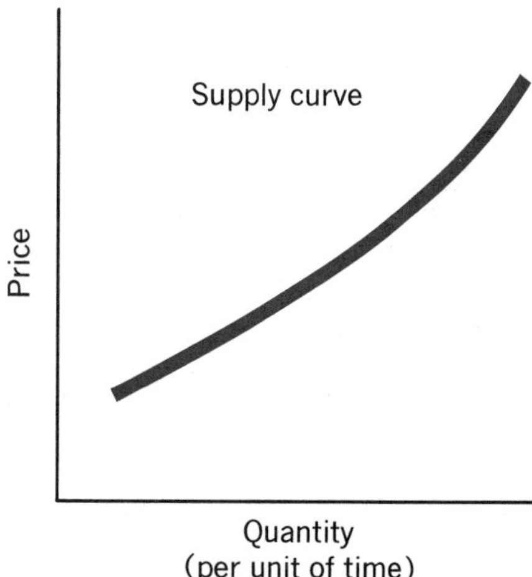

A typical supply curve slopes upward because each additional unit tends to be more difficult or expensive to make, at least in the short run.

FIGURE 7.2 THE SHORT-RUN SUPPLY CURVE

INDIVIDUAL AND COLLECTIVE SUPPLY AND DEMAND

We must add one last word before we investigate the market at work. Thus far we have considered only the factors that make an *individual* more willing and able to buy or less willing and able to sell as prices fall. Generally when we speak of supply and demand we refer to markets composed of *many* suppliers and demanders. That gives us an additional reason for relating price and behavior. If we assume that most individuals have somewhat different willingnesses and abilities to buy, because their incomes and their tastes are different, or they have unequal willingnesses or abilities to sell, then we can see that *a change in price will bring into the market new buyers or sellers:* **As price falls, it will tempt or permit one person after another to buy, thereby adding to the quantity of the good that will be purchased at that price. Conversely, as prices rise, the number of sellers drawn into the market will increase, and the quantity of goods they offer will rise accordingly.**

We can see this graphically in Figure 7.3. Here we show three individuals' demand curves. At the going market price of $2, A is either not willing or not able to buy any of the commodity. B is both willing and able to buy 1 unit. C buys 3 units. If we add up their demands, we get a *collective or market demand curve.* At the indicated market price of $2, the quantity demanded is 4 units. What would it be (approximately) for each buyer, and for the group, at a price of $1?

The same, of course, applies to supply. In Figure 7.4 we show individual supply curves and a collective or market supply curve that is 7 units at $2 market supply. What would total supply be at a price of $1? What would seller A's supply be at $1?

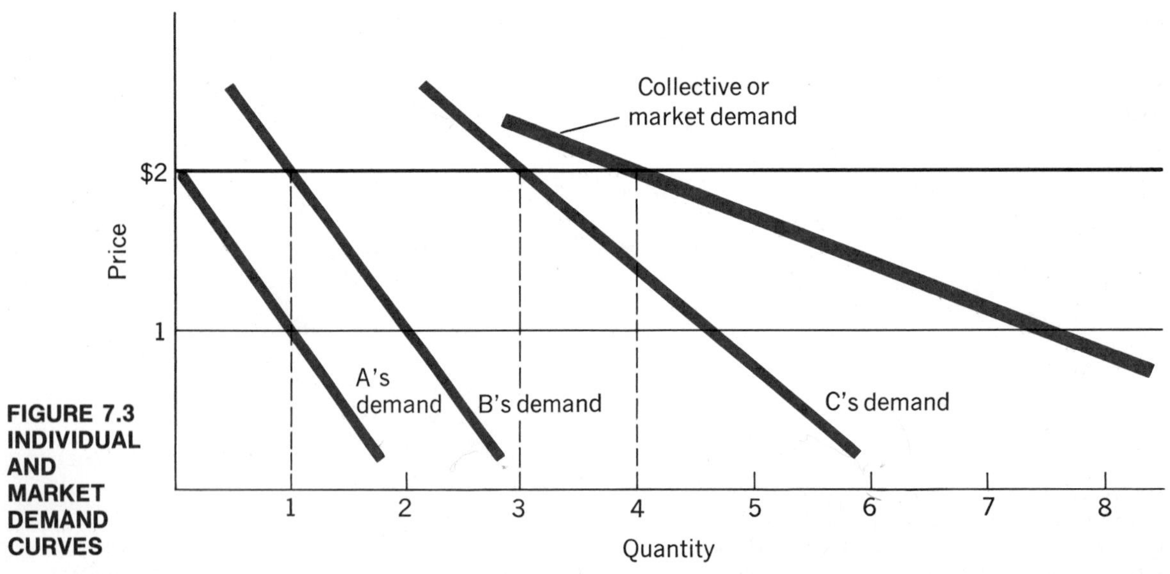

FIGURE 7.3 INDIVIDUAL AND MARKET DEMAND CURVES

The demand curves for a product on a market are nothing but the sum of the individual demand curves for it.

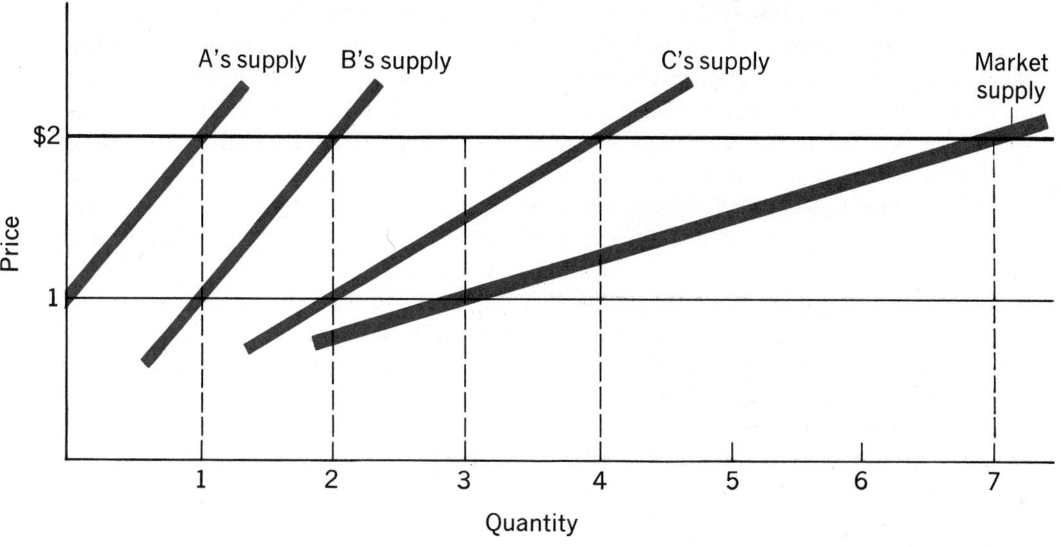

FIGURE 7.4 INDIVIDUAL AND MARKET SUPPLY CURVES

Like market demand curves, market supply curves sum up the willingness and ability of individuals into a market total.

BALANCING SUPPLY AND DEMAND

We are now ready to see how the market mechanism works. Undoubtedly you have already grasped the crucial point on which the mechanism depends. This is the opposing behavior that a change in prices brings about for buyers and sellers. Rising prices will be matched by an increase in the willingness and ability of sellers to offer goods, but in a decrease in the willingness and ability of buyers to take goods.

It is through these opposing reactions that the market mechanism works. Let us examine the process in an imaginary market for shoes in a small city. In Table 7.1 we show the price-quantity relationships of buyers and of sellers: how many thousand pairs will be offered for sale or sought for purchase at a range of prices from $50 to $5. We call such an array of price-quantity relationships a **schedule** of supply and demand.

Price	*Quantity demanded (1,000 prs.)*	*Quantity supplied (1,000 prs.)*
$50	1	125
$45	5	90
$40	10	70
$35	20	50
$30	25	35
$25	30	30
$20	40	20
$15	50	10
$10	75	5
$ 5	100	0

TABLE 7.1 DEMAND AND SUPPLY SCHEDULES

Go down the price schedule and notice that quantities demanded do not equal quantities supplied—until you get to $25. Below $25 they are also unequal. $25 is the equilibrium price.

As before, the schedules tell us that buyers and sellers react differently to prices. At high prices, buyers are either not willing or unable to purchase more than small quantities of shoes, whereas sellers would be only too willing and able to flood the city with them. At very low prices, the quantity of shoes demanded would be very great, but few shoe manufacturers would be willing or able to gratify buyers at such low prices.

If we now look at *both* schedules at *each* price level, we discover an interesting thing. *There is one price—*$25 in our example*—at which the quantity demanded is exactly the same as the quantity supplied.* At every other price, one schedule or the other is larger, but as $25 the amounts in both columns are the same: 30,000 pairs of shoes. We call this balancing price the *equilibrium price.* We shall soon see that it *is* the price that emerges spontaneously in an actual market where supply and demand contend.*

EMERGENCE OF THE EQUILIBRIUM PRICE

How do we know that an equilibrium price will be brought about by the interaction of supply and demand? The process is one of the most important in all of economics, so we should understand it very clearly.

INTERPLAY OF SUPPLY AND DEMAND

Suppose in our example above that for some reason or other the shoe retailers put a price tag on their shoes not of $25 but of $45. What would happen? Our schedules show us that at this price shoe manufacturers will be pouring out shoes at the rate of 90,000 pairs a year, whereas customers would be buying them at the rate of only 5,000 pairs a year. Shortly, the shoe factories would be bulging with unsold merchandise. It is plain what the outcome of this situation must be. In order to realize some revenue, shoe manufacturers will begin to unload their stocks at lower prices. *They do so because this is their rational course as competitive maximizers.*

As they reduce the price, the situation will begin to improve. At $40, demand picks up from 5,000 pairs to 10,000, while at the same time the slightly lower price discourages some producers, so that output falls from 90,000 pairs to 70,000. Shoe manufacturers are still turning out more shoes than the market can absorb at the going prices, although the difference between the quantities supplied and the quantities demanded is smaller than it was before.

Let us suppose that the competitive pressure continues to reduce prices so that shoes soon sell at $30. Now a much more satisfactory state of affairs exists. Producers will be turning out 35,000 pairs of shoes. Consumers will be buying them at a rate of 25,000 a year. Still there is an imbalance. Some shoes will still be piling up, unsold, at the factory. Prices will therefore continue to fall, eventually to $25. At this point, the quantity of shoes supplied by the manufacturers—30,000 pairs—is exactly that demanded by customers. There is no longer a surplus of unsold shoes hanging over the market and acting to press prices down.

*Of course we have made up our schedules so that the quantities demanded and supplied would be equal at $25. The price that actually brought about such a balancing of supply and demand might be some odd number such as $24.98.

THE MARKET CLEARS

Now let us quickly trace the interplay of supply and demand from the other direction. Suppose that prices were originally $5. Our schedules tell us that customers would be standing in line at the shoe stores, but producers would be largely shut down, unwilling or unable to make shoes at those prices. We can easily imagine that customers, many of whom would gladly pay more than $5, let it be known that they would welcome a supply of shoes at $10 or even more. They, too, are trying to maximize their utilities. If enough customers bid $10, a trickle of shoe output begins. Nevertheless, the quantity of shoes demanded at $10 far exceeds the available supply. Customers snap up the few pairs around and tell shoe stores they would gladly pay $20 a pair. Prices rise accordingly. Now we are getting closer to a balance of quantities offered and bid for. At $20 there will be a demand for 40,000 pairs of shoes, and output will have risen to 20,000 pairs. Still the pressure of unsatisfied demand raises prices further. Finally a price of $25 is tried. Now, once again, the quantities supplied and demanded are exactly in balance. There is no further pressure from unsatisfied customers to force the price up further, because at $25 no customer who can afford the going price will remain unsatisfied. The market "clears."

CHARACTERISTICS OF EQUILIBRIUM PRICES

Thus we can see how the interaction of supply and demand brings about the establishment of a price at which both suppliers and demanders are willing and able to sell or buy the same quantity of goods. We can visualize the equilibrating process more easily if we now transfer our supply and demand schedules to graph paper. Figure 7.5 is the representation of the shoe market we have been dealing with.

The graph shows us at a glance the situation we have analyzed in detail. At the price of $25, the quantities demanded and supplied are equal: 30,000 pairs of shoes. The graph also shows more vividly than the schedules why this is an *equilibrium* price.

Suppose that the price were temporarily lifted above $25. If you will draw a horizontal pencil line from any point on the vertical axis above the $25 mark to represent this price, you will find that it intersects the demand curve before it

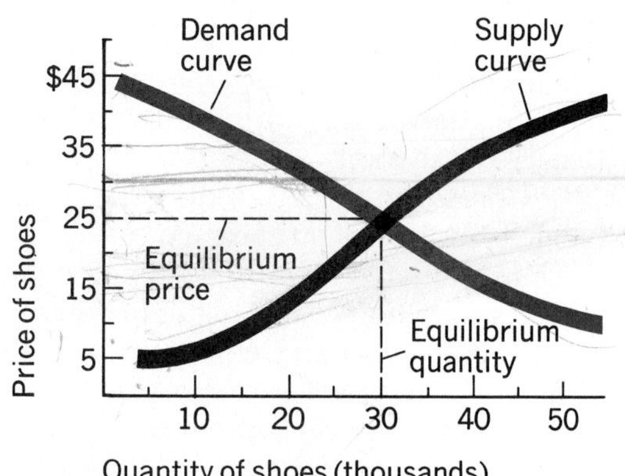

Demand and supply curves only show what the schedule has already revealed: There is one price at which the two quantities are equal. This is the equilibrium price.

FIGURE 7.5 DETERMINATION OF AN EQUILIBRIUM PRICE

reaches the supply curve. In other words, *the quantity demanded is less than the quantity supplied at any price above the equilibrium price, and the excess of the quantity supplied means that there will be a downward pressure on prices, back toward the equilibrium point.*

The situation is exactly reversed if prices should fall below the equilibrium point. Now the quantity demanded is greater than that supplied, and the pressure of buyers will push the price up to the equilibrium point.

Thus equilibrium prices have two important characteristics:

1. They are the prices that will spontaneously establish themselves through the free play of the forces of supply and demand.

2. Once established, they will persist unless the forces of supply and demand themselves change.

DOES "DEMAND EQUAL SUPPLY"?

There is one last thing to be noted carefully about equilibrium prices. They are the prices that bring about an equality in the *quantities demanded* and the *quantities supplied.* They are not the prices that bring about an equality of "supply and demand."

Probably the most common beginning mistake in economics is to say that supply and demand are equal when prices are in equilibrium. If we remember that both supply and demand mean the *relationships* between quantities and prices, we can see that an equality of supply and demand would mean that the demand schedule and the supply schedule for a commodity were alike, so that the curves would lie one on top of the other. In turn, this would mean that at a price of $50, buyers of shoes would be willing and able to buy the same number of shoes that suppliers would be willing to offer at that price, and the same for buyers at $5. If such were the case, prices would be wholly indeterminate and could race high and low with no tension of opposing interests to bring them to a stable resting place.

Hence we must take care to use the words *supply* or *demand* to refer only to relationships or schedules. When we want to speak of the effect of a particular price on our willingness or ability either to buy or sell, we use the longer phrase *quantity demanded* or *quantity supplied.*

THE ROLE OF COMPETITION

We have seen how stable, lasting prices may spontaneously emerge from the flux of the marketplace, but we have silently passed over a basic condition for the formation of these prices. This is the role played by competition in the operation of the market mechanism.

Competition is often discussed as a somewhat unpleasant attribute of economic man. Now, however, we can see that it is an attribute that is indispensable if we are to have socially acceptable outcomes for a market process.

Competition is the regulator that "supervises" the orderly working of the market. But economic competition (unlike the competition for prizes outside economic life) is not a single contest. It is a *continuing process.* It monitors a race that no one ever wins, a race where all must go on endlessly trying to stay in front, to avoid the economic penalties of falling behind.

SUPPLY AND DEMAND, AGAIN

Here is one of the oldest "puzzles" in economics. Suppose that the price of A.T.&T. stock rises. Because the price rises, the demand for the stock falls. Therefore the price of A.T.&T. must decline. It follows that the price of A.T.&T. should never vary or at least should quickly return to the starting point.

Tell that to your broker. Better, tell it to your instructor and show him—and yourself—with a graph of supply and demand, where the fallacy of this puzzle lies. Hint: When the price rises, does the *demand* for A.T.&T. stock fall or does the *quantity demanded* fall? Will the price fall again?

Moreover, unlike the contests of ordinary life, economic *competition involves not just a single struggle among rivals, but two struggles.* One is between the two sides of the markets; the other is among the marketers on each side. The competitive marketplace is not only where the clash of interest between buyer and seller is worked out by the opposition of supply and demand, but also where buyers contend against buyers and sellers against sellers.

TWO NECESSARY ASPECTS OF COMPETITION

It is this double aspect of the competitive process that accounts for its usefulness. A market in which buyers and sellers had no conflict of interest would not be competitive, for prices could then be arranged at some level convenient for both sides, instead of representing a compromise between the divergent interests of the two. Conversely, a market that was no more than a place where opposing forces contended would be only a tug of war, a bargaining contest with an unpredictable outcome, unless we knew the respective strengths and cunning of the two sides.

Competition drives buyers and sellers to a meeting point because each side of the price contest is also contesting against itself. Vying takes place not merely *between* those who want high prices and those who want low ones. On each side of this divide, vying takes place *among* marketers whose self-interest urges them to meet the demands of the other side. If some unsatisfied shoe buyers, although preferring low prices to high ones, did not want shoes enough to offer a little higher price than the prevailing one, and if some unsatisfied sellers, although hoping for high prices, were not driven by self-interest to offer a price a little below that of their rivals, the price would not move to the balancing point where the two sides arrived at the best possible settlement.

Thus, whereas buyers as a group want low prices, each individual buyer has to pay as high a price as he can to get into the market. Whereas sellers as a group want high prices, each individual seller has to trim his prices if he is to be able to meet the competition.

MAXIMIZING SUBJECT TO CONSTRAINTS

Does the extraordinary market mechanism bear a relation to the general notion of maximizing? Indeed it does. Buyers and sellers both are *willing* to respond to price signals because they wish to maximize their incomes or utilities. But neither can maximize at will. Buyers are *constrained* by their budgets, and sellers are *constrained* by their costs. Thus the *ability* of buyers or sellers to respond to price signals is limited by obstacles of budgets or cost.

In addition, buyers and sellers are both constrained by the operation of the market. A seller might like to sell his goods above the market price, and a buyer might like to buy goods below the market price; but the presence of competitors means that a seller who quotes a price above the market will be unable to find a buyer, and a buyer who makes a bid below the market will be unable to find a seller.

Thus the market mechanism is a very important example of what economists call "maximizing subject to constraints." Furthermore, we can see that it is the very interaction of the maximizing drives and the constraining obstacles that leads the market to the establishment of equilibrium prices. We can also see that if we could know these maximizing forces and constraints beforehand, we would know the supply and demand curves of a market and could actually predict what its equilibrium price would be! In actual fact, our knowledge falls far short of such omniscience, but the imaginary example nonetheless begins to open up for us the analytical possibilities of economics.

KEY CONCEPTS

LOOKING BACK

You can now see that the purpose of this chapter is to show how maximizing subject to constraints works in terms of demand and supply. Here are the main points that you should carry away from what you have read:

Demand is the willingness and ability to buy at a given price

1. Demand is a central idea of economics. It means the willingness and ability of any person or group of persons to buy a good or service at a particular price. Your demand schedule reflects your desire to maximize your utilities for that good, within the constraint of your budget.

Marginal utility typically falls

2. Our willingness or ability to buy more of any kind of wealth reflects the marginal utility that another unit of that wealth will yield. The marginal utility means the additional utility—the pleasures of the *next* movie, the *next* pair of shoes, the *next* dollar of income—within a given period of time. A basic assumption of economic reasoning is that the marginal utility of any one thing diminishes: The second movie, pair of shoes, or dollar will not give as much pleasure as the first one.

Therefore typical demand curves fall

3. This gives rise to normal, downward-sloping demand curves, showing that we are only willing to buy more units of the same goods at cheaper prices. These curves represent our schedules in simplified form.

Supply curves typically rise

4. Supply curves typically rise, because suppliers are not able (or willing) to offer more and more goods within a given period of time, except at higher prices.

Supply and demand vs. quantities supplied or demanded

5. Supply and demand refer to the range of goods or services that sellers or buyers will offer at differing prices. At any given price we should refer to the *quantity supplied* or the *quantity demanded.* When we say supply or demand, we mean the whole schedule or the curve that represents that schedule.

The idea of equilibrium where quantities offered are equal to quantities demanded

6. When we compare schedules or plot two supply and demand curves, we can find out if there is an equilibrium price. This is a price where the quantities offered or supplied are equal to the quantities demanded. Economists are often careless and say that at an equilibrium price "supply equals demand," but students should watch their language! In an equilibrium price, the *quantities demanded* equal the *quantities supplied,* and the market clears.

How equilibrium prices emerge and persist

7. Equilibrium prices spontaneously establish themselves through the interplay of supply and demand, and they will persist unless the willingness or abilities of buyers and sellers change.

There is a two-sided aspect of competition

8. There is a double-edged aspect to competition. Competition not only means that buyers oppose sellers, each trying to get the better of the other, but also that buyers have to win out against other buyers and that sellers have to outdo—or do as well as—other sellers.

The price system

9. Lastly, bear in mind that you are learning the remarkable way in which an economic mechanism coordinates the very different objectives and activities of buyers and sellers through only one means—the signal of price. Prices inform people how to maximize rationally. The Invisible Hand does the rest!

ECONOMIC VOCABULARY

Demand 96	**Diminishing marginal utility 97**	**Equilibrium prices 102**
Taste 96	**Supply 99**	**Demand and supply curves 103**
Budget 97	**Schedules 101**	**Competition, two aspects 105**

QUESTIONS

1. Fill out the schedule below by supplying reasonable numbers to show the quantities demanded and supplied for T-shirts in a small town, at prices ranging from $1.00 to $10.00, over a period of, say, one year. (You might assume that there are about 10,000 potential buyers in your market.) Now graph the schedule in the graph space provided. Be sure to indicate the quantities on the horizontal axis.

Schedule of supply and demand for T-shirts, per year.

Price of T-shirts	*Quantity demanded*	*Quantity supplied*
$10		
9		
8		
7		
6		
5		
4		
3		
2		
1		

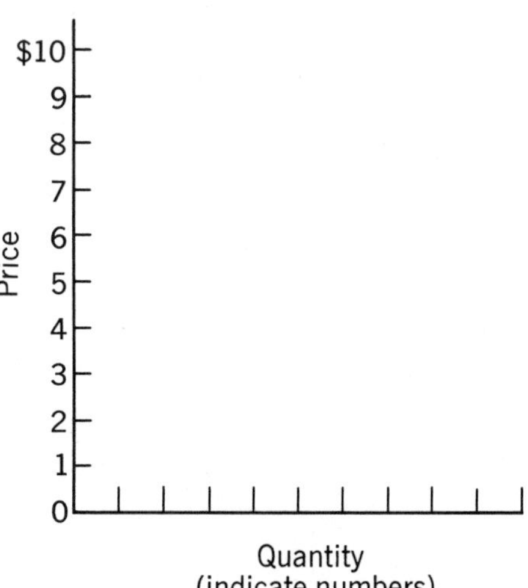

2. Choose any arbitrary price above equilibrium. How will maximizing behavior lead this higher price back toward equilibrium? Does it require a contest among buyers? Sellers? Both? Either?
3. Now do the same thing with a price below the equilibrium.
4. Subtract the quantities in your supply schedule from those in your demand schedule. There will be a plus or minus at all prices except one. Why is that? Does that help explain why an equilibrium price clears a market?
5. Whatever quantity is sold must be bought; whatever is bought must be sold. Then how can we say that only one price will clear the market? Hint: Look again at your answer to question 2.

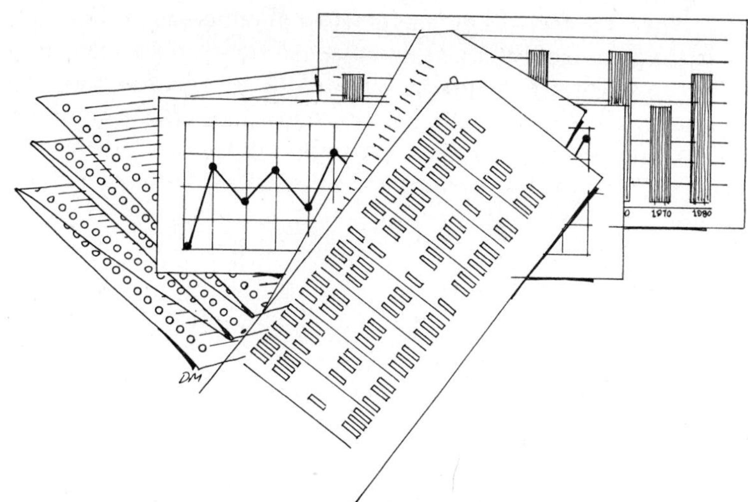

Chapter 8 SIX TOOLS YOU SHOULD KNOW HOW TO HANDLE

A LOOK AHEAD

This is a chapter about concepts and techniques. It isn't about "economics," but about some ideas, simple statistical devices, and other tools with which every economist must be familiar. There is no single, large idea to keep in mind as you go through this chapter. We suspect that for most students it will be very easy; easy or hard, it has to be mastered. Keep a list of the six ideas as they come, and check them off against the review in "Looking Back" after you have finished.

This chapter will give us a series of concepts and techniques that we shall use in thinking clearly about economics. Some of them seem very simple but are more subtle than they appear at first. Others look demanding at first, even though they are actually very simple. There are six of these intellectual tools. Try to master them, for we will be using them continuously from now on.

1. CETERIS PARIBUS

The first concept is the need to eliminate outside influences that might invalidate our efforts to make scientific statements about economic behavior. If we were physicists trying to arrive at the formula for gravitation, for instance, we would have to make allowances for wind or air resistance in calculating the force that gravity really exerts. So, too, in economics we have to eliminate disturbing influences from our observations. We do so by making the assumption that "other things" remain constant while we focus on the particular relationships we're interested in.

This assumption of holding "other things equal" is called by its Latin name, *ceteris paribus.* It is extremely easy to apply in theory and extremely difficult to apply in practice. In our examination of the demand curve, for example, we assume that the *income* and *tastes* of the person (or of the collection of persons) are unchanged while we examine the influence of price on the quantities of shoes they are willing and able to buy. The reason is obvious. If we allowed their incomes or tastes to change, both their willingness *and* their ability would also change. If prices doubled but a fad for shoes developed, or if prices tripled but income quadrupled, we would not find that demand decreased as prices rose.

Ceteris paribus is applied every time we speak of supply and demand and on many other occasions as well. Since we know that in reality prices, tastes, incomes, population size, technology, moods, and many other elements of society are continually changing, we can see why this is a heroic assumption. It is one

STATICS AND DYNAMICS: THE IMPORTANCE OF TIME

Of all the sources of difficulty that creep into economic analysis, none is more vexing than *time.* The reason is that time changes all manner of things and makes it virtually impossible to apply *ceteris paribus.* That is why, for example, we always mean "within a fixed period of time" when we speak of something like diminishing marginal utility. There is no reason for the marginal utility of a meal tomorrow to be less than one today, but good reason to think that a second lunch on top of the first will bring a sharp decline in utilities.

So, too, supply and demand curves presumably describe activities that take place within a short period of time, ideally within an instant. The longer the time period covered, the less is *ceteris* apt to be *paribus.*

This poses many difficult problems for economic analysis, because it means that we must use a "static" (or timeless) set of theoretical ideas to solve "dynamic" (or time-consuming) questions. The method we will use to cope with this problem is called comparative statics. We compare an economic situation at one period with an economic situation at a later period, without investigating in much detail the path we travel from the first situation to the second. To inquire into the path requires calculus and advanced economic analysis. We'll leave that for another course.

that is almost impossible to trace in actual life or to correct for fully by special statistical techniques.

Yet we can also see that unless we apply *ceteris paribus*, at least in our minds, we cannot isolate the particular interactions and causal sequences that we want to investigate. The economic world then becomes a vast Chinese puzzle. Every piece interlocks with every other, and no one can tell what the effect of any one thing is on any other. If economics is to be useful, it must be able to tell us something about the effect of changing *only* price or *only* income or *only* taste or any *one* of a number of other things. We can do so only by assuming that other things are equal and by holding them unchanged in our minds while we perform the intellectual experiment in whose outcome we are interested.

2. FUNCTIONAL RELATIONSHIPS

Economics, it is already very clear, is about relationships—relationships of mankind and nature, and relationships of individuals to one another. The laws of diminishing marginal utility or diminishing returns or supply and demand are all statements of those relationships, which we can use to explain or predict economic matters.

We call relationships that portray the effect of one thing on another *functional relationships*. Functional relationships may relate the effect of price on the quantities offered or bought, or the effect of successive inputs of the same factor on outputs of a given product, or the effect of population growth on economic growth, or whatever.

One important point: Functional relationships are not logical relationships of the kind we find in geometry or arithmetic, such as the square of the hypotenuse of a right triangle being equal to the sum of the squares of the other two sides, or the number 6 being the product of 2 times 3 or 3 times 2. Functional relationships cannot be discovered by deductive reasoning. They are descriptions of real events that we can discover only by empirical investigation. We then search for ways of expressing these relationships in graphs or mathematical terms. In economics, the technique used for discovering these relationships is called *econometrics*.

3. IDENTITIES

Before going on, we must clarify an important distinction between functional relationships and another kind of relationship called an *identity*. We need this distinction because both relationships use the word *equals*, although the word has different meanings in the two cases.

A few pages ahead we shall meet the expression

$$Q_d = f(P)$$

which we read "Quantity demanded (Q_d) *equals* or *is* a function of price ($= f(P)$)." This refers to the kind of relationship we have been talking about. We shall also find another kind of "equals," typified by the statement $P \equiv S$ or purchases equals sales. $P \equiv S$ is *not* a functional relationship, because purchases do not "depend" on sales. They are *the same thing* as sales, viewed from the vantage point of the buyer instead of the seller. *P* and *S* are identities: *Q* and *P* are not. The identity sign is $\equiv$.

Identities are true by definition. They cannot be "proved" true or false, because there is nothing to be proved. On the other hand, when we say that the quantity purchased will depend on price, there is a great deal to be proved. Empirical investigation may disclose that the suggested relationship is not true. It may show that a relationship exists but that the nature of the relationship is not always the same. Identities are changeless as well as true. They are logical statements that require no investigations of human action. The signs $\equiv$ and $=$ do not mean the same things.

Sometimes identities and behavioral equations are written in the same manner with an equal sign ($=$). Technically, identities should be written with an identity sign ($\equiv$). Unfortunately, the sign also reads "equals." Since it is important to know the difference between definitions, which do not need proof, and hypotheses, which *always* need demonstration or proof, we shall carefully differentiate between the equal sign ($=$) and the identity sign ($\equiv$). Whenever you see an equal sign, you will know that a behavioral relationship is being hypothesized. When you see the identity sign, you will know that a definition is being offered, not a statement about behavior.

Identities, being definitions, deserve our attention because they are the way we establish a precise working language. Learning this language, with its special vocabulary, is essential to being able to speak economics accurately.

4. SCHEDULES

We are familiar with the next item in our kit of intellectual tools. It is one of the techniques used to establish functional relationships: the technique of drawing up *schedules* or lists of the different values of elements.

We met such schedules in Chapter 7, in our lists of the quantities of shoes supplied or demanded at various prices. **Schedules are thus the empirical or hypothetical data whose functional interconnection we wish to investigate.** As working economists we would experience many problems in drawing up such schedules in real life. We often use them, however, in economic analysis, as examples of typical economic behaviour.

5. GRAPHS

The depiction of functional relationships through schedules is simple enough, but economists usually prefer to represent these relationships by graphs or equations. This is so because schedules show the relationship only between *specific* quantities and prices or specific data of any kind. **Graphs and equations show *generalized* relationships, relationships that cover all quantities and prices or all values of any two things we are interested in.**

The simplest and most intuitively obvious method of showing a functional relationship in its general form is through a graph. Everyone is familiar with graphs of one kind or another, but not all graphs show functional relationships. A graph of stock prices over time, as in Figure 8.1, shows us the level of prices in different periods. It does not show a behavioral connection between a date and

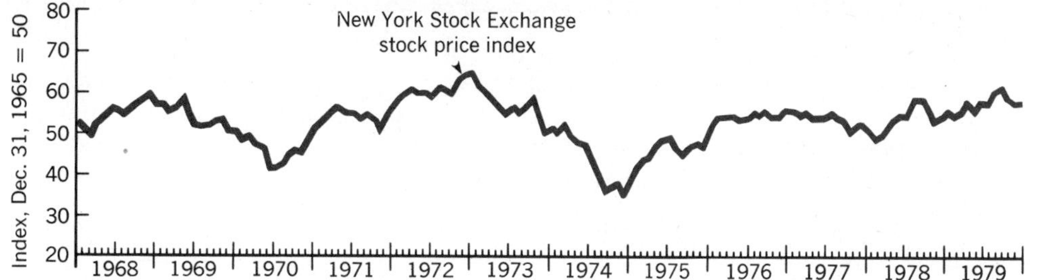

FIGURE 8.1 STOCK MARKET PRICES

Some graphs, like this one, just show how a given variable behaves over time.

a price. Such a graph merely describes and summarizes history. No one would maintain that such and such a date *caused* stock market prices to take such and such a level.

On the other hand, a graph that related the price of a stock and the quantities that we are willing and able to buy *at that price, ceteris paribus,* is indeed a graphic depiction of a functional relation. If we look at the hypothetical graph below, we can note the dots that show us the particular price/quantity relationships. Now we can tell the quantity that would be demanded at any price, simply by going up the price axis, over to the demand curve, and down to the quantity axis. In Figure 8.2, for example, at a price of $50 the quantity demanded is 5,000 shares per day.*

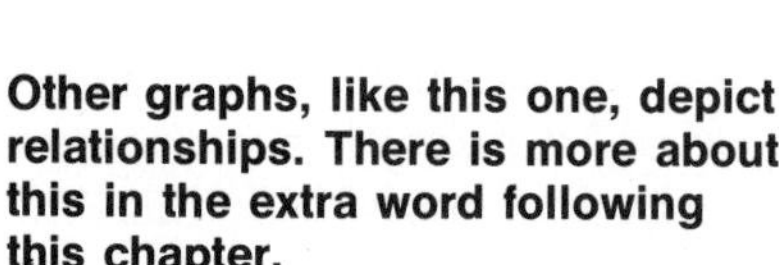

Other graphs, like this one, depict relationships. There is more about this in the extra word following this chapter.

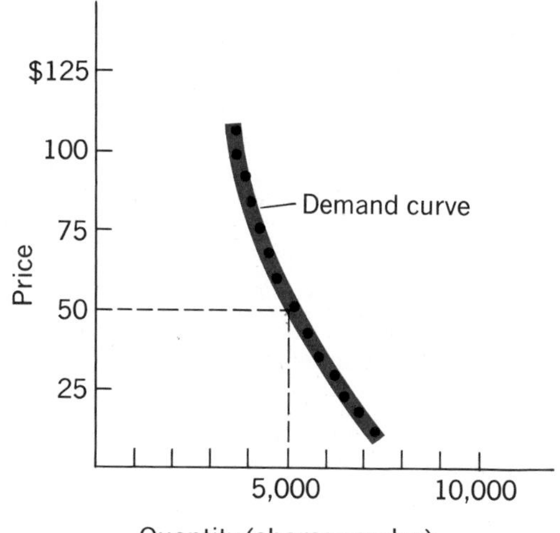

FIGURE 8.2 PRICE/ QUANTITY RELATIONSHIP OF A GIVEN SHARE

*Technically we would need a schedule of survey results showing the quantities demanded for every conceivable price in order to draw a graph. In fact, we obtain results for a variety of prices and assume that the relationship between the unmeasured points is like that of the measured points. The process of sketching in unmeasured points is called *interpolation.*

UPWARD SLOPING DEMAND CURVES

Although most demand curves slope downward, in three interesting cases they don't. The first concerns certain *luxury goods* in which the price itself becomes part of the "utility" of the good. The perfume Joy is extensively advertised as "the world's most expensive perfume." Do you think its sales would increase if the price were lowered and the advertisement changed to read "the world's second-most expensive perfume"?

The other case affects just the opposite kind of good: certain basic staples. Here the classic case is potatoes. In nineteenth-century Ireland, potatoes formed the main diet for very poor farmers. As potato prices rose, Irish peasants were forced to cut back on their purchases of other foods, to devote more of their incomes to buying this necessity of life. More potatoes were purchased, even though their prices were rising, because potatoes were the cheapest thing to eat.

Such goods have upward sloping demand curves. The higher the price, the more you (are forced to) buy. Of course, when potatoes reach price levels that compete with, say wheat, any further price rises will result in a fall in the quantity demanded, since buyers will shift to wheat.

Finally, there is a very important upward sloping curve that relates quantities demanded and *incomes:* the higher our incomes, the more we buy. We will use this special demand relationship a great deal in macroeconomics. However, in microeconomics, the functional relation is mainly between *price* and quantities demanded, not income and quantities demanded. Still, it is useful to remember that the functional relationships involving demand do not all slope in the same direction.

6. EQUATIONS

A third way of representing functional relationships is often used for its simplicity and brevity. **Equations are very convenient means of expressing functional relationships, since they allow us to consider the impact of more than one factor at a time.** A typical equation for demand might look like this:

$$Q_d = f(P)$$

Most of us are familiar with equations but may have forgotten their vocabulary. There are three terms in the equation above: Q_d, f, and P. Each has a name. We are interested in seeing how our quantity demanded (Q_d) is affected by changes in prices (P). In other words, our "demand" is dependent on changes in price. Therefore the term Q_d is called the **dependent variable:** "variable" because it changes; "dependent" because it is the result of changes in P. As we would imagine, the name for P is the **independent variable.**

Now for the term f. The definition of f is simply **"function"** or "function of," so that we read $Q_d = f(P)$ as "quantity demanded is a function of price." If we knew that the quantity demanded was a function of both price *and* income (Y) we would write $Q_d = f(P,Y)$. Such equations tell us what independent variables affect what dependent variables, but they do not tell us *how* Q_d changes with changes in P or Y.

The "how" depends on our actual analysis of actual market behavior. Let us take a very simple case for illustrative purposes. Suppose that a survey of consumer purchasing intentions tells us that consumers would take 100 units of a product if its price were zero—that is, if it were given away free—and that they would buy one-half unit less each time the price went up by $1. The demand equation would then be:

$$Q_d = 100 - .5(P)$$

Thus, if price were $10, buyers would take 100 − .5 × 10, or 95 units.*

We should stop to note one important property of ordinary price/quantity demand or supply functions. It is that they have opposite "signs." A normal demand function is negative, showing that quantities demanded *fall* as prices rise. A supply function is usually positive, showing that quantities supplied *rise* as prices rise. A survey of producers might tell us that the quantity supplied would go up by 2 units for every $1 increase in price, or

$$Q_s = 2(P)$$

Note that the sign of the function 2 is positive, whereas the sign of the demand function was negative, −.5.

ECONOMIC TECHNIQUES REVIEWED

The basic assumptions that economics makes regarding economic society can be summed up in two sets of general propositions or laws—laws about be-

EQUILIBRIUM IN EQUATIONS

It is very easy to see the equilibrium point when we have a supply curve and a demand curve that cross. But since equations are only another way of representing the information that curves show, we must be able to demonstrate equilibrium in equations. Here is a simple example:

Suppose the demand function, as before, is:

$Q_d = 100 - .5\ (P)$, and that the supply function is:

$Q_s = 2(P)$

The question is, then, what value for P will make Q_d equal to Q_s? The answer follows:

If $Q_d = Q_s$, then

$100 - .5(P) = 2(P)$.

Putting all the P's on one side

$2(P) + .5\ (P) = 100$, or $2.5p = 100$. Solving, $P = 40$.

Substituting a price of 40 into the demand equation we get a quantity of 80. In the supply equation we also get 80. Thus 40 must be the equilibrium price.

*Suppose we wanted an equation that would measure the effect on quantity demanded of both price and income (see box). Such an equation might be:

$$Q_d = 100 - .5(P) + .1(Y)$$

where Y = income

In this equation the quantity demanded goes *up* by 100 units whenever incomes rise by $1,000. As before, it goes *down* by ½ unit as prices rise by $1. If incomes were $2,000 and P were $10, the quantity demanded would be (100 − .5 × 10 + .1 × 2,000) = 295 units.

havior and laws about production. What we have been learning in this chapter are the *techniques* of economic analysis—the ways in which economics uses its basic premises.

These techniques, as we have seen, revolve around the central idea of functional relationships. Because behavior or production is sufficiently regular, functions enable us to explain or predict economic activity. Their relationships are presented in the form of graphs or equations derived from the underlying schedules of data.

As we have seen, the ability to establish functional relationships depends critically on the *ceteris paribus* assumption. Unless we hold other things equal, either by econometric means or simply in our heads, we cannot isolate the effect of one variable on another.

ECONOMIC FALLACIES

No chapter on the mode of economic thought would be complete without reference to *economic fallacies.* **Actually there is no special class of fallacies that is called economic. The mistakes we find in economic thought are only examples of a larger class of mistaken ways of thinking that we call fallacies.** But they are serious enough to justify a warning in general and some attention to one fallacy in particular.

The general warning can do no more than ask us to be on guard against the sloppy thinking that can make fools of us in any area. It is easy to fall into errors of false syllogisms,* of trying to prove an argument *post hoc, ergo propter hoc* ("after the fact, therefore the cause of the fact"). An example would be "proving" that government spending must be inflationary by pointing out that the government spent large sums during periods when inflation was present, ignoring other factors that may have been at work.

The gallery of such mistaken conclusions is all too large in all fields. One fallacy that has a special relevance to economics is called the **fallacy of composition.** Suppose we had an island community in which all farmers sold their produce to one another. Suppose further that one farmer was able to get rich by cheating: selling his produce at the same price as everyone else, but putting fewer vegetables into his bushel baskets. Does it not follow that all farmers could get rich if all cheated?

We can see that there is a fallacy here. Where does it arise? In the first example, when our cheating farmer got rich, we ignored a small side effect of his action. The side effect was that a loss in real income was inflicted on the community. To ignore that side effect was proper so long as our focus of attention was what happened to the one farmer. When we broaden our inquiry to the entire community, the loss of income becomes a consideration. Everyone loses as much by being shortchanged as he gains by shortchanging. The side effects have become central effects. What was true for one turns out not to be true for all. Later on, in macroeconomics, we will find a very important example of exactly such a fallacy when we encounter what is called the Paradox of Thrift.

*See the questions at the end of this chapter.

KEY CONCEPTS

LOOKING BACK

This is a chapter about the concepts and techniques of economic analysis, not about the basic assumptions underlying economic theory. We should become familiar with a few of these ideas, or tools.

Ceteris paribus

1. *Ceteris paribus* is the assumption that everything other than the two variables whose relationship is being investigated is kept equal. Without *ceteris paribus* we cannot discern functional relationships.

Functional relationships

2. Functional relationships showing that X depends on Y lie at the very center of economic analysis. They are not logical or deductive relationships but relationships that we discover by *empirical investigation.*

Identities

3. Identities are purely definitional, therefore not subject to proof or to empirical investigation. Such definitions can, however, be very important.

Schedules
Graphs
Equations

4. The three techniques used to represent functional relationships are:

   a. schedules, or lists of data;
   b. graphs, or visual representations;
   c. equations.

5. You should know the meaning of three equational terms: the *independent variable,* the causative element that interests us; the *dependent variable,* the element whose behavior is affected by the independent variable; and the *function,* a mathematical statement of the relation between the two. Read the sentence $x = f(y)$ as "x is a function of y." Here, x is the dependent variable; y is the independent variable.

Fallacy of composition

6. Finally, learn to be on guard against economic fallacies, especially against the fallacy of composition.

ECONOMIC VOCABULARY

Ceteris paribus **110**
Functional relationships 111
Identities 111
Schedules 112
Independent and dependent variables 114
Functions 114
Fallacy of composition 116

QUESTIONS

1. Suppose you would acquire 52 books a year if books were free, but that your acquisitions would drop by 5 books for every dollar that you had to pay. Can you write a demand function for books?
2. Can you write a hypothetical function that might relate your demand for food and the price of food, assuming *ceteris paribus?*
3. "The quantity of food bought equals the quantity sold." Is this statement a functional relationship? If not, why not? Is it an identity?

4. Here is a schedule of supply and demand:

Price	*Units supplied*	*Units demanded*
$1	0	50
2	5	40
3	10	30
4	20	25
5	30	20
6	50	10

Does the schedule show an equilibrium price? Can you draw a graph and approximate the equilibrium price? What is it?

5. How do we read aloud the following? $C = f(Y)$ where C = consumption and Y = income. Which is the independent variable? The dependent?

6. Which of the following statements is a fallacy?

All X is Y
Z is Y
Therefore Z is X

All X is Y
Z is X
Therefore Z is Y

Try substituting classes of objects for the X's and Y, and individual objects for the Z's. Example: All planets (X's) are heavenly bodies (Y). The sun (Z) is a heavenly body (Y). Therefore the sun (Z) is a planet (X). Clearly, a false syllogism. Since Z is Y, however, the sun is a heavenly body.

Other fallacies:

If I can move to the head of the line, all individuals can move to the head of the line.

If I can save more by spending less, all individuals should be able to save more by spending less. Hint: If all spend less, what will happen to our incomes?

The fact that Lenin called inflation a major weapon that could destroy the bourgeoisie indicates that inflations are part of the communist strategy for the overthrow of capitalism.

AN EXTRA WORD ABOUT

GRAPHS AND ECONOMIC CAUSATION

Many students worry a great deal about drawing graphs and worry very little about what graphs show. They are wrong on both counts. The technique of graphing is essentially simple. What graphs show is not.

USES OF GRAPHS

As we have seen on p. 113 some graphs show the movement of a variable over time—for example, stock market prices. No one is perplexed by graphs of this kind. But other graphs show relationships. These are the graphs that worry students. Here are some hints to help you to draw these kinds of graphs.

1. *Always begin by labeling the axes of a graph.* Even the most common supply and demand type of graph should have one label identified as Price (or *P*) and another as Quantity (or *Q*). No mistake is as frequent as omitting *P*'s and *Q*'s or whatever identifying symbols are called for on a graph.

2. *Each point on a graph represents* two *variables.* Each point shows what value of *X* is related to a given value of *Y*—e.g., what quantity is offered (or bought) at a given price. Therefore every point must always be referred to *both* axes. In the figure below for example, point *H* shows *five* units of quantity offered at a price of *six* dollars. Five units and six dollars are called the *coordinates* of point *H*.

3. *Curves show how relationships vary.* A given dot shows the relation of only one pair of coordinates, such as five units and six dollars. A curve shows the relationship of many pairs of coordinates for the function we are interested in. The upward curve *FGH* shows how *P* and *Q* vary for sellers, for instance. An-

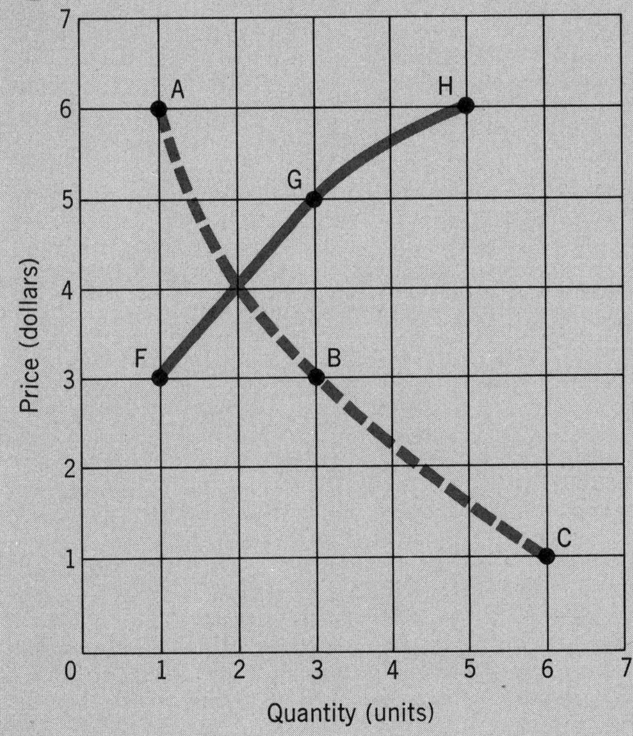

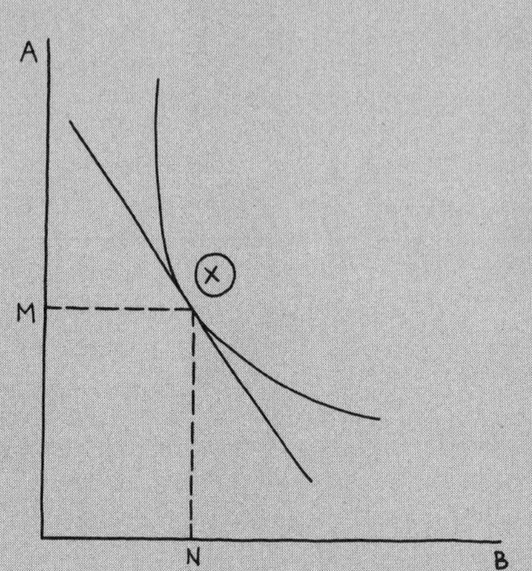

Note that axes are labeled. This graph shows that there is one point (*X*), where there is a common pair of coordinates, *M* and *N,* for two functions or curves.

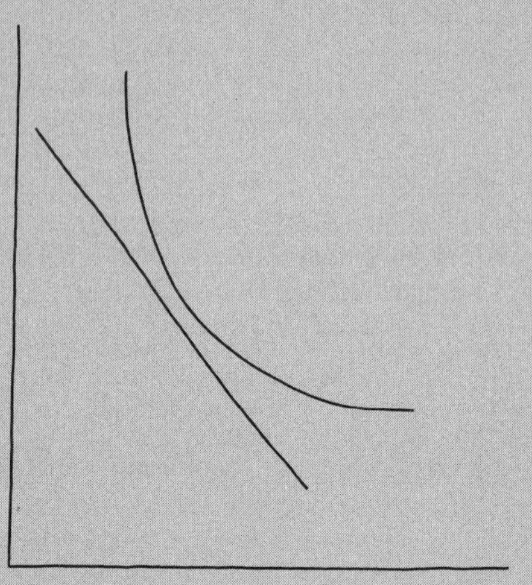

Note axes are not labeled. The graph shows that there is no point where one pair of coordinates relates to both curves. Is that what you want to show?

other curve, *ABC*, shows a relationship with a downward slope, perhaps for buyers. What are the actual values of *P* and *Q* at points *A*, *B*, and *C*? What, if any, coordinates are shared by both curves?

4. *Graphs should be carefully drawn.* Very often a graph represents visually an important idea. It may show that a pair of coordinates lies on *two* curves, as does the equilibrium point in the standard supply/demand graph. Or it may show that one curve touches another at just one point, which also means that the two curves have one pair of coordinates in common. When you draw a curve, you are *describing* a relationship: Be sure you describe it right. Above are two freehand examples for you to study.

5. In his excellent text *Basic Economics,* Professor Edwin Dolan writes: "When you come to a chapter in this book that is full of graphs, how should you study it? The first and most important rule is do *not ever memorize graphs.*"

Professor Dolan is so right! Graphs come last, to capsulize what you know. They never come first, to tell you what you *should* know. Graphs are a pictorial shorthand for ideas, usually ideas about functional relationships (curves) and their interconnections. Learn the economics and the graphs will follow. Learn the graphs—and you will know only geometry.

CORRELATION

That was the easy part of understanding graphs. Now for the hard part. Most students think that graphs "explain" things. They look at a graph of a demand curve and say "The lower price *causes* us to buy more." They look at a graph showing a nice regular pattern between variable *A* and variable *B,* and they assume that this pattern of "correlation" implies an explanation.

Here's an example. On the left, next page, we have plotted the shoe size and the IQs of a group of seniors. No pattern—no "correlation"—is visible.

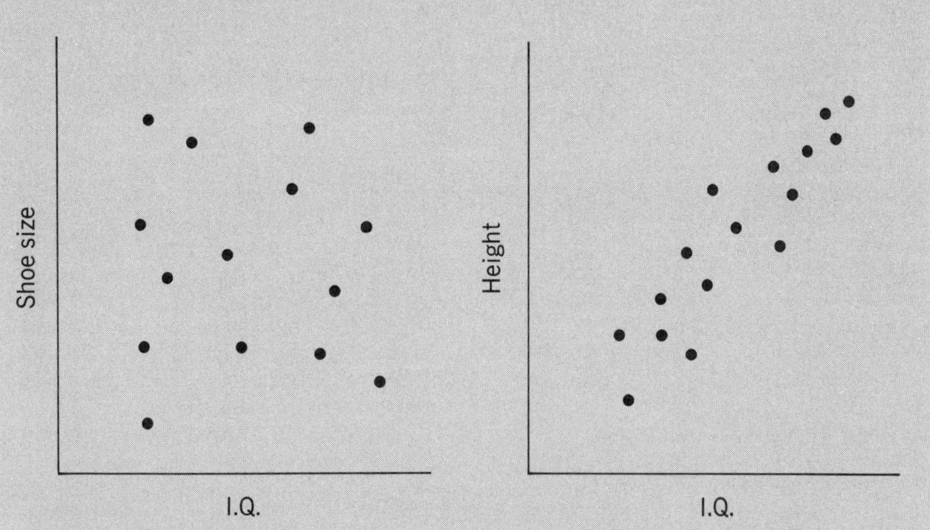

No pattern or correlation exists here.

A clear pattern or correlation is visible.

Hence no one assumes that large shoe sizes cause high IQs. In the graph on the right, we correlate a sample of the heights and the IQs of a number of individuals. There is a clearly visible pattern or correlation.

Does this mean that height causes IQ to increase? Certainly not. Height is associated with age. Our graph happens to cover a population that includes both infants and adults, and so of course there is a correlation, but it is not a causal one. Height does not *cause* IQ. It is associated with IQ through the mediating factor of age and maturity. Lesson: Be very, very careful of jumping to conclusions about causes just from the evidence of associations, or correlations.

Here are a few examples for you to think about.

1. *Wrong-way causation.* It is a statistical fact that there is a positive correlation between the number of babies born in various cities of northwestern Europe and the number of storks' nests in those cities. Is this evidence that storks really do bring babies? The answer is that we are using a correlation to establish a causal connection the wrong way. The true line of causation lies in the opposite direction. Cities that have more children tend to have more houses, which offer storks more chimneys to build their nests in!

2. *Spurious causation.* Suppose there was a positive correlation all during the 1970s between the cost of living in Paris and the numbers of Americans visiting there. Does that imply that American visitors are the cause of price increases in that city?

Here at least there is little danger of getting the causal links back to front. Few people would argue that more Americans visit Paris *because* its prices are going up. It would be equally difficult to argue that American tourists are the cause of rising Parisian prices, simply because the total amount of American spending is small in relation to the total amount of expenditure in Paris.

The answer, then, is that the correlation is spurious in terms of causality, although it is real in terms of sheer statistics. The true explanation for the correlation is that the rising numbers of American visitors and the rising costs of living in Paris are both aspects of a worldwide expansion in incomes and prices. Neither is the "cause" of the other. Both are the results of more fundamental, broader-ranging phenomena.

3. *The problem of* ceteris paribus. Finally, we must consider again the now familiar problem of *ceteris paribus*, the necessity of other things being equal. Suppose we correlate prices and sales, in order to test the hypothesis that lower prices "cause" us to increase the quantities we buy. Now suppose that the correlation turns out to be very poor. Does that disprove the hypothesis? Not necessarily. First we have to find out what happened to income during this period. We also have to find out what, if anything, happened to our tastes. We might also have to consider changes in the prices of other, competitive goods.

As we know, this problem affects all scientific tests, not just those of economics. Scientists cannot test the law of gravitation unless "other things" are equal, such as an absence of air that would cause a feather to fall much more slowly than Galileo predicted. The trouble with the social sciences is that the "other things" are often more difficult to spot—or just to think of—than they are in the laboratory.

WHAT CAN CORRELATION TELL US? These (and still other) pitfalls make economists extremely cautious about using correlations to "prove" causal hypotheses. *Even the closest correlation may not show in which direction the causal influences are working.*

So, too, *the interconnectedness of the economic process often causes many series of data to move together.* In inflationary periods, for example, most prices tend to rise, or in depression many indexes tend to fall, without establishing that any of these series was directly responsible for a movement in another particular series.

Finally, economists are constantly on the lookout for factors that have not been held constant during correlation, so that *ceteris paribus conditions were not in fact maintained.*

Is there an answer to such puzzling problems of correlation and causation? There is a partial answer. We cannot claim that a correlation is proof that a causal relationship exists. But every valid hypothesis—economic or other—*must* show a high and "significant" correlation coefficient between "cause" and "effect," provided that we are reasonably certain that our statistical test has rigorously excluded spurious correlations and unsuspected "other things."

This exclusion is often very difficult, sometimes impossible to achieve with real data. A physicist can hold "other things equal" in his laboratory, but the world will not stand still just so an economist can test his theories. *The net result is that correlations are a more powerful device for* disproving *hypotheses than for proving them.* All we can say on the positive side is that a causal relationship is likely to exist (or at least has not been shown *not* to exist) when we can demonstrate a strong correlation backed by solid reasoning.

Part

Part 3 Macroeconomics: The Analysis of Prosperity and Recession

SECTION 1: The Basic Elements of Growth

A LOOK AHEAD

This chapter introduces us to the subject of gross national product, or GNP—the value of the annual final output of the economic system. Much of macroeconomics focuses on this strategic figure in an effort to discover

(1) how it is determined,
(2) what makes it change, and
(3) how we can help its growth.

Two main ideas run through the pages ahead. First, we learn the very important vocabulary by which we identify the components of GNP. Be sure you grasp the difference between final and intermediate goods, and between consumption and investment goods. Second, we learn the difficulties associated with GNP as a measure of output. GNP is the single most important device for counting overall activity that economics has, but as we will see, it is far from a reliable measure of welfare.

What is "macroeconomics"? The word derives from the Greek *macro* meaning "big," and the implication is therefore that it is concerned with bigger problems than is microeconomics (*micro* = small). Yet microeconomics wrestles with problems that are quite as large as those of macroeconomics. The difference is really not one of scale. It is one of approach, of original angle of incidence. **Macroeconomics begins from a viewpoint that initially draws our attention to aggregate economic phenomena and processes, such as the growth of total output.** Microeconomics begins from a vantage point that first directs our analysis to the workings of the marketplace. Both views are needed to comprehend the economy as a whole, just as it takes two different lenses to make a stereophoto jump into the round. Since we can learn only one view at a time, we now turn to the spectacle of the entire national economy as it unfolds to the macroscopic gaze.

THE MACRO PERSPECTIVE

What does the economy look like from the macro perspective? The view is not unlike that from a plane. What we see first is the fundamental tableau of nature—fields and forests, lakes and seas, with their inherent riches; then the diverse artifacts of humankind—cities and towns, road and rail networks, factories and machines, stocks of half-completed or unsold goods; finally the human actors themselves with all their skills and talents, their energies, their social organization.

Thus our perspective shows us a vast panorama from which we single out for special attention one process that we can see taking place in every corner of the economy. **This process is a vast river of output, a ceaseless flow of production that emerges from the nation's economic activity.**

OUTPUT

How does this flow of production arise? Later, in microeconomics, we shall investigate motives that lead factors of production to offer their services to business firms, and motives that lead entrepreneurs to hire factors. A macro perspective, however, studies the market process from a somewhat different standpoint, one that focuses on the stream of output as a whole, rather than tracing it back to its individual springs and rivulets.

It may help us picture the flow as a whole if we imagine that each and every good and service that is produced—each loaf of bread, each nut and bolt, each doctor's service, each theatrical performance, each car, ship, lathe, or bolt of cloth—can be identified and followed as a radioactive isotope allows us to follow the circulation of certain kinds of cells through the body. Then if we look down on the economic panorama, we can see the continuous combination of land, labor, and capital giving off a continuous flow of "lights" as goods and services emerge in their saleable form.

INTERMEDIATE GOODS

Where do these lights go? Many are soon extinguished. **The goods or services they represent are *intermediate goods* that are incorporated into other products to form more fully finished items of output.** Thus, from our aerial perspective we can follow a product such as cotton from the fields to the spinning mill, where its light is extinguished, for there the cotton disappears into a new product: yarn. In turn, the light of the yarn traces a path as it leaves the spinning mill by way of sale to the textile mill, there to be doused as the yarn disappears into a new good: cloth. Again, cloth leaving the textile mill lights a way to the factory where it will become part of an article of clothing.

FINAL GOODS: CONSUMPTION

And what of the clothing? **Here at last we have what the economist calls a *final* good. Why "final"? Because once in the possession of its ultimate owner, the clothing passes out of the active economic flow.** As a good in the hands of a consumer, it is no longer an object on the marketplace. Its light is now extinguished permanently; or if we wish to complete our image, we can imagine it fading gradually as the clothing disappears into the utility of the consumer. In the case of consumer goods like food or of consumer services like recreation, the light goes out faster, for these items are "consumed" as soon as they reach their final destination.*

We shall have a good deal to learn in later chapters about the macroeconomic behavior of consumers. What we should notice in this first view is the supreme importance of this flow of production into consumers' hands. By this vital process, the population replenishes or increases its energies and ministers to its wants and needs. If the process were halted very long, society would perish. That is why we speak of *consumption* as the ultimate end and aim of all economic activity.

A SECOND FINAL GOOD: INVESTMENT

Nevertheless, for all the importance of consumption, if we look down on the illuminated flow of output we see a surprising thing. Whereas the greater portion of the final goods and services of the economy is bought by the human agents of production for their consumption, we also find that a lesser but still considerable flow of final products is not. What happens to it?

If we follow an appropriate good, we may find out. Watch the destination of steel leaving a Pittsburgh mill. Some of it, like our cotton cloth, will become incorporated into consumers' goods, ending up as cans, automobiles, or household articles. But some will not find its way to a consumer at all. Instead, it will end up as part of a machine or an office building or a railroad track.

Now in a way, these goods are not "final," for they are used to produce still further goods or services. The machine produces output of some kind; the building produces office space, the rail track produces transportation. **Yet there is a difference between such goods, used for production, and consumer goods, like clothing. The difference is that the machine, the office building, and the track are goods that are used by business enterprises as part of their permanent productive equipment.** In terms of our image, these goods slowly lose their light-giving powers as their services pass into flows of production, but usually they are replaced with new goods before their light is totally extinguished.

That is why we call them *capital goods* or *investment goods,* as distinguished from consumers' goods. As part of our capital, they will be preserved, maintained,

*In fact, of course, they are not *really* consumed but remain behind as garbage, junk, wastes, and so on. Economics used to ignore these residuals, but it does so no longer.

and renewed, perhaps indefinitely. Hence the stock of capital, like consumers, constitutes a final destination for output.

GROSS AND NET INVESTMENT

We call the great stream of output that goes to capital **gross investment.** The very word *gross* suggests that it conceals a finer breakdown; and looking more closely, we can see that the flow of output going to capital does indeed serve two distinct purposes. Part of it is used to replace the capital—machines, buildings, track, or whatever—that has been used up in the process of production. Just as the human agents of production have to be replenished by a flow of consumption goods, so the material agents of production need to be maintained and renewed if their contribution to output is to remain undiminished. **We call the part of gross investment whose purpose is to keep society's stock of capital intact, replacement investment, or simply replacement.**

Sometimes the total flow of output going to capital is not large enough to maintain the existing stock, as for example when we allow inventories (a form of capital) to become depleted, or when we simply fail to replace wornout equipment or plant. This running-down of capital we call **disinvestment,** meaning the very opposite of investment. Instead of maintaining or building up capital, we are literally consuming it.

Not all gross investment is used for replacement purposes, however. Some of the flow may *increase* the stock of capital by adding buildings, machines, track, inventory, and so on.* **If the total output consigned to capital is sufficiently great not only to make up for wear and tear but to increase the capital stock, we say there has been new or net investment, or net capital formation.**

CONSUMPTION AND INVESTMENT

A simple diagram may help us picture the flow of final output that we have been discussing. Figure 9.1 calls our attention to these paramount attributes of the output process:

1. **The flow of output is circular, self-renewing, self-feeding.** This circularity is one of the dominant elements in the macroeconomic processes we will study. Consumption output returns to restore or increase our human capital—our ability to work. Investment output restores or increases our material capital.

2. **Societies must make a choice between consumption and investment.** At any given level of output, consumption and investment uses are rivals for the current output of society. Furthermore, we can see that society can add to its capital only the output that it refrains from consuming. Even if it increases its output, it cannot invest the increase except by not consuming it.

3. **Both consumption and investment flows are split between public and private use.** Like consumption and investment, these are also rival uses for output. A society can devote whatever portion of output it pleases to public consumption or public investment, but only by refraining from using that portion for private consumption or investment.

4. **Output is the nation's budget constraint.** Our output is the total quantity of goods and services available for all public and private uses (unless we want to

*Note carefully that increased inventory is a form of investment. Later this will receive special attention.

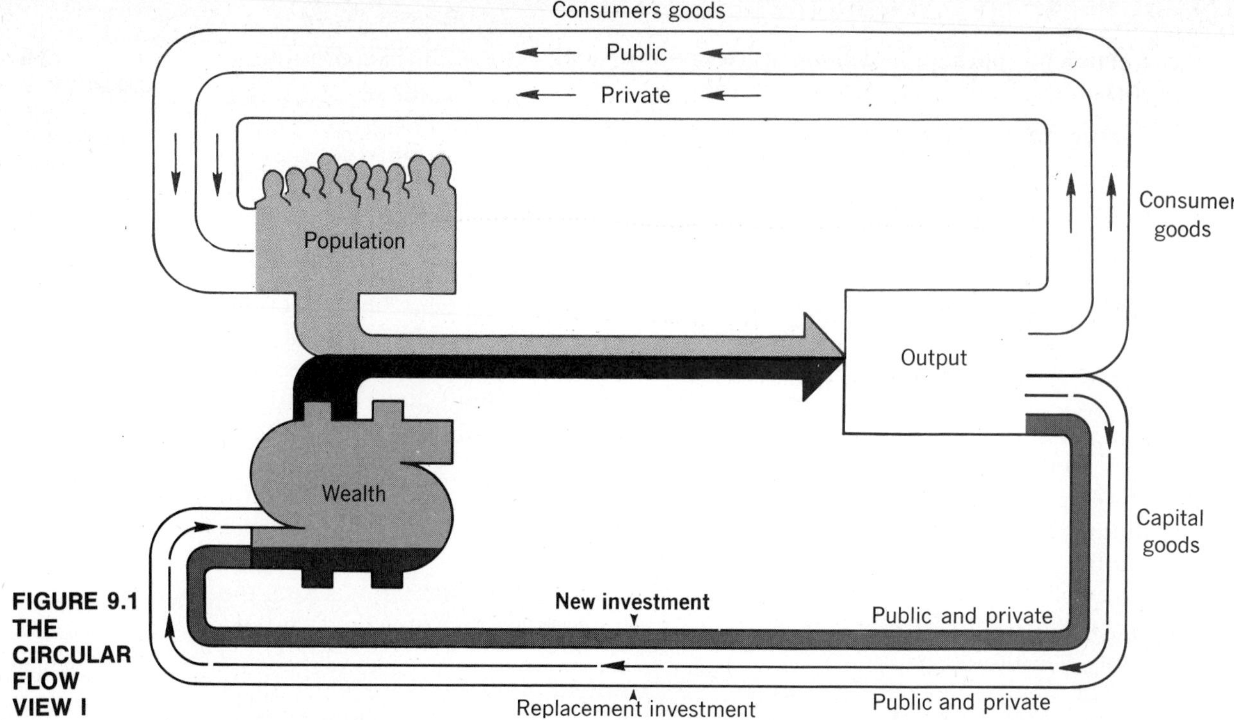

FIGURE 9.1 THE CIRCULAR FLOW VIEW I

The first view of the circular flow shows that output divides into two main streams, consumption and investment—consumption replenishing our human capital, investment replenishing our material capital. Note that there are public and private flows in both consumption and investment output.

use up our past wealth). More goods and services may be desired, but if output is not large enough, they cannot be had.

GROSS NATIONAL PRODUCT

We have had a first view of the overall flow of national output that will play so large a role in our macroeconomic studies. Now we want to look into the flow more closely. Here we can begin by defining gross national product, a term that is already familiar to us from Chapter 5. **We call the dollar value of the total annual output of final goods and services in the nation its gross national product.** The gross national product (or GNP as it is usually abbreviated) is thus nothing but the dollar value of the total output of all consumption goods and of all investment goods produced in a year. We are already familiar with this general meaning, and now we must move on to a more precise definition.

GNP MEASURES FINAL GOODS

We are interested, through the concept of GNP, in measuring the value of the *ultimate* production of the economic system; that is, the total value of all goods and services enjoyed by its consumers or accumulated as new or replacement captial.

Hence we do not count the intermediate goods we have already noted in our economic panorama. We do not add up the value of the cotton *and* the yarn *and* the cloth *and* the final clothing when we compute the value of GNP. That kind of multiple counting might be very useful if we wanted certain information about our total economic activity, but it would not tell us accurately about the final value of output. When we buy a shirt, the price we pay includes the cost of the cloth to the shirtmaker. In turn, the amount the shirtmaker paid for his cloth included the cost of the yarn. In turn, again, the seller of yarn included in his price the amount he paid for raw cotton. Embodied in the price of the shirt, therefore, is the value of all the intermediate products that went into it.

Thus in figuring the value for GNP, we add only the values of all final goods, both for consumption and for investment purposes. Note as well that GNP includes only a given year's production of goods and services. Therefore sales of used car dealers, antique dealers, etc., are not included, because the value of these goods was picked up in GNP the year they were produced.

FURTHER KINDS OF OUTPUT

In our first view of macroeconomic activity we divided the flow of output into two great streams: consumption and gross investment. Now, for purposes of a closer analysis, we must impose a few refinements on this basic scheme.

First we must pay heed to a small flow of production that has previously escaped our notice. That is the net flow of goods or services that leaves this country; that is, the total flow going abroad minus the flow that enters. This international branch of our economy will play a relatively minor role in our analysis for quite a while. We will largely ignore it until Chapters 14 and 34, then we treat it again in Part 6. But we must give it its proper name, *net exports.* Because these net exports are a kind of investment (they are goods we produce but do not consume), we must now rename the great bulk of investment that remains in this country. We will henceforth call it **gross private domestic investment.**

By convention, gross private domestic investment refers only to investments in physical assets such as factories, inventories, homes. Personal expenditures on acquiring human skills, as well as expenditures for regular use, are considered **personal consumption expenditures**—the technical accounting term for *consumption.* As these accounting terms indicate, *public* consumption and investment are included in neither personal consumption expenditures nor gross private domestic investment. Here is our last flow of final output: All public buying of final goods and services is kept in a separate category called **government purchases of goods and services.**

FOUR STREAMS OF FINAL OUTPUT

We now have four streams of final output, each going to a final purchaser of economic output. **Therefore we can speak of gross national product as being the sum of personal consumption expenditure (*C*), gross private domestic investment (*I*), government purchases (*G*), and net exports (*X*), or (to abbreviate a long sentence) we can write that**

$$\text{GNP} \equiv C + I + G + X$$

This is a descriptive identity that should be remembered.

It helps, at this juncture, to look at GNP over the past decades. In Figure 9.2 we show the long irregular upward flow of GNP from 1929 to the present,

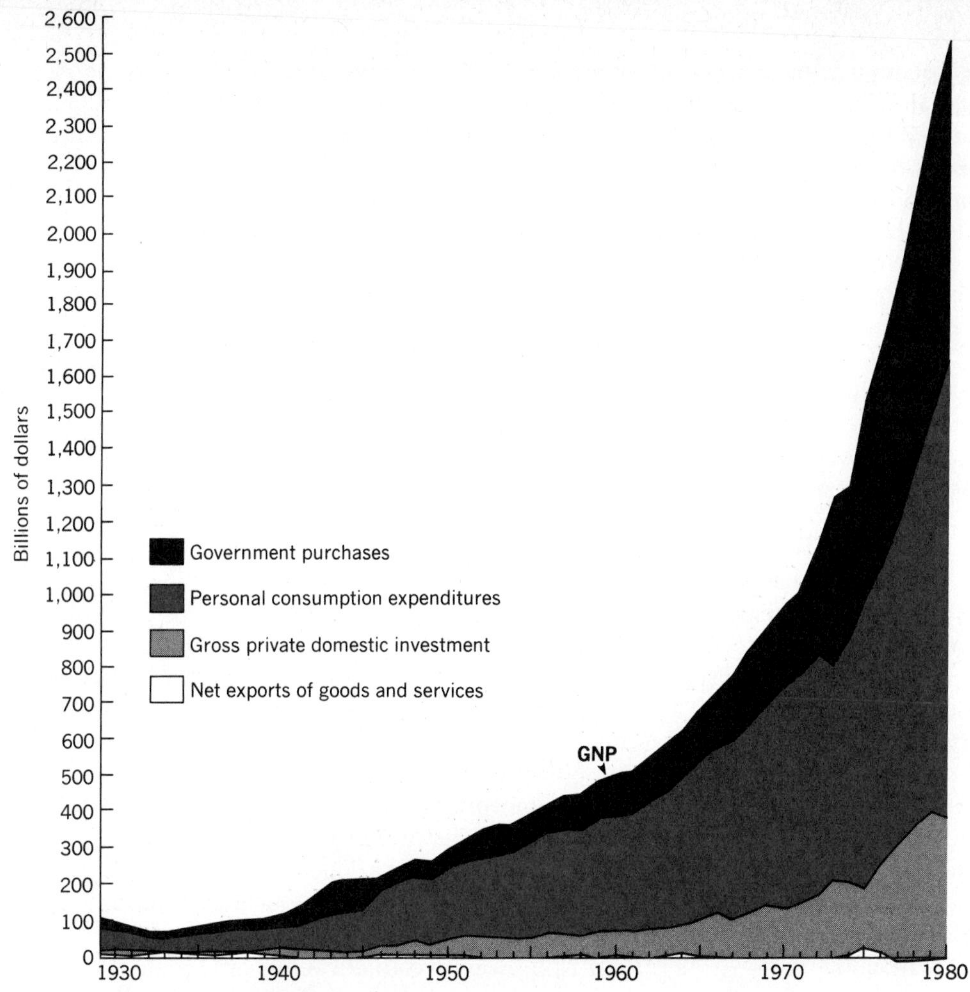

FIGURE 9.2 GNP AND COMPONENTS, 1929–1980
Here we see the historical record of GNP (a graph we have already met) this time with its component parts added.

with the four component streams of expenditure visible. Later we will be talking at length about the behavior of each stream, but first we need to be introduced to the overall flow itself.

GNP AS A MEASURE

GNP is an indispensable concept in dealing with the performance of our economy, but it is well to understand the weaknesses as well as the strengths of this most important single economic indicator.

1. GNP deals in dollar values, not in physical units; we have to correct it for inflation

As we know from Chapter 4, trouble arises when we compare the GNP of one year with that of another to determine whether or not the nation is better off.

If prices in the second year are higher, GNP will appear higher, even though the actual volume of output is unchanged or even lower!

We could correct for this price change easily if all prices moved in the same direction or proportion. We would then choose any year as a "base year," and we could easily establish an index to show whether GNP in another year was really higher or lower than in the base year, and by how much.

Problems arise, however, when there are changes in relative prices, with some prices rising more rapidly than others. Then the choice of a base year will affect our calculations. There is no correct way of choosing a base year. We just have to be aware that our choice affects our results. In Figure 9.3 we have used 1972 as our base.

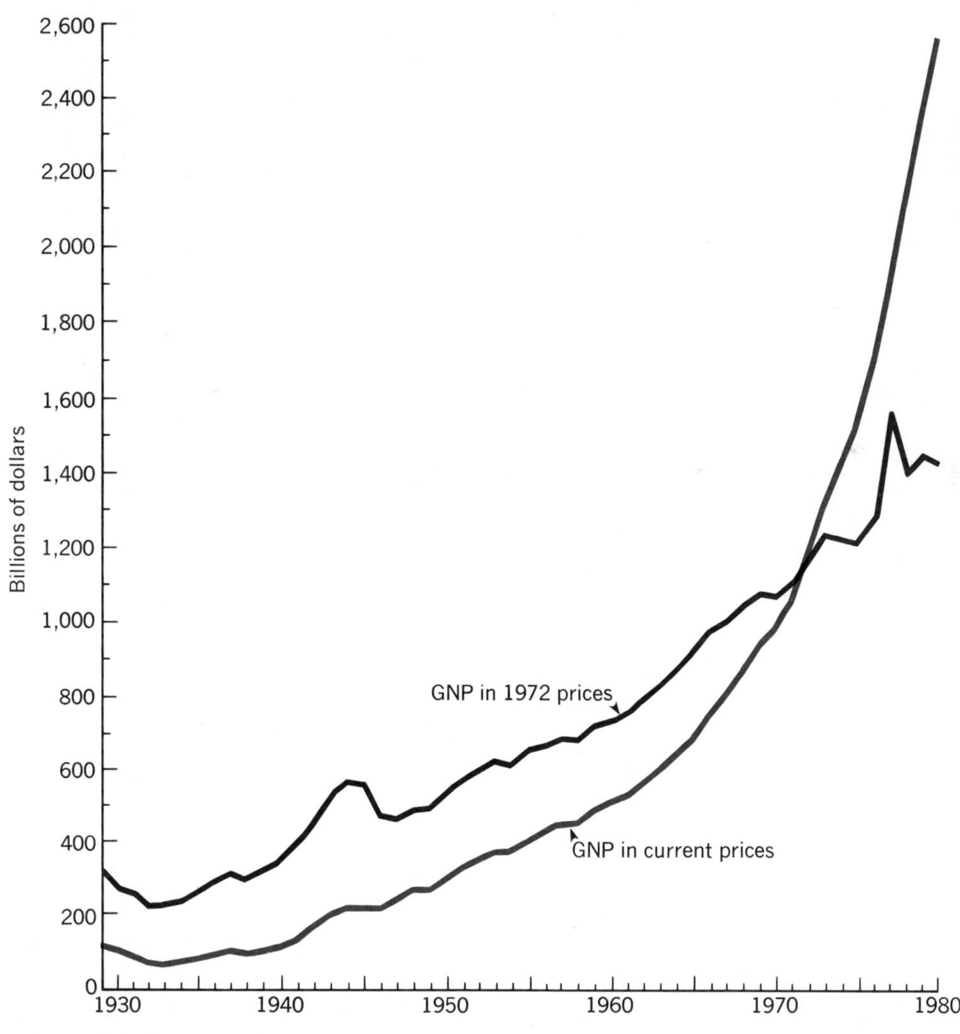

FIGURE 9.3 GNP IN CONSTANT AND CURRENT PRICES 1929–1980

We reduce nominal or current GNP—output measured at existing prices—to real GNP by using a price index. Because relative prices change, it matters which year we use as our base. There is no correct year, but our choice affects our results. Here we use 1972 as our base.

REAL AND CURRENT GNP

It's worth a moment to review the ideas on p. 131.

How do we arrive at a figure for "real" GNP? *The answer is that we "correct" the value of GNP (or any other magnitude measured in dollars) for the price changes that affect the value of our dollars but not the real quantities of goods and services our dollars buy.*

We make this correction by applying a *price index*. Such an index is a series of numbers showing the variation in prices, year to year, from a starting or *base year* for which the price level is set at 100. Thus if prices go up 5 percent a year, a price index starting in year one will read 105 for year two, 110.25+ for year three (105 × 1.05), 115.8 for year four, and so on.

In correcting GNP we use a very complex price index called a GNP *price deflator*. This index, constructed by the Department of Commerce, allows for the fact that different parts of GNP, such as consumer goods and investment goods may change in price at different rates. The present price deflator uses GNP price levels in 1972 as a base. In 1975, the value of the deflator was 126.37. That is, the price index was up 26.37% from 1972.

Now let us work out an actual example. *To arrive at a corrected GNP, we divide the current GNP by the deflator and then multiply by 100.* For example, GNP in current figures was $1,702 billion for 1976; $1,900 billion for 1977; and $2,128 billion for 1978. The deflators for those years were 134, 142, and 152. Here are the results:

$$\frac{\$1702}{134} = 12.70 \times 100 = 1270 \text{ billion}$$

$$\frac{\$1900}{142} = 13.38 \times 100 = 1338 \text{ billion}$$

$$\frac{\$2128}{152} = 14.00 \times 100 = 1400 \text{ billion}$$

Thus the "real value" of GNP in 1978 was $1400 billion, *in terms of 1972 prices,* rather than the $2128 billion of its current value. Two things should be noted in this process of correction. First, the real value of any series will differ, depending on the base year that is chosen. For instance, if we started a series in 1976, the real value of GNP for that year would be $1702, the same as its money value.

Second, the process of constructing a GNP deflator is enormously difficult. In fact there is no single, accurate way of constructing an index that will reflect all the variations of prices of the goods within GNP. To put it differently, we can construct different kinds of indexes, with different weights for different sectors, and these will give us differing results. The point then is to be cautious in using corrected figures. Be sure you know what the base year is. And remember that complex indexes, such as the GNP deflator, are only approximations of a change that defies wholly accurate measurement.

2. Changes in quality of output will not show in GNP

The second weakness of GNP also involves its inaccuracy as an indicator of "real" trends over time. The difficulty revolves around changes in the utility of goods and services. In a technologically advancing society, goods are usually improved from one decade to the next or even more rapidly, and new goods are constantly being introduced. In an urbanizing, increasingly high-density society, the utility of other goods may be lessened over time. An airplane trip today, for example, is certainly preferable to one 30 years ago; a subway ride is not. This year's car costs more than last year's car, but it also gets better gas mileage. How much of the increase in price reflects that improvement in quality and how much of the increase is simply an increase in price? It is difficult for anyone to know, but government statisticians try to adjust GNP statistics for just such changes in quality. Generally speaking, the longer the time period over which comparisons of real GNP are being made, the larger is the quality factor, and therefore the more tentative the results become.

3. GNP does not reflect the purpose of production

A third difficulty with GNP lies in its blindness to the ultimate use of production. If in one year GNP rises by a billion dollars, owing to an increase in expenditure on education, and in another year it rises by the same amount because of a rise in cigarette production, the figures in each case show the same amount of growth of GNP. Even output that turns out to be wide of the mark or totally wasteful—such as the famous Edsel car that no one wanted or military weapons that are obsolete from the moment they appear—all are counted as part of GNP.

The problem of environmental deterioration adds another difficulty. Some types of GNP growth directly contribute to pollution—cars, paper or steel production, for example. Other types of GNP growth are necessary to stop pollution—sewage disposal plants or the production of a clean internal combustion engine. Still other types of GNP have little direct impact on the environment. Most personal services fall into this category.

Our conventional measure of GNP makes no distinction among such outputs. For instance, the cleaning bills we pay to undo damage caused by smoke from the neighborhood factory become part of GNP, although cleaning our clothes does not increase our well-being. It only brings it back to what it was in the first place.

4. GNP does not include most goods and services that are not for sale

Presumably GNP tells us how large our final output is. Yet it does not include one of the most useful kinds of work and chief sources of consumer pleasure—the labor of women in maintaining their households. Yet, curiously, if this labor were paid for—that is, if we engaged cooks and maids and babysitters instead of depending on wives for these services, GNP *would* include their services as final output, since they would be purchased on the market. The labor of wives being unpaid, it is excluded from GNP.*

A related problem is that some parts of GNP are paid for by some members of the population and not by others. Rent, for example, measures the services of landlords for homeowners and is therefore included in GNP, but what of the homeowner who pays no rent? Similarly, what of the family that grows part of its food at home and therefore does not pay for it?

There is no entirely satisfactory solution to such problems. Because no one has devised a way of valuing housewives' services in a manner that appears fair and objective, we just leave the value of these services out of GNP. On the other hand, when it is possible to impute a value to unpaid services, statisticians at the

*An added difficulty here is that we are constantly moving toward purchasing "outside" services in place of home services. Laundries, bakeries, restaurants, etc., all perform work that used to be performed at home. Thus the process of *monetizing* activity gives an upward trend to GNP statistics that is not fully mirrored in actual output.

Department of Commerce do so. For instance, they include in GNP an estimate of the value of the rentals of owner-occupied homes and of food grown at home.

5. GNP does not indicate anything about the distribution of goods and services among the population

Societies differ widely in how they allocate their production of purchasable goods and services among their populations. A pure egalitarian society might allocate everyone the same quantity of goods and services. Many societies establish minimum consumption standards for individuals and families. Few deliberately decide to let someone starve if they have the economic resources to prevent such a possibility. *Yet to know a nation's GNP, or even to know its average (per capita) GNP, is to know nothing about how broadly or how narrowly this output is shared. A wealthy country can have many poor families. A poor country can have some very wealthy families.*

GNP AND WELFARE

All these doubts and reservations should instill in us a permanent caution against using GNP as if it were a clear-cut measure of social contentment or happiness. Economist Edward Denison once remarked that perhaps nothing affects national economic welfare so much as the weather, which certainly does not get into the GNP accounts! Hence, because the U.S. may have a GNP per capita that is higher than that of say, Holland, it does not mean that life is better here. It may be worse. In fact, by the indices of health care or quality of environment, it probably *is* worse.

Yet, with all its shortcomings, GNP is still the simplest way we possess of summarizing the overall level of market activity of the economy. If we want to examine its welfare, we had better turn to specific social indicators of how long we live, how healthy we are, how cheaply we provide good medical care, how varied and abundant is our diet, etc.—none of which we can tell from GNP figures alone. But we are not always interested in welfare, partly because it is too complex to be summed up in a single measure. For better or worse, therefore, GNP has become the yardstick used by most nations in the world. Although other yardsticks are sure to become more important, GNP will be a central term in the economic lexicon for a long time to come.

KEY CONCEPTS

LOOKING BACK

The macro perspective

1. Our introduction to macroeconomics involves a special perspective on the economy, one that emphasizes total output rather than behavior in the marketplace.

Intermediate vs. final goods: consumption and investment

2. Observing the flow of total output, we discover that it can be divided into intermediate goods and final goods. Intermediate goods go *into* final goods. Final goods are those used for consumption or for investment.

Gross investment comprises net investment and replacement

3. Investment can be further divided into gross and net investment. Gross investment is the sum of output not used for consumption. Part of it is for replacement of worn out capital goods. The remainder is net investment.

Output is a circular flow

4. The flow of output has four major characteristics: It is circular, replenishing our human or material wealth; it is used for consumption or investment, but the same item cannot be used for both simultaneously; it has public and private uses, both as consumption and as investment; and it constitutes the budget constraint of the nation.

Gross national product is the value of final output

5. The annual flow of final output, valued at its market price, is called the gross national product, or GNP. Note that it includes only final, not intermediate output.

GNP $\equiv C + I + G + X$

6. The annual output can be described as comprising four distinct flows:

a consumption flow,
an export flow,
a flow of domestic gross investment,
a public flow.

Together they give us the identity GNP $\equiv C + I + G + X$.

GNP is a widely used measure of performance. But GNP does not show quality, usefulness, or nonmarket output, and it ignores income distribution

7. Gross national product is widely used as a measure of economic performance. However, it suffers a number of deficiencies as such a measure. It has even more difficulty as an indicator of welfare or well-being because:

Real GNP is not easy to calculate from nominal GNP; different base years give different results.
GNP gives a very imperfect indication of the quality of output.
The size of GNP does not inform us of its purpose or usefulness.
GNP does not include (or imprecisely includes) any output that is not sold.
GNP gives us no clue as to the distribution of income.

ECONOMIC VOCABULARY

Macroeconomics 125
Intermediate goods 125
Final goods 126
Consumption goods 126
Gross and net investment 127
Disinvestment 127
Capital formation 127
Circular flow 127
GNP 128
Gross private domestic investment 129
Personal consumption expenditures 129
Government purchases 129

QUESTIONS

1. Explain how the circularity of the economic process means that the outputs of the system are returned as fresh inputs.
2. What is meant by net investment? How is it different from gross investment? Does the idea of "net consumption" mean anything? (Suppose there is a minimum amount of consumption needed to keep body and soul together?)
3. Why are investment goods considered final goods and not intermediate ones?
4. Write the basic definitional formula for GNP.
5. Do you think we should develop measures other than GNP to measure our performance? What sorts of measures? After thinking about this, look at the "Extra Word" in this chapter.

AN EXTRA WORD ABOUT
SOCIAL INDICATORS

Many people object to the gross national product on the grounds that it focuses our attention on too narrow a band of human activity. Many of the things that improve or degrade our society are left out. Worse still, because they are left out they are ignored. These are not the previously mentioned items, such as imputed income for housewives or negative economic outputs in the form of pollution, that might be added to the GNP to make it a more comprehensive measure of economic *output.* These omissions are measurements of life expectancy, morbidity, mental illness, crime, social unrest and other areas of human activity.

The Social Indicators movement is an effort to expand our system of social accounts to measure progress (or the lack of progress) in these other dimensions. The GNP would not be eliminated but would be just one of a number of measurements in an expanded set of social accounts, some of them listed in Table 9.1.

First, there are many aspects of human existence that are important to welfare but *unmeasurable.* Consider friendship. Without doubt, social relationships influence our welfare; but could we measure whether the average American has more or fewer friends, better or less helpful friends? Clearly we cannot. Unfortunately, the Social Indicators movement has been so closely linked to the idea of measurement that such problems have led to less and less political interest in the idea.

Second, there is the aggregation problem. We have seen that dollar values are used as the common denominator to aggregate different economic goods and services. What is to be the common denominator used to aggregate life expectancy, crime, and mental illness? Nothing obvious suggests itself. Although there is nothing wrong in presenting three dozen different indices of social progress, one cannot easily say, if indicators point in different directions, whether society is improving.

TABLE 9.1
SOME SOCIAL INDICATORS

Life expectancy at birth	72.8 years (1976)
Days of disability	18 days per year per person (1976)
Violent crimes	467 per 100,000 (1977)
Property crimes	4,588 per 100,000 (1977)
High school graduate rate	75.4 percent (1977)
Job satisfaction	3.44 on a scale of 1 to 4 (1973)
Substandard housing units	7.4 percent (1970)

Ideally, such a wide-ranging set of social accounts would give us a better indication of the trend of general welfare than that provided by simple GNP measurements. Yet, although the federal government now issues a social report every other year, the Social Indicators movement has never had the impact that was imagined when it started in the mid 1960s. There are two fundamental reasons for its weakness.

Lacking an aggregate measure of general welfare, social indicators have had very little impact on public opinion. A declining GNP is front-page news. General welfare may also be declining, but no one social indicator is able to show us this. The net result is that the GNP, for all its shortcomings, is not about to be eclipsed by a more general indicator of social welfare in the near future.

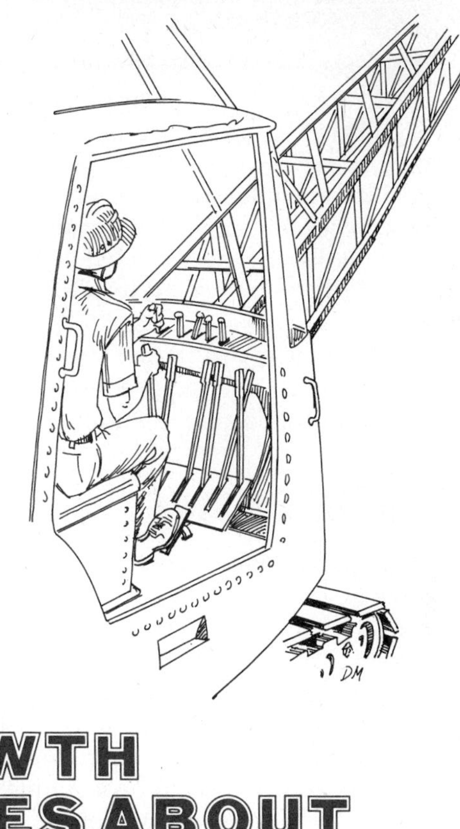

Chapter 10 HOW GROWTH COMES ABOUT

A LOOK AHEAD

We learned some essential macroeconomic vocabulary in our last chapter. Now we are about to learn some essential macroeconomics.

(1) The center of our focus is economic growth, the principal issue with which macroeconomics is concerned. We already know from Chapter 5 that growth comes from increases in the quantity and quality of labor and capital inputs. Here we are going to look into these inputs more closely. We will discover that we cannot easily distinguish increases in the quantity of capital from changes in its quality.

(2) Our discussion will end with a second look at production possibility curves, this time as depictions of the constraints on economic growth.

Macroeconomics is essentially concerned with growth. Chapter 5 opened a discussion of the long upward trend of U.S. output and the reasons for this trend. Recall that our growth trend for nearly 100 years has resulted in an average annual increase in real GNP per capita of about 1.5 percent a year—enough to double per capita income every 47 years. In our last chapter we began to analyze this process by familiarizing ourselves with the way our stock of wealth interacts with our labor force to yield a flow of output that we call gross national product.

Now we are going to push forward by learning much more about the underlying trends and causes of growth in the American economy. That will set the stage for the work that still lies ahead, when we will narrow our focus down to the present and inquire into the reasons for the problems of our macrosystem —unemployment and inflation, booms and busts.

THE SOURCES OF GROWTH

What determines how fast we have grown in the past, and how rapidly we may grow in the future? We already know the basic answer from Chapter 5. Growth comes from increases in the quantity or in the quality of the two major inputs—labor and capital. Of course, it also depends mightily on the resources with which we are endowed and it is influenced by our sheer willingness to work hard. And that willingness in turn is affected by economic policies, such as how much of our incomes go in taxes. Therefore growth is anything but a cut and dried subject that can be disposed of by a simple analysis of the essential inputs of labor and capital. Nevertheless, by looking into these inputs we will learn a lot.

THE LABOR FORCE

Output depends on work and work depends on people working. Thus the first source of growth is the rise in the sheer number of people in the labor force.

Figure 10.1 gives us a picture of the population and the labor force over the past half century. As we would expect, the size of the force has been steadily rising as our population has increased.

But there is more here than quickly meets the eye. One might expect that as our society has grown richer and more affluent, fewer people would seek employment. But that is not the case. Looking back to 1890 or 1900, we find that only 52 out of every 100 persons over 14 sought paid work. Today about 60 out of every 100 persons of working age seek employment. Looking forward is more uncertain; but if we can extrapolate (extend) the trend of the past several decades to the year 2000, we can expect perhaps as may as 65 persons out of 100 to be in the labor market by that date.

PARTICIPATION IN THE LABOR FORCE

The overall trend toward a larger participation rate for the entire population masks a number of significant changes:

1. **Young males entering the labor force are older than were those who entered in the past.**

A larger number of young men remain in high school now or go on to college. Only a third of elementary school pupils now go on to college, but the ratio is steadily growing.

2. **Older males show a dramatic withdrawal from the labor force.**

Almost 7 out of 10 older males used to work. Now only 2 or 3 out of ten work. The reason is the advent of Social Security and private pension plans. It is probable that the proportion of older males in the labor force will continue to fall as the retirement age is slowly reduced.

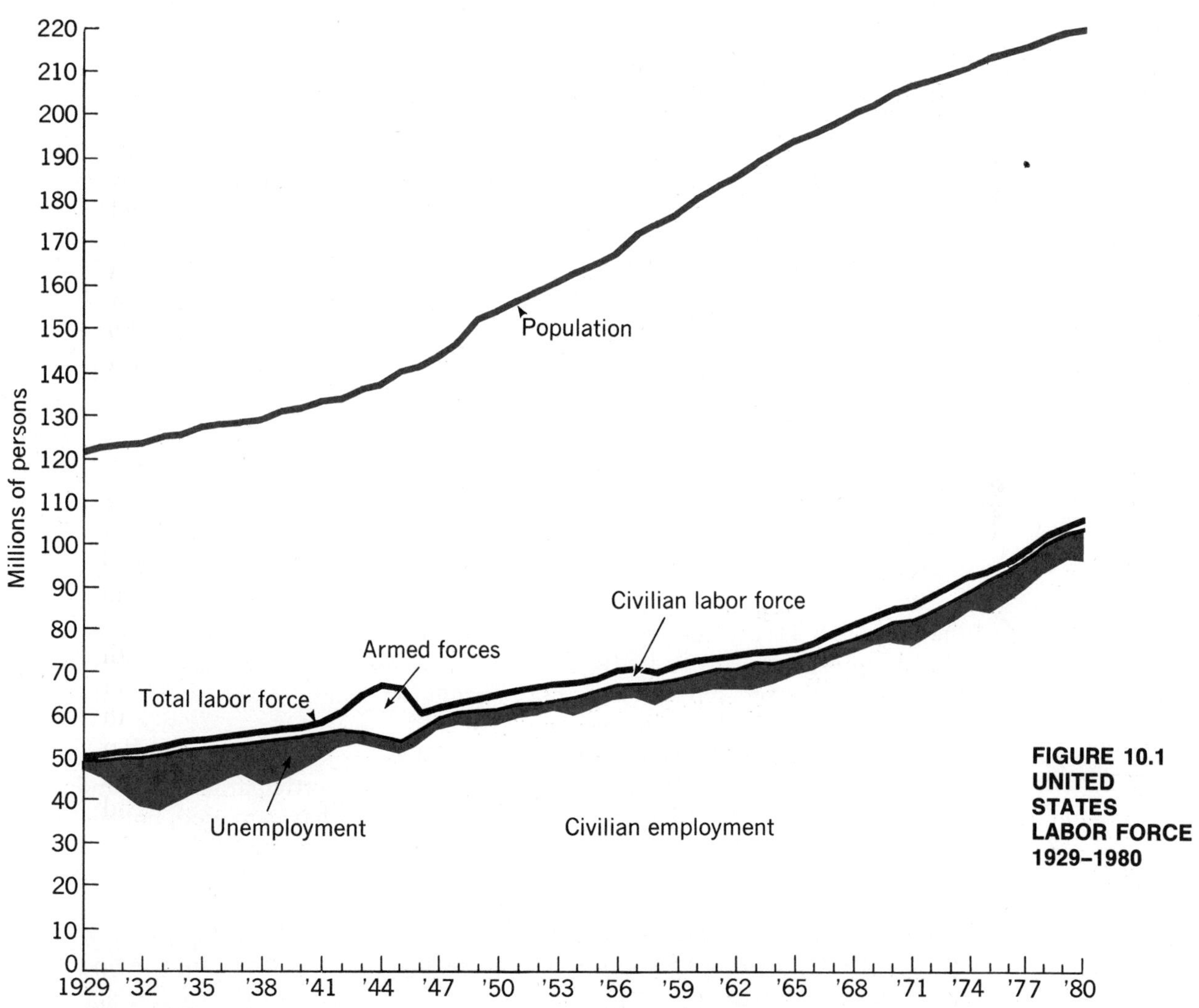

FIGURE 10.1 UNITED STATES LABOR FORCE 1929–1980

Although our eyes cannot easily make it out on the graph, the proportion of the total population seeking work has steadily risen. Today about two-thirds of the *working age* population is in the labor force—at work or looking for work.

3. **Counterbalancing this fall in male participation is a spectacular rise in total female participation. Indeed, the overall trend toward an increasing search for work within the population at large is entirely the result of the mass entrance of women into the labor force.**

This surge of women into the labor market reflects several changing factors in the American scene (many of these changes can be found abroad, as well). One factor is the growth of nonmanual, as contrasted with manual, jobs. Another is the widening cultural approval of working women and working wives. The average American girl who marries today in her early twenties and goes on to raise a family will nevertheless spend 25 *years* of her life in paid employment after her children are grown. Yet another reason for the influx of women is that technology has released them from household work. Finally there is the pressure to raise living standards by having two incomes within the household.

HOURS OF WORK

In addition to deciding whether to participate in the labor force, individuals decide how much labor they wish to contribute as members of the labor force. That is, they must decide how many hours of work they wish to offer during a week or how many weeks they wish to work in a year.

Had we asked this question in the days of Adam Smith, it would have been relatively simple to answer. Wages were so close to subsistence that someone in the labor force was obliged to work extremely long hours to keep body and soul together. Paid vacations were unknown to the employees of the cotton mills. Unpaid vacations would have been tantamount to starvation.

With the slow rise in productivity, working men and women gradually found their income rising above subsistence, and a new possibility came into being: the possibility of deliberately working less than their physical maximum, *using part of their increased productivity to buy leisure for themselves instead of wages.* Thus, beginning in the early nineteenth century we find that labor organizations (still very small and weak) sought to shorten the workweek. In Chapter 2, we saw that a signal victory was won in England in 1847 with the introduction of the Ten Hour Day as the legal maximum for women and children. In America, in the prosperity of the 1920s, the 48-hour week finally became standard. More recently, the two-day weekend has become the general practice. Now we hear of the coming of the three-day weekend.

Thus the total supply of labor-time has not risen as fast as the labor force, because a decline in average hours has offset the rise in participation rates and in population. On balance, the total supply of labor-hours has increased, but the supply of labor-hours *per employee,* male and female, has fallen.

QUANTITY VS. QUALITY

So far we have only looked at changes in the quantity of labor inputs. Now we must get some feeling for the importance of this rising quantity in bringing about economic growth.

We do so by comparing the increase in total hours of labor with the increase in total output. In 1900 our labor force was approximately 30 million men and women who worked approximately 60 hours a week. As a result they expended 94 billion hours of annual labor. By 1980 the total labor force had grown to almost 110 million. The average workweek was now 36 hours. Total man-hours of labor input therefore amounted to roughly 206 billion hours of annual labor.*

Total hours of labor input over this eighty-year period therefore increased by a little more than two-fold. But total economic output over the same period increased by almost ten-fold. Clearly the sheer physical increase in the hours of labor was not sufficient to account for more than a small part of our growth trajectory.

THE QUALITY OF LABOR INPUTS

Where shall we look for the remaining sources of growth? Our first move will be to examine changes in the quality of our labor hours. The 206 billion hours of labor expended in 1980 were in many cases more skillful, more knowledgable, more healthy, than the labor hours of 1900. These changes in the quality of our working abilities have come about in two ways.

1. Growth of human capital

By human capital, we mean the skills and knowledge possessed by the labor force. Even though the measurement of human capital is fraught with difficulties, we cannot ignore this vital contributory element in labor productivity. Ferenc Jánossy, a Hungarian economist, has suggested a vivid imaginary experiment to highlight the importance of skills and knowledge.

Suppose, he says, that the populations of two nations of the same size could be swapped overnight. Fifty million Englishmen would awake to find themselves in, say, Nepal, and 50 million Nepalese would find themselves in England. The newly transferred Englishmen would have to contend with all the poverty and difficulties of the Nepalese economy. The newly transferred Nepalese would confront the riches of England. But the Englishmen would bring with them an immense reservoir of literacy, skills, discipline, and training, whereas the Nepalese would bring the very low levels of human capital that are characteristic of underdeveloped countries. Is there any doubt, asks Jánossy, that growth rates in Nepal, with its new, skilled population, would soon rise dramatically, and that those of England would fall catastrophically?

One way of indicating in very general terms the rising amount of human capital is to trace the additions to the stock of education that the population embodies. Table 10.1 shows the change in the total number of years of schooling of the U.S. population over the past three-quarters of a century, as well as the rise in formal education per capita. While these measures of human capital are far from exact or all-inclusive, they give some dimensions to the importance of skills and knowledge in increasing productivity.

*This is a *very* rough calculation, intended for purposes of illustration. Our estimate makes no allowance for vacations, strikes, illnesses, or unemployment. But it will be legitimate enough to make the central point that soon follows; The *quantity* of labor input cannot possibly account for more than a small portion of our total growth.

TABLE 10.1 STOCK OF EDUCATION, U.S.

	1900	*1980*
Total man-years of schooling embodied in population (million)	228	2728
Percent of labor force with high-school education or more	6	68
Percent of high-school graduates entering college	17	46

Here are three indicators of the huge increase in the education embodied in the labor force.

2. Shifts in the occupations of the labor force

A second source of added productivity results from shifts in employment from low productivity areas to high productivity areas. If workers move from occupations in which their productivity is low to other occupations in which output per man-hour is high, the productivity of the economy will rise even if there are no increases in productivity *within* the different sectors.

A glance at Table 10.2 shows that very profound and pervasive shifts in the location of labor have taken place. What have been the effects of this shift on our long-term ability to produce goods?

The answer is complex. In the early years of the twentieth century, the shift of labor out of agriculture into manufacturing and services probably increased the overall productivity of the economy, since manufacturing was then the most technologically advanced sector. In more recent years, however, we would have to arrive at a different conclusion. Agriculture, although highly productive, is now a very small sector in terms of employment. Moreover, the proportion of the labor force employed in manufacturing is roughly constant, up or down only a few percentage points year to year.

Today, growth in employment takes place mainly in the mixture of occupations we call the service sector: government, retail and wholesale trade, utilities and transportation, professions such as the law, accounting, and the like. The growth of output per capita is less evident in these occupations. Thus the drift of labor into the service sector means that average GNP per worker is growing more slowly today than if labor were moving into manufacturing or agriculture.

Why is this growth-lowering shift taking place? The reason has to do with the changing pattern of demand in an affluent society. There seems to be a natural sequence of wants as a society grows richer: first for food and basic clothing,

TABLE 10.2 PERCENT DISTRIBUTION OF ALL EMPLOYED WORKERS

	1900	*1980*
Agriculture, forests, and fisheries	38.1	3.3
Manufacturing, mining, transportation, construction, utilities	37.7	34.4
Trade, government, finance, professional and personal services	24.2	62.3

Notice the long-term shift out of agriculture, through manufacturing and other goods-related occupations, into services. This has had a dragging effect on national productivity.

then for the output of a wide range of industrial goods, then for recreation, professional advice, public administration, and the enjoyment of other services.

OVERALL CONTRIBUTION OF LABOR

Can we sum up the overall contribution of changes in the inputs of labor to our economic growth? Clearly, changes in the quality of inputs—in our skills and capacities—far outweigh changes in our quantity of inputs—sheer man-hours of effort. When it comes to *measuring* the effect of changes in the quality of inputs, however, we are faced with difficult problems. Partly this is because we must balance the favorable effects of increases in human capital with the unfavorable effects of shifts in occupation. In part it is also because individuals are performing different tasks within each sector, as well as moving from one sector to another.

In the end we are left with little more than the recognition that knowledge and know-how, energy and initiative, enthusiasm and intelligence are powerful motors of economic growth. Indeed, economic growth expresses the gradual accumulation of these qualities of humankind much more than it expresses the increase in its sheer volume of exertion.

CAPITAL

What about capital? It must be apparent that without increases in the quantity of capital we could never achieve much growth. The rising labor force would then have to work with the same amount of machines, buildings, transportation equipment and the like, and diminishing returns would soon lower productivity severely. Therefore we have to **widen capital**—to keep the amount of capital per worker at least abreast of increases in the labor force—if we are to have any significant growth at all.

Actually, a vigorous economy does better than that. It also **deepens capital,** adding to its stock of capital wealth faster than to its labor force, so that each worker has more capital equipment than his or her predecessor, thereby experiencing the same increase in productivity that Adam Smith's workers experienced when new machinery was added to their pin factory.

THE MEASUREMENT PROBLEM

By how much has our stock of capital grown? Right away we come across a problem that we did not have to face when we considered the labor force. When we seek to measure the effects of changing labor inputs, we can at least count heads, or hours, in comparing past and present. But there is no such convenient unit of measurement when we come to capital. Is a power crane comparable to a shovel? Can we measure the amount of capital used by a bookkeeper today and in 1900 by comparing a computer (or even a desk calculator) to a pencil?

Such considerations make it plain that we cannot easily distinguish changes in the size of our capital stock from changes in its quality. Occasionally we can directly measure changes in the amount of capital; for instance we can compare miles of railroad trackage over time. But even here there are changes in quality embodied in the "same" capital—modern rails are welded not riveted, roadbeds are different, trackage is electrified.

TABLE 10.3 CAPITAL WEALTH, 1975 ($ BILLIONS)			
	Structures	$2,555	
	farm		$ 20.9
	residential		952.9
	public		745.2
	institutional		125.6
	other priv. non-res.		710.5
	Equipment	1,041.3	
	priv. business and public		543.7
	consumer durables		496.6
	Inventories	707.2	
	Land	1,284.8	
	Total	5,587.6	

Our total national capital is usually broken down as the table shows. Why do we not include the value of stocks and bonds, or money? The answer is that these are claims on our real wealth; in themselves they are not wealth.

TOTAL CAPITAL STOCK

How large is our modern capital stock? Table 10.3 gives us an overall view.

As we can see, our total national capital amounts to $5.5 trillion dollars, an unimaginably vast sum. If we take only the total for structures and equipment, the figure is $3.5 trillion—about $41,000 worth of capital for every person in the labor force.

This total capital stock is about five or six times as large as the capital stock at the beginning of the century. (Remember: To some extent we are comparing apples and pears here. The smaller sum was not only less capital of the same kind—fewer miles of railroad trackage, if you will—but also very different capital: pencils instead of computers.) **But one thing is indubitable from this general overview. The increase in the quantity and the quality of capital is of critical importance in explaining our national growth. More and better capital are essential elements in increasing our productivity capacity.**

INVESTING AND INVENTING

How do we augment the amount of capital or improve its quality? Actually the two processes generally go hand in hand, for the very act of adding to our capital stock is usually accompanied by an improvement. But it is useful, nonetheless, to separate the two processes in our minds.

We increase the quantity of capital by withholding resources from consumption—saving them—and by using those resources to build capital goods. This is the process of investment that we studied in our last chapter. A great deal of our macroeconomic studies in the chapters immediately ahead will be about this central, vital process.

We improve the quality of our capital by a process for which there is no simple name. Let us call it technology. Technology includes inventing and applying new products and processes, and achieving economies of scale—improvements that arise from sheer size (see p. 88).

SOURCES OF TECHNOLOGY

Technology is probably the single most important factor in determining how fast we grow. One instance of the astonishing power of technology is to compare the period of time it has taken various economies to recover from the devastation of war. In ancient times it could take centuries for a city painfully to rebuild itself: Think of Rome after the "fall"! After the Civil War it required almost a half century before the South could restore its economic vitality. European cities required ten years to pull themselves out of the ruins of the first world war. Following World War II, restoration was accomplished in five years or less. Hiroshima was virtually rebuilt within five years of its "rebirth" in 1950. The reason for this accelerating tempo of reconstruction? Essentially technology.

No one quite understands how technical change comes about. Studies have shown that inventions often follow economic demand—a boom in railroad travel, for example, serving to induce research and development in the expanding industry.* A famous study by Jewkes, Sawers and Stillerman, *The Sources of Invention,* has revealed that most of the major technological breakthroughs of the twentieth century, from penicillin to the jet engine, were the work of individual inventors and tinkers and not of organized laboratory work.†

Thus technology has independent sources over which we have little or no control. **But there is no doubt that technical change can be nurtured by systematic investigation and research and development—R & D, as industry calls it.** In recent years however, R & D expenditures have shown a disquieting fall in the United States. We used to spend about 3 percent of GNP in R & D. Today we are barely investing 2 percent—a drop of one third. Here is a very likely reason for the lagging rate of growth our economy has suffered in recent years. We will go further into this problem at the end of our study of macroeconomics, when we inquire into ways of improving our economic performance.

PRODUCTION POSSIBILITY CURVES

We should now have a fairly clear picture of how growth originates. Let us conclude by translating the material we have covered into a production possibility curve—the graphic depiction of our limits of output that we have already encountered on p. 90.

THE PRODUCTION FRONTIER

Increases in the quantity or quality of labor or capital move our production possibility curve to the right. Do you remember the illustration we used of an economy that produced only milk and grain? In Figure 10.2 we show how changes in the size of our labor force, in its skills or in its equipment can alter the production "frontier." In panel I, we have shown the case where the production of both outputs increases; but II and III make clear that this is not always the case. Sometimes increases in education, new inventions or other changes will affect one kind of output and not the other.

Such a two-commodity diagram may seem unreal, but remember that "milk" and "grain" can stand for consumption and investment (or any other choices available to an economy). In fact, with a little imagination we can construct a three-dimensional production-possibility *surface* showing the limits imposed by scarcity on a society that divides its output among three uses such as consumption, investment, and government. Figure 10.3 shows what such a diagram looks like.

*Jacob Schmookler, *Invention and Economic Growth* (Cambridge: Harvard University Press, 1966).

†John Jewkes, David Sawers, Richard Stillerman, *The Sources of Invention* (London: Macmillan, 1960).

FIGURE 10.2 SHIFTS IN THE PRODUCTION FRONTIER

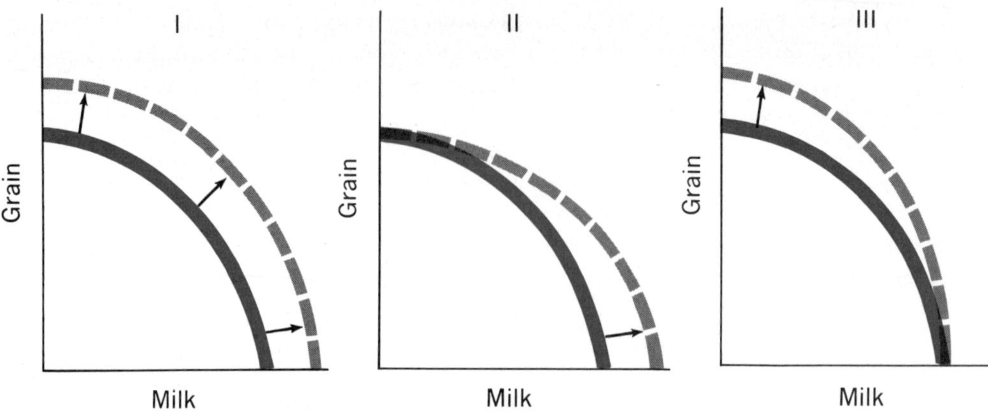

Changes in the quantity or quality of labor and/or capital make growth possible by pushing out our production frontier. As we can see, they may not affect all kinds of outputs equally.

Note how the production-possibility surface swells out from the origin like a windfilled spinnaker sail. Any place on the sail represents some combination of consumption, investment, and government spending that is within the reach of the community. **Any place behind the efficiency frontier represents a failure of the economy to employ all its resources. It is a graphic depiction of unemployment of men or materials.**

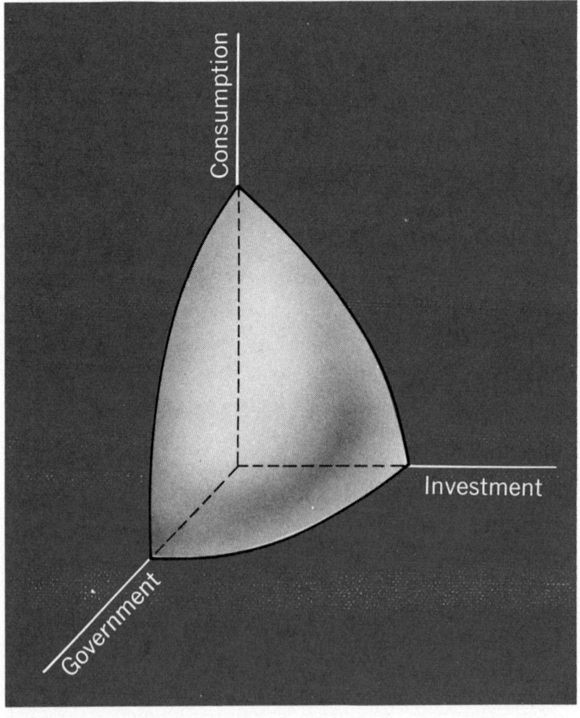

FIGURE 10.3 A PRODUCTION-POSSIBILITY SURFACE

Actually, there is a frontier for every kind of output, but we have no way of depicting such a fantastic array. Here is a three-dimensional P-P surface that shows the frontier for these crucial outputs: consumption, investment, government.

Very few economies actually operate on their efficiency frontiers. Most economies have at least *some* unemployed inputs or are not using their inputs with all possible efficiency. Perhaps only in wartime do we reach the frontiers of our production-possibility map. Nonetheless, we can see that a major job of economic policy makers is to move the economy as close to its frontiers as possible, under normal conditions and to move the frontier out as fast as possible.

LOOKING BACK

KEY CONCEPTS

Growth is the central trend at 1.5 percent a year, per capita

1. Growth is the central concern of macroeconomics and it is a central trend of the economy. In Chapter 5 we saw that our real per capita growth has increased at about 1.5 percent a year, plus or minus 10 percent. This doubles real per capita living standards every 47 years.

Increases in labor inputs reflect population growth and changes in participation rates

2. Growth comes from increases in the quantity or quality of our main inputs, labor and capital. Increases in the quantity of labor have resulted from growth in population and a gradual rise in the over-all participation rate, especially the entrance of women into the labor force.

Total labor hours have roughly doubled 1900–1980

3. Weekly hours have decreased since the turn of the century. Overall, it is likely that total labor hours (labor force times working hours) have slightly more than doubled, 1900–1980.

Labor hours embody more education, but the labor force works in less productive occupations

4. Changes in the quality of labor are more difficult to measure. They include increases in the amount of education embodied in the labor force and adding to the value of our human capital, and also changes in the kinds of work we do. There has been a long-term shift into service occupations which have lower than average productivity.

Total real output is up 10 times, 1900–1980. Much of this comes from capital but we cannot measure increases in quantity vs. quality

5. Total real output between 1900 and 1980 has increased some ten-fold. A major portion of this growth must come from capital inputs. However it is almost impossible to separate changes in the quantity and quality of capital, because capital is always changing.

Investment is the process by which we add to the quantity of capital; technology adds to its quality

6. Although quantity and quality are almost impossible to separate, we speak of increases in the quantity of capital as arising through investment, and increases in its quality as arising through technology. In fact, an act of saving and investment is the means by which invention or innovation takes place.

R & D is a key activity, recently declining as a percent of GNP

7. The sources of technology are not clearly understood. Research and development activities are likely a very important source of technological improvement; recently R&D has been declining in the U.S.

Changes in labor and capital inputs move out the production-possibility frontier

8. Production-possibility curves can now be seen as describing the constraints on growth. We can move the frontiers out by the changes in labor and capital inputs that we have been describing.

ECONOMIC VOCABULARY

QUESTIONS

1. Set up a production-possibilities curve for an economy producing food and steel. Show how some combinations of food and steel cannot be produced, even though each of the goods lies within the limit of production on its own axis. Explain why the P-P curve is bowed. (If you can't, reread p. 90.)
2. Think about ways in which education can improve productivity—and ways in which it cannot. Would you think that going or not going to elementary school would have a greater or lesser effect on output per hour than going to college? In what line of work?
3. Try to think of some kinds of capital that have remained essentially unchanged over the last 50 years. How about ordinary tools, such as those that a carpenter uses? Can you picture in your mind's eye the effect of widening this kind of capital to match a growing force of carpenters, as against equipping the force with new kinds of tools such as power saws?
4. Is it possible for an economy that failed to invest to continue to grow? Suppose it worked harder? Are there limits to such kinds of growth? Are there limits to the growth that new and better capital will bring?

Chapter 11 HOW PRODUCTION IS SUSTAINED

A LOOK AHEAD

Here we move from considerations of long-term growth to a closer understanding of how the economy works. This will involve us in a step-by-step analysis of one central question: How can an economy sustain itself? Or in other words, how can it buy back all its own production?

We will attack the problem by seeing how every item of cost incurred in production becomes someone's income. That is a key part of the answer: Costs are also incomes. But it is not the whole answer. Incomes must thereafter be spent if they are to become demand. And if they are not spent? Then we have trouble, recession, slowdowns in production.

We end with a few definitions that you should be sure to learn. When you finish this chapter you will be ready for the all-important next one on saving and investment. So read this one carefully!

So far, we have talked about GNP from the supply point of view. First we familiarized ourselves with the actual process of production itself—the interaction of the factors of production and the accumulated wealth of the past as they cooperated to bring a flow of output into being. Next we examined the forces that swelled that volume of output over time, mainly the increase in skills and capital equipment and technology that are responsible for our long-term trend of growth.

But we cannot pursue the problem of growth much further before we have understood something about the operation of the economy that is both very simple and surprisingly complex. **How do we know that there will be enough purchasing power to buy the amount of production that the economy creates?** Until we understand how an economy can sustain itself, we will not be able to understand how it can pull itself up by its own bootstraps—that is, how it can grow.

OUTPUT AND DEMAND

The question leads us to understand a fundamental linkage between demand and output. How does output actually come into existence? Anyone in business will give you the answer. The crucial factor in running a business is *demand* or *purchasing power;* that is, the presence of buyers who are willing and able to buy some good or service at a price the seller is willing to accept.

But how does demand or purchasing power come into existence? Any buyer will tell us that dollars come in as part of *income* or cash receipts. But where, in turn, do the dollar receipts or incomes of buyers come from? If we inquire again, most buyers will tell us that they have money in their pockets because in one fashion or another they have contributed to the process of production; that is, because they have helped to make the output that is now being sold.

Thus output is generated by demand—and demand is generated by output! Our quest for the motive force behind the flow of production therefore leads us to discover a great *circular flow* within the economy.

THE CIRCULAR FLOW

At the top of the circle in Figure 11.1 we see payments flowing from households to firms or government units (cities, states, federal agencies, etc.), thereby creating the demand that brings forth production. At the bottom of the circle, we see more payments, this time flowing from firms or governments back to households, as businesses hire the services of the various factors in order to carry out production. **Thus we can see that there is a constant regeneration of demand as money is first spent by the public on the output of firms and governments, and then in turn spent by firms and governments for the services of the public. That is how an economy that has produced a given GNP is able to buy it back.**

This is by no means a self-evident matter. Indeed, one of the most common misconceptions about the flow of economic activity is that there will not be enough purchasing power to buy everything we have produced—that somehow we are unable to buy enough to keep up with the output of our factories. So it is well to understand once and for all how an economy can sustain a given level of production through its purchases on the market.

We start, then, with an imaginary economy in full operation. We can, if we

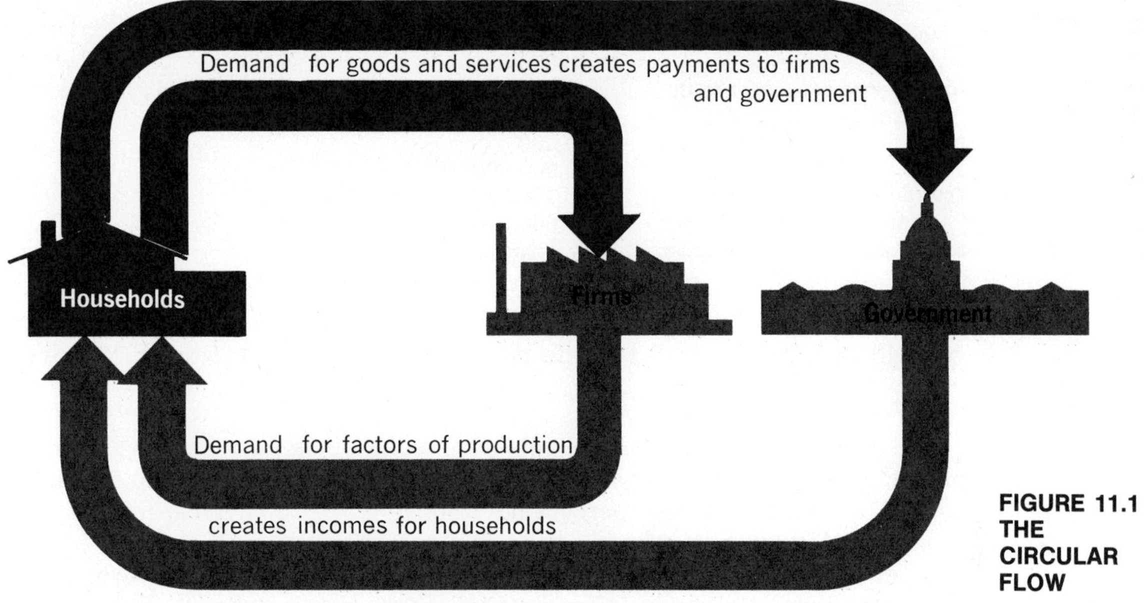

FIGURE 11.1 THE CIRCULAR FLOW

This is the same circular flow concept that we encountered in Figure 9.1. Here we use it to emphasize that the demand for output is itself generated by output.

---

wish, imagine ourselves as having collected a year's output, which is now sitting on the economic front doorstep looking for a buyer. What we must now see is whether it will be possible to *sell* this gross national product to the people who have been engaged in producing it. We must ask whether enough income or receipts have been generated in the process of production to buy back all the products themselves.

COSTS AND INCOMES

How does production create income? Business people do not think about "incomes" when they assemble the factors of production to meet the demand for their product. They worry about *cost.* All the money they pay out during the production process is paid under the heading of *cost,* whether it be wage or salary cost, cost of materials, depreciation cost, tax cost, or whatever. Thus it seems that the concept of cost may offer us a useful point of entry into the economic chain. **If we can show how all costs become incomes, we will have taken a major step toward understanding whether our gross national product can in fact be sold to those who produced it.**

It may help us if we begin by looking at the kinds of costs incurred by business firms in real life. Since governments also produce goods and services, this hypothetical firm should be taken to represent government agencies as well as business firms. Both incur the same kinds of costs; only the labels differ.

Table 11.1, a hypothetical expense summary of General Output Company, will serve as an example typical of all business firms, large or small, and all

TABLE 11.1 GENERAL OUTPUT COMPANY COST SUMMARY

Wages, salaries, and employee benefits	$100,000,000
Rental, interest, and profits payments	5,000,000
Materials, supplies, etc.	60,000,000
Taxes other than income	25,000,000
Depreciation	20,000,000
Total	$210,000,000

government agencies. (If you examine the year-end statements of any business, you will find that costs all fall into one or more of the cost categories shown.)

FACTOR COSTS

Some of these costs we recognize immediately as payments to factors of production. The item for wages and salaries is obviously a payment to the factor *labor.* The item for interest (perhaps not so obviously) is a payment to the factor *capital;* that is, to those who have lent the company money in order to help it carry on its productive operation. The item for rent is, of course, a payment for the rental of *land* or natural resources from their owners.

Note that we have included profits with rent and interest. In actual accounting practice, profits are not shown as an expense. For our purposes, however, it will be quite legitimate and very helpful to regard profits as a special kind of factor cost going to business people for their risk-taking function. Later we shall go more thoroughly into the matter of profits.

FACTOR COSTS AND VALUE OF OUTPUT

Two things strike us about these factor costs. *First, it is clear that they represent payments that have been made to secure production.* In more technical language, they are payments for factor inputs that result in commodity outputs. All the production actually carried on within the company or government agency, all the value it has added to the economy has been compensated by the payments the company or the agency has made to land, labor, and capital. To be sure, there are other costs, for materials and taxes and depreciation, and we shall soon turn to these. But whatever production or assembly or distribution the company or agency has carried out during the course of the year has required the use of land, labor, or capital. **Thus the total of its factor costs represents the value of the total new output that General Output by itself has given to the economy.**

From here it is a simple step to add up *all* the factor costs paid out by *all* the companies and government agencies in the economy, in order to measure the total new *value added* by all productive efforts in the year. This measure is called **national income.** As we can see, it is less than gross national product, for it does not include other costs of output, namely certain taxes and depreciation.

FACTOR COSTS AND HOUSEHOLD INCOMES

A second fact that strikes us is that *all factor costs are income payments.* **The wages, salaries, interest, rents, etc., that were costs to the company or agency were income to its recipients. So are any profits, which will accrue as income to the owners of the business.**

Thus, just as it sounds, national income means the total amount of earnings of the factors of production within the nation. If we think of these factors as constituting the households of the economy, we can see that *factor costs result directly in incomes to the household sector.* If factor costs were the only costs involved in production, the problem of buying back the gross national product would be a very simple one. We should simply be paying out to households, as the cost of production, the very sum needed to buy GNP when we turned around to sell it. A glance at the General Output expense summary shows that this is not the case. There are other costs besides factor costs. How shall we deal with them?

COSTS OF MATERIALS

The next item of the expense summary is puzzling. Called payments for "materials, supplies, etc.," it represents all the money General Output has paid, not to its own factors, but to other companies for other products it has needed. We may even recognize these costs as payments for those *intermediate products* that lose their identity in a later stage of production. How do such payments become part of the income available to buy GNP on the marketplace?

Perhaps the answer is already intuitively clear. When General Output sends its checks to, let us say, U.S. Steel or General Electric or to a local supplier of stationery, each of these recipient firms now uses the proceeds of General Output's checks to pay its own costs.

And what are those costs? What must U.S. Steel or all the other suppliers now do with their checks? The answer is obvious. They must reimburse their own factors and then pay any other costs that remain.

Figure 11.2 may make the matter plain. It shows us, looking back down the chain of intermediate payments, that what constitutues material costs to one

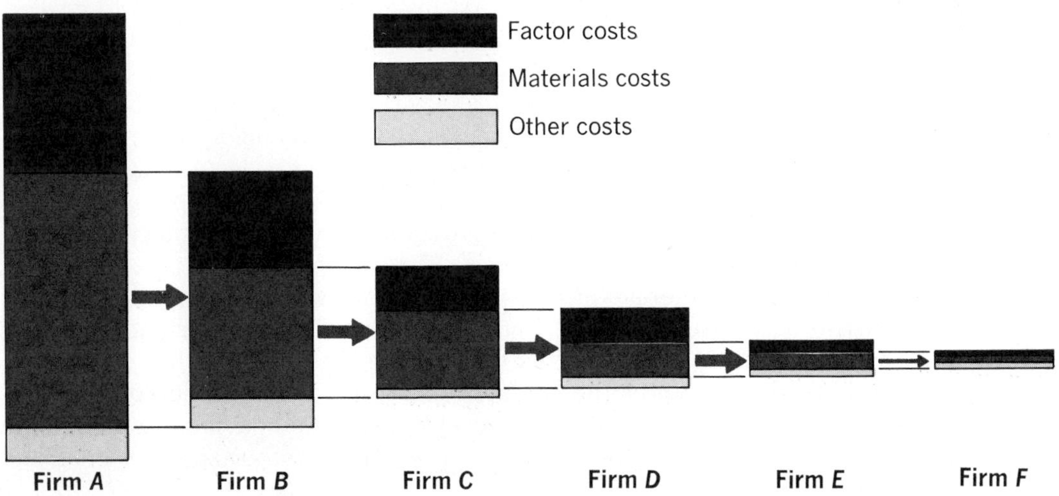

FIGURE 11.2 HOW MATERIALS COSTS BECOME OTHER COSTS

The cost of materials to Firm A consists of Firm B's payments to its factors and other costs, just as Firm B's materials cost is made up of Firm C's factor and other costs. Eventually all costs of materials reduce to payments to labor, capital and land. After all, what other ultimate costs are there?

firm is made up of factor and other costs to another. Indeed, as we unravel the chain from company to company, it is clear that all the contribution to new output must have come from the contribution of factors somewhere down the line. **All the costs of new output—all the value added—must ultimately be resolvable into payments to the owners of land (or natural resources), labor, and capital.**

Another way of picturing the same thing is to imagine that all firms or agencies in the country were bought up by a single gigantic corporation. The various production units of the new supercorporation would then ship components and semifinished items back and forth to one another, but there would not have to be any payment from one division to another. The only payments that would be necessary would be those required to buy the services of factors—that is, various kinds of labor or the use of property or capital—so that at the end of the year, the supercorporation would show on its expense summary only items for wages and salaries, rent, and interest (and as we shall see, taxes and depreciation), but it would have no item for materials cost.

We have come a bit further toward seeing how our gross national product can be sold. **To the extent that GNP represents new output made during the course of the year, the income to buy back this output has already been handed out as factor costs, either paid at the last stage of production or carried along in the guise of material costs.**

But a glance at the General Output expense summary shows that entrepreneurs incur two kinds of costs that we have still not taken into account: taxes and depreciation. Here are costs employers have incurred that have not been accounted for on the income side. What can we say about them?

TAX COSTS

Let us begin by tracing the taxes that General Output pays, just as we have traced its material payments.* In the first instance, its taxes will go to government units—federal, state, and local. But we need not stop there. Just as we saw that General Output's checks to supplier firms paid for the suppliers' factor costs and for still further interfirm transactions, so we can see that its checks to government agencies pay for goods and services that these agencies have produced—goods such as roads, buildings, or defense equipment; or services such as teaching, police protection, and the administration of justice. General Output's tax checks are thus used to help pay for factors of production—land, labor, and capital—that are used in the *public sector.*

In many ways, General Output's payments to government units resemble its payments to other firms for raw material. Indeed, if the government *sold* its services to General Output, charging for the use of the roads, police services, or defense protection it affords the company, there would be *no* difference whatsoever. The reason we differentiate between a company's payment to the public sector and its payments for intermediate products is important, however, and worth looking into.

*For simplicity, we also show government agencies as taxpayers. In fact, most government units do *not* pay taxes. Yet there will be hidden tax costs in the prices of many materials they buy. No harm is done by treating government agencies like taxpaying firms in this model.

The first reason is clearly that with few exceptions, the government does *not* sell its output. This is partly because the community has decided that certain things the government produces (education, justice, or the use of public parks, for instance) should not be for sale but should be supplied to all citizens without direct charge. In part, it is also because some things the government produces, such as defense or law and order, cannot be equitably charged to individual buyers since it is impossible to say to what degree anyone benefits from—or even uses—these communal facilities. Hence General Output, like every other producer, is billed, justly or otherwise, for a share of the cost of government.

There is also a second reason why we consider the cost of taxes as a new kind of cost, distinct from factor payments. It is this. **When business firms have finished paying the factors, they have not yet paid all the sums that employers must lay out. Some taxes, in other words, are an addition to the cost of production.**

INDIRECT VS. DIRECT TAXES

These taxes—so-called *indirect taxes*—are levied on the productive enterprise itself or on its actual physical output. Taxes on real estate, for instance, or taxes that are levied on each unit of output (such as excise taxes on cigarettes) or taxes levied on goods sold at retail (sales taxes) are all payments that entrepreneurs must make as part of their costs of doing business.

This does not mean that all taxes collected by the government are costs of production. Many taxes will be paid, not by the entrepreneurs as an expense of doing business, but by the *factors* themselves. These so-called *direct* taxes (such as income taxes) are *not* part of the cost of production. When General Output adds up its total cost of production, it naturally includes the wages and salaries it has paid, but it does not include the taxes its workers or executives have paid out of their incomes. Such direct taxes transfer income from earners to government, but they are not a cost to the company itself.

In the same way, the income taxes on the profits of a company do *not* constitute a cost of production. General Output does not pay income taxes as a regular charge on its operations but waits until a year's production has taken place and then pays income taxes on the profits it makes *after* paying its costs. If it finds that it has lost money over the year, it will not pay any income taxes—although it will have paid other costs, including indirect taxes. **Thus direct taxes, such as income taxes, are not a cost paid out in the course of production that must be recouped, but a payment made by factors (including owners of the business) from the incomes they have earned through the process of production.**

TAXES AS COST

Now we can see two reasons why taxes are handled as a separate item in GNP and are not telescoped into factor costs, the way materials costs are. One reason is that taxes are a payment to a sector different from that of business and thus indicate a separate stream of economic activity.

The second reason, and the one that interests us more at this moment, is that *certain taxes*—indirect taxes—*are an entirely new kind of cost of production, not previously picked up.* As an expense paid out by entrepreneurs, over and above factor costs (or material costs), these tax costs must be part of the total selling price of GNP.

Will there be enough incomes handed out in the process of production to cover this item of cost? We can see that there will be. The indirect tax costs paid out by firms will be received by government agencies who will use these tax receipts to pay income to factors working for the government. Any direct taxes (income taxes) paid by General Output or by its factors will also wind up in the hands of a government. **Thus all tax payments result in the transfer of purchasing power from the private to the public sector, and when spent by the public sector, they will again become demand on the marketplace.**

DEPRECIATION

But there is still one last item of cost. At the end of the year, when the company is totting up its expenses to see if it has made a profit for the period, its accountants do not stop with factor costs, material costs, and indirect taxes. If they did, the company would soon be in serious straits. In producing its goods, General Output has also used up a certain amount of its assets—its buildings and equipment—and a cost must now be charged for this wear and tear if the company is to be able to preserve the value of its physical plant intact. If it did not make this cost allowance, it would have failed to include all the resources that were used up in the process of production, and it would therefore be overstating its profits.

Yet this cost has something about it clearly different from other costs that General Output has paid. Unlike factor costs or taxes or material costs, depreciation is not paid for by check. When the company's accountants make an allowance for depreciation, all they do is make an entry on the company's book, stating that plant and equipment are now worth a certain amount less than in the beginning of the year.

At the same time, however, General Output *includes* the amount of depreciation in the price it intends to charge for its goods. As we have seen, one of the resources used up in production was its own capital equipment, and it is certainly entitled to consider the depreciation as a cost. Yet it has not paid anyone a sum of money equal to this cost! How, then, will there be enough income in the marketplace to buy back its product?

REPLACEMENT EXPENDITURE

The answer is that in essence it has paid depreciation charges to itself. Depreciation is thus part of its gross income. Together with after-tax profits, these depreciation charges are called a business's *cash flow.*

A business does not *have* to spend its depreciation accruals, but normally it will, to maintain and replace its capital stock. To be sure, an individual firm may not replace its worn-out capital exactly on schedule. But when we consider the economy as a whole, with its vast assemblage of firms, that problem tends to disappear. Suppose we have 1,000 firms, each with machines worth $1,000 and each depreciating its machines at $100 per year. Provided that all the machines were bought in different years, this means that in any given year, about 10 percent of the capital stock will wear out and have to be replaced. It's reasonable to assume that among them, the 1,000 firms will spend $100,000 to replace their old equipment over a ten-year span.*

This enables us to see that insofar as there is a steady stream of replacement expenditures going to firms that make capital goods, there will be payments just large enough to balance the addition to costs due to depreciation. As with all other payments to firms, these replacement expenditures will become incomes to factors, etc., and thus can reappear on the marketplace.

THE THREE STREAMS OF EXPENDITURE

Our analysis is now complete. Item by item, we have traced each element of cost into an income payment, so that we now know there is enough income paid out to buy back our GNP at a price that represents its full cost. Perhaps this was a conclusion we anticipated all along. After all, ours would be an impossibly difficult economy to manage if somewhere along the line purchasing power dropped out of existence, so that we were always faced with a shortage of income to buy back the product we made. But our analysis has also shown us something more unexpected. We are accustomed to thinking that all the purchasing power in the economy is received and spent through the hands of people—usually meaning households. Now we can see that this is not true. There is not only one, but there are *three* streams of incomes and costs, all quite distinct from one another (although linked by direct taxes).

1. Factor costs → Households → Consumers goods

   ↓ Direct Taxes

2. Indirect taxes → Government agencies → Government goods

   ↑ Direct Taxes

3. Depreciation → Business firms → Replacement investment

The one major crossover in the three streams is the direct taxes of households and business firms that go to governments. This flow permits governments to buy more goods and services than could be purchased with indirect taxes alone.

There is a simple way of explaining this seemingly complex triple flow. Each stream indicates the existence of a *final taker* of gross national product: the consumer, government, and business itself.† Since output has final claimants

*What if the machines *were* all bought in one year or over a small number of years? Then replacement expenditures will *not* be evenly distributed over time, and we may indeed have problems. This takes us into the dynamics of prosperity and recession, to which we will turn in due course. For the purpose of our explanatory model, we will stick with our (not too unrealistic) assumption that machines wear out on a steady schedule and that aggregate replacement expenditures therefore also display a steady, relatively unfluctuating pattern.

†We continue to forget about net exports until Chapter 36. They are taken care of quite satisfactorily as a component of gross private investment.

other than consumers, we can obviously have a flow of purchasing power that does not enter consumers' or factors' hands.

THE COMPLETED CIRCUIT OF DEMAND

The realization that factor owners do not get paid incomes equal to the total gross value of output brings us back to the central question of this chapter: Can we be certain that we will be able to sell our GNP at its full cost? Has there surely been generated enough purchasing power to buy back our total output?

We have thus far carefully analyzed and answered half the question. We know that all costs will become incomes to factors or receipts of government agencies or of firms making replacement items. To sum up again, factor costs become the incomes of workers, managements, owners of natural resources and of capital; and all these incomes together can be thought of as comprising the receipts of the household sector. Tax costs are paid to government agencies and become receipts of the government sector. Depreciation costs are initially accrued within business firms, and these accruals belong to the business sector. As long as worn-out capital is regularly replaced, these accruals will be matched by equivalent new receipts of firms that make capital goods.

CRUCIAL ROLE OF EXPENDITURES

What we have not yet established, however, is that these sector receipts will become sector expenditures. That is, we have not demonstrated that all households will now *spend* all their incomes on goods and services, or that government units will necessarily *spend* all their tax receipts on public goods and services, or that all firms will assuredly *spend* their depreciation accruals for new replacement equipment.

What happens if some receipts are not spent? The answer is of key importance in understanding the operation of the economy. A failure of the sectors to spend as much money as they have received means that some of the costs that have been laid out will *not* come back to the original entrepreneurs. As a result, they will suffer losses. If, for instance, our gross national product costs $1 trillion to produce but the various sectors spend only $900 billion in all, then some entrepreneurs will find themselves failing to sell all their output. Inventories of unsold goods will begin piling up, and business people will soon be worried about overproducing. The natural thing to do when you can't sell all your output is to stop making so much of it, so businesses will begin cutting back on production. As they do so, they will also cut back on the number of people they employ. As a result, business costs will go down; but so will factor incomes, for we have seen that costs and incomes are but opposite sides of one coin. As incomes fall, the expenditures of the sectors might very well fall further, bringing about another twist in the spiral of recession.

This is not yet the place to go into the mechanics of such a downward spiral of business. But the point is clear. **A failure of the sectors to bring all their receipts back to the marketplace as demand can initiate profound economic problems. In the contrast between an unshakable equality of costs and incomes on**

THE THREE FLOWS

To help visualize these three flows, imagine for an instant that our money comes in colors (all of equal value): black, gray, and red. Now suppose that firms always pay their factors in red money, their taxes in gray money, and their replacement expenditures in black money. In point of fact, of course, the colors would soon be mixed. A factor that is paid in red bills will be paying some of his red income for taxes; or a government agency will be paying out gray money as factor incomes; or firms will be using black dollars to pay taxes or factors, and gray or red dollars to pay for replacement capital.

But at least in our minds, we can picture the streams being kept separate. A gray tax dollar paid by General Output to the Internal Revenue Service for taxes could go from the government to another firm, let us say in payment for office supplies, and we can think of the office supply firm keeping these gray dollars apart from its other receipts to pay its taxes with. Such a gray dollar could circulate indefinitely from government agencies to firms and back again, helping to bring about production but never entering a consumer's pocket! In the same way, a black replacement expenditure dollar going from General Output to, let us say, U.S. Steel could be set aside by U.S. Steel to pay for *its* replacement needs; and the firm that received this black dollar might, in turn, set it aside for its own use as replacement expenditure. We can imagine a circuit of expenditures in which black dollars went from firm to firm to pay for replacement investment and never ended up in a pay envelope or as a tax payment.

the one hand, and the uncertain connection between incomes and expenditures on the other, we have come to grips with one of the most important problems in macroeconomics.

FROM RECESSION TO INFLATION

We have concentrated on the problem of buying back GNP because that is the best way to understand the circular flow properties of production. But most of us these days are worried about inflation. How does that tie into our analysis?

The answer should be clear enough. If recession arises because there is too little expenditure to cover the costs of producing GNP, inflation arises because there is too much expenditure. We have all heard inflation described as "too much money chasing too little goods"; as a description that is entirely correct, although it fails to explain where "too much money" comes from.

We have something of a problem in going further into an explanation of inflation at this point. We have not yet learned about money, nor have we studied the motivation of expenditure. So we will simply have to wait before we go deeply into the inflationary phenomenon. We will be back to the subject many times.

SOME IMPORTANT DEFINITIONS

We have completed the necessary economic analysis of this chapter, showing how the demand for GNP is generated. But we still need to improve and refine our economic vocabulary. Before we move on, therefore, we must learn some very useful and frequently encountered definitions.

The first of these concerns two ways of looking at GNP. One way is to think of GNP as measuring the value of a year's final output. As we know that value is a sum of costs: factor costs, indirect tax costs, the costs of depreciation. But we also know that these same costs are identical with the incomes or receipts of sectors. Therefore GNP measures total incomes as well as total costs.

GNP AND GNI

To express the equality with the conciseness and clarity of mathematics, we can write two equations. First, GNP as a sum of final outputs:

$$\text{GNP} \equiv C + G + I + X,$$

where C, I, G, and X (exports) are designations of the four categories into which we divide our flow of production.

Next, we write an equation that describes GNP not as a sum of outputs but as a sum of costs:

$$\text{GNP} \equiv F + T + D,$$

where F, T, and D are familiar to us as factor, indirect tax, and depreciation costs. *But we have also learned that all costs are identical with incomes.* It follows, therefore, that we can speak of the sum of these costs as Gross National Income, or GNI. Hence the last set of identities:

Gross National Product ≡ Gross National Income

or **GNP ≡ GNI,**

or $\boldsymbol{C + G + I + X \equiv F + T + D}$.

It is important to remember that these are all accounting identities, true by definition. The National Income and Product Accounts, the official government accounts for the economy, are kept in such a manner as to make them true. As the name implies, these accounts are kept in two sets of books, one on the products produced in the economy and one on the costs of production, which we know to be identical with the incomes generated in the economy. Since both sets of accounts are measuring the same output, the two totals must be equal.

NNP AND NATIONAL INCOME

It is now easy to understand the meaning of two other measures of output. One of these is called **net national product** (NNP). As the name indicates, it is exactly equal to the gross national product minus depreciation. GNP is used much more than NNP, since the measures of depreciation are very unreliable. The other measure, national income, we have already met. It is *GNP minus both depreciation and indirect taxes.* This makes it equal to the sum of factor costs only. Figure 11.3 should make this relationship clear. The aim of this last measure is to identify the net income that actually reaches the hands of factors of production. Consequently, the measure is sometimes called the *national income at factor cost.* Its abbreviation is Y.

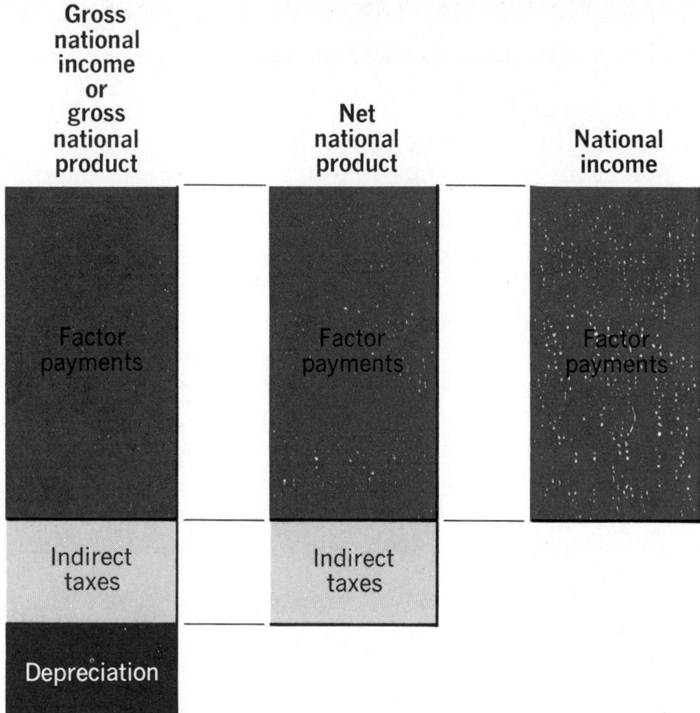

FIGURE 11.3 GNP, NNP, AND NI

GNP, NNP, and NI (or Y) fit into one another like a nest of Chinese boxes. As you can see, the basic unit of measurement of output is national income; net and gross national products are derived by adding specific costs—indirect taxes for NNP and depreciation for GNP.

THE CIRCULAR FLOW AGAIN

The "self-reproducing" model economy we have now sketched out is obviously still very far from reality. Nevertheless, the particular kind of unreality that we have deliberately constructed serves a highly useful purpose. An economy that regularly and dependably buys back everything it produces gives us a kind of bench mark from which to begin our subsequent investigations. We call such an economy, whose internal relationships we have outlined, an economy in **stationary equilibrium,** and we denote the changeless flow of costs into business receipts, and receipts back into costs, a *circular flow.*

We shall return many times to the model of a circular flow economy for insights into a more complex and dynamic system. Hence it is well that we summarize briefly two of the salient characteristics of such a system.

1. A circular flow economy will never experience a recession

Year in and year out, its total output will remain unchanged. Indeed, the very concept of a circular flow is useful in showing us that an economic system can maintain a given level of activity *indefinitely,* so long as all the sectors convert all their receipts into expenditures.

2. **A circular flow economy will never know a boom**

That is, it will not grow, and its standard of living will remain unchanged. That standard of living may be high or low, for we could have a circular flow economy of poverty or of abundance. But in either state, changelessness will be its essence.

THE GREAT PUZZLE

What we have demonstrated in this chapter is an exceedingly important idea. There *can* always be enough purchasing power generated by the process of output to buy back that output.

Yet we all know, from our most casual acquaintance with economics, that in fact there is not always enough purchasing power around, or that on occasions there is too much purchasing power. With too little, we have slumps and recessions; with too much, booms and inflation.

Hence the circular flow sets the stage for the next step in our study of macroeconomics. If there *can be* the right amount of purchasing power generated, why isn't there? Or to put the question more perplexingly: if there *can be* enough purchasing power to buy *any* size output, small or large, what determines how large purchasing power will actually be, and therefore how large output will actually be?

These questions point the way for the next stage of our investigation. We must study the workings of demand much more realistically than heretofore by removing some of the assumptions that were necessary to create a model of a circular flow system.

KEY CONCEPTS

LOOKING BACK

The demand for GNP is generated in the act of production as firms hire factors

1. The question to be grasped is how an economy can sustain itself, how it can generate enough demand to buy back its own output. This leads at once to the origin of demand for output, or purchasing power. In turn we see that purchasing power is generated by the act of production, as firms and government employers hire factors of production. Thus we begin with the concept of a circular flow.

Factor costs are income to the factors of production

2. When factors are hired, they create costs. It is important to see that all costs are necessarily also incomes. We group all costs—including material costs—into three categories. The first category, factor costs—wages, salaries, interest payments, and the like—are obviously incomes for the factors of production who receive them.

Indirect taxes are costs that become receipts of government agencies. (Note: Income taxes are not costs of production)

3. In the second category are the costs of indirect taxation. These are not direct income taxes which are borne by the factors out of their incomes and are not a cost of production. Indirect taxes are simply added onto factor costs as an expense of production. Such indirect taxes become part of the receipts of government agencies.

Depreciation costs accrue to firms and can be used for replacement investment

4. Depreciation costs are the final category of production cost. These costs are received by business firms, who use them to finance replacement investment.

Thus, all costs are incomes, but all incomes may not become expenditures

5. Thus there are three streams of spending in the economy: (1) factor costs which go to the households who spend these "costs" (their incomes) for consumption; (2) indirect taxes which go to government for expenditure on public goods and services; and (3) depreciation costs that accrue to business firms for expenditure as replacement investment. It is important to see that the transition from "cost" to "income" is unbreakable—they are identities. This is not so for the transition from cost (or income) to expenditure. Here is a crucial area of potential malfunction.

GNP ≡ GNI

6. We can express GNP in two ways: as a sum of final outputs or as a sum of incomes. Thus there is an identity between gross national income and gross national product.

A circular flow economy has no growth

7. The model of a circular flow economy elucidates how such an economy can repurchase its own production. But a circular flow system has no vitality, no growth.

ECONOMIC VOCABULARY

Factor costs 152
National income 152
Direct and indirect taxes 155
Depreciation 156
GNP and GNI 160
Circular flow 161
Net national product 160
Stationary equilibrium 161

QUESTIONS

1. What are factor costs? To what sector do they go? Do all factor costs become personal incomes? Do they become personal expenditures? (Careful about this last: Suppose that a household *saves* part of its income!)
2. What are direct taxes? What is "direct" about them? Why are they distinguished from "indirect" taxes? Why is an indirect tax, such as a sales tax, considered an addition to the value of GNP, whereas an income tax is not? Think: Does the value of the goods or services you personally create get bigger if you pay a larger income tax? Does it get larger if the sales tax is increased?
3. To whom are material costs paid? Why do we not count them as a separate part of GNP?
4. Exactly what is depreciation? Why is it a cost? Who pays it, and how? Who receives it? Is it possible that a firm can pay depreciation to itself? How else would you describe a business that made an allowance at the end of the year for the value of the machinery that had been used up in production?
5. Why is the link between an expenditure and a receipt an identity? Why is the link between a receipt and an expenditure not an identity? Can there be any expenditure ever without someone receiving it? Can someone receive a payment but not make an expenditure himself? Be sure you grasp the difference here.

Chapter 12 SAVING AND INVESTMENT

A LOOK AHEAD

This key chapter tells us about the process that injects growth into a circular flow economy—the process of saving and investment.

(1) It shows how the act of saving creates a gap in final demand, a gap that can only be offset by compensatory action from the other sectors. When this compensatory action is undertaken by business it is called investment, and it results in the creation of growth-promoting capital goods.

(2) We trace how savings move from the household sector to the business (or government) sector where they are spent.

(3) We note the effects of transfer payments on the flow of spending, and learn how profits can be returned to create new demand.

Our model of a circular flow economy which buys back all of its output by spending all of its receipts begins to explain how our economic system works—and why sometimes it does not work. Yet it leaves us in the dark with respect to the central question of growth, for an economy that merely bought back all its output by spending all its receipts would not grow. It would remain in place, reproducing itself from year to year. If we want to put growth into the picture we have to add something that has so far been lacking from our exposition.

Moreover, we know what is lacking from our circular flow model. It is the process of saving and investing by which we add more capital and better capital—the key to economic growth. Therefore, in this chapter we are going to connect the previous analysis of how the macrosystem works with our central concern with understanding growth.

THE MEANING OF SAVING

We begin by making sure that we understand a key word—*saving*. Saving, for an economist, cannot be defined just as putting money in the bank. Rather, it is refraining from spending *all or part of income for consumption goods or services*. It should be very clear then why saving is such a key term. In our discussion of the circular flow, it became apparent that expenditure was the critical link in the steady operation of the economy. If saving is not-spending, then it would seem that saving could be the cause of just that kind of downward spiral of which we caught a glimpse in our preceding chapter.

And yet this clearly is not the whole story. The act of investing—of spending money to direct factors into the production of capital goods—requires an act of saving. **We must save—that is, not use all our income for consumption—if we are to have the ability to hire factors to build capital goods. A society that did no saving would have no way of breaking out of a stationary circular flow.**

Hence, saving is clearly necessary for the process of investment. Now, how can one and the same act be necessary for economic expansion and a threat to its stability? This is a problem that will occupy us during much of the coming chapters.

THE DEMAND DIAGRAM

Let us use a diagram to show how saving can create both a "gap" in demand and an "opening" for investment.

In Figure 12.1 we trace the flow of expenditure through the economy from left to right. On the left we start with three blocks showing the factor, tax, and depreciation costs that have been incurred by businesses and government agencies as costs of production. Now we are going to follow those costs as they become incomes to different sectors, and thereafter as they get translated into new demand through the act of expenditure.

Look at the blocks for taxes and depreciation first. Here we see that an amount of taxes becomes the exact equivalent amount of government receipts; and thereafter an equal amount of government expenditure. (We could think of this as a sum of indirect taxes that becomes the income of a city government and thereafter is all paid out as salaries to city employees.) Clearly there is no gap in demand here. But neither is there an opening for investment.

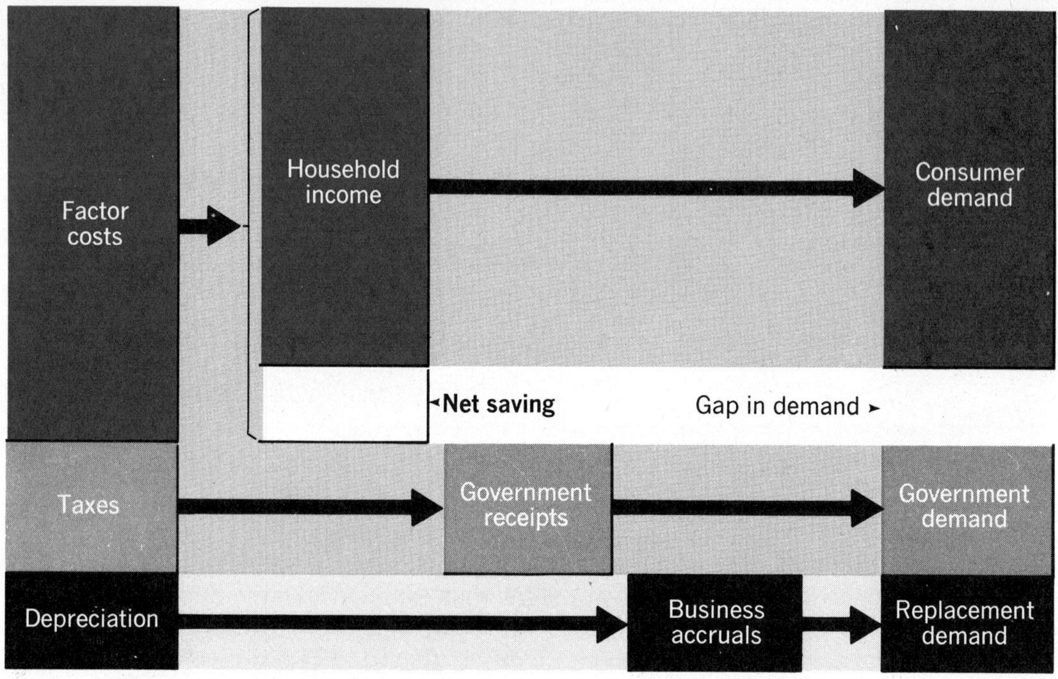

FIGURE 12.1 THE DEMAND GAP

We have used a circular flow type of diagram to show how a demand gap—and also an opening for investment—can arise. We assume that business and government spend all their receipts—of course that assumption may not be true. But it highlights the effects of saving in the household sector. This is the focus of our present investigation.

The same analysis applies to the bottom block. First we see the cost of depreciation, every penny of which becomes a receipt of the business sector, and all of which is spent as replacement investment. No gap here, and no net investment either.

THE GAP

But now look at the top block, representing factor costs. Every penny of those costs becomes factor income, as our diagram shows. This must be the case because all costs, as we know, are incomes. If households now spent all their income, there would be no gap here either, and we would have a stationary, circular flow economy. But our diagram shows that households save a part of their incomes. The result is precisely what we would expect. **There is a gap in demand introduced by the deficiency of consumer spending.** It begins to look as if we are approaching the cause of economic recession and unemployment. Yet whereas we have introduced net saving, we have forgotten about its counterpart, net investment. Cannot the investment activity of a growing economy in some way close the demand gap?

THE DILEMMA OF SAVING

This is indeed, as we shall soon see, the way out of the dilemma. But before we trace the way investment compensates for saving, let us draw some important conclusions from the analysis we have made up to this point.

1. **Any act of saving, in and by itself, creates a gap in demand, a shortage of spending. Unless this gap is closed, there will be trouble in the economic system, for employers will not be getting back as receipts all the sums they laid out.**
2. **The presence of a demand gap forces us to make a choice. If we want a dynamic, investing economy, we will have to be prepared to cope with the problems that net saving raises. If we want to avoid these problems, we can close the gap by urging consumers or corporations not to save. Then we would have a dependable circular flow, but we would no longer enjoy economic growth.**

THE OFFSET TO SAVINGS

How, then, shall we manage to make our way out of the dilemma of saving? The diagram makes clear what must be done. If a gap in demand is due to the savings of households, then *that gap must be closed by the expanded spending of some other sector.* There are only two other such sectors: government and business. Thus in some fashion or other, the savings of one sector must be offset by the increased activity of another.

But how is this offset to take place? How are the resources that are relinquished by consumers to be made available to entrepreneurs in the business sector or to government officials? In a market economy there is only one way that resources or factors not being used in one place can be used in another. Someone must be willing and able to hire them.

Whether or not government and business *are* willing to employ the factors that are not needed in the consumer goods sector is a very critical matter, soon to command much of our attention. But suppose that they are willing. How will they be able to do so? How can they get the necessary funds to expand their activity?

INCREASING EXPENDITURE

There are six principal methods of accomplishing this essential increase in expenditure.

1. **The business sector can increase its expenditures by *borrowing* the savings of the public through the sale of new corporate bonds.**
2. **The government sector can increase its expenditures by *borrowing* savings of the other sectors through the sale of new government bonds.**
3. **Both business and government sectors can increase expenditures by *borrowing* additional funds from commercial banks.***
4. **The business sector can increase its expenditures by attracting household savings into partnerships, new stock, or other *ownership* (*or equity*).**

*Actually, they are borrowing from the public through the means of banks. We shall learn about this in Chapter 18.

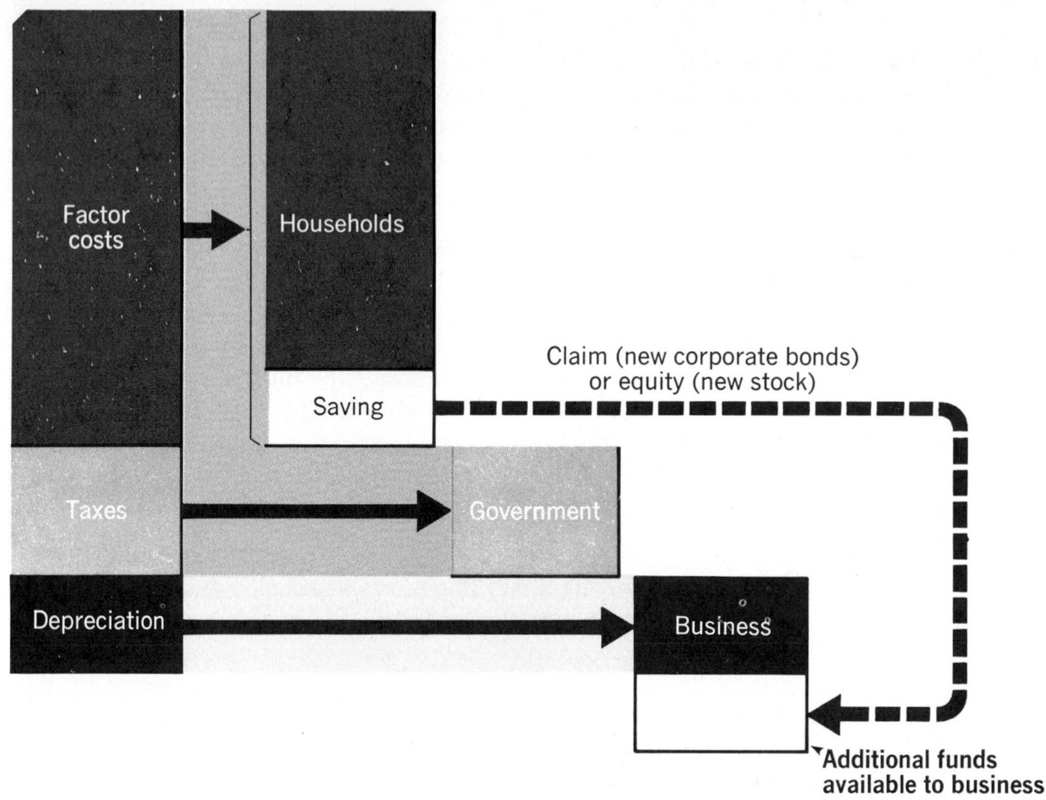

FIGURE 12.2 TWO WAYS OF TRANSFERRING SAVING BETWEEN SECTORS

Here we depict the way a demand gap can be closed by transferring the savings of one sector to another which will spend it. Our diagrams show how savings can go into business, in exchange for claims (bonds or stock) or to government, in exchange for government bonds.

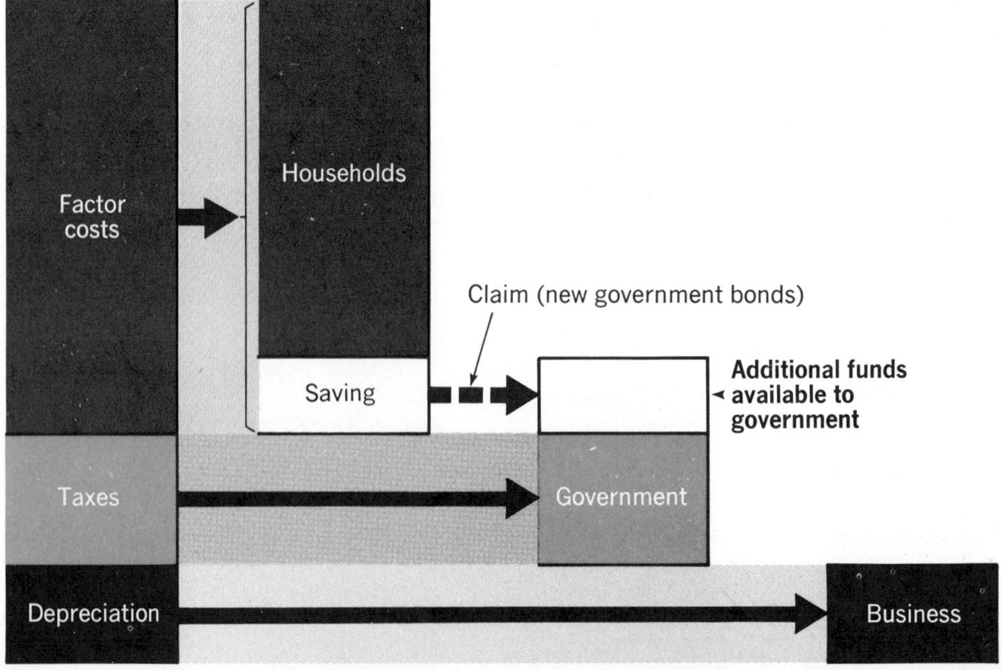

5. **The government sector can increase its expenditures by *taxing* the other sectors. (We will see later why the increase in government spending is likely to be larger than the decreased spending caused by the taxes.)**
6. **Both business and government sectors can increase their expenditures by drawing on *accumulated past savings,* such as unexpended profits or tax receipts from previous years.**

CLAIMS

The first four of these methods have one attribute that calls them especially to our attention. **They give rise to claims that reveal from whom the funds have been obtained and to whom they have been made available, as well as on what terms.** Bonds, corporate or government, show that savings have been borrowed from individuals, banks, or firms by business and government units. Shares of stock reveal that savings have been obtained on an equity (ownership) basis, as do new partnership agreements. Borrowing from banks gives rise to loans that also represent the claims of one part of the community against another.

PUBLIC AND PRIVATE BORROWING

Now let us look at the upper diagram in Figure 12.2. This shows what happens when savings are made available to the business sector by direct borrowing from households. Note the claim (or equity) that arises. If the government were doing the borrowing rather than the business sector, the diagram would look like the lower diagram in Figure 12.2. Notice that the claim is now a government bond.

We have not looked at a diagram showing business or government borrowing its funds from the banking system. (This process will be better understood when we take up the problem of money and banking, in Chapter 17.) The basic concept, however, although more complex, is much the same as above.

COMPLETED ACT OF OFFSETTING SAVINGS

There remains only a last step, which must now be fully anticipated. We have seen how it is possible to offset the savings in one sector, where they were going to cause an expenditure gap, by increasing the funds available to another sector. It remains only to *spend* those additional funds in the form of additional investment or, in the case of the government, for additional public goods and services. The two completed expenditure circuits now appear in Figure 12.3.

While Figure 12.3 is drawn so that the new investment demand or new government demand is exactly equal to net saving, it is important to understand that there is nothing in the economic system guaranteeing that these demands will exactly equal net saving. The desire for new investment or new government goods and services may be either higher or lower than new saving.

INFLATION AGAIN

This last point is absolutely essential. If the offsets of business plus government are not large enough to cover the gap, we will not succeed in buying back GNP at its actual cost and recession will ensue. It follows that if the offsets are larger than the gap, we will be spending more on GNP than it cost to produce and inflation may be the result, if the economy cannot expand its output.

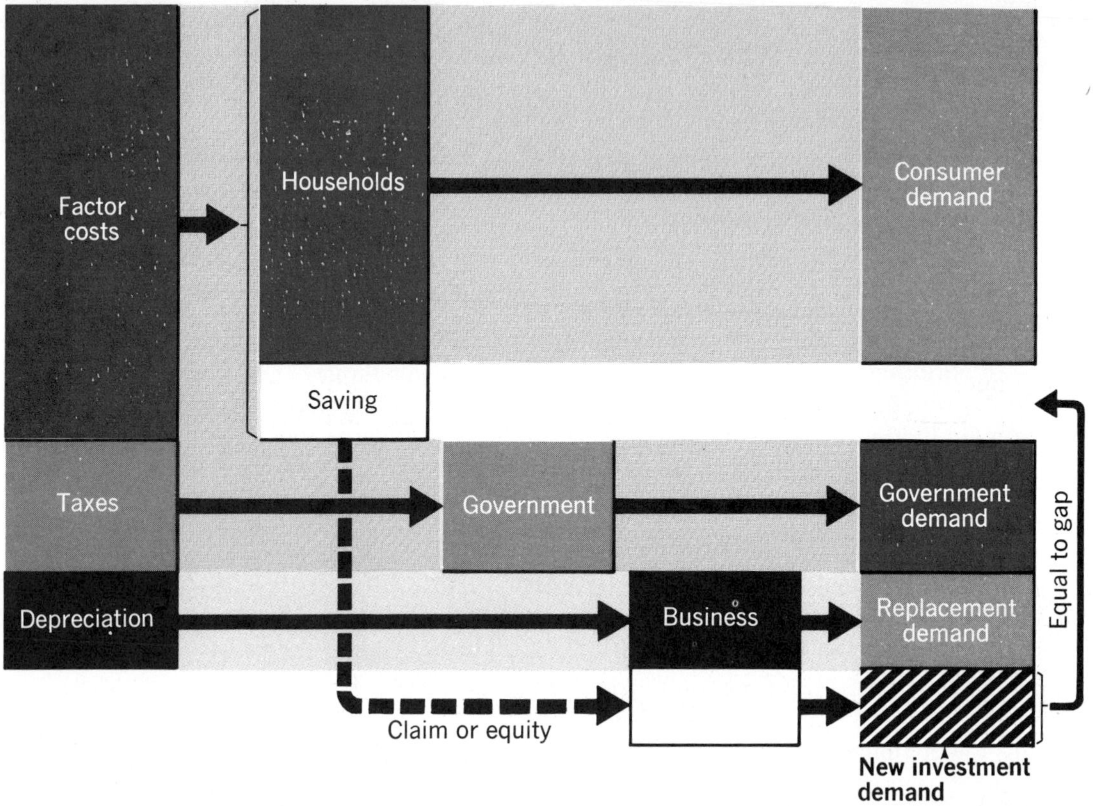

Factor costs
Households
Consumer demand
Saving
Taxes
Government
Government demand
Equal to gap
Depreciation
Business
Replacement demand
Claim or equity
New investment demand

FIGURE 12.3 TWO WAYS OF CLOSING THE DEMAND GAP **There remains only to show how the savings of the household sector, now transferred to business or government, can be spent by these latter sectors to offset the gap in demand in consumption. Note: There is no guarantee that the offsets will just balance the savings. They may be too much, bringing us growth or inflation—or too little, bringing recession.**

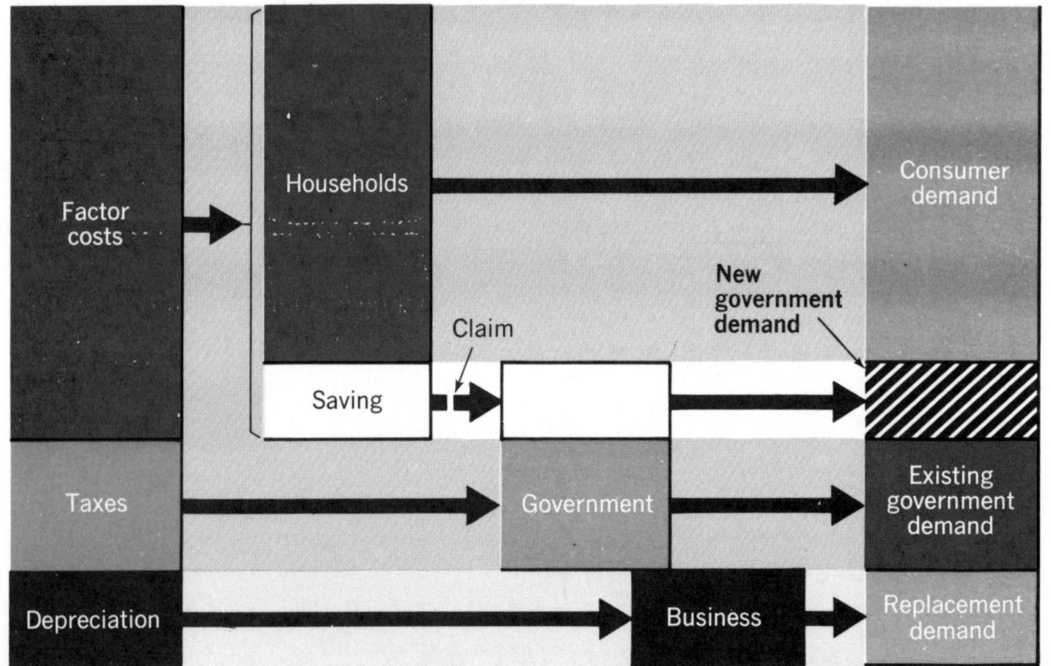

This is not yet a full explanation of either recession or inflation, because it does not explain why (or even how) offsets might be too large or too small. We need to understand more than we yet do about the money mechanism, especially in the case of inflation. But at least we are closer to seeing how the economy works—or fails to work—as a whole.

INTERSECTORAL OFFSETS

We would be getting a little ahead of ourselves if we stopped now to investigate recession or inflation. For we must first grasp the point that an economy which is working normally, in which saving takes place, *must* generate potential demand gaps, and that such an economy *must* offset those gaps if it is to function properly.

Once this simple but fundamental point is clearly understood, much of the mystery of macroeconomics disappears, for we can then begin to see that an economy in movement, as contrasted with one in a stationary circular flow, is one in which sectors must *cooperate* to maintain the closed circuit of income and output. In a dynamic economy, we no longer enjoy the steady translation of incomes into expenditure which, as we have seen, is the key to an uninterrupted flow of output. Rather, we are faced with the presence of net saving and the possibility of a gap in final demand. Difficult though the ensuing problems are, let us not forget that net saving is the necessary condition for the accumulation of capital. The price of economic growth, in other words, is the risk of economic decline.

TRANSFER PAYMENTS AND PROFITS

We have talked about the transfer of purchasing power from savers to investors, but we have not yet mentioned another kind of transfer, also of great importance in the overall operation of the economy. This is the transfer of incomes from sector to sector (and sometimes within sectors).

TRANSFERS

As we already know, income transfers, called *transfer payments,* are a very useful and important means of reallocating purchasing power in society. Through transfer payments, members of the community who do not participate in production are given an opportunity to enjoy incomes that would otherwise not be available to them. Thus Social Security transfer payments make it possible for the old or the handicapped to be given an income of their own (not, to be sure, a currently *earned* income), and unemployment benefits give purchasing power to those who cannot get it through employment.

Not all transfers are in the nature of welfare payments, however. The distribution of money *within* a household is a transfer payment. So is the payment of interest on the national debt.* So is the grant of a subsidy to a private enter-

*As we know, the payment of interest on corporate debt is not considered a transfer payment, but a payment to a factor of production. Actually, much government interest should also be thought of as a factor payment (for the loan of capital for purposes of public output); but by convention, all government interest is classified as a transfer payment.

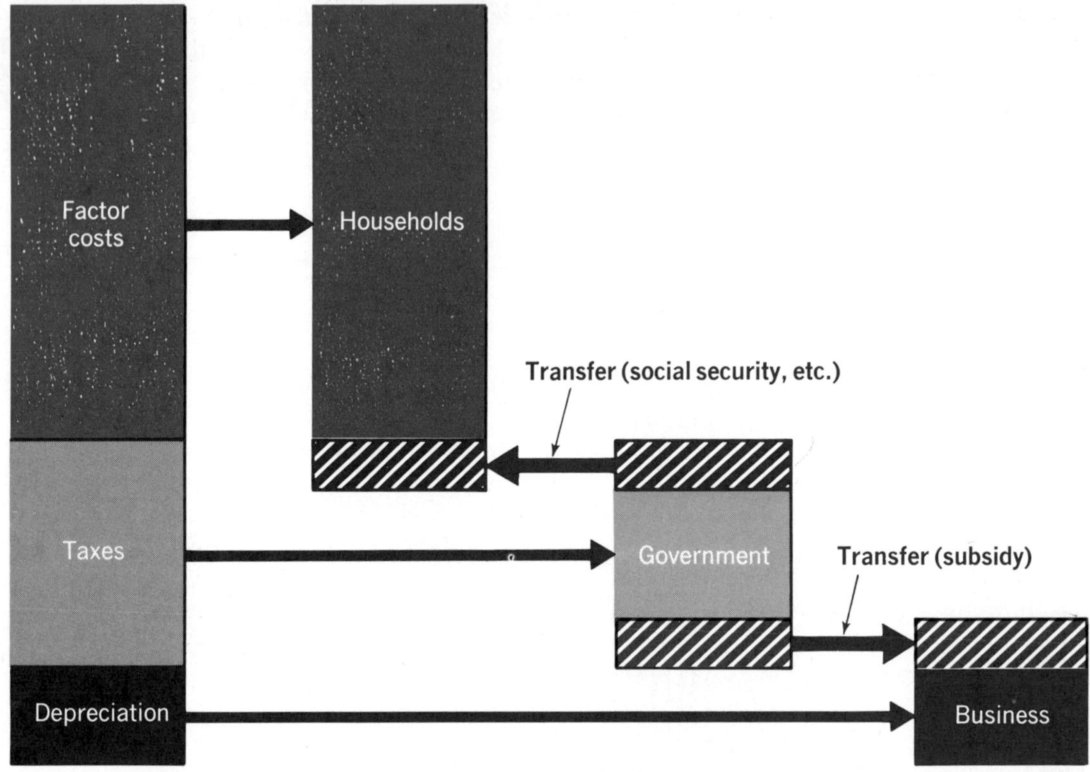

FIGURE 12.4 TRANSFER PAYMENTS

Transfer payments shift spending power from one sector (or group within a sector) to another. They do not increase production and therefore cannot increase incomes. But they can redistribute income, for reasons good and bad.

prise such as an airline, or of a scholarship to a college student. Any income payment that is not earned by selling one's productive services on the market falls in the transfer category.

It may help to understand this process if we visualize it in our flow diagram. Figure 12.4 shows two kinds of transfers. The upper one, from government to the household sector, shows a typical transfer of incomes, such as veterans' pensions or Social Security; the transfer below it reflects the flow of income that might be illustrated by a payment to agriculture for crop support. Transfers *within* sectors, such as household allowances, are not shown in the diagram.

One thing we may well note about transfers is that they can only rearrange the incomes created in the production process; they cannot increase those incomes. Income, as we learned in the last chapter, is inextricably tied to output—indeed, income is only the financial counterpart of output.

Transfer payments, on the other hand, are a way of arranging individual claims to production in some fashion that strikes the community as fairer or more efficient or more decorous than the way the market process allocates them through the production process. As such, transfer payments are an indispensable and often invaluable agency of social policy. But it is important to understand that no amount of transfers can, in themselves, increase the total that is to be shared. That can happen only by raising output itself.

TRANSFER PAYMENTS AND TAXES

We have mentioned, but only in passing, another means of transferring purchasing power from one sector to another: taxation. Heretofore we have often spoken as though all government tax receipts were derived from indirect taxes that were added onto the cost of production.

In fact, this is not the only source of government revenue. Indirect taxes are an important part of state and local revenues, but they are only a minor part of federal tax receipts. Most federal taxes are levied on the income of the factors of production or on the profit of business after the other factors have been paid.

Once again it is worth remembering that the government taxes the consumer (and business) because it is in the nature of much government output

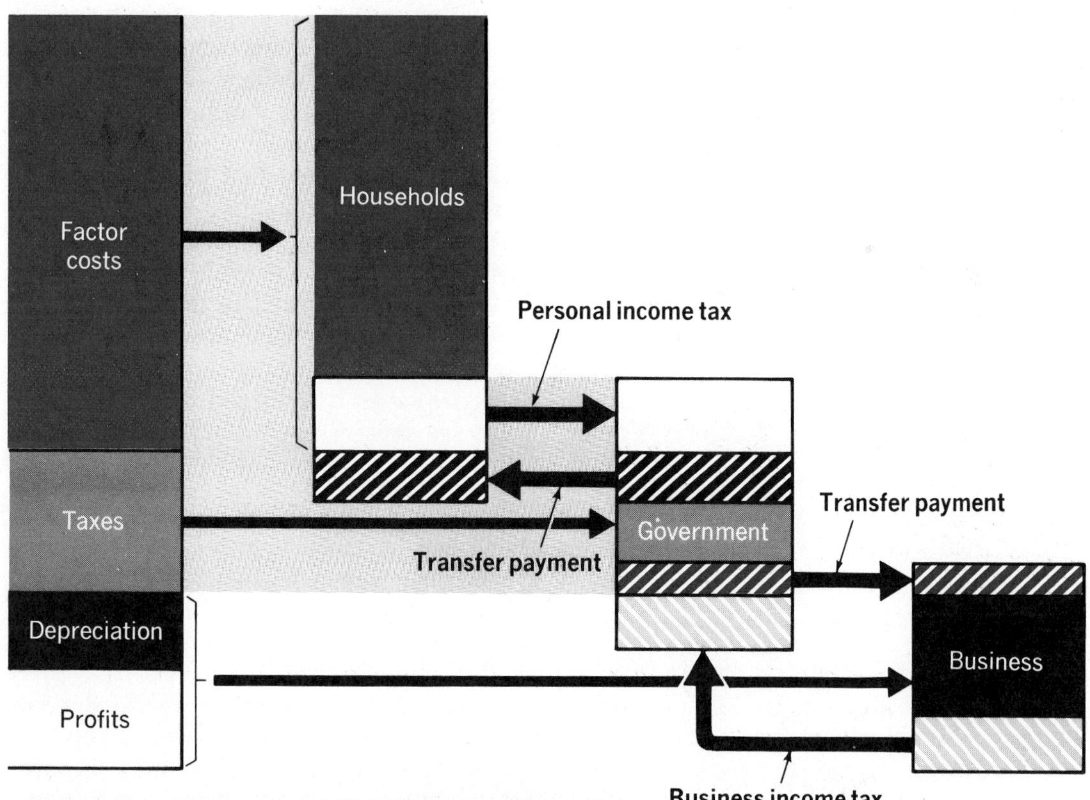

FIGURE 12.5 TRANSFERS AND INCOME TAXES
Direct (income) taxes are a kind of transfer—a redistribution from the private to the public sphere. The chart shows how complex the back-and-forth effect of taxes and transfers can be.

that it cannot be *sold.* Taxes are the way we are billed for our share—rightly or wrongly figured—of government production that has been collectively decided upon. As we can now see, taxes—both on business and on the household sector—also finance many transfer payments. That is, the government intervenes in the distribution process to make it conform to our politically expressed social purposes, taking away some income from certain individuals and groups and providing income to others. Figure 12.5 shows what this looks like in the flow of GNP. (Note that the business sector is drawn with profits, as our next section will explain.)

As we can see, the exchanges of income between the household and the government sector can be very complex. Income can flow from households to government units via taxation and return to the household sector via transfer payments; and the same two-way flows can take place between government and business.

PROFITS AND DEMAND

The last diagram has already introduced a new element of reality into our discussion. Taxes on business *income* presuppose that businesses make *profits.* Let us see how these profits fit into the savings-investment process.

During our discussion of the circular flow, we spoke of profits as a special kind of factor cost—a payment to the factor *capital.* Now we can think of profits not merely as a factor cost (although there is always a certain element of risk-remuneration in profits), but as a return to especially efficient or forward-thinking firms who have used the investment process to introduce new products or processes ahead of the run of their industries. We also know that profits accrue to powerful firms that exact a semimonopolistic return from their customers.

What matters in our analysis at this stage is not the precise explanation we give to the origin of profits, but a precise explanation of their role in maintaining a "closed-circuit" economy in which all costs are returned to the marketplace as demand. A commonly heard diagnosis for economic maladies is that profits are at the root of the trouble, in that they cause a withdrawal of spending power or income from the community. If profits are saved or retained within the firm, this can be true. In fact, however, profits are usually distributed in three ways. They may be

1. **Paid out as income to the household sector in the form of dividends or profit shares, to become part of household spending.**
2. **Directly spent by business firms for new plant and equipment.**
3. **Taxed by the government and spent in the public sector.**

All three methods of offsetting profits appear in Figure 12.6.

Thus, we can see that profits need not constitute a withdrawal from the income stream. Indeed, unless profits are adequate, business will very likely not invest enough to offset the savings of the household sector. They may, in fact, even fail to make normal replacement expenditures, aggravating the demand gap still further in this way.

Thus the existence of profits, far from being deflationary—that is, far from

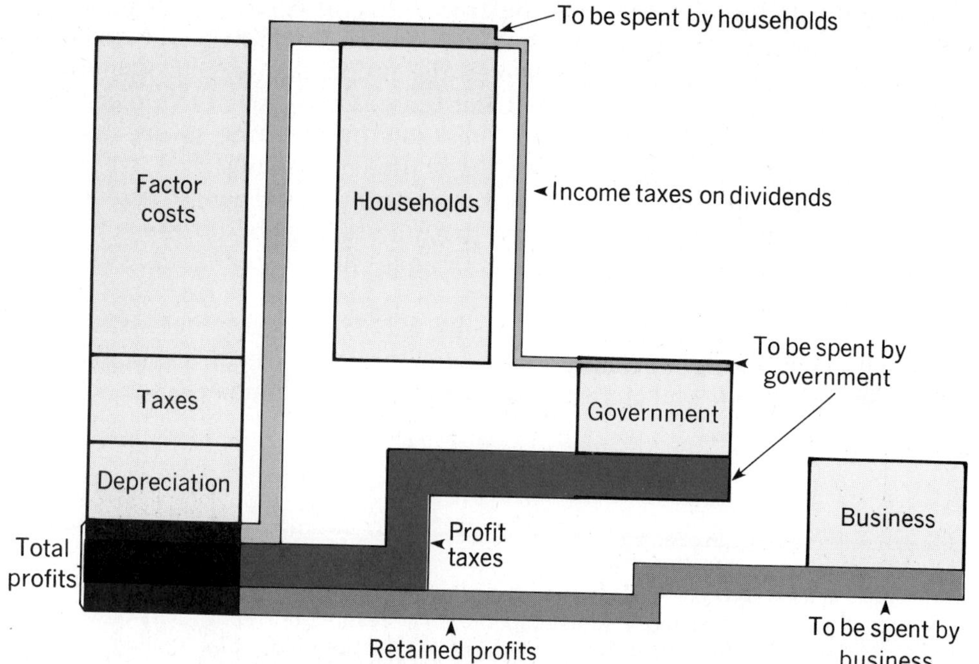

FIGURE 12.6 PROFITS IN THE CIRCULAR FLOW

There are three ways in which profits can be returned to GNP as expenditure: (1) by being distributed as dividends and spent by households; (2) by being taxed away and spent by government, and (3) by being directly spent by business for new investment.

---

causing a fall in income—is, in fact, essential for the maintenance of a given level of income or for an advance to a higher level. Nonetheless, there is a germ of truth in the contention of those who have maintained that profits can cause an insufficiency of purchasing power. **For unless profits are returned to the flow of purchasing power as dividends that are spent by their recipients or as new capital expenditures made by business or as taxes that lead to additional public spending, there will be a gap in the community's demand.** Unspent, hoarded profits are a drag on growth, but not invested profits.* Thus we can think of profits just as we think of saving—an indispensable source of economic growth or a potential source of economic decline.

SAVING, INVESTMENT, AND GROWTH

We are almost ready to leave our analysis of the circle of production and income to proceed to a much closer study of the individual dynamic elements

*Here we must distinguish between the individual firm and all firms together. An individual firm that saves its profits will usually put them in a bank and thereby make them available to other firms. But if all firms collectively hold onto their profits, trouble will result.

that create and close demand gaps. Before we do, however, it is well that we take note of one last fact of the greatest importance. In offsetting the savings of any sector by investment, we have closed the production and income circuit, much as in the stationary circular flow, but there is one crucial difference from the circular flow. Now we have closed the flow by diverting savings into the creation of *additional* capital. Unlike the stationary circular flow where the handing around of incomes did no more than maintain unchanged the original configuration of the system; in our new dynamic saving-and-investment model *each closing of the circuit results in a quantitative change—the addition of a new "layer" of capital.*

Hence, more and more physical wealth is being added to our system; and thinking back to our earlier chapters on the interaction of wealth and population, we would expect more and more productiveness from our human factors. Growth has entered our model.

KEY CONCEPTS

LOOKING BACK

The meaning of saving

1. Saving is indispensable for investment. To save means to refrain from using all our income for consumption, thus freeing resources for use as capital wealth.

Saving is necessary for growth, but creates a demand gap

2. A circular flow economy has no gaps. But if we introduce the act of saving there will be some purchasing power that is not returned to the economy. Thus the act of saving, which is necessary for growth, creates the necessity to offset the gap it leaves in spending.

Intersectoral transfers of saving against claims

3. Demand gaps can only be offset if another sector increases its spending sufficiently to offset the gap. The second sector can do this by issuing claims or equities—such as bonds or stocks—that attract saving for its use.

Transfer payments redistribute income but cannot increase total income

4. Another form of intersectoral (and sometimes intrasectoral) transfer is a direct transfer payment—a redistribution of income from one group to another. Social Security is an example of such a transfer. So are welfare payments, subsidies to business, crop supports, and the like. Transfers may be very important in providing additional income for some persons, but cannot increase total income, because they are not payments that arise from production.

Profits can return to demand via dividends, taxes, or investment

5. Profits can all return to the flow of demand, either as dividend payments, tax revenues, or as expeditures for investment. They are not, therefore, a source of insufficient purchasing power—unless they are not used. Hoarded, unspent profits lower demand; profits which are used do not.

Necessity of sectoral cooperation. Offsets must balance gaps

6. The essential point is that intersectoral cooperation is necessary in any modern economy that has net saving. Saving creates the conditions for growth—and for decline. There must be offsets to demand gaps if GNP is not to decline. And needless to say, if the offsets are too large, inflation will follow.

ECONOMIC VOCABULARY

Saving 165
Demand gap 166
Claims 169
Intersectoral offsets 171
Transfer payment 171

QUESTIONS

1. What do we mean by a demand gap? Show in a diagram. (And draw the diagram very, very carefully.)
2. In the same diagram show how this gap can be offset by business investment. Now show how the gap could have been filled by government spending.
3. Why is saving indispensable for investment? Can you think of any way in which a society could gather together the factors of production to undertake investment unless it had performed an act of saving? From this point of view, what does "saving" mean?
4. Can we have an act of saving without an act of investment?
5. Diagram the three ways in which business profits can be returned to the expenditure flow. What happens if they are not returned?

SECTION 2: The Determination of Income

Chapter 13 CONSUMPTION DEMAND

A LOOK AHEAD

With this chapter we begin to investigate the way in which the different sectors—household, business, and government—"work."

(1) There is one essential economic fact to be mastered in this chapter. It has to do with the basic passivity of consumption—the fact that consumption has generally followed income and has rarely been an independent economic force of its own.

(2) There is a new relationship, and its associated vocabulary, to learn: The propensity to consume describes how we divide our income between consumption and saving. The *average* propensity to consume describes the division of our total income; the *marginal* propensity to consume describes the division of any changes in our income.

(3) Putting together the propensity to consume and the idea of consumption's passivity we will arrive at a consumption function—a simple mathematical way of depicting how the nation's consumption relates to its income.

With a basic understanding of the crucial role of expenditure and of the complex relationship of saving and investment behind us, we are in a position to look more deeply into the question of the determination of gross national product. For what we have discovered so far is only the *mechanism* by which a market economy can sustain or fail to sustain a given level of output through a circuit of expenditure and receipt. Now we must try to discover the *forces* that dynamize the system, creating or closing gaps between income and outgo. What causes a demand for the goods and services measured in the GNP? Let us begin to answer that question by examining the flow of demand most familiar to us—consumption.

THE HOUSEHOLD SECTOR

Largest and in many respects most important of all the sectors in the economy is that of the nation's households—that is, its families and single-dwelling individuals (the two categories together called consumer units) considered as receivers of income and transfer payments* or as savers and spenders of money for consumption.

How big is this sector? In 1979 it comprised some 59 million families and some 21 million independent individuals who collectively gathered in $1920 billion in income and spent $1503 billion. As Figure 13.1 shows, the great bulk of receipts was from factor earnings, and transfer payments played only a relatively small role. **As we can also see, we must subtract personal tax payments from household income (or *personal income* as it is officially designated) before we get *disposable personal income*—income actually available for spending.** It is from disposable personal income that the crucial choice is made to spend or save. Notice the presence of savings in the bar on the right. This is the source of a demand gap that other sectors will have to fill.

SUBCOMPONENTS OF CONSUMPTION

Finally we see that consumer spending itself divides into three main streams. The largest of these is for **nondurable** goods, such as food and clothing or other items whose economic life is (or is assumed to be) short. Second largest is an assortment of expenditures we call consumer **services**, comprising things such as rent, doctors' or lawyers' or barbers' ministrations, theater or movie admissions, bus or taxi or plane transportation, and other purchases that are not a physical good but work performed by someone or some equipment. Last is a substream of expenditure for consumer **durable** goods, which, as the name suggests, include items such as cars or household appliances whose economic life is considerably greater than that of most nondurables. We can think of these goods as comprising consumers' physical capital.

There are complicated patterns and interrelations among these three major streams of consumer spending. As we would expect, consumer spending for durables is extremely volatile. In bad times, such as 1933, it has sunk to less than 8 percent of all consumer outlays; in the peak of good times in the early 1970s,

*Remember that the word "transfer" refers to payments made unilaterally—that is, without any service being performed by the recipient. Social Security (or any pension) is a transfer payment. So are unemployment insurance, or business subsidies, or allowances paid to children.

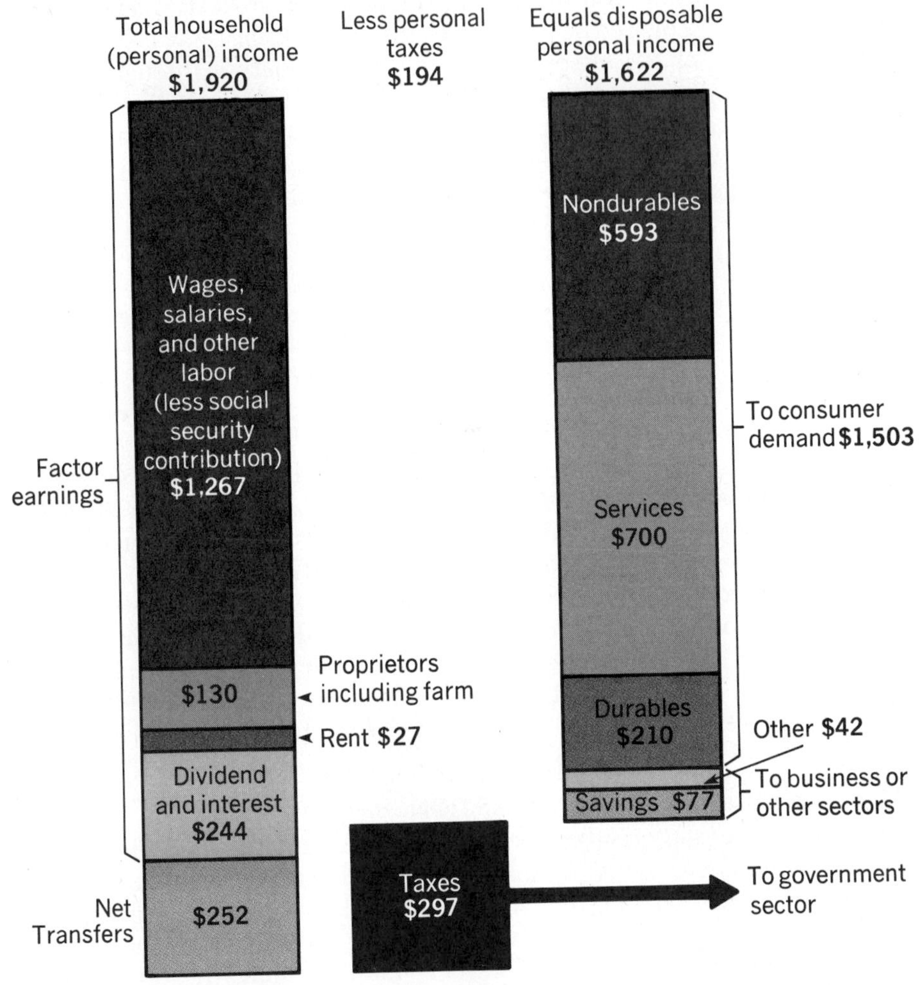

FIGURE 13.1 HOUSEHOLD SECTOR, 1979

** Totals do not always add, owing to rounding*

Notice that the consumption flow chart shows that the sector is a net saver. Here is the source of a demand gap that other sectors must compensate for.

---

it came to nearly double that. Meanwhile, outlays for services have been a steadily swelling area for consumer spending in the postwar economy. As a consequence of the growth of consumer buying of durables and of services, the relative share of the consumer dollar going to soft goods has been slowly declining.

CONSUMPTION AND GNP

The internal dynamics of consumption are of great interest to someone who seeks to project consumer spending patterns into the future—perhaps as an aid to merchandising. But here we are interested in the larger phenomenon of the relationship of consumption as a whole to the flow of gross national product.

Figure 13.2 shows us this historic relationship since 1929. Certain things stand out.

1. Consumption spending is by far the largest category of spending in GNP

Total consumer expenditures—for durable goods such as automobiles or washing machines, for nondurables like food or clothing, and for services such as recreation or medical care—account for approximately two-thirds of all the final buying in the economy.

2. Consumption is not only the biggest, but the most stable of all the streams of expenditure

Consumption is *the* essential economic activity. Even if there is a total breakdown in the social system, households will consume some bare minimum. Further, it is a fact of common experience that even in adverse circumstances, households seek to maintain their accustomed living standards. Thus consumption activities constitute a kind of floor for the level of overall economic activity. Investment and government spending, as we shall see, are capable of sudden reversals; but the streams of consumer spending tend to display a measure of stability over time.

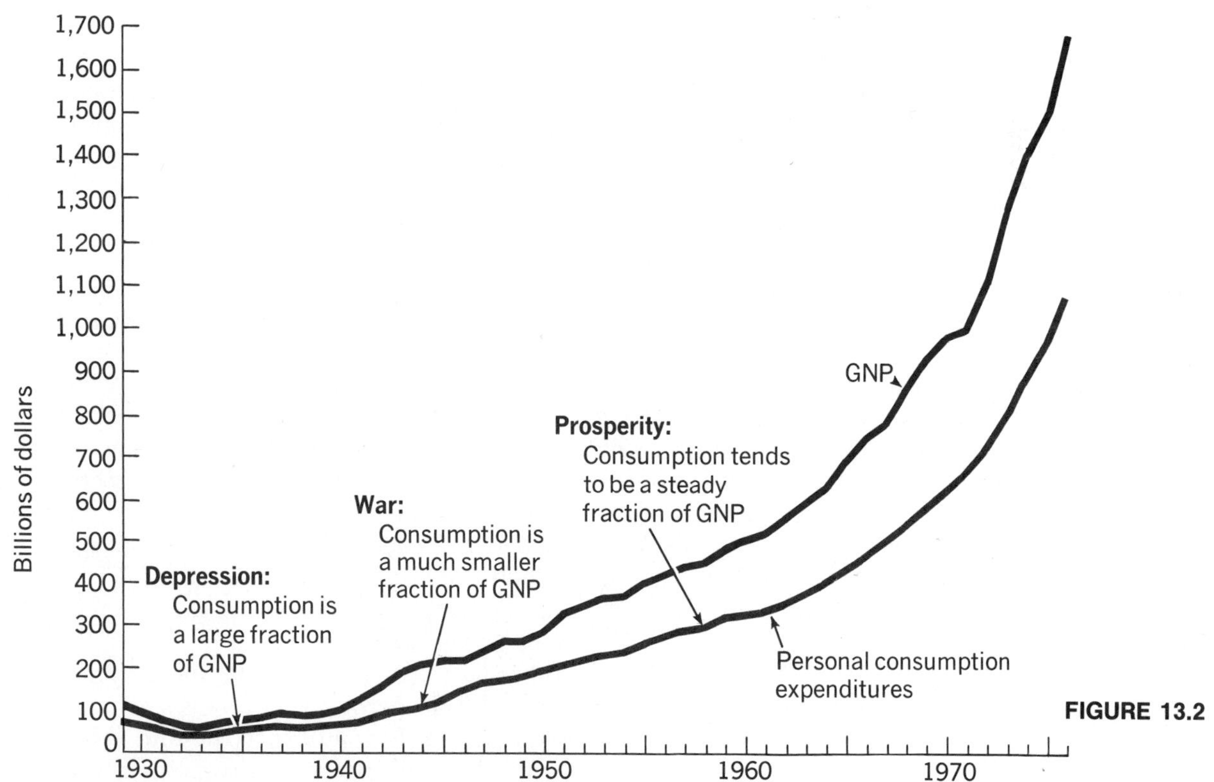

FIGURE 13.2

3. Consumption is nonetheless capable of considerable fluctuation as a proportion of GNP

Remembering our previous diagrams, we can see that this proportionate fluctuation must reflect changes in the relative importance of investment and government spending. And indeed this is the case. As investment spending declined in the Depression, consumption bulked relatively larger in GNP; as government spending increased during the war, consumption bulked relatively smaller. The changing *relative* size of consumption, in other words, reflects broad changes in *other* sectors rather than sharp changes in consuming habits.

To this broad generalization, we must make a partial exception for the behavior of consumption during inflation. As we shall see, consumption can take on a life of its own in periods when consumers buy in advance of their normal needs because they hope to beat expected price rises.

4. Despite its importance, consumption alone will not "buy back" GNP

It is well to recall that consumption, although the largest component of GNP, is still *only* two-thirds of GNP. Government buying and business buying of investment goods are essential if the income-expenditure circuit is to be closed. During our subsequent analysis it will help to remember that consumption expenditure by itself does not provide the only impetus of demand.

SAVING IN HISTORIC PERSPECTIVE

This first view of consumption activity sets the stage for our inquiry into the dynamic causes of fluctuations in GNP. We already know that the saving-investment relationship lies at the center of this problem and that much saving arises from the household sector. Hence, let us see what we can learn about the saving process in historic perspective.

SAVING AND INCOME

We begin with Figure 13.3 showing the relationship of household saving to disposable income—that is, to household sector incomes after the payment of taxes.

What we see here are two interesting facts. First, during the bottom of the Great Depression there were *no* savings in the household sector. In fact, under the duress of unemployment, millions of households were forced to **dissave**—to borrow or to draw on their old savings (hence the negative figure for the sector as a whole). By way of contrast, we notice the immense savings of the peak war years when consumers' goods were rationed and households were urged to save. Clearly, then, the *amount* of saving is capable of great fluctuation, falling to zero or to negative figures in periods of great economic distress and rising to as much as a quarter of income during periods of goods shortages.

In this graph we are struck by another fact. However variable the amounts, the savings *ratio* shows a considerable stability in normal years. This steadiness is particularly noteworthy in the postwar period. From 1950 to the mid 1970s, consumption has ranged between roughly 92 to 95 percent of disposable per-

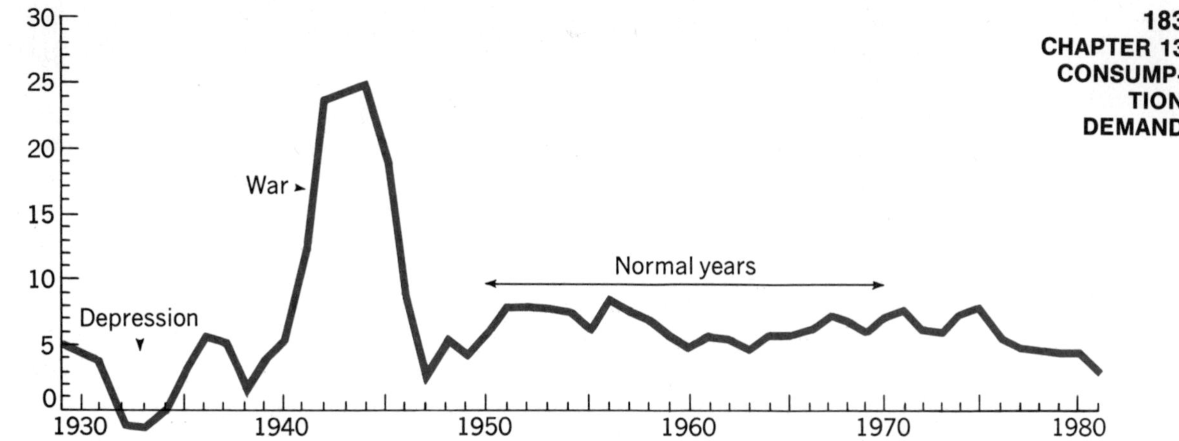

FIGURE 13.3 SAVING AS A PERCENT OF DISPOSABLE INCOME
The ratio of savings to disposable income is remarkably steady. This steadiness will become the basis of an important generalization about the macro behavior of the economy.

sonal income—which is, of course, the same as saying that savings have ranged roughly between 8 percent and 5 percent. **If we take the postwar period as a whole, we can see that in an average year we have consumed a little more than 94 cents of each dollar of income and that this ratio has remained fairly constant even though our incomes have increased markedly.**

SAVINGS AND INFLATION

You will notice, however, a drop in the savings rate starting in 1976. This is almost certainly the consequence of the worsening inflation rate of those years. As consumers came to anticipate rising prices, they tried to get ahead of the inflationary situation by buying in advance of normal needs, or by borrowing. After 1974, when we had our first taste of double-digit inflation, consumer credit rose precipitously, almost doubling from 1975 to 1980. The fall in savings, in other words, did not reflect a drop in real incomes but a shift in the propensity to consume. Whether this will be a permanent shift we will not know for some time.

LONG-RUN SAVINGS BEHAVIOR

The long-run stability of the savings ratio is an interesting, important phenomenon and something of a puzzling one, for we might easily imagine that the savings ratio would rise over time. Statistical investigations of cross sections of the nation show that rich families tend to save not only larger amounts, but larger *percentages* of their income, than poor families do. Thus as the entire nation has grown richer and as families have moved from lower income brackets to higher ones, it seems natural to suppose that they would also take on the higher savings characteristics that accompany upper incomes.

Were this so, the economy would face a very serious problem. In order to sustain its higher levels of aggregate income, it would have to invest an ever larger *proportion* of its income to offset its growing ratio of savings to income. As we shall see in our next chapter, investment is always a source of potential trouble because it is so much riskier than any other business function. If we had to keep on making proportionally larger investments each year to keep pace with our proportionally growing savings, we should live in an exceedingly vulnerable economic environment.

Fortunately, we are rescued from this dangerous situation, because our long-run savings ratio, as we have seen, displays a reassuring steadiness. In fact, there has been no significant upward trend in the savings ratio for the nation's households since the mid-1800s, and there may have been a slight downward trend. (See box.)

THE CONSUMPTION-INCOME RELATIONSHIP

What we have so far seen are some of the historical and empirical relationships of consumption and personal saving to income. We have taken the trouble to investigate these relationships in some detail, since they are among the most important causes of the gaps that have to be closed by investment. But the statistical facts in themselves are only a halfway stage in our macroeconomic inves-

SHORT-RUN VS. LONG-RUN SAVINGS BEHAVIOR

How do we reconcile the stability of the long-run savings ratio with the fact that statistical studies always reveal that rich families save a larger percentage of their incomes than do poor families? As the nation has moved en masse into higher income brackets, why has it not also saved proportionately more of its income?

The explanation for the long-run stability of savings behavior revolves around the importance of *relative* incomes, or "keeping up with the Joneses," in consumption decisions. If a family earned $20,000 in 1940, it was a wealthy family with an income far above the average. It could save a large fraction of its income and still have more than other families in the community had to spend on consumption. By 1980 the family with a $20,000 annual income was simply an average family. To keep up with consumption standards of other families in the community, it needed to spend a large fraction of its income. As a result, the savings rates for families with $20,000 gradually fell over time as the families changed from wealthy to average.

The same relative income effect is seen in the savings rates of black families. For any given income level, the average black family saves more than the average white family. Since black family incomes are lower than white family incomes, any given income has a higher relative position among blacks than it does among whites. To keep up with their peer group, whites must consequently spend more than blacks.

As a result of these and still other motivations, savings behavior in the long run differs considerably from that in the short run. Over the years, American households have shown a remarkable stability in their rate of overall savings. Its importance has already been mentioned. In a shorter period of time, however—over a few months or perhaps a year—households tend to save higher fractions of increases in their incomes than they do in the long run. The very great importance of this fact we shall subsequently note.

tigation. Now we want to go beyond the facts to a generalized understanding of the behavior that gives rise to them. Thus our next task is to extract from the facts certain behavioral *relationships* that are sufficiently regular and dependable for us to build into a new dynamic model of the economy.

If we think back over the data we have examined, one primary conclusion comes to mind. This is the indisputable fact that the *amount* of saving generated by the household sector depends in the first instance upon the income enjoyed by the household sector. Despite the stability of the savings ratio, we have seen that the dollar volume of saving in the economy is susceptible to great variation, from negative amounts in the Great Depression to very large amounts in boom times. Now we must see if we can find a systematic connection between the changing size of income and the changing size of saving.

PROPENSITY TO CONSUME

There is indeed such a relationship, lying at the heart of macroeconomic analysis. We call it the *consumption function* or, more formally, the *propensity to consume*, the name invented by John Maynard Keynes, the famous English economist who first formulated it in 1936* What is this "propensity" to consume? **It means that the relationship between consumption behavior and income is sufficiently dependable so that we can actually *predict* how much consumption (or how much saving) will be associated with a given level of income.**

We base such predictions on a *schedule* that enables us to see the income-consumption relationship over a considerable range of variation. Table 13.1 is such a schedule, a purely hypothetical one, for us to examine.

TABLE 13.1 A PROPENSITY-TO-CONSUME SCHEDULE

BILLIONS OF DOLLARS		
Income	*Consumption*	*Savings*
$100	$80	$20
110	87	23
120	92	28
130	95	35
140	97	43

A typical propensity-to-consume schedule shows that savings and consumption both rise as income rises.

One could imagine, of course, innumerable different consumption schedules; in one society a given income might be accompanied by a much higher propensity to consume (or propensity to save) than in another. But the basic hypothesis of Keynes—a hypothesis amply confirmed by research—was that the consumption schedule in all modern industrial societies had a particular basic configuration, despite these variations. **The propensity to consume, said Keynes, reflected the fact that on the average, people tended to increase their consumption as their incomes rose, but not by as much as their income increased. In other words, as the incomes of individuals rose, so did both their consumption *and their savings.***

*See Chapter 3 for more on Keynes.

Note that Keynes did not say that the *proportion* of saving rose. We have seen how involved is the dynamic determination of savings ratios. Keynes merely suggested that in the short run, the *amount* of saving would rise as income rose—or to put it conversely again, that families would not use *all* their increases in income for consumption purposes alone. It is well to remember that these conclusions hold in going down the schedule as well as up. Keynes' basic law implies that when there is a decrease in income, there will be some decrease in the *amount of saving,* or that a family will not absorb a fall in its income entirely by contracting its consumption.

What does the consumption schedule look like in the United States? We will come to that shortly. First, however, let us fill in our understanding of the terms we will need for our generalized study.

AVERAGE PROPENSITY TO CONSUME

The consumption schedule gives us two ways of measuring the fundamental economic relationship of income and saving. One way is simply to take any given level of income and to compute the percentage relation of consumption to that income. This gives us the *average propensity to consume.* In Table 13.2, using the same hypothetical schedule as before, we make this computation.

The average propensity to consume, in other words, tells us how a society at any given moment divides its total income between consumption and saving. It is thus a kind of measure of long-run savings behavior, for households divide their incomes between saving and consuming in ratios that reflect established habits and, as we have seen, do not ordinarily change rapidly.

TABLE 13.2 CALCULATION OF THE AVERAGE PROPENSITY TO CONSUME

BILLIONS OF DOLLARS		
Income	*Consumption*	*Consumption ÷ Income (Av. propensity to consume)*
$100	$80	.80
110	87	.79
120	92	.77
130	95	.73
140	97	.69

We calculate the average propensity to consume simply by dividing consumption by income.

MARGINAL PROPENSITY TO CONSUME

But we can also use our schedule to measure another very important aspect of saving behavior: the way households divide *increases* (or decreases) in income between consumption and saving. This *marginal propensity to consume* is quite different from the average propensity to consume, as the figures in Table 13.3 (still from our original hypothetical schedule) demonstrate.

Note carefully that the last column in Table 13.3 is designed to show us something quite different from the last column of the previous table. Take a given income level—say $110 billion. In Table 13.2 the average propensity to consume for that income level is .79, meaning that we will actually spend on consumption 79 percent of our income of $110 billion. But the corresponding figure opposite

TABLE 13.3 CALCULATION OF THE MARGINAL PROPENSITY TO CONSUME

BILLIONS OF DOLLARS				
Income	*Consumption*	*Change in income*	*Change in consumption*	*Marginal propensity to consume = Change in consumption ÷ change in income*
$100	$80	—	—	—
110	87	$10	$7	.70
120	92	10	5	.50
130	95	10	3	.30
140	97	10	2	.20

We calculate the marginal propensity to consume by dividing changes in our consumption by changes in our income.

$110 billion in the marginal propensity-to-consume table (13.3) is .70. This does *not* mean that out of our $110 billion income we somehow spend only 70 percent, instead of 79 percent, on consumption. It *does* mean that we spend on consumption only 70 percent *of the $10 billion increase* that lifted us from a previous income of $100 billion to the $110 billion level. The rest of that $10 billion increase we saved.

Much of economics, in micro- as well as macroanalysis, is concerned with studying the effects of *changes* in economic life. It is precisely here that marginal concepts take on their importance. When we speak of the average propensity to consume, we relate all consumption and all income from the bottom up, so to speak, and thus we call attention to behavior covering a great variety of situations and conditions. **But when we speak of the marginal propensity to consume, we are focusing only on our behavior toward *changes* in our incomes.** Thus the marginal approach is invaluable, as we shall see, in dealing with the effects of short-run fluctuations in GNP.

A SCATTER DIAGRAM

The essentially simple idea of a systematic, behavioral relationship between income and consumption will play an extremely important part in the model of the economy we shall soon construct. But the relationships we have thus far defined are too vague to be of much use. We want to know if we can extract from the facts of experience not only a general dependence of consumption on income, but a *fairly precise method of determining exactly how much saving will be associated with a given amount of income.*

Here we reach a place where it will help us to use diagrams and simple equations rather than words alone. So let us begin by transferring our conception of a propensity-to-consume schedule to a new kind of diagram directly showing the interrelation of income and consumption.

The *scatter diagram* (Figure 13.4) shows precisely that. Along the vertical axis on the left we have marked off intervals to measure total consumer expenditure in billions of dollars; along the horizontal axis on the bottom we measure disposable personal income, also in billions of dollars. The dots tell us, for the years enumerated, how large consumption and income were. For instance, if we take the dot for 1966 and look directly below it to the horizontal axis, we can

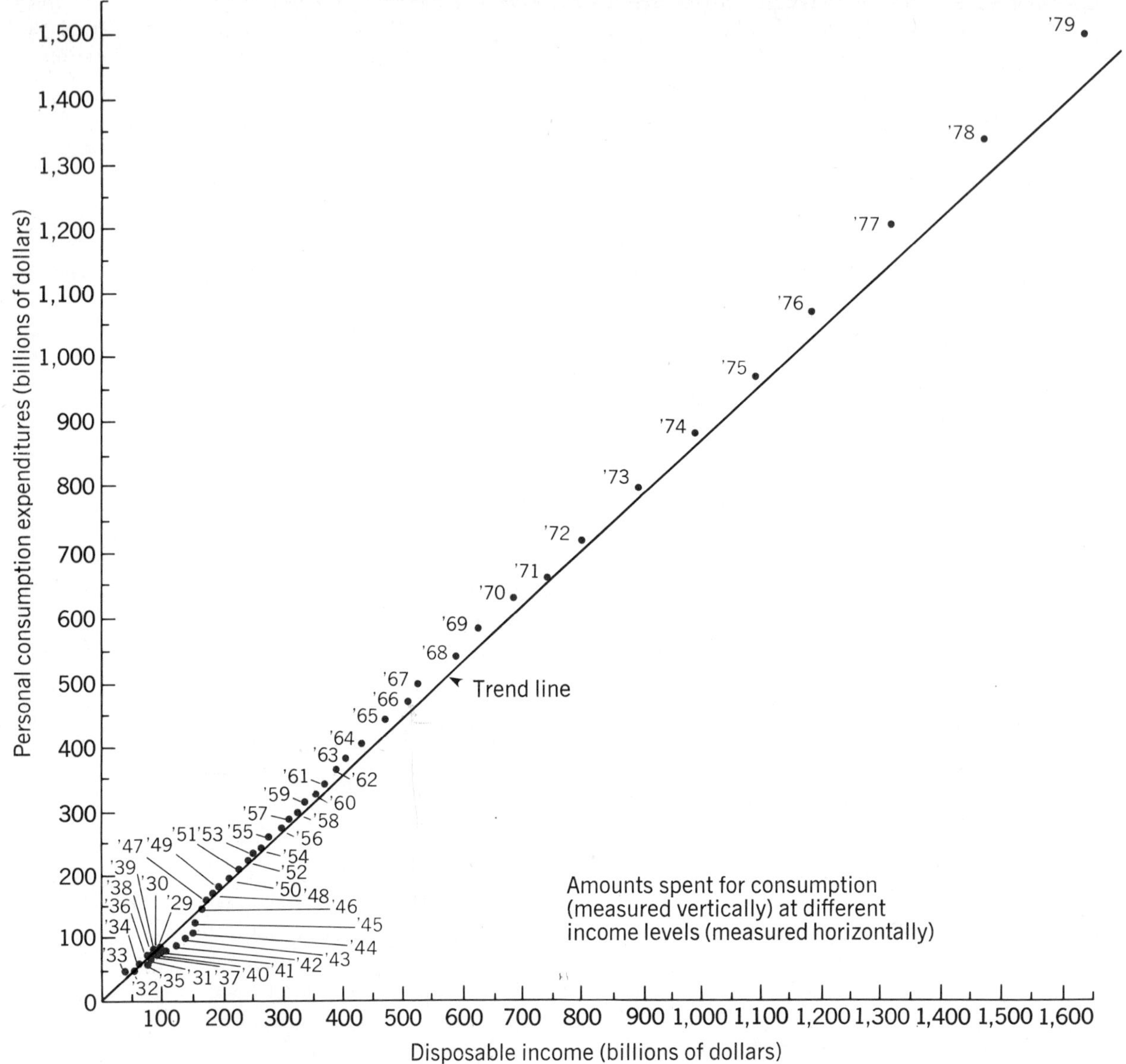

FIGURE 13.4 U.S. PROPENSITY TO CONSUME 1929–1979

A scatter diagram shows the functional relationship between two variables—in this case between consumption and income. The trend line is fitted by a statistical technique known as "the least squares method." The trend line shows us the average propensity to consume. We get a very rough (and not very accurate) idea of the marginal propensity to consume by noting the slope of the line between two consecutive years.

see that disposable personal income for that year was roughly $510 billion. The same dot measured against the vertical axis tells us that consumption for 1966 was a little more than $475 billion. If we now divide the figure for consumption by that for income, we get a value of 93.1 percent for our propensity to consume. If we subtact that from 100, our propensity to save must have been 6.9 percent.*

Returning to the diagram itself, we notice that the black line which fits the trend of the dots does not go evenly from corner to corner. If it did, it would mean that each amount of income was matched by an *equal* amount of consumption—in other words, that there was no saving. Instead, the line leans slightly downward, indicating that as income goes higher, consumption also increases, but not by quite as much.

Does the chart also show us marginal propensity to consume? Not really. As we know, our short-run savings propensities are higher than our long-run propensities. This chart shows our settled position from year to year, after the long-run, upward drift of spending has washed out our marginal (short-run) savings behavior.

Nevertheless, if we look at the movement from one dot to the next, we get some notion of the short-run forces at work. During the war years, for instance, as the result of a shortage of many consumer goods and a general exhortation to save, the average propensity to consume was unusually low. That is why the dots during those years form a bulge below the trend line. After the war, we can also see that the marginal propensity to consume must have been very high. As a matter of fact, for a few years consumption actually rose faster than income, as people used their wartime savings to buy things that were unavailable during the war. Between 1946 and 1947, for example, disposable income rose by some $9.8 billion, but personal outlays rose by almost $18 billion! By 1950, however, the consumption-income relationship was back to virtually the same ratio as during the 1930s.

THE CONSUMPTION FUNCTION IN SIMPLE MATH

There is another way of reducing to shorthand clarity the propensity to consume. Obviously, what we are looking for is a functional relationship between income (Y) the independent variable, and consumption (C), the dependent variable. In mathematical language we write

$$C = f(Y)$$

and we want to discover what f looks like.

Highly sophisticated and complex formulas have been tried to fit values of C and Y. Their economics and their mathematics are both beyond the scope of this book. But we can at least get a clearer idea of what it means to devise a *consumption function* by trying to make a very simple one ourselves. If we look at Figure 13.4 we can see that during the depression years, at very low levels of income, around $50 billion, consumption was just as large as income itself. (In some years it was actually bigger; as we have seen, there was net dissaving in

*It is difficult to read figures accurately from a graph. The actual values are: disposable income, $512 billion; consumption, $479 billion; average propensity to consume, 93.4 percent.

1933). Hence, we might hypothesize that a consumption function for the United States might have a fixed value representing this "bottom," plus some regular fraction designating the amount of income that would be saved for all income over that amount.

A GENERALIZED CONSUMPTION FUNCTION

This is a very important hypothesis. It enables us to describe the consumption function as an amount that represents rock-bottom consumption, to which we add additional consumption spending as income rises. If a is the bottom, and subsequent spending out of additional income is $b(Y)$, where b represents this spending propensity, we can now write the consumption function as a whole as:

$$C = a + b(Y)$$

We have seen that a is \$50 billion, and we know that our actual spending propensity, b, is about 94 percent. Therefore, we can get a *very rough* approximation of consumption by taking \$50 billion and adding to it 94 percent of our disposable income over \$50 billion. In 1973 for example, disposable income was \$883 billion. If we add \$50 billion and .94 (883 − 50), we get \$833. Actual consumption in 1973 was \$828 billion.

Let the reader be warned, however, that devising a reliable consumption function is much more difficult than this simple formula would indicate. The process of translating economics into *econometrics*—that is, of finding ways to represent abstract theoretical relationships in terms of specific empirical relations—is a very difficult one. Nonetheless, even our simple example gives one an idea of what the economist and the econometrician hope to find: a precise way of expressing functional interrelations (like those between consumption and income), so that the relations will be useful in making predictions.

PASSIVITY OF CONSUMPTION

Throughout this chapter we have talked of the dynamics of consuming and saving. Now it is important that we recall the main conclusion of our analysis, the essential passivity of consumption as an economic process. Consumption spending, we will recall, is a function of income. This means it is a *dependent* variable in the economic process, a factor that is acted *on*, but that does not itself generate spontaneous action.

To be sure, it is well to qualify this assertion. For one thing, consumption is so large a fraction of total spending that small changes can bring large results. In 1974 and again in 1979 consumers held back on car purchases for fear of gasoline shortages, and the effect on automobile sales had considerable impact on GNP. And we have already called attention to the push exerted by inflation-induced consumption in the late 1970s.

Yet these are exceptions to the rule. During the normal course of things, no matter how intense wants may be, consumers ordinarily lack the spendable cash to translate their desires into effective demand. Brief swings in consumption—as for automobiles—may give rise to short-run fluctuations in saving, but these savings are short-lived and therefore cannot drive the economy upward or downward for any extended period of time. This is probably true for inflation-induced spending too.

CONSUMER CREDIT

What about consumer credit, someone will ask. Aren't many families in debt up to their ears? Doesn't the ability to buy "on time" enable consumers as a group to spend more than their incomes?

Consumer credit indeed enables families to spend a larger amount than they earn as incomes or receive as transfers, for short periods of time. During the late 1970s consumers have gone on a credit card binge, piling up unprecedented amounts of outstanding credit. Nonetheless, consumers do not use credit to spend more than their total receipts; some consumers do, but consumers as a group do not. We know this is true because the value of all consumption spending includes purchases that are made on credit, such as cars or many other kinds of items bought on household loans or on installment. But this total spending is still less than the total receipts of the consumer sector. Thus there continues to be net household saving, although the *rate* of saving has fallen.

Would there be more saving if there were no credit? In that situation, many families would put income aside until they had accumulated enough to buy cars, refrigerators, houses, and other big items. During the period that they were saving up to buy these goods, their savings rates would certainly be higher than if they had consumer credit at their disposal. But after they had bought their "lumpy" goods, their savings rates would again fall, perhaps below the level of a consumer credit economy, which tempts us to buy lumpy items and to perform our saving through installment payments.

As a result, we would expect to find high savings rates in an economy where desires for lumpy items were increasing but where consumer credit was not available. Economists cite this as one explanation of the fact that Japanese families have savings rates that are more than three times as high as American families, even though Japanese incomes are lower. In Japan you cannot "buy now, pay later"; so you save now and buy later.

This highlights an extremely important point. **Wants and appetites *alone* do not drive the economy upward; if they did, we should experience a more impelling demand in depressions, when people are hungry, than in booms, when they are well off.** Hence the futility of those who urge the cure of depressions by suggesting that consumers should buy more! There is nothing consumers would rather do than buy more, if only they could. Let us not forget, furthermore, that consumers are at all times being cajoled and exhorted to increase their expenditures by the multibillion dollar pressures exerted by the advertising industry.

The trouble is, however, that consumers cannot buy more unless they have more incomes to buy with. Of course, for short periods they can borrow or they may temporarily sharply reduce their rate of savings; but each household's borrowing capacity or accumulated savings are limited, so that once these bursts are over, the steady habitual ways of saving and spending are apt to reassert themselves.

Thus it is clear that in considering the consumer sector we study a part of the economy that, however ultimately important, is not in itself the source of major changes in activity. Consumption mirrors and, as we shall see, can magnify disturbances elsewhere in the economy, but it does not initiate the greater part of our long-run economic fortunes or misfortunes.

LOOKING BACK

KEY CONCEPTS

Consumption spending is the largest and steadiest flow in GNP. Disposable income is factor earnings after direct taxes.

1. The household sector is the largest of the components of GNP. Household income is called disposable personal income—it is factor earnings after taxes. Household expenditures are called consumption. The main categories of consumption are nondurables, durables, and services. Altogether consumption spending is the biggest and the steadiest of the GNP flows.

2. Despite its steadiness and size, however, consumption fluctuates and will not buy back GNP.

Long-run savings habits have been very stable at 5–8 percent a year. Inflation may be discouraging saving

3. Savings behavior is very steady over the long run. We tend to save about 4 to 8 percent of our incomes, except for exceptional periods such as war, depression, or inflation. This long-run stability is probably attributable to the sociological factor known as "keeping up with the Joneses." Inflation may be changing these spending habits.

The propensity to consume is simply a fraction: *C* to *Y*. The hypothesis is that changes in income are always used for both saving and consuming

4. The relation between saving and income is called the propensity to consume. The words themselves simply mean the ratio into which we divide income between consumption and saving. But the behavior hypothesis of the propensity to consume is that *increases* in income are never entirely spent or entirely saved, but are used for both spending and saving in regular, predictable ways.

Average and marginal propensity to consume

5. The measure of the relation between any given level of income and its associated level of consumption is called the average propensity to consume. The relation between a change in income and the associated change in saving or consumption is called the marginal propensity to consume.

$C = a + b(Y)$ where *a* is the "bottom" and *b* is the proportion of *Y* used for consumption

6. The generally accepted hypothesis about consumption behavior is that there is a "bottom"—a level of consumption that will be maintained (for a while) even if income falls below consumer spending by using up past saving to maintain a minimum standard of living. Additional income over this bottom will be divided in some regular way between consumption and saving. The bottom is designated a. The division of income (Y) between consumption and saving is designed b. Thus we write the consumption function as $C = a + b(Y)$.

Consumption is a dependent variable in the GNP flow

7. Although changes in consumption can exert considerable effects on GNP because of the size of total consumption, consumption is usually a passive element in the flow. It is Y that is the independent variable, not C.

ECONOMIC VOCABULARY

QUESTIONS

1. Why are some components of consumption more dynamic than others? Why, for instance, does the demand for durables fluctuate more widely than that for services? (Has *durability* something to do with it?)
2. "The reason we have depressions is that consumption isn't big enough to buy the output of our farms and factories." What is wrong about this statement? Is it *all* wrong?
3. Suppose a family has an income of $10,000 and saves $500. What is its average propensity to consume? Can you tell from this information what its marginal propensity to consume is?
4. Suppose the same family now increases its income to $12,000 and its saving to $750. What is its new propensity to consume? Now can you figure out its marginal propensity to consume?
5. Draw a scatter diagram to show the following:

Family income	*Savings*
$4,000	$ 0
5,000	50
6,000	150
7,000	300
8,000	500

From the figures above, calculate the average propensity to consume at each level of income. Can you calculate the marginal propensity to consume for each jump in income?

AN EXTRA WORD ABOUT
AID IN CASH OR KIND

Over the past 15 years there has been a gradual expansion in the public provision of *private* consumption goods—not roads, but actual consumers' goods. For example, food stamps have risen from $.03 billion in 1965 to $4.6 billion in the 1978 budget. Government medical expenditures rose from $7 billion to $34 billion from 1965 to 1978. Why is the government getting increasingly involved in the distribution of private goods?

Food stamps and medical expenditures can both be viewed as income redistribution measures. Both raise the real incomes of recipients, who are mainly poor. But what arguments can be mustered in favor of giving the poor food or medical aid, rather than cash? Cash, such as welfare payments, could always be used to buy food or medical treatment; and it might yield a much higher real income to the recipient, if he or she did not happen to need food or medical assistance, but something else, such as better housing. Why force the poor to consume things that they may not rank at the top of their lists of needs?

There are two classic arguments in favor of aid-in-kind, rather than aid-in-cash. One is that the poor cannot be trusted to buy what is best for them. They may actually *need* food or medical care, it is said, but if given the money they will spend it on luxuries or liquor. Thus, by "tying" their aid, we are really doing them a favor.

Is this a valid argument? We need hardly point out that it involves value judgments. Indeed, the argument has a patronizing ring to it. To be sure, there probably are people on welfare who *would* spend a cash bonus for luxuries or liquor instead of food or medical help, although the poor are not alone in spending their incomes in ways that maximize short-run pleasures rather than long-run benefits.

The second argument for aid-in-kind is more sophisticated. It revolves around the distinction between luxuries and necessaries. As a society we have quite egalitarian beliefs about how necessaries should be distributed, but we have no such beliefs about luxuries. We look with favor on rationing of a very scarce "necessity," such as a new vaccine, but we easily tolerate a high degree of inequality in the distribution of new Cadillacs. This distinction puts us on the horns of a dilemma. If we distribute welfare through equal amounts of cash, we are helping to bring about a more egalitarian distribution of luxuries, since the poor are free to spend their money on luxuries if they wish. On the other hand, if we distribute cash welfare unequally, we are possibly contributing to the unequal distribution of necessities, where we would like the poor to get a "fair share."

Aid-in-kind is an effort to get around this dilemma. When we distribute medical care equally, we are lending support to the equal sharing of medical care, which we consider a necessity. When we distribute food stamps, we are actually printing a different kind of money, usable only for food, and distributing this money in special ways. Thus aid-in-kind ties egalitarianism to "necessaries."

Does this justify aid-in-kind? Most economists, including ourselves, would prefer to give aid in cash, allowing each recipient to do with it as he or she wished. But to the extent that the preferences of the public are to be taken into account—and the tax-paying public far outnumbers the recipients of aid—the distribution of aid-in-kind may commend itself simply because it seems to accord with the political and social wishes of the public, the supreme arbiter in these matters.

Chapter 14 INVESTMENT DEMAND

A LOOK AHEAD

Warning! This is a chapter that ought to be read twice. It contains ideas that are both new and important. What is more, the vocabulary is one that most of us are not used to.

(1) The vocabulary: Investment, unlike consumption, is not an activity we are familiar with at first hand; we have to learn to think of it in real terms, not financial ones.

(2) There are two new ideas, both much used by economists: a) The idea of the multiplier; you will want to learn the formula for the multiplier and to understand why it is determined by the marginal propensity to save. b) The idea of marginal efficiency; here you need to know about discounting future income—the key to understanding expected profit and the decision-making process behind investment.

(3) Most important of all: Investment gives us the first real insight into why the macro system can be unstable. It is not only the key to growth, but the key to booms and busts. That's the idea that will unify the pages ahead.

In studying the behavior of the consumption sector, we have begun to understand how the demand for GNP arises. Now we must turn to a second source of demand —investment demand. This requires a shift in our vantage point. As experienced consumers, we know about consumption, but the activity of investing is foreign to most of us. Worse, we are apt to begin by confusing the meaning of investment, as a source of demand for GNP, with "investing" in the sense familiar to most of us when we think about buying stocks or bonds.

INVESTMENT: REAL AND FINANCIAL

We had best begin, then, by making certain that our vocabulary is correct. **Investing, or investment, as the economist uses the term in describing the demand for GNP, is an activity that uses the resources of the community to maintain or add to its stock of physical capital.** It is the counterpart of the real activity of saving we learned about in Chapter 12.

Investment may or may not coincide with the purchase of a security. When we buy an ordinary stock or bond, we usually buy it from someone who has previously owned it, and therefore our personal act of "investment" becomes, in the economic view of things, merely a *transfer* of claims without any direct bearing on the creation of new wealth. A pays B cash and takes his General Output stock; B takes A's cash and doubtless uses it to buy stock from C; but the transactions between A and B and C in no way alter the actual amount of real capital in the economy. Only when we buy *newly issued* shares or bonds, and then only when their proceeds are directly allocated to new equipment or plant, does our act of personal financial investment result in the addition of wealth to the community. In that case, A buys his stock directly (or through an investment banker) from General Output itself, and not from B. A's cash can now be spent by General Output for new capital goods, as presumably it will be.

Thus, much of investment, as economists see it, is a little-known form of activity for the majority of us. This is true not only because real investment is not the same as personal financial investment, but because the real investors of the nation usually act on behalf of an institution other than the familiar one of the household. **The unit of behavior in the world of investment is typically the business firm, just as in the world of consumption it is the household.** Boards of directors, chief executives, or small-business proprietors are the persons who decide whether or not to devote business cash to the construction of new facilities or to the addition of inventory; and this decision, as we shall see, is very different in character and motivation from the decisions familiar to us as members of the household sector.

THE INVESTMENT SECTOR IN PROFILE

Before we begin an investigation into the dynamics of investment decisions, however, let us gain a quick acquaintance with the sector as a whole, much as we did with the consumption sector.

Figure 14.1 gives a first general impression of the investment sector in a recent year. Note that the main source of gross private domestic investment expenditure is the retained earnings of business; that is, the expenditures come from depreciation accruals or from profits that have been kept in the business.

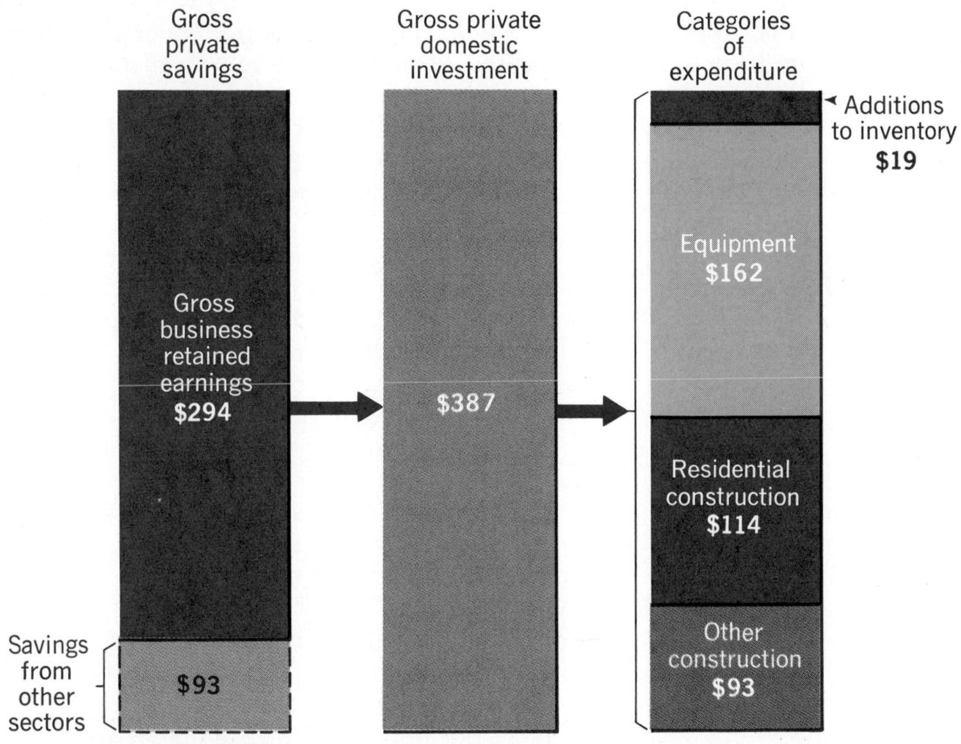

FIGURE 14.1 BUSINESS SECTOR 1979

There is one essential difference between this flow chart and that for consumption. The consumption chart shows net saving—the source of a demand gap. Investment typically shows net spending—an excess of business expeditures over the retained earnings of business.

However, as the next bar shows, gross investment *expenditures* are considerably larger than retained earnings. The difference represents funds that business obtains in the various ways—mainly borrowing or issuing new equity—that we discussed on page 167.

Our chart enables us to see that most gross investment is financed by business itself from its *internal* sources—retained earnings plus depreciation accruals—and that external sources play only a secondary role. In particular, this is true of new stock issues, which, during most of the 1960s and early 1970s, raised only some 3 to 8 percent of the funds spent by the business sector for new plant and equipment.

CATEGORIES OF INVESTMENT

From the total funds at its disposal, the business sector now renews its worn-out capital and adds new capital. Investment, as we know, is one of the main vehicles for growth. Let us say a word concerning some of the main categories of investment expenditure.

1. Inventories

At the top of the expenditure bar in Figure 14.1 we note an item of $19 billion for *additions to inventory*. Note that this figure does not represent total inventories, but only *changes* in inventories, upwards or downwards. If there had been no change in inventory over the year, the item would have been zero, even if existing inventories were huge. Why? Because those huge inventories would have been included in the investment expenditure flow of *previous* years when they were built up.

Inventories are often visualized as completed TV sets sitting in some warehouse. While some inventories are completed goods sitting in storage, most are in the form of goods on display in stores, half-finished goods in the process of production, or raw materials to be used in production. When a steel company adds to its stock of iron ore, it is adding to its inventories.

Investments in inventory are particularly significant for one reason. Alone among the investment categories, inventories can be *rapidly* used up as well as increased. A positive figure for one year or even one calendar quarter can quickly turn into a negative figure the next. **This means that expenditures for inventory are usually the most volatile element of any in gross national product.** A glance at Figure 14.2 shows a particularly dramatic instance of how rapidly inventory spending can change. In the fourth quarter of 1973, we were investing in inventories at an annual rate of over $20 billion. Five quarters later, we were working off inventories—*disinvesting* in inventories—by roughly the same amount. Thus, within a span of a year and a half, there was a swing of almost $50 billion in spending. Rapid inventory swings, although not quite of this magnitude, are by no means uncommon. Look at the change from June 30 to December 31, 1979.

As we shall see more clearly later, this volatility of investment has much significance for business conditions. Note that while inventories are being built up, they serve as an offset to saving—that is, some of the resources released from

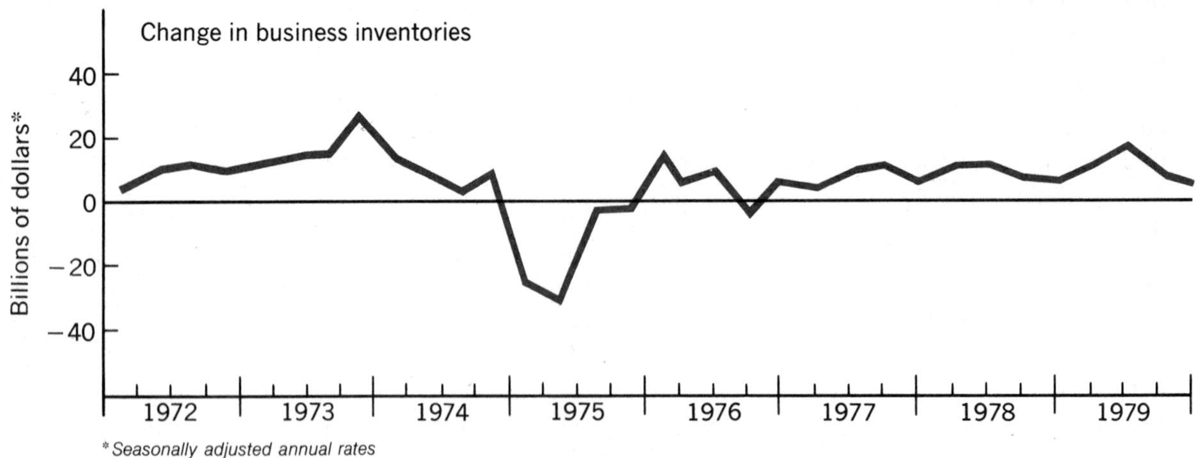

FIGURE 14.2 INVENTORY SWINGS

Inventories are a crucial portion of investment because they can change so rapidly. Compare 3Q (3rd quarter) 1973 with 2Q 1975!

consumption are used by business firms to build up stocks of inventory capital. But when inventories are being "worked off," we are actually making the demand gap bigger. As we would expect, this can give rise to serious economic troubles.

2. Equipment

The next item in the expenditure bar (Figure 14.1) is more familiar: $162 billion for *equipment.* Here we find expenditures for goods of a varied sort—lathes, trucks, generators, computers, office typewriters.* The total includes both *new equipment* and *replacement equipment.*

New equipment is obviously a very important means of widening and deepening capital—that is, of promoting growth. But let us take a moment to consider **replacement investment.** Exactly what does it mean to "replace" a given item of equipment? Suppose we have a textile loom that cost $100,000 and that is now on its last legs. Is the loom replaced by spending another $100,000, regardless of what kind of machine the money will buy? What if loom prices have gone up and $100,000 no longer buys a loom of the same capacity? Or suppose that prices have remained steady but that owing to technological advance, $100,000 now buys a loom of double the old capacity?

Such problems make the definition of "replacement" an accountant's headache and an economist's nightmare. At the moment there isn't even a generally accepted estimate of replacement investment. We need not involve ourselves deeper in the question, but we should note the complexities introduced into a seemingly simple matter once we leave the changeless world of stationary flow and enter the world of invention and innovation.

3. Construction—residential

Our next section on the expenditure bar (Figure 14.1) is total *residential construction,* another big growth item. But why do we include this $114 billion in the investment sector when most of it is represented by new houses that householders buy for their own use?

Part of the answer is that most houses are built by business firms, such as contractors and developers, who put up the houses *before* they are sold. Thus the original expenditures involved in building houses typically come from businesses, not from households. Later, when the householder buys a house, it is an existing asset, and his or her expenditure does not pump new incomes into the economy but only repays the contractor who *did* contribute new incomes.

Actually, this is a somewhat arbitrary definition, since, after all, business owns *all* output before consumers buy it. However, another reason for considering residential construction as investment is that, unlike most consumer goods, houses are typically maintained as if they were capital goods. Thus their durability also enters into their classification as investment goods.

Finally, we class housing as investment because residential purchases behave very much like other items of construction. Therefore it simplifies our

*But *not* typewriters bought by consumers. Thus the same good can be classified as a consumption item or an investment item, depending on the use to which it is put.

understanding of the forces at work in the economy if we classify residential construction as an investment expenditure rather than as a consumer expenditure.

4. Other construction—plant

Last on the bar, $92 billion of *other construction* is largely made up of the "plant" in "plant and equipment"—factories and stores and private office buildings and warehouses. (It does not, however, include public construction such as roads, dams, harbors, or public buildings, all of which are picked up under government purchases.) It is interesting to note that the building of structures, as represented by the total of residential construction plus other private construction, accounts for over half of all investment expenditures, and this total would be further swelled if public construction were included herein. This tells us that swings in construction expenditure can be a major lever for economic change.

INVESTMENT IN HISTORIC PERSPECTIVE

With this introduction behind us, let us take a look at the flow of investment, not over a single year, but over many years.

In Figure 14.3 several things spring to our attention. Clearly, investment demand is not nearly so smooth and unperturbed a flow of spending as consumption. Note that gross investment in the depths of the Depression virtually disappeared—that we almost failed to *maintain*, much less add to, our stock of wealth. (Net investment was, in fact, a negative figure for several years.) Note also investment was reduced during the war years as private capital formation was deliberately limited through government allocations.

Four important conclusions emerge from this examination of investment spending:

First, as we have many times stressed, investment is a major vehicle for growth. The upward sweep of investment is a basic explanation of our long-run rising GNP.

Second, as we have already seen, investment spending contains a component—net additions to inventory—that is capable of drastic, sudden shifts. This accounts for much of the wavelike movement of the total flow of investment expenditure.

Third, investment spending as a whole is capable of more or less total collapses of a severity and degree that are never to be found in consumption.

Fourth, unlike household spending, investment can fluctuate independently of income. It may rise when GNP is low, perhaps to usher in a boom. It can fall when GNP is high, perhaps to trigger a recession. It is an independent variable in the determination of demand.

The prime example of such a collapse was, of course, the Great Depression. From 1929 to 1933, while consumption fell by 41 percent, investment fell by *91 percent,* as we can see in Figure 14.3. At the bottom of the Great Depression in 1933, it was estimated that one-third of total unemployment was directly associated with the shrinkage in the capital goods industry. Conversely, whereas consumption rose by a little more than half from 1933 to 1940, investment in the same period rose by *nine times.*

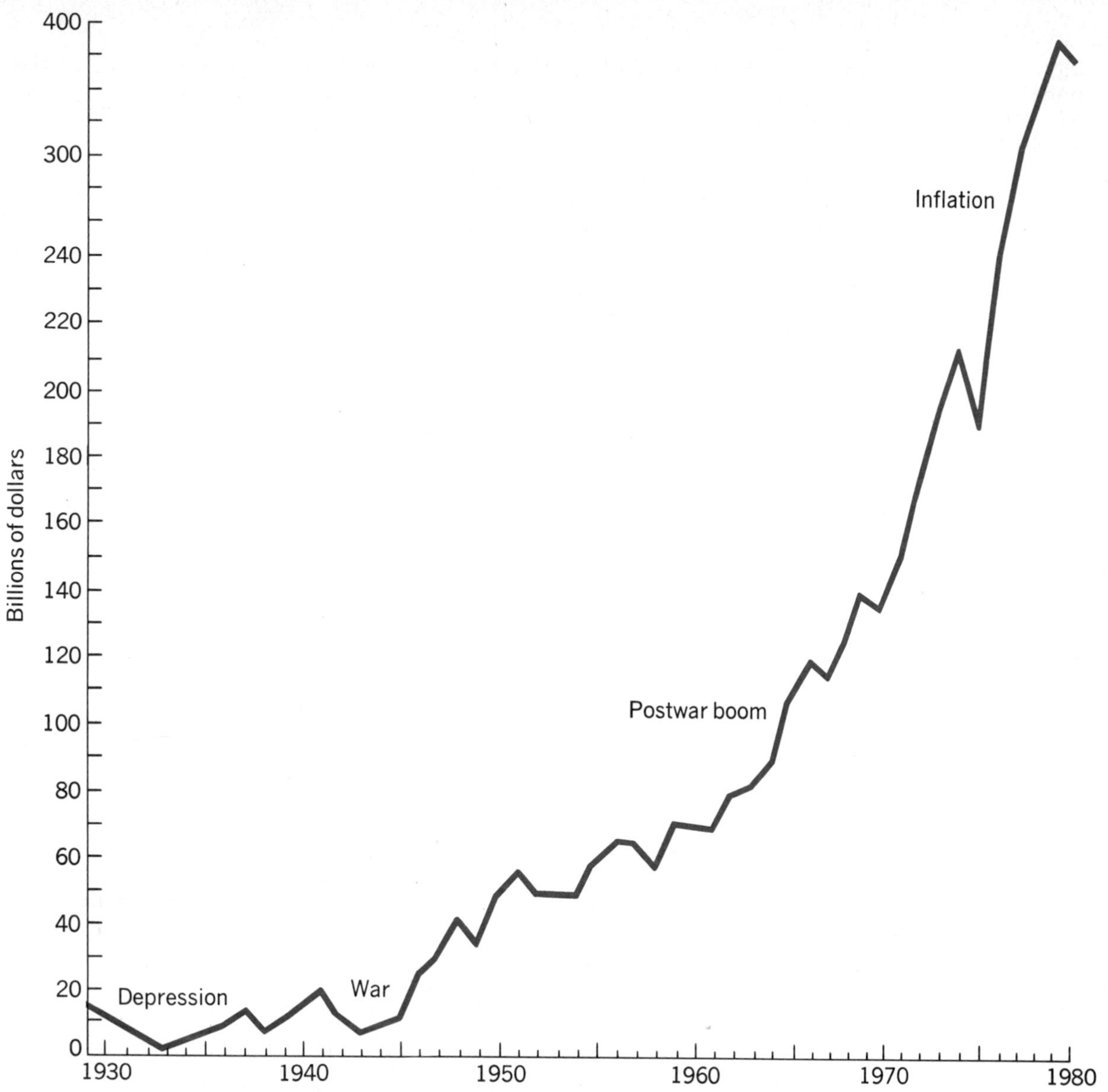

FIGURE 14.3 GROSS PRIVATE DOMESTIC INVESTMENT 1929–1980
It is evident that investment is a much more volatile item than consumption. Look at the collapse in the Great Depression. The World War I trough was different—investment was pushed aside for war spending. Then came the great postwar boom—until the troubled 1970s.

THE MULTIPLIER

We shall look more closely into the reasons for the sensitivity of investment spending. But first a question must surely have occurred to the reader. For all its susceptibility to change, the investment sector is, after all, a fairly small sector. In 1979, total expenditures for gross private domestic investment came to less than one-seventh of GNP, and the normal year-to-year variation in investment spending in the 1960s and 1970s is only about 1 to 2 percent of GNP. To devote so much time to such small fluctuations seems a disproportionate emphasis. How could so small a tail as investment wag so large a dog as GNP?

SNOWBALL EFFECT

The answer lies in a relationship of economic activities known as the *multiplier*. **The multiplier describes the fact that additions to spending (or diminutions in spending) have an impact on income that is greater than the original increase or decrease in spending itself.** In other words, even small increments in spending can *multiply* their effects (whence the name).

It is not difficult to understand the general idea of the multiplier. Suppose that we have an island community whose economy is in a perfect circular flow, unchanging from year to year. Next, let us introduce the stimulus of a new investment expenditure in the form of a stranger who arrives from another island (with a supply of acceptable money) and who proceeds to build a house. This immediately increases the islanders' incomes. In our case, we will assume that the stranger spends $1,000 on wages for construction workers, and we will ignore all other expenditures he may make. (We also make the assumption that these workers were previously unemployed, so that the builder is not merely taking them from some other task.)

Now the construction workers, who have had their incomes increased by $1,000, are very unlikely to sit on this money. As we know from our study of the marginal propensity to consume, they are apt to save some of the increase (and they may have to pay some to the government as income taxes), but the rest they will spend on additional consumption goods. Let us suppose that they save 10 percent and pay taxes of 20 percent on the $1,000 they get. They will then have $700 left over to spend for additional consumer goods and services.

But this is not an end to it. The sellers of these goods and services will now have received $700 over and above their former incomes and they, too, will be certain to spend a considerable amount of their new income. If we assume that their family spending patterns (and their tax brackets) are the same as the construction workers, they will also spend 70 percent of their new incomes, or $490. And now the wheel takes another turn, as still *another* group receives new income and spends a fraction of it.

CONTINUING IMPACT OF RESPENDING

If the newcomer then departed as mysteriously as he came, we would have to describe the economic impact of his investment as constituting a single "bulge" of income that gradually disappeared. The bulge would consist of the original $1,000, the secondary $700, the tertiary $490, and so on. If everyone continued to spend 70 percent of his new income, after ten rounds all that would remain by way of new spending traceable to the original $1,000 would be about $28. Soon, the impact of the new investment on incomes would have virtually disappeared.

But now let us suppose that after our visitor builds his house and leaves, another visitor arrives to build another house. This time, in other words, we assume that the level of investment spending *continues* at the higher level to which it was raised by the first expenditure for a new house. We can see that the second house will set into motion precisely the same repercussive effects as did the first,

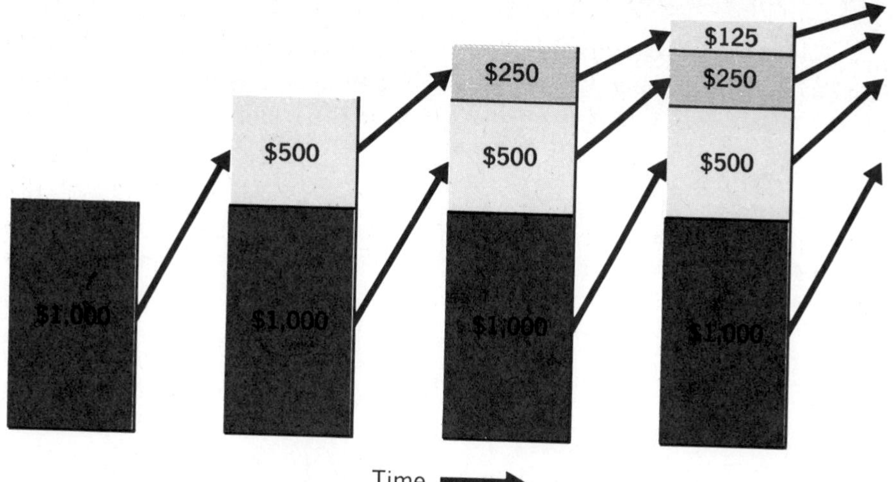

FIGURE 14.4 THE MULTIPLIER

This flow chart shows how respending creates additional income from one period to the next. This addition to income is called the multiplier. The size of the multiplier is the relation between the original new spending ($1,000) and the total new income created ($2,000). In this case the multiplier is 2.

and that the new series of respendings will be added to the dwindling echoes of the original injection of incomes.

In Figure 14.4, we can trace this effect. The succession of colored bars at the bottom of the graph stands for the continuing injections of $1,000 as new houses are steadily built. (Note that this means the level of new investment is only being maintained, not that it is rising.) Each of these colored bars now generates a series of secondary, tertiary, etc., bars that represent the respending of income after taxes and savings. In our example we have assumed that the respending fraction is 50 percent.

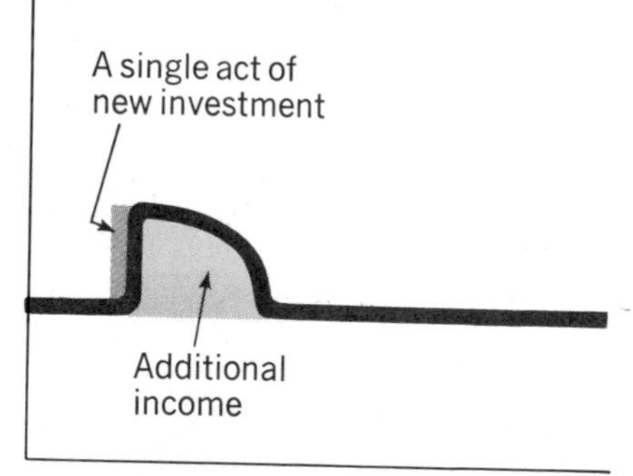

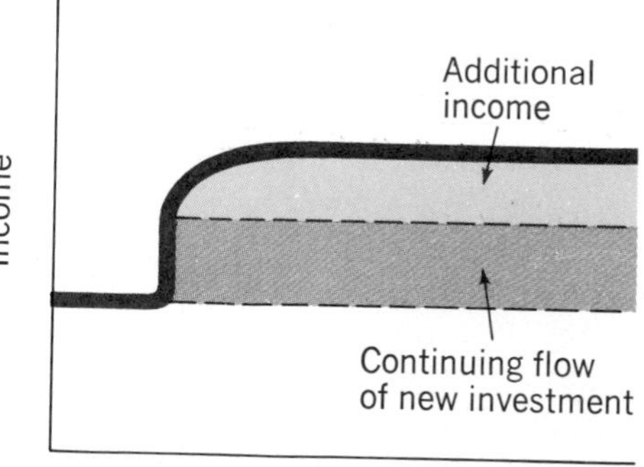

FIGURE 14.5 ONCE-OVER AND CONTINUING EFFECTS OF INVESTMENT

A single act of new spending creates a bulge in income that gradually disappears as successive receivers save part of their receipts and therefore do not respend them. A continuing flow of new spending creates a permanent addition to incomes that is larger than the new investment. Here the gradual retirement of new receipts into saving is offset by pumping out fresh additions to income.

Let us now examine the effects of investment spending in a generalized fashion, without paying attention to specific dollar amounts. In Figure 14.5, we see the effects of a single, *once-and-for-all* investment expenditure (the stranger who came and went), contrasted with the effects of a *continuing* stream of investment.

Our diagrams show us two important things:

1. **A single burst of investment creates a bulge of incomes larger than the initial expenditure, but a bulge that disappears.**

2. **A continuing flow of investment creates a new steady level of income, higher than the investment expenditures themselves.**

MARGINAL PROPENSITY TO SAVE

We can understand now that *the multiplier is the numerical relation between the initial new investment and the total increase in income.* If the initial investment is $1,000 and the total addition to income due to the respending of that $1,000 is $3,000, we have a multiplier of 3; if the total addition is $2,000, the multiplier is 2.

What determines how large the multiplier will be? The answer depends entirely on our marginal consumption (or, if you will, our marginal saving) habits —that is, on how much we consume (or save) out of each dollar of additional income that comes to us. Let us follow two cases in Figure 14.6. In the first, we will

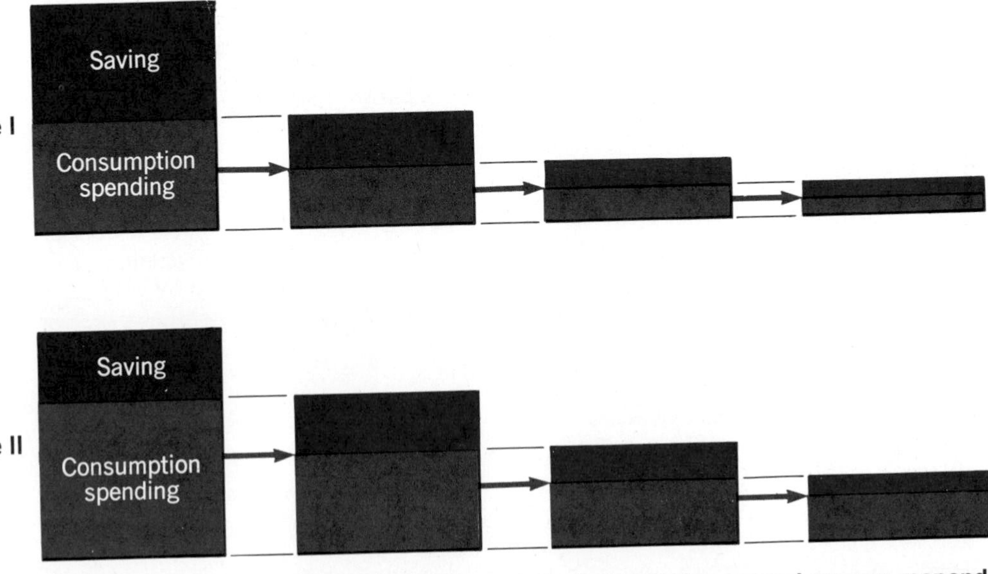

FIGURE 14.6 COMPARISON OF TWO MULTIPLIERS

The graph makes visually apparent the obvious fact that the amount we can respend is determined by the amount we save. Therefore, the lower our savings ratio, the higher the total of our respending. Or vice versa, high marginal propensities to save result in low multipliers.

assume that each recipient spends only one-half of any new income that comes to him, saving the rest. In the second case, he spends three-quarters of it and saves one-quarter.

It is very clear that the amount of income that will be passed along from one receiver to the next will be much larger where the marginal propensity to consume is higher. In fact, we can see that the total amount of new incomes (total amount of boxes below) must be mathematically related to the proportion that is spent each time.

What is this relationship? The arithmetic is easier to figure if we use not the consumption fraction, but the *saving fraction* (the two are, of couse, as intimately related as the first slice of cake and the remaining cake). If we use the saving fraction, the sum of new incomes is obtained by taking the reciprocal of (i.e., inverting, or turning upside down) the fraction we save. Thus, if we save ½ our income, the total amount of new incomes generated by respending will be ½ inverted, or 2 (twice the original increase in income). If we save ¼, it will be the reciprocal of ¼, or 4 times the original change.

BASIC MULTIPLIER FORMULA

We call the fraction of new income that is saved the *marginal propensity to save* (often abbreviated as mps). As we have just seen, this fraction is the complement of an already familiar one, the marginal propensity to consume. If our marginal propensity to consume is 80 percent, our marginal propensity to save must be 20 percent; if our mpc is three-quarters, our mps must be one-quarter. *In brief, mps + mpc ≡ 1.*

Understanding the relationship between the marginal propensity to save and the size of the resulting respending fractions allows us to state a very simple (but very important) formula for the multiplier:

change in income = multiplier × change in investment

Since we have just learned that the multiplier is determined by the reciprocal of the marginal propensity to save, we can write:

$$\text{multiplier} = \frac{1}{\text{mps}}$$

If we now use the symbols we are familiar with, plus a Greek letter Δ, delta, that means "change in," we can write the important economic relationship above as follows:

$$\Delta Y = \left(\frac{1}{\text{mps}}\right) \times \Delta I$$

Thus, if our mps is ¼ (meaning, let us not forget, that we save a quarter of increases in income and spend the rest), then an increase in investment of $1 billion will lead to a total increase in incomes of $4 billion

$$\$4 \text{ billion} = 1/\left(\frac{1}{1/4}\right) \times \$1 \text{ billion}$$

Note that the multiplier is a complex or *double* fraction:

it is 1/(¼) and *not* 1/4.

If the mps is 1/10, $1 billion gives rise to incomes of $10 billion; if the mps is 50 percent, the billion will multiply to $2 billion. And if mps is 1? This means that the entire increase in income is unspent, that our island construction workers tuck away (or find taxed away) their entire newly earned pay. In that case, the multiplier will be 1 also, and the impact of the new investment on the island economy will be no more than the $1,000 earned by the construction workers in the first place.

LEAKAGES

The importance of the size of the marginal savings ratio in determining the effect that additional investment will have on income is thus apparent. Now, however, we must pass from the simple example of our island economy to the more complex behavioral patterns and institutional arrangements of real life. The average propensity to save (the ratio of saving to disposable income) runs around 6 to 7 percent. In recent years, the *marginal* propensity to save (the ratio of additional saving to increases in income) figured over the period of a year has not departed very much from this figure. If this is the case, then, following our analysis, the multiplier would be very high. If mps were even as much as 10 percent of income, a change in investment of $1 billion would bring a $10 billion change in income. If mps were nearer 6 percent—the approximate level of the average propensity to save—a change of $1 billion would bring a swing of over $16 billion. Were this the case, the economy would be subject to the most violent disturbances whenever the level of spending shifted. For example, the $50 billion swing in inventory investment from late 1973 to early 1975 would have produced a sixteenfold fall in GNP—a fall of $800 billion!

Taxes. In fact, however, the impact of the multiplier is greatly reduced because the successive rounds of spending are dampened by factors other than personal saving. One of them we have already introduced in our imaginary island economy. This is the tendency of *taxation* to "mop up" a fraction of income as it passes from hand to hand. This mopping-up effect of taxation is in actuality much larger than that of saving. For every dollar of change in income, federal taxes will take about 30 cents, and state and local taxes another 6 cents.

Business Saving. Another dampener is the tendency of respending to swell *business savings* as well as personal incomes. Of each dollar of new spending, perhaps 10 cents goes into business profits, and this sum is typically saved, at least for a time, rather than immediately respent.

Imports. Still another source of dampening is the tendency of consumers and businesses to increase purchases from abroad as their incomes rise. These rising *imports* divert 3 to 4 percent of new spending to foreign nations and accordingly reduce the successive impact of each round of expenditure.

The Effect of Leakages. All these withdrawals from the respending cycle are called *leakages,* and the total effect of all leakages together (personal savings, business savings, taxes, and imports) is to reduce the overall impact of the multiplier from an impossibly large figure to a very manageable one. In dealing with the multiplier equation ($\Delta Y = 1/\text{mps} \times \Delta I$), we usually interpret mps to mean the total withdrawal from spending due to all leakages. **The combined effect of all leakages brings the actual multiplier in the United States in the 1970s to a little more than 2 over a period of 2 years.**

To be sure—and this is very important—all these leakages *can* return to the income stream. Household saving can be turned into capital formation; business profits can be invested; tax receipts can be disbursed in government spending programs; and purchases from foreign sellers can be returned as purchases *by* foreigners. What is at stake here is the regularity and reliability with which these circuits will be closed. In the case of ordinary income going to a household, we can count with considerable assurance on a "return expenditure" of consumption. In the case of the other recipients of funds, the assurance is much less; hence we count their receipts as money that has leaked out of the expenditure flow, for the time being.

THE DOWNWARD MULTIPLIER

The multiplier, with its important magnifying action, rests at the very center of our understanding of economic fluctuations. Not only does it explain how relatively small stimuli can exert considerable upward pushes, but it also makes much clearer than before how the failure to offset a small savings gap can snowball into a serious fall in income and employment.

For just as additional income is respent to create still further new income, a loss in income will not stop with the affected households. On the contrary, as families lose income, they cut down on their spending, although the behavior pattern of the propensity-to-consume schedule suggests that they will not cut their consumption by as much as their loss in income. Yet each reduction in consumption, large or small, lessens to that extent the income or receipts of some other household or firm.

We have already noted that personal savings alone do not determine the full impact of the multiplier. This is even more fortunate on the way down than on the way up. If the size of the multiplier were solely dependent on the marginal propensity to save, an original fall in spending would result in a catastrophic contraction of consumption through the economy. But the leakages that cushion the upward pressure of the multiplier also cushion its downward effect. As spending falls, business savings (profits) fall, tax receipts dwindle, and the flow of imports declines. We shall discuss this cushioning effect when we look into the government sector.

All of these leakages now work in the direction of mitigating the repercussions of the original fall in spending. The fall in business profits means that less will be saved by business and thus less withdrawn from respending; the decline in taxes means that more money will be left to consumers; and the drop in imports similarly releases additional spending power for the domestic market. Thus, just as the various leakages pulled money away from consumption on the way up, on the way down they lessen their siphoning effect and in this way restore purchasing power to consumers' hands. As a result, in the downward direction as in the upward, the actual impact of the multiplier is about 2, so that a fall in investment of, say, $5 billion will lower GNP by $10 billion.

Even with a reduced figure, we can now understand how a relatively small change in investment can magnify its impact on GNP. If the typical year-to-year change in investment is around $10 billion to $20 billion, a multiplier of 2 will produce a change in GNP of $20 billion to $40 billion, by no means a negligible figure.

THE MULTIPLIER AND INFLATION

Is the multiplier an inflation-breeding process? It is easy to think so, because the very word "multiplier" suggests inflation.

But that is not a correct way of looking at the question. The multiplier itself only describes the outcome of a basic pattern of economic behavior—the fact that we spend part of any additional income we receive. In itself, respending is not inflationary. But two things could make it so:

(1) **If there are no more goods available—if we have reached a ceiling on production—then indeed our efforts to spend more money will only succeed in driving up prices.** Here is really "too much money chasing too few goods." But in that case the inflation-creating condition is the ceiling on production. The effort to use our income for more enjoyments is still perfectly normal.

(2) **If we begin to expect inflation and therefore spend more of our incomes than we ordinarily would, or if we rush to get rid of our income as soon as possible for fear that prices will be higher tomorrow, then indeed our spending pushes us toward inflation.** This kind of panicky spending is a very important perpetuating mechanism for inflation, and we will be considering it more carefully in our chapter devoted to inflation. But even here, it is the scary expectations that are the cause of inflation. The respending itself is a normal part of economic behavior.

THE DEMAND FOR INVESTMENT

Consumption demand, we remember, is essentially directed at the satisfaction of the individual—at providing him with the "utilities" of the goods and services he buys. An increasingly affluent society may not be able to say that consumer expenditure is any longer solely geared to necessity, but at least it obeys the fairly constant promptings of the cultural and social environment, with the result that consumer spending, in the aggregate, fluctuates relatively little, except as income fluctuates.

PROFIT EXPECTATIONS

A quite different set of motivations drives the investment impulse. Whether the investment is for replacement of old capital or for the installation of new capital, the ruling consideration is not apt to be the personal use or satisfaction that the investment yields to the owners of the firm. Instead, the touchstone of investment decisions is *expected profit.*

Note the stress on *expectations*. One firm may be enjoying large profits on its existing plant and equipment at the moment; but if it anticipates no profits from the sale of goods that an *additional* investment would make possible, the firm will make no additions to capital. Another firm may be suffering current losses; but if it anticipates a large profit from the production of a new good, it may launch a considerable capital expenditure. The view is never backward, but always forward.

There is a sound reason for this anticipatory quality of investment decisions. Typically, the capital goods bought by investment expenditures are expected to last for years and to pay for themselves only slowly. In addition, they are often highly specialized. If capital expenditures could be recouped in a few weeks or months, or even in a matter of a year or two, or if capital goods were easily transferred from one use to another, they would not be so risky and their dependence on expectations not so great. But it is characteristic of most capital goods that they *are* durable, with life expectancies of ten or more years, and that they tend to be limited in their alternative uses, or to have no alternative uses at all. You cannot spin cloth in a steel mill or make steel in a cotton mill.

The decision to invest is thus always forward-looking. Even when the stimulus to build is felt in the present, the calculations that determine whether or not an investment will be made necessarily concern the flow of income to the firm in the future. These expectations are inherently much more volatile than the current drives and desires that guide the consumer. Expectations, whether based on guesses or forecasts, are capable of sudden and sharp reversals of a sort rare in consumption spending. Thus in its orientation to the future we find a main cause for the volatility of investment expenditures.

THE DETERMINANTS OF INVESTMENT

We speak of consumption as a function of income because we know that there is a behavioral pattern that relates the flow of consumer spending to household incomes. Can we speak of a similar investment function relating capital spending to corporation incomes?

No such simple function exists. This is because the forward-looking nature of investment makes it inherently independent of past influences. Some investment is "induced" by past consumption—inventories, for example, may follow sales—but other investment is "autonomous"—quite independent of consumption. Much investment depends on technology, which is largely unpredictable. And other erratic or unknowable events also bring their effects to bear—the gyrations of the stock market, changes in the inflationary outlook, the ups and downs of foreign relations, and the like.

THE ACCELERATION PRINCIPLE

Nevertheless, investment expenditure is not just a random variable. There are patterns in investment, even though they may be upset by sudden, unforeseen shifts in total investment spending.

One such pattern of considerable importance is called the *acceleration principle*, or sometimes just the accelerator. The name springs from the fact that investment often depends upon the rate of growth of the economy.

Year	Sales (millions)	Existing capital (millions)	Needed capital (2 × sales) (millions)	Replacement investment (millions)	Induced new investment (2 × addition to sales) (millions)	Total investment
1	$100	$200	$200	$20	—	$20
2	120	200	240	20	$40	60
3	130	240	260	20	20	40
4	135	260	270	20	10	30
5	138	270	276	20	6	26
6	140	276	280	20	4	24
7	140	280	280	20	—	20
8	130	280	260	—	—	0
9	130	260	260	20	—	20

TABLE 14.1 A MODEL OF THE ACCELERATOR

The accelerator model shows how investment spending can fall, even though sales are rising. Compare the total amount of investment in the last column with the change in sales in the second column. In the third year sales are up by $10 million. But investment spending is down by $20 million!

Table 14.1 is a model that explains this phenomenon. It shows us an industry whose sales rise for six years, then level off, and finally decline. We assume it has no unused equipment and that its equipment wears out every ten years. Also, we will make the assumption that it requires a capital investment of $2 to produce a flow of output of $1.

Now let us see the accelerator at work.

In our first view of the industry, we find it in equilibrium with sales of, let us say, $100 millions, capital equipment valued at $200 millions, and regular replacement demand of 20 millions, or 10 percent of its stock of equipment. Now we assume that its sales rise to $120 millions. To produce $120 millions of goods, the firm will need (according to our assumptions) $240 millions of capital. This is $40 millions more than it has, so it must order new equipment. Note that its demand for capital goods now shoots from $20 millions to $60 millions: $20 millions for replacement as before, and $40 millions for new investment. Thus investment expenditures *triple*, even though sales have risen but 20 percent!

Now assume that in the next year sales rise further, to $130 millions. How large will our firm's investment demand be? Its replacement demand will not be larger, since its new capital will not wear out for ten years. And the amount of new capital needed to handle its new sales will be only $20 millions, not $40 millions as before. Its total investment demand has *fallen* from $60 millions to $40.

What is the surprising fact here? It is that *we can have an actual fall in induced investment, though sales are still rising!* In fact, as soon as the *rate of increase* of consumption begins to fall, *the absolute amount* of induced investment declines. Thus a slowdown in the rate of improvement in sales can cause

an absolute decline in the orders sent to capital goods makers. This helps us to explain how weakness can appear in some branches of the economy while prosperity seems still to be reigning in the market at large. It will play a role when we come to explain the phenomenon of the business cycle.

Now look at what happens to our model in the eighth year, when we assume that sales slip back to 130 millions. Our existing capital (280 millions) will be greater by 20 millions than our needed capital. That year the industry will have no new orders for capital goods and may not even make any replacements, because it can produce all it needs with its old machines. Its orders to capital goods makers will fall to zero, even though its level of sales is 30 percent higher than at the beginning. The next year, however, if sales remain steady, it will again have to replace one of its old machines. Its replacement demand again jumps to 20 millions. No wonder capital goods industries traditionally experience feast or famine years!

There is, in addition, an extremely important point to bear in mind. **The accelerator's upward leverage usually takes effect only when an industry is operating at or near capacity.** When an industry is not near capacity, it is relatively simple for it to satisfy a larger demand for its goods by raising output on its underutilized equipment. Thus, unlike the multiplier, which yields its effects on output only when we have unemployed resources, the accelerator yields its effects only when we do *not* have unemployed capital.

INTEREST RATES AND COST OF INVESTMENT

There is a second element in the economy that imposes a certain degree of orderliness on investment. This is the influence of interest rates on investment.

Interest rates affect investment in two ways. The first is to change the costs of investment. If businesses must borrow to make capital expenditures, a higher rate of interest makes it more expensive to undertake an investment. For huge firms that target a return of 15 to 20 percent on their investment projects, a change in the interest rate from 10 to 11 percent may be negligible. But for certain kinds of investment—notably utilities and home construction—interest rates constitute an important component of the cost of investment funds. To these firms, the lower the cost of borrowed capital, the more stimulus for investment. The difference in *interest costs* for $1 million borrowed for 20 years at 10 percent (instead of 11 percent) is $200,000, by no means a negligible sum. Since construction is the largest single component of investment, the interest rate therefore becomes an important influence on the value of total capital formation.

INTEREST RATES AS A GUIDE TO DISCOUNTING

A second guide is offered to business not directly seeking to borrow money for investment but debating whether to invest the savings (retained earnings) of the firms. This problem of deciding on investments introduces us to an important idea: the discounting of future income.

Suppose that someone gave you an ironclad promise to pay you $100 a year hence. Would you pay him $100 *now* to get back the same sum 365 days in the future? Certainly not, for in parting with the money you are suffering an *opportunity cost* or a cost that can be measured in terms of the opportunities that your

THE STOCK MARKET AND INVESTMENT

How does the stock market affect business investment? There are three direct effects. One is that the market has traditionally served as a general barometer of the expectations of the business-minded community as a whole. We say "business-minded" rather than "business," because the demand for, and supply of, securities mainly comes from securities dealers, stockbrokers, and the investing public, rather than from nonfinancial business enterprises themselves. When the market is buoyant, it has been a signal to business that the "business climate" is favorable, and the effect on what Keynes called the "animal spirits" of executives has been to encourage them to go ahead with expansion plans. When the market is falling, on the other hand, spirits tend to be dampened, and executives may think twice before embarking on an expansion program in the face of general pessimism.

This traditional relationship is, however, greatly lessened by the growing power of government to influence the trend of economic events. Business once looked to the market as the key signal for the future. Today it looks to Washington. Hence, during the past decade when the stock market has shown wide swings, business investment in plant and equipment has remained basically steady. This reflects the feelings of corporate managers that government policy will keep the economy growing, whatever "the market" may think of events.

A second direct effect of the stock market on investment has to do with the ease of issuing new securities. One of the ways in which investment is financed is through the issuance of new stocks or bonds whose proceeds will purchase plant and equipment. When the market is rising, it is much easier to float a new issue than when prices are falling. This is particularly true for certain businesses—A.T. & T. is a prime example—that depend heavily on stock issues for new capital rather than on retained earnings.

Finally, when the market is very low, companies with large retained earnings may be tempted to buy up other companies, rather than use their funds for capital expenditure. Financial investment, in other words, may take the place of real investment. This helps successful companies grow, but does not directly provide growth for the economy as a whole.

action (to pay $100 now) has foreclosed for you. Had the going rate of interest been 10 percent, for example, you could have loaned your $100 at 10 percent and had $110 at the end of the year. Hence, friendship aside, you are unlikely to lend your money unless you are paid something to compensate you for the opportunities you must give up while you are waiting for your money to return. **Another way of saying exactly the same thing is that we arrive at the *present value* of a specified sum in the future by discounting it by some percentage.** If the discount rate is 10 percent, the present value of $100 one year in the future is $100 ÷ 110, or approximately $90.90.

DISCOUNTING THE FUTURE

This brings us back to the business that is considering whether or not to make an investment. Suppose it is considering investing $100,000 in a machine that is expected to earn $25,000 a year for 5 years, over and above all expenses, after which it will be worthless. Does this mean that the expected profit on the machine is therefore $25,000—the $125,000 of expected earnings less the $100,000 of original cost? No, it does not, for the expected earnings will have to be discounted by some appropriate percentage to find their present value. Thus the first $25,000 to be earned by the machine must be reduced by some discount rate; and the second $25,000 must be discounted *twice* (just as $100 to be repaid in *two* year's time will have to yield the equivalent of *two* years' worth of interest); the third $25,000, three times, etc.*

Clearly, this process of discounting will cause the present value of the expected future returns of the machine to be less than the sum of the undiscounted returns. If, for example, its returns are discounted at a rate of 10 percent, the business will find that the present value of a five-year flow of $25,000 per annum comes not to $125,000 but to only $94,700. This is *less* than the actual expenditure for the machine ($100,000). Hence, at a discount rate of 10 percent, the business would not undertake the venture.

On the other hand, if it used a discount rate of 5 percent, the present value of the same future flow would be worth (in round numbers) $109,000. In that case, the machine *would* be a worthwhile investment.

MARGINAL EFFICIENCY OF INVESTMENT

What rate should our business use to discount future earnings? Here is where the rate of interest enters the picture. Looking out at the economy, the business manager sees that there is a whole spectrum of interest rates, ranging from very low rates on bonds (usually government bonds) where the element of risk is very small, to high rates on securities of the same maturity (that is, coming due in the same number of years) where the risk is much greater, such as "low-grade" corporate bonds or mortgages. Among this spectrum of rates, there will be a rate at which he or she can borrow—high or low, depending on each one's credit worthiness in the eyes of the banking community. By applying that rate the manager can discover whether the estimated future earning from the venture, properly discounted, is actually profitable or not.

We can see the expected effect of interest rates on investment in Figure 14.7. Suppose that a businessman has a choice among different investment projects from which he anticipates different returns. The technical name for these discounted returns is the **marginal efficiency of investment.** Suppose he ranks those projects, as we have in Figure 14.7, starting with the most profitable (A) and proceeding to the least profitable (G). How far down the list should he go? The rate of interest gives the answer. Let us say that the rate (for projects of comparable risk) is shown by OX. Then all his investment projects whose marginal efficiency is higher than OX (investments A through D) will be profitable, and all

*The formula for calculating the present value of a flow of future income that does not change from year to year is:

$$\text{Present value} = \frac{R}{(1 + i)} + \frac{R}{(1 + i)^2} + \cdots + \frac{R}{(1 + i)^n}$$

where R is the annual flow of income, i is the interest rate, and n is the number of years over which the flow will last.

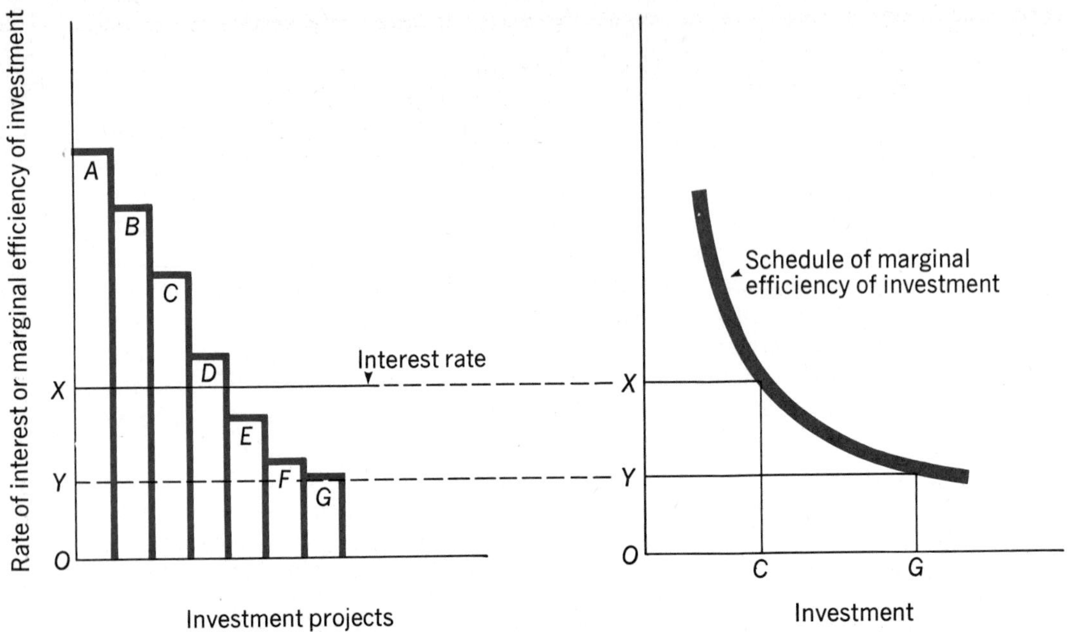

FIGURE 14.7 MARGINAL EFFICIENCY OF CAPITAL

A businessman calculates profitability by discounting the expected returns of various ventures. This gives him the marginal efficiency of those ventures. By comparing these marginal efficiencies with the rate of interest for projects of the same degree of risk, he can tell whether the opportunity cost of putting his money into the venture is worthwhile or not.

---

those whose marginal efficiency falls below *OX* (*E* through *G*) will be discarded or at least postponed.

Note that if the interest rate falls, more investments will be worthwhile; and that if it rises, fewer will be. As the figure on the right shows in generalized form, a fall in the rate of interest (e.g., from *OX* to *OY*) induces a rise in the quantity of investment (from *OC* to *OG*).

INTEREST AND INVESTMENT

Thus, whether we figure interest as a cost or as a guideline against which we measure the expected returns of a capital investment, we reach the important conclusion that low interest rates should encourage investment spending—or in more formal language, that investment should be inversely related to the rate of interest.

To be sure, the fact that a given investment, such as project *B* above, has a marginal efficiency higher than the interest rate is no guarantee that a business actually will undertake it. Other considerations—perhaps political, perhaps psychological—may deter management, despite its encouraging calculations. But assuredly a business will not carry out a project that yields less than the interest rate, because it can make more profit by lending the money, at the same degree of risk, than by investing it.

LOOKING BACK

KEY CONCEPTS

Real vs. financial investment

1. By the term investment, economists usually refer to the use of resources to create new capital, not to using money to buy assets. Investment is crucial as the key to growth.

Four main forms of investment expenditure. Inventories as a source of investment instability

2. There are four main kinds of investment expenditure: equipment, residential construction, plant, and inventories. Equipment and construction, both for residential and nonresidential purposes, are important for growth. Inventory investment is often the cause of cyclical swings.

Differences of investment and consumption: expectations a key factor

3. Investment is in large degree an independent, not a dependent, variable. It is subject to swings or even collapses of a kind unknown to consumption. Above all, investment is keyed to expectations of future profit, and not to past income.

Investment exerts an upward or downward multiplier. The multiplier is determined by the respending fraction, mpc or its reciprocal mps.
mps ≡ 1–mpc

Respending in itself is not inflationary

4. Investment exerts a larger effect on GNP than the direct change in investment spending. This is because income created by new investment (or income reduced by a fall in investment) is multiplied. The multiplier depends on the degree to which the original change in investment is respent. This respending fraction is the marginal propensity to consume, or its reciprocal, the marginal propensity to save. Respending is normal, not inflationary. It creates inflation only when there is too little production or when respending becomes panicky.

$$\Delta Y = \frac{1}{\text{mps}} \times \Delta I$$

5. The effect of a change of investment on GNP therefore depends on the mpc or the mps. The simplest way to calculate the multiplier is to use the formula $Y = 1/\text{mps}$. Do not forget that mps is itself a fraction: If mps = ¼, then the multiplier is 1 ÷ ¼ = 4.

Leakages:
- **savings**
- **imports**
- **taxes**
- **business profits—**
- **lower multiplier to about 2**

6. The actual mps is not just determined by our personal savings. Imports, marginal taxes, and business savings also absorb increases in income and therefore lower respending. These are all leakages, which together reduce the actual effect of the multiplier to about 2 over the period of a year.

The acceleration principle links investment to increases in output. Investment may fall even though output is still rising

7. Although investment can be highly unstable, it does have some internal patterns and regularities. One of these is the accelerator or acceleration principle. This is a wave-like pattern that is induced in investment, to the extent that increases in output require ("induce") increases in investment. As output rises, induced investment at first rises faster; then investment may actually fall even though output is still growing.

Interest rates affect investment through cost

8. Interest rates also influence investment spending. One obvious effect is that interest is a cost of investment.

Future income must be discounted to allow for opportunity cost. Interest rates are the guide to whether the marginal efficiency of a given investment is profitable

9. Interest rates are also a guide to investment profitability. Businessmen discount the expected future earnings of investment, because future income represents an opportunity cost. Interest rates show the returns available for various kinds of risk. A businessman compares the discounted earnings of any project—its marginal efficiency—with the interest rate to see if it is worth the opportunity cost.

Low interest rates encourage investment

10. Whether as a cost, or as a guide to marginal efficiencies, interest rates encourage investment when they go down, discourage it when they go up.

ECONOMIC VOCABULARY

Real vs. financial investment 196
Replacement investment 199
Multiplier 201
Marginal propensity to save 204
Leakages 206
Acceleration principle 209
Discounting 212
Marginal efficiency of investment 213

QUESTIONS

1. If you buy a share of stock on the New York Stock Exchange, does that create an equal amount of investment?
2. Why are inventories subject to such sudden shifts?
3. Why do we face the possibility of a large-scale collapse in investment spending but not in consumption spending?
4. Draw a diagram of boxes showing the multiplier effect of $100 expenditure when the marginal propensity to spend is one-tenth. Draw a second diagram showing the effect when the mps is nine-tenths. The larger the savings ratio, the larger or smaller the multiplier?
5. Calculate the impact on income if investment rises by $10 billion and the multiplier is 2. If it is 3. If it is 1.
6. A simple problem: Income is $500 billion. Inventories decline by $5 billion. The multiplier is 2. What is the new level of income?
7. Suppose you had the following leakages: mps, 10 percent; marginal taxation, 20 percent; marginal propensity to import, 5 percent; marginal addition to business saving, 15 percent. What will be the size of the second round of spending, if the first round is $1 billion? What will be the size of the third round? What will be the final total of new spending?
8. Explain the relationship between the marginal propensity to consume and the marginal propensity to save. Why must these two fractions always add up to 1?
9. Complete the following accelerator model, assuming that you need $2 of equipment to produce $1 of output, and that replacement is at 20 percent per year. Check back on page 210 if you need guidance.

Year	*Output*	*Replacement investment*	*New equipment needed*	*Total investment*
1	100	20	0	—
2	120	—	40	—
3	130	—	—	—
4	135	—	—	—

10. If the rate of interest were 10 percent, what would be the present value of $100 due a year hence? Two years hence? Remember: the first year's discounted value has to be discounted a second time.

AN EXTRA WORD ABOUT

THE EXPORT SECTOR

Before we go on to the problem of public demand, we must mention, if only in passing, a sector we have so far largely overlooked. This is the foreign sector, or more properly the sector of net exports.

If we lived in Europe, South America, or Asia, we could not be so casual in our treatment of foreign trade, for this sector constitutes the very lifeline of many, perhaps even most, countries. Our own highly self-sustained economy in which foreign trade plays only a small quantitative (although a much more important qualitative) role in generating total output is very much the exception rather than the rule.

In part, it is the relatively marginal role played by foreign trade in the American economy that allows us to treat it so cavalierly. But there is also another problem. The forces that enter into the flows of international trade are much more complex than any we have heretofore discussed. Not alone the reactions of American consumers and firms, but those of foreign consumers and firms must be taken into account. Thus comparisons between international price levels, the availability of foreign or domestic goods, credit and monetary controls, exchange rates—a whole host of other such considerations—lie at the very heart of foreign trade. To begin to unravel these interrelationships, one must study international trade as a subject in itself, and that we will defer until Chapter 34 and Part 6. Nevertheless, we should try to understand the main impact of foreign trade on the demand for GNP, even if we cannot yet investigate the forces and institutions of foreign trade as thoroughly as we might like.

IMPACT OF FOREIGN TRADE

We must begin by repeating that our initial overview of the economic system, with its twin streams of consumption and investment, was actually incomplete. It portrayed what we call a "closed" system, an economy with no flows of goods or services from within its borders to other nations or from other nations to itself.

Yet such flows must, of course, be taken into account in computing our national output. Let us therefore look at a chart that shows us the main streams of goods and services that cross our borders. (see Figure 14.8).

First a word of explanation. Exports show the total value of all goods and services we sold to foreigners. Imports show the total value of all goods and services we bought from foreigners. Our bottom line shows the net difference between exports and imports, or the difference between the value of the goods we sold abroad and the value we bought from abroad. This difference is called *net exports,* and it constitutes the net contribution of foreign trade to the demand for GNP.

If we think of it in terms of expenditures, it is not difficult to see what the net contribution is. When exports are sold to foreigners, their expenditures add to American incomes. Imports, on the contrary, are expenditures that we make to other countries (and hence that we do not make at home). If we add the foreign expenditures made here and subtract the domestic expenditures made abroad, we will have left a net figure that will show the contribution (if any) by foreigners to GNP.

THE EXPORT MULTIPLIER

What is the impact of this net expenditure on GNP? It is much the same as net private domestic investment. If we have a rising net export balance, we will have a net increase in spending in the economy.

Conversely, if our net foreign trade balance falls, our demand for GNP will decline, exactly as if the demand for domestic investment fell. Thus, even though we must defer for a while a study of the actual forces at work in international trade, we can quickly include the effects of foreign trade on the level of GNP by considering the net trade balance as a part of our investment demand for output.

One point in particular should be noted. If there is a rise in the net demand generated by foreigners, this will have a *multiplier effect,* exactly as an increase in investment will have. Here is, in fact, our illustrative story of an individual visiting an island (p. 202) come to life. Additional net foreign spending will generate new buying; and decreased net foreign spending will diminish incomes, with a similar train of secondary and tertiary effects. We will look into this problem again when we study the foreign trade difficulties of the United States in Chapter 34.

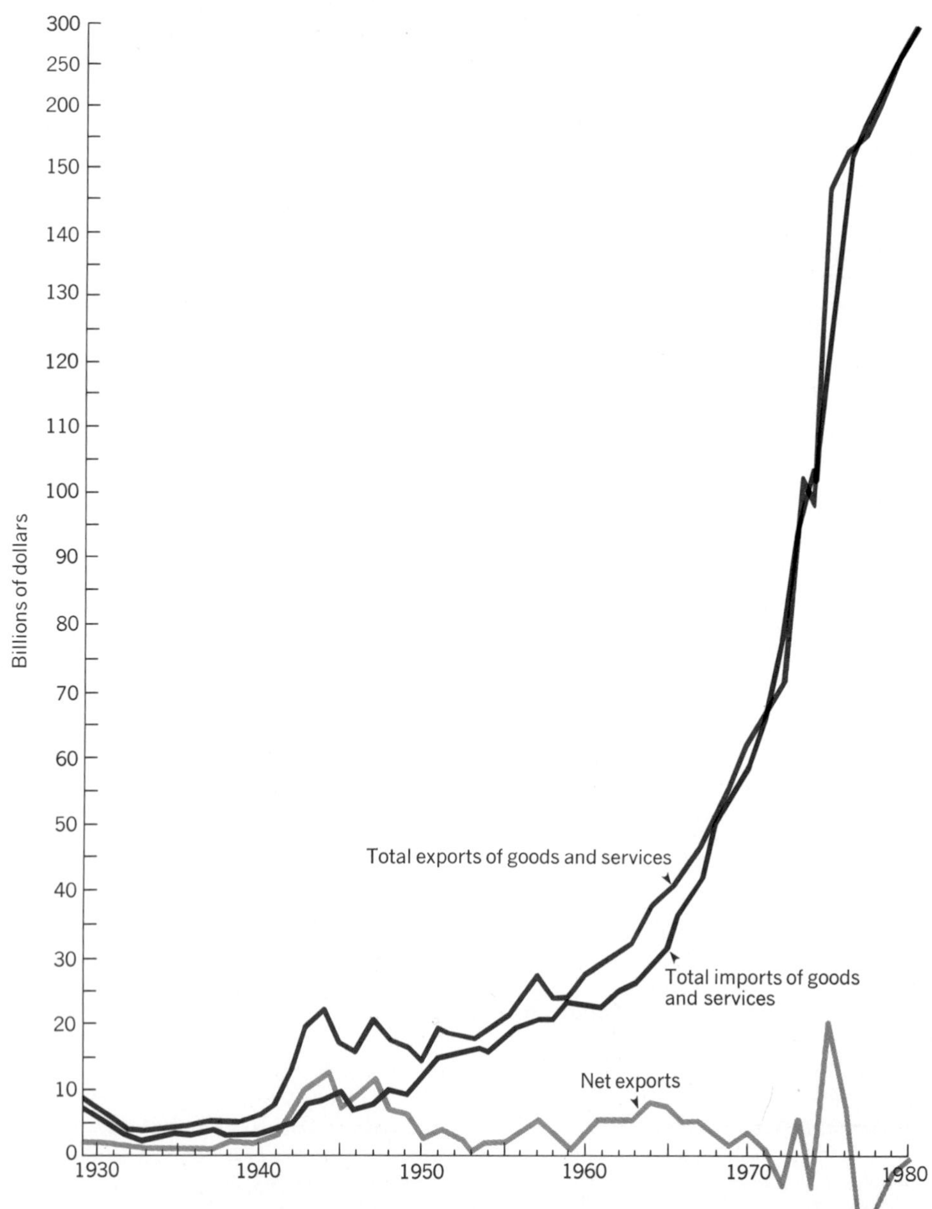

**FIGURE 14.8
EXPORTS,
IMPORTS,
AND NET
EXPORTS**

Chapter 15 GOVERNMENT DEMAND

A LOOK AHEAD

This chapter covers three main ideas:

(1) The way in which the public sector can offset a demand gap. Since the mechanics are exactly the same as the mechanics of the business sector, there will be no difficulty here.

(2) The question of how we finance a government deficit. Because national debts are not at all like the debts of households and businesses, there is something surprising to learn here.

(3) The question of how the government sector can be used to quicken or slow down the flow of GNP.

As we shall see, there are many problems in "demand management."

THE PUBLIC SECTOR

The government sector, taken as a whole, has changed from a very small sector to a very large one. In 1929, total government purchases of goods and services were only half of total private investment spending; in 1979 total government purchases were almost 25 percent *larger* than private investment. In terms of its contributions to GNP, government is now second only to consumption. Thus, the public sector, whose operation we will have to examine closely, has become a major factor in the economy as a whole.

KINDS OF GOVERNMENT SPENDING

Let us begin by learning to distinguish carefully among various aspects of what we call "government spending." As we shall see, it is very easy to get confused between "*expenditures*" and "*purchases*"; between *federal* spending and *total government* spending (which includes the states and localities); and between *war* and *nonwar* spending.

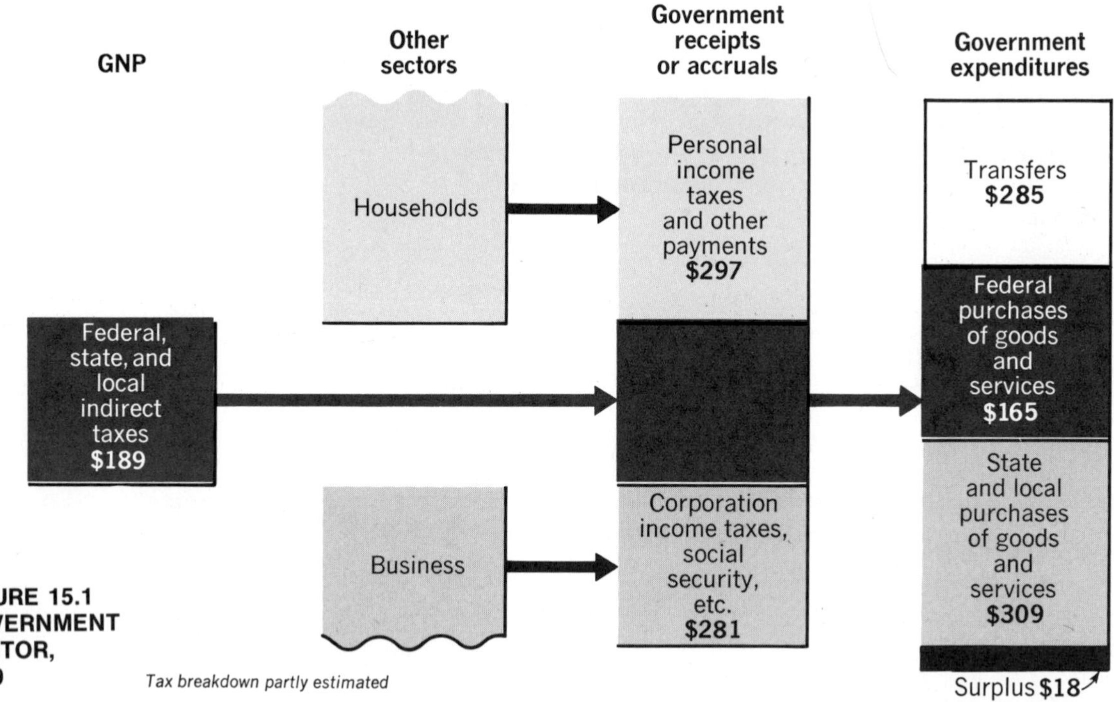

FIGURE 15.1 GOVERNMENT SECTOR, 1979

This familiar flow chart is different in one vital respect from those for consumption and investment. The consumption flow has a normal demand gap. The investment flow has a normal net contribution to demand. But the government flow can have either. It is possible to run the public sector at a surplus or a deficit. That is actually the theme of this chapter.

1. Government expenditures vs. purchases of goods and services

When we speak of government spending, we must take care to specify whether we mean total *expenditures of the government* or *purchases of goods and services.* The difference lies in the category we have called *transfer payments,* payments that are made to redistribute income, not to pay for work or for economic activity.

Transfers are a very important part of government spending. As Figure 15.1 shows, in 1979 the public sector spent $285 billion for transfer purposes. This includes Social Security payments, unemployment insurance, various agricultural and business subsidies, and the like. When we add up all the expenditures of government, including these transfers, the total is over $759 billion, or about one-third of GNP.

However we must remember that transfer payments only rearrange incomes. They do not directly create incomes through new production. Therefore if we want to measure the impact of government spending on GNP, we should exclude transfers. This gives us a total of $474 billion or about 20 percent of GNP.

2. Federal vs. state and local spending

The second distinction we must make is to differentiate between federal and nonfederal spending. If we take the total purchases of goods and services, we should note that $309 billion—just under two-thirds—arises from the expenditures of state and local governments, and only the remaining third from federal spending. **Federal spending is larger than state and local only if we include transfers. When these payments are added in, federal spending becomes about a third larger than nonfederal.**

It also makes a big difference whether we are speaking of federal or total government when we consider the deficit of the public sector. In Fig. 15.1 we can see a surplus of $18 billion for the public sector as a whole. That year, the federal budget was in deficit to the tune of $11 billion. But the public sector showed a surplus because state and local surpluses outweighed the federal budget enough to change the balance. To complicate things still more, the reason for the state and local surplus was partly the consequence of federal grants to the states. If the federal government had not helped out the states and localities, there would have been a federal surplus and a state and local deficit.

3. Welfare vs. warfare

A last caution has to do with the nature of federal spending. Much of the flow of federal purchases is connected with arms. Two-thirds of federal purchases in 1980 was for defense purposes. Despite the cry of an expanding federal government, Table 15.1 shows that federal purchases of total goods and services are hardly a larger percentage of GNP than in 1940!

Then why the outcry? The reason lies in the very marked growth of welfare services, many of them financed by state and local government as well as by federal government. These include health and medical programs, public educa-

Selected years	1929	1933	1940	1950	1960	1970	1976	1977	1978	1979	1980
Federal Purchases	1.4	3.8	6.1	6.5	10.6	9.7	8.1	7.6	7.1	7.0	6.9
Federal Expenditures (Purchases plus transfers)	2.5	7.2	10.0	14.3	18.4	20.8	23.3	22.2	21.6	21.4	22.5

TABLE 15.1 FEDERAL NONDEFENSE PURCHASES AND EXPENDITURES AS PERCENT OF GNP

The proportion of government spending for total purchases is still a small part of GNP. The relation of government expenditures (including transfers) has risen very much faster.

tion and housing, welfare assistance and Social Security. **Total welfare expenditures today come to about 20 percent of GNP, compared with less than 1 percent in 1929.**

TOO MUCH WELFARE?

Is this too high a level? There is no doubt that there exists a very strong anti-government sentiment in many parts of the nation today, evidenced in the tax revolt that has surfaced in a number of states. Much of this anti-government sentiment, it is only fair to point out, has a strong flavor of self-interest. City dwellers do not think that government spends too much on urban problems, but country dwellers do. Country dwellers do not think that government spends too much on agricultural problems, but city dwellers do. Couples with children do not want school expenditures cut, but childless couples do. Older people want higher Social Security benefits, but not younger people.

An economist has no special expertise that enables him to solve these essentially *political* problems. Economists can speak with some knowledge about the effects of various kinds of welfare spending—for example, the effects of unemployment insurance in making it less costly for someone to quit a job—but they cannot really pronounce on whether the effect is good or bad. That is a matter where value judgments come into play. We have set aside Chapter 33, "Taxing and Spending," to examine some of the issues in this tangled problem.

ECONOMICS OF THE PUBLIC SECTOR

However one feels about what government *should* do, it is vital to understand what it *does* do. This brings us away from the value-laden, political aspect of government spending to its objective, economic aspect. Economists who disagree sharply about the best government policy for the country can still agree in their understanding of how the public sector works. (Where they do not agree, we'll point out the bone of contention.)

MOTIVATIONS

Here the appropriate place to begin seems to be in the difference in *motivations* that guide public, as contrasted with private, spending. We recall that the motivations for the household sector and the business sector are lodged in the free decisions of their respective units. Householders decide to spend or save their incomes as they wish, and we are able to construct a propensity-to-consume schedule only because there seem to be spending and saving patterns that emerge spontaneously from the householders themselves. Similarly, business firms exercise their own judgments on their capital expenditures, and as a result we have seen the inherent variability of investment decisions.

But when we turn to the expenditures of the public sector, we enter an entirely new area of motivation. It is no longer fixed habit or profit that determines the rate of spending, but *political decision*—that is, the collective will of the people as it is formulated and expressed through their local, state, and federal legislatures and executives.

As we shall soon see, this does not mean that government is therefore an entirely unpredictable economic force. There are regularities and patterns in the government's economic behavior, as there are in other sectors. **Yet the presence of an explicit political will that can direct the income or outgo of the sector as a whole (especially its federal component) gives to the public sector a special significance. This is the only sector whose expenditures and receipts are open to deliberate control. We can exert (through public action) very important influences on the behavior of households and firms. But we cannot directly alter their economic activity in the manner that is open to us with the public sector.**

THE GOVERNMENT AS A BALANCING SECTOR

The basic idea behind modern fiscal policy is simple enough. We have seen that economic recessions have their roots in a failure of the business sector to offset the savings of the economy through sufficient investment. If savings or leakages are larger than intended investment, there will be a gap in the circuit of incomes and expenditures that can cumulate downward, at first by the effect of the multiplier, thereafter, and even more seriously, by further decreases in investment brought about by falling sales and gloomy expectations.

But if a falling GNP is caused by an inadequacy of expenditures in one sector, our analysis suggests an answer. Could not the insufficiency of spending in the business sector be offset by higher spending in another sector, the public sector? Could not the public sector serve as a supplementary avenue for the transfer of savings into expenditure?

As Figure 15.2 shows, a demand gap can indeed be closed by transferring savings to the public sector and spending them. The diagram shows savings in the household sector partly offset by business investment and partly by government spending. It makes clear that at least so far as the mechanics of the economic flow are concerned, the public sector can serve to offset savings or other leakages equally as well as the private sector.

How is the transfer accomplished? It can be done much as business does it, by offering bonds that individuals or institutions may buy with their savings. Unlike business, the government cannot offer stock, for it is not run as a profit-making enterprise. However, government has a source of funds quite different from business; namely, *taxes*. **In effect, government can commandeer purchasing power in a way that business cannot.**

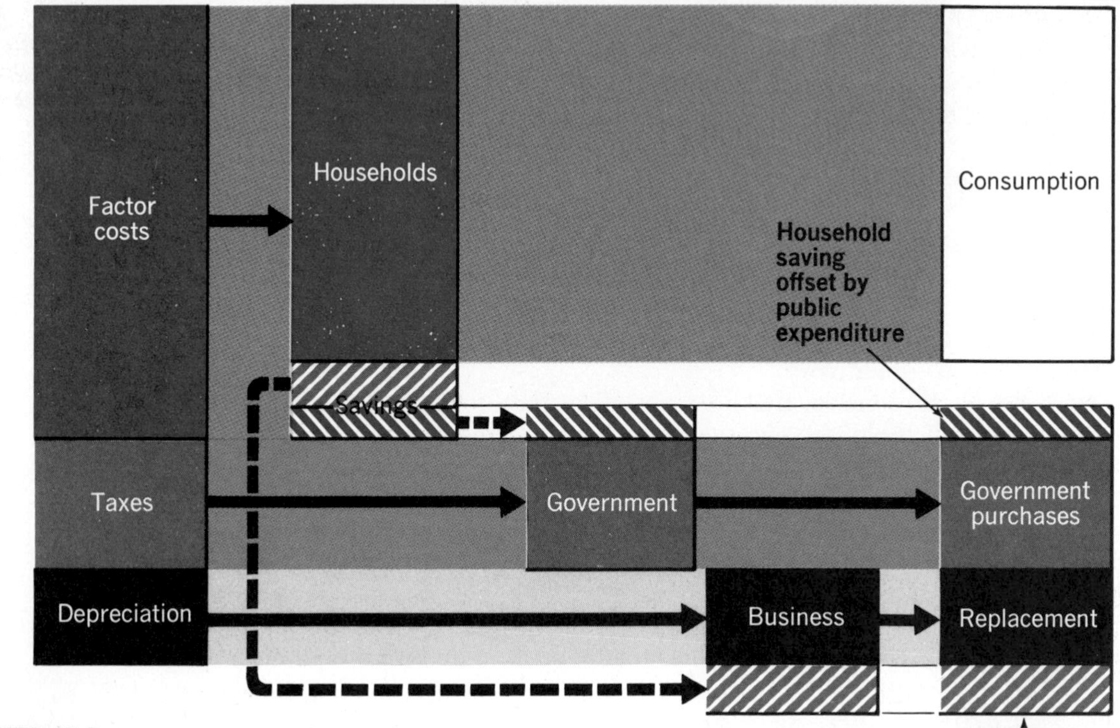

FIGURE 15.2 PUBLIC EXPENDITURE AND THE DEMAND GAP

The "economics" of filling a demand gap by government spending are exactly like those of investment spending. The "politics" are not.

DEFICIT SPENDING

But isn't it inflationary when the government borrows money? It certainly can be, but economists of all shades of opinion agree that it need not be: It depends on many factors that we will take up, some in this chapter, some later.

First, however, we must understand exactly what it means for the government to borrow. **Any government that uses its budget as a stabilizing device must be prepared to spend more than it takes in in taxes. On occasion it must purposefully plan a budget in which outgo exceeds income, leaving a negative figure called a *deficit*.**

That raises a problem that alarms and perplexes many people. Like a business or consumer, the government cannot spend money it does not have. Therefore it must *borrow* the needed funds from individuals, firms, or banks in order to cover its deficit. Deficit spending, in other words, means the spending of borrowed money, money derived from the sale of government bonds.

DEFICITS AND LOSSES

Can the government safely run up a deficit? Let us begin to unravel this important but perplexing question by asking another: can a private business afford to run up a deficit?

There is one kind of deficit that a private business *cannot* afford: a deficit that comes from spending more money on current production than it will realize from its sale. This kind of deficit is called a *business loss;* and if losses are severe enough, a business firm will be forced to discontinue its operations.

But there is another kind of deficit, although it is not called by that name, in the operations of a private firm. This is an excess of expenditures over receipts brought about by spending money on *capital assets.* When the American Telephone and Telegraph Company or the Exxon Corporation uses its own savings or those of the public to build a new plant and new equipment, it does not show a loss on its annual statement to stockholders, even though its total expenditures on current costs and on capital may have been greater than sales. Instead, expenditures are divided into two kinds, one relating current costs to current income, and the other relegating expenditures on capital goods to an entirely separate capital account. Instead of calling the excess of expenditures a deficit, they call it investment.*

DEBTS AND ASSETS

Can A.T. & T. or Exxon afford to run deficits of the latter kind indefinitely? The answer is yes! To be sure, after a stated number of years, A.T. & T.'s or Exxon's bonds will come due and must be paid back. Perhaps the companies can do that out of their accumulated earnings. Usually, however, when a bond becomes due, a corporation issues *new* bonds equal in value to the old ones. It then sells the new bonds and uses the new money it raises to pay off its old bondholders.

Many big corporations such as Exxon or A.T. & T. do, in fact, continuously "refund" their bond issues, paying off old bonds with new ones, and never paying back their indebtedness as a whole. A.T. & T., for instance, actually increased its total indebtedness almost ten-fold between 1929 and 1980. Exxon ran up its debt from $170.1 million in 1929 to over $4 billion in 1980. And the credit rating of both companies today is as good as, or better than, it was in 1929.

GOVERNMENT DEFICITS

Can government, like business, borrow "indefinitely"? The question is important enough to warrant a careful answer. Hence, let us begin by comparing government borrowing and business borrowing.

One difference that springs quickly to mind is that businesses borrow in order to acquire productive assets. That is, matching the new claims on the busi-

*Investment does not *require* a deficit, since it can be financed out of current profits. But many expanding companies do spend more money on current and capital account than they take in through sales, and thereby incur a deficit for at least a part of their investment.

ness sector is additional real wealth that will provide for larger output. From this additional wealth, business will also receive the income to pay interest on its debt or dividends on its stock. But what of the government? Where are its productive assets?

We have already noted that the government budget includes dams, roads, housing projects, and many other items that might be classified as assets. During the 1960s, federal expenditures for such civil construction projects averaged about $5 billion a year. Thus the total addition to the gross public debt during the 1960s (it rose from roughly $240 billion in 1960 to $301 billion in 1969) could be construed as merely the financial counterpart of the creation of public assets.

Why is it not so considered? Mainly because, as we have seen, the peculiar character of public expenditure leads us to lump together all public spending, regardless of kind. In many European countries, however, public capital expenditures are sharply differentiated from public current expenditures. If we had such a system, the government's deficit on capital account could then be viewed as the public equivalent of business's deficit on capital account. Such a change might considerably improve the rationality of much discussion concerning the government's deficit.

SALES VS. TAXES

But there is still a difference. Private capital enhances the earning capacity of a private business, whereas most public capital, save for such assets as toll roads, does not make money for the public sector. Does this constitute a meaningful distinction?

We can understand, of course, why an individual business insists that its investment must be profitable. The actual money that the business will pay out in the course of making an investment will almost surely not return to the business that spent it. A shirt manufacturer, for instance, who invests in a new factory cannot hope that the builders of that factory will spend all their wages on the firm's shirts. The manufacturer knows that the money spent through investment will soon be dissipated throughout the economy and that even strenuous selling efforts will only recapture part of it.

Not so with a national government, however. Its income does not come from sales but from taxes, and those taxes reflect the general level of income of the country. Thus any and all money that government lays out, just because it enters the general stream of incomes, redounds to the taxing capacity or, we might say, the "earning capacity" of government.

Under today's normal conditions, the government will recover about half or a little more of its expenditure.* But in any event, note that the government does not lose its money in the way that a business does. Whatever goes into the income stream is always *available* to the government as a source of taxes; whereas

*We can make a rough estimate of the multiplier effect of additional public expenditure as 2 and of the share of an additional dollar of GNP going to federal taxes as about ⅓ (see p. 206). Thus $1 of public spending will create $2 of GNP, of which 67¢ will go back to the federal government.

whatever goes into the income stream is not necessarily available to any single business as a source of sales.

This reasoning helps us understand why federal finance is different from state and local government finance. An expenditure made by New York City or New York State is apt to be respent in many other areas of the country. Thus taxable incomes in New York will not, in all probability, rise to match local spending. As a result, *state and local governments must look on their finances much as an individual business does.* The power of full fiscal recapture belongs solely to the federal government.

INTERNAL AND EXTERNAL DEBTS

This difference between the limited powers of recoupment of a single firm and the relatively limitless powers of a national government lies at the heart of the basic difference between business and government deficit spending. It helps us understand why the government has a capacity for financial operation that is inherently of a far higher order of magnitude than that of business. We can sum up this fundamental difference in the contrast between the *externality of business debts* and the *internality of national government debts.*

What do we mean by the externality of business debts? We simply mean that business firms owe their debts to someone distinct from themselves—someone over whom they have no control—whether this be bondholders or the bank from which they borrowed. Thus, to service or to pay back its debts, business must transfer funds from its own possession into the possession of outsiders. If this transfer cannot be made, if a business does not have the funds to pay its bondholders or its bank, it will go bankrupt.

The government is in a radically different position. Its bondholders, banks, and other people or institutions to whom it owes its debts belong to the same community as that whence it extracts its receipts. In other words, the government does not have to transfer its funds to an outside group to pay its bonds. It transfers them, instead, from some members of the national community over which it has legal powers (taxpayers) to other members of the *same* community (bondholders). The contrast is much the same as that between a family that owes a debt to another family, and a family in which the husband has borrowed money from his wife; or again between a firm that owes money to another, and a firm in which one branch has borrowed money from another. **Internal debts do not drain the resources of one community into another, but merely redistribute the claims among members of the same community.**

To help bring home the point, imagine that you and your roommate exchange $1,000 IOUs. Each of you now has a $1,000 asset (an IOU from the other person) but each of you also has a $1,000 liability (the IOU each owes the other). The total debt of the room is now $2,000. But is your room richer or poorer, or is any individual in the room richer or poorer? The answer is obviously no. No one is better or worse off than before. And what happens if you now each pay off your IOUs? Once again no one is richer or poorer than before. The same thing is true at the national level. The national debt makes us neither richer nor poorer, since we (as taxpayers) owe it to ourselves (as bondholders).

THE POWER TO PRINT MONEY

Ultimately the federal government has the power to incur an unlimited deficit because it has the power to print money. If a local government such as New York City incurs too much debt, investors lose confidence in the ability of the city to buy back its bonds when they come due. Therefore they will refuse to buy the city bonds and the municipality can go bankrupt.

This cannot happen to the federal government because by constitutional authority it has the power to create money. It could, therefore, simply print up the money needed to buy back its own obligations!

Needless to say, this is a cure that might well be worse than the disease. We hear about "rolling the printing presses" as the worst symptom of inflation. If the government actually began printing money wholesale to buy its own bonds, there would be a flight from the currency—maybe from the country!—and the spectre of a runaway inflation might become a reality. We will discuss printing money again in Chapter 19. But we must recognize that the *unused* power of the printing press still reassures investors that they will never face default on a federal bond. It is odd, isn't it: The power to print money is the most important safeguard for government bonds—as long as it isn't used!

PROBLEMS OF GOVERNMENT SPENDING

We have spent enough time in gaining an understanding of the question of government deficit. It is time to return to the central question of this chapter—using the public sector as a means of keeping the economy moving ahead.

DEFICITS AND INFLATION

Again the pressing question is raised: Isn't government spending inflationary? We are now close enough to an overall understanding of macroeconomics so that we can see why economists agree that the answer is: sometimes yes, sometimes no. The reason is that government spending in itself is really no different from any other kind of spending. The check you receive from the Internal Revenue Service goes into your pocket—and out of it—exactly the same way as does the check you receive from your employer. Somewhat as in the case of the multiplier, we must see that a government *expenditure* in and of itself, whether financed by taxes or borrowing, is no different from a private expenditure which may be financed by selling output or by borrowing money from the public.

Then what could make government spending inflationary? Two things:

1. If government spending is financed by borrowing from the Federal Reserve system, this may create monetary pressures that have inflationary consequences. We will have to defer consideration of this until we get to Chapters 19 and 31.

2. If government spending adds to total national expenditure at a time when there is already too much consumer and business spending, the added flow of public spending will certainly send up prices. Government spending to buy war supplies is a typical example of this.

Therefore government spending *can* be inflationary in certain cases. But there are also clear cases where it will not be inflationary. If there is a large amount of slack in the economy—unemployed men and women and unused equipment—more expenditure of any kind will be welcome, and prices are not likely to rise appreciably.

OTHER PROBLEMS: REDISTRIBUTION

We will be back to inflation again many times. Here we still want to clear up the economics of the public sector. And that requires us to take brief notice of two other problems that are brought by public spending.

One of these problems is that the people or institutions from whom taxes are collected are not always exactly the same people and institutions to whom interest is paid, so that servicing a government debt often poses problems of *redistribution of income.* For instance, if all government bonds were owned by rich people and if all government taxation were regressive (i.e., proportionately heavier on low incomes), then servicing a government debt would mean transferring income from the poor to the rich. Considerations of equity aside, this would also probably involve distributing income from spenders to savers and would thereby intensify the problem of closing the savings gap.

In addition, a debt that a government owes to foreign citizens is *not* an internal debt. It is exactly like a debt that a corporation owes to an outside public, and it can involve payments that can cripple a nation. Do not forget that the internality of debts applies only to *national* debts held as bonds by members of the same community of people whose incomes contribute to government revenues. About 20 percent of the U.S. debt is held by foreigners.

THE DISCOURAGEMENT OF PRIVATE SPENDING

Finally we must pay heed to one more problem. A rising public debt may cause indirect but nonetheless serious harm if it discourages private investment.

This could be a very real cost of government debts, were such a reaction to be widespread and long-lasting. It may well be (we are not sure) that the long drawn out and never entirely successful recovery from the Great Depression was caused, to a considerable extent, by the adverse psychological impact of government deficit spending on business investment intentions. Business did not understand deficit spending and interpreted it either as the entering wedge of socialism (instead of a crash program to save capitalism) or as a wasteful and harebrained economic scheme. To make matters worse, the amount of the government deficit (at its peak $4 billion), while large enough to frighten the business community, was not big enough to begin to exert an effective leverage on total demand, particularly under conditions of widespread unemployment and financial catastrophe.

Today, however, it is much less likely that deficit spending would be attended by a drop in private spending. A great deal that was new and frightening in thought and practice in the 1930s is today well-understood and tested. World War II was, after all, an immense laboratory demonstration of what public spending could do for GNP. The experience of recent years gives good reason to believe that deficit spending does not cause a significant slowdown in private investment expenditure: There has been no statistical evidence that federal spending has discouraged or **crowded out** private investment.

DEMAND MANAGEMENT

We have spent a lot of time discussing the problems of the public sector. Now we shall familiarize ourselves with the possibilities of using that sector to stabilize, or to spur on, the economy.

PUBLIC PROPENSITIES

We shall start by discovering something surprising about public spending. Despite the fact that it is politically determined, public spending reveals propensities, much like private spending.

The reason for these propensities is that both government income and government outgo are closely tied to private activity. Government receipts are derived in the main from taxes, and taxes—direct or indirect—tend to reflect the trend of business and personal income. If fact, we can generalize about tax payments in much the same fashion as we can about consumption, describing them as a predictable function of GNP. To be sure, this assumes that tax *rates* do not change. But since rates change only infrequently, we can draw up a general schedule that relates tax receipts and the level of GNP. The schedule will show not only that taxes rise as GNP rises, but that they rise *faster* than GNP.

Why faster? Largely because of the progressive structure of the federal income tax. As household and business incomes rise to higher levels, the percentage "bite" of income tax increases. Thus as incomes rise, tax liabilities rise even more. Conversely, the tax bite works downward in the opposite way. As incomes fall, taxes fall even faster, since households or businesses with lowered incomes find themselves in a less steep tax bracket.

PERSONAL DEBTS AND PUBLIC DEBTS

In view of the fact that our national debt today figures out to approximately $2,880 for every man, woman, and child, it is not surprising that we frequently hear appeals to "common sense," telling us how much better we would be without this debt, and how our grandchildren will groan under its weight.

Is this true? We have already discussed the fact that internal debts are different from external debts, but let us press the point home from a different vantage point. Suppose we decided that we would pay off the debt. This would mean that our government bonds would be redeemed for cash. To get the cash, we would have to tax ourselves (unless we wanted to roll the printing presses), so that what we would really be doing would be transferring money from taxpayers to bondholders.

Would that be a net gain for the nation? Consider the typical holder of a government bond—a family, a bank, or a corporation. It now holds the world's safest and most readily sold paper asset from which a regular income is obtained. After our debt is redeemed, our families, banks, and corporations will have two choices: (1) They can hold cash and get *no* income, or (2) they can invest in other securities that are slightly *less* safe. Are these investors better off? As for our grandchildren, it is true that if we pay off the debt they will not have to carry its weight. But to offset that, neither will they be carried by the comfortable government bonds they would otherwise have inherited. They will also be relieved from paying taxes to meet the interest on the debt. Alas, they will be relieved as well of the pleasure of depositing the green Treasury checks for interest payments that used to arrive twice a year.

Government expenditures also show certain propensities, which is to say some government spending is also functionally related to the level of GNP. A number of government programs are directly correlated to the level of economic activity in such a way that spending *decreases* as GNP *increases*, and vice versa. For instance, unemployment benefits are naturally higher when GNP is low or falling. Many payments such as food stamps, aid to dependent children, or various welfare programs are highly sensitive to unemployment: in 1976, for example, when unemployment neared 9 percent, such outlays were $20 billion higher than if unemployment had been 5 percent. So, too, disbursements to farmers under various agricultural programs vary inversely with good and bad crop years.

AUTOMATIC STABILIZERS

All these automatic effects taken together are called the *automatic stabilizers* or the *built-in stabilizers* of the economy. What they add up to is an automatic government counterbalance to the private sector. As GNP falls because private spending is insufficient, taxes decline even faster and public expenditures grow, thereby automatically causing the government sector to offset the private sector to some extent. In similar fashion, as GNP rises, taxes tend to rise even faster and public expenditures decline, thereby causing the government sector to act as a brake.

The public sector therefore acts as an automatic compensator, even without direct action to alter tax or expenditure levels, pumping out more public demand when private demand is slowing, and curbing public demand when private demand is brisk.

How effective are the built-in stabilizers? It is estimated that the increase in transfer payments plus the reduction in taxes offset about 35¢ of each dollar of original decline in spending. Here is how this works. Suppose that private investment were to fall by $10 billion. If there were no stabilizers, household spending might fall by another $10 billion (the multiplier effect), causing a total decline of $20 billion in incomes.

The action of the stabilizers, however, will prevent the full force of this fall. First, the reduction in incomes of both households and firms will lower their tax liabilities. Since taxes take about 35¢ from each dollar, the initial drop of $10 billion in incomes will reduce tax liabilities by about $3.5 billion. Most of this—let us say $3 billion—is likely to be spent. Meanwhile some public expenditures for unemployment insurance and farm payments will rise, pumping out perhaps $1 billion into the consumption sector, all of which we assume to be spent by its recipients.

Thus, the incomes of firms and households, having originally fallen by $10 billion, will be offset by roughly $4 billion—$1 billion in additional transfer incomes and $3 billion in income spent by households because their taxes are lower. As a result, the decline in expenditure will be reduced from $10 billion to about $6 billion (actually $6.5 billion, according to the calculations of the Council of Economic Advisers).

This is certainly an improvement over a situation with no stabilizers. Yet if the drop in investment is not to bring about some fall in GNP, it will have to be *fully* compensated by an equivalent increase in government spending or by a fall in taxes large enough to induce an equivalent amount of private spending. This will require public action more vigorous than that brought about automatically. Indeed, it requires that the government take on a task very different from any we have heretofore studied, the task of *demand management,* or acting as the *deliberate* balancing mechanism of the economy.

FISCAL VS. MONETARY POLICY

It has two basic alternatives: fiscal and monetary policy. We will have to defer a consideration of the second alternative until a later chapter. **Here we will focus on fiscal policy, by which we mean two courses of action:**

1. **increasing or decreasing government spending;**
2. **raising or lowering taxes.**

We have already looked into the mechanics of the first option in Figure 15.2, where we showed that government expenditure fills a demand gap exactly like private expenditure. It follows that a decrease in government spending will also create a decrease in final demand, just as a drop in the spending of any other sector.

Our diagram did not show the direct effect of tax changes simply because it is difficult to draw such a diagram clearly. But it is not difficult to understand the effect of a tax change. When the government lowers taxes it diminishes the transfer of income from households or firms into the public sector. Households and firms therefore have more income to spend. Conversely, in raising taxes a government withdraws spending power from households and firms. As a result, we can expect that private spending will fall.

FULL EMPLOYMENT BUDGETS

The direct effects of expenditures and taxes are thus easy to picture, and the rule for demand management should be simple: Establish a government budget that will have an expansionary influence when GNP is too low and a restraining influence when it is too high; and balance the budget when GNP is at desired levels.

But this seemingly obvious guideline is not as simple as it looks. Suppose that we are suffering from mild unemployment and the President's advisers accordingly recommend a level of expenditure that, combined with existing tax rates, would produce a small deficit. Isn't this following the proper guide?

The answer is: not necessarily. For if we calculate the flow of tax receipts that the government would be receiving *if we were operating at full employment,* the planned level of expenditure may in fact be so small that it would not even produce a neutral budget, but a deflationary one at the *desired* level of GNP! A glance at Figure 15.3 shows that this can indeed be the case. In 1974, for example, the actual budget was in substantial deficit, as the colored line shows. But if we calculate the budget *at full employment levels* of tax receipts, we find that our flow of expenditure was far too short of the levels needed to spend our receipts *at that level.* As the black line shows, our flows of taxes and expenditures at full employment would have given us a surplus! Therefore the $12 billion deficit was too little to give us the stimulus we needed to reach full employment. A true full-employment budget would have raised expenditures (or cut taxes) to bring the economy up to a high level of operation.

Paradoxically, although this would have required more expenditures or a

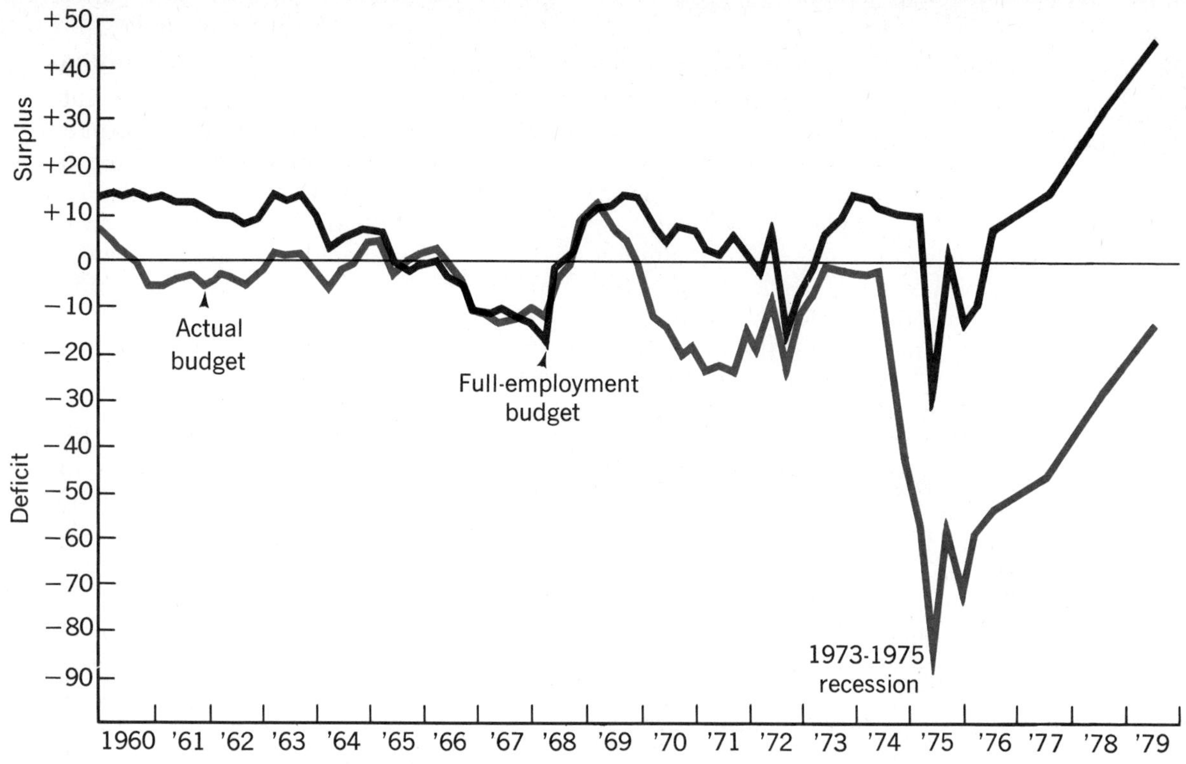

FIGURE 15.3 FULL EMPLOYMENT AND ACTUAL BUDGET DEFICITS

lower tax rate, the effect at full employment might have been a government budget that was balanced, rather than one in deficit.

In other words, wise fiscal policy—whether of stimulus or restraint—must be figured on a basis of full employment *because that is the only way to get us there.*

TAX CUTS VS. EXPENDITURES

Which of the two direct methods of managing demand—taxes or spending—is preferable? The question basically asks us which we need more: public goods or private goods. But there are a number of technical economic criteria that we must also bear in mind.

First, tax cuts and expenditures tend to favor different groups. Tax cuts benefit those who pay taxes, and expenditures benefit those who receive them. This simple fact reveals a good deal about the political and economic pros and cons of each method. Tax cuts are of little direct benefit to poor families whose incomes are so low that they pay little or no income taxes. Expenditure programs *can* benefit these disadvantaged groups or areas—for example, by slum clearance in specific cities, training programs, or simply higher welfare payments. Expenditure programs can also help special groups, such as military or road contractors, or middle-income families who usually benefit from housing programs.

The difference, then, is that tax programs have a widespread impact, whereas expenditure programs tend to have a concentrated impact: **Tax cuts or increases are diffused across the economy, exerting their influences on different income strata, whereas expenditure programs are often concentrated geograph-**

ically or occupationally. (Some expenditure programs, such as Social Security or medical aid, can have a broad "horizontal effect" as well.)

Second, expenditure programs tend to be more reliable as a means of increasing demand, whereas tax programs tend to be effective in decreasing demand. The reason is clear enough. If the government wishes to increase final demand and chooses to lower taxes, it makes possible a higher level of private spending, but there is no guarantee that firms or households will in fact spend all their tax savings. Indeed, the marginal propensity to consume leads us to be quite certain that firms and households will not spend all their tax reductions, at least for a time. Thus if the government wants to increase demand by say $7 billion, it may have to cut taxes by about $10 billion.

On the other hand, tax increases are a very reliable method of decreasing demand. Individuals or firms *can* "defy" tax increases and maintain their former level of spending by going out and borrowing money or by spending their savings, but it is unlikely they will do so. If the government tries to hold back total demand by cutting its own expenditure programs, however, there is the chance that firms and individuals will undo the government's effort to cut demand by borrowing and spending more themselves.

There is no magic formula that will enable us to declare once and for all what policy is best for demand management. It is often impossible to raise taxes for political reasons, in which case a decrease in expenditures is certainly the next best way to keep total demand from rising too fast. So, too, it may be impossible to push through a program of public expenditure because public opinion or congressional tempers are opposed to spending. In that case, a tax cut is certainly the best available way to keep demand up if the nation is threatened with a recession.*

RESPONSIBILITY OF PUBLIC DEMAND

All these considerations point out how difficult it is to conduct demand management as smoothly in practice as in textbooks. There was a time not too long ago when economists talked rather glibly of "fine-tuning" the economy. That was in the first flush of triumph of the *idea* of managed demand, before the hard realities of full-employment budgets and other problems had been fully faced. Economists are a good deal more modest in their claims these days.

Nevertheless, the basic idea of using the government as a balancing mechanism for the economy remains valid, however difficult it may be to realize the perfect balance in fact. It is valid because the federal sector is the only sector whose operations we can collectively control. There is no way for business to determine how much it should spend as a sector, no way for consumers to concert their activity. More important, even if there were such a way, business and consumer actions might not accord with the needs of the macroeconomy. Only the public sector can act consciously on behalf of the public interest; only the public sector can attempt to reconcile the needs of all groups. However exasperating or inefficient or clumsy public demand management may be, it remains a major accomplishment, both in theory and fact, of twentieth-century economics.

*We should add that there is a school of economic thought that holds futile all efforts to steer the economy away from its self-determined track. We will discuss the ideas of this school of "rational expectations" in Chapter 20.

KEY CONCEPTS

Public sector defined as purchases or expenditures

Public sector can be used to fill demand gaps

Public deficits differ from private debts insofar as governments have tax powers to commandeer receipts, and because government debts may be internal

Deficit spending can but need not be inflationary, especially in a situation of economic slack

Automatic stabilizing characteristics of the public sector

Demand management uses monetary or fiscal policy to influence the level of GNP

Taxes and expenditures have different uses and effects. Both should be calculated on a full employment basis

Through fiscal demand management we influence GNP

LOOKING BACK

1. The public sector is second in size only to consumption. We must learn to distinguish the sector as defined by purchases—a net contribution to GNP—and as defined by expenditures (purchases plus transfers).

2. The public sector can be used to offset a demand gap exactly as the business sector can. The difference is that the public sector can be deliberately used to manage the economy in a way that the private sector cannot.

3. The public sector typically borrows money to finance its gap-filling expenditures. This creates deficits, or an excess of expenditures over tax receipts. These deficits differ from private debts in two ways. First, the government has the power to capture revenues through taxation, which no business can do. Second, a government debt may be internal—owed by the community to itself. This may create problems of redistribution, but the internality of debt avoids the external drain, or burden, that is imposed on all non-national borrowers.

4. Deficit spending may be, but need not be, inflationary. It is inflationary if financed in an inflationary manner, as we shall later see, or if government spending is increased at a time when the economy is already tight. But deficit spending when the economy is slack will mainly add to output, not to price rises.

5. Although the public sector is an independent variable determined by political decision, it has propensity-like attributes. Because tax receipts rise faster (and fall more slowly) than GNP, and because welfare-type expenditures fall when GNP rises and vice versa, the public sector acts as an automatic stabilizer, exerting an influence against the movement of GNP.

6. There are two basic means of demand management—monetary and fiscal policy. We will study monetary policy shortly. Fiscal policy uses government spending or taxing to influence the level of national economic activity. In the choice between taxes and expenditure, advantages lie on both sides. Higher taxes are a better way to hold back GNP than expenditure cuts; higher expenditures are more directly aimed at needy groups. Expenditure increases are a stronger boost to a weak economy. In figuring the appropriate change needed, tax or expenditure, the authorities must calculate on the basis of a full employment situation.

7. The fiscal management of demand is full of difficulties but it is the only manner in which we can attempt to influence the behavior of GNP.

ECONOMIC VOCABULARY

QUESTIONS

1. What are the main differences between the public and private sectors? Are these differences economic or political?
2. Show in a diagram how increased government spending can offset a demand gap. Can you show how decreased taxation can do the same?
3. Show how the automatic stabilizers might work if we had an increase of investment of $20 billion and the multiplier were two, and if the increase in taxes and the *decrease* public expenditure associated with the rise in investment were $3 billion and $1 billion respectively.
4. If the government is going to go into debt, does it matter whether it spends money for roads or for relief? For education or weapons? Is there a connection between the economic effects of government spending and the welfare effects? How about the various kinds of things we could buy with $10 billion of private investment?
5. Why is the internality of debts so important?
6. Could you explain to a conservative that government spending was (a) safe and (b) not "socialistic"? Or do you think that it is not safe and that it *is* socialistic? All government spending?

AN EXTRA WORD ABOUT

STATE AND LOCAL FINANCES

State and local finances are very sensitive to the condition of the economy. When national output goes down, state and local revenues (in real terms) also decline. Occasionally a state goes up against the national trend, but usually a national slowdown pulls down all state and local revenues. As household incomes fall, state and local income taxes decline. As household spending weakens, sales tax receipts fall. As employment worsens, revenues from payroll taxes fall off. All this results in pressure to cut back state and local budgets. And this, in turn, adds its undertow to the national picture, giving the recession additional force.

One suggested remedy for this built-in weakness of state and local finance is *countercyclical revenue sharing.* This remedy would automatically authorize federal grants-in-aid to state and local governments when times were bad. Such grants would be sufficiently large to maintain state and local spending at the levels they would have reached if the recession had not occurred. This would allow state and local governments to make long-range plans without having to worry about short-run fluctuations in their revenues, and it would also prevent these governments from inadvertently worsening a national recession by cutting back on their own expenditures.

A difficulty in countercyclical revenue sharing lies in different regional growth rates. Incomes and output have been growing faster in the West and South, for example, than in the Midwest or Northeast. This uneven pace has been going on for some years, but has recently been exaggerated by high energy prices. The slower-growing Northeast and Midwest have to use expensive oil, whereas the faster-growing South and West have available to them the relatively cheaper energy source of natural gas.

As a result, the lucky states in high-growth regions may show budget surpluses when the unlucky states in slow-growth regions show deficits. Countercyclical revenue sharing would then have to make the difficult choice of whether or not to seek to equalize differences or to ignore them.

TABLE 15.2 RATIO OF FEDERAL EXPENDITURES TO FEDERAL TAX COLLECTIONS, 1975

Northeast	.86
Midwest	.76
South	1.14
West	1.20

Source: *National Journal,* June 26, 1976, p. 881.

There is a natural tendency to say "Ignore them," because such differences hardly seem a matter of federal concern. But a second look shows us that the matter is not as simple as this. For the federal government itself is a partial cause of some of these very differences! When we look at federal individual income taxes received and grants-in-aid paid out in different areas, it is clear that the federal government is taking net spending power out of the slow-growing Northeast and Midwest and injecting it in the fast-growing South and West.

Thus the federal government is contributing to the differences in growth rates, although we should stress that this is only one cause of the differences, and certainly not the main one.

What should the federal government do? Beginning with Franklin Roosevelt, it has followed a deliberate policy of trying to equalize regional differentials. TVA is probably the most well-known effort to aid one particular region, but actually nearly all federal programs are structured to give more help to low-income states than to high-income ones. If the South, for example, has been, and still is, favored in federal policy it is because, despite its rapid growth, its average family income remains below that of the Northeast, $15,657 compared to $17,680 in 1978.

Most people favor this federal equalizing role. The question today is whether, and to what degree, the policy should now be extended within states to localities. New York City, for example, lies in the middle of one of the richest regions in the nation, but it is a pocket of serious poverty. If the federal government decides that it wants to help low-income localities, as well as low-income states, how should this be done? By federalizing welfare? By relieving localities of hospital expenses through federal health insurance? By giving federal aid to primary education in low-income cities? These are some of the suggestions that have been put forth. None of them is without problems. But at issue is the basic question whether we want the federal government to play the same role with localities that it has long played with regions. Once that issue is clarified, the problems will begin to take care of themselves.

THE NEW YORK CITY DEBT CRISIS

New York City's 1976 debt crisis was a vivid illustration of how even very large and seemingly rich government institutions *that are not national in scope* have limits to the amount of deficit finance they can safely undertake. Because any resident can leave New York, all the city's debt is potentially external to it.

As Table 15.3 shows, New York City's debt had been building up for a long period. But over most of these years its bonds were rated very highly by various companies, such as Standard and Poor's, that give ratings (risk designations) to private and public bonds. We can also see that the debt build-up accelerated after 1970, partly the consequence of financially imprudent actions on the part of New York City officials, partly the result of the 1974–1975 recession that hit many northeastern cities hard.

To pay its bills, the city had to borrow larger and larger sums at the very time that the federal government had created a very tight situation in the money markets—a "credit crunch"—as part of its efforts to curb inflation. In a tight-money period, everyone has trouble borrowing, and banks and other lenders reexamine their credit applicants to determine who should be first in line and who should be last.

In this reexamination, New York City fared very badly. Its bond ratings suddenly fell. Overnight it became apparent to everyone that its debt and deficit had reached levels that could not be sustained in the long run. As a result, New York suddenly found itself unable to borrow. Not only was no one willing to lend funds to cover its current deficit, which had reached a staggering $700 million for the year 1974, but banks or other lenders would not even lend the city money to finance its outstanding debt. That is, the normal process of rolling over the debt by replacing bonds that had become due with new bonds was impossible.

What were the city's options at this point? All were unpleasant. One was to slash expenditures to the point at which the deficit would be eliminated, and revenues would cover debt repayments. This would have required so drastic a cut in expenditures (something on the order of 25 percent) that city officials

TABLE 15.3 NEW YORK CITY'S DEBT ($ BILLIONS)

1950	$ 3
1960	6
1970	8
1974	14
1976	16

feared the city could not be safely operated—too few police, firemen, sanitation workers, teachers.

Another option was to raise taxes by the amount needed to cover debt repayment. There were two problems here. First, this course would have required additional taxing powers for the city, which the state legislature was loathe to hand over. Second, city taxes, already among the highest in the nation, would have soared to such astronomical levels that many taxpayers would have voted with their feet, by moving out of the city to the suburbs or to neighboring states.

A third option was to default on debt repayments—simply not to honor the old bonds that came due. Here the difficulties were obvious. A default would still have left the city short of funds to cover its current deficit. And, of course, a default would have terribly damaged its prospects for selling bonds in the future. Once burned, twice shy in the bond market. Then, too, many worried lest a default in New York's bonds might not set off a series of defaults in other municipal bonds, giving rise to a serious panic in the capital markets.

Last was the hope that the federal government would save the situation, and city officials pleaded with the Ford administration to add a federal guarantee to city bonds, thereby assuring their saleability, or for outright federal loans or grants to cover the deficit. But the Ford administration was not eager to rescue the city on easy terms. It felt that the city was itself responsible for much of its financial plight and that a rescue operation for New York could lead to requests from many other hard-pressed cities.

What happened in the end? All options were used to some extent. The city did cut its services. City taxes were raised. Default was technically avoided, but holders of city bonds were forced to exchange their securities for long-term bonds that carried lower interest rates. And the federal government made some necessary loans.

As part of the rescue operation, city finances were placed under the scrutiny of a committee of state, federal, and private representatives who monitor its union contracts and other expenditures, its taxes, and its budgets. Since that time of crisis the city has staggered along, managing to postpone a second crisis, but not really achieving financial solidity. Other cities, such as Cleveland, have experienced similar or even more drastic financial crunches. It is likely that many cities are going to be financially troubled for a long time, unless the federal government relieves them of burdens such as welfare or local hospital costs.

Is it all a cautionary tale, warning us of the profligacy of local governments and the shortsightedness of politicians? To some extent it is because the sins of both commission and omission by various city mayors have been great. But it is not *just* that. While New York, Newark, Detroit, and Cleveland have suffered, Houston, Dallas, and the sun-belt cities in general have prospered. Is this because their politicians are more honest, their government structures more efficient? More likely it is because these cities are the recipients of a movement of labor and capital away from the frost belt to sunnier climes. The eastern cities are located in a region which is experiencing a relative decline. Expenses are high because many of these cities were pioneers in offering social services, but today their revenues are dwindling. They are in for a long season of tribulation unless the federal government acts to mitigate this drift.

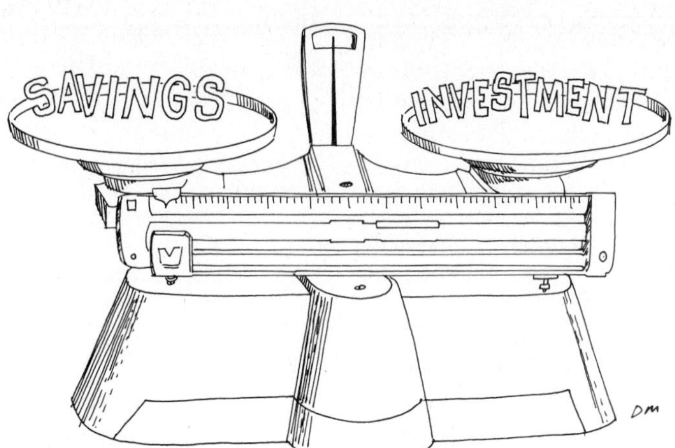

Chapter 16 THE DETERMINATION OF GNP

A LOOK AHEAD

We have gradually assembled the parts of the puzzle. We now have a good idea of the way that the various sectors behave and interact. It remains only to piece them together to get a picture of how GNP is determined. That is what we do in this chapter.

(1) We will clarify the idea of a supply curve for GNP—a curve that will establish the costs of producing a larger or smaller output within our production possibility frontier.

(2) We will add a demand curve for GNP—a curve that will show how much output the sectors will want to buy at different levels of utilization.

(3) Putting the curves together will give us an equilibrium GNP. We will take a look at how this GNP can move upward or downward as the sectors alter their activity.

We have reached the destination toward which we have been traveling for several chapters. We are finally in a position to understand how the forces of supply and demand determine the actual level of GNP that confronts us in daily life—"the state of the economy" that affects our employment prospects, our immediate well-being, our satisfaction or dissatisfaction with the way things are going.

SUPPLY AND DEMAND IN MACRO

As we have begun to see, the short-run level of GNP is determined by the outcome of two opposing tendencies of supply and demand, just as the level of prices and quantities in a marketplace is set by the counterplay of these forces. **In fact, the opposition of supply and demand plays just as central a role in macroeconomics as in microeconomics. The crucial difference is that in macroeconomics we talk of supply and demand in relation to GNP, whereas in microeconomics we speak of them mainly in relation to price.**

THE UTILIZATION OF OUR POTENTIAL

What determines the supply of GNP? For the long run, the answer hinges on the quantity and quality of our inputs, a question we looked into in Chapter 10. These inputs determine the limits of our productive power—the production possibility frontiers that constrain our capacity to produce.

But in the short run our supply of GNP depends on how much of our production potential we actually use. Here we come up against the impossibility of going beyond the production possibility curve. **Therefore it is the degree of utilization of our production capacity—the extent to which we achieve full employment of human and material capital—that determines how close we come to the production frontier.**

What will we use as supply and demand curves to establish where that point will be? The demand curve is easy to imagine—it will be determined by the amount of expenditure the community generates at different levels of employment and utilization. Obviously, the more fully we employ our manpower, the more incomes individuals will have and the more output they will want. We shall shortly see how the demand for output can be represented in graphic form.

But what about the supply of output? Here we want to show how the value of output will change as we use more or less of our available productive power. The supply curve will show how much output costs at different levels of utilization. **The supply curve will therefore relate output and costs, and the demand curve will relate output and expenditure.**

THE SUPPLY CURVE OF INCOME

What does such a supply curve look like? **Here we make use of an identity that we learned in Chapter 11. Incomes and output are always the same. The amount of income made available to the community must rise, dollar for dollar, with the amount of production, because every dollar going into production must become income to some individual or institution.**

Our supply curve must show this identity, and Figure 16.1 makes clear that the resulting curve will be a 45° line. Notice that $OX = OY$, $OX' = OY'$, and so on. Notice also that this supply curve is fixed, in that the relation between in-

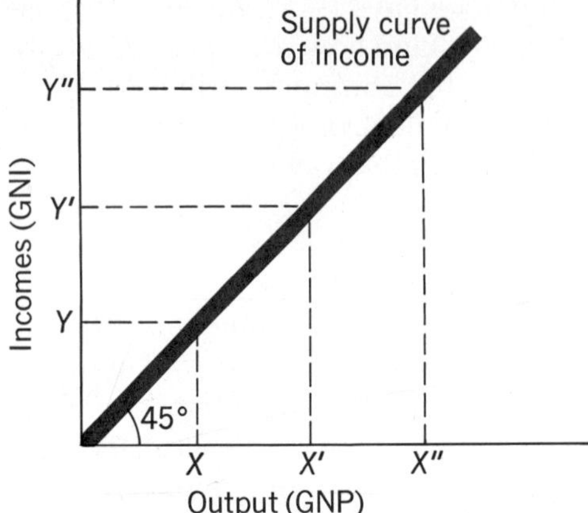

FIGURE 16.1 SUPPLY CURVE OF INCOME

The supply curve of income makes use of the identity between output ($C+I+G+X$) and income ($F+T+D$). Every unit of output generates incomes that exactly match its costs. This identity gives rise to a 45° line, which lies equidistant between the two axes at all points.

These panels show the amounts of spending that will take place in each sector (and then the three combined) as the degree of utilization increases. Spending rises in the household sector because of the propensity to consume. The accelerator and various governmental "propensities" give a slight positive slope to spending in those sectors as well.

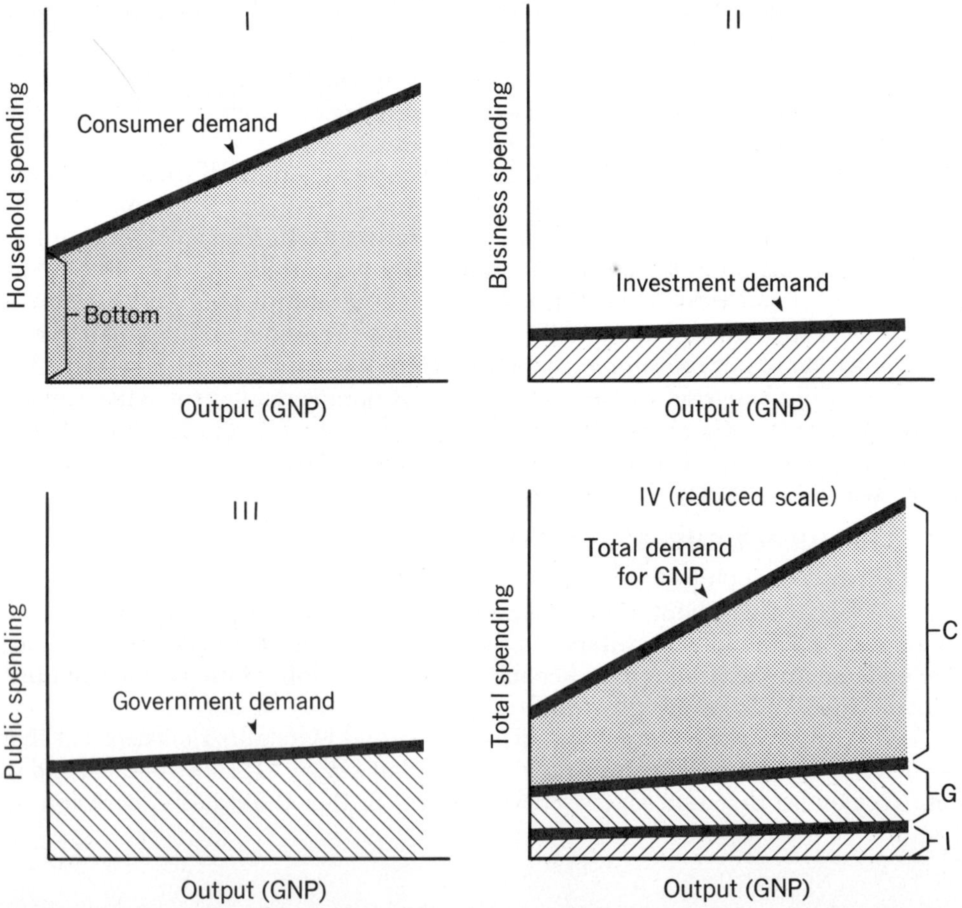

I
Household spending
Consumer demand
Bottom
Output (GNP)

II
Business spending
Investment demand
Output (GNP)

III
Public spending
Government demand
Output (GNP)

IV (reduced scale)
Total spending
Total demand for GNP
C
G
I
Output (GNP)

FIGURE 16.2 THE DEMAND FOR GNP

Here the supply curve shows the amount of income associated with different amounts of output. They are identical. The demand curve shows the amount of spending at different levels of output. Where spending equals income we have an equilibrium level of GNP.

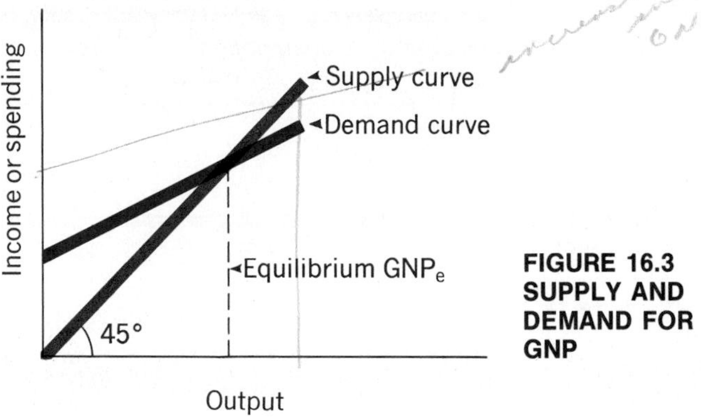

FIGURE 16.3 SUPPLY AND DEMAND FOR GNP

comes (GNI) and output (GNP) is always the same—identical. Again, for each dollar that we increase output, we add a dollar to income. Thus the supply of income is identical with the value of output.

DEMAND CURVE FOR GNP

Now what about the demand for GNP? **We already know that the demand curve will show us the amount of spending (demand for output) that will be generated by the community as output rises from zero to the full utilization of existing resources.**

Of course such a curve will slope upward. In Figure 16.2 we see why this is so. Panels I through IV sum up the demand of consumption, investment, and government. *They show that total spending will rise as output rises: Here is our upward sloping demand curve.*

It now remains only to put the demand and supply curves together, as in Figure 16.3.

This equilibrium shows us the money value of GNP brought about by the flow of demand against supply. It might, for example, indicate that this value of GNP was $1.5 trillion. It does *not* tell us whether $1.5 trillion is a *good* size for GNP, any more than a price of $20 for a commodity tells us whether that is a good or bad price from the viewpint of buyers, producers, or the economy at large. We shall return to this critical point at the end of our chapter.

ANOTHER VIEW OF EQUILIBRIUM

SAVING AND INVESTMENT

Equilibrium is always a complicated subject to master, so let us fix the matter in our minds by going over the problem once more. Suppose that by means of a questionnaire we are going to predict the level of GNP for an island community. To simplify our task, we will ignore government and exports, so that we can concentrate solely on consumption, saving, and investment.

We begin by interrogating the island's business community about their intentions for next year's investment. Now we know that some investment will be induced and that, therefore, investment will partly be a result of the island's

TABLE 16.1

Income	Consumption	Saving	Investment
	(In millions)		
$100	$75	$25	$30
110	80	30	30
120	85	35	30

The interplay of saving and investment reveals the equilibrium output just as schedules of supply and demand show an equilibrium price.

level of income; but again for simplification, we assume that businesses have laid their plans for next year. They tell us they intend to spend $30 million for new housing, plant, equipment, and other capital goods.

Next, our team of pollsters approaches a carefully selected sample of the island's householders and asks them what their consumption and savings plans are for the coming year. Here the answer will be a bit disconcerting. Reflecting on their past experience, our householders will reply: "We can't say for sure. We'd *like* to spend such-and-such an amount and save the rest, but really it depends on what our incomes will be." Our poll, in other words, will have to make inquiries about different possibilities that reflect the island's propensity to consume.

Now we tabulate our results, and find that we have the schedule shown in Table 16.1.

INTERPLAY OF SAVING AND INVESTMENT

If we look at the last two columns of Table 16.1, those for saving and investment, we can see a powerful cross play that will characterize our model economy at different levels of income, for the forces of investment and saving will not be in balance at all levels. At some levels, the propensity to save will outrun the act of purposeful investment; at others, the motivation to save will be less than the investment expenditure made by business firms. In fact, our island model shows that at only one level of income—$110 million—will the saving and investment schedules coincide.

What does it mean when intended savings are greater than the flow of intended investment? It means that people are *trying* to save out of their given incomes a larger amount than business is willing to invest. Now if we think back to the exposition of the economy in a circular flow, it will be clear what the result must be. The economy cannot maintain a closed circuit of income and expenditure if savings are larger than investment. This will simply give rise to a demand gap, the repercussions of which we have already explored.

But a similar lack of equilibrium results if intended savings are less than intended investment expenditure (or if investment spending is greater than the propensity to save). Now business will be pumping out more than enough to offset the savings gap. The additional expenditures, over and above those that compensate for saving, will flow into the economy to create new incomes—and out of those new incomes, new savings.

Income and output will be stable, in other words, only when the flow of intended investment just compensates for the flow of intended saving. Investment and saving thus conduct a tug of war around this pivot point, driving the economy upward when intended investment exceeds the flow of intended saving; down-

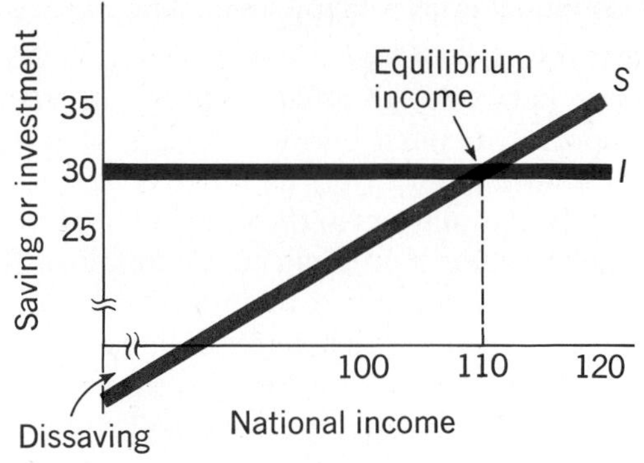

FIGURE 16.4 SAVING AND INVESTMENT

Here we simply put into graphic form the schedules of saving and investment (or leakages and injection). The equilibrium point is easy to see.

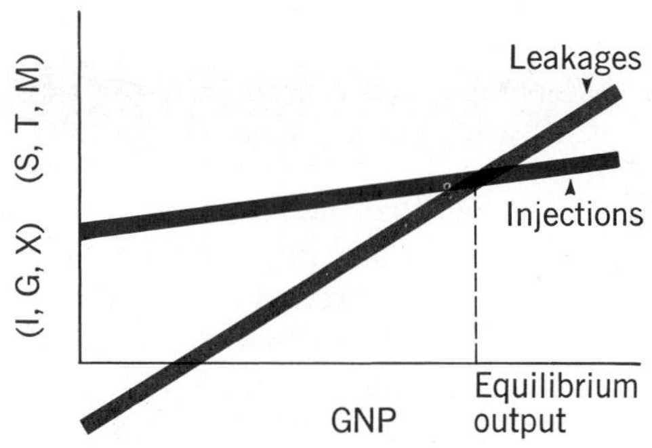

FIGURE 16.5 LEAKAGES AND INJECTIONS

ward when it fails to offset saving. In Figure 16.4 we show this crosscurrent in schematic form. Note that as incomes fall very low, householders will *dissave.*

INJECTIONS VS. LEAKAGES

We can easily make our graph more realistic by adding taxes (T) and imports (M) to savings, and exports (X) and government spending to investment. The vertical axis in Figure 16.5 now shows all *leakages and injections.*

We recall that leakages are any acts, such as savings, increased taxes, profits, or imports that reduce spending. Similarly, injections are any acts, such as investment or higher government spending or rising exports or even a spontaneous jump in consumption, that lead to higher spending. And just to introduce another feature of the real world, we will tilt the injection line upward, on the assumption that induced investment will be an important constituent of total investment. The leakages curve will not be exactly the same shape as the savings curve, but it will reflect the general tendency of savings and imports and taxes to rise with income.

INTENDED AND UNINTENDED S AND I

The careful reader may have noted that we speak of *intended* savings and *intended* investment as the critical forces in establishing equilibrium. This is because there is a formal balance—an identity—between *all* saving and investment (or all leakages and all injections) at every moment in the economy. In the same way, purchases in any market must exactly equal sales at each and every moment, but that does not mean the market is in equilibrium at all times.

Economists distinguish between the formal identity between total saving and investment (or between all leakages and all injections) and the active difference between *intended* savings and investment (or *intended* saving, *intended* imports, *intended* business saving, etc., and *intended* additional expenditures of all kinds).

What matters in the determination of GNP are the *actions* people are taking—actions that lead them to try to save or to invest or that make them struggle to get rid of unintended inventories or to build up desired inventories. These are the kinds of activities that will be moving the economy up and down in the never-ending "quest" for its equilibrium point. The fact that at each moment past savings and investment are identical from the viewpoint of the economy's balance sheet is important only insofar as we are economic accountants. As analysts of the course of future GNP, we concentrate on the inequality of future, intended actions.

THE PARADOX OF THRIFT

The fact that income must always move toward the level where the flows of intended saving and investment are equal leads to one of the most startling—and important—paradoxes of economics. **This is the so-called paradox of thrift, a paradox that tells us that the attempt to increase intended saving may, under certain circumstances, lead to a fall in actual saving.**

The paradox is not difficult for us to understand at this stage. An attempt to save, when it is not matched with an equal willingness to invest or to increase government expenditure, will cause a gap in demand. This means that business will not be getting back enough money to cover costs. Hence, production will be curtailed or costs will be slashed, with the result that incomes will fall. As incomes fall, savings will also fall, because the ability to save will be reduced. Thus, by a chain of activities working their influence on income and output, the effort to *increase* savings may end up with an actual *reduction* of savings.

This frustration of individual desires is perhaps the most striking instance of a common situation in economic life, the incompatibility between some kinds of individual behavior and some collective results. An individual farmer, for instance, may produce a larger crop in order to enjoy a bigger income; but if all farmers produce bigger crops, farm prices are apt to fall so heavily that farmers end up with less income. So, too, a single family may wish to save a very large fraction of its income for reasons of financial prudence; but if all families seek to save a great deal of their incomes, the result—unless investment also rises—will be a fall in expenditure and a common failure to realize savings objectives. The paradox of thrift, in other words, teaches us that the freedom of behavior available to a few individuals cannot always be generalized to all individuals.*

*The paradox of thrift is actually only a subtle instance of a type of faulty reasoning called the fallacy of composition. The fallacy consists of assuming that what is true of the individual case must also be true of all cases combined. The flaw in reasoning lies in our tendency to overlook "side effects" of individual actions (such as the decrease in spending associated with an individual's attempt to save more, or the increase in supply when a farmer markets his larger crop) which may be negligible in isolation but which are very important in the aggregate.

An increase of injections of *AB* leads to a larger increase in GNP, *XY*. This is a graphic presentation of the multiplier. It is important to understand why *AB* creates *XY*. The reason is that the leakage curve slopes. And why does it slope? Because its slope represents the marginal propensity to save. And *that* is the cause of the multiplier.

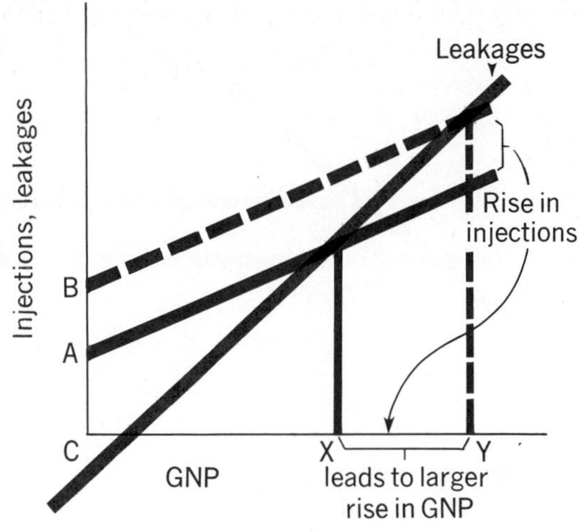

FIGURE 16.6 MULTIPLIER IN GRAPHIC FORM

THE MULTIPLIER

There remains only one part of the jigsaw puzzle to put into place. This is the integration of the *multiplier* into our analysis of the determination of GNP.

We remember that the essential point about the multiplier was that changes in investment, government spending, or exports resulted in larger changes in GNP because the additions to income were respent, creating still more new incomes. Further, we remember that the size of the multiplier effect depended on the marginal propensity to consume, the marginal propensity to tax, and the marginal propensity to buy imports as GNP rises. Now it remains only to show how this basic analytic concept enters into the determination of equilibrium GNP.

Let us begin with the diagram that shows injections and leakages, and let us now draw a new line showing an increase in injections (Figure 16.6). Notice that the increase in GNP is larger than the increase in injections. *This is the multiplier itself in graphic form.*

SLOPE OF THE LEAKAGE CURVE

Both diagrams also show that the relation between the original increase in injections and the resulting increase in GNP depends on the *slope* of the leakage line. Figure 16.7 shows us two different injection-GNP relationships that arise from differing slopes.

Notice how the *same* increase in spending (from *OA* to *OB* on the injections axis) leads to a much smaller increase in panel I GNP (from *OX* to *OY*), where the leakage slope is high, than in panel II (from *OX′* to *OY′*), where the slope is more gradual.

Why is the increase greater when the slope is more gradual? The answer should be obvious. The slope represents the marginal propensity to save, to tax, to import—in short, all the marginal propensities that give rise to leakages. If these propensities are high—if there are high leakages—then the slope of the leakage curve will be high. If it is low, the leakage curve will be flat.

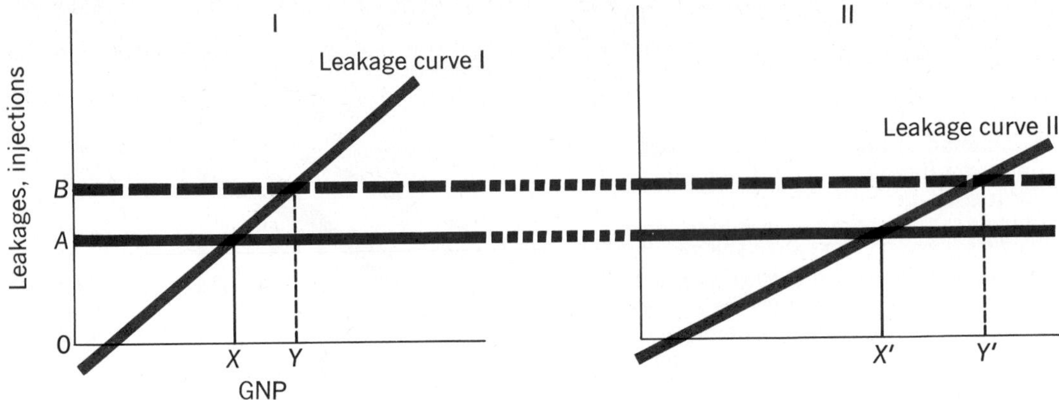

FIGURE 16-7 TWO MULTIPLIERS

Here is another chance to relate the graphics of the multiplier to the underlying behavior that causes the multiplier. The two differently sloped leakage curves generate different multipliers. This is because their different slopes picture different patterns of spending and saving.

A LAST LOOK AT EQUILIBRIUM

Thus we finally understand how GNP reaches an equilibrium position after a change in demand. Here it is well to reiterate, however, that the word "equilibrium" does not imply a static, motionless state. Nor does it mean a desired state. We use the word only to denote the fact that *given* certain behavior patterns, there will be a determinate point to which their interaction will push the level of income; and *so long as the underlying patterns of injections and leakages remain unchanged, the forces they exert will keep income at this level.*

In fact, of course, the flows of spending and saving are continually changing so that the equilibrium level of the economy is constantly shifting, like a Ping-Pong ball suspended in a rising jet of water. Equilibrium can thus be regarded as a target toward which the economy is constantly propelled by the push-pull between leakages and injections. The target may be attained but momentarily before the economy is again impelled to seek a new point of rest. What our diagrams and the underlying analysis explain for us, then, is not a single determinate point at which our economy will in fact settle down, but the *direction* it will go in quest of a resting place as the dynamic forces of the system exert their pressures.

EQUILIBRIUM AND FULL EMPLOYMENT

Like the market for any single good or service, the market for all goods and services will find its equilibrium where the total quantity of goods demanded equals that supplied. But now we must note something of paramount importance. While the economy will automatically move to this equilibrium point, the point need not bring about the full employment of the factors of production, particularly labor. In Figure 16.8, the economy at equilibrium produces a GNP indicated by GNP_e, but as our diagram indicates, this may be well short of the volume of production needed to bring about full employment (GNP_f). Equilibrium

This last, simple-looking graph is perhaps the most important of all. It shows that equilibrium GNP_e may not be full utilization GNP_f—that we may be at rest far behind production possibility.

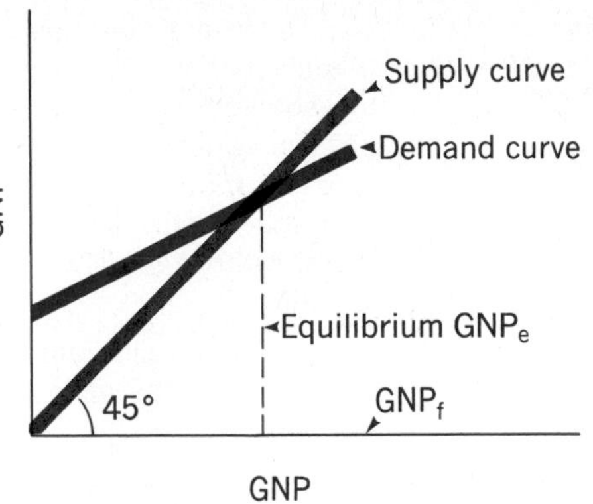

FIGURE 16.8 SUPPLY AND DEMAND FOR GNP

can thus occur at any level of capacity utilization. All we can say about it—exactly as in the market for goods and services—is that it is the level toward which the system will move, and from which it will not budge unless the demand curve shifts. It is certainly not necessarily the "right" level in any sense, and it may indeed be a very poor or unsatisfactory level, as during the Great Depression.

The aim of macroeconomic policy making is therefore to raise or lower the demand curve for GNP so that it crosses the supply curve at, or near, full employment or some other desired level of output. As we have already seen, this is an objective that is exceedingly difficult to accomplish; but at least we possess, in the body of macroeconomics itself, the basic intellectual tools needed to understand the nature of the task.

LOOKING BACK

KEY CONCEPTS

Actual output depends on the degree of utilization of human and other resources

1. The potential output of the economy is determined by its production possibilities. But the amount actually produced depends on how close we can get to the production possibility frontier. This depends on the degree to which we utilize our human and other resources.

Demand for GNP relates spending and output. Supply and GNP relates cost and output

2. The degree of utilization depends on the demand and supply for GNP. The demand for GNP is determined by the amounts the sectors will want to buy at different levels of utilization. The supply of GNP will relate the cost of GNP to its level of output.

The identity of cost and income means that the supply curve will be a 45° line

3. The supply curve of GNP uses the identity between costs and incomes to show that at all levels of utilization, output will generate incomes equal to its cost. The relation of identity between cost and income means that the supply curve of GNP will be a 45° line. Whatever the level of output, the supply of income (or spending power) will be identical with the cost of producing that output.

Equilibrium GNP is most easily shown as the level of output where S = I, or leakages equal injections

4. Equilibrium GNP is determined by the interplay of the supply of and demand for GNP. It is most easily depicted in terms of the interaction of the savings and investment, or leakage and injection, schedules. At equilibrium, saving must equal investment, and leakages must equal injections.

Investment or injection determine the level of income, via the multiplier. Attempts to increase S without increasing income will fail

5. In the interplay between S and I (or leakages and injections), it is investment (or injections) that play the critical role in establishing the equilibrium level of output. Saving or leakages are dependent, passive variables in the process. Changes in intended investment will lead, via the multiplier, to changes in income that permit the economy to save the amount that matches intended investment. Attempts to save more, without boosting income first, are doomed to failure—the paradox of thrift.

Equilibrium GNP may not be full utilization GNP

6. An equilibrium GNP may not be a socially satisfactory GNP. The economy may be at rest although it is well behind its production frontiers.

ECONOMIC VOCABULARY

Utilization 241
Injections and leakages 245
Intended and unintended S and I 245
Paradox of thrift 246

QUESTIONS

1. Suppose an economy turns out to have the following consumption and saving schedule (in billions): (You can fill in the missing numbers.)

income	*saving*	*consumption*
$400	$50	$350
450	—	395
—	60	440
550	70	—
600	85	—

Now suppose that firms intend to invest $60 billion. What will be the level of income? If investment rises to $85 billion, what will be the new level of income? What would be the multiplier?

2. Diagram the model above assuming that I = 60, then that I = 85.
3. Show in the diagram that the multiplier is determined by the slope of the leakage curve. What does this slope represent?
4. Copy diagram 16.3 showing the supply and demand curves that establish where equilibrium GNP will be. Now draw a new, higher demand curve, and drop a perpendicular line to the horizontal axis to show where the new equilibrium GNP will be. Measure the distance showing the rise in the demand for GNP and the distance showing the change in equilibrium GNPs. Can you see that GNP will increase by more than the rise in demand? And that this is simply another way of showing the multipler? And that as in Figure 16.7, the multiplier will depend on the slope of the leakage curve, here depicted as its twin, the marginal propensity to spend?

SECTION 3: Money and Growth

Chapter 17 MONEY

A LOOK AHEAD

With this chapter we open a new section in our macro studies—an investigation into the nature and function of money. It is necessary to begin by learning the definitions and terms that make up the economic vocabulary we will use (as we did with GNP). Much of this chapter consists of an introduction to the meaning of money, which is not just the currency and coins we offhand think of as money.

In addition we shall learn how banks use the money we deposit with them to carry on lending and investing operations. The central process we shall trace is the manner in which banks *create* money through their normal business operations.

We have almost completed our analysis of the major elements of macroeconomics, and soon we can bring our analysis to bear on some major problems of the economy. But first there is a matter that we must integrate into our discussion. This is the role that money plays in fixing or changing the level of GNP, along with the other forces that we have come to know.

Actually, we have been talking about money throughout our exposition. After all, one cannot discuss expenditure without assuming the existence of money. But now we must look behind this unexamined assumption and find out exactly what we mean when we speak of money. This will entail two tasks. In this chapter we shall investigate the question of what money *is*—for money is surely one of the most perplexing inventions of human society. Then in our next chapter, once we have come to understand what currency and gold and bank deposits are and how they come into being, we will look into the effect that money has on our economic operations.

THE SUPPLY OF MONEY

Let us begin by asking "What is money?" Coin and currency are certainly money. But are checks money? Are the deposits from which we draw checks money? Are savings accounts money? Government bonds?

The answer is somewhat arbitrary. Basically, money is anything we can use to make purchases with. But there exists a spectrum of financial instruments that serve this purpose—a continuum that varies in liquidity, or the ease with which it can be used for purchasing. By law, coin and currency are money because they are defined by law as "legal tender": a seller *must* accept them as payment. Checks do not have to be accepted (we have all seen signs in restaurants saying, "WE DO NOT ACCEPT CHECKS"), although in fact checks are overwhelmingly the most prevalent means of payment. In some states checks can be written on savings accounts as well as on checking accounts. On occasion, government bonds are accepted as a means of payment.

Thus, a variety of things can be counted as money. By far the most important general definition is the sum of all cash in the hands of the public plus all demand deposits. This amount is called M1-A by the Federal Reserve, which also keeps track of M1-B (M1-A plus some additional checking accounts at thrift institutions), M-2, M-3 and still further expanded definitions. The distinctions between these definitions are important for the monetary authorities but not for us. We will simply use the letter M to refer to the money supply, meaning cash in the hands of the public plus demand deposits.

CURRENCY

Money, then, is mainly currency and checking accounts. In 1979 for example, M was $382 billion, of which $107 billion was currency in the hands of the public, and $275 billion was the total of checking accounts, or demand deposits, to give them their technical name.

Of the two kinds of money, currency is the form most familiar to us. Yet there is a considerable mystery even about currency. Who determines how much currency there is? How is the supply of coins or bills regulated?

CREDIT CARDS

Money serves as a mechanism for storing potential purchasing power and for actually purchasing goods and services. Since cash and personal checks are the principal means for making these purchases, money has come to be defined as cash outside banks plus checking accounts. But what about credit cards. Shouldn't they be considered money?

Credit cards clearly can be used to make purchases, so that they appear on the surface to have a vital attribute of money. But a moment's reflection shows that in fact they *substitute* for cash or checks in which payment is finally made. The moment you pay your credit card bill, or the moment the credit card company pays the local merchant, the credit card is replaced by standard money. *Thus credit cards play the role of money only to the extent that credit bills are unpaid!*

In this role credit cards are not unique. Any unpaid bill or charge account is like money, in that you are able to purchase goods and services in exchange for your personal IOU. In a sense, each person is able to "print" money to the extent that he can persuade people to accept his IOUs. For most of us, that extent is very limited.

From an economist's point of view, the value of all outstanding trade credit (unpaid bills, unpaid charge accounts, or credit cards) *should* be considered money. It is not included in the official statistics for two reasons. First, it is difficult or impossible to figure how much trade credit is outstanding at any moment. Second, fluctuations in trade credit do not have a big impact on the economy. Ordinarily, the value of trade credit does not vary much, and therefore trade credit does not give rise to substantial changes in the effective money supply.

We often assume that the supply of currency is set by the government that issues it. Yet when we think about it, we realize that the government does not just hand out money, and certainly not coins or bills. When the government pays people, it is nearly always by check.

Then who does fix the amount of currency in circulation? You can answer the question by asking how you yourself determine how much currency you will carry. If you think about it, the answer is that you cash a check when you need more currency than you have, and you put the currency back into your checking account when you have more than you need.

What you do, everyone does. The amount of cash that the public holds at any time is no more and no less than the amount that it *wants* to hold. When it needs more—at Christmas, for instance—the public draws currency by cashing checks on its own checking accounts; and when Christmas is past, shopkeepers (who have received the public's currency) return it to their checking accounts.

Thus the amount of currency we have bears an obvious, important relation to the size of our bank accounts, for we can't write checks for cash if our accounts will not cover them.

Does this mean, then, that the banks have as much currency in their vaults as the total of our checking accounts? No, it does not. But to understand that, let us follow the course of some currency that we deposit in our banks for credit to our accounts.

BOOKKEEPING MONEY

When you put money into a commercial bank,* the bank does not hold that money for you as a pile of specially earmarked bills or as a bundle of checks made out to you from some payer. The bank takes notice of your deposit simply by crediting your account, a bookkeeping page recording your present balance. After the amount of the currency or check has been credited to you, the currency is put away with the bank's general store of vault cash and the checks are sent to the banks from which they came, where they will be charged against the accounts of the people who wrote them.

There is probably no misconception in economics harder to dispel than the idea that banks are warehouses stuffed with money. In point of fact, you might search as hard as you pleased in your bank, but you would find no money that was yours other than a bookkeeping account in your name. This seems like a very unreal form of money; and yet, the fact that you can present a check at the teller's window and convert your bookkeeping account into cash proves that your account must nonetheless be real.

But suppose that you and all the other depositors tried to convert your accounts into cash on the same day. You would then find something shocking. There would not be nearly enough cash in the bank's till to cover the total withdrawals. In 1979 for instance, total demand deposits in the United States amounted to about $275 billion. But the total amount of coin and currency held by the banks was only $11 billion!

At first blush, this seems like a highly dangerous state of affairs. But second thoughts are more reassuring. After all, most of us put money into a bank because we do *not* need it immediately, or because making payments in cash is a nuisance compared with making them by check. Yet, there is always the chance—more than that, the certainty—that some depositors *will* want their money in currency. How much currency will the banks need then? What will be a proper reserve for them to hold?

FEDERAL RESERVE SYSTEM

For many years, the banks themselves decided what reserve ratio constituted a safe proportion of currency to hold against their demand deposits. Today, however, most large banks are members of the Federal Reserve, a central banking system established in 1913 to strengthen the banking activities of the nation. Under the Federal Reserve System, the nation is divided into twelve districts, each with a **Federal Reserve Bank** owned (but not really controlled) by the member banks of its district. In turn, the twelve Reserve Banks are themselves coordinated by a seven-member Federal Reserve Board in Washington. Since the President, with the advice and consent of the Senate, appoints members of the board for fourteen-year terms, they constitute a body that has been purposely established as an independent nonpolitical monetary authority.†

*A commercial bank is a bank that is empowered by law to offer checking services. It may also have savings accounts.

†The independence of the Federal Reserve is a perennially controversial issue. See "An Extra Word" at the end of Chapter 18.

One of the most important functions of the Federal Reserve Board is to establish reserve ratios for different categories of banks, within limits set by Congress. Historically these reserve ratios have ranged between 13 and 26 percent of demand deposits for city banks, with a somewhat smaller reserve ratio for country banks. Today, reserve ratios are determined by size of bank and by kind of deposit, and they vary between 18 percent for the largest banks and 8 percent for the smallest. The Federal Reserve Board also sets reserve requirements for time deposits (the technical term for savings deposits). These range from 1 to 6 percent, depending on the ease of withdrawal.

THE BANKS' BANK

Yet here is something odd! We noticed that in 1979 the total amount of deposits was $275 billion and that banks' holdings of coin and currency were only $11 billion. This is much less than the 16 percent reserve against deposits established by the Federal Reserve Board. How can this be?

The answer is that cash is not the only reserve a bank holds against deposits. Claims on other banks are also held as its reserve.

What are these claims? Suppose, in your account in Bank A, you deposit a check from someone who has an account in Bank B. Bank A credits your account and then presents the check to Bank B for payment. Bank A does not expect to be paid coin and currency, however. Instead, Bank A and Bank B settle their transaction at still *another* bank where both Bank A and Bank B have their own accounts. These accounts are with the twelve Federal Reserve Banks of the country, where all banks who are members of the Federal Reserve System (and this accounts for banks holding most of the deposits in our banking system) *must* open accounts. Thus at the Federal Reserve Bank, Bank A's account will be credited, and Bank B's account will be debited, in this way moving reserves from one bank to the other.*

The Federal Reserve Banks serve their member banks in exactly the same way as the member banks serve the public. Member banks automatically deposit in their Federal Reserve accounts all checks they get from other banks. As a result, banks are constantly clearing their checks with one another through the Federal Reserve System, because their depositors are constantly writing checks on their own banks payable to someone who banks elsewhere. **Meanwhile, the balance that each bank maintains at the Federal Reserve—that is, the claim it has on other banks—counts, as much as any currency, as part of its reserve against deposits.**

In 1979, therefore, when demand deposits were $275 billion and cash in the banks only $11 billion, we would expect the member banks to have had heavy accounts with the Federal Reserve banks. And so they did—$33 billion in all. Thus, total reserves of the banks were $44 billion ($11 billion in cash plus $30 billion in Federal Reserve accounts), enough to satisfy the legal requirements of the Fed.

*When money is put into a bank account, the account is credited; when money is taken out, the account is debited.

FRACTIONAL RESERVES

Thus we see that our banks operate on what is called a *fractional reserve system.* That is, a certain specified fraction of all demand deposits must be kept on hand at all times in cash or at the Fed. The size of the minimum fraction is determined by the Federal Reserve, for reasons of control that we shall shortly learn. It is *not* determined, as we might be tempted to think, to provide a safe backing for our bank deposits. For under *any* fractional system, if *all* depositors decided to draw out their accounts in currency and coin from all banks at the same time, the banks would be unable to meet the demand for cash and would have to close. We call this a "run" on the banking system. Needless to say, runs can be terrifying and destructive economic phenomena.*

Why, then, do we court the risk of runs, however small this risk may be? What is the benefit of a fractional banking system? To answer that, let us look at our bank again.

LOANS AND INVESTMENTS

Suppose its customers have given our bank $1 million in deposits and that the Federal Reserve Board requirements are 20 percent, a simpler figure to work with than the actual one. Then we know that our bank must at all times keep $200,000 either in currency in its own till or in its demand deposit at the Federal Reserve Bank.

But having taken care of that requirement, what does the bank do with the remaining deposits? If it simply lets them sit, either as vault cash or as a deposit at the Federal Reserve, our bank will be very "liquid," but it will have no way of making an income. Unless it charges a very high fee for its checking services, it will have to go out of business.

And yet there is an obvious way for the bank to make an income while performing a valuable service. The bank can use all the cash and check claims it does not need for its reserve to make *loans* to businesses or families or to make financial *investments* in corporate or government bonds. It will thereby not only earn an income, but it will assist the process of business investment and government borrowing. Thus the mechanics of the banking system lead us back to the concerns at the very center of our previous analysis.

INSIDE THE BANKING SYSTEM

Fractional reserves allow banks to lend, or to invest in securities, part of the funds that have been deposited with them. But that is not the only usefulness of the fractional reserve system. It works as well to help enlarge or diminish the supply of investible or loanable funds, as the occasion demands. Let us follow the workings of this process. To make the mechanics of banking clear, we are going to look at the actual books of the bank—in simplified form, of course—so that we can see how the process of lending and investing appears to the banker himself.

*A "run" on the banking system is no longer so much of a threat as in the past, because the Federal Reserve could supply its members with vast amounts of cash. We shall learn how, later in this chapter.

ASSETS AND LIABILITIES

We begin by introducing two basic elements of business accounting: *assets* and *liabilities*. Every student at some time or another has seen the balance sheet of a firm, and many have wondered how total assets always equal total liabilities. The reason is very simple. Assets are all the things or claims a business owns. Liabilities are claims against those assets—some of them the claims of creditors, some the claims of owners (called the *net worth* of the business). Since assets show everything that a business owns, and since liabilities show how claims against these self-same things are divided between creditors and owners, it is obvious that the two sides of the balance sheet must always come to exactly the same total. The total of assets and the total of liabilities are an identity.

T ACCOUNTS

Businesses show their financial condition on a *balance sheet* on which all items on the left side represent assets and all those on the right side represent liabilities. By using a simple two-column balance sheet called a "T account" (because it looks like a T), we can follow very clearly what happens to our bank as we deposit money in it or as it makes loans or investments. (See Table 17.1.)

ORIGINAL BANK	
Assets	*Liabilities*
$1,000,000 (cash and checks)	$1,000,000 (money owed to depositors)
Total $1,000,000	**Total $1,000,000**

TABLE 17.1

T accounts always balance, because liabilities show claims on assets.

We start off with the example we have just used, in which we open a brand new bank with $1 million in cash and checks on other banks. Accordingly, our first entry in the T account shows the two sides of this transaction. Notice that our bank has gained an asset of $1 million, the cash and checks it now owns, and that it has simultaneously gained $1 million in liabilities, the deposits it *owes* to its depositors (who can withdraw their money).

ORIGINAL BANK			
Assets		*Liabilities*	
Vault Cash	$100,000	Deposits	$1,000,000
Deposit at Fed	900,000		
Total	**$1,000,000**	**Total**	**$1,000,000**

TABLE 17.2

This is how the T account looks after checks have been cleared through the Federal Reserve. If you will examine some bank balance sheets, you will see these items listed as "Cash and due from banks." This means, of course, cash in their own vaults plus their balance at the Federal Reserve.

As we know, however, our bank will not keep all its newly gained cash and checks in the till. It may hang on to some of the cash, but it will send all the checks it has received, plus any currency that it feels it does not need, to the Fed for deposit in its account there. Table 17.2 shows the resulting T account.

EXCESS RESERVES

Now we recall from our previous discussion that our bank does not want to remain in this very liquid, but very unprofitable, position. **According to the law, it must retain only a certain percentage of its deposits in cash or at the Federal Reserve—20 percent in our hypothetical example. All the rest it is free to lend or invest.** As things now stand, however, it has $1 million in reserves—$800,000 more than it needs. Hence, let us suppose that it decides to put these *excess reserves* to work by lending that amount to a sound business risk. (Note that banks do not lend the excess reserves themselves. These reserves, cash and deposits at the Fed, remain right where they are. Their function is to tell the banks how much they may loan or invest.)

MAKING A LOAN

Assume now that the Smith Corporation, a well-known firm, comes in for a loan of $800,000. Our bank is happy to lend them that amount. But making a loan does not mean that the bank now pays the company in cash out of its vaults. Rather, *it makes a loan by opening a new checking account for the firm* and by crediting that account with $800,000. (Or if, as is likely, the Smith firm already has an account with the bank, it will simply credit the proceeds of the loan to that account.)

Now our T account shows some interesting changes (see Table 17.3).

There are several things to note about this transaction. First, our bank's reserves (its cash and deposit at the Fed) have not yet changed. The $1 million in reserves are still there.

Second, notice that the Smith Corporation loan counts as a new asset for the bank because the bank now has a legal claim against the company for that amount. (The interest on the loan is not shown in the balance sheet; but when it is paid, it will show up as an addition to the bank's cash.)

Third, deposits have increased by $800,000. Note, however, that this $800,000 was not paid to the Smith firm out of anyone else's account in the bank.

TABLE 17.3

ORIGINAL BANK

Assets		*Liabilities*	
Cash and at Fed	$1,000,000	Original deposits	$1,000,000
Loan (Smith Corp.)	800,000	New deposit (Smith Corp.)	800,000
Total	**$1,800,000**	**Total**	**$1,800,000**

The bank has used its excess reserves to make a loan. The loan itself is a signed IOU which is a new asset for the bank. The corresponding liability is the new deposit opened in the name of the borrower.

It is a new checking account, one that did not exist before. As a result, the supply of money is also up! More about this shortly.

THE LOAN IS SPENT

Was it safe to open this new account for the company? Well, we might see whether our reserves are now sufficient to cover the Smith Corporation's account as well as the original deposit accounts. A glance reveals that all is well. We still have $1 million in reserves against $1.8 million in deposits. Our reserve ratio is much higher than the 20 percent required by law.

It is so much higher, in fact, that we might be tempted to make another loan to the next customer who requests one, and in that way further increase our earning capacity. But an experienced banker shakes his head. "The Smith Corporation did not take out a loan and agree to pay interest on it just for the pleasure of letting that money sit with you," he explains. "Very shortly, the company will be writing checks on its balance to pay for goods or services; and when it does, you will need every penny of the reserve you now have."

That, indeed, is the case. Within a few days we find that our bank's account at the Federal Reserve Bank has been charged with a check for $800,000 written by the Smith Corporation in favor of the Jones Corporation, which carries its account at another bank. Now we find that our T account has changed dramatically. Look at Table 17.4.

ORIGINAL BANK

Assets		*Liabilities*	
Cash and at Fed	$ 200,000	Original deposits	$1,000,000
Loan (Smith Corp.)	800,000	Smith Corp. deposits	0
Total	**$1,000,000**	**Total**	**$1,000,000**

SECOND BANK

Assets		*Liabilities*	
Cash and at Fed	$800,000	Deposit (Jones Corp.)	$800,000
Total	**$800,000**	**Total**	**$800,000**

TABLE 17.4

The borrower uses the loan, and its deposits fall to zero. But the assets (and deposit liabilities) of another bank have risen.

Let us see exactly what has happened. First, the Smith Corporation's check has been charged against our account at the Fed and has reduced it from $900,000 to $100,000. Together with the $100,000 cash in our vault, this gives us $200,000 in reserves.

Second, the Smith Corporation's deposit is entirely gone, although its loan agreement remains with us as an asset.

Now if we refigure our reserves we find that they are just right. We are required to have $200,000 in vault cash or in our Federal Reserve account against our $1 million in deposits. That is exactly the amount we have left. Our bank is now fully "loaned up."

CONTINUING EFFECTS

But the banking *system* is not yet fully loaned up. So far, we have traced what happened only to our bank when the Smith Corporation spent the money in its deposit account. Now we must trace the effect of this action on the deposits and reserves of other banks.

We begin with the bank in which the Jones Corporation deposits the check it has just received from the Smith Corporation. Another look at Table 17.4 will show you that the Jones Corporation's bank now finds itself in exactly the same position as our bank was when we opened it with $1 million in new deposits, except that the addition to this second generation bank is smaller than the addition to the first generation bank.

As we can see, our second generation bank has gained $800,000 in cash and in deposits. Since it needs only 20 percent of this for required reserves, it finds itself with $640,000 excess reserves, which it is now free to use to make loans as investments. Suppose that it extends a loan to the Brown Company and that the Brown Company shortly thereafter spends the proceeds of that loan at the Black Company, which banks at yet a third bank. The two T accounts in Table 17.5 show how the total deposits will now be affected.

TABLE 17.5

SECOND BANK
(after Brown Co. spends the proceeds of its loan)

Assets		*Liabilities*	
Cash and at Fed	$160,000	Deposits (Jones Corp.)	$800,000
Loan (to Brown Co.)	640,000	Deposits (Brown Co.)	0
Total	**$800,000**	**Total**	**$800,000**

THIRD BANK
(After Black Co. gets the check of Brown Co.)

Assets		*Liabilities*	
Cash and at Fed	$640,000	Deposit (Black Co.)	$640,000
Total	**$640,000**	**Total**	**$640,000**

Here is a repetition of the same process, as the Second Bank uses its lending capacity to finance Brown Co.

As Figure 17.1 makes clear, the process will not stop here but can continue from one bank to the next as long as any lending power remains. Notice, however, that this lending power gets smaller and smaller and will eventually reach zero.

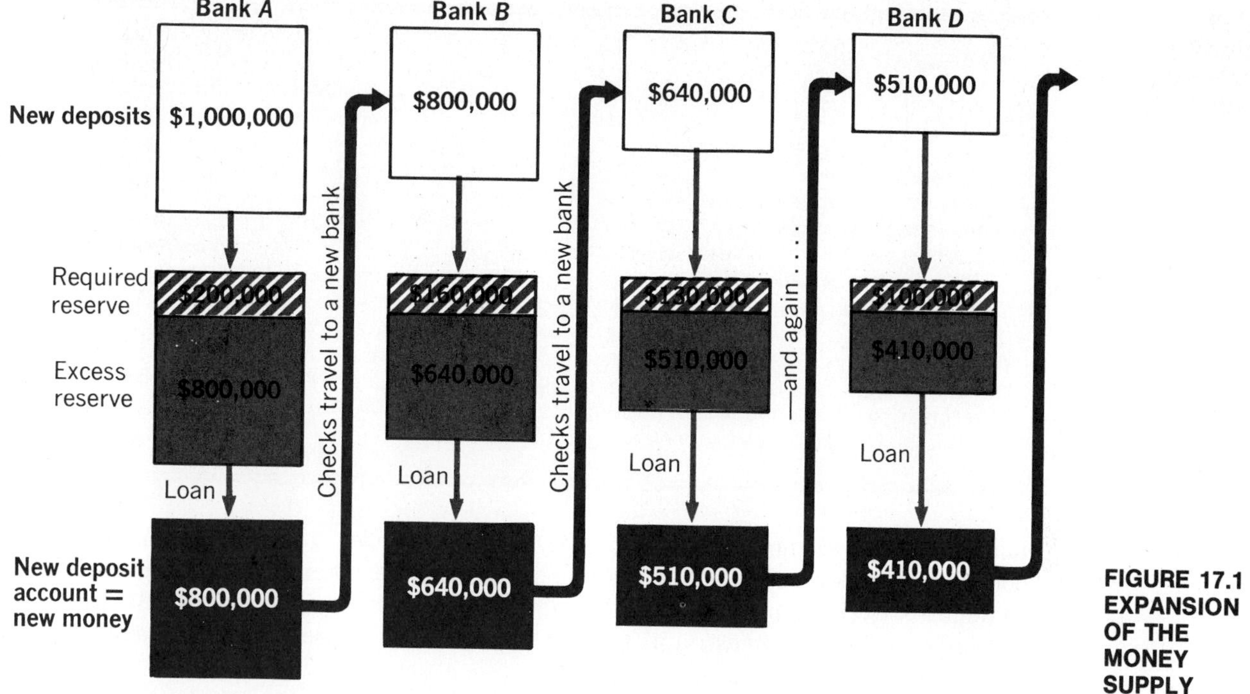

FIGURE 17.1 EXPANSION OF THE MONEY SUPPLY

As the relending process continues, successive banks add to their deposits, and the money supply increases. Note the resemblance to the multiplier process.

EXPANSION OF THE MONEY SUPPLY

If we now look at the bottom of Figure 17.1 we will see something very important. **Every time any bank in this chain of transactions has opened an account for a new borrower,** ***the supply of money has increased.*** Remember that the supply of money is the sum of currency outside the banking system (i.e., in our own pockets) plus the total of demand deposits. As our chain of banks kept opening new accounts, it was simultaneously expanding the total check-writing capacity of the economy. Thus, money has materialized, seemingly out of thin air.

Now how can this be? If we tell any banker in the chain that he has "created" money, he will protest vehemently. The loans he made, he will insist, were backed at the time he made them by excess reserves as large as the loan itself. Just as we had $800,000 in excess reserves when we made our initial loan to the Smith Corporation, so every subsequent loan was always backed 100 percent by unused reserves when it was made.

Our bankers are perfectly correct when they tell us that they never, never lend a penny more than they have. Money is not created in the lending process because a banker lends money he doesn't have. **Money is created because you and I generally pay each other by checks that give us claims against each other's bank.** If we constantly cashed the checks we exchanged, no new money would be

MONEY AND DEBT

All this gives us a fresh insight into the question of what money is. We said before that it is whatever we use to make payments. But what do we use? The answer is a surprising one. We use *debts*—specifically, the debts of commercial banks. Deposits are, after all, nothing but the liabilities that banks owe their customers. Furthermore, we can see that one purpose of the banking system is to buy debts from other units in the economy, such as businesses or governments, in exchange for its own debts (which are money). For when a bank opens an account for a business to which it has granted a loan or when it buys a government bond, what else is it doing but accepting a debt that is *not* usable as money, in exchange for its deposit liabilities that *are* usable as money. And why is it that banks create money when they make loans, but you or I do not, when we lend money? Because we all accept bank liabilities (deposits) as money, but we do not accept personal or business IOUs to make payments with.

created. But we do not. We deposit each other's checks in our own bank acacounts; and in doing so, we give our banks more reserves than they need against the deposits we have just made. These new excess reserves make it possible for our banks to lend or invest, and thereby to open still more deposit accounts, which in turn lead to new reserves.

LIMITS ON THE EXPANSION

This all sounds a little frightening. Does it mean that the money supply can go on expanding indefinitely from a single new deposit? Wouldn't that be extremely dangerous?

It would of course be very dangerous, but there is no possibility that it can happen. For having understood how the supply of money can expand from an original increase in deposits, we may now understand equally well what keeps an expansion within bounds.

1. Not every loan generates an increase in bank deposits

If our bank had opened a loan account for the Smith Corporation at the same time that another firm had paid off a similar loan, there would have been no original expansion in bank deposits. In that case, the addition of $800,000 to the Smith account would have been exactly balanced by a decline of $800,000 in someone else's account. Even if that decline would have taken place in a different bank, it would still mean that the nation's total of bank deposits would not have risen, and therefore no new money would have been created. **Thus, only net additions to loans have an expansionary effect.** We will shortly see how such net additions arise in the first place.

2. There is a limit to the rise in money supply from a single increase in deposits

As Figure 17.1 shows, in the chain of deposit expansion each successive bank has a smaller increase in deposits, because each bank has to keep some of its newly gained cash or checks as reserve. Hence the amount of *excess* reserves, against which loans can be made, steadily falls.

Further, we can see that the amount of the total monetary expansion from an original net increase in deposits is governed by the size of the fraction that has to be kept aside each time as reserve. **In fact, we can see that just as with the multiplier, the cumulative effect of an increase in deposits will be determined by the reciprocal of the reserve fraction.** If each bank must keep one-fifth of its increased deposits as reserves, then the cumulative effect of an original increase in deposits, when it has expanded through the system, is five times the original increase. If reserves are one-fourth, the expansion is limited to four times the original increase, and so on.*

3. The monetary expansion process can work in reverse

Suppose that the banking system as a whole suffers a net loss of deposits. Instead of putting $1 million into a bank, the public takes it out in cash. The bank will now have too few reserves and it will have to cut down its loans or sell its investments to gain the reserves it needs. In turn, as borrowers pay off their loans, or as bond buyers pay for their securities, cash will drain from other banks who will now find *their* reserves too small in relation to their deposits. In turn, they will therefore have to sell more investments or curtail still other loans, and this again will squeeze still other banks and reduce their reserves, with the same consequences.

Thus, just as an original expansion in deposits can lead to a multiple expansion, so an original contraction in deposits can lead to a multiple contraction. The size of this contraction is also limited by the reciprocal of the reserve fraction. If banks have to hold a 25 percent reserve, then an original fall of $100,000 in deposits will lead to a total fall of $400,000, assuming that the system was fully loaned up to begin with. If they had to hold a 20 percent reserve, a fall of $100,000 could pyramid to $500,000.

4. The expansion process may not be fully carried through

We have assumed that each bank in the chain always lends out an amount equal to its excess reserve, but this may not be the case. The third or fifth bank along the way may have trouble finding a credit-worthy customer and may decide—for the moment, anyway—to sit on its excess reserves. Or borrowers along the chain may take out cash from some of their new deposits and thereby reduce the banks' reserves and their lending powers. Thus the potential expansion may be only partially realized.

5. The expansion process takes time

Like the multiplier process, the expansion of the money supply encounters many "frictions" in real life. Banks do not instantly expand loans when their reserves

*If M is the money supply, D is net new deposits and r is the reserve ratio, then $\Delta M = 1/r \times \Delta D$. Notice that this formula is exactly the same as that for the multiplier.

rise; bank customers do not instantly spend the proceeds of bank loans. The time lags in banking are too variable to enable us to make an estimate of how long it takes for an initial increase in new deposits to work its way through the system, but the time period is surely a matter of months for two or three rounds.

WHY BANKS MUST WORK TOGETHER

There is an interesting problem concealed behind this crisscrossing of deposits that leads to a slowly rising level of the money supply. Suppose that an imaginary island economy was served by a single bank (and let us forget about all complications of international trade, etc.), and this bank, which worked on a 20 percent reserve ratio, was suddenly presented with an extra one million dollars worth of reserves—let us say newly mined pure gold. Our bank could, of course, increase its loans to customers. By how much? *By five million dollars!*

In other words, our island bank, all by itself, could use an increase in its reserves to create a much larger increase in the money supply. It is not difficult to understand why. Any borrower of the new five million, no matter where he spent his money on the island, would only be giving his checks to someone who also banked at the single, solitary bank. The whole five million, in other words, would stay *within* the bank as its deposits, although the identity of those depositors would, of course, shift. Indeed, there is no reason why such a bank should limit its expansion of the money supply to five million. As long as the soundness of the currency was unquestioned, such a bank could create as much money as it wanted through new deposits, since all of those deposits would remain in its own keeping.

The imaginary bank makes it plain why ordinary commercial banks *cannot* expand deposits beyond their excess reserves. Unlike the monopoly bank, they must expect to *lose* their deposits to other banks when their borrowers write checks on their new accounts. As a result they will also lose their reserves, and this can lead to trouble.

OVERLENDING

This situation is important enough to warrant taking a moment to examine. Suppose that in our previous example we had decided to lend the Smith Corporation not $800,000 but $900,000, and suppose as before that the Smith Corporation used the proceeds of that loan to pay the Jones Corporation. Now look at the condition of our bank after the Smith payment has cleared (Table 17.6).

TABLE 17.6

ORIGINAL BANK			
Assets		*Liabilities*	
Cash and at Fed	$ 100,000	Original deposits	$1,000,000
Loan (Smith Corp.)	900,000	Smith Corp. deposit	0
Total	**$1,000,000**	**Total**	**$1,000,000**

A bank that lends an amount larger than its excess reserve will be in trouble. Its reserves will fall below the level required by law.

Our reserves would now have dropped to 10 percent! Indeed, if we had loaned the company $1,000,000 we would be in danger of insolvency.

Banks are, in fact, very careful not to overlend. If they find that they have inadvertently exceeded their legal reserve requirements, they quickly take remedial action. One way that a bank may repair the situation is by borrowing reserves for a short period (paying interest on them, of course) from another bank that may have a temporary surplus at the Fed; this is called borrowing *federal funds.* Or a bank may quickly sell some of its government bonds and add the proceeds to its reserve account at the Fed. Or again, it may add to its reserves the proceeds of any loans that have come due and deliberately fail to replace these expired loans with new loans. Finally, a bank may borrow reserves directly from its Federal Reserve Bank and pay interest for the loan. We shall shortly look into this method when we talk about the role of the Federal Reserve in regulating the quantity of money.

The main point is clear. A bank is safe in lending only an amount that it can afford to lose to another bank. But of course one bank's loss is another's gain. That is why, by the exchange of checks, the banking system can accomplish the same result as the island monopoly bank, whereas no individual bank can hope to do so.

INVESTMENTS AND INTEREST

If a bank uses its excess reserves to buy securities, does that lead to the same multiplication effect as a bank loan?

It can. When a bank buys government securities, it usually does so from a securities dealer, a professional trader in bonds.* Its check (for $800,000 in our example) drawn on its account at the Federal Reserve will be made out to a dealer, who will deposit it in his bank. As a result, the dealer's bank suddenly finds itself with an $800,000 new deposit. It must keep 20 percent of this as required reserve, but the remainder is excess reserve against which it can make loans or investments as it wishes.

Is there a new deposit, corresponding to that of the borrower? There is: the new deposit of the securities dealer. Note that in his case, as in the case of the borrower, the new deposit on the books of the bank has not been put there by the transfer of money from some other commercial bank. The $800,000 deposit has come into being through the deposit of a check of the Federal Reserve Bank, which is not a commercial bank. Thus it represents a new addition to the deposits of the private banking system.

Let us see this in the T accounts. Table 17.7 shows what our first bank's T account looks like after it has bought its $800,000 in bonds (paying for them with its Federal Reserve checking account).

As we can see, there are no excess reserves here. But look at the bank in which the seller of the government bond has deposited the check he has just received from our bank (Table 17.8). Here there are excess reserves of $640,000 with which additional investments can be made. It is possible for such new deposits, albeit diminishing each time, to remain in the financial circuit for some

*The dealer may be only a middleman, who will in turn buy from, or sell to, corporations or individuals. This doesn't change our analysis, however.

TABLE 17.7

ORIGINAL BANK			
Assets		*Liabilities*	
Cash and at Fed	$ 200,000	Deposits	$1,000,000
Government bonds	800,000		
Total	**$1,000,000**	**Total**	**$1,000,000**

Excess reserves can be used to buy bonds as well as to finance loans.

TABLE 17.8

SECOND BANK			
Assets		*Liabilities*	
Cash	$800,000	New deposit of bond seller	$800,000
Total	**$800,000**	**Total**	**$800,000**

When the seller of the bond deposits his check, the same money-expanding process will be set into motion.

time, moving from bank to bank as an active business is done in buying government bonds.

YIELDS

Meanwhile, however, the very activity in bidding for government bonds is likely to raise their price and thereby lower their rate of interest.

This is a situation that you will probably be faced with in your personal life, so you should understand it. A bond has a *fixed* rate of return and a stated face value. If it is a 9 percent, $1,000 bond, this means it will pay $90 interest yearly. If the bond now sells on the marketplace for $1,200, the $90 yearly interest will be less than a 9 percent return ($90 is only 7.5 percent of $1,200). If the price should fall to $900, the $90 return will be more than 9 percent ($90 is 10 percent of $900). Thus the *yield* of a bond varies inversely—in the other direction—from its market price.

When the price of government bonds changes, all bond prices tend to change in the same direction. This is because all bonds are competing for investors' funds. If the yield on "governments" falls, investors will switch from governments to other, higher-yielding bonds. But as they bid for these other bonds, the prices of these bonds will rise—and their yields will fall, too!

In this way, a change in yields spreads from one group of bonds to another. A lower rate of interest or a lower yield on government securities is quickly reflected in lower rates or yields for other kinds of bonds. In turn, a lower rate of interest on bonds makes loans to business look more attractive. Thus, sooner or later, excess reserves are apt to be channeled to new loans as well as new investments. Thereafter the deposit-building process follows its familiar course.

KEY CONCEPTS

LOOKING BACK

The supply of money is usually defined as cash in the public's hands, plus demand deposits

1. The supply of money is generally defined as the cash in the possession of the public (not the cash in bank vaults) plus checking deposits, technically known as demand deposits. The total is called M (technically M1–A). Other measures of money include savings accounts and other liquid assets.

Banks must keep stated fractions of reserves against their deposits. These reserves are cash or accounts at a Federal Reserve Bank. Banks can lend or invest sums equal to excess reserves

2. Banks are required by the Federal Reserve Act to maintain stated proportions of actual cash (in their own vaults) or claims on other banks as reserves against their deposits. These reserves are largely maintained as accounts with one of the twelve Federal Reserve banks of the country. This is called the fractional reserve system. It permits banks to use excess reserves, above the legal requirement, to make loans or investments.

Banks make loans by opening deposits for the borrower. These deposits, when spent, become new deposits for other banks, enabling them in turn to expand their loans or investment

3. When a bank makes a loan against its excess reserve, it opens a deposit in the name of the borrower. That deposit is normally used for business purposes, and thereby becomes a new deposit in some other bank. In turn that bank must keep a legal reserve to cover part of its new deposit, but is free to lend or invest an amount equal to its excess reserve.

The process of successive relending expands the money supply

The banking system can increase M, although no bank by itself could long do so

4. The successive spending of loans creates additional deposits through the system, acting like a multiplier. These new deposits are additions to the money supply. No single bank on its own would dare to expand the total of deposits, but working together as a system, the member banks can increase this supply to the extent that fractional reserve requirements permit.

The expansion process has limits, set by the reserve fraction. It only applies to net loans. And it may work in reverse

5. The money expansion has several limits: Only net loans create new money, not loans that are offset by repayments; expansion is controlled by the reserve fraction, just like the multiplier process; monetary expansion can work in reverse if repayments exceed new loans; the expansion process may not be carried all the way through; and the process takes time.

Using excess reserves to buy bonds also increases the money supply

6. A bank that uses its excess reserve to buy bonds also creates new deposits when the seller of the bond deposits his check. This too can expand the money supply.

As bond prices change, bond yields also change. The higher the price, the lower the yield.

7. As bonds are bought and sold, their price changes. Because bonds have fixed interest obligations, a higher or lower price for a bond changes its yield. As bond prices rise, yields fall, and vice versa.

ECONOMIC VOCABULARY

Money Supply—M_1, M_1+, M_2 252
Federal Reserve system 254
Fractional reserves 256
Assets and liabilities 257
T accounts 257
Excess reserves 258
Overlending 264
Yields 266

QUESTIONS

1. Why do we not count cash in the tills of commercial banks in the money supply? When you deposit currency in a commercial bank, what happens to it? Can you ask for your particular bills again? If you demanded to see "your" account, what would it be?
2. What determines how much vault cash a bank must hold against its deposits? Would you expect this proportion to change in some seasons, such as Christmas? Do you think it would be the same in worried times as in placid times? In new countries as in old ones?
3. What are excess reserves? Suppose a bank has $500,000 in deposits and that there is a reserve ratio of 30 percent imposed by law. What is its required reserve? Suppose it happens to hold $200,000 in vault cash or at its account at the Fed. What, if any, is its excess reserve?
4. If the bank above wanted to make loans or investments, how much would it be entitled to lend or invest? Suppose its deposits increased by another $50,000. Could it lend or invest this entire amount? Any of it? How much?
5. If a bank lends money, it opens an account in the name of the borrower. Now suppose the borrower draws down his new account. What happens to the reserves of the lending bank? Show this in a T account.
6. Suppose the borrower sends his check for $1,000 to someone who banks at another bank. Describe what happens to the deposits of the second bank. If the reserve ratio is 20 percent, how much new lending or investing can it do?
7. If the reserve ratio is 20 percent, and the original addition to reserves is $1,000, what will be the total potential amount of new money that can be created by the banking system? If the ratio is 25 percent?

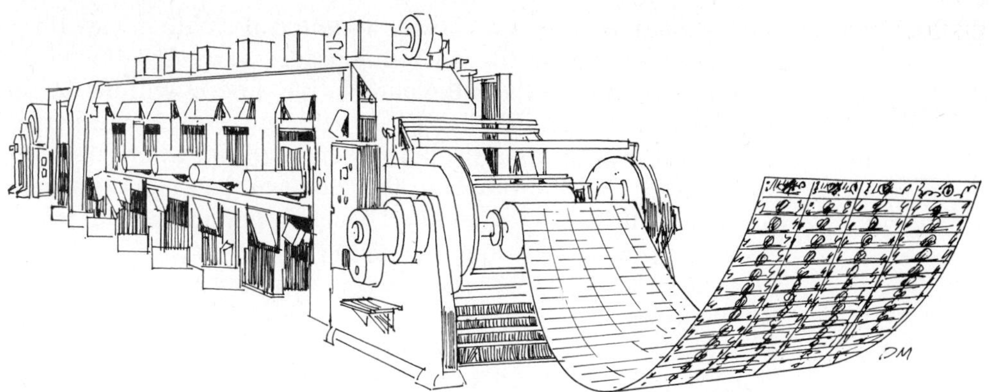

Chapter 18 CONTROLLING THE MONEY SUPPLY

A LOOK AHEAD

In our last chapter we learned what money was and how the money supply could be increased. But we have not yet investigated the methods by which the national government exercises control over the money supply; this we shall do here.

(1) First we look into the workings of the Federal Reserve System, particularly with respect to the three ways in which it can loosen or tighten the monetary strings. The question of how much money the Federal Reserve *should* create is taken up in the next chapter; the material here prepares us to understand it.

(2) Second, we explore a question everyone is curious about: What exactly is the connection between money and gold?

(3) Finally we will trace the process by which money is actually made and distributed. Here we take a look at the printing presses and catch a glimpse of Fort Knox.

We have now seen how a banking system can create money through the creation of excess reserves. But the key to the process is the creation of the *original* excess reserves, for without them the cumulative process will not be set in motion. We remember, for example, that a loan will not result in an increase in the money supply if it is offset by a decline in lending somewhere else in the banking system; neither will the purchase of a bond by one commercial bank if it is only buying a security sold by another. **To get a net addition to loans or investments, however, a banking system—assuming that it is fully loaned up—needs an increase in its reserves.** Where do these extra reserves come from? That is the question we must turn to next.

ROLE OF THE FEDERAL RESERVE

In our example we have already met one source of changes in reserves. When the public needs less currency, and it deposits its extra holdings in the banks, reserves rise, as we have seen. Contrariwise, when the public wants more currency, it depletes the banks' holdings of currency and thereby lowers their reserves. In the latter case, the banks may find that they have insufficient reserves behind their deposits. To get more currency or claims on other banks, they will have to sell securities or reduce their loans. This might put a very severe crimp in the economy. Hence, to allow bank reserves to be regulated by the public's fluctuating demand for cash would seem to be an impossible way to run our monetary system.

But we remember that bank reserves are not mainly currency; in fact, currency is a relatively minor item. Most reserves are the accounts that member banks hold at the Federal Reserve. Hence, if these accounts could somehow be increased or decreased, we could regulate the amount of reserves—and thus the permissible total of deposits—without regard to the public's changing need for cash.

This is precisely what the Federal Reserve System is designed to do. Essentially, the system is set up to regulate the supply of money by raising or lowering the reserves of its member banks. When these reserves are raised, member banks find themselves with excess reserves and are thus in a position to make loans and investments by which the supply of money will increase further. Conversely, when the Federal Reserve lowers the reserves of its member banks, they will no longer be able to make loans and investments, or they may even have to reduce loans or get rid of investments, thereby extinguishing deposit accounts and contracting the supply of money.

MONETARY CONTROL MECHANISMS

How does the Federal Reserve operate? There are three ways.

1. Changing reserve requirements

It was the Federal Reserve itself, we will remember, that originally determined how much in reserves its member banks should hold against their deposits. Hence by changing that reserve requirement for a given level of deposits, it can give its member banks excess reserves or can create a shortage of reserves.

This has two effects. First, it immediately changes the lending or investing capacity of all banks. In our imaginary bank we have assumed that reserves were set at 20 percent of deposits. Suppose now that the Federal Reserve determined to lower reserve requirements to 15 percent. It would thereby automatically create extra lending or investing power for our *existing* reserves. Our bank with $1 million in deposits and $200,000 in reserves could now lend or invest an additional $50,000 without any new funds coming in from depositors. On the other hand, if requirements were raised to, say, 30 percent, we would find that our original $200,000 reserve was $100,000 short of requirements, and we would have to curtail lending or investing until we were again in line with requirements.

Second, the new reserve requirements raise or lower the reserve multiplier —expanding or contracting the limits of the flexible money system. Because these new reserve requirements affect *all* banks, changing reserve ratios is a very effective way of freeing or contracting bank credit on a large scale. But it is an instrument that sweeps across the entire banking system in an undiscriminating fashion. It is therefore used only rarely, when the Federal Reserve Board feels that the supply of money is seriously short or dangerously excessive and needs remedy on a countrywide basis.

2. Changing discount rates

A second means of control uses interest rates as the money-controlling device. Recall that member banks that are short on reserves have a special privilege, if they wish to exercise it. They can *borrow* reserve balances from the Federal Reserve Bank itself and add them to their regular reserve account at the bank.

The Federal Reserve Bank, of course, charges interest for lending reserves, and this interest is called the **discount rate.** By raising or lowering this rate, the Federal Reserve can make it attractive or unattractive for member banks to borrow to augment reserves. Thus, in contrast with changing the reserve ratio itself, changing the discount rate is a mild device that allows each bank to decide for itself whether it wishes to increase its reserves. In addition, changes in the discount rate tend to influence the whole structure of interest rates, either tightening or loosening money. When interest rates are high, we have what we call **tight money.** This means not only that borrowers have to pay higher rates, but that banks are stricter and more selective in judging the credit worthiness of business applications for loans. Conversely, when interest rates decline, money is called easy, meaning that it is not only cheaper but literally easier to borrow.

Although changes in the discount rate can be used as a major means of controlling the money supply and are used to control it in some countries, they are not used for this purpose in the U.S. The Federal Reserve Board does not allow banks to borrow whatever they would like at the current discount rate. The discount "window" is a place where a bank can borrow small amounts of money to cover a small deficiency in its reserves, but it is not a place where banks can borrow major amounts of money to expand their lending portfolios. **As a result, the discount rate serves more as a signal of what the Federal Reserve would like to see happen than as an active force in determining the total borrowings of banks.**

3. Open-market operations

Most frequently used, however, is a third technique called open-market operations. This technique permits the Federal Reserve Banks to change the supply of reserves by buying or selling U.S. government bonds on the open market.

How does this work? Let us suppose that the Federal Reserve authorities wish to increase the reserves of member banks. They will begin to buy government securities from dealers in the bond market, and they will pay these dealers with Federal Reserve checks.

Notice something about these checks: *They are not drawn on any commercial bank!* They are drawn on the Federal Reserve Bank itself. The security dealer who sells the bond will, of course, deposit the Federal Reserve's check, as if it

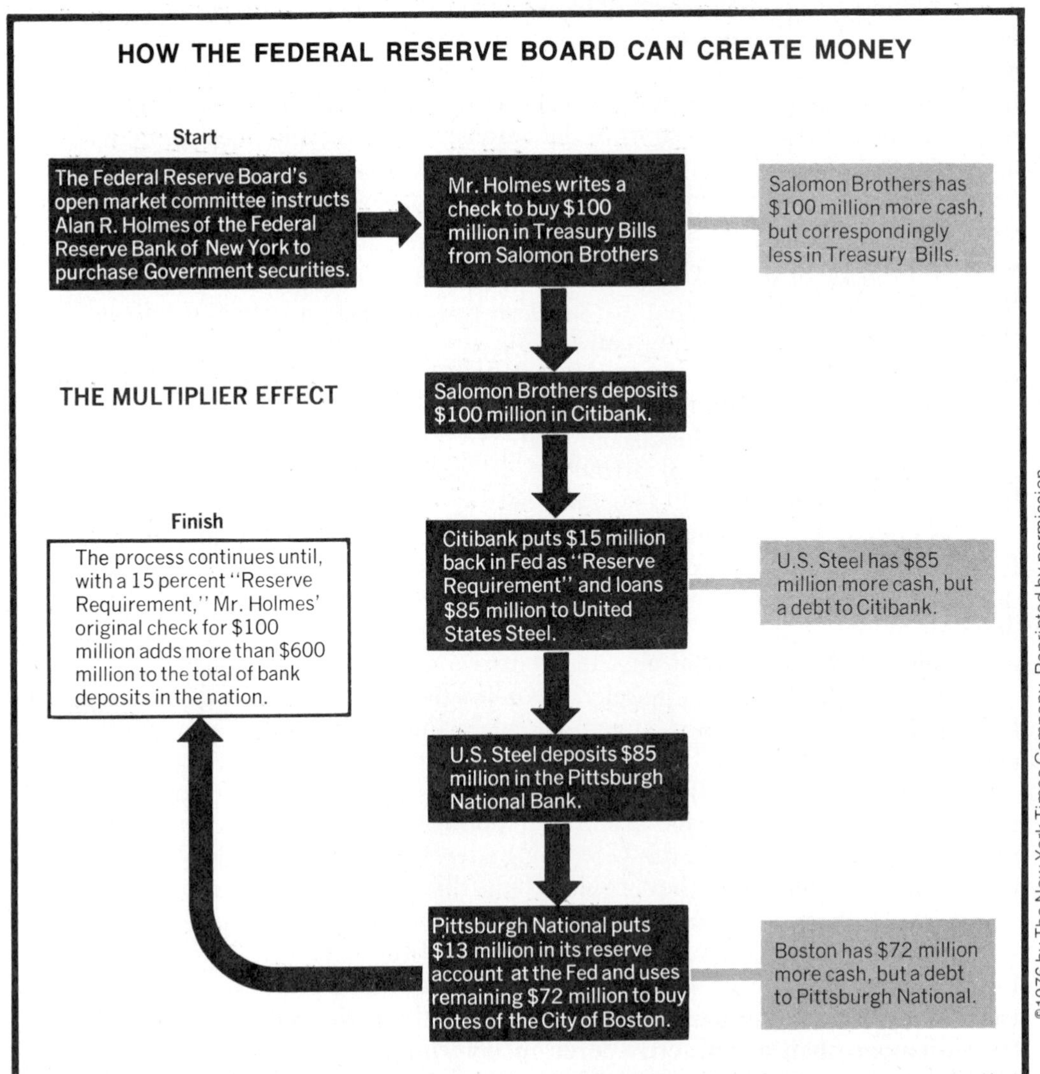

were any other check, in his own commercial bank; and his bank will send the Federal Reserve's check through for credit to its own account, as if it were any other check. *As a result, the dealer's bank will have gained reserves, although no other commercial bank has lost reserves.* On balance, then, the system has more lending and investing capacity than it had before. In fact, it now has *excess* reserves and these, as we have seen, will spread out through the system. **Thus by buying bonds the Federal Reserve has, in fact, deposited money in the accounts of its members, thereby giving them the extra reserves that it set out to create** (see box).

Conversely, if the authorities decide that member banks' reserves are too large, they will sell securities. Now the process works in reverse. Security dealers or other buyers of bonds will send their own checks on their own regular commercial banks to the Federal Reserve in payment for these bonds. This time the Fed will take the checks of its member banks and charge their accounts, thereby reducing their reserves. **Since these checks will not find their way to another commercial bank, the system as a whole will have suffered a diminution of its reserves.** By selling securities, in other words, the Federal Reserve authorities lower the Federal Reserve accounts of member banks, thereby diminishing their reserves. Isn't this, you might ask, really the same thing as raising or lowering the reserve ratio? If the Fed is really just putting money into member bank accounts when it buys bonds and taking money out when it sells them, why does it bother to go through the open market? Why not just tell the member banks that their reserves are larger or smaller?

Analytically, you are entirely right. There are however cogent reasons for working through the bond market. The open-market technique allows banks to *compete* for their share of the excess reserves that are being made available or taken away. Banks that are good at attracting depositors will thereby get extra benefit from an increase in the money supply. Thus, rather than assigning excess reserves by executive fiat, the Fed uses the open market as an allocation device.

In addition, open-market operations allow the Fed to make very small changes in the money supply, whereas changes in reserve requirements would be difficult to adjust in very fine amounts.

ASYMMETRIC CONTROL

How effective are all these powers over the money supply? The Federal Reserve Board's capacity to control money is often compared to our ability to manipulate a string. If the Federal Reserve Board wishes to *reduce* the money supply, it can increase the discount rate or sell bonds. Sooner or later, this tends to be effective. If banks have free or excess reserves, they will not immediately have to reduce their lending portfolios; but eventually, by pulling on the string hard enough, the Fed can force a reduction in bank loans and the money supply.

The Federal Reserve Board's capacity to increase the money supply is not equally great. It can reduce reserve rates and buy bonds, but it cannot *force* banks to make loans if they do not wish to do so. Banks can, if they wish, simply increase their excess reserves. Normally, banks wish to make loans and earn profits; but if risks are high, they may not wish to do so. Such a situation occurred in the Great Depression. Banks piled up vast reserves rather than make loans, since the risk of default was too high to make most loans an attractive economic gamble. In terms of our analogy, the Federal Reserve Board can pull, but it cannot push on its string of controls.

STICKY PRICES

We are almost ready to look into the dynamics of money in our next chapter, but we must examine a question that we have heretofore passed over in silence. We have taken for granted that we need a larger supply of money in order to expand output. But why should we? Why could we not grow just as well if the supply of money were fixed?

Theoretically we could. If we cut prices as we increased output, a given amount of money (or a given amount of expenditure) could cover an indefinitely large real output. Furthermore, as prices fell, workers would be content not to ask for higher wages (or would even accept lower wages), since in real terms they would be just as well or better off.

It is not difficult to spot the flaw in this argument. In the real world, prices of many goods cannot be cut easily. If the price of steel rose and fell as quickly and easily as prices on the stock exchange or if wages went down without a murmur of resistance or if rents and other contractual items could be quickly adjusted, then prices would be flexible and we would not require any enlargement of our money supply to cover a growing real output.

In fact, as we know, prices are extremely "sticky" in the downward direction. Union leaders do not look with approval on wage cuts, even when living costs fall. Contractual prices cannot be quickly adjusted. Many big firms administer their prices and carefully avoid price competition: Note, for example, that the price of many customer items is printed on the package months before the item will be sold.

Thus we can see that a fixed supply of money would put the economy into something of a straitjacket. As output tended to increase, business would need more money to finance production, and consumers would need more money to make their larger expenditures. If business could get more money from the banks, all would be well. But suppose it could not. Then the only way it could get a larger supply of cash would be to persuade someone to lend the money, and persuasion would be in the form of a higher rate of interest. But this rising interest rate would discourage other businesses from going ahead with their plans. Hence the would-be-boom would be stopped dead in its tracks by a sheer shortage of spending power.

A flexible money supply obviates this economic suffocation. The fact that banks can create money (provided that they have excess reserves) enables them to take care of businesses that wish to make additional expenditures. The expenditures themselves put additional money into the hands of consumers. And the spending of consumers in turn sends the enlarged volume of purchasing power back to business firms to complete the great flow of expenditure and receipt.

HIGH POWERED MONEY AND INFLATION

A flexible money supply rescues the system from suffocation. But does it expose it to the dangers of hyperventilation? Does an expandable money supply threaten us with inflation?

In our next chapter we will directly tackle the relation between the money supply and the level of prices. But we ought to say a preliminary word here. **For clearly bank reserves have an inflationary potential in a fractional reserve system, simply by virtue of the fact that they are capable of creating a multiple of themselves. That is why bank reserves are called *high powered money,* and why economists pay careful attention to the volume of reserves when they are considering the extent of the inflationary dangers facing an economy.**

But the fact that high powered money *can* become the basis for inflation is not at all the same as saying that inflation is directly caused by high powered money. It merely tells us that the existence of a flexible money supply poses a problem of monetary management—the theme of the chapter to come.

There is, however, a special source of inflationary increases in bank reserves that we should know about. If a nation becomes the recipient of large inflows of foreign gold, as the United States was during the 1930s; or if foreigners put their money in its banks, as has been the case with Germany and Switzerland in modern times, banks will find their deposits rising. Unlike the case in which deposits increase because of central bank action, this rise may take place despite efforts of the central bank to hold down the quantity of high powered money. The remedy for such inflationary inflows of gold and foreign money takes us into the area of international finance, not a subject for this chapter. But we ought to be aware that such problems can arise, and that they may be difficult to cope with.

PAPER MONEY AND GOLD

Finally, let us clear up one last mystery of the monetary system—the mystery of where currency (coin and bills) actually comes from and where it goes. If we examine most of our paper currency, we will find that it has "Federal Reserve Note" on it: That is, it is paper money issued by the Federal Reserve System. We understand, by now, how the public gets these notes: It simply draws them from its checking accounts. When it does so, the commercial banks, finding their supplies of vault cash low, ask their Federal Reserve district banks to ship them as much new cash as they need.

And what does the Federal Reserve Bank do? It takes packets of bills ($1 and $5 and $10) out of its vaults, *where these stacks of printed paper have no monetary significance at all,* charges the requisite amount against its member banks' balances, and ships the cash out by armored truck. So long as these new stacks of bills remain in the member banks' possession, they are still not money! But soon they will pass out to the public, where they will be money. Do not forget, of course, that as a result the public will have that much *less* money left in its checking accounts.

Could this currency-issuing process go on forever? Could the Federal Reserve print as much money as it wanted to? Suppose that the authorities at the Federal Reserve decided to order a trillion dollars worth of bills from the treasury mints. What would happen when those bills arrived at the Federal Reserve Banks? The answer is that they would simply gather dust in their vaults. There would be no way for the Federal Reserve to "issue" its money unless the public wanted cash. And the amount of cash the public could want is always limited by the amount of money in its checking accounts.

Thus the spectre of "rolling the printing presses" has to be looked at skeptically. In a nation such as pre-Hitler Germany, where most individuals were paid by cash, not by check, it was easier to get the actual bills into circulation than it would be in a highly developed check money system such as ours. The roads to inflation are many, but the actual printing of money is not likely to be one of them.*

THE GOLD COVER

Are there no limitations on this note-issuing or reserve-creating process? Until 1967 there *were* limitations imposed by Congress, requiring the Federal Reserve to hold gold certificates equal in value to at least 25 percent of all outstanding notes. (Gold certificates are a special kind of paper money issued by the U.S. Treasury and backed 100 percent by gold bullion in Fort Knox.) Prior to 1964 there was a further requirement that the amount of gold certificates also be sufficient to give a 25 percent backing as well to the total amount of member bank deposits held by the Fed. Thus the legal obligation not to go beyond this 25 percent gold cover provided a strict ceiling on the amount of member bank reserves the Federal Reserve system could create or on the amount of notes it could ship at the request of its member banks.

All this presented no problem in, say, 1940, when the total of member bank reserves plus Federal Reserve notes came to only $20 billion, against which we held gold certificates worth almost $22 billion. Trouble began to develop, however, in the 1960s when a soaring GNP was accompanied by a steadily rising volume of both member bank reserves and Federal Reserve notes. By 1964, for example, member bank reserves had grown to $22 billion, and outstanding Reserve notes to nearly $35 billion. At the same time, our gold stock had declined to just over $15 billion. With $57 billion in liabilities ($22 billion in member bank reserves plus $35 billion in notes) and only $15 billion in gold certificates, the 25 percent cover requirement was clearly imperiled.

Congress thereupon removed the cover requirement from member bank reserves, leaving all our gold certificates available as backing for our Federal Reserve notes. But even that did not solve the problem. Currency in circulation contined to rise with a record GNP until it exceeded $40 billion in 1967. Our gold stock meanwhile continued to decline to $12 billion in that year and threatened to fall further. The handwriting on the wall indicated that the 25 percent cover could not long be maintained.

There were basically two ways out. One would have been to change the gold cover requirements from 25 percent to, say, 10 percent. That would have made our gold stock more than adequate to back our paper money (and our member bank deposits, too).

*We have all seen pictures of German workers being paid their wages in wheelbarrow loads of marks. The question is this: Why didn't the German authorities simply print paper money with bigger denominations, so that someone who was paid a billion marks a week could get ten 100 million mark notes, not ten thousand 1 million mark notes? The answer is that it takes time to go through the bureaucratic process of ordering a new print run of higher denomination notes. Imagine a young economist at the finance ministry suggesting to his chief that they ought to stock up on billion mark notes to be put into circulation six months hence. His superior would certainly be horrified. "You can't do that," he would protest. "Why, an order for billion mark notes would be—inflationary!"

GOLDFINGER AT WORK

Some years ago a patriotic women's organization, alarmed lest the Communists had tunneled under the Atlantic, forced an inspection of the gold stock buried at Fort Knox. It proved to be all there. An interesting question arises as to the repercussions, had they found the great vault to be bare. Perhaps we might have followed the famous anthropological example of the island of Yap in the South Seas, where heavy stone cartwheels are the symbol of wealth for the leading families. One such family was particularly remarkable insofar as its cartwheel lay at the bottom of a lagoon, where it had fallen from a canoe. Although it was absolutely irretrievable and even invisible, the family's wealth was considered unimpaired, since everyone knew the stone was there. If the Kentucky depository had been empty, a patriotic declaration by the ladies that the gold really was in Fort Knox might have saved the day for the United States.

The second way was much simpler: *eliminate the gold cover entirely.* With very little fuss, this is what Congress did in 1967.

GOLD AND MONEY

Does the presence or absence of a gold cover make any difference? From the economist's point of view it does not. Gold is a metal with a long and rich history of hypnotic influence, so there is undeniably a psychological usefulness in having gold behind a currency. But unless that currency is 100 percent convertible into gold, *any* money demands an act of faith on the part of its users. If that faith is destroyed, the money becomes valueless; so long as it is unquestioned, the money *is* "as good as gold."

Thus the presence or absence of a gold backing for currency is purely a psychological problem, so far as the value of a domestic currency is concerned. But the point is worth pursuing a little further. Suppose our currency *were* 100 percent convertible into gold—suppose, in fact, that we used only gold coins as currency. Would that improve the operation of our economy?

A moment's reflection should reveal that it would not. We would still have to cope with a very difficult problem that our bank deposit money handles rather easily. This is the problem of how we could increase the supply of money or diminish it, as the needs of the economy changed. With gold coins as money, we would either have a frozen stock of money (with consequences that we shall trace in the next chapter), or our supply of money would be at the mercy of our luck in goldmining or the currents of international trade that funneled gold into our hands or took it away. And incidentally, a gold currency would not obviate inflation, as many countries have discovered when the vagaries of international trade or a fortuitous discovery of gold mines increased their holdings of gold faster than their actual output.

MONEY AND BELIEF

How, then, do we explain the world-wide rush to buy gold—a rush that has raised the dollar price of gold from $35 an ounce—its official price as late as 1971—to over $800 an ounce in 1979, before it fell again to half that level.

Once again, the economist offers no rational explanation for such a phenomenon. There is nothing in gold itself that possesses more value than silver, uranium, land, or labor. Indeed, judged strictly as a source of usable values, gold is rather low on the spectrum of human requirements. **The sole reason why people want gold—rich people and poor people, sophisticated people and ignorant ones—is that gold has been for centuries a metal capable of catching and holding our fancy, and in troubled times it is natural enough that we turn to this enduring symbol of wealth as the best bet for preserving our purchasing power in the future.**

Will gold in fact remain valuable forever? And if so, how valuable? There is absolutely no way to answer such a question.

As we cautioned at the outset, money is a highly sophisticated and curious invention. At one time or another nearly everything imaginable has served as the magic symbol of money: whales' teeth, shells, feathers, bark, furs, blankets, butter, tobacco, leather, copper, silver, gold, and (in the most advanced nations) pieces of paper with pictures on them, or simply numbers on a computer printout. In fact, anything is usable as money, provided that there is a natural or enforceable scarcity of it, so that men can usually come into its possession only through carefully designated ways. Behind all the symbols, however, rests the central requirement of faith. **Money serves its indispensable purposes as long as we believe in it. It ceases to function the moment we do not. Money has well been called "the promises men live by."**

But the creation of money and the control over its supply is still only half the question. We have yet to trace how our money supply influences the flow of output itself—or to put it differently, how the elaborate institutions through which men promise to honor one another's work and property affect the amount of work they do and the amount of new wealth they accumulate. This is the subject to which our next chapter will be devoted.

LOOKING BACK

KEY CONCEPTS

The Federal Reserve is the source of most of the net increases (or decreases) in deposits

1. The volume of demand deposits can only increase if there is an increase in deposits that is not matched by a decrease elsewhere. This net increase in deposits and reserves mainly comes from the Federal Reserve system. In the same way the money supply will only contract if a fall in deposits at one bank is not balanced by a rise elsewhere. Again, the Federal Reserve is the source of such net decreases.

Three methods of changing the money supply:
1. Raising or lowering reserve requirements. This is a powerful but undiscriminating weapon

2. The Fed has three methods by which it can change the net total of deposits. The first is by changing the reserve requirement. This directly freezes or frees a portion of the reserves of each bank and also changes the deposit multiplier. This is a potent means of bringing about large changes in money supply but it exerts its effect across the board in an undiscriminating fashion.

2. Changing discount rates signals a policy of tighter or easier money

3. Second, the Federal Reserve can change discount rates—the rate at which member banks can borrow. This action not only directly encourages or discourages member bank borrowing, but is widely regarded as a signal to the financial world that the Fed is eager to make money tight or easier.

3. Open market operations are an important week-to-week means of control. When the Fed buys government bonds it creates net deposits; selling bonds reduces total deposits

4. Third and most important in week-to-week activities are open market operations. These operations are the buying and selling of government bonds conducted by the New York Federal Reserve Bank in the bond market. When the Fed buys bonds it pays for them by its own check. This check, when deposited in a bank, creates a new deposit that is not gained from another bank. It is a net increase in money supply. Selling a bond withdraws deposits in the same way. Open market operations enable banks to compete for their share of the new deposits that will be created.

Asymmetric controls makes it easier to tighten than to expand loans and investments

5. The controls over the money supply are not evenly balanced, but asymmetric. It is easier for the Reserve to pull on the string and reduce lending or investing capacity than to push on the string and assure an increase in loans or investments.

A flexible money system is necessary for an economy with sticky prices

6. The flexible monetary system is necessary because prices are sticky. This is the consequence of long-term contracts, wage agreements, and similar institutional rigidities that make it impossible for prices to fall so that a fixed money supply could finance a growing volume of real output.

High powered money has an inflationary potential

7. Bank reserves are high powered money which creates an inflationary potential. This is a challenge for monetary management.

Paper money has no gold backing. It only passes into use when the public converts its demand deposits into cash

8. Printed money is not actually money until it passes into the hands of the public. The amount depends on the public's demand for cash and the size of its checking accounts. There is no longer a gold cover behind printed money.

Gold is valuable because of its long symbolic importance

9. Gold has long held a special place in the human imagination and this accounts for its value. There is no way of knowing whether gold will continue to hold that special place.

ECONOMIC VOCABULARY

Changing reserve requirements 237
Discount rates 271
Tight money 271
Open market operations 272
Asymmetric control 273
Sticky prices 274
High powered money 274
Gold cover 276

QUESTIONS

1. Suppose that a bank has $1 million in deposits, $100,000 in reserves, and is fully loaned up. Now suppose the Federal Reserve System lowers reserve requirements from 15 percent to 10 percent. What happens to the lending capacity of the bank? What happens to the deposit multiplier?
2. The Federal Reserve Banks buy $100 million in U.S. Treasury notes on the open market. How do they pay for these notes? What happens to the checks? Do they affect the reserves of member banks? Will buying bonds increase or decrease the money supply?

3. Now explain what happens when the Fed sells Treasury notes. Who buys them? How do they pay for them? Where do the checks go? How does payment affect the accounts of member banks at their Federal Reserve bank?
4. Why do you think gold has held such a prestigious place in people's minds?
5. Explain why monetary policy is a better instrument for slowing down an economy than for revving it up. Is this still true if we include inflation as part of revving up? Why is real output more difficult to attain than high prices?

AN EXTRA WORD ABOUT

INDEPENDENCE OF THE FED

The Federal Reserve Board is run by 7 governors, each appointed to a 14-year term by the President with the approval of Congress. The governors of the Federal Reserve System cannot be removed during their terms of office except for wrongdoing. Thus, although fiscal policy is located in the executive and legislative branches of the government, monetary policy is vested in an independent board.

There were two initial justifications for this institutional arrangement. The first was that monetary policies were necessarily subject to quick changes. Second, it was felt that monetary policies ought to be insulated from the political process.

Are these reasons still valid? Some economists think so; others, including ourselves, think not. To take the first argument: It is true that Congress cannot be expected to operate an efficient open-market system on a daily basis. But this is not an argument for divorcing the responsibility for such operations from the *executive* branch. In most of the world's governments, Central Banks (the equivalent of the Fed) are located within the executive establishment, usually as a part of the Treasury or Finance ministries or departments. These banks have no trouble making quick decisions. Moreover, even if Congress could not be expected to approve of every jiggle in monetary measures, there is no reason why it could not endorse or direct the major thrust of monetary strategy toward an expansionary or a contractive general objective.

The argument about "insulation" depends on one's view of democracy, where values once again reign supreme. There is a curious inconsistency, however, in trying to insulate only monetary policies, not fiscal policies. Why should we trust the democratic mechanism to establish expenditures and taxes, but not the supply of money?

As in most institutional debates, dramatic changes are unlikely, although we seem to be moving in a more democratic direction in our monetary management. Congress now expects to be briefed every quarter on the Fed's monetary targets for the following year. There are also bills pending in Congress to integrate the Fed more fully by altering the tenure of the Chairman to be concomitant with that of the President; or to require the Fed to issue an economic report directly after the President's Economic Report, stating what differences, if any, lie between them, and justifying the Fed's course of action if it differs from that of the administration.

Meanwhile, a high degree of integration exists in fact, although not in law. More and more, the Fed bows to public pressure or to pressure from the administration. This is hardly surprising. As we shall see in our next chapter, we live at a time when the importance of money in the economy is more highly regarded than it used to be. The idea of an independent Fed does not sit so well in an era when we think of the Fed as bearing a prime responsibility for our economic well-being. Having created the Federal Reserve Board in the first place, Congress can alter it, as it wishes; and it undoubtedly would alter it, were the Fed to risk a direct confrontation with congressional or presidential economic objectives. The more important money management becomes, the more powerful are the pressures to place it within, not outside the main political mechanisms of the nation.

MONEY AND THE MACRO SYSTEM

A LOOK AHEAD

In our preceding chapter, we found out something of what money is and how it comes into being. Now we must turn to the much more complicated question of how money works.

(1) What happens when the banks create or destroy deposits?

(2) Can we directly raise or lower incomes by altering the quantity of money?

(3) Can we control inflation or recession by using the monetary management powers of the Federal Reserve System?

These extremely important questions will be the focus of discussion in this chapter.

THE QUANTITY THEORY OF MONEY

QUANTITY EQUATION

One relation between money and economic activity must have occurred to us. It is that the quantity of money must have something to do with *prices.* Does it not stand to reason that if we increase the supply of money, prices will go up, and that if we decrease the amount of money, prices will fall?

Something very much like this belief lies behind one of the most famous equations (really identities) in economics. The equation looks like this:

$$MV \equiv PT$$

where

M = *quantity of money* (currency outside banks plus demand deposits)
V = *velocity of circulation,* or the number of times per period or per year that an average dollar changes hands
P = *the general level of prices,* or a price index
T = *the number of transactions made in the economy* in a year, or a measure of physical output

If we think about this equation, its meaning is not hard to grasp. What the quantity equation says is that the amount of *expenditure* (M times V, or the quantity of money times the frequency of its use) equals the amount of *receipts* (P times T, or the price of an average sale times the number of sales). Naturally, this is an identity. In fact, it is our old familiar circular flow. What all factors of production receive (PT) must equal what all factors of production spend (MV).

Just as our GNP identities are true at every moment, so are the quantity theory of money identities true at every instant. They merely look at the circular flow from a different vantage point. And just as our GNP identities yielded useful economic insights when we began to inquire into the functional relationships within those identities, so the quantity theory can also shed light on economic activity if we can find functional relationships concealed within its self-evident "truth."

ASSUMPTIONS OF THE QUANTITY THEORY

To move from identities to functional relationships, we need to make assumptions that lend themselves to investigation and evidence. In the case of the GNP $\equiv C + G + I + X$ identity, for instance, we made a critical assumption about the propensity to consume, which led to the multiplier and to predictive statements about the influence of injections on GNP. In the case of $MV \equiv PT$, we need another assumption. What will it be?

The crucial assumptions made by the economists who first formulated the quantity theory were two: (1) The velocity of money—the number of times an average dollar was used per year—*was constant;* and (2) transactions (sales) *were always at a full-employment level.* If these assumptions were true, it followed that the price level was a simple function of the supply of money:

$$P = \frac{V}{T} \cdot M$$

$$P = kM$$

where k was a constant defined by V/T.

If the money supply went up, prices went up; if the quantity of money went down, prices went down. Since the government controlled the money supply, it could easily regulate the price level.

TESTING THE QUANTITY THEORY

Is this causal relation true? Can we directly manipulate the price level by changing the size of our stock of money?

The original inventors of the quantity equation, over half a century ago, thought this was indeed the case. And of course it *would* be the case if everything else in the equation held steady while we moved the quantity of money up or down. In other words, if the velocity of circulation, V, and the number of transactions, T, were fixed, changes in M would have to operate directly on P.

Can we test the validity of this assumption? There is an easy way to do so. Figure 19.1 shows us changes in the supply of money compared with changes in the level of prices.

A glance at Figure 19.1 answers our question. Between 1929 and 1979 the supply of money in the United States increased over eleven-fold, while prices rose only a little more than four-fold. Clearly, something *must* have happened to

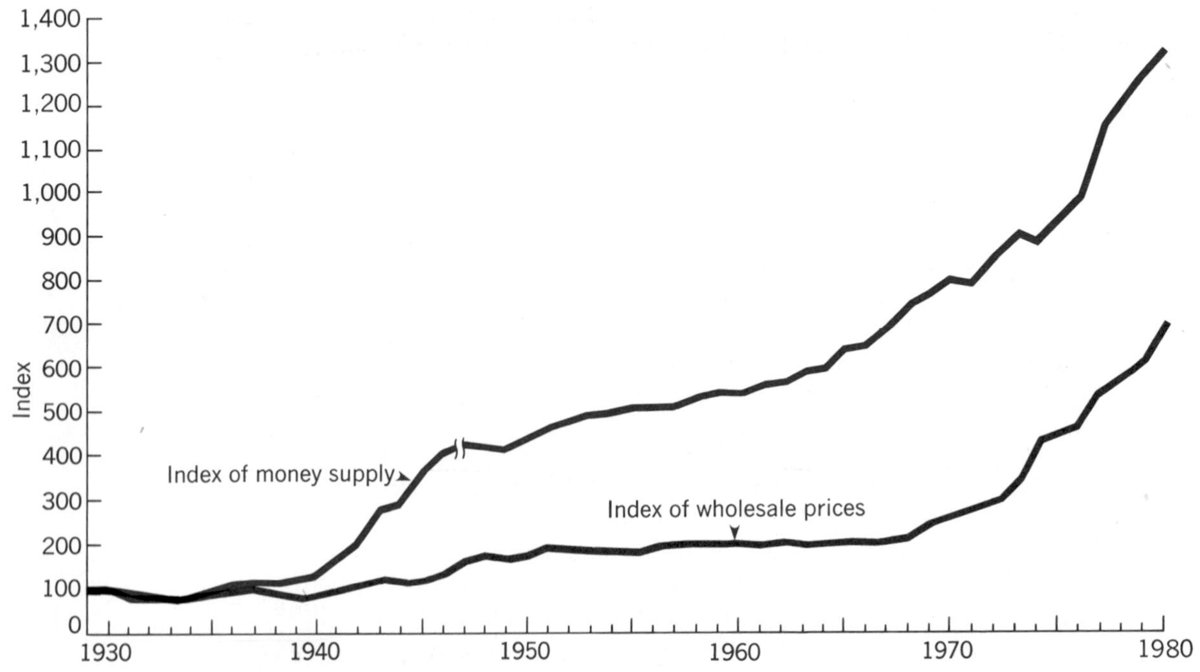

FIGURE 19.1 MONEY SUPPLY AND PRICES

Money supply has risen faster than price levels, proof that there is no iron linkage between *M* and *P*. *V* and *T* must be taken into account.

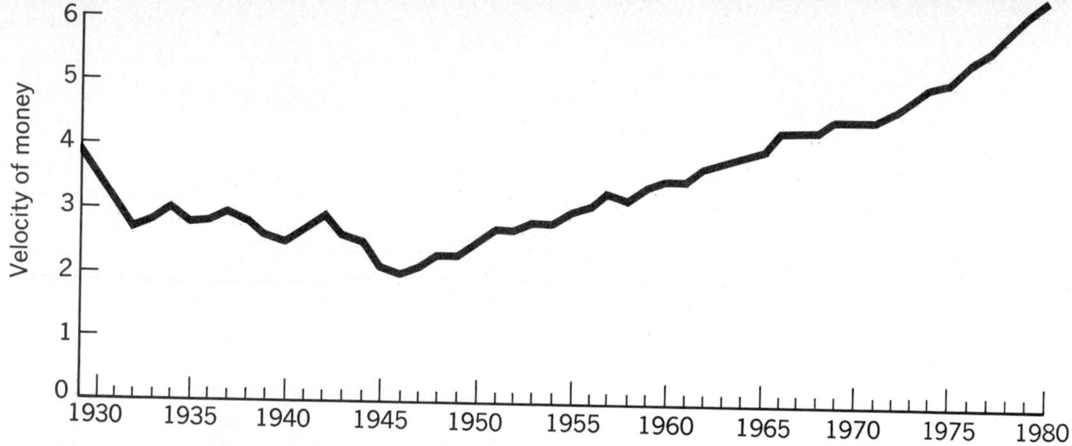

FIGURE 19.2 VELOCITY OF MONEY

Velocity is an important source of change. The quicker we spend money, the more dollars we send chasing after goods.

V or to *T* to prevent the eleven-fold increase in *M* from bringing about a similar increase in *P*. Let us see what those changes were.

CHANGES IN *V*

Figure 19.2 gives us a first clue as to what is wrong with a purely mechanical interpretation of the quantity theory. In it we show how many times an average dollar was used to help pay for each year's output.* We derive this number by dividing the total expenditure for each year's output (which is, of course, the familiar figure for GNP) by the actual supply of money—currency plus checking accounts—for each year. As the chart shows, the velocity of money fell by 50 percent between 1929 and 1946, only to rise above the 1929 level over the postwar years.

We shall return later to an inquiry into why people spend money less or more quickly, but it is clear beyond question that they do. This has two important implications for our study of money. First, it gives a very cogent reason why we cannot apply the quantity theory in a mechanical way, asserting that an increase in the supply of money will *always* raise prices. For if people choose to spend the increased quantity of money more slowly, its impact on the quantity of goods may not change at all, whereas if they spend the same quantity of money more rapidly, prices can rise without any change in *M*.

Second and more clearly than we have seen, the variability of *V* reveals that money itself can be a destabilizing force—destabilizing because it enables us to do two things that would be impossible in a pure barter economy. We can:

1. **Delay between receiving and expending our rewards for economic effort.**
2. **Spend more or less than our receipts by drawing on, or adding to, our cash balances.**

*Note that final output is not quite the same as *T*, which embraces *all* transactions, including those for intermediate goods. But if we define *T* so that it includes only *transactions that enter into final output, PT* becomes a measure of gross national product. In the same way, we can count only those expenditures that enter into GNP when we calculate *MV*. It does no violence to the idea of the quantity theory to apply it only to final output, and it makes statistical computation far simpler.

Classical economists used to speak of money as a "veil," implying that it did not itself play an active role in influencing the behavior of the economic players. But we can see that the ability of those players to vary the rate of their expenditure—to hang onto their money longer or to get rid of it more rapidly than usual—makes money much more than a veil. Money (or rather, people's wish to hold or to spend money) becomes an independent source of change in a complex economic society. **To put it differently, the use of money introduces an independent element of uncertainty into the circular flow.***

CHANGES IN *T*

Now we must turn to a last and perhaps most important reason why we cannot relate the supply of money to the price level in a mechanical fashion. This reason lies in the role played by *T*; that is, by the volume of output.

Just as the early quantity theorists thought of *V* as essentially unvarying, so they thought of *T* as a relatively fixed term in the quantity equation. In the minds of nearly all economic theorists before the Depression, output was always assumed to be as large as the available resources and the willingness of the factors of production would permit. While everyone was aware that there might be minor variations from this state of full output, virtually no one thought they would be of sufficient importance to matter. **Hence the quantity theory implicitly assumed full employment or full output as the normal condition of the economy.** With such an assumption, it was easy to picture *T* as an unimportant term in the equation and to focus the full effect of changes in money on *P*.

The trauma of the Great Depression effectively removed the comfortable assumption that the economy naturally tended to full employment and output. At the bottom of the Depression, real output had fallen by 30 percent. Aside from what the Depression taught us in other ways, it made unmistakably clear that changes in the volume of output (and employment) were of crucial importance in the overall economic picture, and that the economy does *not* naturally gravitate to full employment levels.

A MODERN QUANTITY THEORY?

It is clear, then, that the old-fashioned quantity theorists were mistaken. (For an explanation of *why* they erred, see the box on p. 287.)

Does this mean that there is *no* relation between the quantity of money and the rate of inflation? Certainly no one would go that far. There is not the faintest doubt that we could create a terrific inflation by recklessly increasing the money supply, or that we would bring inflation to a stop (along with the whole economy) by ruthlessly pulling on the string of monetary control.

The problem is whether we can find a functional relationship that will enable us to predict, with tolerable accuracy, the effects of ordinary increases or decreases in *M* on *P*. This would mean replacing the assumption of a fixed *V* with a variable *V* related in some fashion to other elements in the system, and

*Technically, the standard economic definition of money is that it is both a means of exchange and a store of value. It is the latter characteristic that makes money a potentially disturbing influence.

WHY THE OLD QUANTITY THEORISTS ERRED

Modern economists can easily show that the velocity of money is not constant and that the volume of transactions (GNP) is not always at full employment. But it should not be thought that the originators of the quantity theory were stupid or too lazy to look up the basic data. Most of the numbers on which economists now rely were simply not in existence then. The national income, for example, was not calculated until the early 1930s, and the GNP was not "invented" until the early 1940s. You cannot calculate the velocity of money unless you know the national income or the gross national product.

Neither did the original quantity theorists have accurate measures of unemployment or capacity utilization. They used the only method available to them: direct observation of the world, a method that is notoriously inaccurate when one's view is much smaller than "the world." The idea of mass involuntary unemployment required the idea of an equilibrium output that would be less than a full-employment output, an idea completely foreign to pre-Keynesian thought.

it would also require finding a way of relating increases in *MV* to *T* as well as to *P*.

There has been a very active search for such precise relationships, but so far none have been found. Therefore we do not yet have a new quantity equation—a way of predicting how much *P* will change as we change *M*, or of foretelling how a given change in *MV* will be split between *P* and *T*. Until we find such functional relationships, a new quantity theory remains a hope, not an achievement.

OUTPUT AND PRICES

How does our modern emphasis on the variability of output and employment fit into the overall question of money and prices? The answer is very simple, but very important. We have come to see that the effect of more money on prices cannot be determined unless we also take into account the effect of spending on the volume of transactions or output.

It is not difficult to grasp the point. Let us picture an increase in spending, perhaps initiated by a business launching a new investment program or by the government inaugurating a new public works project. These new expenditures will be received by many other entrepreneurs as the multiplier mechanism spreads the new spending through the economy. But now we come to the key question. What will entrepreneurs do as their receipts increase?

It is at this point that the question of output enters. For if factories or stores are operating *at less than full capacity,* and if there is an *employable supply of labor available,* the result of their new receipts is almost certain to be an increase in output. That is, employers will take advantage of the rise in demand to produce and sell more goods and services. They may also try to raise prices and increase their profits further; but *if their industries are reasonably competitive, it is doubtful that prices can be raised very much.* Other firms with idle plants will simply undercut them and take their business away. An example is provided

MAXIMUM VS. FULL EMPLOYMENT

What is "full" employment? Presumably government spending is guided by the objectives of the Employment Act of 1946, which declares the attainment of "maximum employment" to be a central economic objective of the government.

But what is maximum employment? Does it mean zero unemployment? This would mean that no one could quit his job even to look for a better one. Or consider the problem of inflation. Zero unemployment would probably mean extremely high rates of inflation, for reasons we will look into more carefully later. Hence no one claims that full employment is maximum employment in the sense of an absence of *any* unemployment whatsoever.

But this opens the question of how much *unemployment* is accepted as consistent with maximum employment. Under Presidents Kennedy and Johnson, the permissible unemployment rate was 4 percent. Under Presidents Nixon, Ford, and Carter the permissible unemployment rate rose to a range of 4.5 to 5 or even 6 percent, largely because inflation had worsened. Hence the meaning of full employment is open to the discretion of the economic authorities, and their policies may vary from one period to another.

by the period 1934 through 1940 when output increased by 50 percent while prices rose by less than 5 percent. The reason, of course, lay in the great amount of unemployed resources, making it easy to expand output without price increases.

FULL EMPLOYMENT VS. UNDEREMPLOYMENT

This is a very important finding for macroeconomics, for it helps us see that policies that make sense in one economic situation make no sense in another. This is particularly the case with policies that promote spending of any kind—public spending or private spending, spending out of earned income or deficit spending. If an economy is suffering from large numbers of unemployed workers and from large amounts of underutilized capacity, it *must* spend more if it is to move back to its production frontiers. As we have learned in Chapter 11, expenditure is the necessary precondition for output. Unless we spend more, we are doomed to remain permanently underemployed.

But spending more will not bring us more output if we are at, or close to, the production frontier. Then more spending—for consumption or investment, for private use or public use—can only send prices higher, with little or no effect on the volume of output.

Until recently, this distinction between the beneficial effects of expenditure when unemployment was high, and the bad effects of expenditure when unemployment was low, was a central premise of modern macroeconomics. Today, the distinction is not so sharp as it once was, for we seem to have moved into a condition in which spending sends up prices even though we are certainly not in a state of full employment or utilization. This is a problem that we will study more closely in Chapter 31, which is devoted to the dilemmas of modern inflation.

MONEY AND EXPENDITURE

We have almost lost sight of our subject, which is not yet inflation but how money affects GNP. And here there is an important point. How does an increased supply of money get into GNP? People who have not studied economics often discuss changes in the money supply as if the government put money into circulation, mailing out dollar bills to taxpayers. The actual connection between an increase in *M* and an increase in *MV* is much more complex. Let us look into it.

1. The transactions demand for money

From our previous chapter we know the immediate results of an increased supply of money, whether brought about by open-market operations or a change in reserve ratios. **The effect in both cases is a rise in the lendable or investible reserves of banks. *Ceteris paribus,* this will lead to a fall in interest rates as banks compete with one another in lending their additional unused reserves to firms or individuals.**

As interest rates decline, some firms and individuals will be tempted to increase their borrowings. It becomes cheaper to take out a mortgage, to buy a car on an installment loan, to finance inventories. Thus, as we would expect, the demand curve for spending money, like that for most commodities, slopes downward. As money gets cheaper, people want to buy (borrow) more of it. To put it differently, the lower the price of money, the larger the quantity demanded. We speak of this demand curve for money to be used for expenditure as the *transactions demand for money.*

2. Financial demand

But there is also another, quite separate source of the demand for money. This is the demand for money for *financial purposes,* to be held by individuals or corporations as part of their assets.

What happens to the demand for money for financial purposes as its price goes down? Financial demand also increases, although for different reasons. When interest rates are high, individuals and firms tend to keep their wealth as fully invested as possible, in order to earn the high return that is available. But when interest rates fall, the opportunity cost of keeping money idle is much less. If you are an investor with a portfolio of $10,000, and the rate of interest is 10 percent, you give up $1,000 a year if you are very liquid (i.e., all in cash), whereas if the interest rate is only 6 percent, your opportunity cost for liquidity falls to $600.

LIQUIDITY PREFERENCE

Economists call this increased willingness to be in cash as interest rates fall *liquidity preference.* The motives behind liquidity preferences are complex—partly speculative, partly precautionary. With low opportunity costs for holding money, we can afford to hold cash for any good investment or consumption opportunity that happens to come along. Similarly, it is cheaper to hold more money to protect ourselves against any unexpected emergencies.

In this way, both the speculative and precautionary motives make us more and more willing or eager to be in cash when interest rates are low, and less and less willing when rates are higher. Thus the financial demand for cash, like the transactions demand, is a downward sloping demand curve.

If we now put together the transactions and the financial demands for money and add the supply curve of money—the actual stock of money available—the result looks like Figure 19.3.

Our diagram shows us that at interest rate *OA*, there will be *OX* amount of money demanded for transactions purposes and *OY* amount demanded for li-

PRECAUTIONARY AND SPECULATIVE DEMAND

Both the precautionary and the speculative demand for money can be illustrated in the problem of buying or selling bonds. Most bonds are a promise to pay a certain stated amount of interest and to repay the principal at some fixed date. To simplify things, forget the repayment for a moment and focus on the interest. Suppose that you paid $1,000 for a perpetual bond that had a "coupon"—an interest return—of $100 per year with no date of repayment. And suppose that you wanted to sell that bond. What would it be worth?

The answer depends wholly on the current market rate of interest for bonds of equal risk. Suppose that this rate of interest were 10 percent. Your bond would then still be worth $1,000, because the coupon would yield the buyer of the bond 10 percent on his money. But suppose that interest rates had risen to 20 percent. You would now find that your bond was only worth $500. A buyer can go into the market and purchase other bonds that will give him a 20 percent yield on his money. Therefore he will pay you only $500 for your bond, because your $100 coupon is 20 percent of $500. If you want to sell your bond, that is the price you will have to accept.

On the other hand, if interest rates have fallen to 5 percent, you can get $2,000 for your bond, for you can show the buyer that your $100 coupon will give him the going market return of 5 percent at a price of $2,000. (If you were to buy a *new* $1,000 bond at the going 5 percent interest rates, it would carry a coupon of only $50.)

These calculations also show that it can be very profitable at times to hold money. When interest rates are rising, bond prices are falling. Therefore, the longer you wait before you buy, the bigger will be your chances for a capital gain if interest rates turn around and go the other way. This means that we tend to get "liquid" whenever we think that interest rates are below normal levels and bonds are too high; and that we tend to get out of money and into bonds whenever we think that interest rates are above normal levels, and therefore bonds are cheap. The trick, of course, is being right about the course of interest rates before everyone else.

Actual operations in the bond market are complicated, because we must take into account not only interest rates but the time left until a bond becomes mature (i.e., is repaid). The closer it is to maturity, the less its price will depart from its face value or principal. Nonetheless, very great gains and losses can be made in bonds that have some years to go before maturity. Even the most conservative bonds, such as government bonds, will swing in price as our speculative and precautionary impulses incline us now toward liquidity, now toward a fully invested position.

The demand for money has a negative slope, whether we want money to spend or to hold as a liquid investment: The lower interest rates fall, the more money we will seek. The supply of money, as we can see, is a fixed quantity in the short run.

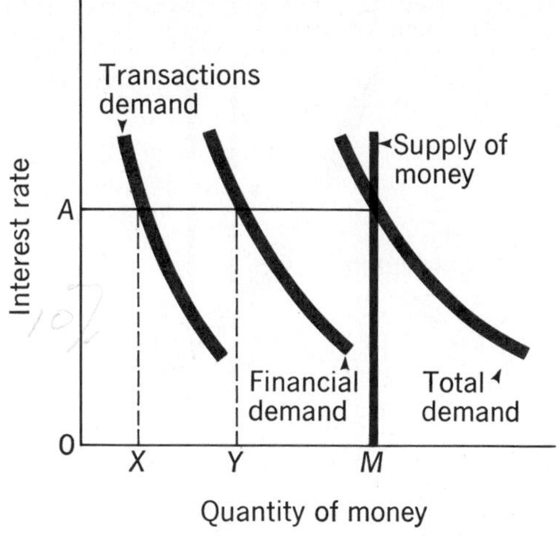

FIGURE 19.3 TRANSACTIONS AND FINANCIAL DEMANDS FOR MONEY

quidity purposes. The total demand for money will be OM ($= OX + OY$), which is just equal to the total supply.

CHANGING THE SUPPLY OF MONEY

Let us suppose that the monetary authorities reduce the supply of money. We show this in Figure 19.4. Now we have a curious situation. The supply of money has declined from *OM* to *OM′*. But notice that the demand curve for money shows that firms and individuals want to hold *OM* at the given rate of interest *OA*. *Yet they cannot hold amount* OM, *because the monetary authorities have cut the supply to* OM′. What will happen?

The answer is very neat. As bank reserves fall, banks will tighten money—raise lending rates and screen loan applications more carefully. Therefore in-

The Fed reduces the money supply from *OM* to *OM′*. *OA* is no longer a price for money that will clear the market. Now see Figure 19.5.

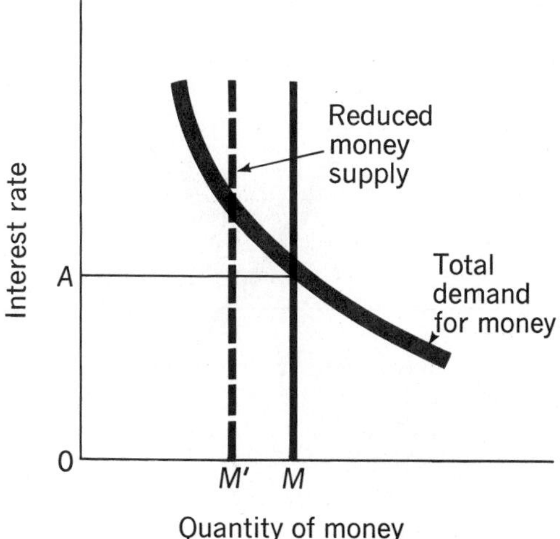

FIGURE 19.4 REDUCING THE SUPPLY OF MONEY

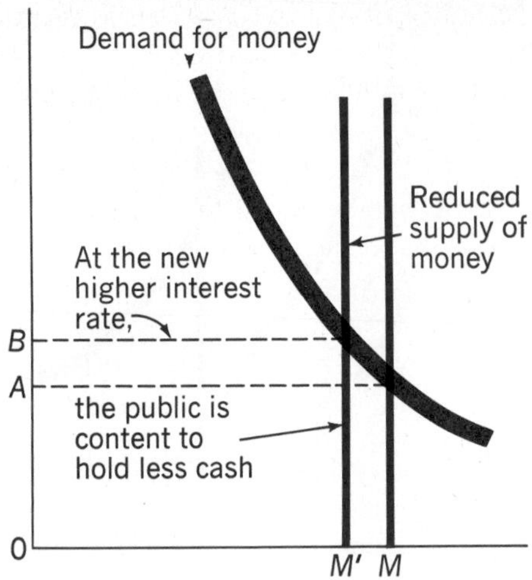

FIGURE 19.5 DETERMINATION OF NEW EQUILIBRIUM

When the quantity of money shrinks, the public will try to acquire money by selling bonds. As they do so, bond yields rise. As yields rise, the demand for money falls. The market now finds a new clearing price (*OB*) for its smaller quantity of *OM′*.

dividuals and firms will be competing for a reduced supply of loans and will bid more for them. At the same time, individuals and firms will feel the pinch of reduced supplies of cash and will try to get more money to fulfill their liquidity desires. The easiest way to get more money is to sell securities, to get out of bonds and into cash. **Note, however, that selling securities does not create a single additional dollar of money. It simply transfers money from one holder to another. But it does change the rate of interest. As bonds are sold, their price falls; and as the price of bonds falls, the interest yield on bonds rises (see p. 266).**

Our next diagram (Figure 19.5) shows what happens. As interest rates rise, the public is content to hold a smaller quantity of money. Hence a new interest rate, *OB*, will emerge, at which the public is *willing* to hold the money that

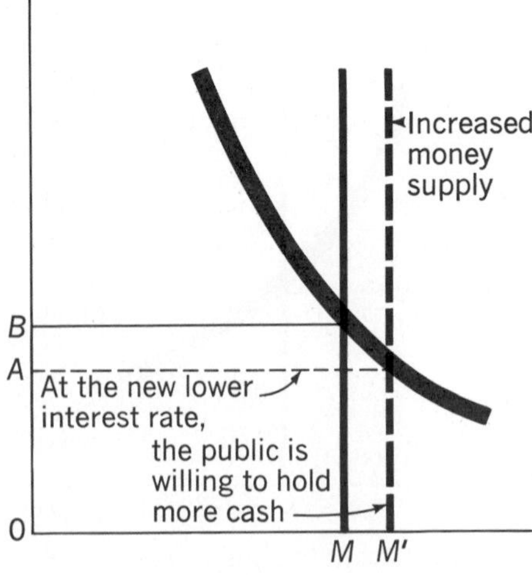

FIGURE 19.6 INCREASING THE SUPPLY OF MONEY

Here is the opposite story. The Fed increases *M* to *OM′*. Individuals do not want more money at the old price (*OB*). They use the new supply of money to buy bonds. Bond prices rise, yields fall. At a lower interest rate (*OA*) the public will be willing to hold *OM′*.

there *is to hold.* The attempt to become more liquid ceases and a new equilibrium interest rate prevails.

Suppose the authorities had increased the supply of money. In that case, individuals and firms would be holding more money than they wanted at the going rate of interest. They would try to get out of money into bonds, sending bond prices up and yields down. Simultaneously, banks would find themselves with extra reserves and would compete with one another for loans, also driving interest rates down. As interest rates fell, firms and individuals would be content to hold more money either for transactions or liquidity purposes until a new equilibrium was again established. Figure 19.6 shows the process at work.

DETERMINATION OF INTEREST RATES

This gives us the final link in our argument. We have seen that interest rates determine whether we wish to hold larger or smaller balances, either for transactions or financial (liquidity) purposes. But what determines the interest rate itself?

The Federal Reserve can, of course, raise or lower the discount rate, and big banks from time to time can announce a new "prime rate"—the rate at which they will lend to their best customers. But neither the Fed nor the biggest bank could make a rate "stick" if there were no bidders for money at that level, or conversely, if everyone converged on the bank for a loan. Although rates are announced by the monetary authorities or by big banks, they must accord with the forces of the marketplace if they are to hold steady. And we can now see that the forces of the marketplace are summed up in the interplay of supply and demand that we have been discussing.

Our demand for money is made up of our transactions demand curve and our financial (liquidity) demand curve. The supply of money is given to us by the monetary authorities. The price of money—interest—is therefore determined by the demand for, and supply of, money, exactly as the price of any commodity is determined by the demand and supply for it.

MONEY AND EXPENDITURE

What our analysis enables us to see, however, is that once the interest rate is determined, it will affect the use to which we put a given supply of money. Now we begin to understand the full answer to the question of how changes in the supply of money affect GNP (and prices). Let us review the argument one last time.

1. Suppose that the monetary authorities want to increase the supply of money. They will lower reserve ratios or buy government bonds on the open market.

2. Banks will find that they have larger reserves. They will compete with one another and lower lending rates.

3. Individuals and firms will also find that they have larger cash balances than they want at the going rate of interest. They will try to get rid of their extra cash by buying bonds, thereby sending bond yields down.

4. As interest rates fall, both as a result of bank competition and rising bond prices, the new, larger supply of money will find its way into use. *Part of it will*

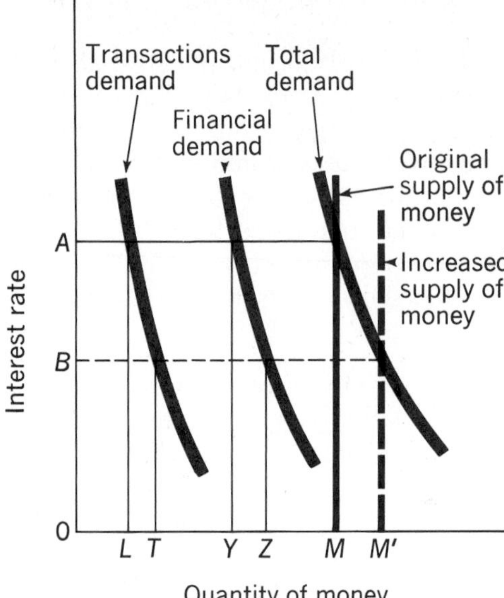

FIGURE 19.7 USING MONEY FOR TWO PURPOSES

This is exactly the same situation as that shown in Figure 19.6, but here we show how the increased supply of money is divided between transactions (LT) and financial uses (YZ).

be used for additional transactions purposes, as individuals and firms take advantage of cheaper money and increase their borrowings. Part of it will be used for larger financial balances, as the public's desire for liquidity grows with falling interest rates.

We can see the process very clearly in Figure 19.7. We begin with *OM* money supply and a rate of interest *OA*. As we can see, *OL* amount of money is held for liquidity purposes, and *OY* for transactions purposes. Now the stock of money is increased to *OM′*. The interest rate falls, for the reasons we now understand, until it reaches *OB*. At the new interest rate, liquidity balances have increased to *OT*, and transactions balances to *OZ*.

Exactly the same process would take place in reverse if the stock of money were decreased from *OM′* to *OM*. Can you see that the decreased supply of money will result partly in smaller transactions balances and partly in smaller liquidity balances? Do you understand that it is the higher rate of interest that causes the public to hold these smaller balances?

MONETARISM

In recent years much controversy has been generated by a new approach to money management called *monetarism*, an approach originally advanced by Nobel Laureate Milton Friedman. Monetarism has three interesting propositions:

1. **Increases or decreases in the supply of money affect spending directly, not just indirectly via their effects on the rate of interest**

Monetarists believe this to be the case because they hold that the public has a strong propensity to keep a fixed proportion of its income in liquid form, and will therefore spend any "excess" cash that is thrust upon it: If you find that your bank account is unexpectedly large, you will tend to buy something rather than hold the cash.

2. Only monetary policy can influence the course of GNP

Monetarists hold that increases in public expenditure only displace, or **crowd out,** private expenditure. Therefore fiscal policy comes to naught, except to shift resources from private to public purposes. Fiscal policy cannot increase the level of GNP because an increase in public spending will be offset by a decrease in private spending.

3. There is a natural tendency to stability in the economy

Monetarism strongly espouses the belief that the market mechanism is a powerful and efficient regulator of economic activity, and that left to itself it will steer the economy on a steady, high employment course. Moreover, most efforts to alter this course, by correcting for minor dips and swings for example, only aggravate small instabilities and make them into big ones. In fact, Professor Friedman holds that the depth and persistence of the Great Depression was entirely the consequence of the erroneous policies followed by the Federal Reserve during the 1930s.

This does not mean that the government should follow no policy. On the contrary, Friedman urges that a steady automatic increase in the money supply, geared to increases in productivity, would be the best way of urging and assisting the natural processes of expansion. He seeks an unvarying growth in money, not a varying one—a growth determined by rules, not by decisions.

Are the monetarists right? We do not really know. A great deal of interest has been stirred up by their bold and provocative ideas, and without doubt economists have become more interested in, and concerned about, money as a result of Friedman's work. But the matter is not yet settled scientifically. It is not easy to demonstrate that a crowding out effect actually takes place. It is not by any means clear that the Depression would have ended sooner had the Federal Reserve not followed its probably wrong-headed policies.

We are not going to pass judgment on monetarism here. Rather, in our next chapter we will return to the question as part of a larger issue—the issue of how much control we are able to exert over our path of economic growth.

THE ART OF MONETARY MANAGEMENT

Whether the monetarists are finally shown to be correct or not, we do not today have anything like a steady or automatic increase in money supply. On the contrary, the members of the Federal Reserve Boards meet regularly to discuss what changes in monetary policy seem advisable—whether money should be tightened or loosened, and what means should be used to reach their targets. Thus the art of money management is very much with us.

Why "art"? Is not the task of the monetary authority very clear? By increasing the supply of money, it pushes down interest rates and encourages expenditure. Hence all it has to do is to regulate the quantity of money to maintain a level of spending that will keep us at a high, but not too high, level of employment.

SHIFTING LIQUIDITY PREFERENCES

Unfortunately, things are not that simple. Suppose that the Fed is concerned about an acceleration of inflation and decides to tighten money to hold back the pressure on prices. But suppose that at the same time the public's liquidity preferences are going down because they too expect higher prices and want to spend their dollars "while they're still good."

The result may be a shift that frustrates the intentions of the Fed. In Figure 19.8 we can see that the Fed has reduced *M*, obviously in the hope of sending interest rates up from *OA* to *OB*. But the public has meanwhile shifted its demand curve to the left so that interest rates remain unchanged.

Shifts such as these that make the demand for money change in the "wrong" way (from the Reserve's point of view) enormously complicate the money management task.

CREDIT CRUNCHES

Suppose now that the monetary authorities are convinced that the brakes have to be applied swiftly and firmly to the money supply. They know from past experience that they may create a *credit crunch.* When the brakes are slammed on, not all parts of the economy suffer alike. Mortgage loans, for example, may be very hard to get. Little customers are much more likely to get turned down by the banks than big customers.

This uneven reduction in lending was very marked in the crunch of 1974. While residential and state and municipal borrowing declined by 24 percent, corporate borrowing rose by 114 percent. Even these figures understate the differences among sectors of the economy. Large corporations were not only able to gain more domestic loans than small business or local governments, but they also had access to international money markets. Thus to some extent they were exempt from the control of domestic monetary authorities. Many large firms, for instance, borrowed in West Germany to make investments in the United States.

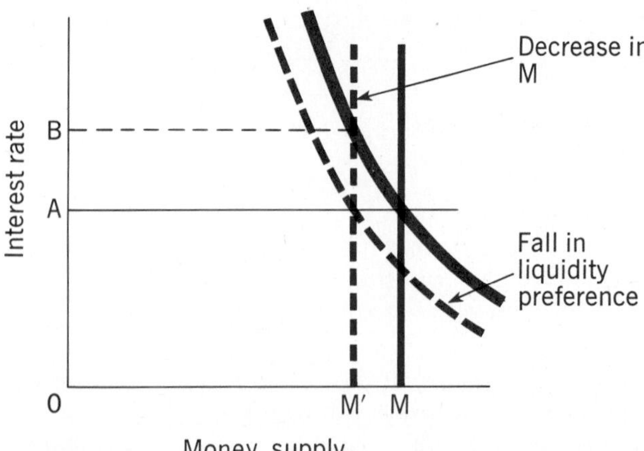

FIGURE 19.8 A SHIFT IN LIQUIDITY PREFERENCE

The Fed cuts the money supply from *OM* to *OM′*. It hopes to raise interest rates from *OA* to *OB*; and it would —if liquidity preferences were unchanged. But the downward shift in the demand curve for money frustrates the Fed. Interest rates remain at *OA*.

But even large corporations can run into trouble during credit crunches. In the 1968 crunch the Chrysler Corporation almost collapsed. And the Penn Central did collapse. **Such disasters together with the uneven effects of a crunch, place a limit on monetary policies. Very stringent restraints seem both institutionally and politically impossible.** After the 1969–1970 credit crunch, efforts were made to develop financial intermediaries that would lend to the sectors most severely hurt and thus spread the effects of monetary policies more evenly across the economy. During the 1974 recession, however, these intermediaries proved to be ineffective. A painful credit crunch occurred despite these new institutions. Will we have another bad crunch as we enter the 1980s? There are some signs that we will in housing and other industries especially hard hit by high interest rates.

A CONTINUING PROBLEM

All these problems help us understand why money management is an art, not a science. Much depends on the "feel" of the economy, on experience, on mature judgment. There is very little that can be reduced to a pat formula.

Could money management become a science? Only if we were to adopt a monetarist position and abandon all efforts to intervene in the economy, trusting entirely to the effects of a steady, unvarying, automatic growth in the money supply. In our next chapter we will look into this question further, for it is one of the central issues of our day.

LOOKING BACK

KEY CONCEPTS

1. The quantity theory, in its original formulation, directly related increases in *M*, the stock of money, to increases in *P*, the price-level. The formula for the theory was $MV = PT$, where *V*, velocity, and *T*, transactions (output) were assumed to be unchanging.

Originally the quantity theory was formulated as $MV = PT$, where *P* and *T* were taken as fixed. We know that they are not

2. Empirical evidence, not available at the time of the original formulation, has made it clear that *V* and *T* are both variables, not constants. This is particularly the case with *T*, which can no longer always be assumed to tend to full utilization levels.

Modern quantity theory seeks a way of relating *V* to *M*, and *MV* to both *P* and *T*

3. A modern quantity theory would relate *V* to *M*, and would divide the effects of *MV* between *P* and *T*. No such reliable formulation has yet been achieved.

More spending should not send up prices when unemployment is high. This is less true in an inflationary economy

4. As a general rule, increases in spending will generate additional output, with or without price increases, as long as there is large unused capacity in the labor and capital markets. But additional spending, private or public, will generate only price rises and no more output as we reach full employment. This distinction is somewhat blurred in today's inflationary economy.

Money supply affects expenditure two ways. As interest rates fall, more is borrowed for ordinary spending

5. Increases (or decreases) in the money supply affect expenditure in two different ways. The demand for money for ordinary transactional purposes is negatively sloped, like most demand curves. As interest rates fall, individuals and businesses borrow more money for transaction motives.

The demand for money for liquidity purposes also increases as interest rates fall

6. A second source of demand on the money supply is for financial purposes. As interest rates fall the opportunity cost of liquidity also falls. Accordingly, individuals sell bonds to get into cash. This demand curve is known as liquidity preference. Changes in the supply of money are therefore partly absorbed by changes in transaction balances and partly by changes in liquidity balances.

When the Fed changes the stock of *M*, individuals find themselves holding more money, or less money, than desired. They will buy or sell bonds, and in so doing will change yields. Thus the rate of interest is set by *S* and *D* for money

7. By changing the stock of money, the authorities create more or less money than the public wants to hold at existing interest rates. The public will buy bonds to get out of money or sell them to get into cash. Buying and selling will not change the amount of money, but it will change bond yields. Thus interest rates are determined by the supply and demand for money.

Monetarism has 3 basic tenets:
(1) Changes in the quantity of money directly affect spending
(2) Public spending crowds out private, so that only monetary policy can alter GNP
(3) The best monetary policy is steady, automatic, unchanging growth

8. Monetarism is a theory that suggests that changes in the supply of money affect spending directly, even without changing interest rates, because individuals tend to spend excess cash. The monetarist position also holds that the system responds only to monetary, not fiscal, policy. This is because monetarists believe that public spending displaces or crowds out private spending, leaving total GNP largely unaffected in size. And last, monetarism holds the system to be inherently stable, and blames monetary policy for destabilizing it. The best monetary policy would be a steady automatic increase in *M*, geared to productivity.

Money management is an art. Liquidity shifts and potential credit squeezes limit its effectiveness

9. Monetary management is an art, not a science. Shifts in liquidity preference and potential credit crunches, among other problems, can frustrate or limit the effectiveness of monetary policy.

ECONOMIC VOCABULARY

Quantity theory 283	**Liquidity preference** 289	**Monetarism** 294
Quantity equation 283	**Transactions demand** 289	**Crowding out** 295
Velocity of circulation 283	**Financial demand** 289	**Credit crunch** 296

QUESTIONS

1. Why is the quantity equation a truism? Why is the interpretation of the quantity equation that *M* affects *P* not a truism?
2. If employment is full, what will be the effects of an increase in private investment on prices and output, supposing that everything else stays the same?
3. In what way can an increase in excess reserves affect *V* or *T*? Is there any certainty that an increase in reserves will lead to an increase in *V* or *T*?

4. Suppose that you had $1,000 in the bank. Would you be more willing to invest it if you could earn 5 percent or 8 percent? What factors could make you change your mind about investing all or any part at, say, 8 percent? Could you imagine conditions that would make you unwilling to invest even at 10 percent? Other conditions that would lead you to invest your whole cash balance at, say, 3 percent?
5. Suppose that the going rate of interest is 7 percent and that the monetary authorities want to curb expenditures and act to reduce the quantity of money. What will the effect be in terms of the public's feeling of liquidity? What will the public do if it feels short of cash? Will it buy or sell securities? What would this do to their price? What would thereupon happen to the rate of interest? To investment expenditures?
6. Suppose that the monetary and fiscal authorities want to encourage economic expansion. What are the general measures that each should take? What problems might changing liquidity preference interpose?
7. Do you unconsciously keep a "liquidity balance" among your assets? Suppose that your cash balance rose. Would you be tempted to spend more?
8. Show in a diagram how a decrease in the supply of money will be reflected in lower transactions balances and in lower financial balances. What is the mechanism that changes these balances?
9. Do you understand (a) how the rate of interest is determined; (b) how it affects our willingness to hold cash? Is this in any way different from the mechanism by which the price of shoes is determined or the way in which the price of shoes affects our willingness to buy them?

Chapter 20 GROWTH AND ITS PROBLEMS

A LOOK AHEAD

Here we reach the final chapter of our basic macro studies, returning to the issue with which we began: economic growth. There are three main problems discussed in the pages to follow.

(1) The first is an investigation into the characteristics and possible causes of the business cycle.

(2) The second is the matter of trying to reach our maximum potential growth.

(3) The third is the complex question: Can we improve our growth rate?; can we intervene effectively in the macro system? We shall look into arguments on both sides of the matter before summing up the problem as we see it.

From the very first pages of our study of macroeconomics, growth has been at the center of our focus. Now, in this final chapter on that subject, we must return explicitly to the problem, adding to our previous knowledge and reflecting on issues that we have not yet had an opportunity to explore in depth.

UNEVEN GROWTH

Let us begin by investigating an aspect of growth that we have heretofore ignored. It is the uneven pace at which the historic trajectory of growth proceeds. If you will take a moment to look back at the chart of national growth on p. 64, you will notice its long, almost uninterrupted upward slope; or again, a glance at p. 66 will show the same thing.

SHORT VS. LONG RUN

But these long-run charts, on which only very large movements are visible, conceal from our view another aspect of the growth process that is of very great importance. In any short-run period, the long-run consistency fades from view and the economy is marked by sharp ups and downs in the growth in output.

Take the years 1895 to 1905, very smooth-looking on the chart on p. 67. As Table 20.1 reveals, those years were, in fact, anything but steady.

TABLE 20.1 U.S. RATES OF GROWTH 1895–1905

1895–1896	−2.5%	1900–1901	+11.5%
1896–1897	+9.4	1901–1902	+ 1.0
1897–1898	+2.3	1902–1903	+ 4.9
1898–1899	+9.1	1903–1904	− 1.2
1899–1900	+2.7	1904–1905	+ 7.4

Source: *Long-Term Economic Growth* (U.S. Dept of Commerce, 1966), p. 107.

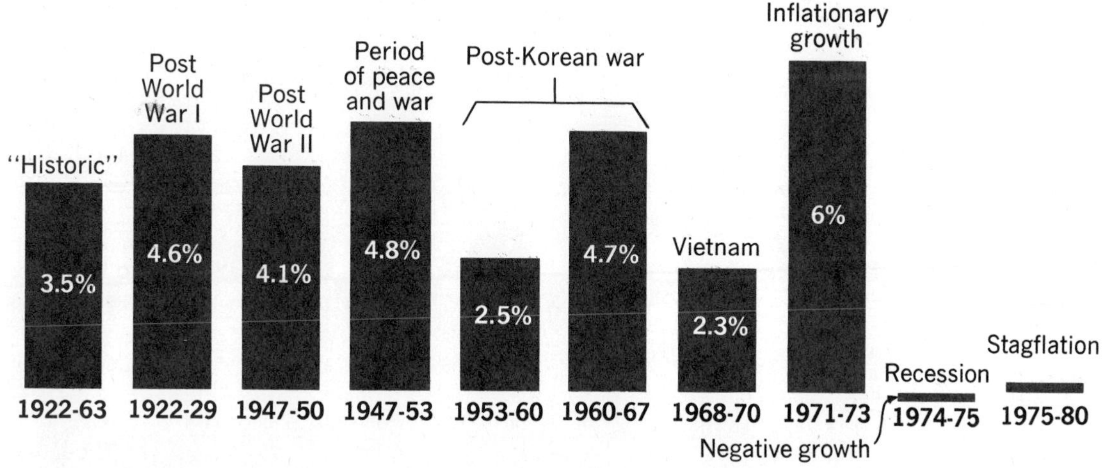

FIGURE 20.1 SHORT-TERM VARIATIONS IN THE RATE OF GROWTH

Except in periods of real recession, such as 1974–75 or 1979–80, the economy always shows growth. But the rate of growth varies considerably, as we can see.

Or examine a more recent period, not year by year, but in groups of years. As we can see in Figure 20.1 the rate of growth has varied greatly over the last fifty years. At times, such as the 1974–1975 recession, the economy has even shown negative rates of growth. These episodes may show up only as small dips in the graph of our long-term advance, but they have meant suffering and deprivation for millions of persons who were robbed of work or income as a consequence of these dips.

BUSINESS CYCLES

This sequence of ups and downs, periods of growth followed by doldrums, introduces us to the question of business cycles. For if we inspect the profile of the long ascent carefully, we can see that its entire length is marked with irregular tremors or peaks and valleys. Indeed, the more closely we examine year-to-year figures, the more of these tremors and deviations we discover, until the problem becomes one of selection: Which vibrations shall we consider significant and which shall we discard as uninteresting.

The problem of sorting out the important fluctuations in output (or in statistics of prices or employment) is a difficult one. Economists have actually detected dozens of cycles of different lengths and amplitudes. Cycles vary from the very short rhythms of expansion and contraction that can be found, for example, in patterns of inventory accumulation and decumulation, to large background pulsations of 17 or 18 years in the housing industry. Possibly (the evidence is

FIGURE 20.2 THE BUSINESS CYCLE

This chart, prepared by the Cleveland Trust Company, vividly shows our swings. Note that the swings lie around a base line called "long-term trend." That is actually an upward tilting line reflecting our long-term growth rate of 1.5 percent per capita.

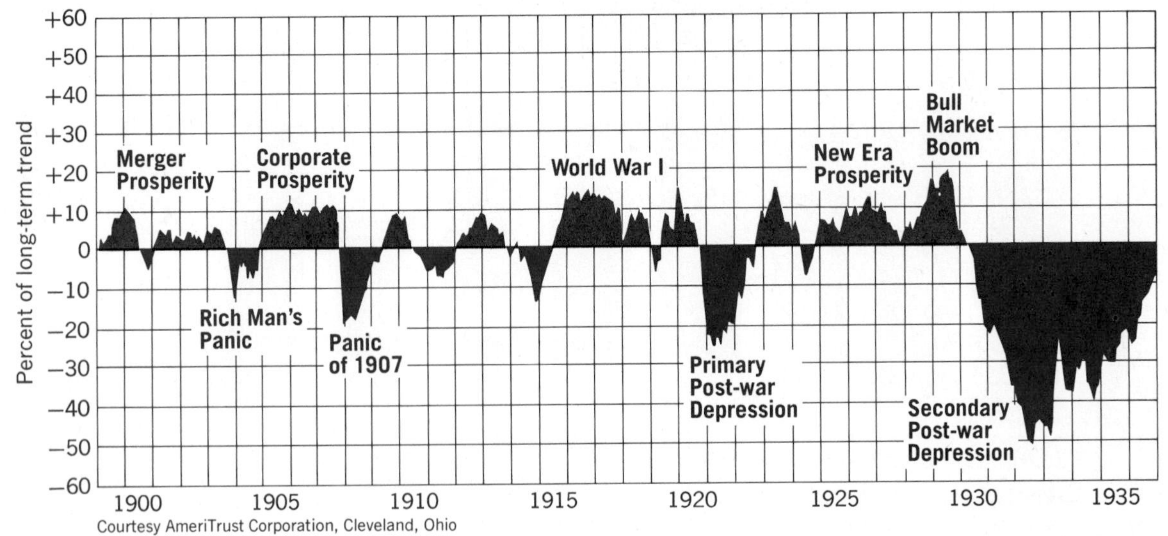

Courtesy AmeriTrust Corporation, Cleveland, Ohio

unclear) there are swings of 40 to 50 years in the path of capitalist development as a whole, called Kondratief cycles after their Russian discoverer.

Generally, however, when we speak of the business cycle we refer to a wavelike movement that lasts, on the average, about 7 to 11 years. In Figure 20.2 this major oscillation of the American economy stands forth very clearly, for the chartist has eliminated the underlying tilt of growth, so that the profile of economic performance looks like a cross section at sea level rather than a cut through a long incline.

STYLIZED CYCLES

In a general way we are all familiar with the meaning of business cycles, for the alternation of "boom and bust" or prosperity and recession (a polite name for a mild depression) is part of everyday parlance. It will help us study cycles, however, if we learn to speak of them with a standard terminology—**peak, contraction, trough, recovery.** We can do this by taking the cycles from actual history, superimposing them, and drawing the general profile of the stylized cycle that emerges. It looks like Figure 20.3. This model of a typical cycle enables us to speak of the length of a business cycle as the period from one peak to the next or from trough to trough. If we fail to measure from *similar* points on two or more cycles, we can easily get a distorted picture of short-term growth—for instance, one that begins at the upper turning point of one cycle and measures to the trough of the next. Much of the political charge and countercharge about growth rates can be clarified if we examine the starting and terminating dates used by each side.

FIGURE 20.2 (continued)

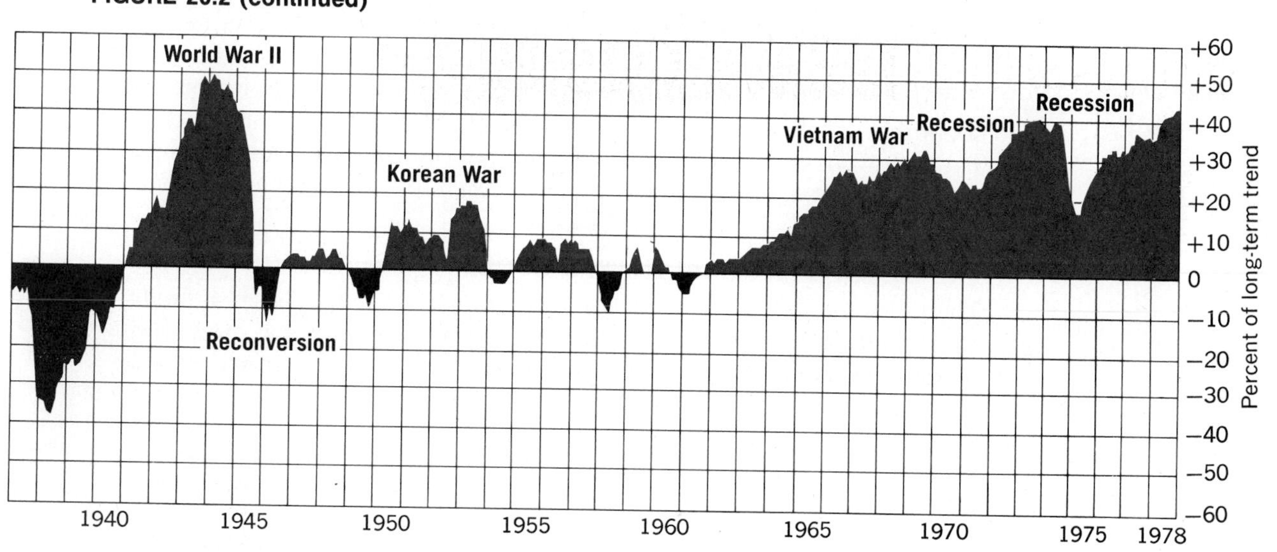

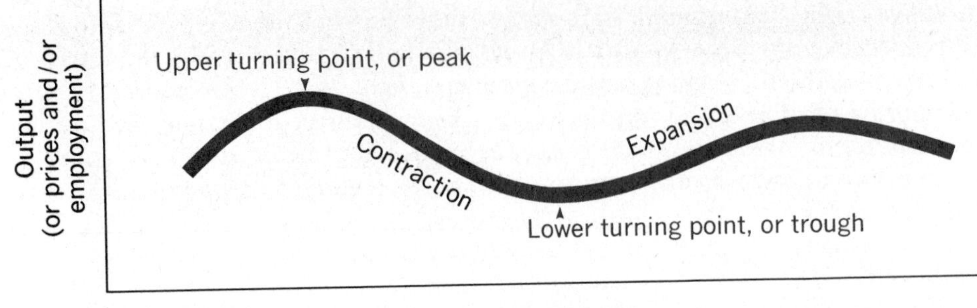

FIGURE 20.3 THE STYLIZED CYCLE

An idealized cycle serves to give us standard nomenclature, so that we can compare two or more cycles.

CAUSES OF CYCLES

What lies behind this more or less regular alternation of good and bad times?

Innumerable theories, none of them entirely satisfactory, have been advanced to explain the business cycle. A common business explanation is that waves of optimism in the world of affairs alternate with waves of pessimism—a statement that may be true enough, but that seems to describe the sequence of events rather than to explain it. Hence economists have tried to find the underlying cyclical mechanism in firmer stuff than an alternation of moods. One famous late-nineteenth-century economist, W. S. Jevons, for example, explained business cycles as the consequence of sunspots—perhaps not as occult a theory as it might seem, since Jevons believed that the sunspots caused weather cycles that caused crop cycles that caused business cycles! The trouble was that subsequent investigation showed that the periodicity of sunspots was sufficiently different from that of rainfall cycles to make the connection impossible.

Other economists have turned to causes closer to home: to variations in the rate of gold mining (with its effects on the money supply); to fluctuations in the rate of invention; to the regular recurrence of war; and to yet other factors. There is no doubt that many of these events can induce a business expansion or contraction. The persistent problem, however, is that not one of the so-called underlying causes itself displays an inherent cyclicality—much less one with a periodicity of 7 to 11 years.

THE MULTIPLIER-ACCELERATOR CYCLE

Then how do we explain cycles? **Economists no longer seek a single explanation of the phenomenon in an exogenous (external) cyclical force. Rather, they tend to see cycles as our own eye first saw them on the growth curve—as variations in the rate of growth that tend to be induced by the dynamics of growth itself.**

We can gain considerable insight into this uneven pace of growth if we combine our knowledge of the multiplier and the accelerator—the latter, we recall, showing us the investment induced by the growth of output.

Boom and bust. Let us, then, assume that some stimulus such as an important industry-building invention, has begun to increase investment expenditures. We can easily see how such an initial impetus can generate a cumulative and self-feeding boom. As the multiplier and accelerator interact, the first burst of investment stimulates additional consumption, the additional consumption induces more investment, and this in turn reinvigorates consumption. Meanwhile, this process of mutal stimulation serves to lift business expectations and to encourage still further expansionary spending. Inventories are built up in anticipation of larger sales. Prices firm up, and the stock market rises. Optimism reigns. A boom is on.

What happens to end such a boom? There are many possible reasons why it may peter out or come to an abrupt halt. It may simply be that the new industry will get built and thereafter an important stimulus to investment will be lacking. Or even before it is completed, wages and prices may have begun to rise as full employment is neared, and the climate of expectations may become wary. ("What goes up must come down," is an old adage in business, too.) Meanwhile, perhaps tight money will choke off spending plans or make new projects appear unprofitable.

Or investment may begin to decline because consumption, although still rising, is no longer rising at the earlier *rate* (the acceleration principle in action). We have already noticed that the action of the accelerator, all by itself, could give rise to wavelike movements in total expenditure (see p. 210). The accelerator, of course, never works all by itself, but it can exert its upward and downward pressures within the flux of economic forces and in this way give rise to an underlying cyclical impetus.

Contraction and recovery. It is impossible to know in advance what particular cause will retard spending—a credit shortage, a very tight labor market, a saturation of demand for a key industry's products (such as automobiles). But it is all too easy to see how a hesitation in spending can turn into a general contraction. Perhaps warned by a falling stock market, perhaps by a slowdown in sales or an end to rising profits, business begins to cut back. Whatever the initial motivation, what follows thereafter is much like the preceding expansion, only in reverse. The multiplier mechanism now breeds smaller rather than larger incomes. Downward revisions of expectations reduce rather than enhance the attractiveness of investment projects. As consumption decreases, unemployment begins to rise. Inventories are worked off. Bankruptcies become more common. We experience all the economic and social problems of a recession.

But just as there is a natural ceiling to a boom, so there is a more or less natural floor to recessions. The fall in inventories, for example, will eventually come to an end, for even in the severest recessions, merchants and manufacturers must have *some* goods on their shelves and so must eventually begin stocking up. The decline in expenditures will lead to easy money, and the slack in output will tend to a lower level of costs; and both of these factors will encourage new investment projects. Meanwhile, the countercyclical effects of government fiscal policy will slowly make their effects known. Sooner or later, in other words, expenditures will cease falling, and the economy will tend to bottom out.

GOVERNMENT-CAUSED CYCLES

We have spoken about business cycles as if they were initially triggered by a spontaneous rise in investment or by a natural cessation of investment. But our acquaintance with the relative sizes of the components of GNP should make us wary of placing the blame for recessions solely on industry. More and more, as government has become a major source of spending, cycles have resulted from variations in the rate of government spending, not business spending. Cycles these days, more often than not, are made in Washington.

Take the six recessions (periods of decline in real GNP lasting at least six months) since World War II. Every one of them can be traced to changes in government budgetary policies. The first four recessions—in 1949, 1954, 1957–1958, and 1960–1961—resulted from changes in the military budget. In each case, the federal government curtailed its rate of military expenditure without taking compensatory action by increasing expenditure elsewhere or by cutting taxes. The result in each instance was a slackening in the rate of growth.

The 1969–1970, the 1974–1975, and the 1980 recessions are even more interesting. They represent cases in which the federal government deliberately created a recession through fiscal and monetary policies aimed at slowing down the economy. The purpose, as we know, was to dampen inflation. The result was to reverse the trend of growth. Thus it is no longer possible, as it once was, to discuss business cycles as if they were purely the outcome of the market process.

There is no doubt that the market mechanism has produced cycles in the past, and would continue to produce them if the government were miraculously removed from the economy. But given the size of the public sector these days, we need to look first to changes in government spending as the initiating source of a cycle.

POTENTIAL GROWTH

Can we curb the business cycle? We shall see. But the idea of a fluctuation-free path of growth directs our attention once again to the long historic trajectory with which we began our study of growth. If we multiply the rise in our year-to-year hours of labor input by an index of the rising productivity of that labor, we can easily derive a curve showing our *potential output over time.* The question is therefore how much of that potential output we do in fact produce.

Through much of the 1950s and 1960s, potential output ran well ahead of the output we actually achieved. Figure 20.4 shows that between 1974 and 1979 the amount of lost output represented by this gap came to the staggering sum of $310 billion. In 1979 we could have added another $30 billion to GNP—$136 per person—if we had brought unemployment down from the actual level of 5.8 percent to 5.1 percent, the level now used to calculate potential GNP. In the recession year of 1980 the loss was far greater still.

REASONS FOR SLOW GROWTH

Why have we fallen so far short of our potential growth? There are two reasons. The first is that we have deliberately pursued policies of tight money and fiscal restraint, hoping to hold down the rate of inflation. That is a problem to

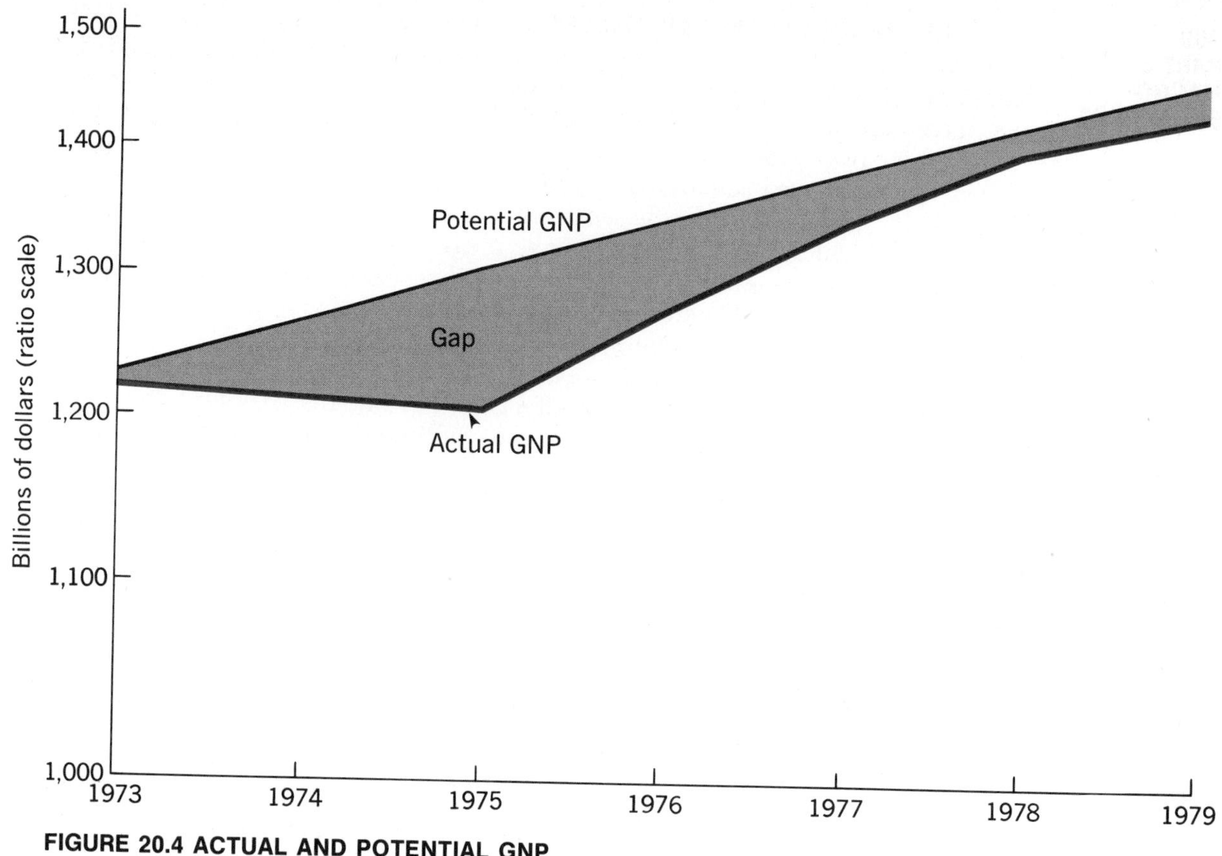

FIGURE 20.4 ACTUAL AND POTENTIAL GNP

which we will return shortly, when we ask whether we could make up this shortfall by different economic policies.

But there is a second, more long-run, reason for our disappointing performance. **It is that our productivity has been dropping for some years. In the period 1973-1978, industrial productivity rose about 4 percent per year in West Germany, about 5 percent per year in Japan—but only one percent annually in the United States. This drop in productivity actually became negative during 1979, when output per manhour in the nonfarm private business sector *fell* for a brief period at an annual rate of 2.3 percent.** If that decrease continued, the Joint Economic Committee of Congress warned, Americans would suffer a drastic decline in real living standards.*

*Our international position has already worsened because of the long relative fall in our productivity. We are no longer the nation with the world's highest standard of living, but the nation with the fifth highest standard, outranked by Switzerland, Denmark, West Germany, and Sweden, with Japan only 7 percent behind. Such international comparisons are always treacherous because tastes and styles differ so much among countries. But the basic fact that American living standards are now shared—or bettered—abroad is indisputable.

Why has our productivity fallen? The long-term reasons are fairly clear. We have been devoting a smaller fraction of our GNP to new plant and equipment than have our major economic competitors. Over the last decade, our investment has been roughly 10 percent of GNP. West Germany's rate has been 15 percent; Japan's 20 percent. In addition, our R & D expenditures have not only fallen, but may have been aimed less advantageously than those of our competitors. Mounting concern over the environment has dictated costly antipollution expenditures which add to cost but not to measured output. Finally, we have a much larger military establishment than any other Western nation. Over a quarter of our national R & D effort goes for military purposes, compared with 7 percent for West Germany and 4 percent for Japan.* A strong defense establishment may be a national necessity, but it exacts a price in slower growth. It takes a while before these causes exert their effects, but eventually they pull down our rate of production per manhour. That is the condition from which we are suffering today.

RECENT POOR PERFORMANCE

The reasons for our recent precipitous decline into negative productivity rates is something else, however. Here one main cause is simply the poor performance of the economy itself. When the rate of utilization sags, we do not typically lay off managers, research departments, salesmen, maintenance staff and the like, even though we may not be able to use their potential inputs fully. The result is a drop in productivity because there is a lot of unused manpower per unit of output. Conversely, when we move out of recession, productivity runs ahead of the economy because we can greatly increase production for a while without adding much to overhead.

Probably 30 percent of our productivity slowdown stems from this factor. Another 20 percent comes from a changing mix of our outputs. In the U.S. there are large differences in productivity among industries. In 1978 an hour of work produced not quite $6 worth of output in services (valued at 1972 prices), $8.70 in manufacturing, and $11.56 in agriculture. With so wide a range, shifts in our composition of output will have significant effects on our average productivity. And after 1972, such a shift occurred. Output grew largely in the low productivity service sectors rather than in high productivity areas like electronics or agriculture.

Another 30 percent of our decline in growth can be traced to problems in specific industries—mining, construction and utilities. Utilities have suffered because of high fuel prices which have lead to sluggish growth and resulting sluggish productivity. Mining is an industry beset with health and safety problems which affect its working force and the environment. We are now moving more rapidly than in the past to remedy these problems, but falling productivity is one of the prices we must pay. Construction has also been a very poor performer on the productivity scale. Perhaps this is only because its output is diffi-

*B. Depalme and others, *Science and Technology in the New Socioeconomic Context,* OECD, Paris, 1980 (forthcoming).

cult to measure. Perhaps it is because we are building fewer large-scale projects where efficiency is high and more small ones where it is lower. Perhaps it is because zoning and other laws make building more expensive.

That accounts for 80 percent of our productivity decline. The source of the remaining 20 percent remains a mystery.

RAISING THE GROWTH RATE

Obviously there is no quick fix to our productivity problem. But it is equally obvious that there are policies that would gradually, if not immediately, improve our annual rate of potential growth. There is no doubt that measures to increase our rate of capital formation will sooner or later yield more output per manhour. So will efforts to raise, or to direct more skillfully, our R & D expenditures. So will policies to assist industries such as mining to modernize their operations, or policies to enable other unproductive industries, such as textiles, to "disinvest" —shrink back their size.

But such policies are easier to devise than to implement. Raising investment expenditures in industry may mean cutting them back elsewhere—for example in urban renewal. Is that what we want to do? Spurring investment will probably necessitate higher corporate profits, which many will oppose. Allowing unproductive industries to fade away will impose heavy burdens on their employees who will fight with all their power to prevent their livelihoods from also fading away. Relaxing environmental protection standards will boost productivity—but at what social cost?

Thus problems abound. Nonetheless, with all the difficulties, no one disputes that it is within our national capacity to raise the rate of long-term growth by improving the quality and quantity of our key inputs. **Finally, we ought to bear in mind that there is often a trade-off between efficiency and equity**—a point stressed by Arthur Okun, former Chairman of the Council of Economic Advisers. Policies that encourage growth may do so at the expense of well-being: We would certainly grow faster if we transferred all insurance workers into factories. Assuming that *they* wouldn't mind the switch, would we welcome a world without insurance? How about a world of highly efficient houses, all built with cookie-cutter duplication? A world of high output per mine worker, but also high accident rates and high pollution? Productivity is very important, but it is not the only thing that is very important.

THE SHORT RUN

Recall, however, that much of the recent decline in productivity is the result of our disappointing economic performance rather than the cause of it. To accelerate our short-run growth rate, we have to move up to the production frontier rather than move the frontier further out. And here the question becomes more complex and more interesting. For economists are by no means unanimous that we can change our degree of utilization by using the conventional measures we have learned about—expansive fiscal policies or increases in the money supply. We remember that the monetarists have even asserted that the efforts of the Federal Reserve to intervene in the market typically make things worse, not better!

Thus we find ourselves today in the midst of a debate over the efficacy of intervention. Can we significantly improve our rate of growth? Let us first examine the arguments against, then those in favor, and finally try to strike a balance.

ARGUMENTS AGAINST INTERVENTION

Why do some economists feel that the conventional ways of improving our performance are futile? There are three reasons:

1. TIME LAGS

One cogent argument is the problem of time lags. The argument is very simple and entirely true. It takes time to collect data. It takes time to interpret data. It takes time to convince people who look at data that the situation has—or has not—changed. It takes time to devise a new policy. It takes time to implement a policy by action. It takes time for the new policy—expenditure, taxes, interest rates, or whatever—to exert its effect.

Various estimates have been made of some of these time lags. Table 20.2 shows an estimate for a Federal Reserve stimulus:

TABLE 20.2 ESTIMATED TIME LAGS

Type of lag	*Estimated length (months)*
data	2.0
recognition	2.0
legislative	0.5
transmission	1.0
effectiveness	8.5

Source: Robert Gordon, *Macroeconomics* (Boston: Little Brown, 1978), p. 471.

The disconcerting result of this lag is that by the time the remedy has arrived on the scene, the illness may have changed. Indeed, there is even the possibility that the underlying situation will have markedly changed and that the remedy will only make the problem worse.

2. RATIONAL EXPECTATIONS

A second argument against the effectiveness of intervention is called the theory of rational expectations. **Essentially it claims that government intervention cannot change the outcome of a market economy, because the market will have already anticipated government action and will have taken steps that will nullify it.**

We have already seen such nullifying actions when we noted that shifts in liquidity preferences could offset Federal Reserve intentions (see page 295). Now we must add the possibility that investors or market participants will deliberately change their behavior because they expect that the government will undertake a certain policy. We all read the newspapers and magazines, watch TV and hear radio. We all know, long before the event, that the government is considering raising or lowering taxes, tightening or loosening money. Will we not, then, pursue our best economic advantage by taking these expectations into account as we plan our economic activity?

Suppose, for example, that investors read about pressure on the Federal Reserve to increase the money supply and lower interest rates. Will not a rational investor buy bonds immediately, in order to sell them at a profit when yields fall? In that case, when the Fed actually does increase the money supply, there is no change in interest rates because the change has already occurred in anticipation of government policy!

What the theory of rational expectations tells us is that well-informed mass action can make it very difficult for the government to bring about a desired economic change in any area of the economy. According to the theory it will be as difficult or impossible to change the level of employment as to change the level of spending because the actors on the marketplace will always manage to attain their objectives. In fact, government intervention is likely to bring about undesired changes. Take the well known case of the banker who makes a public statement assuring his depositors that their money is safe. Perhaps it *was* safe before he made the pronouncement, but his words instill anxiety and the next thing you know there is a run on his bank. In the same way, a highly placed administration official can assure the American public that there will be plenty of gasoline, but his very assurance may stir up enough anxiety so that the next day we find lines at the gas pumps.

Such perversely self-fulfilling prophecies are an example of rational expectations. Each person is driven to maximize his or her self-interest in a market system —indeed, that is how the system gets its energy. **But that very driving force, coupled with a continuous search for as much information as possible, makes it very difficult to force the market to yield a solution different from its natural, spontaneous outcome. What the theorists of rational expectations are telling us is that the market mechanism is a much more powerful, self-steering process than interventionists tend to believe.**

3. NATURAL STABILITY AND MOMENTUM

We have already encountered the third main argument of the noninterventionists when we looked into monetarism. The contention is that the economy is essentially a stable, growing process, and that efforts to alter its course are likely to destabilize or depress, not steady or strengthen its inherent momentum.

At bottom, this view also rests on the dynamics of the maximizing, competitive process. In the view of the noninterventionists the constant tendency of all markets is to seek equilibria—prices that will clear the quantities offered and sought. So, too, the noninterventionists emphasize the tendency of the market process as a whole to express the main elements within it—the search for work, the incentive for profit, the level of skill and industrial technique. **These real forces, they believe, will determine the degree of utilization that prevails, and efforts to change that level cannot produce lasting effects because they cannot change the underlying drives and technical realities of our situation.**

One important instance of this emphasis on the natural stability of the system involves the crowding out phenomenon we mentioned in our last chapter. The noninterventionists believe that the amount of investment in the nation will be limited to the amount of saving it can generate—that is, the resources it can divert from consumption. When the government absorbs some of those savings into the public sector, whether by taxing them or by attracting them into public bond issues, it lowers the availability of savings for the private sector. There will be a shift of national effort from the production of private goods to the production of public goods, but there will not be any more growth because added public expenditure will be offset by lowered private spending.

NONINTERVENTIONIST POLICY

What sort of government policy do the noninterventionists advocate? They all agree that we can improve our long-run growth potential by adopting measures that will improve the quantity and quality of inputs. Therefore noninterventionists advocate encouragement to investment and R & D, for instance, by changing the tax laws to promote saving and profit-making. Needless to say, their opponents accuse them of pursuing highly interventionist policies in the name of noninterventionism!

Second, noninterventionists believe in encouraging the natural stability and expansiveness of the economy by establishing automatic increases in the money supply, as we have previously discussed. And that is essentially all. Noninterventionists would balance the full employment budget. They would eliminate all Federal Reserve policies to raise or lower reserve ratios or discount rates, or to act in the open market, with the possible exception of policies needed to cope with international pressures on the dollar, a matter we discuss in Chapter 34, "Defending the Dollar."

Thus in place of an active fiscal and monetary policy, noninterventionists advocate a firm but unchanging monetary policy. We have tried to improve the economy, they claim, but we have not succeeded. Now it is time to let it manage itself.

ARGUMENTS FOR INTERVENTION

There is, of course another side to the story. Here is the problem as the interventionists see it:

1. THE POWER OF PREDICTION

Interventionists do not fault their opponents when they call attention to the problem of time lags and the mischief they can cause. They claim, however, that the record of *short-run* predictions is good enough so that we should be able to circumvent what has been a source of trouble in the past. During the 1970s, according to economist Robert J. Gordon, "Forecasters have been able to predict accurately a year in advance the direction of most changes in unemployment, even though they failed badly in predicting the magnitude of the increase in unemployment following the 1973–74 supply shock episode."*

Interventionists know that policy decisions got us into as much trouble as they got us out of during the past decade or so; but they believe that it would be foolish to abandon all efforts to ward off, or to correct, poor economic performance on that account. Most monetary policy lags are about a year in length.

*Robert J. Gordon, *Macroeconomics* (Boston: Little, Brown & Co., 1978) p. 476.

Interventionists now think we can make reliable forecasts for such periods, so that policy decisions will work their eventual effects in the direction we want them to, and not against it.

2. REMEDYING IMPERFECT MARKETS

We recall that a second major plank in the noninterventionist platform was that markets tended to frustrate the intentions of government policy makers because market participants always beat them to the punch. But this theory is clearly only valid for markets where there exists a great deal of information and mobility. That is emphatically not the case with many of the market processes into which government seeks to intervene.

Take as an instance the difference between the financial market and the labor market. The financial market is a quivering network of information. You can prove that by going into any brokerage house and finding out what the going price is for any of two or three thousand securities. If you wish to buy those securities you can always do so by bidding a fraction more than the market, and you can always sell by offering them at a fraction less. Compare the labor market. If you walk into an employment office, you will have difficulty learning about the price or quantity of employment available outside your city, or outside a few standard trades or professions. If you offer your skills for sale at a fraction less than the going rate, the chances are very great that this price advantage will not suffice to get you a job.

In such imperfect markets, which make up a great deal of the economy, it makes no sense to apply a theory of rational expectations. The participants in the labor market do not behave in the same way as those in the financial markets. Therefore the market for employment does not maximize in the same manner as the market for capital funds. The government can improve employment and the degree of utilization, argue the interventionists, because nothing like a network of information or mobility exists.

3. THE DANGER OF INSTABILITY

Third, the interventionists stress the instability, not the inherent steadiness, of the private sector. They do not argue with the noninterventionists that capitalism is a dynamic system always seeking to grow, or that its market mechanism is a powerful force for clearing its supplies and demands (with the caution, noted above, that not all markets work the way the noninterventionists claim). Their own position centers on two major claims.

First, they point to the historic record of boom and bust that marked the course of capitalism long before the existence of government as an intervening force. In the 1890s for instance, we had a depression in which almost a fifth of the labor force was thrown out of work. That kind of instability, the interventionists assert, is the consequence of capitalism's dynamism: New industries are built up and peak out; booms develop momentum and slide to a halt; external shocks such as war or natural disaster shake it out of its routines. Moreover, the interventionists go on to claim, the instability of the system is much greater—and much more dangerous—in an economy of giant businesses than in one of shopkeepers and local handicrafts. The economy of the nineteenth century, they say, was stable as a pile of sand is stable even when it receives a blow. The late twentieth-century system is unstable as a great tower of blocks, each block a giant company, would be unstable if it were to receive a similar blow.

Second, the interventionists argue that we no longer have the social or political option of not intervening. In the great depressions of the past the public accepted a passive government response because it was generally believed that government had no right (as well as no capacity) to deal with economic misfortunes. That point of view is now as dead as the dodo, interventionists insist. When growth slows down or inflation speeds up, the public cry is that government should "do something." To be told that doing nothing is the best response to economic trouble is an idea that no Western electorate would accept, and that no Western government would propose. Therefore an interventionist response is forced on us, the activists say, and the attitude of those who advocate noninterventionism is simply irresponsible.

THE UPSHOT OF THE ARGUMENT

Is it possible to sum up the pros and cons of this complex argument? Perhaps we can suggest two conclusions that award some recognition to each side and that present the issue as we see it.

1. **Unquestionably we are going to pursue interventionist economic policies, both in the short and the long run**

The last argument of the interventionists seems to us irrefutable. It is no longer imaginable that any modern government would take a passive stance toward such problems as inflation, unemployment, energy, productivity, and a dozen similar issues. Many of these problems can be addressed in different ways, and later in this book, especially in Part 5, we discuss what some of these alternative policies might be. But there is no doubt in our minds that some form of active policy will be followed.

2. **Our policy determinations will be seriously hampered by the kinds of problems raised by the noninterventionists**

Thus we are going to try to improve our short-run economic performance. But how well will we succeed in doing so? The objections raised by the noninterventionists suggest that efforts to accelerate or decelerate, redirect or guide the economy will be much more difficult than we have thought in the past. It was not so very long ago that economists spoke of "fine tuning" the economy as if it were a vast hi-fi set that could be regulated with precision by turning the knobs labeled "fiscal policy" and "monetary policy." We now know that this cannot be done. Some knobs are stuck; others turn without much affecting the quantity or quality of sound; still others seem to set up feedback that distorts the results we seek.

But this is not to say that we cannot regulate the economy at all. Our own belief is that we can intervene to our collective benefit, provided that we have realistic expectations of what it lies within our power to do. Modern industrial economies are very complex systems and we should not expect that we can fiddle with them like radios. But some success is better than none—and some success seems possible. That takes us, however, to the arena of public policy and the array of giant problems confronting us there; to this matter we devote all of Part 5.

LOOKING BACK

KEY CONCEPTS

The business cycle exhibits the fluctuating rhythm of economic growth

1. Growth is not an even process, but is marked by fluctuations that we designate as a business cycle. There are many kinds of cycle, of varying periodicities (durations). We speak of their phases as four: upper turning point or peak, contraction, lower turning point or trough, and expansion.

The 7- to 11-year cycle is analyzed in terms of a multiplier-accelerator interaction, often triggered by government action

2. No entirely satisfactory explanation has been found for the 7- to 11-year periodicity of the principal business cycle. Economists analyze the alternation of boom and bust mainly in terms of the interaction of the multiplier and accelerator. The cause of the cyclical pattern lies as much in government action as in the spontaneous behavior of the business economy.

Potential growth focuses attention on the output that full employment would yield. Actual growth has fallen seriously short of this in recent years

3. The attention of economists today is focused less on cycles than on the difference between potential and actual growth. Potential growth is the trend of output that would result from the continuous full employment of the labor force. Actual growth is the value of GNP in fact produced. In recent years there has been a serious growth gap.

Growth and productivity have lagged because of low investment and R & D, shifts to less productive occupations, and the inefficiency of recessions

4. The growth gap is attributed to a slowdown in productivity, and to anti-inflation measures that have curbed economic activity. Productivity in the U.S. has been falling for a decade. The reasons are numerous: relatively low investment, low R & D expenditures, nonproductive expenses such as the installation of pollution controls, shifts in occupations, and the tendency to build up overhead costs during recession. In addition, certain important industries have been beset with performance problems.

Growth can almost surely be aided by long-term policies to boost investment and R & D

5. Raising the growth rate involves long- and short-run policies. Most economists would agree that long-run institutional changes, such as increasing R & D, or raising the investment rate, would assist growth.

Can short-term growth be affected by fiscal and monetary policy? Noninterventionists say no because of the problems of time lags, rational expectations, and the natural stability of the system

6. There are divergent views as to whether growth can be boosted in the short run by fiscal and monetary policy. The noninterventionists argue that such policies have little effect for three reasons: (1) Time lags make proper timing difficult or impossible: (2) rational expectations lead to frustration of government plans because the market anticipates such plans or sidesteps them; and (3) there is a natural stability and momentum to the economy that government policies cannot change.

Interventionists place their faith in short-run forecasts, in the inapplicability of rational expectations to markets such as the labor market, and in the belief that instability is politically intolerable

7. Interventionists argue that time lags can be offset by reasonably dependable short-run forecasting; that rational expectations only work in near-perfect markets such as finance, not in the labor market where employment is immediately affected; and that the history of capitalism shows a great deal of instability. They argue, moreover, that in modern times it is not politically feasible for government to stand aside.

8. Our own belief is that interventionism is a fact of life, but that the effective implementation of policy will be more difficult than was once believed for the reasons raised by the interventionists.

ECONOMIC VOCABULARY

Business cycles 301
Peak, contraction, trough, recovery 303
Multiplier-accelerator 304
Potential growth 306
Time lags 310
Rational expectations 311

QUESTIONS

1. Explain how the interaction of the multiplier and the accelerator can give rise to cycles. Why does not such a multiplier-accelerator interaction shed light on the question of periodicity? Have you any ideas as to why the typical cycle is 8–10 years long? Suppose that capital goods tended to wear out in this period of time: Would this give rise to a cycle if their replacement were bunched in time?
2. Try to get hold of a time series, such as a short of stock market prices or GNP over the last 20 years. Can you spot a cyclical pattern at all? How do you think you would go about locating such a cycle?
3. What are the sources of growth for potential GNP? Explain how potential GNP is a kind of production possibility curve through time.
4. Can you suggest ways in which we might empirically investigate the reasons for the decline in growth? Suppose that your city was lagging in employment and prosperity, and that you were asked to determine why. How would you try to discover whether part of the reason was a relative decline in local productivity?
5. If you follow the newspapers, how long do you think it takes you, on the average, to spot a trend—say in the performance of a baseball team? How long does it take you to change your mind that a trend you thought you had identified was in fact incorrect? If you were going to change the performance of a team, how far ahead would you have to forecast its results to compensate for the time lags involved in spotting trends and in changing your mind?
6. Have you ever changed your actual economic behavior to achieve a result you wanted, *before* some anticipated government action made that impossible? If you felt that rationing were coming, would you stock up on gasoline? Would you buy diamonds if you believed that diamond purchases would be declared illegal in the future? Would you change your college program if you had reason to believe that government was going to change the training requirements for various professions?
7. What is your own appraisal of the willingness of the public to accept economic reversals without calling for government to "do something"? Do you think it is less tolerant of inaction in the case of inflation or unemployment?

Part

Microeconomics: The Anatomy of a Market System

SECTION 1: How Markets Work

Chapter 21 INTRODUCTION TO THE MICROECONOMY

A LOOK AHEAD

In this short introduction to microeconomics we learn one simple but central thing: The market mechanism is a device for organizing the production and distribution activities of society. It does so through two vast market networks:

(1) The factor market, in which businesses, households, and government agencies are brought together to produce and distribute wealth.

(2) The goods market, in which products and services are allocated.

Notice as we go along that each institution will enter the two markets on different sides. The household, for example, *sells* its services on the factor market and *buys* goods and services on the goods market, whereas business *buys* factors of production on the factor market and *sells* goods and services on the goods market. In the end we will discover that the two markets are connected.

THE MARKET SYSTEM

We began our study of macroeconomics by learning how the economy looked from a macro perspective. Now that we are about to start a study of microeconomics, there is no more effective way to illustrate the difference between the two approaches than to look over the economic panorama from our new vantage point.

Once again our eye is caught by the enormous flux of activity taking place in the offices, factories, and fields of the nation. But now our micro perspective brings a hitherto unnoticed aspect of the process to the fore. We are no longer much interested in the river of total output or its component parts, consumption, and investment. Instead, we direct our attention to the activity taking place in a thousand corners of the economy where individuals and firms are conducting their daily business. We look at the economic flow as a *vast web of transactions* into which virtually everyone enters as either a buyer or a seller.

PRODUCTION

We are all familiar with this market system in which we participate as buyers of goods and services. We are not as used to thinking about it as a mechanism for organizing production. Yet that is actually one of the two vital services that the market performs.

Figure 21.1 shows us how the market takes charge of production. Let us first look at the blue arrows that go clockwise from households to business, and then from business to households. These arrows represent the movement of *actual services or products* from one place to another. Starting from households, these services consist of the skills and energies of labor (and the physical services of capital goods or land) that householders produce and make available to business.

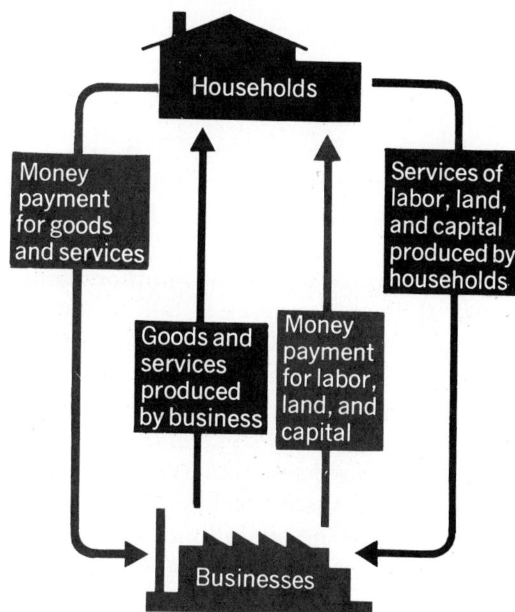

This diagram shows us two loops. The blue loop represents production. Real labor and other services leave households for business firms and return as real goods and services. The brown loop represents distribution. Money payments leave businesses for households and return as payments for business output.

FIGURE 21.1 THE BASIC MARKET MECHANISM

Thereafter, as the blue arrows show, the products that business has made from these services of labor and resources move back to the households, where they will be consumed.

Thus we can see that the market mechanism organizes the indispensable economic activity of production. The market mechanism is a great circular motion of economic activity converting labor, land, and capital—the factors of production (recall p. 15)—into commodities that will renew and sustain the owners of these resources.

DISTRIBUTION

The other vital service that the market performs is allocation, for the goods and services which have been produced must be shared out in the community. We must therefore see how money payments are used in the market mechanism as a device for organizing the sharing out activity of the nation. This leads us to take notice of a second loop in Figure 21.1 which goes in the opposite direction from the production loop. This is the flow of money payments. With every individual market transaction, goods or services move in one direction and money moves in the other.

Our brown arrows show us this second circular flow of payments going in the opposite direction to the flow of real activity. With every household purchase of a business product, money moves from the hands of householders to the hands of business. And with every purchase of the services of the factors of production, money moves from business into the owners of these factors—wages and salaries going to labor, rent to landowners, profit or interest to owners of capital resources. **Thus we can see that in addition to organizing production, the market mechanism organizes the distribution or sharing-out incomes.**

Of course, Figure 21.1 does not depict the entire market mechanism. It has omitted a vital flow of goods and services from one business to another, matched by a return flow of payments from business to business. No less vital, government has been left out, both as a buyer of goods and services and as a producer of outputs of its own, thereby linking the government with households and business. Figure 21.2 shows these complicated interlocks.

TWO KINDS OF MARKETS

Another way of revealing how the market mechanism works is to divide its activities into two kinds of market: a factor market and a goods market, as in Figure 21.3.

The factor market is another name for the loop where production takes place. Here the services of labor, land, and capital are bought and sold, hired and fired, offered and withheld in a vast number of transactions whose outcome is the production of goods and services.

The market for goods and services is the loop where allocation is organized. Here shoes and ships and sealing wax are sold to, and thereby distributed among, the buyers of society.

Breaking the market system down into two kinds of market further clarifies the working of the overall mechanism. **For we can see that households and firms (including government units) both participate in each of the two basic markets, but on different sides of each market.** In the market for goods, the household is a

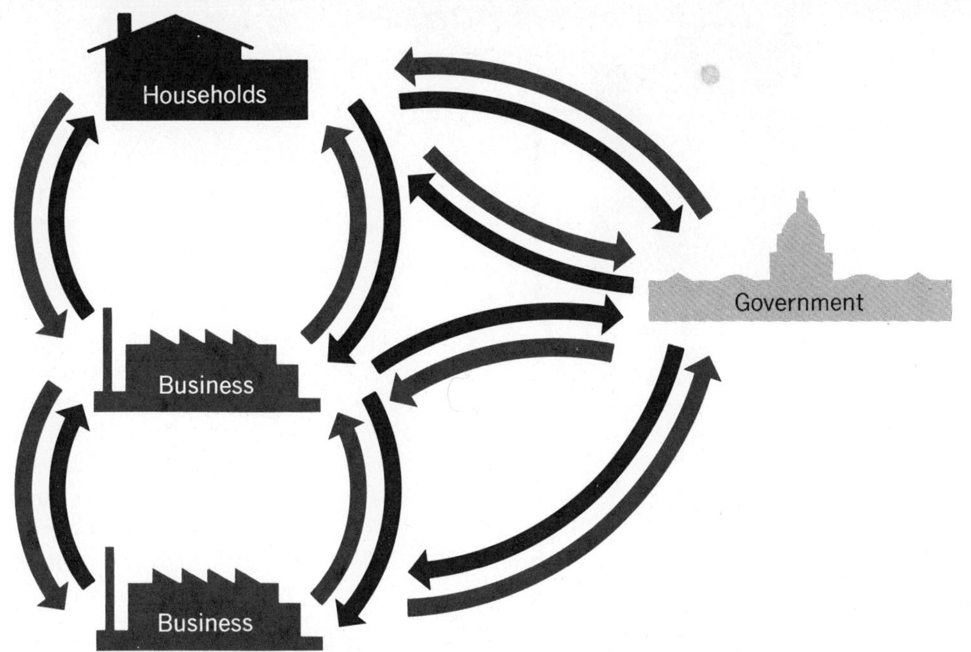

FIGURE 21.2 THE COMPLETE BUSINESS MECHANISM

Here we begin to get some idea of how complex the flow of the market mechanism actually is. But notice that the brown and blue flows are essentially the same as in Figure 21.1.

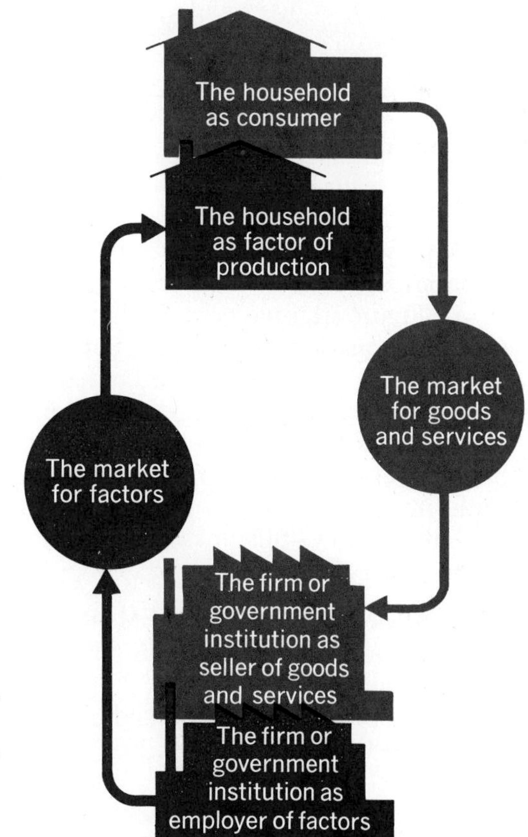

FIGURE 21.3 CIRCULAR FLOW IN TWO MARKETS

Here we see how households, businesses, and government agencies participate in two markets, acting as buyer in one and as seller in the other.

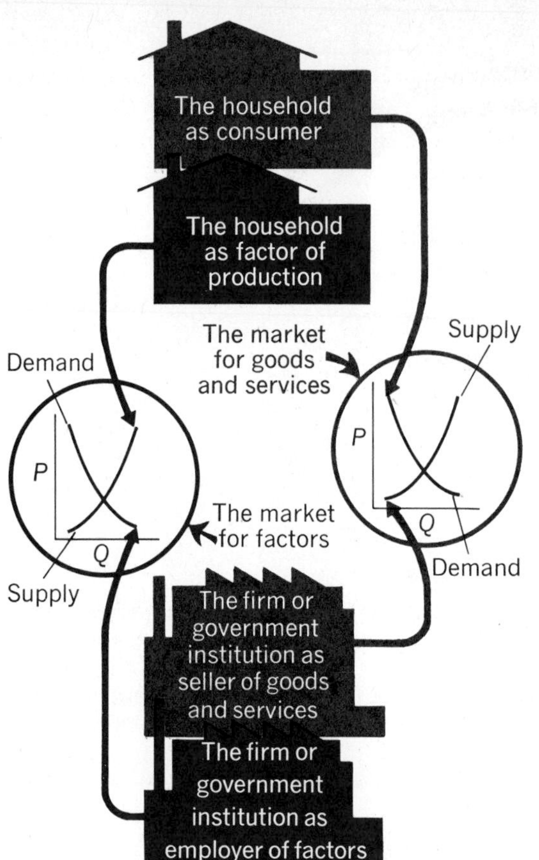

FIGURE 21.4 DEMAND AND SUPPLY CURVE IN THE CIRCULAR FLOW

Our final diagram shows how supply and demand curves represent the activities of the participants in the market mechanism. Notice especially that the household is the source of the demand curve in the goods market and of the supply curve in the factor market. What is the role of business?

---

buyer. In the market for factors, the household is a seller as its members offer their services for hire. In the market for goods, the firm is a seller. In the market for factors, the firm buys. Thus we can redraw our model of the circular flow with supply and demand curves that show the twofold participation of each of the basic participants in the two markets.

In Figure 21.4 we can see that the household is the source of the demand curve in the market for goods. We also see it is the source of the supply curve in the market for factors. On the other hand, the firm shapes the supply curve in the goods market, and the demand curve in the factor market.

Thus, far from being a chaos of buying and selling, the market system is a seamless web—a network of transactions with demand on one market reflected in supply in another, and supply in one market reflected in demand on another. This circular flow—this linkage of demand and supply—will be one of the main keys to understanding how the economy works as a whole.

LOOKING AT THE SYSTEM AS A WHOLE

Now for a last important insight. The two markets—for factors and for goods—are also connected.

This is because the household income that will be spent in the goods market is earned in the factor market. For businesses, the income that will be spent on hiring factors has to be earned in the goods market. **Production and distribution are therefore mutually dependent, not wholly independent, activities.** The outcome of the production circuit determines how the distribution circuit will operate; and the outcome of the distribution circuit determines the ability of business firms to enter the factor market.

Thus once again we see the market mechanism as a complex system, a network of actions that impose order and pattern on the economic life of society.

Like many models, ours operates at a very high level of abstraction. It lumps together the richest investor and the poorest laborer in the market for factors. It jumbles the sale of caviar and hospital care into one undifferentiated market for goods and services. Nevertheless, this abstract conception begins to untangle the flux of market activities in the world around us. It even clarifies our task in the chapters ahead. We must study the two different markets and the two different institutions, one at a time, to find out the actions and motivations characteristic of each. We begin in our next chapter by taking a searching look at households and their demand for goods and services.

LOOKING BACK

KEY CONCEPTS

Market mechanism: two loops or circuits

The central idea of this chapter has been to show that the vast array of buying and selling activity we call "the market" is actually a *system*—that is, a social institution that displays regular, orderly patterns of operation. We follow the operations of this mechanism by observing that it can contain two loops or circuits, one having to do with production, one with distribution.

The production loop: business buys factor services and makes goods that are used by the factors

1. First, production. The market network is the means by which a market society organizes its factors of production so as to bring about production. This shows up as a flow of services (labor power, or the services of capital or land) from households that own them to businesses that put them to productive use. The loop is completed when the goods that business produces return to the household to be consumed or put to further use.

The distribution loop: payments to factors who buy business's output

2. The distribution loop is a circuit of money payments, not of real services or goods. It goes in the opposite direction to the production loop as businesses pay households for their services as factors of production and as households pay businesses for the products they buy.

Two kinds of markets

3. Another way of revealing the connectedness of the market mechanism is to divide the complex totality of market activity into two kinds of markets: the market for factors and the market for goods (and services). The factor market regulates production; the goods market organizes allocation.

Households enter the factor market as sellers; business enters it as a buyer

4. In the factor market, households offer their services to business as labor or as owners of land and capital. Their activities therefore shape the supply curves in that market.

In the goods market, households shape the demand curve and business actions determine the supply curve

5. It is just the reverse in the market for goods and services. Here it is business that shapes the supply curve because businesses are the sellers in this market, whereas demand is formed by the factors of production (behaving as households).

The two are connected: production and distribution are interdependent

6. Finally, we can see that the two markets—for factors and for goods—are interconnected. This is the same as saying that the activities of production and distribution are interconnected. Incomes earned in production determine how large will be the shares of each factor; and the amount of revenue earned in the goods market, where distribution takes place, will help determine the ability of firms to bid for factor services.

ECONOMIC VOCABULARY

Production 319
Distribution 320
Factor market 320
Goods market 320

QUESTIONS

1. What is the difference between the market for goods and for factors? Can a household be a buyer in the market for factors? Suppose it hires a maid? Are a maid's services a factor of production, or a kind of service? Can a household be a seller in the goods market? Suppose it sells homegrown vegetables? In that case, is it acting as a household or a firm?
2. Can you describe other ways in which the factor and the goods markets interact? Will a firm's behavior on the goods market (its supply curve) be affected by a household's behavior on the factor market (the household supply curve or the price that a household asks for its services)? How about a firm's behavior as a buyer of factors being determined by a household's behavior as a buyer of goods?
3. What is meant by describing the market as a "system"? What exactly do we mean by a system? Does it imply that there is something mechanical—machinelike—about the way a social organism works? Can you see that all these words, such as "system," "mechanism," even "works," imply a regular, orderly, predictable process?

AN EXTRA WORD ABOUT
PRIVATE MARKETS AND PUBLIC "MARKETS"

In our analysis of the circular flow we skipped a little hastily over the difference between two flows of income and output. One flow comes from the interplay of households and private firms. The other comes from the interplay of households and government agencies. Let us look into a few of the differences.

1. In the private part of the economy incomes are very different, depending on individual skills, inheritance, luck, and so forth. *In the public part of the system we all have the same "income"—one vote.*

2. In the private part of the system we spend as much or as little of our incomes as we wish in each market. *In the public part we spend all or nothing.* We use all of our vote for one side (or person) or the other, or we do not vote at all.

3. In the public section of the system we buy goods and services such as education, defense, and justice just as we do in the private section, but we buy them in a curious, indirect manner. First, we use our equal incomes (votes) to support or oppose politicians who promise to institute or diminish the public goods we want. We vote for (or against) defense-minded or education-minded representatives. We cannot, however, actually buy the public output we want unless 51 percent of the public also spends its votes the same way. *There is no way of buying* some *public education or* some *defense or* some *justice just for ourselves. It is all or none, quite unlike the situation in the private portion of the system.*

4. Furthermore, having voted for a public good, we have not yet determined the outcome of the public process. Pressure groups can influence the expenditures that our representatives make. Much also depends on the kinds of taxes that the government chooses. Taxes inevitably favor some groups over others. Here again, *the decision of the majority is imposed on all of us. There is no legal way of not paying taxes, even though you voted against them in the first place.*

5. Yet although taxes are an involuntary expenditure for each individual, they are voluntary from the point of view of society as a whole! We could, after all, vote to have no education, no defense. And although private expenditures are voluntary in one sense—if we don't like a good, we just don't buy it—in another sense they are more compulsory than public goods. *It is possible to get a "free ride" on public goods, for example, by enjoying the nation's public output even though you may pay no taxes whatsoever. There is almost no way of enjoying private output without spending your own income.*

We will have many occasions, as we go on, to look into the problems created by these two kinds of income. Perhaps you can see that there are moral dilemmas connected with the highly egalitarian distribution of "voting income," just as there are with the highly unequal distribution of money income.

Chapter 22 PRICES AND ALLOCATION

A LOOK AHEAD

One of the most important ideas in microeconomics unfolds in this chapter: It is how the market *rations* (or allocates) goods and services. The price mechanism is a way of determining who shall participate in economic activity, as buyer or seller, and who shall not. Bear in mind, as you read the chapter, that all societies must find some means of solving this rationing or allocation problem. The things to look for here are the strong points and the weak points of *price* rationing.

As part of the price-rationing system we also meet two familiar situations: shortages and surpluses. We don't have to tell you that these are important terms. Their meaning may surprise you, however.

Finally, for those who want to go a little more deeply into the theory of market behavior we have a special section on using the price mechanism to maximize utilities. You will find it in the "Extra Word" following the chapter.

THE ALLOCATION PROBLEM

From Chapter 7, "Supply and Demand", we know how prices are formed on the marketplace. Although we cannot look very fully into supply curves until we probe the operations of the firm, we understand in general that prices for goods reflect the interplay of the demand schedules of consumers and the supply schedules of producers. In our next chapter, changes in demand will affect prices, and various characteristics of demand will exert different influences on the price structure.

Before we turn to the dynamics of supply and demand, let us use the price mechanism to shed more light on the problems of microeconomics. For our understanding of that price mechanism reveals how the market system solves a crucial problem: how to *ration* goods or services among the many claimants and uses for them.

RATIONING

In one form or another, rationing—or the allocation of goods among claimants—is a disagreeable but inescapable task that every economic system must carry out; for in all societies, the prevailing reality of life has been the inadequacy of output to fill the wants and needs of the people. In traditional economies, rationing is performed by a general adherence to rigidly established rules. Whether by caste or class or family position or whatever, these rules determine the rights of various individuals to share in the economic product. In command societies, the division of the social product is carried out in a more explicitly directed fashion, as the governing authorities determine the rights of various groups or persons to share in the fruits of society.

A market society, as we know, minimizes the heavy hand of tradition and the authoritative one of command. It cannot escape some system of rationing, though, to prevent what would otherwise be an impossibly destructive struggle among its citizens. This critical allocative task is also accomplished by the price mechanism. One of the prime functions of a market is to determine who shall be allowed to acquire goods and who shall not.

HOW THE MARKET RATIONS

Imagine a market with ten buyers, each willing and able to buy one unit of a commodity, but each having a different maximum price that is agreeable to him. Imagine ten suppliers, each also willing and able to put one unit of supply on the market, again each at a different price. Such a market might look like Table 22.1.

Remember that the maximum prices may differ because different people have different desires for the commodity or because they have different incomes. The person who is willing to pay the highest prices may not desire the commodity the most. He or she may simply have the most income and be willing and able to pay more for everything.

As we can see, the equilibrium price will lie at $6, for at this price there will be five suppliers of one unit each and five purchasers of one each. Now let us make a graph and let each bar stand for one person. The height of the bar tells us the maximum each person will be willing to pay for the unit of the commodity

Price	$11	$10	$9	$8	$7	$6	$5	$4	$3	$2	$1
Number willing and able, at above price, to											
buy one unit	0	1	2	3	4	5	6	7	8	9	10
sell one unit	10	9	8	7	6	5	4	3	2	1	0

TABLE 22.1

The table shows a line-up of buyers and sellers, each one with a different maximum or minimum price (also called a "reservation price"). Can you see why $6 is an equilibrium price?

or the minimum he or she would sell it for. If we line up our marketers in order of their demand and supply capabilities, our market will look like Figure 22.1.

What we have drawn is in fact nothing but a standard supply-and-demand diagram. But look what it shows us. All the buyers who can afford and are willing to pay the equilibrium price (or more) will get the goods they want. All those who cannot will not. So, too, all the sellers who are willing and able to supply the commodity at its equilibrium price or less will be able to consummate sales. All those who cannot will not.

Thus the market, in establishing an equilibrium price, has in effect allocated the goods among some buyers and withheld it from others. It has permitted some sellers to do business and denied that privilege to others. In our case in Chapter 7 anyone who could pay $25 or more got a pair of shoes. Those who could not pay that much were unable to get shoes. All producers who could turn out shoes for $25 or less were able to do business, and those who could not meet that price were unable to make any sales at all.

Note that the market is in this way a means of excluding certain people from economic activity; namely, customers with too little money or with too weak desires or suppliers unwilling or unable to operate at a certain price.

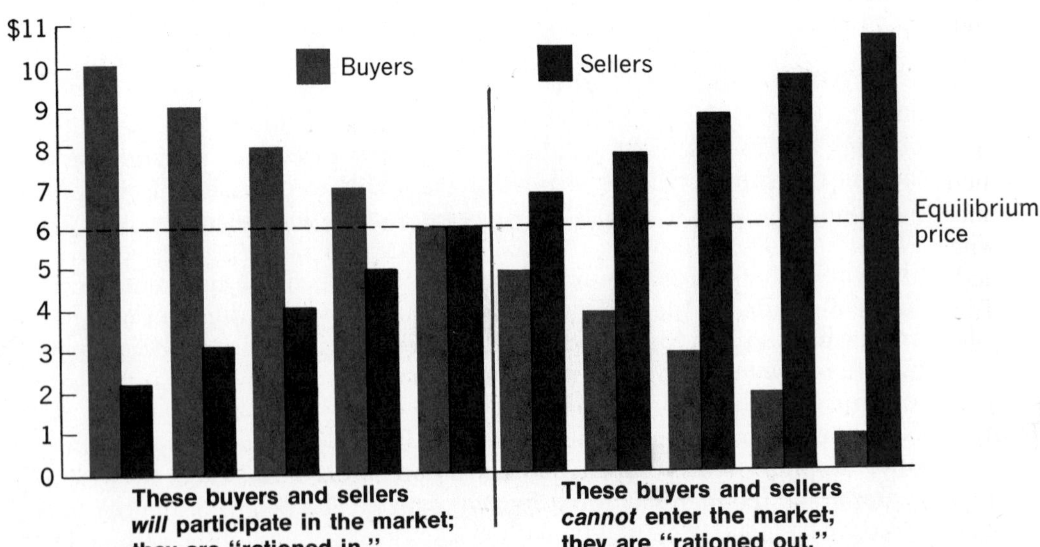

FIGURE 22.1 HOW THE MARKET RATIONS

Later we will see that the market mechanism allocates incomes in much the same way as it allocates goods. Those who successfully enter the market as factors of production get paid wages, rents, or interest. Those who do not, don't.

PRICE VS. NONPRICE RATIONING

The rationing system of the market is both its triumph and its trouble.

Let us look first at the triumphs. Nonmarket systems typically suffer from two difficulties. If they are run mainly by tradition, they tend to be inert, passive, changeless. It's very hard to get things done in a traditional economy, if anything has to be done in a new way.

A command system has a different inherent problem. It is good at getting things done but it acquires its problem-solving capacity at a price. The price is the presence of political power in the economic mechanism, either as a large bureaucracy or as an authority capable of sticking its nose into daily life.

Against these two difficulties, the price system has two great advantages: (1) *it is highly dynamic*, and (2) *it is self-enforcing*. That is, on the one hand it provides an easy avenue for change to enter the system; on the other, it permits economic activity to take place without anyone overseeing the system.

The second (self-enforcing) attribute of the market is especially useful with regard to the rationing function. In place of ration tickets with their almost inevitable black markets or cumbersome inspectorates or queues of customers trying to be first in line, the price system operates without any kind of visible administration apparatus or side effect. The energies that must go into planning or the frictions that come out of it are alike rendered unnecessary by the self-policing market mechanism.

MARKET PROBLEMS

On the other hand, the system has the defects of its virtues. If it is efficient and dynamic, it is also devoid of values. It recognizes no valid claim to the goods and services of society except those of wealth and income. Those with income and wealth are entitled to the goods and services that the economy produces; those without income and wealth receive nothing.

This blindness of the market to any claim on society's output except wealth or income creates very serious problems. It means that those who inherit large incomes are entitled to large shares of output, even though they may have produced nothing themselves. It means that individuals who have no wealth and who cannot produce—perhaps because they are ill, or simply because they cannot find work—have no way of gaining an income through the economic mechanism. To abide just by the market system of distribution we would have to be willing to tolerate individuals starving on the street.

Therefore every market society interferes to some extent with the outcome of the price rationing system. In times of emergency it issues special permits that take precedence over money and thereby prevents the richer members of society from buying up all the supplies of scarce and costly items. In depressed areas, it may distribute basic food or clothing to those who have no money to buy them. To an ever increasing extent it uses its taxes and transfer payments to redistribute the ration tickets of money in accordance with the prevailing sense of justice.

SHORTAGES

Our view of the price system as a rationing mechanism helps to clarify the meaning of two words we often hear as a result of intervention into the market-rationing process: *shortage* and *surplus.*

What do we mean when we say there is a *shortage* of housing for low-income groups? The everyday meaning is that people with low incomes cannot find enough housing. Yet in every market there are always some buyers who are unsatisfied. We have previously noted, for instance, that in our shoe market, all buyers who could not or would not pay $25 had to go without shoes. Does this mean there was a shoe shortage?

Certainly no one uses that word to describe the outcome of a normal market, even though there are always buyers and sellers who are excluded from that market because they cannot meet the going price. Then what does a "shortage" mean? **We can see now that shortage usually refers to a situation in which some nonmarket agency, such as the government, fixes the price below the equilibrium price.**

An Example in Gasoline. Figure 22.2 shows us such a situation in gasoline. Note that the price established by the oil companies and the government is below the price that would clear the market. As a result, the quantity of gas demanded

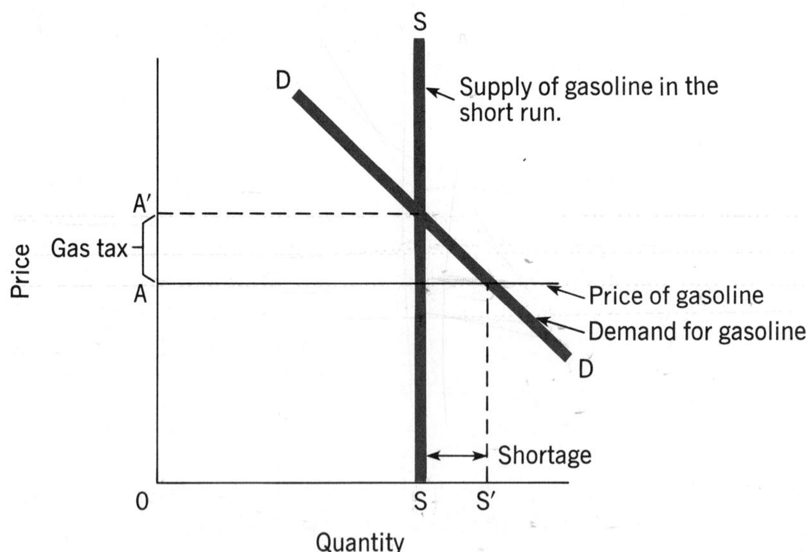

**FIGURE 22.2
THE GAS
SHORTAGE**

Here is a graphic portrait of the gas shortage. The supply of gas in the short run is fixed, as the vertical supply curve SS shows. (We'll discuss vertical curves in our next chapter.) The demand for gas (*DD*) indicates that quantity *OS′* is sought at the going price *OA*. There isn't that much gas. A shortage of *SS′* exists, creating gas lines. Suppose the government puts on a gas tax *AA″*, raising gas prices from *OA* to *OA′*. At the new higher price the quantity demanded is *OS*, just equal to supply. There is no more shortage. But there is a lot of complaint about high prices!

The graph makes clear that a "shortage" means that prices are not able to rise to equilibrium levels, so that quantity demanded exceeds quantity supplied.

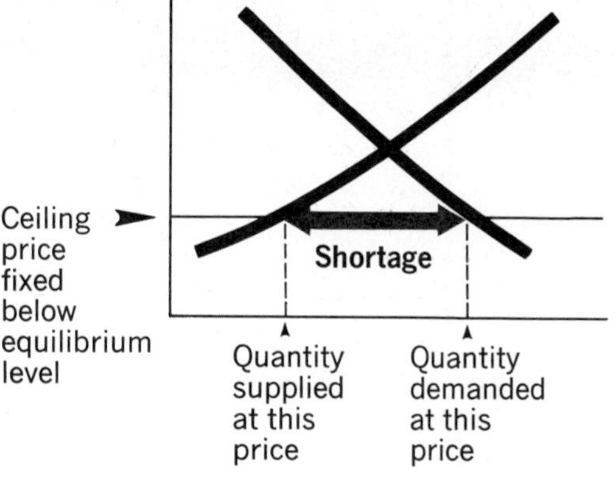

FIGURE 22.3 SHORTAGES

(OS′) is greater than the quantity supplied (OS). The result of this is that we wait in line at the gas pumps and that some people who fail to get to the pumps on time have to go without gas.

How could the shortage be "cured"? Obviously by raising the price to an equilibrium level. Suppose that we did not want the oil companies to raise prices and make larger profits, and instead greatly increased the taxes on gasoline. That would raise the price to a level at which the quantities demanded would be equal to quantities supplied. At a price of, say, \$3 a gallon, the quantity of gas that people bought would be cut back enough so that the lines would disappear.

Why not do that? Many people think it would be a sensible move. But the public would probably object vehemently to paying such high prices. People would rather wait in line and take their chances of going without gas than pay the amount necessary to remove the shortage.

PRICE CONTROLS

This bears directly on the problem of price controls. The problem with such controls is that they tend to fix prices that are below the level that would be established in a free market. As a result, some buyers who would ordinarily have been priced out of the market remain *in* the market, although there are not enough goods offered to satisfy their demands. The result tends to be queues in stores to buy things before they are gone, under-the-counter deals to get on a preferred list, or black or gray markets selling goods illegally at higher prices than are officially sanctioned. We show this in Figure 22.3.

SURPLUSES

The opposite takes place with a surplus. In Figure 22.4 we see a price floor fixed above the equilibrium price. That happens when the government supports a crop above its free market price.

In this situation, the quantity supplied is greater than that demanded (note that we should *not* say that "supply is greater than demand"). In a free market, the price would fall until the two quantities were equal. If the government continues to support the commodity, then the quantity bought by private industries will not be as large as the quantity offered by farmers. Unsold amounts will be a surplus, bought by government.

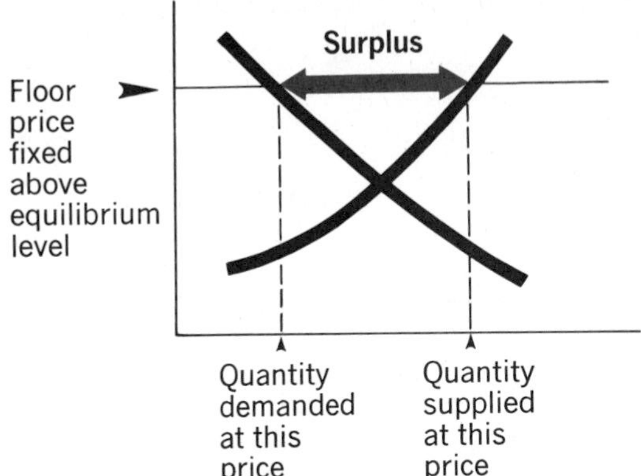

FIGURE 22.4 SURPLUSES

A surplus is just the opposite of a shortage. Now prices are prevented from falling to a clearing level. Therefore, $Q_S > Q_D$.

Thus the words *shortage* and *surplus* mean situations in which there are sellers and buyers who are willing and able to enter the market at the going price but who remain active and unsatisfied because the price mechanism has not eliminated them. This is very different from a free market where there are unsatisfied buyers and sellers *who cannot meet the going price* and who are therefore not taken into account. Poor people, who have no demand for fresh caviar at $60 per pound, do not complain of a caviar shortage. If the price of fresh

RATIONING BABIES

Because the market is such an efficient distributive mechanism, it has been proposed as a means to achieve Zero Population Growth, assuming that this were the declared national policy. Since a sizeable minority (probably about 15 percent) of all families voluntarily choose to have no children or only one, a country can achieve ZPG even if some families have more than two children. The question is how to decide which families should be allowed to have the extra children. Professor Kenneth Boulding has ventured an answer that leans heavily on the market mechanism. He proposes that each girl and boy at adolescence be given 110 green stamps, stamps, of which 100 are required if a woman is to have a legal child. (The penalty for having an illegal child would be very severe.) Unwanted or surplus stamps would then be sold in a market organized for that purpose. It can be seen that the total number of stamps would permit the population as a whole to have 2.2 children per family—the ZPG rate. The market would therefore serve to ration the extra stamps, making them available to those with higher incomes or a greater desire for children. "As an incidental benefit," writes Boulding, tongue in cheek, "the rich will have loads of children and become poor, and the poor have few children and become rich."

When this scheme was first published, it provoked a storm of criticism. Commenting on its reception, Boulding observes: "This modest and humane proposal, so much more humane than that of Swift, who proposed that we eat the surplus babies, has been received with so many cries of anguish and horror that it illustrates the extraordinary difficulty of applying rational principles to processes involving human generation."*

*Kenneth E. Boulding, *Economics as a Science* (New York: McGraw-Hill, 1970), p. 39.

GAS RATIONING, WITH AND WITHOUT TEARS

Although we now understand that the price system is a rationing system, when we say "rationing" we usually mean a system of coupons or publicly determined priorities. If there were a permanent shortage of gasoline—meaning that at going prices, the quantity of gas sought would be larger than the quantity offered—we might ration by allowing each car owner an equal amount or by assuring that certain vehicles, such as ambulances, always had first crack at supplies.

No sooner do we begin to think about rationing by coupon or by priority than we begin to see the complexity of the problem. Clearly, the purpose of rationing is to prevent rich people from riding about in Cadillacs while poor people can't afford the gas to ride to work in their Volkswagens.

Imagine that you were in charge of nonprice rationing. Suppose that the number of gallons of gas expected to be available were 100 billion. Would you now determine the basic ration by dividing this number by the population, giving each person an equal allotment? That would enormously benefit a family with one car and many children, and penalize a single person who might desperately depend on his car. And what would a family do if it got its coupons but did not own a car? Would you perhaps ration supplies per car owner, rather than per person? Here, of course, the trouble is that you would be giving the same allotment to all car owners, without knowing their respective needs. Some owners, such as Hertz and Avis, would be desperate for supplies. Other owners, who hardly used their cars, would not need all their coupons.

Might these very difficulties prompt you to follow a scheme that resembles Boulding's proposal for rationing babies? Suppose you issued to each adult a book of coupons entitling him to his basic allotment of gallons, and *you allowed individuals to buy or sell these coupons!* To be sure, rich citizens would now be in a position to buy up coupon books, but poor citizens would not have to sell their books. If they needed their basic allotment, they would keep their coupons. If they did not need their allotment, they could supplement their income by selling it.

The point of such a plan is to use the market as a means by which individuals can determine their own economic activities according to their marginal utilities, and to combine that use with the overall fairness that a market may not attain. The ration books would insure a basically democratic sharing of one part of the national wealth, but they would permit individuals to maximize their surpluses in a way that rationing alone would not.

caviar were set by government decree at $1 a pound, there would soon be a colossal "shortage."

WHEN PRICE RATIONING FAILS

What about the situation with low-cost housing? Essentially what we mean when we talk of a shortage of inexpensive housing is that we view the outcome of this particular market situation with noneconomic eyes and pronounce the result distasteful. By the standards of the market, the poor who cannot afford to buy housing are simply buyers at the extreme lower right end of the demand curve. Their elimination from the market for housing is only one more example of the rationing process that takes place in *every* market. When we single out certain goods or services (such as a doctor's care or higher education) as being in "short supply," we imply that we do not approve of the price mechanism as the appropriate means of allocating scarce resources in these particular instances. Our disapproval does not imply that the market is not as efficient a distributor as ever. What we do not like is the outcome of the market rationing process. The underlying distribution (or maldistribution) of income clashes with other standards of the public interest that we value more highly than efficiency.

LOOKING BACK

KEY CONCEPTS

The market as rationing or allocation mechanism

This short and simple chapter is one of the most important in this entire section, for the idea of the market as a rationing system—a means of allocating output (or, as we will later see, income)—is fundamental to understanding our form of economic society.

Price as rationer

1. The rationing device used by the market is simplicity itself. Price determines who will and who will not enter the market, whether as buyer or seller. Those who cannot or do not wish to sell or buy at existing prices are rationed out of the marketplace.

Strengths of the market system: flexibility and self-governance

2. The price system of allocation has two great advantages. It avoids the stodginess and unresponsiveness of tradition-bound systems, and it makes unnecessary the bureaucracy or political intervention of command-run systems. Markets govern themselves. Those who are rationed in and those who are rationed out usually—although not always—acquiesce in the market's determinations.

Weaknesses: no social conscience

3. Price rationing has one great disadvantage: It recognizes no claim on output except the ability to enter the market. Therefore it has no "heart," no social conscience. As a result all market systems make allowances for those whom it considers are unfairly kept out of the market.

Shortages: when prices are below equilibrium, quantities demanded exceed quantities supplied

4. The function of price as an allocator throws light on shortages and surpluses. What we mean by a shortage is that price is held below an equilibrium or clearing level by government or other means. As a result the quantity demanded is greater than that supplied. The result of this is queues or black markets or a scramble to get to the front of the line.

Surpluses are just the opposite

5. A surplus comes about just the other way. When prices are held up above clearing levels by price supports or some other means, more is supplied to the market than is demanded. The supply for which there are no buyers at the support price is called a surplus.

Problems of nonprice allocation

6. The idea of shortage and surplus is not difficult to master but it should be mulled over. Reread the box above about rationing gasoline and think about the difficulties of devising a rationing system that would create *less* fuss or fury than the mechanism of price. The problems of nonprice allocation are very great indeed, as the "Extra Word" about voting in Chapter 21 also made clear.

ECONOMIC VOCABULARY

Rationing 327
Allocation 328
Shortage 330
Surplus 331

QUESTIONS

1. Why is rationing an inescapable problem in our kind of society? Is it inescapable even in traditional societies, like the Eskimo? How is it solved there?
2. Explain how the market rations automobiles. What other means of allocating cars could you imagine in a capitalist society? In a socialist one?
3. Under what circumstances is the market not regarded as a good rationer? Take a newly perfected vaccine as an example. Why would people object to selling it to the highest bidder? Why don't the same arguments apply to aspirin?
4. Is there a shortage of low-cost housing? High-cost housing? What do we mean by the term?
5. Would you be in favor of a gas tax that would remove any shortages or do you prefer rationing on a nonprice basis? Which basis strikes you as best?

AN EXTRA WORD ABOUT

OPTIMAL ALLOCATION OF INDIVIDUAL INCOME

There is another way in which a market allows us to allocate income efficiently. Let us see how the market mechanism maximizes the total utilities of a person who shops in many markets for many goods.

An intuitive example may help us begin. Suppose that you had to spend your weekly income each Monday, but that you had to make up your shopping list, once and for all, before leaving your house. If you had enough price catalogs, that would not be impossible to do, although you might debate the merits of this item versus that one. *Suppose you had to make up the list without knowing what prices were!*

Two problems would present themselves. First, you would not know how many goods you could buy, *in toto,* because you would not know whether your income would suffice to buy a few goods or many. Second, you would have no way of ranking the priority of your purchases. Knowing the prices of bread and cake, you can decide how much you want to spend on each. Not knowing these prices, how could you make a rational decision whether to buy many units of bread and no cake or fifty-fifty or some other combination?

You might think, perhaps, that a rational man would buy bread first, then cake. But suppose after he had made his irrevocable decision he found that bread was very expensive and cake very cheap. He might then regret having decided to buy so much bread and dearly wish he had chosen cake instead.

This seemingly trivial example contains more than may at first meet the eye, for it shows us how the existence of prices enables us to behave as rational maximizers in disposing of our incomes. Therefore let us pursue our line of reasoning a little further.

In Figure 22.5 we show our reservation prices for three commodities. *Reservation price* is a term meaning the highest price that we are willing to offer as buyers, or the lowest price we'd take as sellers. In each case, our reservation price for another unit of the same good diminishes because the good gives us less marginal utility. At the same time, as the diagram makes clear, the schedule of reservation prices is very different for each good. Good A

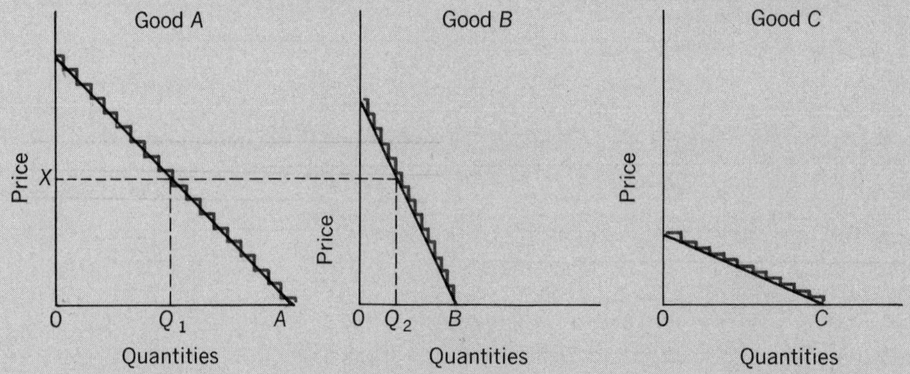

FIGURE 22.5
ALLOCATING INCOME

The graph shows us different schedules of reservation prices (the most we would pay) for successive units of three commodities. At price *OX* we will just be tempted to buy an amount OQ_1 of good *A*, OQ_2 of good *B*, but none of good *C*. At zero price, how much do we want of each?

is very important to us, so our initial reservation price is very high; Good B less so; Good C still less. (We have drawn our reservation prices in step-like fashion and overlaid a generalized schedule of reservation prices, which is, of course, our familiar demand curve.)*

MARGINS VS. TOTALS

The question we want to elucidate is this: *how much of each good will we buy to get the largest possible satisfaction from our income?*

Suppose we had an unlimited income. This is the same thing as supposing that the goods were free, that their prices were zero. How much of Goods A, B, and C would we then acquire? An unlimited amount? Certainly not. As our diagram shows, we don't want unlimited quantities of A, B, and C. Beyond a certain point, their marginal utilities are negative. They are nuisances. We could even have negative reservation prices: We would pay someone to take the stuff away. Thus, with no budget constraint, we consume quantities *OA* + *OB* + *OC*.

Now notice something interesting about this unlimited consumption. The three demand curves reflect differing marginal utilities of the three goods. Looking at these curves, we see that the *total* utility we get from A will be greater than that we get from B or C, and that the *total* utility of B will be greater than that of C. Why then don't we take more of A and B, since their total utility is so large? The answer, also apparent from the graph, is that after we have acquired quantity *OA* of Good A *we don't get any further utility from it.* The same is true of B after we have *OB* of it, and of course of C, after *OC.*

*Remember that each of these schedules of reservation prices depends on our initial income as well as our tastes. With a different income, we might have a different set of desires for the three goods.

This begins to clarify a very important point. To get the maximum amount of enjoyment from our income—even from an *unlimited* income—we need pay no attention to the total utilities we get from various commodities. Their marginal utilities are all we need to know. We will reach a maximum of satisfaction from our total expenditure when we get as much utility from the marginal unit of one good as from another. *Indeed, the rule for maximizing our total satisfaction is to acquire goods until their marginal utilities per dollar of expenditure are equal.*

THE EQUIMARGINAL RULE

This equimarginal rule has many applications in economics, for it has an astonishing property. It means that we don't have to stop to compare totals when we maximize values. *We need compare only margins.* Later we will see that this applies to entrepreneurs trying to maximize total revenues and to minimize total costs. They too will need to look at only marginal costs and incomes. For ourselves as consumers, it means that we do not have to try to compare whether we get more "total" satisfaction out of bread or out of cake. All we have to do is worry about whether we want one more loaf of bread or one more piece of cake. If we buy whichever we want more of at the moment, we will automatically be maximizing our total well-being. When we equally desire another unit of each, we have spent our income as efficiently as possible.

BUDGET CONSTRAINTS

So far, we have imagined that we had no budget constraint. Of course we do have such constraints. Our incomes are limited, and prices are not zero. Then how does the equimarginal principle apply?

If you will turn back to Figure 22.5 you will see an *X* on the price axis of Good A. If you draw a line parallel to the quantity axis all the way across the diagram, we can imagine that this is the price of Goods A, B, and C. We picture them having the same price: e.g., $5 for a basket of fruit (Good A), a necktie (Good B), a movie ticket (Good C). (We could draw different prices for each good, but that would only complicate the diagram without changing the principle.)

Now how much of A, B, and C do we buy? If you will drop a line from the point where price intersects the demand curve, you will see that we buy (approximately) OQ_1 of Good A, and OQ_2 of Good B. We buy none of Good C. Why? Because the price is higher than our top reservation price. We don't want to go to the movies at $5, given our budget constraint.

Now look at Goods A and B. You obviously have much more total utility from A than from B. Why then don't you buy more of A and less of B? The answer is that you are getting as much satisfaction *at the margin* for Good A as for Good B. If you bought another unit of Good A, and one less unit of Good B, you would be giving up more utility than you would be getting. *Thus budget constraints limit the amount of goods we can buy, but we still maximize our well-being by seeking equal marginal utilities from those we buy.*

EQUALIZING MARGINAL UTILITIES

Now let us take one last step. We have just seen that we maximize our personal well-being by equalizing the marginal utilities of goods, not their total utilities. *We can then see that we will spend our income optimally when we get the same satisfaction from a dollar spent on each good.* If the marginal utility of a dollar's worth of bread is equal to that of a dollar's worth of cake, we have obviously achieved our aim.

When we speak of "a dollar's worth" of bread, we are speaking of its price. Therefore we can set up a formula that will describe the way we allocate our incomes to maximize our satisfactions.

$$\frac{\text{Marginal Utility of Good A}}{\text{Price of Good A}} = \frac{\text{Marginal Utility of Good B}}{\text{Price of Good B}}$$

or in more abstract terms:

$$\frac{MU_1}{P_1} = \frac{MU_2}{P_2} = \frac{MU_n}{P_n}$$

where *MU* stands for the marginal utilities of Goods 1, 2 . . . *n*, and $P_1, P_2 \ldots P_n$ stand for their respective prices.

Here is the equimarginal principle at work. We are maximizing our well-being by equating the *marginal* utilities of different goods in proportion to their prices, so that each dollar of expenditure for each good gives us the same enjoyment. We may still get a much larger amount of enjoyment from one kind of good than from another, but we will only decrease our total welfare if we lose sight of the equimarginal principle.

Chapter 23 THE MARKET IN MOVEMENT

A LOOK AHEAD

This chapter will give us an understanding of the most useful single analytic tool of microeconomics—perhaps of all economics: supply and demand in action.

(1) We begin by learning to distinguish shifts of supply and demand curves from movements along those curves. It is the shifts of the curves themselves that are the causes of price change.

(2) That quickly brings us to the subject of elasticity—our responsiveness as buyers or sellers to price changes. We will learn how differing elasticities can alter the price outcome of demand or supply shifts.

(3) The last topic is why elasticities differ. Here we discover the central concept of substitution, the decisive factor that makes a commodity either a "necessity" or a "luxury".

You can see that this is a very important chapter. To learn it well, we suggest that you read it through and then review it by going back over the diagrams. If you can explain them in words, you will have mastered the subject.

Equilibrium prices, emerging from the wholly unsupervised interaction of competing buyers and sellers, are now a part of our understanding. These prices, once formed, silently and efficiently perform the necessary social task of allocating goods among buyers and sellers. Yet our analysis is still too static to resemble the actual play of the marketplace, for one of the attributes of an equilibrium price, we remember, is its lasting quality, its persistence. Things are different in the real world around us, where prices are often in movement. How can we introduce this element of change into our analysis of microeconomic relations?

The answer is that the word *equilibrium* does not imply changelessness. Equilibrium prices last only as long as the forces that produce them do not change. To put it differently, if we want to explain why any price changes, we must always look for changes in the forces of supply and demand that produced the price in the first place.

SHIFTS IN DEMAND AND SUPPLY

What makes supply and demand change? If we recall the definition of those words, we are asking: What might change our willingness or ability to buy or sell something at any given price? Having asked the question, it is not difficult to answer it. If our incomes rise or fall, that will clearly alter our *ability* to buy. Similarly, a change in the prices of other commodities will alter our real income and thus our ability to buy. When food goes up, we go to the movies less often. Finally, a change in tastes will change our *willingness* to buy.

On the seller's side things are a bit more complicated. If we are owners of the factors of production (labor, land, or capital), changes in incomes or tastes will also change our ability and willingness to offer these factors on the market. If we are making decisions for firms, changes in *cost* will be the main determinant. We shall study these changes when we turn to the firm in later chapters.

SHIFTS IN CURVES VS. MOVEMENTS ALONG CURVES

Thus changes in tastes or prices or in income or wealth will shift our whole demand schedule. The same changes, plus any change in costs, will shift our whole supply schedule.

Note that this is very different from a change in the quantity we buy or sell when *prices* change. **In the first case, as our willingness and ability to buy or sell is increased or diminished, the whole demand and supply schedule (or curve) shifts bodily. In the second place, when our basic willingness and ability is unchanged, but prices change, our schedule (or curve) is unchanged, but we move back or forth along it.**

Here are the two cases to be studied carefully in Figure 23.1. Note that when our demand schedule shifts, we buy a *different amount at the same price.* If our willingness and ability to buy is enhanced, we will buy a larger amount; if they are diminished, a smaller amount. Similarly, the quantity a seller will offer will vary as his willingness and ability are altered. Thus demand and supply curves can shift about, rightward and leftward, up and down, as the economic circumstances they represent change. In reality, these schedules are continuously in change, since tastes and incomes and attitudes and technical capabilities (which affect costs and therefore sellers' actions) are also continuously in flux.

CHANGES IN QUANTITIES DEMANDED OR SUPPLIED vs . . . . . . CHANGES IN DEMAND OR SUPPLY

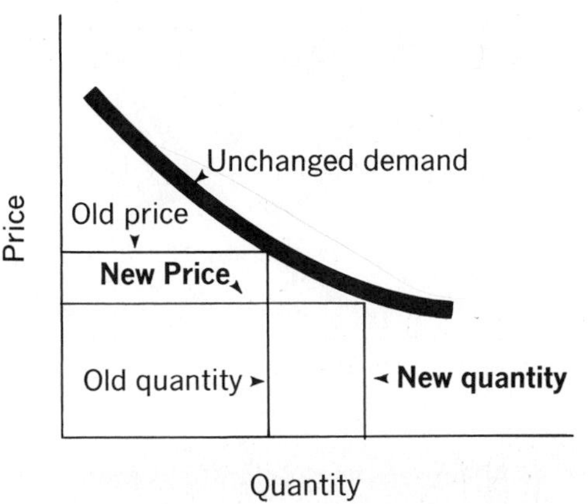

A change in price alone changes the *quantity* we demand or supply.

New demand
Old demand
Unchanged price
New quantity demanded (at same price)
Price
Old quantity demanded
Quantity

A change in our willingness or ability changes our whole *demand schedule.*

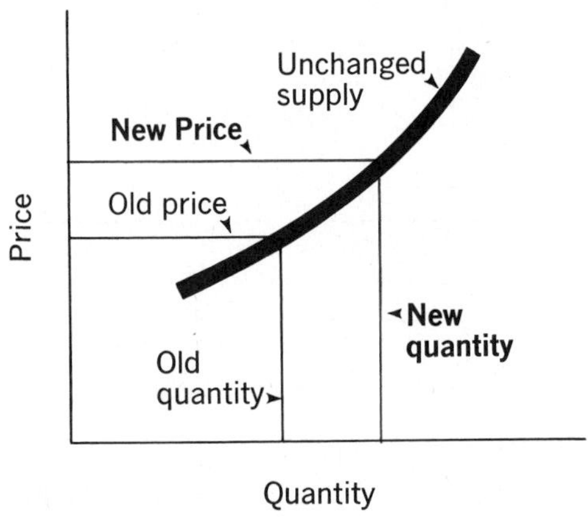

A change in price alone changes the *quantity* we supply.

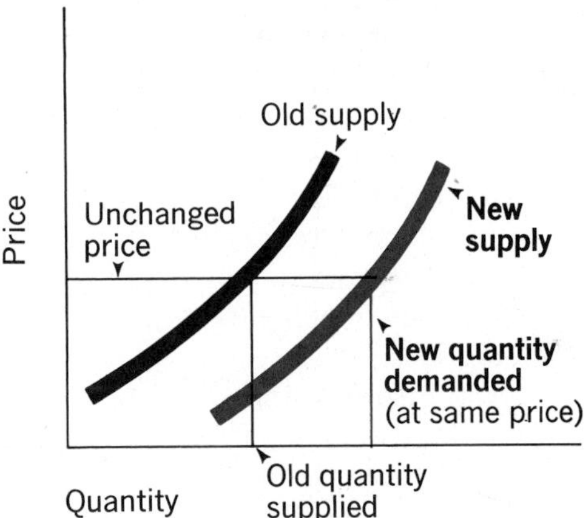

A change in our willingness or ability to sell changes our whole *supply schedule.*

FIGURE 23.1

PRICE CHANGES

How do changes in supply and demand affect prices? We have already seen the underlying process at work for shoes. Changes in supply or demand will alter the *quantities* that will be sought or offered on the market at a given price. An increase in demand, for instance, will raise the quantity sought. Since there are not enough goods offered to match this quantity, prices will be bid up by unsatisfied buyers to a new level. At that level, quantities offered and sought will again balance. Similarly, if supply shifts, there will be too much or too little put on the market in relation to the existing quantity of demand, and competition among sellers will push prices up or down to a new level at which quantities sought and offered again clear.

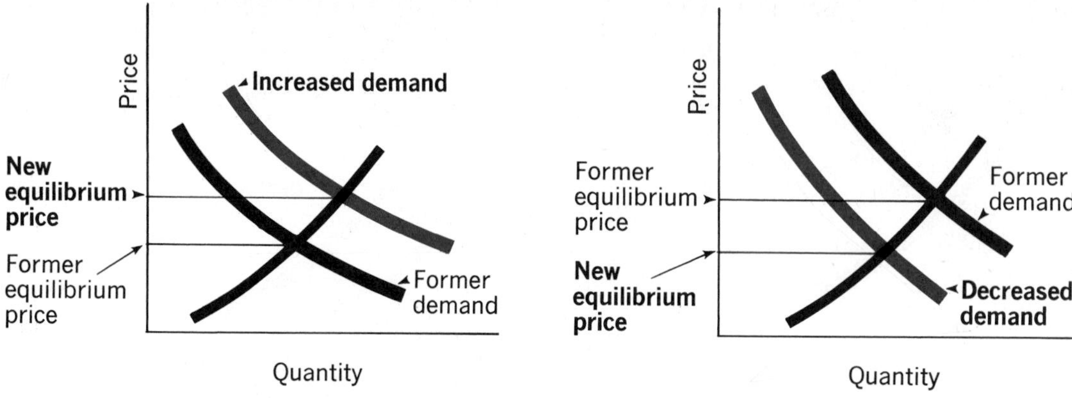

FIGURE 23.2 SHIFTS IN DEMAND
An increase or decrease in our demand schedule changes the equilibrium price, raising it in the first case, lowering it in the second.

In Figure 23.2, we show what happens to the equilibrium price in two cases: first, when demand increases (perhaps owing to a sudden craze for the good in question); second, when demand decreases (when the craze is over). Quite obviously, a rise in demand, other things being equal, will cause prices to rise; a fall will cause them to fall.

We can depict the same process from the supply side. In Figure 23.3, we show the impact on price of a sudden rise in supply and the impact of a fall. Again the diagram makes clear what is intuitively obvious: an increased supply (given an unchanging demand) leads to lower prices; a decreased supply to higher prices.

And if supply and demand *both* change? Then the result will be higher or lower prices, depending on the shapes and new positions of the two curves; that is, depending on the relative changes in the willingness and ability of both sides.

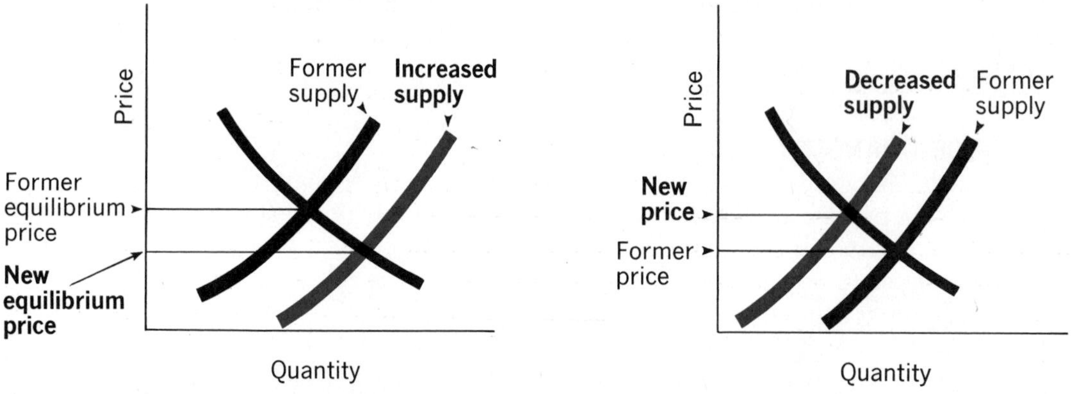

FIGURE 23.3 SHIFTS IN SUPPLY
Shifts in supply also change equilibrium prices. Increased supplies lower them; decreased supplies raise them.

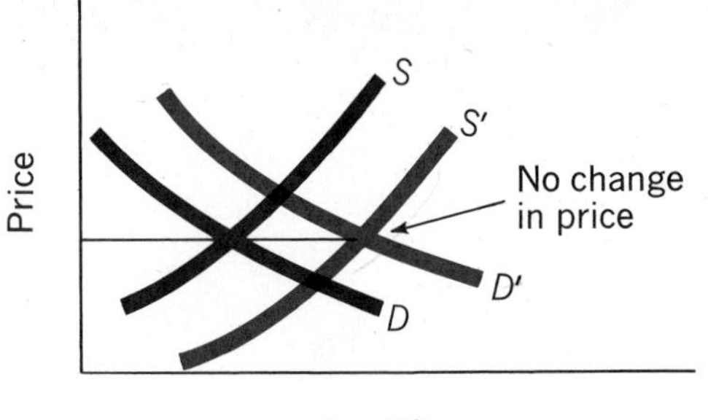

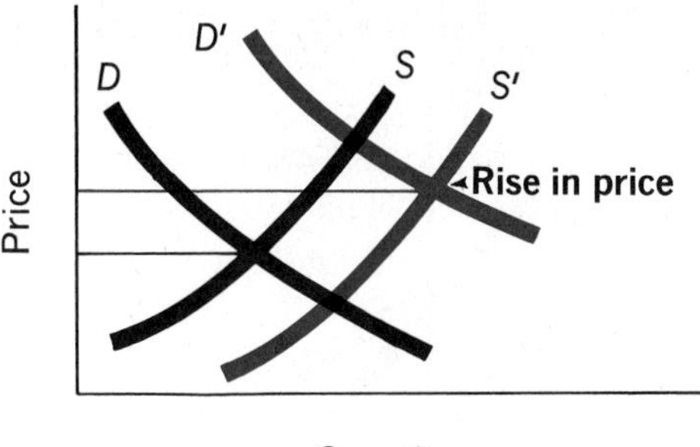

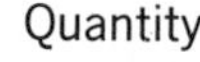

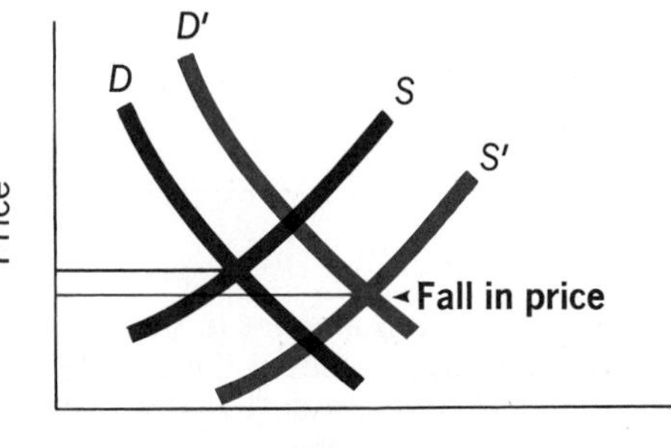

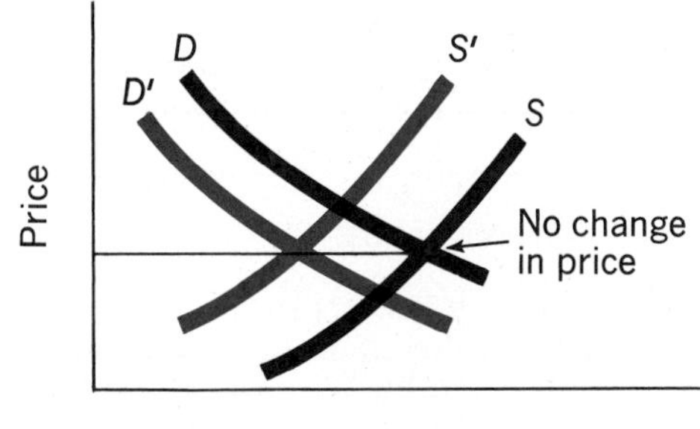

FIGURE 23.4 SHIFTS IN BOTH SUPPLY AND DEMAND

When both supply and demand change, prices may rise, fall, or remain unchanged. The outcome is determined by the intersection of *both* curves, so that we can never tell what will happen to price if we only know what has happened to one curve, but not to the other.

Figure 23.4 shows a few possibilities, where S and D are the original supply and demand curves, and S' and D' the new curves.

LONG AND SHORT RUN

There is one point we should add to conclude our discussion of supply and demand. Students often wonder which "really" sets the price—supply or demand. Alfred Marshall, the great late-nineteenth-century economist, gave the right answer: *both do*, just as both blades of scissors do the cutting.

Yet, whereas prices are always determined by the intersection of supply and demand schedules, we can differentiate between the *short run*, when demand tends to be the more dynamic force, and the *long run*, when supply is the more important force. In Figure 23.5 we see (on the left) short-run fixed supply, as in the instance of fishermen bringing a catch to a dock. Since the size of the catch cannot be changed, the supply curve is fixed in place, and the demand curve is the only possible dynamic influence. Broken lines show that changes in demand alone will set the price.

Now let us shift to the long run and draw a horizontal supply curve representing the average cost of production of fish (and thus the supply price of fish) in the long run. Fluctuations in demand now have no effect on price, whereas a

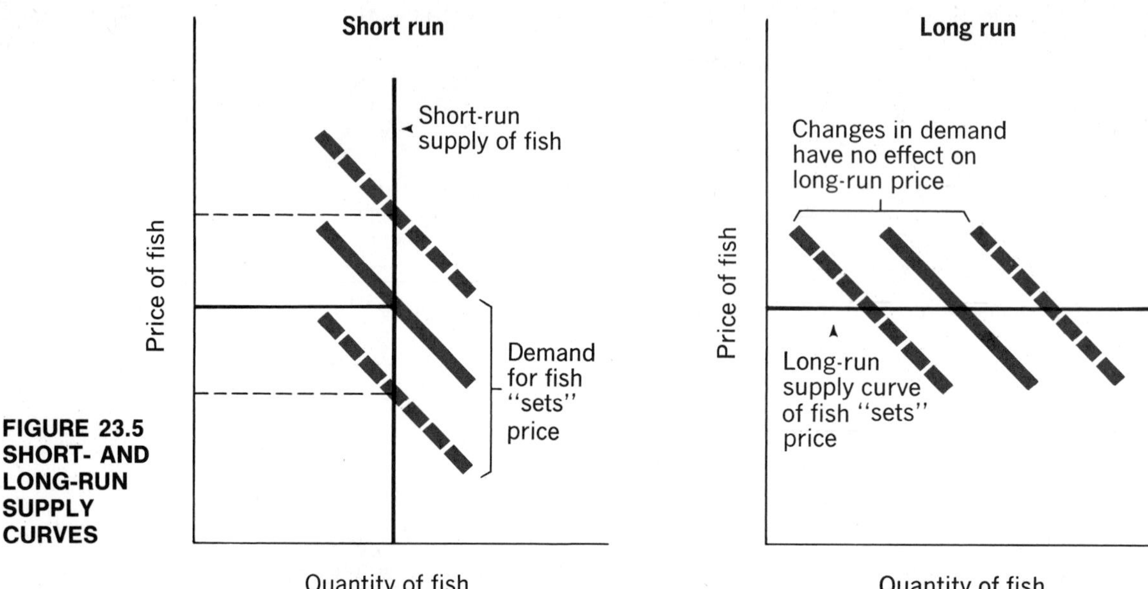

FIGURE 23.5 SHORT- AND LONG-RUN SUPPLY CURVES

Short-run supply is represented by a vertical curve since the same amount is offered no matter what the price. Here, demand "sets" the price, although without the supply curve there would be no price. In the long run, supply is horizontal, and demand has no effect on price. Yet without a demand curve there would be no sales of fish—and therefore no price at all! Both supply and demand are essential for all prices.

change in fishing costs that would raise or lower the supply curve would immediately affect the price.

In all cases, do not forget, *both* demand and supply enter into the formation of price. In the short run, as a rule, changes in demand are more likely to affect changes in prices, whereas in the long run, changes in supply are apt to be the predominant cause of changes in price.

ELASTICITY

We have seen how shifts in demand or supply affect price, but *how much* do they affect price? Suppose, for example, that demand schedules have increased by 10 percent. Do we know how large an effect this change will have on price?

These questions lead us to a still deeper scrutiny of the nature of supply and demand, by way of a new concept called *elasticity* or, more properly, *price elasticity*. Elasticities describe the shapes of supply and demand curves and thereby tell us a good deal about whether a given change in demand or supply will have a small or large effect on price. Figure 23.6 illustrates the case with two supply curves. Our diagrams show two commodities selling at the same equilibrium prices and facing identical demand schedules. Note, however, that the two commodities have very different supply curves. In both cases, demand now increases by the same amount. Notice how much greater is the price increase for the good with the inelastic (steep) supply curve.

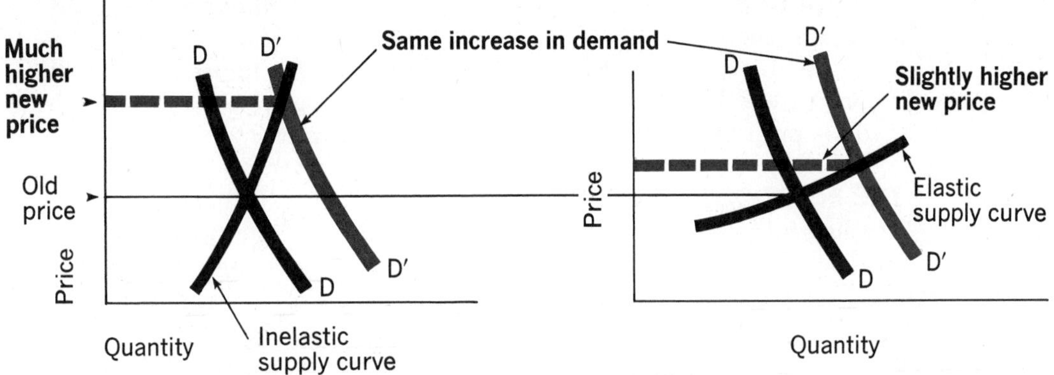

FIGURE 23.6 ELASTICITY OF SUPPLY

Elasticity describes the shapes of supply or demand curves. These shapes in turn represent the sensitivity of buyers or sellers to price changes. On the left we have an inelastic supply curve. The increase in demand from *DD* to D′D′ brings about a big jump in prices (much like the effect on the short-run market for fish, Figure 23.5). On the right, the same increase in demand coaxes forth a lot of additional supply. Therefore price rises much less than in the first case.

Similarly, the price change that would be associated with a change in supply will be greater for a commodity with an inelastic demand curve than for one with an elastic (gently sloping) demand curve. Figure 23.7 shows two identical supply curves matched against very different demand curves. Notice how the commodity with **inelastic demand** suffers a much greater fall in price.

Elasticities are powerful factors in explaining price movements, because the word *elasticity* refers to our sensitivity of response to price changes. An elastic demand (or supply) means that changes in price strongly affect buyers' or sellers' willingness or ability to buy or sell. When schedules are inelastic, the

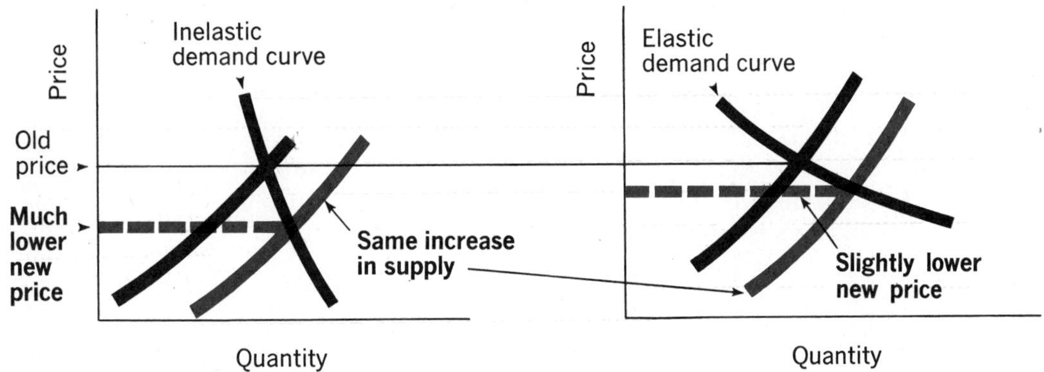

FIGURE 23.7 ELASTICITY OF DEMAND

Elasticity obviously affects demand curves as well as supply curves. Rule: The *more* elastic demand is, the less will a given shift in supply change prices.

effect of price is small. In more precise terms, an elastic demand (or supply) is one in which a given percentage change in prices brings about a larger percentage change in the quantity demanded (or supplied). An inelastic schedule or curve is one in which the response in the quantities we are willing and able to buy or sell is proportionally less than the change in price.

THE ELASTICITY FORMULA

It is helpful to have a very precise idea of how we measure elasticity. The method is simple enough. We compare the percentage change in the quantity demanded over the percentage change in price. If the percentage change in quantity demanded is greater than that of price, our measure of elasticity will be greater than unity, and we have an elastic curve. If it is less than unity, we have an inelastic curve. If the two variables are equal, we have unit elasticity.

In algebra:*

$$\frac{\Delta Q/Q}{\Delta P/P} = \text{measure of elasticity, where}$$

ΔQ is the *change* in quantity demanded
Q is the *original* quantity demanded
ΔP is the *change* in price,
P is the *original* price.

It helps if we see what elasticities of different kinds look like. Figure 23.8 is a family of supply and demand curves that illustrates the range of buying and selling responses associated with a change in prices.

ELASTICITIES AND BUSINESS FORTUNE

Later, in Chapter 33 we will discover a very important effect of elasticities in determining the incidence of taxation—that is, who pays a given tax. But while we are still studying the marketplace, we should note that elasticities have a very great effect on the fortunes of buyers and sellers. It makes a great deal of difference to a buyer whether the supply curve of a commodity he wants is elastic or not, for that will affect very drastically the amount he will have to spend on that particular commodity if its price changes. It makes an equal amount of difference to a seller whether the demand curve for his output is elastic or not, for that will determine what happens to his total revenues as prices change.

Here is an instance in point. Table 23.1 shows three demand schedules: elastic, inelastic, and of unit elasticity. Let us see how these three differently constituted schedules would affect the fortunes of a seller who had to cater to the demand represented by each.

*A footnote to the mathematically inclined student. You have probably noticed that the change in quantity is likely to be a positive number when the change in price is a negative number—we buy more when the price goes down. Therefore the measure of elasticity will also be a negative number. For convenience sake, economists disregard this and speak as if the measure were positive. You should also note that there are a number of refinements in measuring elasticity which we do not go into here. The main one concerns the difference between measuring elasticity at a single point and measuring it along a section of the curve.

FIGURE 23.8 A FAMILY OF SUPPLY AND DEMAND CURVES

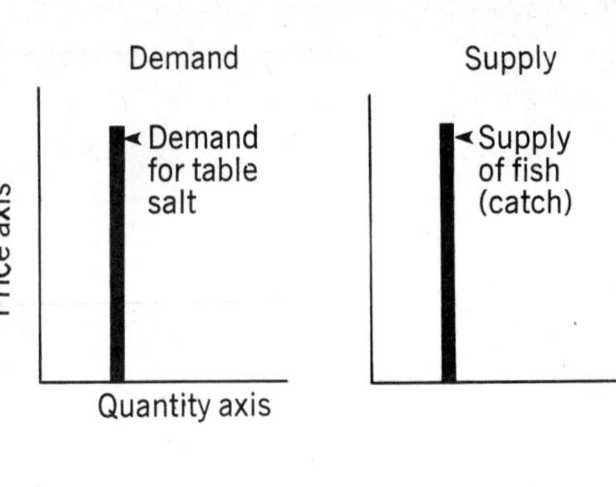

totally inelastic demand or supply. **The quantity offered or sought is unchanged despite a change in price. Examples: Within normal price ranges there is probably no change at all in the quantity of table salt bought. Similarly, a fisherman landing a catch of fish will have to sell it all at any price within reason.**

inelastic demand or supply. **Quantity offered or sought changes proportionately less than price. Examples: We probably do not buy twice as much bread if the price of bread drops to half. On the supply side, the price of wheat may double, but farmers are unable (at least for a long time) to offer twice as much wheat for sale.**

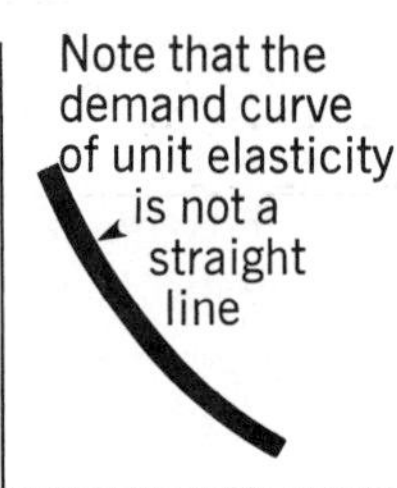

unit elasticity. **This is a special case in which quantities demanded or supplied respond in exact proportion to price changes. (Note the shape of the demand curve, a rectangular hyperbola.) Examples: Many goods may fit this description, but it is impossible flatly to state that any one good does so.**

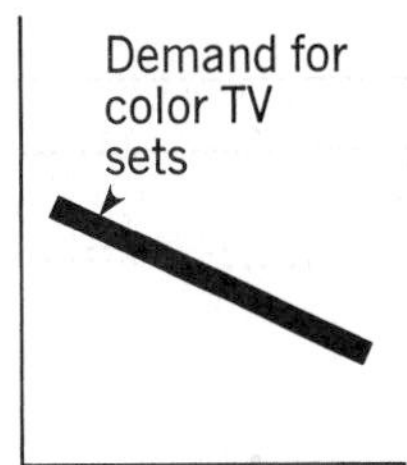

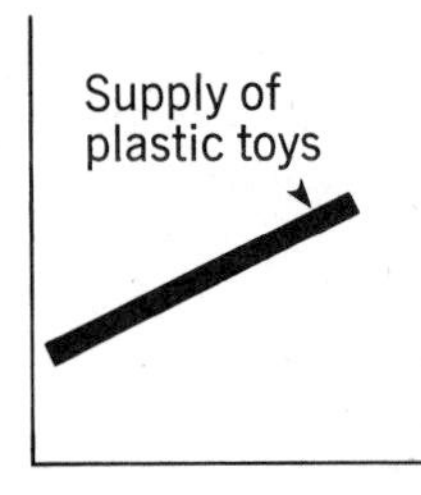

elastic demand or supply. **Price changes induce proportionally larger changes in quantity. Examples: Many luxury goods increase dramatically in sales volume when their price is lowered. On the other side, elastic supply usually affects items that are easy to produce, so that a small price rise induces a rush for expanded output.**

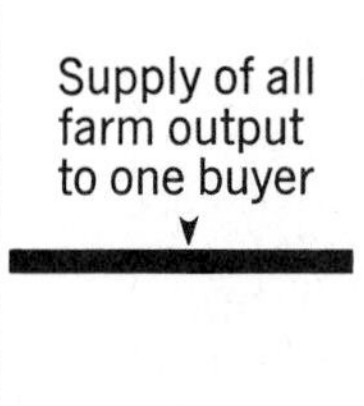

totally elastic demand or supply. **The quantity supplied or demanded at the going price is "infinite." Examples: This seemingly odd case turns out to be of great importance in describing the market outlook of the typical small competitive firm. Merely as a hint: For an individual farmer, the demand curve for his output at the going price looks horizontal because he can sell all the grain he can possibly grow at that price. A grain dealer can also buy all he wants at that price.**

TABLE 23.1 DEMAND SCHEDULES FOR THREE GOODS

Price	Quantities demanded: Inelastic demand	Unit elasticity	Elastic demand
$10	100	100	100
9	101	111 1/9	120
8	102	125	150
7	103	143	200
6	104	166 2/5	300
5	105	200	450
4	106	250	650
3	107	333 1/3	900
2	108	500	1,400
1	109	1,000	3,000

The three demand schedules are different in elasticity because each reveals a different ability or willingness to buy as prices change. Compare the percentage response of the three buyers to a 10 percent drop of price from $10 to $9.

A very interesting result follows from these different schedules. The amounts spent (price times quantity) are in Table 23.2. **The total amount spent for each commodity (and thus the total amount received by a firm) will be very different over the indicated range of prices.**

To a seller of goods, it makes a lot of difference whether or not the demand he faces is elastic. *If demand is elastic and he cuts his price, he will take in more revenue.* If his demand is inelastic and he cuts his price, he will take in *less* revenue.

Conversely, a business that raises its price will be lucky if the demand for its product is inelastic, for then receipts will actually increase. Compare the fortunes of the two businesses depicted in Figure 23.9. Note that by blocking in the change in price times the change in quantity, we can show the change in receipts. (Because we have ignored changes in costs, we cannot show changes in profits.)

Our figure shows something else. If we reverse the direction of the price change, our businesses' fortunes take a sharp change. A demand curve that is elastic spells bad news for a business that seeks to raise prices, but the same demand curve brings good fortune to one that intends to cut prices. Just the op-

TABLE 23.2 TOTAL EXPENDITURES (OR RECEIPTS)

Price	Goods with demand schedules that are: Inelastic	Unit elastic	Elastic
$10	1,000	1,000	1,000
9	909	1,000	1,080
8	816	1,000	1,200
7	717	1,000	1,400
6	612	1,000	1,800
5	525	1,000	2,250
4	424	1,000	2,600
3	321	1,000	2,700
2	216	1,000	2,800
1	109	1,000	3,000

Compare what happens to receipts of the three goods when price drops from $10 to $9.

INCOME ELASTICITIES

We should notice that we can use another term—*income elasticity*—to describe how our willingness or ability to buy or sell responds to a change in *income,* rather than price. With many commodities, income elasticities of both demand and supply are more significant than price elasticities in actual economic life.

The idea of income elasticity is exactly the same as price elasticity. Sales of an income-elastic good or service rise proportionately *faster* than income. Sales of an income-inelastic commodity rise *less than proportionately* with income. These relationships are graphed in the accompanying figure.

Do not be fooled into thinking that these are supply curves because they slope upwards. "Income" demand curves show a functional relation different from that of "price" demand curves. In the curves shown, we assume that prices are unchanged, otherwise we would not have *ceteris paribus.*

As an exercise, try drawing an income-elastic and an income-inelastic supply curve.

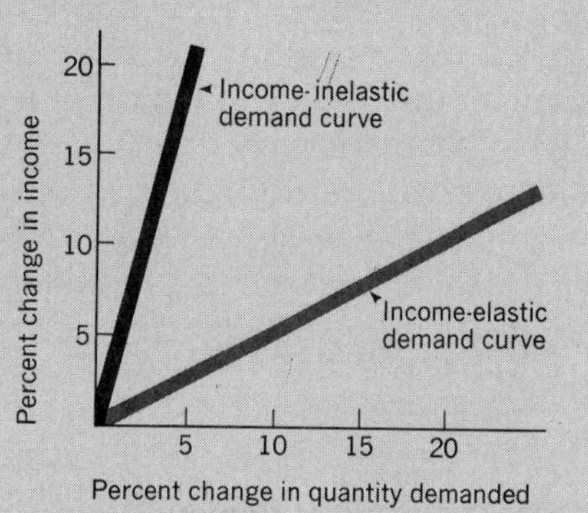

INCOME ELASTICITIES

posite is the case with an inelastic demand curve: Now the condition of demand is favorable for a price rise, since the seller will hold most sales even at the higher price; but inelastic demand is bad for one who cuts prices, since it will gain few additional customers (or the old ones will increase their purchases only slightly) when prices fall.

Obviously, what all business people would like to have is a demand for their product that was inelastic in an upward direction and elastic at lower than existing prices, so that they stood to gain whether they raised or lowered prices. As we shall see when we study pricing under oligopoly, just the opposite is apt to be the case.

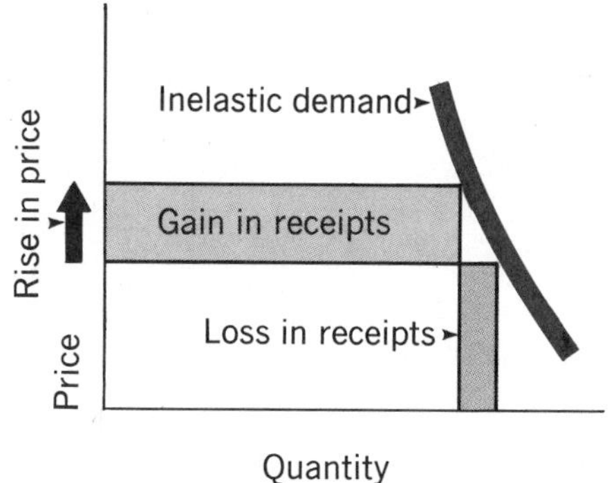

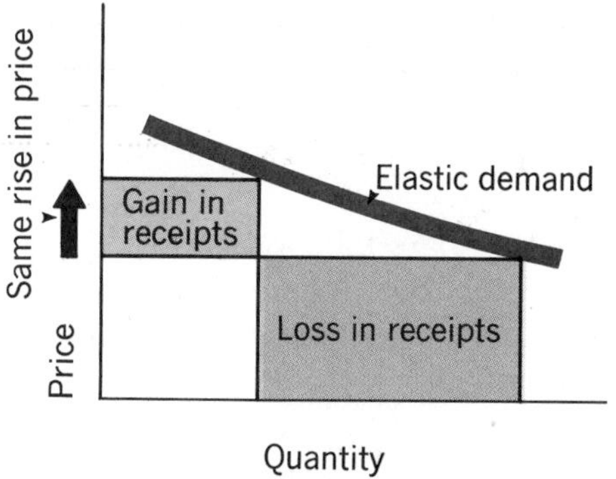

FIGURE 23.9 ELASTICITIES AND RECEIPTS

Notice the striking difference in the receipts of two businesses facing demand curves of different elasticities if each firm raises price by the same amount.

BEHIND ELASTICITIES OF DEMAND: SUBSTITUTION

Because elasticities are so important in accounting for the behavior of prices, we must press our investigation further. We must leave the supply side of elasticity to be studied when we look into the behavior of factors and firms. Here we will ask why are demand curves shaped the way they are? Why is our price (or income) sensitivity for some commodities so great and for others so slight?

If we think of a good or service for which our demand might be very inelastic—say eyeglasses (assuming we need them)—and compare it with another for which our demand is apt to be highly elastic—say a trip to Europe—the difference is not difficult to grasp. One thing is a necessity; the other is a luxury. But what do we mean by *necessity* and *luxury?*

One attribute of a necessity is that it is not easily replaced by a substitute. If we need eyeglasses, we will spend a great deal of money, if we must, to acquire a pair. Hence such a necessity has a very inelastic demand curve.

MARGINAL UTILITY AGAIN

Necessities are never absolute in the sense that nothing can be substituted for the commodity in question. High enough prices will drive buyers to *some* substitute, however imperfect.* Just when will the buyer be driven to the "next best thing"? As we know, economists say that the decision will be made by a comparison of the marginal utility derived from a dollar's worth of the high-priced item with that derived from the lower-priced substitute. As the price of champagne goes up and up, there comes a point at which we would rather spend our next dollar for a substantial amount of beer than a sip of champagne.

NECESSITIES AND ELASTICITY

We have seen that necessities have inelastic demand curves, so that we stick to them as prices rise. What about when they fall? Won't we rush to buy necessities, just because they *are* necessities? Won't that make their demand curves elastic?

Surprisingly, we do not rush to buy necessities when their prices fall. Why? The answer is that necessities are the things we buy *first*, just because they are necessities. Having bought what we needed before the fall in price, we are not tempted to buy much more, if any more, after the fall. Bread, as we commented before, is a great deal more valuable for life than diamonds are: but we ordinarily have enough bread, so that the marginal utility of another loaf is no greater than that of an equivalent expenditure on any other good. Thus, as the price of bread drops, the quantity we seek expands only slightly. So, too, with eyeglasses.

Compare the case with a luxury, such as a trip to Europe. There are many

*What *would* be the substitute for eyeglasses? For a very nearsighted person, the demand for one pair of glasses would be absolutely inelastic over a considerable price range. But when glasses got to be, say $500 a pair, substitutes would begin to appear. At those prices, one could hire someone to guide him around or to read aloud. Admittedly this is less satisfactory than having glasses; but if the choice is between spending a very large amount on glasses and on personal help, the latter might seem preferable. Of course, there are some goods without any substitutes—air, for example. Such goods are "free goods," because no one owns them. If a good such as air could be owned, it would have to be subject to stringent public control, to prevent its owners from exacting a horrendous price for it.

THE SEARCH FOR SUBSTITUTES

The search for substitutes is a complicated process that can lead to equally complicated supply-and-demand reactions. Just after a taxi strike in New York City, when fares went up 50 percent, people switched to substitutes (they rode buses, subways, or walked) and the taxi business suffered severely. Then after the shock of the increase wore off, business revived. People got used to higher fares; that is, they discovered that the marginal utility of a high-priced taxi ride was still greater than the marginal utility of the money they saved by using other transportation, plus the marginal utility of the time they wasted or the business they lost because they weren't taking taxis. In other words, the substitutes weren't satisfactory. Gradually, people began taking more cab rides, and taxi receipts were higher than before the fare hike. The quantity of taxi service consumed was down somewhat, but not by as much as the original drop. In this case, demand proved to be more *inelastic* over time than it was in the very short run.

substitutes for such a trip: trips out West, trips South, or some other kind of vacation. As a result, if the price of a European trip goes up, we are easily persuaded to switch to some alternative plan. Conversely, when the price of a European trip gets cheaper, we are quick to substitute *it* for other possible vacation alternatives, and our demand accordingly displays its elastic properties.

Do not make the mistake, however, of thinking that elasticity is purely a function of whether items are expensive or not. Studies have shown that the demand for subway transportation in New York City is price-elastic, which hardly means that riding in the subways is the prerogative of millionaires. The point, rather, is that the demand for subway rides is closely affected by the comparative prices of substitutes—bus fares and taxis. **Thus it is the ease or difficulty of substitution that always lies behind the various elasticities of demand schedules.**

THE IMPORTANCE OF SUBSTITUTES

Time also plays an important role in shaping our demand curves. Suppose, for example, that the price of orange juice suddenly soared owing to a crop failure. Would the demand for orange juice be elastic or inelastic?

In the short run, it would generally be more inelastic than in the longer run. Lovers of orange juice would likely be willing to pay a higher price for their favorite juice because (they would believe) there was really no other juice quite as good. As weeks went by, they might be tempted to try other breakfast juices, and no doubt some of these experiments would take. Substitutes would be found, after all.

The point is that it takes time and information for patterns of demand to change. Thus demand curves generally become more elastic as time goes on and the range of discovered substitutes becomes larger.

Because substitutes form a vast chain of alternatives for buyers, changes in the price of substitutes change the position of demand curves. Here is a new idea to be thought about carefully. Our existing demand curve for bread or diamonds has the shape (elasticity) it does because substitutes exist at various prices. When the prices of those substitutes *change,* the original commodity suddenly looks "cheaper" or "more expensive." If the price of subway rides rises from 50 cents to 65 cents, while the price of taxi rides remains the same, we will be tempted to switch part of our transportation from subways to taxis. If subway rides went to $1, there would be a mass exodus to taxis. Thus we should add changes in taste and in income when we consider the possible causes of a shift in demand. If the price of a substitute commodity rises, the demand for the original commodity will rise. As the price of substitutes falls, demand for the original commodity will fall. This may, of course, bring changes in the price of the original commodity.

COMPLEMENTS

In addition to substitution, there is another connection between commodities. This is the relationship of *complementarity*. Complementarity means that some commodities are technically linked, so that you cannot very well use one without using the other, even though they are sold separately. Automobiles and gasoline are examples of such complementary goods, as are cameras and film.

Here is another instance of change in the price of one good actually affecting the position of the demand curve for the other. If the price of film goes up, it becomes more expensive to operate cameras. Hence the demand for cameras is apt to drop. Note that the price of cameras has not changed in the first instance. Rather, when the price of the complementary good, the film, goes up, the whole demand curve for cameras shifts to the left. Thereafter, the price of cameras is apt to fall, too.

BEHAVIOR AND NATURE, AGAIN

There is a last point we should make before we leave the subject of elasticity. We have seen that the substitutability of one product for another is the underlying cause of elasticity. Indeed, more and more we are led to see products themselves as bundles of utilities surrounded with other competing bundles that offer a whole range of alternatives for a buyer's satisfaction.

What is it that ultimately determines how close the substitutes come to the commodity in question? As with all questions in economics that are pursued to the end, the answer lies in two aspects of reality before which economic inquiry comes to a halt. One of these is human behavior, with its tastes, drives, and wants. One person's substitute will not be another's.

The other ultimate basing point is the technical and physical nature of the world that forces certain constraints upon us. Cotton may be a substitute for wool because they both have the properties of fibers, but diamonds are not a substitute for the same end-use, because they lack the requisite physical properties. Diamonds, as finery, may be a substitute for clothes made out of cotton; but until we learn how to spin diamonds, they will not be a substitute for the cloth itself.

KEY CONCEPTS

Demand (or supply) vs. quantity demanded (or supplied)

LOOKING BACK

1. This chapter is called "The Market in Movement" and its central idea is how prices change. This introduces us to the basic distinction between a change in demand (or supply) and a change in the quantity demanded (or supplied). Here you must be absolutely certain that you

understand that by a change in demand we mean a new demand schedule, a shift in our demand curve. Thus we will buy more (or less) at the same price. *Ceteris paribus,* a change in price alone will alter the quantity demanded, not the demand schedule itself.

Elasticity measures our quantity response to price changes:

$$\frac{\Delta Q/Q}{\Delta P/P}$$

2. The use of curves gives us a quick, graphic sense of the market at work. In particular, it highlights our responsiveness as buyers or sellers to changes in price (or income). We call this responsiveness the elasticity of our supply or demand curves. You should learn the formula for this elasticity and the definition of elastic and inelastic curves.

Elasticities affect receipts and expenditures

3. Elasticities greatly affect the way markets work. One important effect is the relation between elasticities and business receipts. A firm facing an elastic demand curve will be glad to raise prices, sad to lower them. Why? A buyer with an inelastic demand for a commodity will be sad when prices go up, glad when they go down. Again why? (If you don't know, review page 346.)

Substitution lies behind elasticity

Necessities and luxuries are created by ease of substitution

4. Finally, we go behind elasticity to find the all important element of substitution. It is the ease of finding substitutes that shapes our behavior as buyers and sellers. If we can't find substitutes, we change our buying habits relatively little even if prices go up. This is another way of describing a necessity. If substitutes abound, even a small price rise will bring a larger reduction in the quantity we consume—we have given up a luxury.

It has been said that substitution is the law of economic life, the key to everything. Think about the kinds of substitutes we have for even the most necessary items. What are the substitutes for water? Bread? There are surprisingly many. Indeed, it is hard to find items like eyeglasses, for which substitutes are very few.

5. *Last, be sure you do the questions to this chapter.* They will help you discover what you know—and don't yet know.

ECONOMIC VOCABULARY

Shifts in curves vs. movements along curves 340
Elasticity 344
Inelastic demand 345
Substitute 351
Complement 352

QUESTIONS

1. What changes in your economic condition would increase your demand for clothes? Draw a diagram to illustrate such a change. Show on it whether you would buy more or less clothes at the prices you formerly paid. If you wanted to buy the same quantity as before, would you be willing and able to pay prices different from those you paid earlier?
2. Suppose that you are a seller of costume jewelry. What changes in your economic condition would decrease your supply curve? Suppose that costs dropped. If demand were unchanged, what would happen to the price in a competitive market?

3. Draw the following: an elastic demand curve and an inelastic supply curve; an inelastic demand curve and an elastic supply curve; a demand curve of infinite elasticity and a totally inelastic supply curve. Now give examples of commodities that each one of these curves might represent.
4. Show on a diagram why elasticity has so much effect in determining price changes. (Refer back to the diagrams on p. 345 to be sure that you are right.)
5. Draw a diagram that shows what we mean by an increase in the quantity supplied; another diagram to show what is meant by an increase in supply. Now do the same for a decrease in quantity supplied and in supply. (Warning: It is very easy to get these wrong. Check yourself by seeing if the decreased supply curve shows the seller offering less goods at the same prices.) Now do the same exercise for demand.
6. Show on a diagram (or with figures) why you would rather be the seller of a good for which demand was elastic, if you were in a market with falling prices. Suppose prices were rising—would you still be glad about the elasticity of demand?
7. How does substitution affect elasticity? If there are many substitutes for a product, is demand for it elastic or inelastic? Why?
8. If you were a legislator choosing a product on which to levy an excise tax, would you choose a necessity or a luxury? Which would yield the larger revenue? Show how your answer hinges on the different elasticities of luxuries and necessities.
9. By and large, are luxuries apt to enjoy elastic or inelastic demands? Has this anything to do with their price? Can high-priced goods have inelastic demands?
10. Why is demand more apt to become elastic over time?
11. The price of pipe tobacco rises. What is apt to be the effect on the demand for pipes? On the demand for cigars?

Chapter 24 WHERE THE MARKET FAILS

A LOOK AHEAD

We have been learning about how the market works as an efficient allocator of goods. Now we must learn about how the market fails to work in certain instances. Two general categories of cases will interest us in this chapter.

(1) The first has to do with situations in which the market operates badly or inefficiently.

(2) The second concerns a class of transactions that entirely escape the market's organizing powers. In the second class we come across the very important problem of pollution and we will consider ways of coping with it.

Up to this point we have been concerned with learning about the ways in which the market operates as a self-enforcing mechanism for allocating goods. We have noted that the results of its allocation may not necessarily please us because the market has a very mercenary attitude toward allocation, but we have made a point of stressing how efficiently and effectively it operates compared with other rationing systems.

In this chapter we must round out our understanding of the market by probing two areas of economic activity where the market works very inefficiently or not at all. One of these has to do with instances where marketers have no way of making intelligent decisions and where, therefore, the results of the market will reflect ignorance, luck, or accident rather than informed maximizing behavior. The second case involves a large category of production that we call public goods—goods that escape the ministrations of the market entirely.

INFORMATION PROBLEMS

The whole market system, we recall from Chapter 6, is built on the assumption that individuals are *rational maximizers.* But buried in that assumption is the implicit expectation that marketers will have at least roughly accurate information about the market. A good example is the situation faced by the tourist in a bazaar of a country where he or she doesn't know a word of the language. Such a buyer has no way of knowing what the price of an article "ought" to be. That's why tourists so often return triumphantly with their bazaar trophies—only to discover that they were for sale in their hotel at half the price.

THE PREVALENCE OF IGNORANCE

Without correct or adequate information marketers obviously cannot make correct decisions. But typically marketers do not have adequate information. Consumers guide themselves by hearsay, by casual information picked up by random sampling, or by their susceptibility to advertising. Who has time to investigate which brand of toothpaste is really best or even tastes best? Even professional buyers, such as industrial purchasing agents, cannot know every price of every product, including all substitutes.

The lack of information can be remedied, at least up to a point; but the remedy costs money or its equivalent—time. Few of us have the resources or patience to do a complete research job on every item we buy. Would it even be rational to do so? **Thus a certain amount of ignorance always remains in all markets, causing prices and quantities to differ from what they would be if we had complete information.** These differences can be very great, as anyone knows who has ever discovered, with sinking heart, that he or she paid "much too much" for a given article or sold it for "much too little."

MARKET INSTABILITY

One important class of market failure that stems from inadequate information is market instability. We have concentrated thus far on the tendency of markets to gravitate toward an equilibrium price. But markets may not equilibrate if the information marketers have is faulty; instead they may gyrate or race back

See text for the explanation of this cobweb. If expectations and information remain unchanged, producers will go on chasing their tails forever.

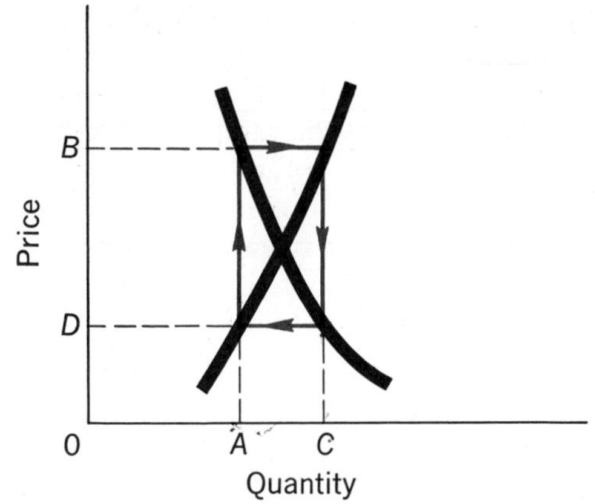

FIGURE 24.1 THE COBWEB

and forth as does the stock market when investors are particularly "nervous" or uninformed about the future.

COBWEBS

One interesting kind of market instability is called a *cobweb,* for reasons that become clear when we look at Figure 24.1. In this graph we show the supply and demand curves for some commodity that is produced a long time before it is sold, so that producers can't quickly change their outputs to correspond with the state of the market. They have to gear production to the demand that they *expect* six months or even longer into the future. If these expectations are unfounded, trouble can ensue.

In Figure 24.1 we begin by supposing that Christmas tree growers initially put the quantity *OA* on the market. We can see that quantity *OA* will sell at price *OB*. Figuring that this will be *next year's* price, tree growers now plant the amount they are willing and able to offer at price *OB*—quantity *OC*. Alas, when

The cobweb on the left spirals into an equilibrium and the one on the right "explodes." The reason in both cases lies in the position and shape of the supply and demand curves. In other words, if supply and demand are favorable, a cobweb can lead to stability. If they are wrong, terrible instability can result.

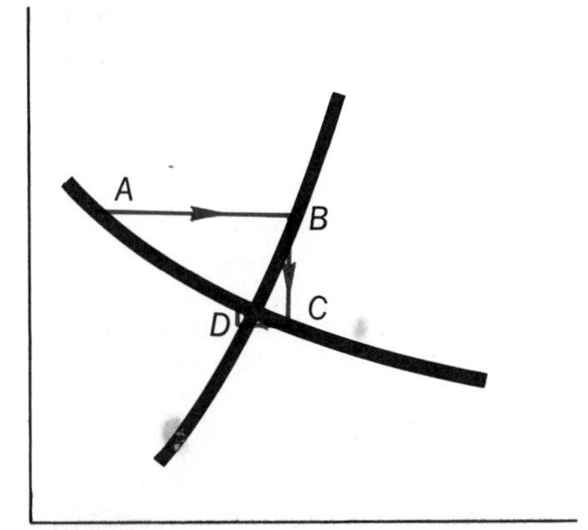

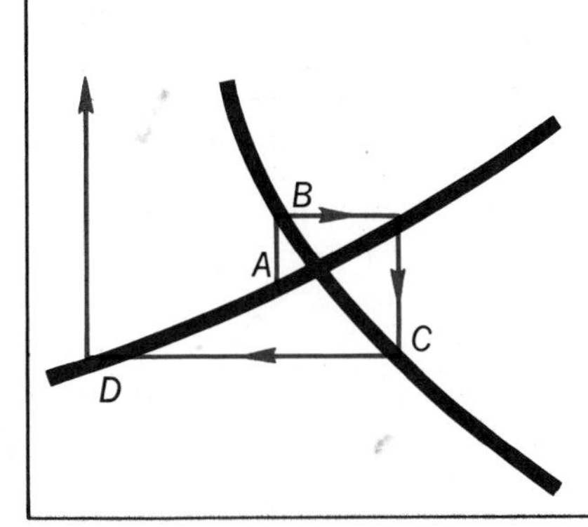

FIGURE 24.2 STABILIZING AND EXPLOSIVE COBWEBS

the harvest comes, it is found that quantity *OC* will fetch only price *OD*. Now the process goes into reverse. Growers will figure that next year's price will be *OD*, and they plant amount *OA*, since at price *OD* the quantity they wish to supply is no more than that. Thereupon, next harvest time the price goes back to *OB* and around we go. If the supply and demand schedules were differently sloped, we could have a cobweb that converged toward equilibrium, as we show on the left of Figure 24.2; and we could have one that "exploded" as we see in the diagram on the right.

EXPECTATIONS AND INFLATION

Expectations are so important in making markets work smoothly that we must spend a little more time with them.

Let us quickly learn how expectations work. Suppose that buyers of a commodity discover that its price is rising. If they expect that this rise in price will be short-lived or even if they think that the new higher price will persist for a fairly long time, they will behave the way textbooks say they should. In the face of higher prices, quantities demanded will decline, a new equilibrium price will be established, and that will be that. The market will have performed its task.

PERVERSE REACTIONS

Now suppose that the rise in prices sets off expectations that prices will rise still more. This is a very common experience in inflationary times, when the mounting prices of goods lead us to believe that prices will be still higher tomorrow, not that they will be lower or remain at their new levels. **In this case of inflationary expectations, we do not behave as normal demanders. Instead of curtailing our willingness to buy, the rise in prices spurs it on. Better to buy more today than wait till tomorrow when prices will be higher still. Thus, expectations can induce perverse reactions in the marketplace.** Of course, the same kinds of perverse reactions can affect the supply curves of sellers. Ordinarily, a rise in prices brings about an increase in the quantities offered. Not, however, if expectations point in the direction of still higher prices. Then sellers will hold back, causing the supply curve to shift leftward.

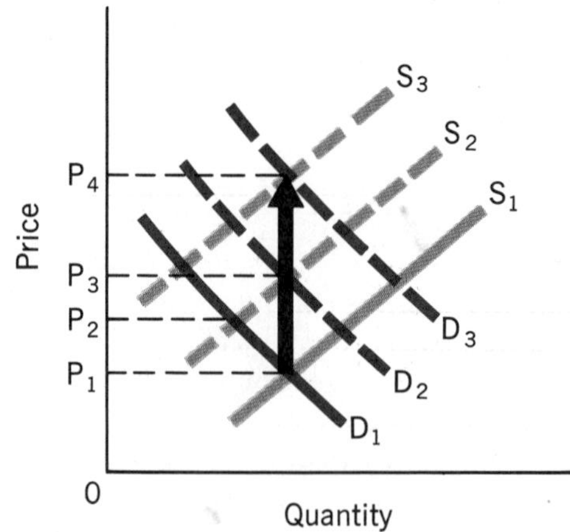

FIGURE 24.3 A SELF-FEEDING PRICE RISE

Suppose we have a market in which D_1 is the demand curve and S_1 the supply curve, with price at P_1. Now suppose that supply shifts to S_2, as OPEC countries (for example) raise their prices. If D_1 did not change we would simply have a new stable market with price at P_2. But if the change in supply serves as a trigger to move demand upward, price will rise to P_3. And if OPEC sellers, seeing that the market is buoyant, charge even more—the S_3 supply curve—prices will continue to go up, if demand also shifts to D_3.

The result, as we can see in Figure 24.3, is that prices can move violently upward and that the movement of prices can continue to feed upon itself, because demand and supply curves (D_1, D_2, D_3 and S_1, S_2, S_3) are themselves being shifted by the very fact that prices have changed. In deflationary times, the same process can work in reverse.

Such perverse price movements can lead to very dangerous consequences. They play a major role in the cumulative, self-sustaining processes of inflation or collapse. They can cause commodity prices to shoot to dizzying heights or plummet to the depths. At their worst, perverse behavior threatens to make an entire economy go out of control, as in the case of hyperinflations or panics. At best, they disrupt smooth, orderly markets and bring shocks and dislocations to the economy.

REMEDYING INFORMATION LACKS

Can these market failures be remedied? Some can; some cannot. Ignorance can certainly be reduced by better economic reporting or by truth-in-advertising laws. Cobwebs can be mitigated by accurate economic forecasting. Perverse behavior can be lessened by persuasive pronouncements from important public figures.

But we must recognize that there is a residue of arbitrariness even in the best intentioned remedies. Take the matter of consumer information. We "inform" the consumer, through labels on cigarette packages, that smoking is dangerous, but we do not prohibit the advertising of cigarettes. We spread "market information" by having the incomprehensible contents of medications printed on their containers, but we allow the consumer to be misinformed through advertising that claims superiority of one kind of aspirin over another.

Why? There is no clear rationale in these cases. Essentially we are trying to repair omissions in the market system—injecting information, so that consumers can make better choices—without becoming paternalistic. Perhaps we think it is better to allow the consumer to make some mistakes than to allow the government to make them for him.

That is perhaps as it should be. But the consequence is that the market will continue to produce less than wholly satisfactory or efficient results because a residue of ignorance or misinformation is allowed to remain—or remains despite our best efforts.

PUBLIC GOODS

Now we must turn to the range of problems that derive from the fact that certain kinds of output in our system do not have the characteristics of ordinary goods or services because they are not sold. That is, they never enter the market system in the first place, so it is not surprising that the market cannot allocate them. We call such outputs public goods. Since public goods are not easy to define, let us start by illustrating the properties of goods such as defense, the national weather service, or lighthouses. Such goods have these peculiar characteristics:

1. **The consumption of a public good by one individual does not interfere with its consumption by another.** A lighthouse is as effective for ten boats as for one. A weather service is as useful for 100 million TV viewers as for 100. By way

of contrast, private goods cannot be consumed in the same way. Food, clothing, or doctors' services that I use cannot also be consumed by you.

2. No one can be excluded from the use of a public good. I can deny you the use of my car. There is no way of denying you the use of "my" national defense system.

3. Most important of all, public goods can be provided only by collective decisions. My private consumption depends on my individual decision to spend or not spend my income. But there is no way that I can, by myself, buy defense, weather services, or a lighthouse service.* We must not only agree to buy the public good or services, but agree *how much* to buy!

Not all public goods are entirely "pure." Highways, education, the law courts, or sanitation services are not so universally available as lighthouses or defense. The amount of education, road space, court time, or garbage service that I consume does affect the amount left over for you. It is possible to exclude some citizens from schools or roads. But even these less perfect examples share in the third basic attribute of public goods. They must all be produced by collective decisions, usually by the voting system of the community.

FREE RIDING

Because of their characteristics, all public goods share a common difficulty. ***Their provision cannot be entrusted to the decision-making mechanism of the market.***

In the use of ordinary goods, each person can consume only as much as that person buys. Here the market works very well. **By way of contrast, in the use of public goods each person will not buy an amount that he or she really wants, because each can enjoy the goods that someone else buys.** Do not forget that there is no way of excluding others from the use of a pure public good (or from most not-so-pure ones). Therefore each of us would try to get a free ride if we attempted to use the market to determine the level of output.

An example may help. Lighthouse service is a pure public good. Why couldn't we make it a private good? The answer is that no boatowner would be willing to pay what the lighthouse is actually worth to him. Why should he? So long as someone else builds a lighthouse, the boatowner can enjoy its services free!

VOTING INSTEAD OF BUYING

How do we then determine the level of provision of such goods? By eschewing the useless market mechanism and availing ourselves of another means of decision-making: voting. We vote for the amount of public goods we want; and because voting is a curious mechanism (see "An Extra Word" in Chapter 21), sometimes we oversupply ourselves with these goods, and sometimes we undersupply ourselves. We swim in defense and starve in prison reform because defense has "friends in Congress" and prisons do not.

Is there a remedy for the problem? Some economists have suggested that

*Not even if I were immensely rich or an absolute monarch? In that case we would not have a market system, but a command economy catering to one person. Then indeed there would be no distinction between public and private goods.

we should try to bring as many public goods as possible into the market system by getting rid of their "public" characteristics. We could charge admission to the city's parks, so that we could produce only as much park service as people were willing to buy. We could charge tolls on all roads, even streets, and limit the building or repair of highways to the amount of private demand for road services. We might limit the use of law courts to those who would hire the judge and jury, or ask the police to interfere on behalf of only those citizens who wore a badge attesting to their contribution to the police fund.

PRIVATIZING PUBLIC GOODS?

Such a privatization of public goods might indeed bring the level of their production up, or down, to the amount that we would consume if they were strictly private goods, like cars or movie tickets. The problems are twofold. First, there are innumerable technical difficulties in making many public goods into private ones. Imagine the problems in charging a toll for each city street!

Second, and more arresting, the idea offends our sense of justice. Suppose that we could convert defense into a private good. The defense system would then defend only those who bought its services. Presumably the more you bought, the better you would be defended. Few believers in democracy would like to see our national defense converted into a bastion for the rich. Nor would we remove from public use the law courts, the schools, the police, and so on. Unlike private goods, which we have the *privilege* of buying from our incomes, public goods are thought of as our *rights.*

There are valid arguments and clever techniques for returning *some* public goods into the market's fold. The main point to keep in mind is that it is impossible to make all goods private; and for the ones that should remain public, the market cannot be used to establish a desirable level of output. Here the market mechanism must give way to a political method of making economic decisions.

EXTERNALITIES

Our next instance of market failure is closely connected with the attributes of public goods. It is the problem of allowing for the "externalities" of production; that is, for the effects of the output of private goods and services on persons other than those who are directly buying or selling or using the goods in question.

POLLUTION

Externalities bring us to one of the most vexing and sometimes dangerous problems in our economic system—controlling pollution.

What is pollution, from an economic point of view? It is the production of wastes, dirt, noise, congestion, and other things that we do not want. Although we don't think of smoke, smog, traffic din, and traffic jams as part of society's "production," these facts of economic life are certainly the consequence of producing things we do want. Smoke is part of the output process that also gives us steel or cement. Smog arises from the production of industrial energy and heat, among other things. Traffic is a by-product of transportation. In current jargon, economists call these unwanted by-products "bads" to stress their relation to things we call "goods."

"BADS" ESCAPE THE MARKET

Why do externalities exist? The basic answer is technological: We do not know how to produce goods "cleanly"; i.e., without wastes and noxious by-products such as smoke. But the economic answer calls our attention to another aspect of the problem. **Externalities refer to the fact that the output of bads does not pass through the market system.** A factory may produce smoke, etc., without having to pay anyone for producing these harmful goods. So, too, certain inputs used by firms—air, water, even space in an esthetic rather than economic sense—are available without charge, so that there is no constraint to urge a firm to use air or water sparingly or to build a handsome rather than an ugly factory or building.*

In other words, pollution exists because it is the cheapest way to do many things, some having to do with producing goods, some with consuming them. It is cheaper to litter than to buy waste cans (and less trouble, too); cheaper to pour wastes into a river than to clean them up. That is, it is cheaper for the individual or the firm, but it may not be cheaper for the community. A firm may dump its wastes "for free" into a river, but people living downstream from the firm will suffer the costs of having to cope with polluted water.

MARGINAL PRIVATE AND SOCIAL COSTS

The point is so fundamental it is worth elaborating. In back of the conception of the marketplace as an *efficient* allocator of goods and incomes is a silent assumption. **It is that all the inputs going into the process are owned by some individual and that all the outputs are bought by some person or firm or agency. Presumably, then, the price at which commodities are offered will include all the costs that are incurred in the process.** Presumably also, the price that will be offered will reflect all the prospective benefits accruing to the buyer. In other words, prices established in the marketplace are supposed to take into account *all* the disutilities involved in the process of production, such as fatigue or unpleasantness of work, and *all* the utilities ultimately gained by the final consumer of those goods.

What the problem of pollution has brought home is that the market is not a means for effectively registering a great many of these costs and benefits. The examples of the damage wrought by smoke that is not charged against the factory or of a neighborhood nuisance such as a bar or a hideous advertising sign are instances of economic activities in which *private costs are less than social costs.* These "social" costs are, of course, private costs incurred by other people. Contrariwise, when a person spends money to educate himself, he benefits not only himself but also the community, partly because he becomes a more productive citizen and partly because he presumably becomes a more responsible one. Thus the *social benefits* of some expenditures may be greater than their *private benefits.*

*Some externalities are not "bads," but "goods." A new office building may increase the property value of a neighborhood. Here is a positive externality. The benefit gained by others results from the new building but is not paid to the owners of that building. Such externalities give some private goods the partial attributes of public goods.

CONTROLLING EXTERNALITIES

How can we bring the process of pollution under social control? Basically, we can attack the problem in three ways. We can

1. Regulate the activity that creates it
2. Tax the activity that creates it
3. Subsidize the polluter, to stop (or lessen) his activity

1. REGULATION

Faced with the ugly view of smoke belching from a factory chimney, sludge pouring from a mill into a lake, automobiles choking a city, or persons being injured by contaminants, most ecologically concerned persons cry for regulation: "Pass a law to forbid smoky chimneys or sulfurous coal. Pass a law to make mills dispose of their wastes elsewhere or purify them. Pass a law against automobiles in the central city."

What are the economic effects of regulation? **Essentially the idea behind passing laws is to internalize a previous externality. That is, a regulation seeks to impose a cost on an activity that was previously free for the individual or firm, although not free, as we have seen, for society.** This means that individuals or firms must stop the polluting activity entirely or bear the cost of whatever penalty is imposed by law, or else find ways of carrying out their activities without giving rise to pollution.

Costs of regulation. Let us take the case of a firm that pollutes the environment as a joint product of producing goods or services. Suppose a regulation is passed, enjoining that firm to install antipollution devices—smoke scrubbers or waste-treatment facilities. Who bears this cost?

The answer seems obvious at first look: The firm must bear it. But if the firm passes its higher costs along in higher selling prices, we arrive at a different answer. Examine Figure 24.4. Our firm's original marginal cost (or supply) curve is S_1. The need to install new antipollution equipment raises it by an amount *ac* to S_2. Now a little economic analysis will show us that the cost is in fact borne by three groups, not just by the firm. First, the firm will bear some of the cost be-

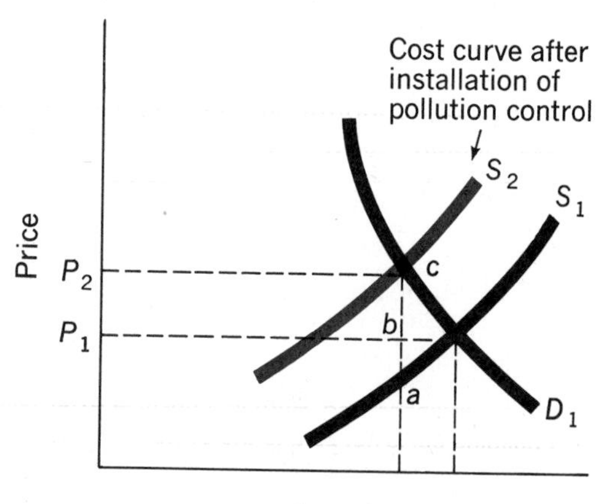

Regulation imposes costs on buyers, sellers, and employees. See text if you don't understand why.

FIGURE 24.4 EFFECTS OF REGULATION

cause at the higher price, it will sell less output. How much less depends on the elasticity of demand for its product. But unless demand is totally inelastic (a vertical line), its sales and income must contract.

Two other groups also bear part of the cost. One group is the factors of production. Fewer factors will be employed because output has fallen. Their loss of income is therefore also a part of the economic cost of antipollution regulation. Last, of course, is the consumer. Prices will rise from P_1 to P_2. Note that the rise in price *bc* is less than the full rise in costs *ab* so that the consumer will not bear all the costs (unless, once again, we have vertical demand curves).

Gains from regulations. Offsetting all these costs is the fact that each of these three groups and the general public now have a better environment. There is no reason, however, why each of these three groups, singly or collectively, should think that *its* benefit outweighs *its* costs. Most of the benefit is likely to go to the general public, rather than to the individuals actually involved in the production or consumption of the polluting good or service.

Thus a regulation forcing car manufacturers to make cleaner engines will cost the manufacturers some lost sales, will cost the consumer added expense for a car, and will cost lost income for whatever land, labor, and capital is no longer employed at higher production costs. As part of the public, all three groups will benefit from cleaner air, but each is likely to feel its specific loss more keenly than its general gain.

Is regulation useful? Regulations are good or bad, mainly depending on their ease of enforcement. Compare the effectiveness of speed limits, which attempt to lessen the externality of accidents, and of regulations against littering. It is difficult enough to enforce speed laws, but it is almost impossible to enforce antilittering laws. On the other hand, regulation of the disposal of radioactive wastes is simpler to enforce because the polluters are few and easily supervised.

This in turn is largely a matter of cost. If we were prepared to have traffic policemen posted on every mile of highway or every city block, regulation could be just as effective for speed violations or littering as for radioactive disposal. Obviously the cost would be horrendous, and so would most people's reaction to being overpoliced.

2. TAXATION

A second way to cope with pollution is to tax it. When a government decides to tax pollution (often called effluent charges), it is essentially creating a price system for disposal processes. If an individual company found that it could clean up its own pollutants more cheaply than paying the tax, it would do so, thereby avoiding the tax. If the company could not clean up its own pollutants more cheaply than the tax cost (which is often the case because of economies of scale in pollution control), it would pay the necessary tax and look to the state to clean up the environment.

The effluent charge looks like, but is not, a license to pollute. It is a license that allows you to give some of your pollutants to the state *for a price.*

As a result of effluent charges, an activity that was formerly costless is no longer so. Thus, in terms of their economic impacts, these charges are just like

government regulations. In fact, they are a type of government regulation. They raise the supply curve for the good in question, with all of the corresponding ramifications. The difference is that each producer can decide whether it pays to install clean-up equipment and not pay the tax, or to pollute and pay whatever tax costs are imposed.

Antipollution taxes vs. regulations. Which is better, regulation or taxation? As we have seen, regulation affects all polluters alike, and this is both its strength and its weakness. Taxation enables each polluter to determine what course of action is best. Some polluters will achieve low pollution targets more cheaply by installing anti-pollution equipment, thereby avoiding taxes on their effluents, while other polluters will find it more profitable to pay the tax.

Here practical considerations are likely to be all important. For example, taxation on effluents discharged into streams is likely to be more practical than taxation on smoke coming from chimneys. The state can install a sewage treatment plant, but it cannot clean up air that is contaminated by producers who find it cheaper to pay a pollution tax than to install smoke-suppressing equipment. Moreover, to be effective, a pollution tax should vary with the amount of pollution—a paper mill or a utility plant paying more taxes if it increases its output of waste or smoke. One of the problems with taxation is that of installing monitoring equipment. It is difficult to make accurate measurements of pollution or to allow for differences in environmental harm caused by the same amount of smoke coming from two factories located in different areas.

3. SUBSIDIES

The third way of dealing with pollution is to subsidize polluters to stop polluting. **In this case the government actually pays the offending parties to clean up the damage they have caused or to stop causing it.** For example, a township might lessen the taxes on a firm that agreed to install filters on its stacks. This is, of course, paying the firm to stop polluting.

Economists typically object to subsidies because they camouflage the true economic costs of producing goods and services cleanly. When regulations or taxes increase the price of paper or steel, the individual or firm becomes aware that the environment is not free and that there may be heavy costs in producing goods in a way that will not damage the environment. The increased price will lead him to demand less of these goods. But when he gets clean environment through the allocation of a portion of his taxes, he has no price signal to show him the cost of pollution associated with particular commodities.

Nevertheless, there are cases when subsidies may be the easiest way to avoid pollution. For example, it might be more effective to pay homeowners to turn in old cans and bottles than to try to regulate their garbage disposal habits or to tax them for each bottle or can thrown away. Subsidies may therefore sometimes be expedient means of achieving a desired end, even if they may not be the most desirable means from other points of view.

EXTERNALITIES IN REVIEW

In one way, the problem of externalities differs markedly from the problem of public goods. The difference is that it is possible to allow the market system itself to handle the otherwise hidden costs of pollution by using the various techniques we have examined.

Therefore, in offsetting externalities in the production of private goods, we avoid some of the arbitrariness that troubles us in the provision of public goods. We can internalize the costs of pollution in a way that we cannot privatize the costs or benefits of pure public goods.

Nonetheless, we must keep in mind one theme of this chapter. It is that a market system has weak spots or ineffective areas peculiar to its institutional nature. **Its inability to put a price on external effects or to give a producer the rewards of producing external benefits means that the system, left to itself, may work poorly or even dangerously. The remedy requires political intervention of one kind or another—regulation, taxation, or subsidy—for there is no recourse other than political action when the self-regulating economic mechanism fails.**

MARKET STRENGTHS AND WEAKNESSES

This is not a conclusion that should be interpreted as a kind of general plea for more government. Many economists who severely criticize the market want less government—certainly less bureaucratic, nonparticipatory, nondemocratic government. The point, however, is to recognize that the existence and causes of market malfunction make some government intervention inescapable. We can then seek to use government power to repair individual market failures in order to strengthen the operation of the system as a whole.

After so much criticism of the market system, perhaps it is well to conclude by recalling its strengths. Basically they are two. **First, the market encourages individuals to exert energies, skills, ambition, and risk-taking in the economic pursuits of life. This gives to market systems a high degree of flexibility, vitality, inventiveness, changefulness.** For all their failures, the market economies have displayed astonishing growth, and the source of that growth lies ultimately in the activities of their marketers.

Second, the system minimizes the need for government supervision, although for reasons we now understand it cannot dispense with it. It would be a mistake to suppose that every instance of government intervention is an abridgment of freedom, or that every area of market activity is an exemplar of liberty. The truth is that government and market are equally capable of promoting liberty or giving rise to oppression. Nonetheless, in a world in which the concentration of government power has been one of the greatest scourges of mankind, there is clearly something to be said for the existence of a mechanism capable of handling the basic economic tasks of society with but a minimal dependence on political authority.

KEY CONCEPTS

LOOKING BACK

This chapter is a very important complement to our previous chapters. There we have stressed the advantages of the market as a rationing device. Here we point out its shortcomings or inadequacies.

Inadequate information yields poor market results

1. The first class of serious market failure arises from inadequate or erroneous information. Without correct information marketers cannot make correct decisions and market results may be seriously deficient.

Cobwebs are a form of instability that results from erroneous expectations

2. One consequence of inadequate information is a tendency to generate instability under certain conditions. The most interesting of these is the cobweb, where prices may rise and fall and may never zero in on equilibrium.

Expectations can also lead to inflationary markets

3. Cobwebs in turn reveal the importance of expectations in making markets work smoothly. When expectations are inflationary we get perverse behavior where rising prices make the entire demand curve shift outward. This can be a very important element in perpetuating inflation.

Public goods escape the market and cause free riding

Privatization is sometimes possible but may offend our sense of rights

4. A second large category of market failure arises when the market cannot allocate at all because outputs have no price. One of these cases concerns public goods—goods collectively bought. Public goods result in free riding. In some cases this can be corrected by privatizing public outputs. Often, however, we do not wish to sell public goods because they are deemed to be a citizen's right, and therefore felt to be properly available without specific charge.

Externalities are "bads" that exist because there is no charge based on polluting behavior

5. Externalities have certain of the attributes of public goods. The production of "bads" is a kind of free ride for polluters. Pollution arises because there is no way of charging for the "bads" that production or consumption creates—the litter a consumer throws on the road, the smoke a factory generates, the congestion to which each automobile adds, the lethal wastes made by a nuclear plant.

Regulation, taxation, and subsidy are the three ways of coping with externalities

6. There are three basic ways of coping with externalities. The first is to regulate; the second is to tax; the third is to subsidize. No one of these is always superior to the others, but each has its strengths and weaknesses. Each situation must be judged separately to discover which method is most likely to be effective.

ECONOMIC VOCABULARY

Cobwebs 357
Perverse reactions 358
Public goods 359
Free riding 360
Externalities 361
Bads 362
Regulation 363
Taxation 364
Subsidies 365

QUESTIONS

1. As a seller who seeks to maximize, would you increase or decrease your offerings if prices rose and you expected them to rise further? Suppose you expected them to fall—then what is your rational maximizing response?
2. Can you imagine an industrial process that might result in a cobweb? How about a process in which you had to make heavy commitments in plant and equipment long before production actually took place? Suppose that hydroponic farming takes over, so that agriculture becomes more industrialized and less dependent on seasons. Would you expect the cobweb type of reaction to become less common? Why?
3. Explain the mechanism of a free ride. Are there free rides in private goods? How about window displays? Skywriting?

4. Explain carefully why the market system will not work in supplying the appropriate level of goods that have "public" characteristics.
5. What kinds of public goods do you think should be made private? The national parks? Public schools? Public beaches? Public hospitals? (By "private," we mean charging a user-fee sufficient to cover costs). Explain your preference in each case.
6. Can you think of an externality imposed by a producer on a consumer? (That's easy.) Of one imposed on a producer by a consumer? One imposed by one producer on another? One consumer on another?
7. What do you think would be the best way to handle the following externalities: (1) a smoky factory, (2) roadside littering, (3) overfishing a pond, (4) noise from an airport, (5) radiation hazards in a hospital, (6) billboards, (7) pornography, (8) overcutting forests, (9) noise from motor cycles, (10) disruption to traffic caused by parades. In each case, discuss the relative usefulness of regulation, taxation, and subsidy.

SECTION 2: The Economics of Business

A LOOK AHEAD

We are now going to leave the market in order to look inside the operations of its most important institution—the enterprise or firm. We will first visit a competitive firm, a firm so small that it cannot affect its own market by its operations. Here we meet the entrepreneur, a new personage in our micro studies. Our task in this chapter is to analyze the three main tasks the entrepreneur must carry out:

(1) deciding on the scale of operations;
(2) combining the factors of production as profitably as possible; and
(3) determining the volume of output.

In this visit we do no more than familiarize ourselves with the entrepreneur's task in general terms. In our next chapter we return, pad and pencil in hand, to calculate the firm's course.

Most of us have firsthand knowledge of the household, whose role is crucial in determining the demand for goods. We know a lot less about the firm, whose function is to supply us with goods. In this chapter, we enter the gates of a competitive firm for a quick look around. We will come back in our next chapter to study the operation in greater detail.

ECONOMICS OF THE FIRM

The first person we encounter inside the factory gates is an economic personage we have not previously studied. It is the boss of the works, the organizer of the firm, the *entrepreneur.*

ENTREPRENEURSHIP

An entrepreneur is not necessarily a capitalist; that is, the person who has supplied capital to the business. The entrepreneur may act as the risker of capital, but so may a bank. The capitalist may be a group of people who have lent money to the business but never visited the premises. **An entrepreneur provides a service that is essentially different from that of putting up capital. His or her contribution is *organizational.*** Indeed, some economists have suggested that it is proper to think of four factors of production: labor, land, capital, and entrepreneurship, instead of the traditional first three alone.

ECONOMIC PROFIT

As a fourth factor of production, the entrepreneur is paid a wage, *the wage of management.* It can, of course, be very high, since entrepreneurship is a valuable skill, the skill of maximizing a firm's *economic profit.*

This is not the profit of everyday usage. In ordinary usage we call "profit" any sum left over after a firm has paid its wages and salaries, rents, costs of materials, taxes, etc. Included in that ordinary profit is an amount that an economist excludes from his definition of a true economic profit. This is the interest that is owed to the capitalist for the use of his or her capital. In other words, if a firm has a plant and equipment worth $1 million and makes a profit of $50,000, an economist, before declaring the $50,000 to be a true economic profit, would first ask whether the firm had taken into account the interest owing to it on this capital. If interest rates were 5 percent, and no such allowance had been made (and it usually is not the ordinary accounting practice when the firm owns its own capital), an economist would say that no real economic profits were earned. **Economic profit, in other words, refers to the residual—if there is one. It includes the *implicit costs* of interest, as well as *explicit costs* that are directly paid out.**

Our analysis shows us how an entrepreneur tries to create economic profits after appropriately remunerating all the factors, including capitalists, and how the operation of the market constantly tends to make this economic profit disappear, despite the best entrepreneurial efforts. (That will become clear in our next chapter, rather than in this one.)

One last point. Who gets the residual? It goes to the owner of the business, who is legally entitled to any profits it enjoys. That owner, as we have said, may or may not be the entrepreneur. In a cooperatively owned factory it might be the work force. Usually it is a proprietor, a group of partners, or shareholders. In all cases, this residual economic profit is over and above any recompense for the services these factors supply, including the service of making capital available.

THE TASKS OF THE ENTREPRENEUR

What does our entrepreneur do for his wages of management? In actual practice, he or she will do many things: bargaining with labor unions, establishing credit lines with a bank, arranging complex real estate deals, hiring production and design experts, gauging "what the market will bear" when it comes to pricing and selling output. Some of these tasks we shall investigate in Chapter 27 when we look into the operation of firms that are not perfectly competitive.

But we must begin with a simpler model. We are going to start by analyzing the basic tasks of an entrepreneur in an environment of *pure competition*. As we shall see later, this is more the exception than the rule. Nevertheless, studying the operation of a firm in pure competition reveals more clearly than any other model the essential tasks of entrepreneurship.

PURE COMPETITION

Exactly what do we mean by "pure competition"? In general, economists mean three things:

1. Large numbers of sellers or firms

A monopoly, as we shall see in Chapter 27, means that there is only one firm in an industry. An oligopoly means that there are a few firms. **But a competitive market means that there are many firms—so many that no single firm by itself can affect the prices that it pays for the factors of production or the prices that it receives for its output, regardless of how much or how little it produces.**

Are there such markets? Of course. Farms operate in a market situation that is very close to that of pure competition. So do many small businesses, where the field is so numerous that each entrepreneur knows that he or she has no power to influence the market for the firm's outputs.

2. Easy entry and exit

A competitive industry is not only characterized by large numbers of firms. **It is also an industry into which new firms can move with ease and out of which unsuccessful firms can easily exit.**

This has very important consequences for the conduct of business. We can readily see why: In a competitive industry, if profits are high there will soon be an invasion of entrepreneurs from other fields seeking to reap some of that profit. If business is bad, on the other hand, there will be a general exodus into greener pastures.

3. The outputs of competitive firms are undifferentiated

A differentiated output is one that is recognizable as belonging to its producer. A cereal with a brand name, an automobile with a distinctive look, and fashion garments with their labels are all differentiated goods. The ability of a producer to differentiate his output gives him the ability to gain a loyal clientele and to charge prices that may differ from those of competitors.

No such advantage of differentiation exists in a market characterized by pure competition. One output is exactly like another. Thus, wheat is wheat and bears no identification of the farm it comes from; paper clips are paper clips (although they may have differentiated boxes); coal is coal; one taxi ride is like another.

The absence of product differentiation carries a consequence of great importance. It means that competition among firms must be carried out entirely by trying to beat the prices offered by rivals. There is no way of attracting buyers to a particular output except by price.

PURE COMPETITION AND THE ENTREPRENEUR

As we can see, the conditions for pure competition are stringent indeed. In effect, they rob the entrepreneur, as the chief executive of his business, of much of the power that he would like to have (and that he *does* have in industries that are not so competitive, as we shall see). In fact, in a market of pure competition—farming, much wholesale trading, or small retail business for example—the operating powers of an entrepreneur are reduced to three:

1. The entrepreneur can decide on the scale of the enterprise
2. He can determine how best to combine the factors of production
3. He can choose the level of output that will maximize profits

And that is all he can do. There is no chance of striking a special arrangement with the factors of production, such as signing a "sweetheart" contract with a labor union. There is no point in hiring a design expert or an advertising firm because it is impossible to differentiate his firm's corn, or paper notebooks, or wire coat hangers from his competitors'. There is no strategy in pricing because if he is as much as a penny over his competitors, he will not sell any of his production.

HOW AN ENTREPRENEUR OPERATES

What does an entrepreneur actually do under such demanding conditions?

TASK NO. 1: THE DECISION ON SCALE

The first task lies in the determination of the scale of output—how big the firm is to be. In each industry a certain minimum size, mainly dictated by technology, is needed to operate in the existing market. Suppose that we were considering opening a bookstore. A bookstore may be very small, but it must occupy *some* space. It must stock a reasonable number of books and employ at least one person to sell them. If we were in agriculture, we would need a farm of at least a certain area, depending on our crop, and a basic amount of capital in the form of buildings, equipment, fertilizer, seed. If we were in manufacturing, there would be a minimum size of plant or machinery essential for our operation. If we were in a mass-production business, such as steel, the smallest efficient plant might run into an investment of millions of dollars and a work force of thousands; but that would take us well out of the world of atomistic competition to which we are still devoting our attention.

A curve of average unit costs usually falls at first and then rises. We call such curves "dish-shaped" or "U-shaped." Remember that they show how average costs per unit change as we vary output. Total cost is shown by multiplying average cost per item by the number of units produced. At output *OX*, total cost is *OY* × *OX*.

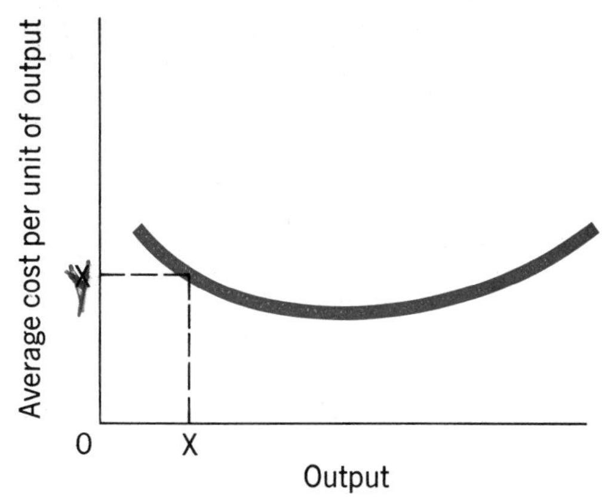

FIGURE 25.1 TYPICAL AVERAGE UNIT COST CURVE

In other words, the first decision of an entrepreneur involves the physical (or engineering) fact that there is a certain amount of each factor that we must hire for technical reasons. This is what we mean by minimum scale. If problems of scale did not exist, we could produce television sets as efficiently in a garage as in a vast plant or raise cattle as cheaply in our back yard as on a range.

Economies of Scale. The choice of a scale of operation has very important consequences for the costs that the entrepreneur's firm will incur. Every plant has a cost curve that describes how much it costs to produce one unit of output at various levels of production. In Figure 25.1 we see such a curve. Notice that when we are producing only small quantities (such as *OX*), the cost for each unit of output is high (*OY*); and that costs per unit typically fall as production increases, after which they eventually rise again. This produces a dish-shaped curve.

We will learn a lot more about cost curves as we move along. Here we should note that a cost curve applies to a given scale of output. A bigger plant may well lower unit costs because it can utilize technologies in large scale pro-

Cost curves change as the scale of output changes. This long-run cost curve, or "envelope" curve, shows how a larger scale first lowers unit costs, then increases them. These curves refer to individual plants, not to firms.

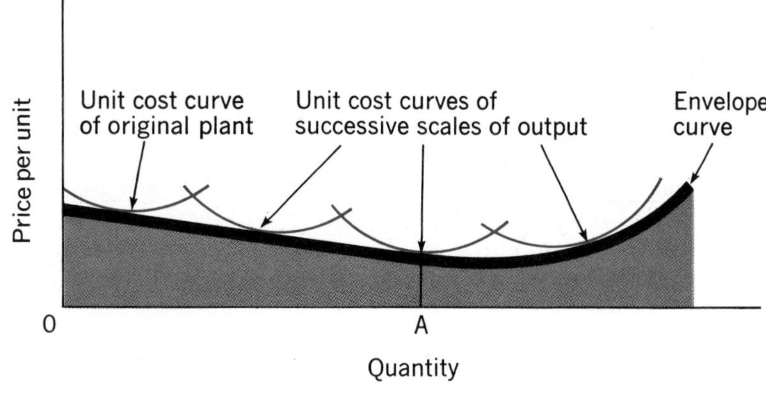

FIGURE 25.2 LONG-RUN COST CURVE

duction that are unavailable to small producers. If a small firm is successful it may be able to gain these *economies* of scale by building a larger plant. In Figure 25.2 we show how successively bigger plants can reduce costs, at least up to a point where the limits of efficiency are reached and mounting costs per unit of output are encountered, creating *diseconomies of scale.*

The actual choice of an appropriate scale of plant is more important for big, oligopolistic firms than for small, competitive ones. But even in atomistic competition there are decisions to be made with regard to scale. A farmer has to decide whether to build another barn. A stationery store owner has to decide whether to buy additional space. The decision as to scale, with its economies and its diseconomies, is a very important first task of entrepreneurship.

TASK NO. 2: COMBINING THE FACTORS

Having chosen the appropriate scale, our entrepreneur now has to make two decisions on how to combine labor, land, and capital; or in more ordinary business language, how much to pay in wages, rent, and interest.

The Profitability Rule: **MR > MC.** The first decision is whether it is profitable to hire a given factor, say an additional salesperson or an additional amount of inventory. This decision is very simple to make. Our entrepreneur merely compares two figures: (1) the cost of adding the additional factor; and (2) the income that he expects to gain from the additional factor. In economic language, he compares the marginal cost of a factor with the marginal revenue he expects from the factor.

By "marginal" we mean the additional cost or the additional revenue in question. If he is thinking of taking on a salesperson and the wage for salesclerks is $8,000, then the marginal cost of such a unit of labor is $8,000. Obviously the person will not be hired unless the entrepreneur expects that the clerk will bring into the firm at least $8,000 of marginal revenue—that is, of additional income.

Hence the cardinal rule for hiring is: Compare marginal cost and marginal revenue. If marginal revenue is greater than marginal cost, hire the factor. If not, get rid of the factor because it is costing more than its keep.

Comparing Factor Returns. And now for the second decision. Assuming that marginal revenue is greater than marginal cost for all factors, the entrepreneur has to decide whether to spend the firm's money on one factor or another. Suppose that an additional salesperson costs $8,000 and is expected to bring in $10,000 of additional income; that a hundred square feet of space would rent for $1,000 and would yield $1,200 of new income; and that a new piece of equipment would cost $10,000 but would increase revenues by $15,000.

Here all the factors are profitable buys. But which is the *most* profitable? The answer is not difficult. Our entrepreneur simply compares the return per dollar for each factor. A dollar of additional labor cost brings in $1.25 ($10,000 of revenue divided by $8,000 of cost); a dollar of space brings in $1.20 ($1,200 divided by $1,000); and a dollar of capital expense yields $1.50. Clearly the most profitable use of the firm's money will be to use it all on equipment as long as the ratios of marginal cost and marginal revenue stay the same.

Maximizing Profits. Will they stay the same? No, for reasons we will investigate more closely in our next chapter, they will not. As the entrepreneur hires more and more equipment (or more and more of any one factor) its marginal revenue will eventually decline because it will be used beyond the point of greatest efficiency. Our entrepreneur will then switch to some other factor that has become more profitable at the margin. In the end, he will maximize his profits by mixing factors so that their marginal returns are all equal, with no special advantage accruing to any one.

Here is a rule to remember. The entrepreneur maximizes profits first by seeking equal marginal revenues.* If returns at the margin are not equal, there must exist opportunities for greater profit by adding more of the factor whose marginal return is higher. This is true whether the entrepreneur is running a competitive business or a monopoly. It is how the entrepreneur ensures that the firm will be as efficient as possible, getting as much return as possible from every dollar that it spends.

TASK NO. 3: DETERMINING THE LEVEL OF OUTPUT

Now we come to the last and most complicated part of the entrepreneur's task. We have seen how he or she determines the initial scale of the enterprise, and how he or she decides whether to hire factors, and if so, which factors to hire. Now we must see how the entrepreneur determines how much output to produce.

The basic rule for determining output is very simple, and resembles the basic rule for hiring factors. **An entrepreneur is constantly comparing marginal costs and marginal revenues for his output, just as he is comparing them for the factors he hires.** The price at which he sells his last unit of output is his marginal revenue. The amount that it costs him to produce that last unit of output is his marginal cost.

It's not difficult to see that he will decide on his volume of production by comparing the two. **If marginal revenue (*MR*) is greater than marginal cost (*MC*), he will be making money on that unit of output and he will want to increase his production to make more money. If *MR* is less than *MC*, he will be losing money on his marginal output and he will want to contract production.**

The Marginal Revenue Curve. It is possible to describe this task of the entrepreneur in a very revealing and helpful graph. Let us start by showing what marginal revenue looks like to a farmer, small businessman, or other competitive entrepreneur.

Remember, the conditions of pure competition rule out any possibility that the small firm, by itself, could affect the level of prices. The prices of wheat or corn, paper clips or coal are just *there* and the entrepreneur has no choice but to take them as the market offers them. Therefore, the demand curve for his product looks to him like Figure 25.3. *It is a horizontal line showing that the market will absorb all the corn or paper clips he can make at a given price.* (The price

*This is just like a consumer seeking to maximize his total utilities by equating the marginal enjoyments of different goods. See "An Extra Word" to Chapter 22.

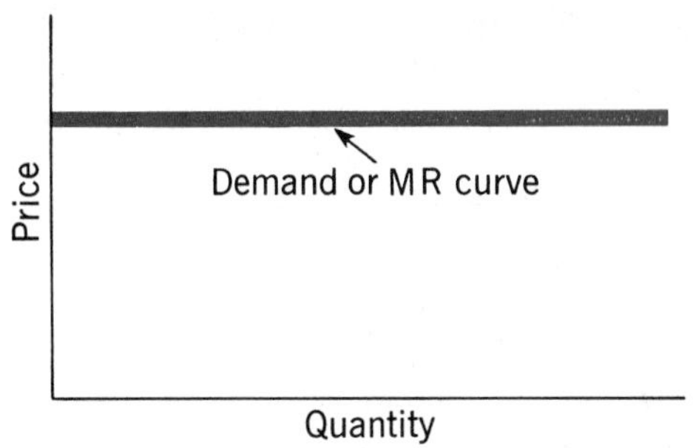

FIGURE 25.3 DEMAND CURVE FOR A COMPETITIVE FIRM

Because a competitive firm by definition cannot affect the market whether it sells all or nothing at all, each unit of item will fetch the same price. Therefore the marginal revenue of each unit will be the same. This means that the demand curve and the marginal revenue curve are one and the same—perfectly elastic, horizontal lines.

may not be a profitable one, but that is another matter into which we will look in our next chapter.)

The point is that the competitive firm's selling price does not change, whatever its levels of output. Each unit therefore brings in exactly as much revenue as the one before or after. That is why its marginal revenue curve is a horizontal line. When we study monopolies and oligopolies we will see that this is not the case for them.

The Marginal Cost Curve. Perhaps we can anticipate what comes next. We are going to discover what the marginal cost curve looks like, and by putting that curve against the marginal revenue curve, we will find out how the entrepreneur solves his third task, determining the level of output.

We already know that *average* costs per unit of output give us a dish- or U-shaped curve (refer back to Figure 25.1 if you've forgotten). Not until the next chapter will we analyze the reasons for the similar shape of the marginal cost curve. But in this first look around a competitive plant, it will suffice if we intuitively understand that it's likely to cost an entrepreneur a lot to start up production, so that marginal costs per unit—the cost of each additional unit—are apt to start out high. We can further see that it is plausible for marginal costs to fall as output gets up to the levels for which the scale of the plant is designed;

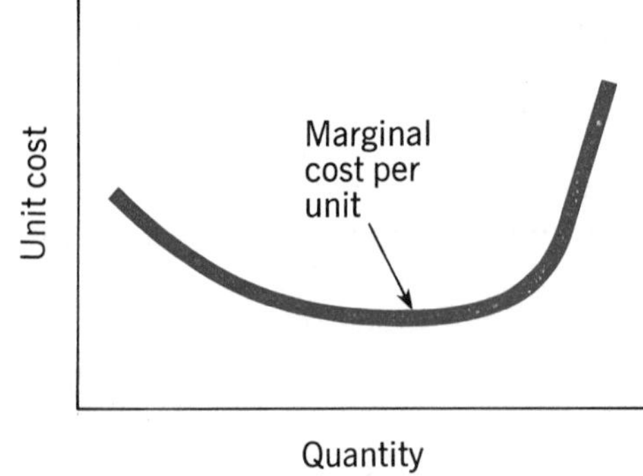

FIGURE 25.4 A TYPICAL MARGINAL COST CURVE

A marginal cost curve shows the additional costs of each unit as we increase output. Usually the marginal cost of the first units is high; then it falls; and finally rises, often sharply. Our next chapter will analyze this curve more carefully.

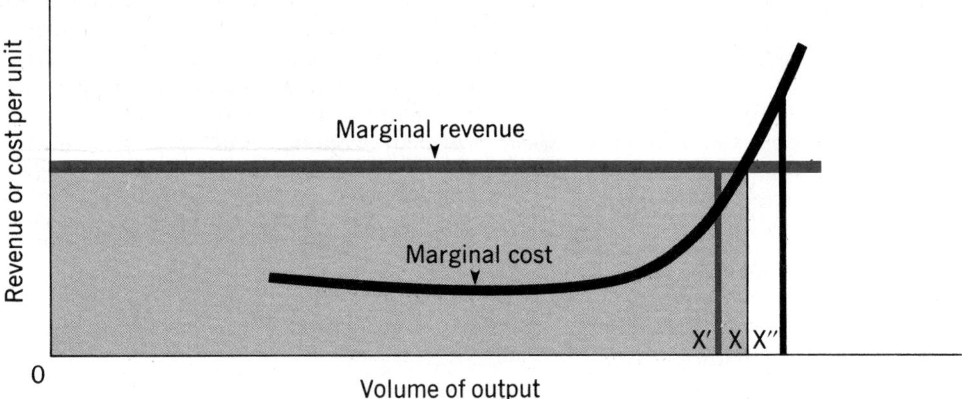

FIGURE 25.5 POINT OF OPTIMUM OUTPUT
Marginal cost and marginal revenue provide the guide to the level of output where profit is maximized. Think about costs and revenues for units marked *X′* and *X″* Can you see why *X′* makes money and *X″* does not? What should the entrepreneur do in each case?

and that marginal costs are likely to rise beyond that point. Thus we get the idea that a marginal cost curve will look like Figure 25.4.

Marginal Revenue and Marginal Cost. Finally we have all the information we need to understand how an entrepreneur performs the last of his three basic tasks. We have a marginal cost profile that tells us what happens to unit costs as we hire or fire factors. We have a marginal revenue profile that tells us what happens to the firm's income as we do the same. It remains only to put the two together to discover just how much output a firm should make to maximize its profits.

We can do this very simply by superimposing the revenue diagram on top of the cost diagram. **The point where marginal revenue and marginal cost meet indicates exactly where the most profitable volume of output lies.** If our entrepreneur was producing to the left of this point, he would be missing the chance of making more money by expanding output. We can see that this is the case because up to point *OX* in Figure 25.5 each additional (marginal) unit of production will bring in more than it costs. If production goes beyond *OX*, on the other hand, the entrepreneur will have miscalculated, because each unit of output beyond *OX* will cost more than it yields.

END OF THE TOUR

There is a great deal that remains to be explained. Is our firm making money? Why do the curves have the shapes they do? Is there an equilibrium level of operation for the firm?

These questions will necessitate a second trip with pad and pencil in hand, ready to do some calculations. Our first visit has prepared the way by showing us in bold terms what the entrepreneur has to do; now we should be ready to put ourselves more directly into his shoes.

KEY CONCEPTS

LOOKING BACK

The entrepreneur seeks an economic profit

1. The key person within the firm is the entrepreneur, the organizer of production. The entrepreneur (who may or may not be a capitalist) seeks to make an economic profit. An economic profit is a residual—what is left after paying all costs, including the implicit costs of interest on the firm's capital.

Three conditions of pure competition: large numbers; easy entry and exit; no product differentiation. Competition by price alone

2. We are first going to study the entrepreneur's task under pure competition. Pure competition refers to a market in which three conditions prevail: a large number of firms; easy entry or exit of firms; and no differentiated products. The only competitive weapon available to the firm is therefore price.

Three entrepreneurial tasks: choosing the right scale

3. The entrepreneur in such a competitive milieu has only three variables under his command. The first is scale. A plant must be the right size to achieve available economies of technology. Often important economies of scale are reduced by achieving larger size.

Hiring factors if their *MR* > *MC*. The factor whose profitability is highest is always hired

4. Second, the entrepreneur must combine factors as profitably as possible to get costs as low as possible. He does so by applying two simple rules. (1) He only hires a factor if its marginal revenue is greater than its marginal cost (if *MR* > *MC*). (2) He always hires the factor whose profitability is greatest, giving the largest return per dollar of cost.

Expanding output until *MC* = *MR*

5. Third, the entrepreneur determines the level of output. He does this by comparing the marginal cost of each unit of additional output with the marginal revenue obtained from that unit. The marginal cost of most firms has a dish or U shape. We shall investigate the reasons for this more carefully in the next chapter. By expanding output until marginal revenue equals marginal cost, the entrepreneur maximizes the firm's profit.

ECONOMIC VOCABULARY

Entrepreneur 370
Economic profit 370
Pure competition 371
Entry and exit 371
Undifferentiated output 371
Scale 372
Economies of scale 373
Marginal cost 374, 375
Marginal revenue 374, 376
Profitability rule: *MR* > *MC* 375

QUESTIONS

1. Suppose that you were about to open a small business—say a drugstore. What do you think would be the factors critical in determining the scale of your operation? Suppose it were a farm? A factory?
2. Why does pure competition require a large number of sellers? Does this mean that a drugstore is not competitive, if it is the only such store in town? What does this suggest about the difficulties of defining a market?
3. Which of the three conditions for pure competition do you think is missing from the following industries: (1) aircraft construction; (2) fashion design; (3) gold mining?

4. Suppose a manufacturer had the following alternatives. It would be possible to
   - spend $1,000 on a machine that would add 115 units to sales (each unit selling at $10)
   - spend $5,000 to hire a new worker who would increase output by 510 units
   - rent new space for $10,000 that would make possible an increase in output of 1,100 units

   How would one know which was the best factor to hire? Show that the manufacturer would begin by asking what the dollar return would be per dollar of cost for each factor. What is this in the case of the machine? The new worker? The land?
5. Why is the demand curve the same as the marginal revenue curve for a manufacturer of wire coat hangers? Draw the demand curve for such a firm. Draw a separate diagram for its marginal revenue curve. Are they exactly the same? (They should be.)
6. Superimpose a firm's MR curve on its MC curve and explain carefully why the point of highest profit is where the curves intersect.

AN EXTRA WORD ABOUT
HELPING THE FARMER

The farmer is the very prototype of the entrepreneur of a competitive firm. But farming is an industry with very special problems. Traditionally, it has been a trouble-ridden occupation. All through the 1920s, the farmer was the "sick man" of the American economy. Each year saw more farmers going into tenantry, until by 1929 four out of ten farmers in the nation were no longer independent operators. Each year the farmer seemed to fall further behind the city dweller in terms of relative well-being. In 1910 the income per worker on the farm had been not quite 40 percent of the nonfarm worker. By 1930, it was just under 30 percent.

Part of this trouble on the farm, without question, stemmed from the difficult heritage of the past. Beset now by drought, now by the exploitation of powerful railroad and storage combines, now by his own penchant for land speculation, the farmer was proverbially an ailing member of the economy. In addition, the American farmers had been traditionally careless of the earth, indifferent to the technology of agriculture. They were not model entrepreneurs. Between 1910 and 1920, for instance, while nonfarm output per worker rose by nearly 20 percent, output per farm worker actually fell. Between 1920 and 1930, farm productivity improved somewhat, but not nearly so fast as productivity off the farm. For the great majority of the nation's agricultural producers, the trouble appeared to be that they could not grow or raise enough to make a decent living.

INELASTIC DEMAND

If we had looked at farming as a whole, however, a very different answer would have suggested itself. Suppose that farm productivity *had* kept pace with that of the nation. Would farm income as a whole have risen? The answer is disconcerting. The *demand* for farm products was quite unlike that for manufactured products generally. In the manufacturing sector, when productivity rose and costs accordingly fell, the cheaper prices of manufactured goods attracted vast new markets, as with the Ford car. Not so with farm products, however. When food prices fell, people did not tend to increase their actual consumption very greatly. Increases in over-all farm output resulted in much lower prices but not in larger cash receipts for the farmer. Faced with an *inelastic demand,* a flood of output only leaves sellers *worse* off than before, as we saw in Chapter 23.

That is very much what happened during the 1920s. From 1915 to 1920, the farmer prospered because World War I greatly increased the demand for his product. Prices for farm output rose, and his cash receipts rose as well; in fact, they more than doubled.

Following the war, when European farms resumed production, American farmers' crops simply glutted the market. Although prices fell precipitously (40 percent in the single year 1920–21), the purchases of farm products did not respond in anything like equal measure. As a result, the cash receipts of the farmer toppled almost as fast as prices. In turn, an ailing farm sector contributed to a general economic weakness that would culminate in the Great Depression.

THE NEW DEAL

At its core, the trouble with the farm sector was that the market mechanism did not yield a satisfactory result for farmers. Two causes were evident. One was the inelastic demand for food. The second was the inability of a vast, highly competitive industry like agriculture to limit its own output, so that it would not constantly "break the market" every time a bumper crop was harvested.

This chronic condition of agriculture was one of the first problems attended to by Franklin Roosevelt's New Deal administration. The New Deal could not alter the first cause, the inelasticity of demand, for that arose from the nature of the consumer's desire for food. It could change the condition of supply, which hurled itself, self-destructively, against an unyielding demand. One of the earliest pieces of New Deal legislation—the Agricultural Adjustment Act—sought to establish machinery to be used by farmers, as a group, to accomplish what they could not do as competitive individuals: curtail output.

The curtailment was sought by offering payments to farmers who agreed to cut back their acreage or in other ways hold down their output. In the first year of the act, there was no time to cut back acreage, so that every fourth row of growing cotton had to be plowed under, and 6 million pigs were slaughtered. In a nation hungry and ill-clad, such a spectacle of waste aroused sardonic and bitter comment. Yet, if the program reflected an appalling inability of a society to handle its distribution problem, its attack on overproduction was not without results. In both 1934 and 1935 more than 30 million acres were taken out of production in return for government payments of $1.1 billion. Farm prices rose as a result. Wheat, having slumped to 38¢ a bushel in 1932, rose to $1.02 in 1936. Cotton doubled in price, hog prices tripled, and the net income of the American farmer climbed from the fearful low of $2.5 billion in 1932 to $5 billion in 1936.

SUPPORT PRICES

Later the New Deal sought to raise farm incomes by establishing *support prices* at which the government would, if necessary, buy farm output. Because the New Deal sought to raise incomes, not to stabilize production, these prices were set at a level *higher* than equilibrium market prices. Given these support prices, farmers could confidently plan their future production, since they knew their output would be bought. But because prices were above equilibrium levels, they chose to grow more than the consumer was willing to consume at the support price. In other words, surpluses emerged, as in Figure 25.6.

To avoid these surpluses, the government limited the acreage that farmers

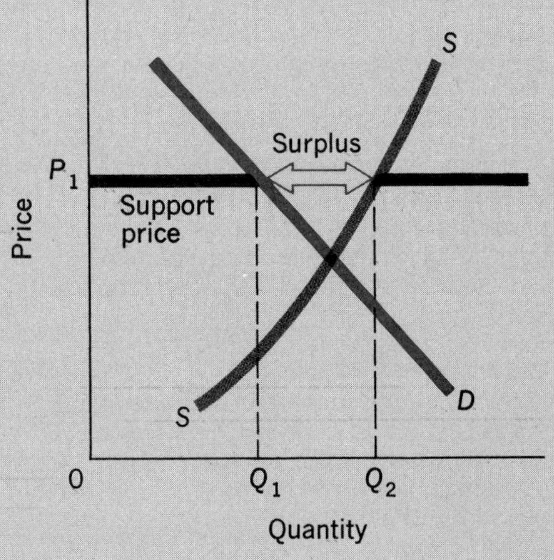

FIGURE 25.6 PRICE SUPPORT SURPLUS

At support price P_1 consumers want to buy quantity Q_1. Farmers, however, produce quantity OQ_2. The difference, Q_1Q_2, has to be bought and stored by the government. In 1960, government warehouses bulged with unsold crops worth $6 billion.

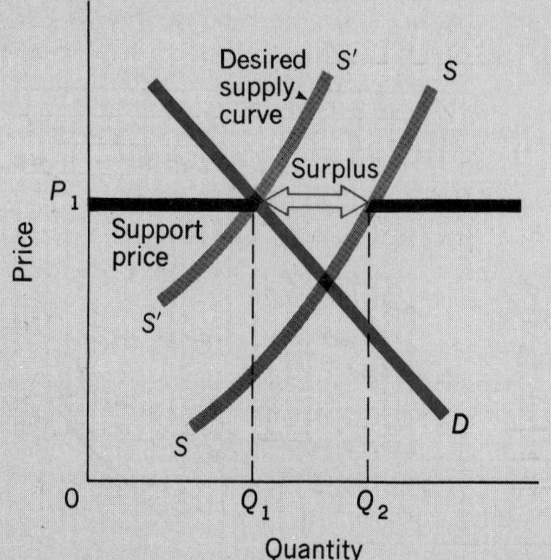

FIGURE 25.7 THE EFFORT TO LIMIT SUPPLY

The government tried to eliminate the surplus by restricting acreage. It sought to move *SS* to *S'S'* to bring about equilibrium output OQ_1.

could plant if they wanted to qualify for support payments, as Figure 25.7 shows. The strategy might have worked were it not for the extraordinary increase in agricultural productivity resulting from new technologies. Between 1940 and the late 1960s, harvested acreage declined by 15 percent, but the yield per acre increased by over *70 percent.* The result was a flood of output. Huge quantities had to be purchased and stored by the government. Only the massive distribution of these supplies to the underdeveloped lands during the early 1960s prevented the surplus problem from becoming a permanent national embarrassment.

INCOME SUPPORT

To avoid these unwanted and politically unwelcome effects, the Nixon administration in 1973 finally adopted a plan that had been proposed almost a quarter-century earlier by Charles Brannan, Secretary of Agriculture under President Truman. The so-called Brannan Plan supports farm *incomes,* not prices. A "target price" is established by law for various crops, but this target price does not apply to the actual selling prices of the crops. The free play of forces on the market allows prices to reach whatever levels supply and demand dictate.

The farmer is fully protected, nonetheless. If actual market prices are below target prices, the government will send a farmer a check for the difference that results from selling his crop below the target level. (Moreover, there is a limit of $20,000 per farmer in these support income payments, whereas there was no limit under previous plans that sent enormous sums to some very large farm operators). Two results follow:

1. When production is high and prices fall, consumers get the benefit of cheaper food prices, although as taxpayers they will still have to give up a certain amount of income to be transferred to farmers.

2. Because target prices are fairly high, farmers can plan with assurance for high outputs, without worrying about "breaking the market." In an era of world food shortages and high domestic food prices, this helps assure a high level of farm output.

THE FARMER AND INFLATION

Since 1973 food prices have soared, doubling in less than ten years. This has been the consequence of many factors.

The demand for food has been very high owing to world food shortages and consequent large agricultural exports. Rising world incomes have induced a global shift towards the consumption of meat. At home, food stamp programs to aid low income families have also helped work off the surplusses that once threatened to overhang the market forever.

Actually the farmer has not benefitted from higher food prices to anything like the degree of their increase. While the prices he has received have risen, so have the prices he has paid—fertilizer and feed, farm machinery and interest costs. The parity ratio that relates an index of prices received to prices paid rose in the farmers' favor in 1973, but has since declined to 1971 levels. Because the volume of farm marketing is up, however, the average income per farm is now over $12,000, compared with $5,000 in 1971. (Adjusting for inflation, it is up about 50 percent.) Certainly the median farmer does not have a large income, although his land may be worth a lot.

Because retail food prices have increased so dramatically, the possibility of freezing retail food prices is often raised. Would that help the situation?

PROBLEMS OF PRICE CONTROLS

If all prices were at or above their equilibrium when controls were imposed and if these equilibrium levels were not changing, price freezes would have no immediate impact, since they would be the same prices that the market would have sooner or later set. Let us assume that this is not the case and that the controls are going to hold some prices below their equilibrium level, as in Figure 25.8.

As we have seen, whenever prices are held below their equilibrium level, shortages will occur; that is, people will want to buy more of the commodity than suppliers are willing to supply. Since price is not being used to ration the existing supplies, some other technique must be found. The only alternatives are to distribute goods and services on a first-come, first-served basis or to establish formal rationing. Note that if the government control procedures break down and black markets are established, *we are right back to rationing by prices.* The only difference is that in the black market, prices are illegal. Purchasers or sellers at these illegal prices can be thrown in jail.

If formal rationing is used, governments seek to reduce the demand curve for the commodity by insisting that you must have both money *and* ration coupons to buy a pound of beefsteak. By limiting the amount of beef covered by ration coupons to the known supply of beef, it becomes possible to push the

As we learned in Chapter 22, price ceilings below equilibrium create shortages.

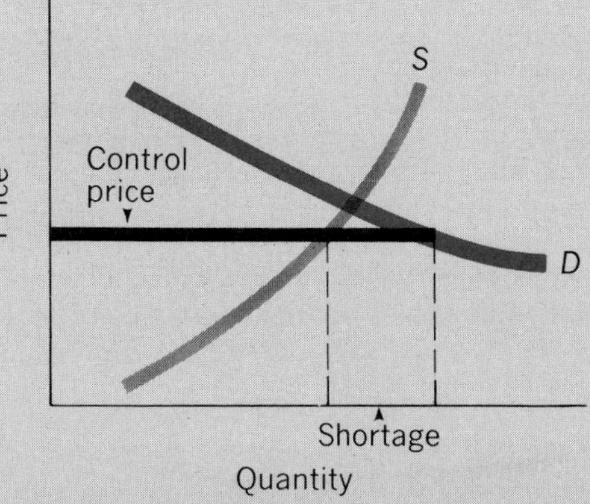

**FIGURE 25.8
PRICE
CONTROLS**

demand curve back to the point where it just crosses the supply curve at the desired price. The problem with this procedure is that the farmer now has no incentive to expand his production. The only way he will produce more is if he is able to get a higher price. Thus the controls that reduce the price of food retard the expansion of the food supply.

Suppose, instead, that we ration on a first-come, first-served basis. Now the problem is the opportunity cost of shopping time. The price of purchasing a good is now the money you must pay plus the time you must wait in line to get what you want. For most people, beefsteak that sells for 50¢ per pound but requires a 2-hour wait in line is not cheap beefsteak.

Now let's assume that the farmer has the option of selling his production to foreigners as well as to Americans. A freeze on retail prices is not a freeze on prices on the farm. Foreign buyers can therefore offer farmers more than American retailers can. Accordingly, farmers sell their crops to foreign buyers. This not only leads to greater U.S. shortages, but it can also create other problems. After the freeze is established, suppose soybean prices rise because of foreign demand. With higher soybean prices, U.S. chicken growers may find that chickens sell below the cost of feeding them. If this occurs, they will stop raising chickens and further aggravate the shortage of meat. Another possibility is that producers may simply hang onto their production, waiting for the freeze to be lifted. If cattle are withheld from the market, for example, shortages are once again exacerbated.

As a result, there are a host of adverse consequences stemming from the effort to control the increase in retail food prices. If retail controls are to be effective in holding prices below their equilibrium levels, they require formal rationing as a complement to price ceilings, plus some nonprice effort to increase the supply of foodstuffs. Eliminating acreage controls would be one nonprice action to increase production in the face of a price freeze.

THE FARM PICTURE IN PERSPECTIVE

As any agricultural economist can tell you, the farmer leads anything but a serene life. He must make difficult guesses about the course of prices years into the future. Prices take large swings, seldom settle into stable patterns, and may be a very good guide to the future.

Efforts to correct these difficulties have not been marked by great success. The original price-support program was costly, inefficient, and not always equitable. The new income-support program hopes to avoid many of these problems, but it may be expensive if market prices fall and target prices are set too high, under political pressure.

Yet, in all this, it is important to gain a sense of long-term perspective. We have seen that the farmer, unable to control economic swings, has traditionally been their victim. What we have tried to do in the last four decades is to intervene in the market process to make it yield results more in accord with our conceptions of social justice. Despite all the difficulties we have discussed, the results are impressive. Agriculture, as an income-producing activity, has benefited substantially—especially for the million-odd successful farmers who produce 90 percent of our marketed farm products. Between 1940 and 1964, farm operator families enjoying the use of electricity increased from 33 percent to more than 95 percent; telephones increased from 25 percent to 76 percent; refrigerators from 15 percent to more than 90 percent. In the West, Midwest, and Northeast, the independent farm operator is today closer than ever before to urban middle class living standards. In the South, traditionally a laggard area, farm incomes are rising faster than the national average. The important lesson is that it is possible to intervene in the market process to bring about desired social ends, although as our chapter has made abundantly clear, the process of intervention is far from simple and is full of unexpected pitfalls.

Chapter 26 OPERATING A COMPETITIVE FIRM: A Second Look

A LOOK AHEAD

In this chapter we will go over some of the material we have already covered, but much more carefully. There are a lot of numbers and a lot of graphs, but you should already be generally familiar with the situation that they analyze.

There are three big questions that tie together the chapter.

(1) Why do unit costs rise, after their initial fall? This will bring us to the very important role of the law of diminishing returns.

(2) What are the conditions for equilibrium of the competitive firm? This will again bring home the need to equate MC and MR and will introduce a new criterion for equilibrium in the industry: Average cost must equal average revenue (or price).

(3) How can profit be earned by a firm in a competitive setting? Here we will learn about intra-marginal earnings, or quasi rents.

Keeping these three main ideas in mind will help you move steadily through the analysis to come.

Once again let us become imaginary entrepreneurs. Since we are familiar with the firm's calculations in regard to buying factor services, let us extend our knowledge into a full appreciation of what the cost problem looks like to us.

FIXED AND VARIABLE COSTS

We know that a firm's total costs must rise as it hires additional factors. Yet, as business people, we can see that our total costs will not rise proportionally as fast as our additional factor costs, because some costs of production will not be affected by an increase in factor input. Real estate taxes, for example, will remain unchanged if we hire one person or 100—so long as we do not acquire additional land. We can assume that the depreciation cost of machinery will not be affected by additions to land or labor. Rent will be unchanged unless the premises are expanded. The cost of electric light will not vary appreciably despite additions to labor or machinery. Neither will the salary of the president. **Thus some costs, determined by legal contract or by usage or by the unchanging use of one factor, do not vary with output. We call these fixed costs.**

In sharp contrast with fixed costs is another kind of cost that does vary directly with output. Here are many factor costs, for generally we vary inputs of labor and capital (and sometimes land) every time we seek a new level of production. To increase output almost always requires the payment of more wages and the employment of more capital (if only in the form of inventories or goods in process) and sometimes the rental of more space. **All costs that vary with output are called variable costs.**

FIXED COSTS PER UNIT

There is certainly no difficulty in picturing what happens to fixed costs per unit of output as output rises. By definition, they must fall. Suppose a manufacturer has fixed costs (rent, certain indirect taxes, depreciation, and overhead) of $10,000 a year. If 5,000 units of the product are produced per year, each unit will have to bear $2 of fixed cost as its share. If output rises to 10,000 units, the unit share of fixed costs will shrink to $1. At 100,000 units it would be a dime. Thus a curve of fixed costs per unit of output would look like Figure 26.1.

We notice that the curve of fixed costs per unit falls steadily. This stands to reason, because the costs *are* fixed, and they are spread over an ever larger output. But this does not explain why the cost curve eventually turns up—why it has a dish or U shape. That question brings us to the question of variable costs.

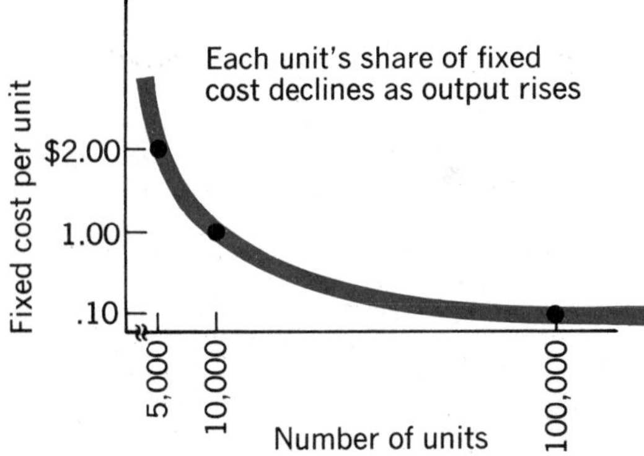

FIGURE 26.1 PROFILE OF FIXED COSTS PER UNIT

As output increases, fixed costs are spread over a larger number of units, and therefore fixed costs per unit steadily decline.

VARIABLE COSTS AND DIMINISHING RETURNS

Variable costs must be the reason that cost curves eventually turn up. This means that variable costs per unit—wages, for example—must rise after a time. Why should that be the case?

The answer takes us away from the firm, for a moment, to think again about a constraint of nature that we have encountered in Chapter 6—the law of diminishing returns.

Let us begin with a case that is very simple to imagine. Suppose we have a farmer who has a farm of 100 acres, a certain amount of equipment, and no labor at all. Now let us observe what happens as he hires one man, then a second man of the same abilities, then a third, and so on. Obviously, the output of the farm will grow. What we want to find out, however, is whether it will grow in some clearly defined pattern that we can attribute to the changing amount of the factor that is being added.

What would such a curve of productivity look like? Assume that one man, working the 100 acres alone as best he can, produces 1,000 bushels of grain. A second man, helping the first, should be enormously valuable, because the two men can begin to specialize and divide the work, each doing the jobs he is better at and saving the time formerly wasted by moving from one job to the next. As a consequence of this division of labor, output may jump to 3,000 bushels.*

MARGINAL PRODUCTIVITY

Since the *difference* in output is 2,000 bushels, we speak of the *marginal productivity* of labor, when two men are working, as 2,000 bushels. Note that we should not (although in carelessness we sometimes do) speak of the marginal productivity of the *second* man. Alone, his efforts are not more productive than those of the first man; if we fired the first man, worker number 2 would produce only 1,000 bushels. What makes the difference is the jump in the combined productivity of the *two* men, once specialization can be introduced. Hence we should speak of the changing marginal productivity of *labor*, not of the individual.

It is not difficult to imagine an increasing specialization taking place with the third, fourth, and fifth man, so that the addition of another unit of labor input in each case brings about an output larger than was realized by the average of all the previous men. Remember that this does not mean the successive factor units themselves are more productive. **It means that as we add units of one factor, the total mix of these units plus the fixed amounts of other factors, forms an increasingly efficient technical combination.** Remember Adam Smith's pin factory! (p. 32).

We call the range of factor inputs, over which average productivity rises, a range of *increasing average returns*. It is, of course, a stage of production that is highly favorable for the producer. Every time he adds a factor, efficiency rises. (As a result, as we shall shortly see, costs per unit of output fall.) The rate of

*With each additional man, the proportions of land, labor, and capital are altered, so that the change in the level of output should rightfully be ascribed to new levels of efficiency resulting from the interaction of *all three factors*. But since labor is the factor whose input we are varying, it has become customary to call the change in output the result of a change in "labor productivity." If we were altering land or capital alone, we would call the change the result of changes in their productivities, even though, as with labor, the real cause is the changing efficiency of *all* factors in different mixes.

increase will not be the same, for the initial large marginal leaps in productivity will give way to smaller ones. But the overall trend of productivity, whether we measure it by looking at *total* output or at *average* output per man, will still be up. All this keeps on happening, of course, because the factor we are adding has not yet reached its point of maximum technical efficiency with the given amount of other factors.

DIMINISHING RETURNS

At a certain point, the farmer notices a disconcerting phenomenon. Marginal output no longer rises when he adds another man. Total output will still be rising, but a quick calculation reveals that the last man on the team has added less to output than his predecessor.

What has happened is that we have overshot the point of maximum technical efficiency for the factor we are adding. Labor is now beginning to crowd land or equipment. Opportunities for further specialization have become nonexistent. **We call this condition of falling marginal performance a condition of decreasing or diminishing returns.** As the words suggest, we are getting back less and less as we add the critical factor—not only from the "marginal" man, but from the combined labor of all men.

If we now go on adding labor, we will soon reach a point at which the contribution of the marginal man will be so small that average output per man will also fall. Now, of course, costs will be rising per unit. If we went on foolishly adding more and more men, eventually the addition of another worker would add nothing to total output. In fact, the next worker might so disrupt the factor mix that *total* output would actually fall and we would be in a condition of negative returns.

TOTAL, AVERAGE, AND MARGINAL PRODUCT

This changing profile of physical productivity is one of the most important generalizations that economics makes about the real world. It will help us to think it through if we now study the relationships of marginal and average productivity and of total output in Table 26.1. All three columns are integrally related to one another, and it is important to understand the exact nature of those relationships.

1. The column for total output is related to the column for marginal productivity, because the rise in total output results from the successive marginal increments. For instance, the reason total output goes from 7,800 bushels with 4 men to 9,800 with 5 men is that the marginal output associated with the fifth man is 2,000 bushels. Thus, if we know the schedule of total outputs, we can always figure the schedule of marginal productivity simply by observing how much total output rises with each additional unit of factor input.

2. It stands to reason, therefore, that if we know the schedule of marginal productivity, it is simple to figure total output: We just add up the marginal increments.

3. Finally, the meaning of average productivity is also apparent. It is simply total output divided by the number of men (or of any factor unit in which we are interested).

Number of men	Total output	Marginal productivity (change in output)		Average productivity (total output ÷ no. of men)	
1	1,000	1,000	Increasing marginal productivity	1,000	Increasing average productivity
2	3,000	2,000		1,500	
3	5,500	2,500		1,833	
4	7,800	2,300	Decreasing marginal productivity	1,950	
5	9,800	2,000		1,960	
6	11,600	1,800		1,930	Decreasing average productivity
7	13,100	1,500		1,871	
8	14,300	1,200		1,790	

TABLE 26.1

It is important to understand the relation between the three columns. If you only knew the successive totals, how would you calculate the marginal products? If you knew the marginal column, how do you figure the total? From there, how do you get the average?

One thing must be carefully studied in this example. Note that marginal productivity begins to diminish with the fourth man, who adds only 2,300 bushels to output, and not 2,500 as did his predecessor. Average productivity, however, rises until we hire the sixth man, because the fifth man, although producing less than the fourth, is still more productive than the average output of all four men. Thus marginal productivity can be falling while average productivity is still rising.

The three curves in Figure 26.2 all show the same phenomenon, only in a graphic way. The top curve shows us that as we add men to our farm, output at first rises very rapidly, then slowly, then actually declines. The marginal productivity curve shows us *why* this is happening to total output. As we add men, the contribution they can make to output changes markedly. At first each man

The graph simply enables us to visualize the relationships of Table 26.1. Note that marginal productivity falls before average productivity.

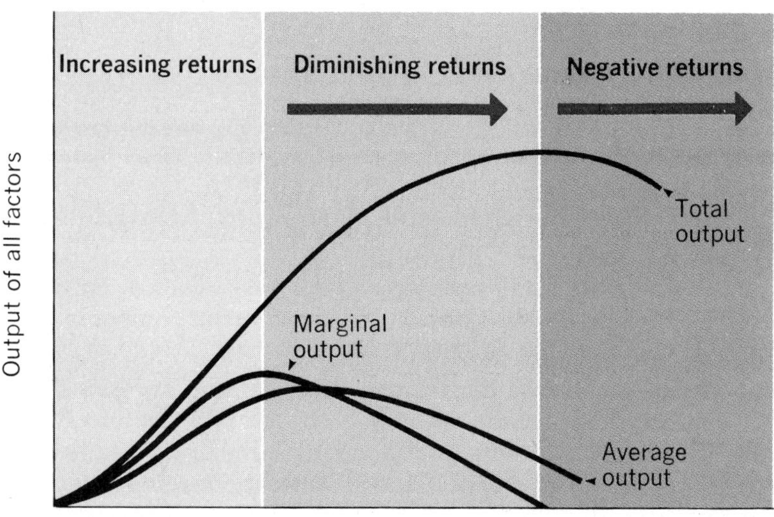

FIGURE 26.2 THE LAW OF VARIABLE PROPORTIONS

adds so much that average output grows rapidly. Thereafter marginal output falls, although average output still rises. Finally, each man adds so little that he actually pulls down the average that obtained before his hiring. The average curve, as we have just indicated, merely sums up the overall output in an arithmetical way by showing us what the average person contributes to it.

THE LAW OF VARIABLE PROPORTIONS

To sum up: If we add successive units of one factor to fixed amounts of others, marginal productivity will at first increase and then decrease. We call this the law of diminishing returns, or the law of variable proportions.

Bear in mind two things about the law. (1) It applies to all factors, land and capital as well as labor; and (2) we can't speak of the law in operation if we don't hold all factors fixed except one. Otherwise, we do not know what is the cause of any change in output.

VARIABLE COSTS PER UNIT

Perhaps we can already anticipate that the law of variable proportions will explain why average costs per unit turn up, despite falling unit fixed costs. Nonetheless, let us work our way through the actual figures.

We will begin by setting up a hypothetical schedule of output for our manufacturer (Table 26.2). As in the case of our farmer, once again we see the law of variable proportions at work. The total number of units produced will rise at first rapidly, then more slowly, with the addition of labor input to the plant.

TABLE 26.2

Number of men	*Total output (units)*	*Marginal product*
0	0	
1	5,000	5,000
2	13,000	8,000
3	23,000	10,000
4	32,000	9,000
5	39,000	7,000
6	44,000	5,000
7	47,000	3,000
8	49,000	2,000

Can you see the law of diminishing returns at work in these figures?

To convert this schedule of physical productivity into a curve of average unit costs, we must do two things:

1. Calculate total variable cost for each level of output.
2. Then divide the total variable cost by the number of units, to get average variable cost per unit of output.

Table 26.3 shows the figures (assuming that the going wage is $5,000).

Notice that average variable costs per unit decline at first and thereafter rise. The reason is by now clear enough. Variable cost increases by a set amount: $5,000 per man, as factors are added. Output, however, obeys the law of variable proportions, increasing rapidly at first and then displaying diminishing returns.

Number of men	Total variable cost @ $5,000 per man	Total output (units)	Average variable cost per unit of output (cost ÷ output)
1	$ 5,000	5,000	$1.00
2	10,000	13,000	.77
3	15,000	23,000	.65
4	20,000	32,000	.63
5	25,000	39,000	.64
6	30,000	44,000	.68
7	35,000	47,000	.74
8	40,000	49,000	.82

TABLE 26.3

Average unit costs first fall, then rise. Why? Because changing marginal productivity first makes output rise rapidly, then more slowly. Variable cost at first gets spread ever more thinly, then (starting with the 5th man), the share of variable costs per unit begins to rise.

It stands to reason, then, that the variable cost *per unit* of output will be falling as long as output is growing faster than costs, and that it will begin to rise as soon as additions to output start to get smaller.

If we graph the typical variable cost curve per unit of output, it will be the familiar dish-shaped or U-shaped profile that Figure 26.3 shows.

TOTAL COST PER UNIT

We can now set up a complete cost schedule for our enterprise by combining fixed and variable costs, as in Table 26.4. Notice how marginal costs begin to turn up *before* average costs.

If we graph the last two columns of figures—average and marginal cost per unit—we get the very important diagram in Figure 26.4.

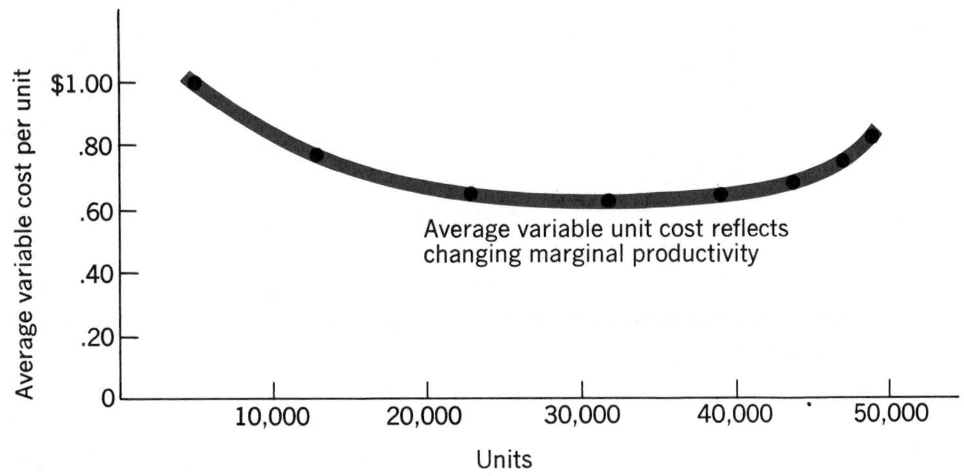

FIGURE 26.3
PROFILE OF CHANGING VARIABLE COSTS PER UNIT

This is simply a graph of the last column in Table 26.3. We now see that the upward slope of the dish-shaped curve is the result of the law of diminishing returns.

TABLE 26.4

			COST PER UNIT OF OUTPUT			
Number of men	Total cost ($10,000 fixed cost + $5,000 per man)	Output (units)	Average (total cost ÷ output)		Marginal (changes in cost ÷ change in output)	
1	$15,000	5,000	$3.00	Falling avg. cost	$	Falling marginal cost
2	20,000	13,000	1.54		.63	
3	25,000	23,000	1.09		.50	
4	30,000	32,000	.94		**.55**	Rising marginal cost
5	35,000	39,000	.90		**.71**	
6	40,000	44,000	**.91**	Rising avg. cost	**1.00**	
7	45,000	47,000	**.96**		**1.67**	
8	50,000	49,000	**1.02**		**2.50**	

Here we show total cost—fixed plus variable—and total output. It's simple thereafter to figure average and marginal costs. Technical note: Ideally, we should like to show how marginal cost changes with *each* additional unit of output. Here our data show the change in costs associated with considerable jumps in output as we add each man. Hence we estimate the marginal cost per unit by taking the *change in total costs* and dividing this by the *change in total output.* The result is really an "average" marginal cost, since each individual item costs actually a tiny fraction less, or more, than its predecessor. We have shown the data this way since it is much closer to the way businessmen figure.

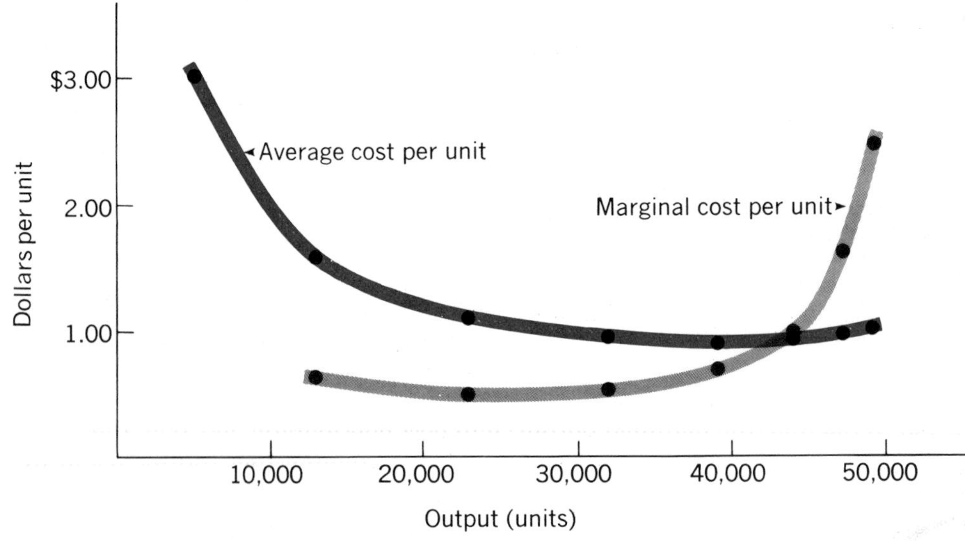

FIGURE 26.4 AVERAGE AND MARGINAL COST PER UNIT

When we graph average and marginal costs we really see what a difference the phenomenon of diminishing returns makes.

THE COST PROFILE

We have reached the end of our cost calculations, and it will help to take stock of what we have done. Actually, despite all the figures and diagrams, the procedure has been quite simple.

1. We began by seeing what would happen to our *fixed costs* per unit as we expanded output. Since fixed costs, by their nature, do not increase as production increases, the amount of fixed cost that had to be charged to each unit of output fell sharply as output rose.

2. Next we calculated the *variable costs* that would have to be borne by each unit as output increased. Here the critical process at work was the law of variable proportions. As the marginal productivity of factors increased, variable cost per unit fell. When the inevitable stage of diminishing returns set in, variable costs per unit had to rise.

3. Adding together fixed and variable costs, we obtained the *total unit cost* of output. Like the variable cost curve, average total unit costs are dish-shaped, reflecting the changing marginal productivity of factors as output grows.

4. Finally, we show the changing *marginal cost per unit*—the increase in total costs divided by the increase in output. As before, it is the changing marginal costs that the entrepreneur actually experiences in altering output. It is the increase at the margin that alters total cost and therefore determines average cost.

AVERAGE AND MARGINAL COSTS

Actually, the cost profile that we have worked out would be known by any businessperson who had never studied microeconomics. Whenever a firm starts producing, its average cost per unit of output is very high. A General Motors plant turning out only a few hundred cars a year would have astronomical costs per automobile.

As output increases, unit costs come down steadily, partly because overhead (fixed costs) is now spread over more units, partly because the factors are used at much greater efficiency. Finally, after some point of maximum factor efficiency, average unit costs begin to mount. Even though overhead continues to decline, it is now so small a fraction of cost per unit that its further decline does not count for much, while the rising inefficiency of factors steadily pushes up variable cost per unit. If General Motors tries to jam through more cars than a plant is designed to produce, the cost per auto will again begin to soar.

So much for the *average* cost per unit. By directing our attention to the changes that occur in total cost and total output every time we alter the number of factors we engage, the *marginal* cost curve per unit simply tells us why all this is happening. In other words, as our plant first moves into high gear, the cars we add to the line (the marginal output) will cost considerably less than the average of all cars processed previously. Later, when diminishing returns begin to work against us, we would expect the added (marginal) cars to be high-cost cars, higher in cost than the average of all cars built so far.

Since the cost of marginal output always "leads" the cost of average output in this way, we can understand an important relationship that all marginal and

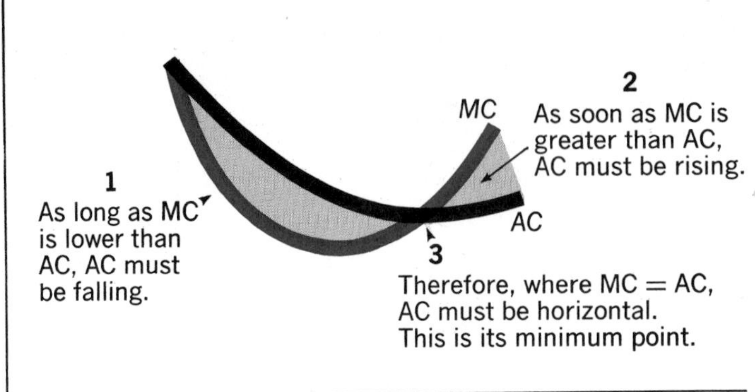

FIGURE 26.5 RELATION OF MARGINAL AND AVERAGE COST PER UNIT

The marginal cost curve cuts the average cost curve at its lowest point. For reasons, read the information on the graph.

average cost curves bear to each other. The marginal cost curve always cuts the average cost curve at the lowest point of average cost.

Why? Because as long as the additional cars are cheaper than the average of all cars, their production must be *reducing* average cost; that is, as long as the marginal cost curve is lower than the average cost curve, the average cost curve must be falling. Conversely, as soon as additional output is more expensive than the average for all previous output, that additional production must *raise* average costs. Again (look at the previous diagram), as soon as marginal cost is above average cost, average cost must begin to rise. Hence it follows that the *MC* (marginal cost) curve must cross the *AC* (average cost) curve at the minimum point of average cost. This relationship has nothing to do with economics, as such, but with simple logic, as Figure 26.5 may elucidate.*

FROM COST TO REVENUE

The cost profile gives us a clear picture of what happens to unit costs as our firm hires additional factors. But that is only half the information we need for understanding how a firm operates with one foot in the factor market and the other in the market for goods. Now we need a comparable profile of what happens to revenues as the firm sells the output its factors have made for it.

AVERAGE AND MARGINAL REVENUE

We already know what the demand curve looks like for a competitive firm. It is a horizontal line, reflecting the fact that the firm's output is too small to affect the market price of the good. Let's now assume that our firm makes such a competitive product—say a metal stamping, whose price is $1.50.

*It follows that the marginal productivity curve always crosses the average productivity curve at its peak. Look at Figure 26.2. As long as marginal productivity is *higher* than average productivity, the average curve must be *rising.* As soon as additional (marginal) output is *less than* the preceding average output, the lower marginal output must *diminish* the average. The relation is exactly that of Figure 26.5, only upside down.

Output (units	Price per unit	Marginal revenue per unit	Total revenue	Average revenue per unit
5,000	$1.50	$1.50	$ 7,500	$1.50
10,000	1.50	1.50	15,000	1.50
20,000	1.50	1.50	30,000	1.50
40,000	1.50	1.50	60,000	1.50

TABLE 26.5

The entrepreneur can easily calculate his revenue curves, knowing that there is a limitless demand for his product.* Each unit will sell at the same price as the one before or the one afterward. The revenue brought in by each unit—the marginal revenue—will therefore be unchanged. So will the average revenue per unit, which is the same thing as the selling price. As the schedule of Table 26.5 and the graph of Figure 26.6 show, marginal and average revenues are the same. (They won't be when we get to less-than-competitive markets in our next chapter.)

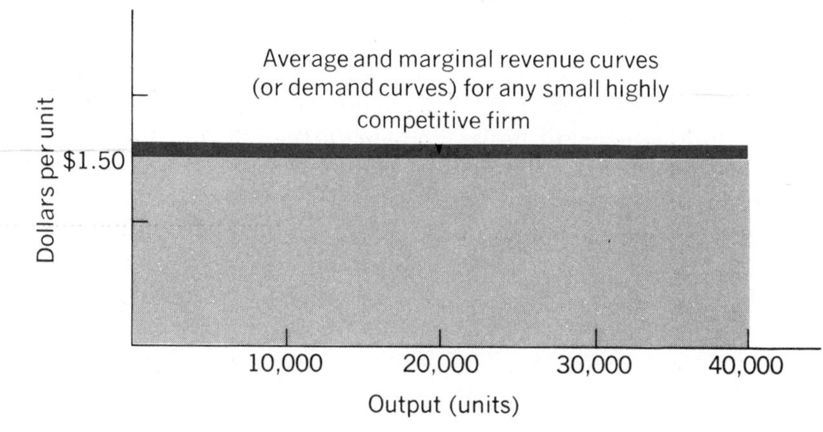

FIGURE 26.6
AVERAGE AND MARGINAL REVENUES UNDER COMPETITION

This is the same flat curve we saw in our previous chapter. We reproduce it here because its flatness holds the key to analyzing the competitive firm's situation. (Can you anticipate why the marginal and average revenue curves will not be flat, and will not be the same, when we get to monopolistic markets?)

MARGINAL COST AND SUPPLY

Now we have all the information we want. We have a cost profile that tells us what happens to unit costs as we hire or fire factors. We have a revenue profile that tells us what happens to unit revenues as we do the same. It remains only to put the two together to discover just how much output the firm should make to maximize its profits. As we can see in Figure 26.7, it is just about at 45,000 units.

We already know why this is the most profitable level of output. But we can now see a new meaning for the marginal cost curve. The marginal cost curve is the firm's supply curve.

*So why doesn't an ambitious firm produce a limitless amount and become limitlessly rich? Because rising unit costs will soon bring it limitless losses.

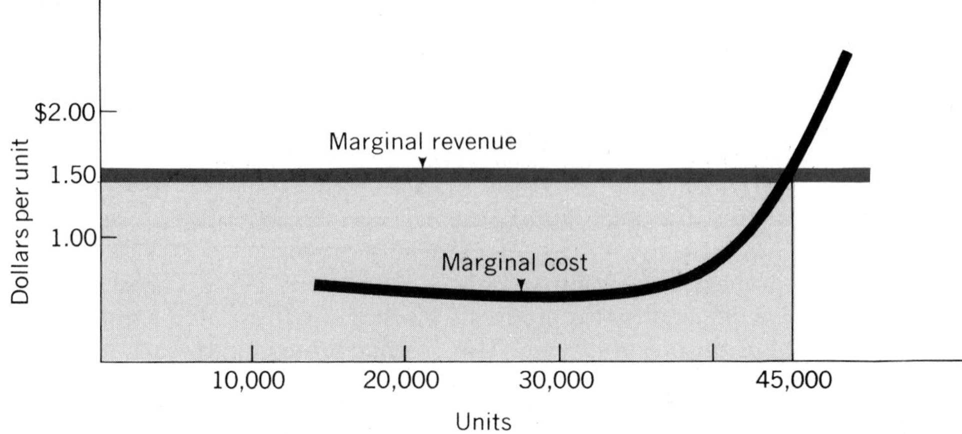

FIGURE 26.7 THE POINT OF OPTIMUM OUTPUT

Here is the same *MC* = *MR* diagram we used in the previous chapter, this time calibrated to show the actual number of units at optimal output.

Suppose price rises from P_1 to P_2 in Figure 26.8. As far as the firm is concerned, it does not matter where its average cost is. What counts is whether additional production will be profitable. Further, it will be profitable only if the marginal cost of that additional production does not exceed marginal revenue. Therefore, when price rises, the firm's output increases from Q_1 to Q_2, a point determined by the intersection of the *MC* curve and the new price.

The point we must bear in mind is more than just a geometrical demonstration. It is that marginal costs, not average costs, determine most production decisions. When prices rise or fall, the change in quantity will reflect the ease or difficulty of adding to or diminishing production, as that ease or difficulty is reflected in the shape of its *MC* schedule.

PROFITS

Now let us return to the firm producing the quantity of stampings that just equates marginal cost and marginal revenue. What is the total amount of economic profit at the firm's best level of output? This is very difficult to tell from diagrams that show only marginal costs and marginal revenues. As we have just

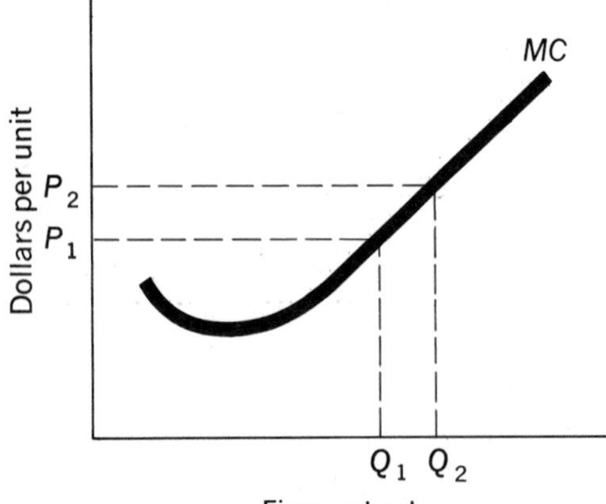

FIGURE 26.8 THE FIRM'S SUPPLY CURVE

We have often talked about a firm's supply curve. Now we can see that it is its marginal cost curve.

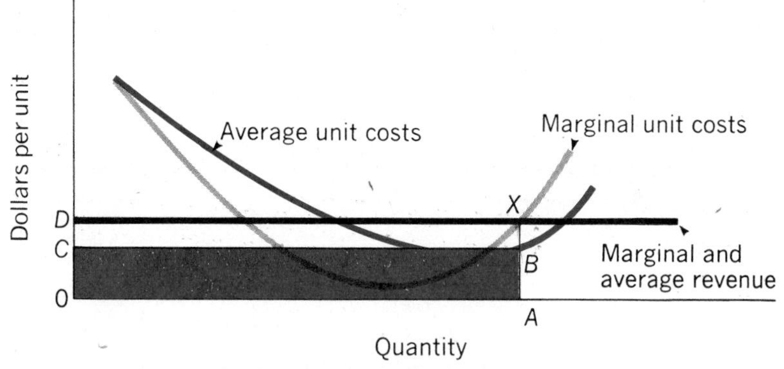

FIGURE 26.9 THE FIRM IN EQUILIBRIUM WITH PROFITS

How well is our firm doing? Total costs = *OABC:* output times average costs. Total revenues = *OAXD:* output times average revenue. Profits equal the difference, or *CBXD*—a profit of *BX* per unit times the number of units.

seen, these curves tell us how large *output* will be. But we must add another curve to enable us quickly to see what the *profit* will be at each level of output.

This is our familiar average cost curve. Average costs, we know, are nothing but total costs reduced to a per-unit basis. Average revenues are also on a per-unit basis. **Hence, if we compare the average unit revenue and cost curves at any point, they will tell us at a glance what total revenues and costs look like at that point.**

Figure 26.9 reveals what our situation is at the point of optimum output. (This time we generalize the diagram rather than putting it into the specific terms of our illustrative firm.)

The diagram shows several things. First, as before, it indicates our most profitable output as the amount *OA*—the output indicated by the point *X*, where the marginal revenue and marginal cost curves meet. **Remember: We use marginal costs and marginal revenues to determine the point of optimum output.**

Second, it shows us that at output *OA*, our *average cost* is *OC* (= *AB*) and our *average revenue* is *OD* (= *AX*), the same as our marginal revenue, since the demand curve for the firm is horizontal. Our profit on the *average* unit of output must therefore be *CD* (= *BX*), the difference between average costs and average revenues at this point. The *total* profit is therefore the rectangle *CDXB*, which is the average profit per unit (*CD*) times the number of units. **Remember again: We use average costs and average revenues to calculate profits.**

WORKING OUT AN EXAMPLE

We can translate this in terms of our firm. At the point where *MC* = *MR*, it is making about 45,000 stampings, as Figure 26.7 shows, at an average cost that we will estimate at 92¢ per unit. (Table 26.4 does not show us the exact cost at 45,000 units, but we will assume it is 1¢ more than the 91¢ cost of making 44,000 units.) Since the selling price is $1.50, we are now taking in a total of $1.50 × 45,000 units, or $67,500, while our total cost is 92¢ × 45,000 units or $41,400. Our profit is the difference between total revenues and total costs or $26,100.

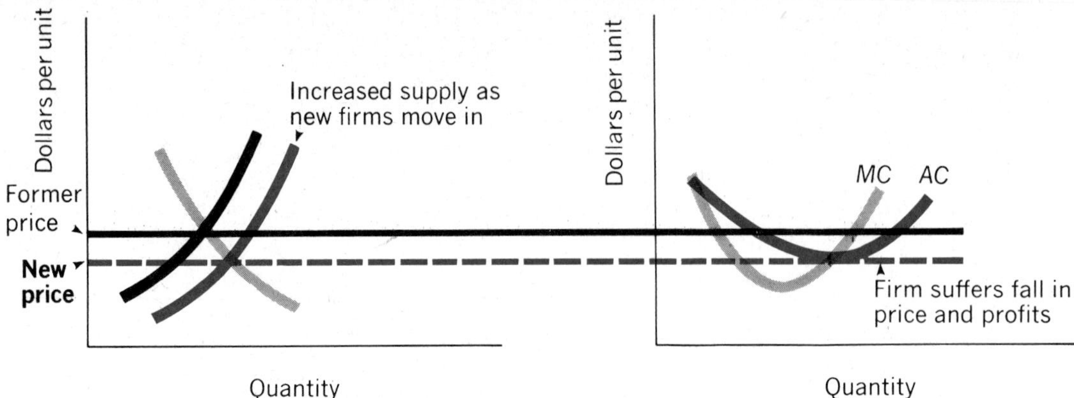

FIGURE 26.10 INDUSTRY IN ADJUSTMENT TO PROFITS
On the left we see that supply and demand lower the price as new firms move in. On the right we see how this affects each individual firm.

ENTRY AND EXIT

However satisfactory from the point of view of the firm, this is not yet a satisfactory stopping point from the point of view of the system as a whole. If our firm is typical of the metal stamping industry, then small firms throughout this line of business are making profits comparable to ours. In other lines of endeavor, though, numerous businesses do not make $26,100 in economic profit. Hence entrepreneurs in these lines will now begin to move into our profitable industry.

Perhaps we can anticipate what will happen now. As other firms move into our line of business, output will increase. The supply curve of the industry will move to the right. The price of our product will therefore fall as Figure 26.10 shows.

How long will this influx of firms continue? Suppose that it continues until price falls *below* the average cost curve of our representative firm. Now its position looks like Figure 26.11. Output will still be set where $MC = MR$ (it always is), but now the average cost curve is above the average revenue curve at this point. The unavoidable result is a loss for the firm, as the diagram shows.

If price sinks too low, the firm will seek optimum output (*MR* = *MC*), but its price will fail to cover average costs. It will make a loss.

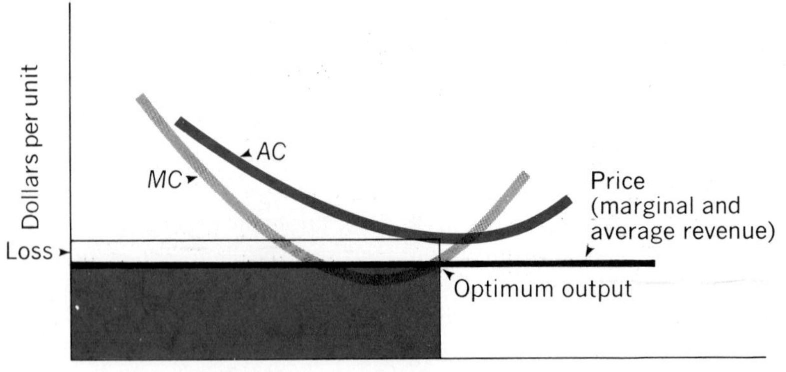

FIGURE 26.11 THE FIRM SUFFERING A LOSS

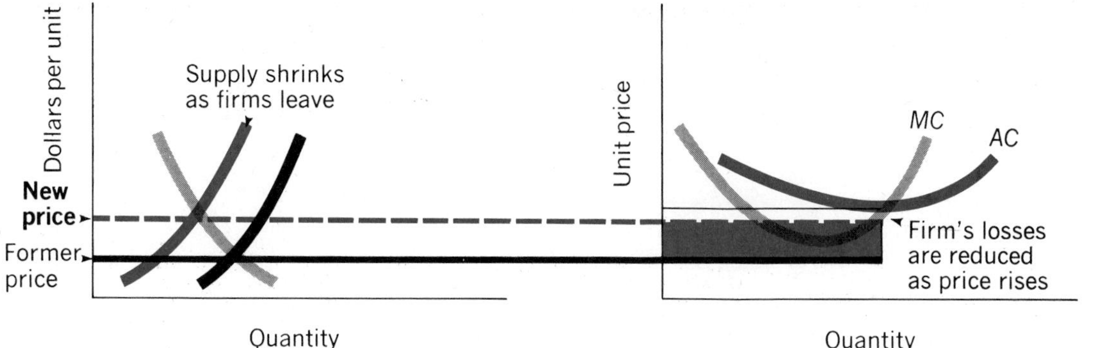

FIGURE 26.12 INDUSTRY ADJUSTMENT TO LOSSES
As firms gradually leave an industry, the supply curve moves to the left, prices rise, and firms' losses are reduced.

What will happen? Clearly, we need a reverse adjustment process—an exodus of firms into greener pastures, so that the supply curve for our industry can move to the left, bringing higher prices for all producers. This may not be a rapid process. Eventually, the withdrawal of producers should bring about the necessary adjustment shown in Figure 26.12.

MINIMIZING LOSSES

The process of minimizing losses (which is as close as an unfortunate entrepreneur can get to maximizing profits) is worth a careful look. Figure 26.13 shows two curves: *AC* is our familiar curve of average costs. *AVC* is the curve of average variable costs (Figure 26.3). It is not *total* cost because it does not include the items like rent that go into fixed cost.

Suppose that price falls to P_1. Should the firm quit? No, because it covers its out-of-pocket expenses (*AVC*) and even makes a little over to cover some, although not all, fixed cost. As long as price is high enough to cover variable costs, a firm will continue to produce. Only when price fails to cover out of pocket *AVC* costs will it be rational to shut down.

How long can a firm go on incurring losses? The answer depends on how rapidly it can terminate its fixed costs, such as getting rid of its buildings, machinery, etc., or how long it can incur losses without going bankrupt. The firm may limp along for an extended period, continuing to add production to the market and thereby delaying the leftward shift of the industry's supply curve.

If price is at P_1 the firm is covering variable costs although not total costs. Perhaps it makes enough to cover its wages and some of its rent. It stays in business despite its economic loss. At price P_2 it can't even cover out-of-pocket costs. It has to shut down.

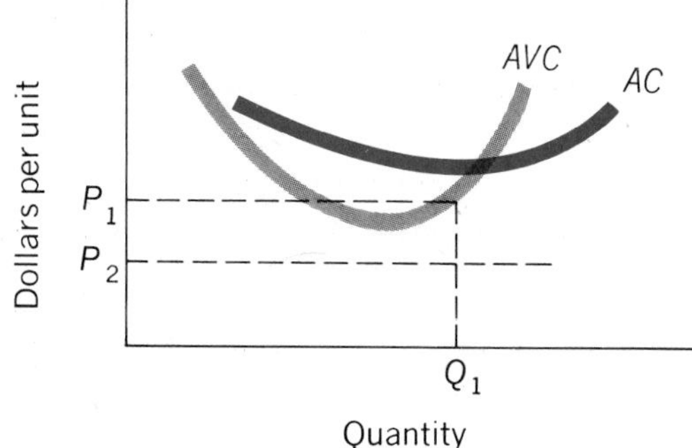

FIGURE 26.13 ADJUSTING TO LOSSES

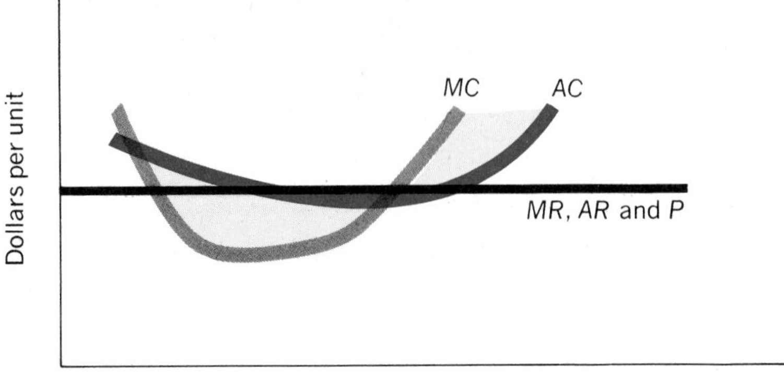

FIGURE 26.14 MARGINAL FIRM IN EQUILIBRIUM WITH NO PROFITS

Here is a diagram to be fully grasped. It shows the conditions for equilibrium of the competitive firm: (1) No incentive to change output (*MR* = *MC*). (2) No incentive for entry or exit (*AC* = *P*).

LONG-RUN EQUILIBRIUM

Sooner or later, whether through the entry of new firms or the gradual withdrawal or disappearance of old ones, we reach a point of equilibrium both for the firm and the industry. It looks like Figure 26.14.

Note that this position of equilibrium has two characteristics for the firm.

1. Marginal cost equals marginal revenue, so there is no incentive for the individual entrepreneur to alter his own output.

2. Average cost equals average revenue (or price), so there is no incentive for firms to enter or leave the industry.

Thus we can state the condition for the equilibrium resting point of our firm and industry as being a four-way equality:

$$MC = MR = AC = P$$

Marginal cost	=	Marginal revenue	=	Average cost	=	Price (average revenue)

We have reached an equilibrium both for the firm and for the industry. It is certainly an uncomfortable one for ourselves as typical manufacturers; for in the final resting point of the firm, it is clear that *profits have been totally eliminated.*

We are driven to the conclusion that in a "perfect" competitive market, the forces of competition would indeed press toward zero the returns of the *marginal* firms in all industries, so that the cost and revenue profile of the last firms able to remain alive in each industry would look like our diagram.

QUASI RENTS

Note, however, that these are marginal firms. Here is a clue to how profits can exist even in a highly competitive situation. In Figure 26.15 we show the supply curve of an industry broken into the individual supply curves of its constituent firms. Some of these firms, for reasons that we will discuss below, will be lower-cost producers than others. When the industry equilibrium price is finally established, they will be the beneficiaries of the difference between the going price, which reduces the profits of the *marginal* firm to zero, and the lower unit costs attributable to their superior efficiency. Industry equilibrium leaves them in the enviable position of the firm shown in Figure 26.9.

These intramarginal profits are called quasi rents.* They are the only true economic profits that we find in competitive industries.

SOURCES OF QUASI RENTS

Where do these quasi rents arise? From several sources. One source may be personnel. Workers hired at the same wage are not always equally productive. A superior manager will recruit or organize a superior work force and gain rents as a result. Another source can be location. Not all prices adjust quickly to changed conditions. A retail store may enjoy a movement of population into its area. The value of its location increases, but its actual rental payments may not rise until a new lease is signed. Third, just plain luck or the uncertainties of the business world constantly create positive or negative quasi rents. An entrepreneur goes into a business having calculated costs and revenues, then finds that costs have fallen or revenues risen, for reasons that could not be anticipated. Positive or negative quasi rents—profits or losses—will ensue. Uncertainty is, in fact as well as in proverb, fundamental to life and a major source of the good or bad fortune that besets the best-laid plans of entrepreneurs.

Thus, economic profits enter the competitive world from changes in the economic setting, from random runs of good and bad luck, from unequal distributions of talent or resources. As a general rule, these sources of quasi rent are ephemeral, and the normal, profit-seeking movement of the industry will erode and eventually erase them. Badly run firms will go out of business or hire a better manager. Badly located firms will pick up and move. Contracts will come to an end and be renegotiated to remove quasi rents. Movements of the marketplace

Even though the marginal firm makes no profit, intramarginal firms may realize quasi rents. Entry into the industry will tend to eliminate them.

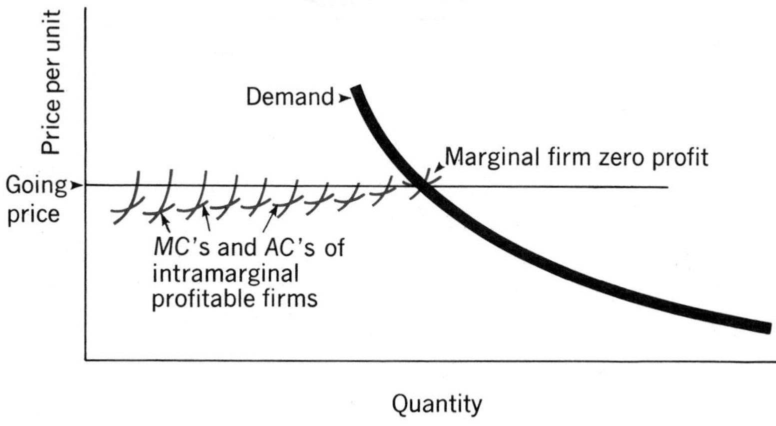

FIGURE 26.15 QUASI OR ECONOMIC RENTS

*Sometimes they are called "economic rents" or even plain "rents".

that create positive rents one year will create negative ones the next. Luck evens out. Thus in the long run, we can expect a tendency in a competitive market to eliminate existing quasi rents, although new ones may be created as conditions change.

KEY CONCEPTS

LOOKING BACK

There are a great many graphs and tables in this chapter, but they all dovetail into an overall concept. The concept is the idea of the competitive firm seeking to maximize its profit. Keeping that in mind will help organize your understanding.

Fixed and variable cost

1. All firms have two kinds of costs, fixed and variable. Fixed costs, which do not vary with output, decline when figured on a per unit basis as output grows. Variable costs display the familiar U shape.

Law of diminishing returns gives first increasing, then diminishing returns

2. Variable costs rise because of the law of diminishing returns—also called the law of variable proportions. This law tells us that as we add more and more of any one factor to a fixed amount of other factors, output will first rise—increasing returns—and then fall—diminishing returns.

This gives falling, then rising variable costs per unit

3. This change in productivity means that costs per unit first fall, then rise, as we add variable costs—usually labor—to a fixed amount of plant and equipment.

Eventually average and marginal cost both rise. *MC* curve always cuts *AC* curve at lowest point

4. If we add variable to fixed costs, we get the dish-shaped curve we are familiar with. As output increases, eventually both average and marginal cost per unit will rise, marginal cost more sharply. The marginal cost curve always cuts the average cost curve at its lowest point.

***AC* and *MR* curves are identical**

5. Average and marginal revenues for a competitive firm are identical and horizontal, as we know. This is because the firm's output is too small to affect price, whether it expands or contracts output.

$MC = MR$ is always optimal output

6. The firm maximizes its own profit by setting output where $MC = MR$. The marginal cost curve always determines the point of optimal output. It is the firm's supply curve.

Entry and exit will change the supply curve for the industry, raising or lowering prices and profits. A firm will produce as long as $AR > AVC$

7. $MC = MR$ is the "solution" for the firm, but it may not be the equilibrium for the industry. If the firm is making profits there will be entry from other firms. Supply will increase. Price will drop. Profits will tend to disappear. If there are losses, some firms will leave the industry. Supply will diminish, prices will rise, losses will be cut. A firm will continue to produce as long as price (average revenue) is greater than average variable cost (out of pocket expenses).

Long-run equilibrium: $MC = MR = AC = P$

8. Long-run equilibrium requires that the firm be at the $MC = MR$ point and that it also have $AC = AR$ (or price). The firm must have no incentive to change output and there must be no incentive to enter or leave the industry.

Quasi rents are intramarginal profits

9. Profits at the margin thus tend toward zero. But intramarginal profits, called quasi rents, may persist.

ECONOMIC VOCABULARY

Fixed costs 386
Variable costs 386
Costs per unit 386
Diminishing returns 388
Marginal productivity 387
Average productivity 388
Law of variable proportions 390
Average and marginal costs per unit 393
Average and marginal revenue 394
Quasi rents 400

QUESTIONS

1. If you were a retail grocer, what kind of costs would be fixed for you? If you were a manufacturer who owned a large computer, would its maintenance be a fixed cost? If you *rented* the computer, would maintenance be a fixed cost?
2. Assume that your fixed costs are $500 a week and that your output can vary from 100 to 1,000 units, given the scale of your enterprise. Graph what happens to fixed costs per unit. Is this diminishing returns?
3. Assume that your plant hires 6 workers successively and that output changes as follows:

Number of workers	1	2	3	4	5	6
Total units of output per week	100	300	550	700	750	800

   What is the marginal product of each worker? The average product? If each worker costs $100 per week, what is the variable cost per unit as you add personnel? Explain the relation between the shape of the curve and the law of variable proportions.
4. If you add fixed costs of $500 per week to the variable cost you have just ascertained, what is the average cost per unit? What is the marginal cost per unit? (Remember, this is figured by dividing the *change in total cost by the change in total output.*)
5. Graph the curve of average total unit costs and marginal unit costs. Why does the marginal unit cost curve cross the average unit cost curve at its lowest point?
6. What does average revenue mean and what is its relation to price? What is meant by marginal revenue? Why is marginal revenue the same as average revenue for a competitive firm?
7. Suppose (in the example above) you sell the output of your firm at $1.35 per unit. Draw in such a marginal revenue curve. Now very carefully indicate where the *MR* and *MC* curves meet. Show on the diagram the output corresponding to this point. What is the approximate average cost at this output? Is there a profit here? Indicate by letters the rectangle that shows the profit per unit of output and the number of units. Is it a quasi rent?
8. What will be the result, in a competitive industry, of such a profit? Draw a diagram showing how an influx of firms can change the ruling market price. Will it be higher or lower?

9. Draw a diagram showing how price could drop below the lowest point on the average total unit cost curve and indicate the low the firm would suffer. Explain, by means of a diagram, why a manufacturer may remain in business even though the firm cannot sell its output for the full cost of producing it. What will determine whether or not it is worth the firm's while to quit entirely?
10. Carefully draw a diagram showing the equilibrium position for the firm. Explain how *MR* and *MC* are all the firm is concerned with. How do *AR* and *AC* enter the picture? Why do *MR* and *MC*, by themselves, fail to give an equilibrium price in a competitive industry?
11. Suppose that you are a druggist and you know that the least efficient druggist in town makes virtually no profit at all. Assuming that you both sell in the same market at the same prices, and that you hire factors at the same prices, what causes could bring about a profit to your enterprise? What would you expect to be the trend of these profits?

Chapter 27 OPERATING A BIG BUSINESS

A LOOK AHEAD

In this chapter we move from the world of perfect competition to that of imperfect competition—monopolies, oligopolies, and monopolistically competitive businesses. We shall study the operation of these business firms and compare it with the operation of the perfectly competitive firm we have already studied.

The crucial difference, as we shall soon see, is that firms operating in conditions of imperfect competition have falling marginal revenue curves rather than horizontal ones. This means that at optimum output, where $MR = MC$, average cost will not equal average revenue or price. The main objective of this chapter is to see what difference this makes.

In the next chapter we shall make a social assessment of big business and consider various ways to deal with the problems it presents.

MOTIVES AND MARKETS

Monopoly (and nowadays oligopoly) are bad words to most people, just as competition is a good word, although not everyone can specify exactly what is good or bad about them. Often we get the impression that the aims of the monopolist are evil and grasping, while those of the competitor are wholesome and altruistic. Therefore the essential difference between a world of pure competition and one of very impure competition seems to be one of motives and drives—of well-meaning competitors and ill-intentioned monopolists.

The truth is that exactly the same motives drive the monopoly and the competitive firm. Both seek to maximize their profits. Indeed, the competitive firm, faced with the necessity of watching costs and revenues in order to survive, is apt to be, if anything, more pennypinching and more intensely profit-oriented than the monopolist who (as we shall see) can afford to take a less hungry attitude toward profits. The lesson to be learned—and to remember—is that motives have nothing to do with the problem of less-than-pure competition. **The difference between a monopoly, an oligopoly, and a situation of pure competition is entirely one of market structure; that is, of the number of firms, ease of entry or exit, and the degree of differentiation among their goods.**

PRICE TAKERS VS. PRICE MAKERS

We have noted a very precise distinction between the competitive situation (numerous firms, undifferentiated goods) and markets with few sellers or highly differentiated goods. In the competitive case, as we have seen, each firm caters to so small a section of the market that the demand curve for its product is, for all intents and purposes, horizontal. By way of contrast, in a monopolistic or oligopolistic market structure there are so few firms that each one faces a downward sloping demand curve. Each monopoly firm, in fact, faces the demand curve of its own industry. That means that each firm, by varying its output, can affect the price of its product.

Another way of describing this difference is to call purely competitive firms, who have no control over their price, *price takers* and to label monopolies or oligopolies or any firm that can affect the price of its product, *price makers.*

"PURE" MONOPOLIES

Before examining the economic problems of a "pure" monopoly, let us see how such a price maker operates. Why do we place the word "pure" in quotes? Because monopoly is not as easy to define as one might think. Essentially, the word means that there is only *one* seller of a particular good or service. The trouble comes in defining the "particular" good or service. In a sense, any seller of a differentiated good is a monopolist, for no one else dispenses *quite* the same utilities as he does. Each shoe-shine boy has his "own" customers, some of whom would probably continue to patronize his stand even if he charged slightly more than his competition.

Thus, at one end of the difficulty is the fact that there is an element of monopoly in many seemingly competitive goods, a complication we shall come back to later. At the other end of the problem there are so-called "natural" monopolies, where economies of scale lead to one seller supplying the whole

HOW MONOPOLISTIC IS A MONOPOLY?

How do we recognize a monopoly? Because of the problem of substitutes, there is no very clear sign, except in a few cases such as the "natural" monopolies. Usually when we speak of monopolies we mean (a) very large businesses with (b) much higher than competitive profits and (c) relatively little direct product competition. Not many firms satisfy all three conditions. Exxon is a monopoly by criteria *a* and *b*, but not by *c;* Polaroid by *b* but not *a*, and perhaps not by *c* (Kodak is its direct product competitor). Note, furthermore, that even small businesses can be monopolies, like "the only gambling house in town" famed in all Westerns.

An interesting case in point is the telephone company. Most people assume that A.T. & T. is a monopoly if ever there was one. Yet in fact, although the Bell Telephone system provides 82 percent of all telephone service in the country, there are actually 1800 telephone companies, quite independent of the Bell System.

market, such as a local utility company. Yet even here there are substitutes. If power rates become exorbitant, we *could* switch from electric light to candlelight. Hence, before we can draw conclusions from the mere fact that a company provides the "only" service of its kind, we need to know how easy or difficult it would be to find substitutes, however imperfect, for its output.

LIMITS OF MONOPOLY

Evidently the problem of defining a "pure" monopoly is not easily resolved. Let us, however, agree to call the local power company a monopoly, because no one else sells gas and electricity to the community. In Figure 27.1 we show what the demand curve of such a monopoly looks like.

One point is immediately clear. **The monopolistic firm faces the same kind of demand curve that the competitive industry faces.** That is so because both cater to *all* the demand for that particular product. A corollary follows. The demand curve itself imposes a fundamental limitation of the monopolist's power to control the market. Suppose a monopoly is selling quantity *OX* at price *OA* as shown in Figure 27.2. The firm would prefer to sell quantity *OY* at price *OA*, but there is no way of forcing the market to take a larger quantity of its product—unless it lowers the price to *OB*.

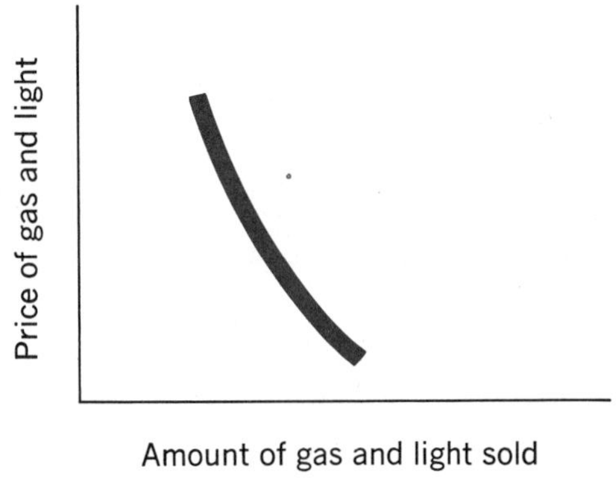

Price of gas and light

Amount of gas and light sold

FIGURE 27.1 DEMAND CURVE FOR A MONOPOLY

A monopolist's demand curve is never horizontal. It slopes like the demand curve of a competitive industry.

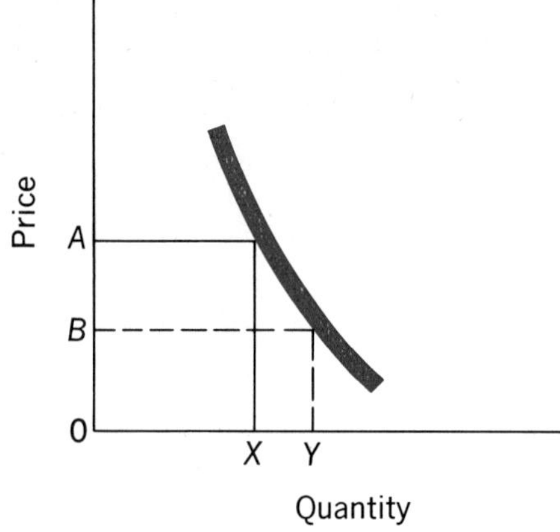

FIGURE 27.2 DEMAND CURVE OF A MONOPOLIST

A demand curve constrains the monopolistic *firm* as decisively as it constrains the competitive *industry*.

The situation is very similar (on the seller's side) to a *union*. A union can raise the price of labor since it controls the supply of labor, but it cannot force employers to hire more labor than they want. Hence the question "Can unions raise wages?" must be answered "Yes," insofar as those who continue to be hired are concerned. But until we know the elasticity of the demand for labor, we cannot say if unions can raise the total amount of labor's revenues. (More on that subject in "An Extra Word" following Chapter 30.)

ADVERTISING

There is one thing a monopoly can do, however, that neither a union nor a purely competitive firm can do. **A monopoly can advertise and thereby seek to move to the right, or change the slope of, the demand curve for its product.** Advertising does not "pay" in a purely competitive firm selling undifferentiated goods, for such a firm has no way of being sure that *its* goods—and not a competitor's—will benefit. But advertising *can* be profitable for a monopoly that will get all the demand it can conjure up. We can think of advertising as an attempt to sell larger quantities of a good or service without reducing prices, by shifting the demand curve itself. Figure 27.3 shows us this important effect, and we will talk about it further in a moment.

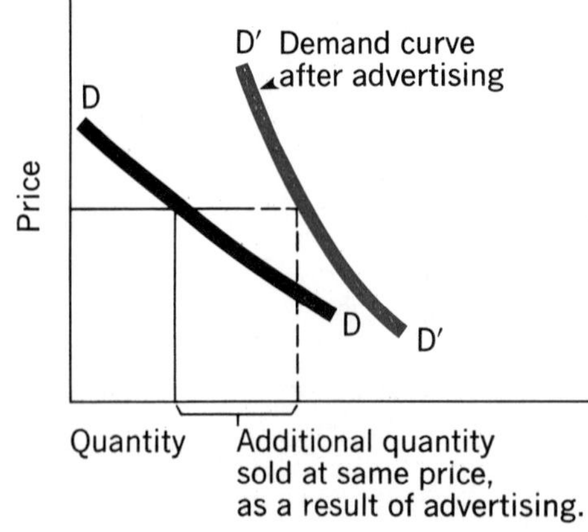

FIGURE 27.3 ADVERTISING AND DEMAND

Any firm that advertises tries to do two things: (1) move *DD* to the right, and (2) make *D'D'* more inelastic than *DD* was.

COST CURVES FOR THE MONOPOLIST

We have seen in what way the shape of the demand curves faced by monopolists differ from those faced by competitive firms. Are cost curves similarly different?

In general, they are not. We can take the cost profile of a monopoly as being essentially like that of a competitive firm. The monopoly, like the competitive firm, buys factors and exerts no control over their prices. A.T. & T. does not affect the level of wages or the price of land or capital by its decision to expand or not to expand production. The monopolist, like the competitive entrepreneur, experiences the effects of changing productivity as he hires additional factors and, again like the competitive firm, shops for the best buy in the factor markets. Thus the same U-shaped average cost curve and the same more steeply sloped marginal cost curve will describe the cost changes experienced by a monopolist quite as well as those of a competitive firm.

FROM COST TO REVENUE

MONOPOLY REVENUES

It is when we come to the revenue side of the picture that we meet the critical distinction of monopoly. **Unlike a competitive firm, a monopoly has a marginal revenue curve that is different from its average revenue curve.** The difference arises because each time a monopoly sells more output, it must reduce the price, not on just the last unit sold, but on *all* units, whereas a competitive firm sells its larger output at the same price. Therefore, as the monopoly's sales increase, its *marginal* revenues will fall.

A table may make this clear. Let us suppose we have a monopoly that is faced with an average revenue or price schedule as in Table 27.1.

Quantity sold	Price	Total revenue	Marginal revenue
1	$20	$20	$20
2	19	38	18
3	18	54	16
4	17	68	14
5	16	80	12
6	15	90	10

As price, *AR*, falls, *MR* falls even more rapidly

TABLE 27.1

The graph of such a marginal revenue curve looks like Figure 27.4. Note that at an output of 6 units, *AR* (price) = $15; *MR* = $10.

What determines the shape of the marginal revenue curve? Obviously, the change in quantity demanded that will be brought about by a drop in price. In turn, this reflects—as we remember from our discussion in Chapter 23—the elasticity of demand which, in turn, hinges on our tastes and the availability of substitutes. The more inelastic the demand the faster the marginal revenue curve will fall. Note especially that the *MR* curve lies below the *AR* curve because the

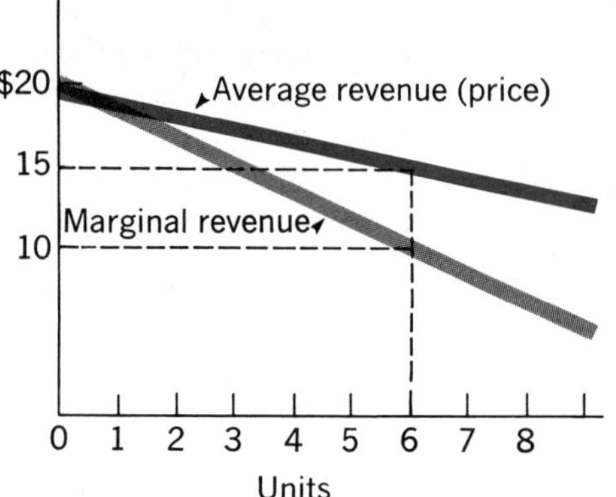

FIGURE 27.4 AVERAGE AND MARGINAL REVENUE FOR A MONOPOLIST

When we graph the monopolist's situation we can see how a sloping demand curve creates an *MR* curve different from the *AR* curve.

monopolist must lower prices on *all* units sold, not on just the marginal unit. Thus each additional item drags down the revenue of all output.

EQUILIBRIUM FOR THE MONOPOLY

The next step is obvious. We must superimpose the cost and the revenue profiles to determine the equilibrium position for the monopolist. We can see it in Figure 27.5.

What will be the equilibrium position? **The monopoly seeking to maximize profit is guided by exactly the same rule as the competitive firm: It adds factors so long as the marginal revenue they bring in is greater than their marginal cost.** Hence we look for the intersection of the *MC* and *MR* curves on Figure 27.5 to discover its optimum output and price.

We can see that optimum output is *OQ*. What about price? To discover this, we go up from the intersection of *MC* and *MR* to the *AR* (price) curve, and then over to the price axis. Optimum price obtainable for output *OQ* is *OA*.

As always, profit reflects the spread between average cost and average revenue. As we can see, this spread is *AZ*, the difference between average cost at output *OQ* and average revenue at that output. Total profit is therefore *AZ* times *OQ*, the rectangle we have shaded in.

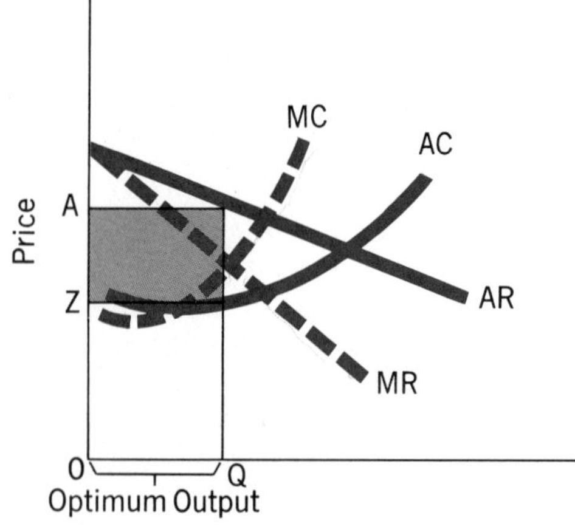

FIGURE 27.5 MONOPOLY EQUILIBRIUM

The intersection of *MR* and *MC* here tells us three things: (1) best output, *OQ;* (2) price at *OQ* = *OA;* and (3) average cost at *OQ* = *OZ.* Profit is the spread between price and cost (*AZ*) times the number of units sold (*OQ*).

MONOPOLY VS. COMPETITIVE PRICES

What is the difference between this price and that of a purely competitive market? We remember the formula for the equilibrium price of such a market: $MC = MR = AC =$ Price. In the monopoly situation, MC still equals MR (this is always the profit-maximizing guide), but price certainly does not equal AC. Whereas the competitive firm is forced to price its goods at the lowest point on its cost curve, the monopolist will sell at a price above cost. If this were the case in a competitive market, we know what the remedy would be. An influx of firms would move the supply curve to the right. As a result, prices would fall until excess profits had been wiped out. **But in a monopoly situation, by the very definition of a monopoly, there is no entry into the market. Hence the monopoly is able to restrict its output to the amount that will bring in the high profit it enjoys.** In our next chapter we shall discuss what we can do about monopoly profits.

OLIGOPOLY

Monopoly in its pure form is a rarity. Most big corporations operate in a market structure of oligopoly rather than monopoly. **In an oligopolistic market situation, a few sellers divide the bulk of the market.** Sometimes there is a long tail of smaller competitors who share the leftovers.

The aircraft industry is a typical oligopoly. In 1972 there were 141 manufacturers of planes or airframes in the United States, but the top four accounted for two-thirds of all sales. There were over 500 makers of soaps and detergents but the top four in that industry accounted for 62 percent of the market. In tires and tubes, 136 companies made up the industry, but the top four cornered three quarters of all sales. In automobiles, the top four manufacturers out of 165 had 93 percent of the market. (Since then, GM and Ford have elbowed American Motors and Chrysler aside, but have lost ground to foreign imports.)

OLIGOPOLY COST AND DEMAND

What does a typical oligopoly look like under the lens of price theory? On the cost side, it is much the same as a monopoly, with a dish-shaped cost curve that includes selling expense. There is, however, an essential difference between the demand curve of a monopolist and that of an oligopolist. The demand curve for a monopolist, since it comprises the entire demand for the commodity, has the familiar downward sloping shape. The demand curve for the oligopolist, although also downward sloping, does not have the clear-cut position of the monopolist's curve.

On the contrary, the essence of the oligopoly's demand curve is that it is uncertain; and moreover, that its position depends on what the oligopoly and its competitors do. Like the monopoly, the oligopoly is free to raise or lower its price. Unlike the monopoly, the oligopoly does not do so against a fixed demand curve. If one oligopoly raises its price, its competitors may meet competition by raising theirs. Or they may keep their prices unchanged. Or an oligopoly may eschew price raises or cuts and lure business away by altering the product or simply by changing its image in advertising. Each of these responses will have a different impact on the demand curves of all its competitors.

THE FIGHT FOR MARKET SHARES

This extreme indeterminacy brings its effects to bear on the character of oligopolistic competition. It makes price competition the least favored rather than the standard mode of competition. Instead of price wars, a fight for shares of the market becomes the normal mode of competition. This is, of course, totally unlike the other market structures we have examined. **No competitive firm fights for a share of the market, because its output is insignificant. A monopoly does not worry about its share, because it has the whole market for itself. But a fight for shares is the very heart of the oligopolistic struggle.**

Moreover, because each producer tries to be better than its main competitors in one way or another, the fight usually takes the form of winning customers to a carefully *differentiated* product. A Ford is made to be distinguishable from a Chevy; a Chevy from a Chrysler.

In the fight for market shares, price cutting becomes a much feared means of competing. Each oligopolist thinks he is better than the competition at designing or advertising or at serving customers. No one thinks he is better at price cutting. Moreover, each oligopolist fears that a price cut will be met by retaliatory price cuts, leaving market shares more or less unchanged and everyone worse off.

THE KINKED DEMAND CURVE

Thus we can see that it is not possible to arrive at neat models of oligopolistic behavior that predict how big companies will respond. But one among many models of behavior has been worked out and is worth familiarizing ourselves with, because it allows us to show graphically why oligopolists do not like to resort to price competition.

Suppose that you were the president of a large company that, along with three other very similar companies, sold roughly 80 percent of a certain commodity. Suppose also that a price had been established for your commodity. It yielded you and your competitors a reasonable profit, but you and your fellow officers were trying to increase that profit.

One possibility that would certainly be discussed would be to raise the price of your product and hope that your customers would continue to be loyal to you. Your company economists might point out that their analyses showed a very elastic demand for your product *if you raised your price, but your competitors did not.* That is, at the higher price, many of your "loyal" customers would switch to a competitive brand, so that your revenues would fall sharply and your profits decline.

Suppose, then, you took the other tack and gambled on that very elasticity of demand by cutting your prices. Would not other firms' customers switch to you and thereby raise your revenues and profits? This time your advisors might point out that if you cut your price, your competitors would almost certainly do the same, to prevent you from taking a portion of their market. As a result, with prices cut all around, you would probably find demand very much less elastic.

As Figure 27.6 shows, you are facing a "kinked" demand curve. In this situation, you might well be tempted to sit tight and do nothing, for a very in-

CONCENTRATION RATIOS: WHAT IS AN INDUSTRY?

Economists generally measure the degree of concentration by comparing the ratio of total sales or total assets of the top 4 or the top 8 companies to the total sales or assets of their industry. But immediately we encounter the difficult problem of defining *industry*. For example, the top 4 companies make 81 percent of a commodity for which there is really no adequate substitute: salt. Yet if we put salt into an industrial classification called "chemical preparations not elsewhere specified," the share of the top 4 companies falls to a paltry 23 percent of the output of that larger group of products.

Take another example. A housewife shopping for salad dressing is a consumer in an "industry" in which the top 4 producers sell 57 percent of the product. If she thinks of herself as a consumer browsing in an industry called "pickles and sauces," the top 4 salad dressing makers' share of output is only 29 percent. So, too, a farmer, looking for a tractor is buying in a "market" in which the top 4 companies make 72 percent of the total output: but if we think of a tractor as belonging to a larger industry called "farm machinery and equipment," the share of the top 4 is only 44 percent.

How *should* we draw lines around industries or products? One way is by measuring how much the sales of product A increase if the price of product B rises. Here is the idea of substitution (p. 350) applied to an important problem of economic policy. We call the measure of interproduct influence *the cross-elasticity of substitution*. If a rise in the price of A leads *many* customers to switch to B, there is at least a prima facie case for drawing the line of the industry to include both. Of course, the argument then arises as to how many consumers it takes to make "many" of them.

teresting thing happens to the marginal revenue curve that is derived from a kinked demand curve.

In Figure 27.7 we now get two marginal revenue curves: one applicable to the upper, elastic section of the demand curve; the other applicable to the lower, inelastic section. At the point of the kink, the marginal revenue curve is discontinuous, dropping vertically from the end of one slope to the beginning of the next. As a result, there is no single point of intersection of the marginal revenue and marginal cost curves. This means that an oligopoly's costs can change considerably before it is forced to alter its optimum volume of output or selling price.

The kinked demand curve is a graphic way of showing why oligopolies tend to shy away from price cutting. Their demand curve is elastic going up, inelastic going down—exactly the opposite of what they would like it to be.

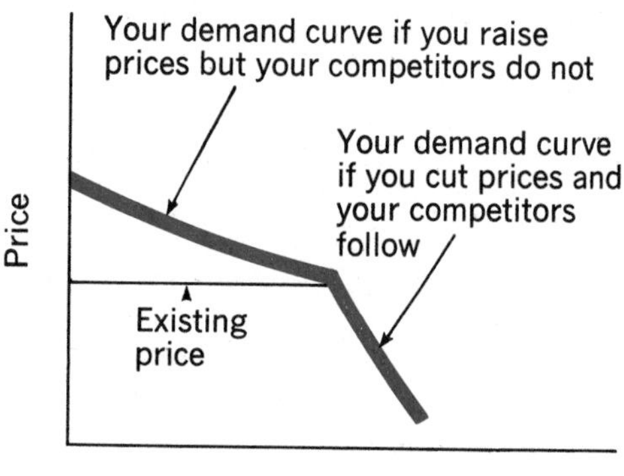

FIGURE 27.6 KINKED DEMAND CURVE

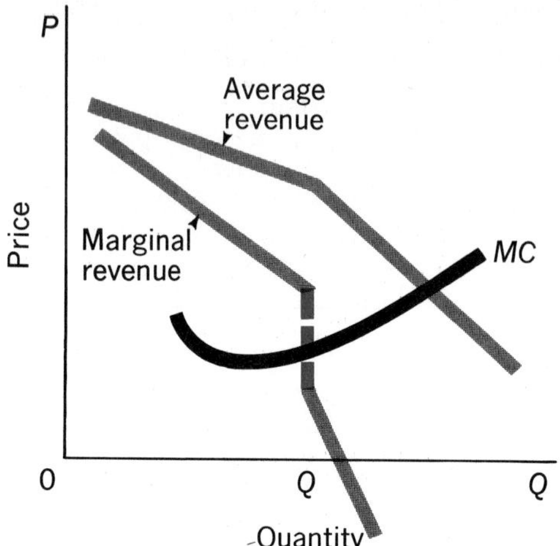

FIGURE 27.7 DISCONTINUOUS *MR* CURVE

The kinked *AR* curve gives rise to a strangely shaped *MR* curve with a vertical discontinuity. Hence costs can change considerably without altering optimum output, *OQ*.

GAME THEORY

A competitive firm has no strategy, because it has no options. It is forced to maximize its short-run profits, or it will soon be forced out of business. But the introduction of market imperfections opens the way for numerous strategies.

The problems of strategy have led to the development of game theory, a new approach to economic analysis. Suppose that we have two arch-rival firms who dominate an industry. The board of directors of Firm A meets one day to decide on price policy. The president opens with, "Trustworthy sources I am unable to reveal inform me that if we raise our prices, Firm B, our main competitor, will raise its prices. I calculate that Firm B and ourselves will each boost profits by $10 million as a consequence. Therefore, I recommend that we raise prices immediately."

At this point, the president is interrupted by the company treasurer, who is a graduate of the Harvard Business School. "I must recommend against this proposal on two counts. First, Firm B may well be baiting a trap for us. If we raise our prices, they will *not* raise theirs. We will thereupon lose a vast amount of business to B. I estimate that this will cause us a loss of $10 million, and that Firm B will make a profit of $20 million.

"Second, suppose that firm B *does* raise prices. Then, as profit-maximizing directors, we should certainly not raise ours; for in that case, by keeping our prices low, we will steal away a great deal of business from B, and we will make a profit of $20 million, while they lose $10 million."

"Well reasoned," says the chairman of the board. "It is not only clear that we should not raise prices, but I suggest that we inform Company B—discreetly, of course—that we *will* raise prices, as they suggest, in order to tempt them to do so. That will make our strategy foolproof."

In due course, this information is transmitted to Firm B, where a similar discussion takes place. Firm B resolves to "accept" Firm A's offer, but in fact not to raise prices at all. Result: neither firm raises prices, because neither trusts the other. Instead of each gaining $10 million, which would have been the result of a price rise by both firms, the two firms stand pat and accept the much smaller profits that accrue from *minimizing risk.*

The kinked demand curve helps explain why oligopoly prices are often so unvarying even without collusion among firms. It does not really explain how the existing price is arrived at; for once cost or demand conditions have changed enough to overcome oligopolistic inertia, a new kink will again appear around the changed price. The kinked curve thus shows what forces affect *changes* in the oligopolistic situation, rather than how supply and demand originally determine the going price.

COLLUSION AND PRICE LEADERSHIP

Another way of avoiding price competition has probably already occurred to the reader. It is for the dominant firms to agree not to undersell one another.

Such agreements have existed, undoubtedly do exist, and certainly minimize price cutting. They are, however, illegal under the antitrust laws. When unearthed, they lead to prosecution, fines, and even jail sentences. Therefore, outright collusion is probably only used as a last resort. Moreover, outright collusion is often not necessary because a kind of tacit collusion called *price leadership* can do just as well.

Price leadership exists when one company sets prices for the entire industry. For years, CPC International set the price of corn starch. From time to time, when the market situation seemed to warrant it, CPC would announce a change in price. Immediately thereafter its two or three big competitors and its host of small fry competition would change their prices.

Did CPC confer with its major competitors over lunch before changing its price? Probably not. Its competitors were glad to follow the leader, because all recognized that this was the best way to maximize profits for the industry as a whole.*

EXCESS CAPACITY AND PRICE WARS

Price leadership may lead to comfortable price relations within an industry, and it is a very common mode of pricing in oligopolistic markets. From time to time, however, the system breaks down. As long as business is good, firms gladly abide by a live and let live philosophy that permits competition to focus on the relatively safe means of product differentiation.

When business is poor, price leadership is not always accepted. This difference is generated by the fact that prices above the equilibrium for a competitive market lead to a condition known as *excess capacity*. Each seller within the industry is tempted to enlarge his production capacity to the size that the "administered" price indicates. The result, as Figure 27.8 shows, is excess capacity; that is, the ability to supply more output (Q_1) than the market will take at that price (Q_2). In desperation, the rivals turn to price cutting, and price wars are apt to break out until stability is once more achieved.

THE DRIVE FOR GROWTH

We have concentrated on the tactics of competition among oligopolies, but we must not leave this form of industrial market structure without paying heed

*How are price leaders "chosen"? The situation varies from one industry to another. Sometimes it is the biggest firm; sometimes the most aggressive. Sometimes leadership shifts around. There is no fixed pattern.

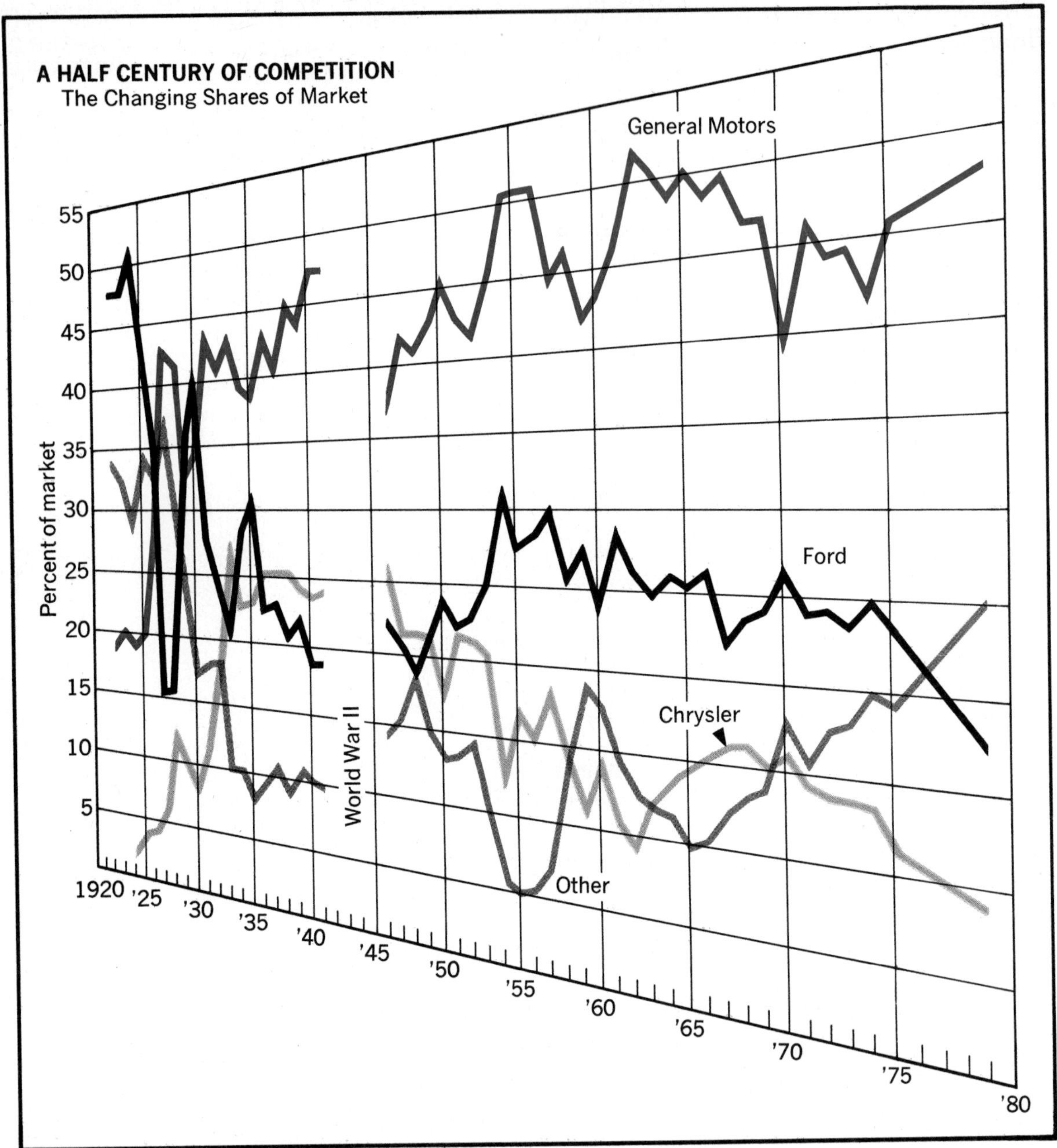

Source: Joe Argenziano for *Fortune* Magazine.

***Fortune* magazine writes: During the last half century, the auto industry has reached a few crucial turning points that affected the fortunes of competitors for many years. In the 1920s, Alfred Sloan of General Motors wrested the lead from Henry Ford. Then, when car production resumed after World War II, Henry Ford II restored his company to a strong No. 2 position. The "other category" now includes mainly imports plus American Motors, which holds less than 5 percent of the market. The chart is based on R. L. Polk & Company's compilation of new-car registration figures.**

The ability of oligopolies to establish prices above equilibrium or clearing prices results in excess capacity. This is just like the surplus in Figure 22.4.

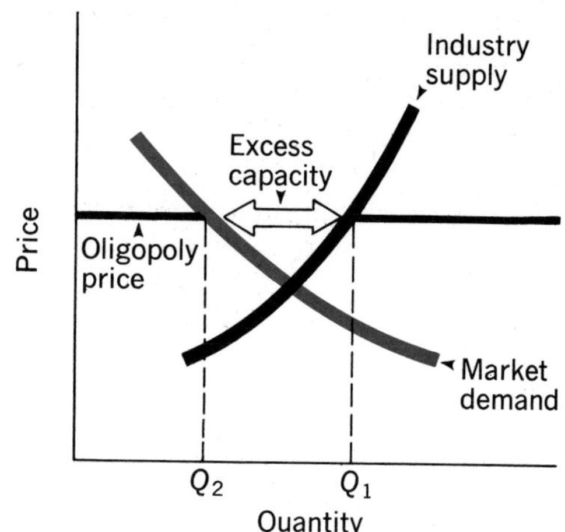

FIGURE 27.8 EXCESS CAPACITY

to a central aspect of oligopolistic life. This aspect is the drive for growth that characterizes virtually all oligopolistic firms.

To be sure, all firms in a market system seek to grow. But small competitive firms are hampered in their efforts because their rising marginal cost curves do not permit a single plant or business to expand very far. Monopolies, as we have seen, are few; and their growth, by definition, is limited to expansion of their industries. The growth situation is very different for an oligopoly. To begin with, because an oligopoly is a large firm, it normally has many plants and therefore tends to enjoy economies of scale or long-run unit cost curves that are horizontal rather than upward-climbing. Thus there is no cost impediment to growth, at least not for a long time.*

Second, the typical oligopolist is not as highly concentrated as the auto or tire manufacturers. The share of the industry served by the top 4 companies is frequently less than 50 percent, and the biggest single company often serves only about a quarter or less of the business. Thus the field for expansion is very great, and the drive to widen one's share correspondingly powerful. Growth may be the dream of the small business in a competitive industry, but it is the stuff of daily life for the oligopolist.

GROWTH WITHIN MARKETS

How is growth achieved? Usually by plowing back profits into more capital equipment or by buying up the ready-made plant and equipment of smaller companies in the field. It is virtually impossible to expand sales without an in-

*We recall from page 373 that long-run cost curves turned up at high levels of output. This is because they referred to economies and eventually diseconomies of scale for a *given plant.* It is indeed likely that unit costs increase in a given plant, because eventually it becomes so large that it is no longer convenient to administer.

An oligopoly or a monopoly may, however, decide to build a new plant rather than to push an existing one beyond its economical size. Do big oligopolistic firms that spread production among several plants also experience rising unit costs? We really do not know. It may be that the new technology of information retrieval has so increased the efficiency of management that multiplant firms *never* experience rising unit costs. For all practical purposes their long-run cost curves are horizontal or perhaps even falling.

crease in capital assets, and therefore we find all successful oligopolies steadily building up the value of their capital.

For a considerable period a successful oligopoly can increase its share of the market in this way. But at a certain point, further growth within the market becomes difficult. The cost of gaining additional business rises, as indifferent customers are wooed and other customers remain loyal to competitive brands. Or the specter of an antitrust suit may loom because a company threatens, by virtue of its growth, to monopolize a market.

MNCs AND CONGLOMERATES

Two responses are open to the successful oligopoly. First, it may transfer its fight for market shares from a national to an international basis. This is the basic thrust behind the growth of the multinational corporations (MNCs), to which we devote "An Extra Word" following Chapter 28.

Or the oligopolist may decide to become a conglomerate; that is, to acquire capital in other industries. By diversifying its sales, it not only escapes the eye of the justice department antitrust lawyers, but it also avoids putting all its eggs in one basket.

The rise of the conglomerate helps explain a curious and seemingly contradictory state of affairs that we noticed in Chapter 5. There we saw that the share of total assets coming under the control of giant companies—virtually all of them oligopolists—had risen dramatically, so that the top 100 industrial companies in 1970 owned about 50 percent of all the assets of all manufacturing companies, about the same share as the top 200 companies had owned in 1948. We also noted that the concentration of sales did not parallel that of assets. Actually, a study of the nation's markets shows no overall drift toward a more highly concentrated pattern *within* markets.

Now we can understand the dynamics of this phenomenon. The concentration of assets is partly explained by the continued growth of some companies within their industries, and by the very rapid rise of conglomerates, often through mergers. Between 1951 and 1960 one-fifth of the biggest companies disappeared, absorbed within the remaining four-fifths! At the same time, the thrust overseas and the diversification of growth have allowed oligopolies to grow without causing marked changes in their dominance within their local markets.

MONOPOLISTIC COMPETITION

We shall return to the world of oligopolies in our next chapter, but we must first continue our survey of competition in the real world. For oligopoly, although perhaps the most significant departure from the ideal of pure competition, is not the most common departure. Once we pass from the manufacturing to the retail or service sectors where competition is still intense and characterized by numerous small units, we encounter a new kind of market situation, equally strange to the pages of a text on pure competition. **This is a situation in which there are many firms, with relatively easy entrance and exit, but where each firm sells a product slightly differentiated from that of every other.** Here is the world of the average store or the small competitive manufacturer of a brand-name product—

indeed, of all sellers who can identify their products for the public and who must face the competition of many other makers of similar but not exactly identical products.

Economists call this market situation tinged by monopoly imperfect competition or monopolistic competition. How does it differ from pure competition? Once again, there is no difference on the cost side. That is the same for both a perfectly competitive and an imperfectly competitive firm, except for the presence of selling costs in imperfect competition. The difference, again, comes in the nature of the demand curve.

We recall that the special attribute of the demand curve facing a firm in a purely competitive situation is its horizontal character. By way of contrast, **in a market of imperfect competition, the demand curve facing each seller slopes gently downward** because one seller's good or service is not exactly like that of competitors, and because the seller therefore has some ability to raise price without losing all his business.

EQUILIBRIUM IN MONOPOLISTIC COMPETITION

What is the equilibrium position of such an imperfectly competitive firm—say a dress manufacturer? In Figure 27.9 on the left, an imperfect competitor is obviously making substantial profits. Note that the firm's best position where $MR = MC$ is *exactly* like that of any firm, monopolies included.

But our firm is not a monopolist and its profits are therefore not immune to erasure by entry into its field. In Figure 27.9 we show the same firm after *other entrepreneurs have moved into the industry* (with additional similar, although not identical, products) and thereby have taken away some of our firm's market and *moved its demand curve to the left.*

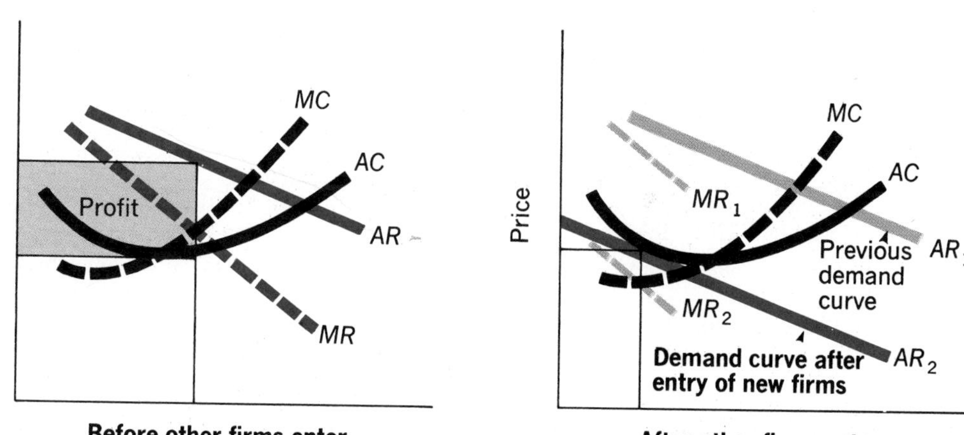

FIGURE 27.9 MONOPOLISTIC COMPETITION

Here we can see that initial equilibrium for a small dress manufacturer looks exactly the same as equilibrium for A.T.&T. In both cases *MC* and *MR* determine output. But unlike the case for A.T.&T., the dress manufacturer experiences the competition of entry. His demand curve AR_1 moves to the left to AR_2. Again, he seeks $MC = MR$, but now there is no spread between *AC* and *AR*. He has no profit and no advantage from his monopolistic *MR* curve.

Note that our final position for the marginal dress firm has no more profit than that of a purely competitive seller because $AC = AR$. On the other hand, because its demand curve slopes, the equilibrium point cannot be at the lowest point on the average cost curve, nor will output have reached optimum size. (Of course, intramarginal firms can be more profitable than the marginal case we have graphed.)

This outcome clearly dissipates economic well-being. The fact that firms are forced to operate to the left of the optimums on their cost curves means that they have not been able to combine factors to yield their greatest efficiency. This failure penalizes factors, once when they are paid too little because their potential marginal productivity has not been reached, and again as consumers when they are forced to pay too much for products that have not been produced at lowest possible cost. In addition, wastage is incurred because the attempt to differentiate products leads in many instances to too many small units; for example, four gas stations at one intersection.

Inefficient though it may be, monopolistic competition yields no profit for the marginal firm in an industry. The entrepreneur therefore feels fully as hard-pressed as would the producer of an undifferentiated commodity. The difference is that a monopolistic competitive businessperson has the possibility of *further differentiating* a product, hoping thereby to tilt the demand curve in a more inelastic position. In turn, this might permit a slight price rise, to squeeze out a tiny "pure monopoly" profit. The result is that monopolistic competition fosters a tremendous variety of goods—the ladies garment industry being a prime example.

SOCIAL CONSEQUENCES

Are monopolies as evil as their reputations? Are oligopolies a bad thing? Are monopolistically competitive industries simply wasteful?

These are questions of major importance, but they take us outside the firm to a public point of view. We shall take up these issues in our next chapter.

KEY CONCEPTS

LOOKING BACK

Markets vs. motivation

Price makers vs. price takers

1. Imperfect competition—monopoly, oligopoly, and imperfect competition—refers to different kinds of market structure than pure competition; it does *not* refer to different motivations. Competitive firms have no option but to take existing prices. Firms in imperfect competition can make prices—although not entirely as they would like.

Monopoly demand curves are like those of competitive industry; advertising may improve them

2. Monopolies are firms that cater to all the demand of a given market. They face the same demand curve as a competitive industry. By advertising, a monopolist hopes to move his demand curve out and to make it more inelastic.

$MR < AR$ for a monopolist

3. Because a monopoly faces a sloping demand curve, its marginal revenue curve is not horizontal, but falling. This is because it must cut price to increase sales. For a competitive firm $MR = AR$; for a monopoly, $MR < AR$.

Monopoly equilibrium:
MR* = *MC
***AR* > *AC* = profit**

4. Monopoly equilibrium is determined by the intersection of *MR* and *MC*. This gives optimum output. Optimum output indicates selling price. Profit is determined by the spread between selling price and average cost at point of optimum output. This profit is not subject to erosion by entry because by definition our firm is the only one—a monopoly.

An oligopoly has a kinked demand curve reflecting competitors' reactions

5. Oligopoly is much more frequent than monopoly. It is a market structure in which a few firms dominate the market. An oligopolist's demand curve is likely to be kinked. The kink simply tells us that each firm's price policy invites a response, so that if it raises prices, competitors won't, whereas if it cuts them, they will.

The fight for market shares, diversification and multinationals

6. Oligopolies often use price leadership to avoid price competition. The fight for market shares is the most conspicuous feature of their strategies. To avoid undue concentration, oligopolies may diversify or go multinational.

Monopolistic competition: entry removes monopoly profits

7. Monopolistic competition refers to market situations in which each firm has a monopoly (a sloping demand curve), but where entry is easy. The result is that demand is pushed to the left and equilibrium is reached without any monopoly profit.

ECONOMIC VOCABULARY

Price takers vs. price makers 406
Monopoly 406
Oligopoly 411
Kinked demand curve 412
Price leadership 415
Market shares 412
Excess capacity 415
Conglomerates 418
Monopolistic competition 418
Differentiated product 418

QUESTIONS

1. How would you define a monopoly? Are monopolies necessarily large? What constraints does a demand curve put on the behavior of a monopoly?
2. Suppose that you were the only seller of a certain kind of machinery in the nation. Suppose further that you discovered that your demand curve looked like this:

Price	$100	$90	$80	$70
Quantity of machines sold	1	2	3	4

   What is the average revenue at each price? What is the marginal revenue at each price? Draw a diagram showing the marginal and average revenues.
3. Now superimpose on this diagram a hypothetical cost profile for your business. Where is the point of equilibrium for the monopolist? Is this the same, in terms of *MC* and *MR*, as the point for the competitive firm? Now show the equilibrium output and price.
4. Does the equilibrium output of the monopolist yield a profit? What are the relevant costs for figuring profit, average cost per unit, or marginal cost? Show on your diagram the difference between average cost and selling price.

5. Why will a monopolist's selling price not be pushed to the lowest point on the cost curve?
6. What is the difference between monopoly and oligopoly? Between oligopoly and pure competition? Between pure competition and monopolistic (or imperfect) competition? Between the latter and oligopoly? Can these differences be expressed in demand curves?
7. What is a differentiated commodity? Give examples. Draw the demand curve for a farmer selling wheat and that for a toy manufacturer selling a special kind of doll. What will happen if the doll manufacturer makes a large profit? What will the dollmaker's final point of equilibrium look like if there are many competitors?
8. Is excess capacity possible in a truly competitive industry? A monopoly? Why in an oligopoly?

AN EXTRA WORD ABOUT

THE BIGGEST COMPANY ON EARTH

BY N. R. KLEINFIELD

It grows even faster than the United States. Every working day, its installers plug in 100,000 more telephones, its customers moving so often that it must put in seven to gain one. Its long limbs connect 135 million phones (48,000 of them in cars and trucks) and by the year 2000 it expects to have a hundred million more.

Every day, a torrent of 493 million calls bolts through its trunks. Long-distance talking, if the projections of its planners are right, will swell by 8 percent a year for the next two decades, overseas chatter, by 21 percent.

Its revenues represent 1.8 percent of the gross national product, and are growing at twice the rate of the G.N.P. Its assets—all its phones and spaghetti strings of cable, its clicking electronic switching systems and horn-like microwave towers—are valued at $103 billion. Planners expect assets to balloon to $400 billion by 2000. It boasts more employees than the number who served with United States forces in Europe during World War II. Its stock has attracted the dollars of so many shareholders—a swarm of three million—that 200 of them die every day.

Making a product that can't be bought and thriving on a commodity that can't be seen, the American Telephone and Telegraph Company keeps rolling along. Many people have tried to drop a wet blanket over it. Legislators and lawyers have attempted to dismantle it for decades (it has 40 separate antitrust suits pending against it right now), but its pulse beats strong. It is a company that has never suffered a loss for any financial quarter.

In the more than 100 years of its existence, the sprawling Bell System has extended its service to virtually every American who desires it, at a price almost every American can afford.

"Phones are more pervasive than bathtubs," one analyst says.

The nation seems essentially telephone-saturated—there are even phone booths in the middle of forests to oblige talkative hunters—but call volumes still spiral upward, at a far faster rate than population growth.

In fact, having a phone is no longer enough. People want more. Bell promises they are going to get it.

As the nation hurtles into the years of the "information society," Bell people say, all manner of ingenious capabilities will be common. The phone will automatically put through a wake-up call to you in the morning. It will electronically snap on the lights and air-conditioner (or heat) shortly before you saunter through your office door. When you take off at the end of the day, the phone will lock up. Dash off a staff memo at your desk and it will be automatically transmitted to receiving devices attached to phones throughout your company.

On your lunch hour, you'll call home and get the clothes washer going. Later on, you'll have to momentarily interrupt a meeting to call the drier. An hour before you wrap up for the day, you'll phone the microwave oven to start the Yankee pot roast.

Pull into the gas station and run your credit card through a device. The gadget will dial a number over the phone lines to a data base that validates your card. The pump unlocks. You put in your 12 gallons of unleaded and are charged $50.

Other things. You will vote by phone. Electric and gas companies will read meters over the phone. And the mail will come by phone; no more postman with pouch slung over his shoulder.

Still other things. "I'll want to repair my 1956 Granada," says Howard Anderson, president of the Yankee Group, a consulting group, "I'll call the specifics into a data bank and out will pour instructions on how to do it. I'll be out there in my driveway, flat on my back, all greasy, and I'll be shouting into my telephone, 'Now I've taken off the wheel, what do I do next?' And the phone will respond, 'Now take out the bearings.' At night, I'll be doing my income taxes and there will be a computer program I can call to explain the horrendous mess to me. All of this from A.T. & T."

DIAL THE LETTERS OF THE NAME

There might be a visual display on everybody's phone that prints out the number of the calling party. (Oh, no, it's Aunt Corky again! Let it ring. Better yet, punch a button that causes the phone to deliver a recorded message reporting that you have, on short notice, been sent to prison.)

Matters may be arranged so that there will be no phone books and no directory assistance operators. You want a person's number? Dial the letters of the name and the number flashes on your display.

The phone may be wedded to the TV set, or else to a wall screen (which, when not in use, can display an electronic picture of, say, ships on a shimmering ocean). That way, you can do your shopping at home by calling up mops and looking them over on your screen. Call up the Sears catalogue on the phone and order away. Do your banking by phone. You want to read the newspaper? Dial it up on the phone.

HOW BIG?

It seems inevitable to many Bell students, though, that the biggest company on earth must at some point finally address the question of how big is too big. If A.T. & T. continues its galloping growth, by the year 2000 it may be 5 percent of the G.N.P. Bell watchers figure the company might have revenues then of a staggering $200 billion, earnings of $20 billion. Some shrewd Bell watchers think it is just a matter of time before its Western Electric manufacturing arm gets taken away.

Robert La Blanc, vice chairman of Continental Telephone, says: "There's a social question in my mind whether any company can be 5 percent of the G.N.P. Man, is that big! I think they've done a pretty good job discharging their social responsibilities, as big as they are now. I'd rather have them handle electronic mail than the Post Office. But there's a worry whether this country will let something get as big as the phone company is going to get."

STOCK RARELY DOES POORLY

As an investment, A.T. & T. has almost always been a secure one, though never a particularly wondrous one. The value of the stock today is slightly more than double what it was in 1900, while the cost of living has more than quintupled. But if the stock rarely outperforms the market, it rarely does poorly during times when the market sinks. So brokers figure that its flock of shareholders—not just its widows and orphans, but its bachelors and young marrieds—will probably continue to place their savings and hopes in Mother Bell.

A.T. & T. has survived wars, depression, floods, earthquakes, scandal, lawsuits, competition, bad jokes and squirrels that gnaw its cable. And, as Mr. Brown says, "If all the problems we face today are solved by the end of my term" as chairman, "I think it is accurate to say that just as many new ones will arise to replace them." New solutions, he adds, will run them down.

"The Bell System is like the sea," one veteran observer said late one afternoon. "Sometimes it is very quiet and peaceful. It's soothing to admire it. Other times it gets angry and rages up and sometimes wreaks havoc. And then it retreats again. We pollute it and we build barriers to it, but we can't live without it, and I'm not sure we can really control it. It is so big that no one can ever truly understand its immensity. No matter what else happens, it is always there. It is just always there."

Chapter 28 THE COST OF MARKET IMPERFECTION

A LOOK AHEAD

We leave the premises of the firm for the perspective of the public. This chapter is devoted to an examination of the social cost of market imperfection and the various ways in which that cost can be reduced.

There is no single analytical problem addressed here. Instead, the central theme is power—economic power in the marketplace. As we shall see, the problem of power is neither so easy to define, nor to offset, as we sometimes tend to believe. The purpose of the chapter is to make you aware of the complexity of a public policy issue of great importance.

Our previous chapter was devoted to the problem of market imperfection from the firm's point of view: How should a monopoly price its products to maximize income? What is an oligopolist's best strategy? What can a monopolistically competitive firm do to hang onto its minuscule market advantage?

Now we address ourselves to the issue of market imperfection from the public's point of view. And here the place to begin is with a simple question: Why oppose monopoly or any other form of market imperfection? What difference does it make?

CONSUMER SOVEREIGNTY

In theory, the answer is very clear. In a purely competitive market, the consumer is king. Indeed, the rationale of such a market is often described as *consumer sovereignty.*

The term means two things. First, in a purely competitive market the consumer determines the allocation of resources by virtue of his or her demand. Second, the consumer enjoys goods that are sold as cheaply and produced as abundantly as possible. As we have seen, in a purely competitive market there exist no profits (except transitory intramarginal rents). Each firm is producing the goods that consumers want, in the largest quantity and at the lowest cost possible, given its cost curves.

In an imperfectly competitive market the consumer loses much of this sovereignty. Firms have *strategies,* including the strategy of influencing consumer demand. Profits are not competed away, so consumers' surplus is transferred to producers. Output is not maximized but is reduced by whatever amounts results from higher-than-competitive prices.

EFFECT OF ADVERTISING

No one contests these general conclusions. How valid are they, however, in actuality? Here the problem becomes muddier.

Take the question of consumer demand. In 1867 we spent an estimated $50 million to persuade consumers to buy products. In 1900 advertising expenditures were $500 million. In 1978 they were $38 *billion*—roughly two-thirds as much as we spend on primary and secondary education. Indeed, advertising expenditures can be considered as a vast campaign to educate individuals to be good consumers.

To what extent does advertising infringe on consumer sovereignty? The question is perplexing. For one thing, it is no longer possible to think of consumers as having "natural" tastes, once we go beyond a subsistence economy. For that reason, much advertising has a genuine informational purpose. People do have to be made aware that it is possible (and imaginable) for, say, a factory worker to take a vacation by airplane rather than in the family car.

Moreover, numerous efforts to create tastes have failed. In the mid-1950s the Ford Motor Company poured a quarter of a billion dollars into a new car, the Edsel, and performed prodigies of advertising to make the American public like it. The public did not, and the car had to be discontinued. So, too, consumers spontaneously decided to buy small sports cars, beginning in the 1950s; and after valiant efforts to turn the tide, the major American manufacturers have capitulated and admitted that American car buyers do want small cars.

Yet it is obvious that all advertising is not informational and that consumers' tastes are manipulated to a considerable (although not clearly measurable) degree. We are mainly creatures of brand preference not because we have sampled all the choices and made up our minds but as a result of advertising exposure. It is difficult to contemplate the battles of aspirin, soap (up to 10 percent of the price of soap is selling expense), cars, and cigarettes without recognizing that much of this represents a waste of resources, including the very scarce resource of talent, which is largely devoted to nullifying the talent in a different advertising agency.

IS PRODUCT DIFFERENTIATION A GOOD THING?

Product differentiation is also an ambiguous case. Few would deny that the proliferation of models is often carried to the point of absurdity—and more important, to the point of substantial economic waste.

Yet, as with advertising, the question is where to draw the line. Where product differentiation results in variations in the actual product and not merely in its image, one must ask whether an affluent society should aim to produce the largest possible quantity of a standardized product at the least possible cost or to offer an array of differing products that please our palates, admittedly at somewhat higher cost. Few consumers in a rich society would prefer an inexpensive uniform to more expensive, individualized clothes. From this point of view, even the wasteful parade of car styles has a certain rationale.

Thus, as with advertising, *some* production differentiation plays a useful and utility-increasing function. The question is how much? It is difficult to form a purely objective judgment, for even if the amount of "useless" product differentiation is relatively small, its impact on the public taste may be disproportionately large. The problem is perhaps particularly acute insofar as much of our taste for style seems to be the product of the deliberate advertising efforts of manufacturers. No doubt there is a real aesthetic pleasure in variety, although one doubts that it would take the form of a yearning for "this year's model" without a good deal of external stimulation. Product differentiation thus becomes in part an effort to maximize the public's utilities. It is also in part an effort to create those "utilities" in order to maximize the producers' profits.

MONOPOLY AND INEFFICIENCY

What about the second main attribute of consumer sovereignty—the ability to buy goods as cheaply as possible? To what extent does oligopoly introduce inefficiency into the system?

Once again the evidence in fact is murkier than in theory. For one thing, we tend to leap to the conclusion that a competitive firm, which has managed to combine its factors as profitably as possible, has also reached the frontiers of technological efficiency. Is this really so? Suppose that the competitive firm cannot afford the equipment that might lead to economies of large-scale production. Suppose it cannot afford large expenditure on research and development. Suppose that its workers suffer from low morale and therefore do not produce as much as they might.

These are not wild suppositions. There is good evidence that many large firms are more efficient, in terms of productivity per man-hour, than small firms, although of course some large, monopolistic firms tolerate highly inefficient practices simply because of the lack of competition. **Big businesses generate higher rates of technical progress than small, competitive firms, and may well justify their short-run monopoly profits by long-run technical progress.***

Once again, however, we must consider the other side. **Profits in monopolistic industries as a whole are 50 to 100 percent higher than those in competitive industries. In certain fields, such as prescription medicines, there is evidence that consumers are sometimes badly exploited.** Brand name aspirins, for example, sell for up to three times the cost of non-brand versions of the same product. Certain medicines, such as antibiotics and the like, have enjoyed enormous profits—which is to say, have forced consumers to pay far more than they would have had to pay were the rate of profit a competitive one.

To turn the coin over once more, a further complication is introduced by virtue of the fact that oligopolies have often provided more agreeable working conditions, more handsome offices, and safer plants than have small competitive firms. Thus some of the loss of consumers' well-being is regained in the form of lessened disutilities of work. Needless to say, this is not solely the result of a kindlier attitude on the part of big producers but reflects their sheltered position against the harsh pressures of competition. Nonetheless, the gains in work conditions and morale are real and must be counted in the balance.

BUSINESS AND POWER

Thus the economic balance sheet is by no means simple to draw up. The advantages are not all on one side, the disadvantages on the other. Although we take the model of pure competition as a baseline for efficiency and economic "virtue," we find in fact that the world is more complicated than that.

There is, however, one final consideration. It concerns power. Economists do not speak much about power because in the competitive situation which is taken as the norm, power disappears. At the core of the idea of consumer sovereignty is the idea that the firm does not have power, that business cannot impose its will either on those it hires or on those it serves.

Clearly this is not true in the real world of imperfect competition. That is why the issue of how to control power becomes of increasing consequence—not just in the sphere of government, where it has always been a central concern of philosophers and political thinkers, but in the private spheres of business and labor. The question is what to do about it? Here are some of the answers.

*The evidence is not clear that leading technical advances *arise* mainly in the laboratories of big business. The solo inventor, tinkerer, and inspired genius continue to make significant contributions. (See Jewkes, Sawers, and Stillerman, *The Sources of Invention* (1960) for a fascinating discussion of this.) Wherever they originate, however, technical advances are usually put into the economic mainstream through big companies that buy the rights to these inventions. Small companies simply cannot afford to do so.

A CONSERVATIVE VIEW

The first suggestion is most prominently associated with the name of Nobel laureate Milton Friedman. Professor Friedman is a philosophic conservative whose response to the question of what a corporation should do to discharge its social responsibility is very simple: Make money.

The function of a business organization in society, argues Friedman, is to serve as an efficient agent of production, not as a locus of social improvement. It serves that productive function best by striving after profit—conforming, while doing so, to the basic rules and legal norms of society. It is not up to business to "do good"; and it is up to government to prevent it from doing bad.

Moreover, says Friedman, as soon as a businessman tries to apply any rules other than moneymaking, he takes into his own hands powers that rightfully belong to others, such as political authorities. Friedman would even forbid corporations to give money to charities or universities. Their business, their responsibility to society, he insists, is *production.* Let the dividend-receivers give away the money the corporations pay them, but do not let corporations become the active social welfare agencies of society.

THE CORPORATION AS SOCIAL ARBITER

Friedman's position has a number of weaknesses, especially in its assumption that stockholders' claims to corporate profits are more valid than are the claims of a corporation's management and workers. This view dismisses the fact that management and workers have done more to create those profits than stockholders have done.

It is interesting to note that few corporate heads espouse Friedman's position. They take the view that the corporation, by virtue of its immense size and strength, has power thrust upon it, whether it wishes to have it or not. The solution to this problem, as these men see it, is for corporate executives to act "professionally" in using this power, doing their best to judge fairly among the claims of the many groups to whom they are responsible: labor, stockholders, customers, and the public at large.

There is no doubt that many top corporate executives think of themselves as the referees among contending groups, and no doubt many of them use caution and forethought in exercising the power of decision. But the weaknesses of this argument are also not difficult to see. There are no criteria for qualifying as a responsible corporate executive (see p. 430). Nor is there any clear guideline, even for the most scrupulous executive, defining the correct manner in which to exercise responsibility. Should an executive's concern for the prevention of pollution take precedence over concern for turning in a good profit statement at the end of the year? Or for giving wage increases? Or for reducing the price of the product? Is the company's contribution to charity or education supposed to represent the executive's preferences or those of customers or workers? Has Xerox a right to help the cause of public broadcasting; the makers of firearms to help support the National Rifle Association?

These questions begin to indicate the complexity of the issue of social responsibility and the problems implicit in allowing important *social* decisions to be made by private individuals who are not publicly accountable for their actions.

PORTRAIT OF A CHIEF EXECUTIVE

A capsule profile of the chief executives of the biggest 500 industrial corporations

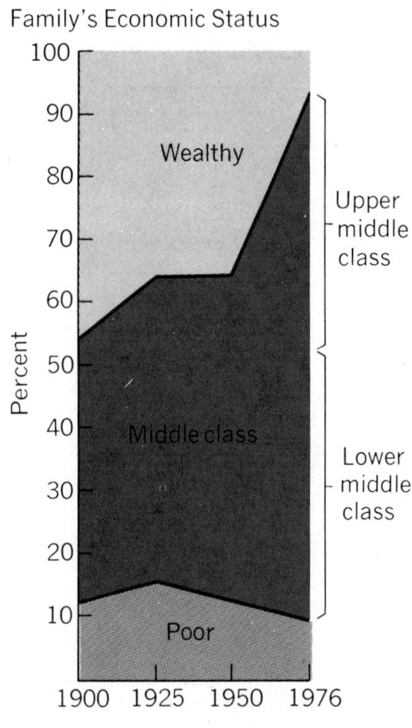

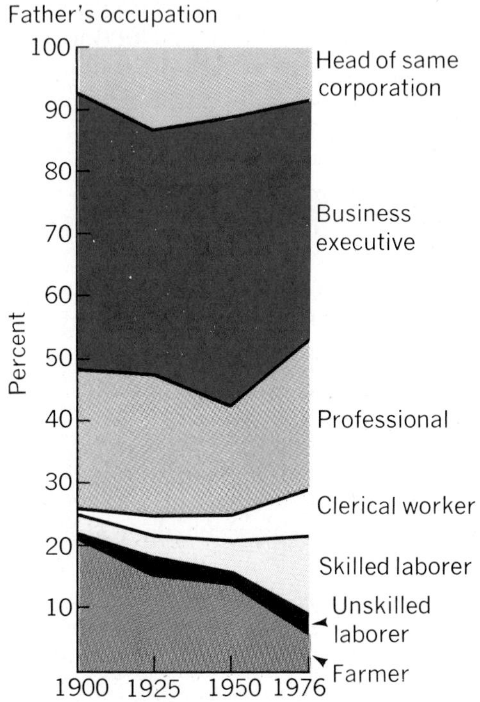

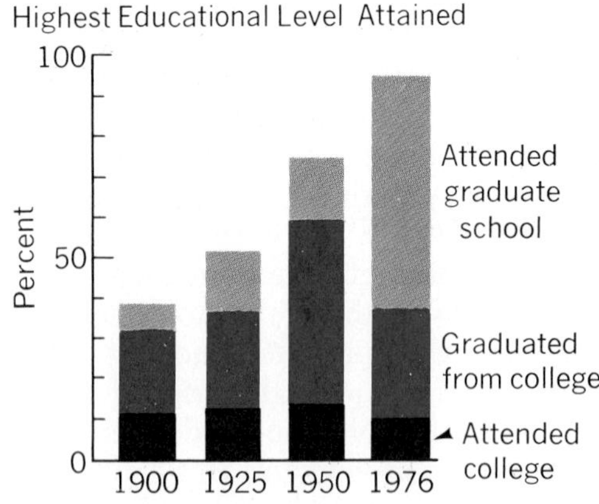

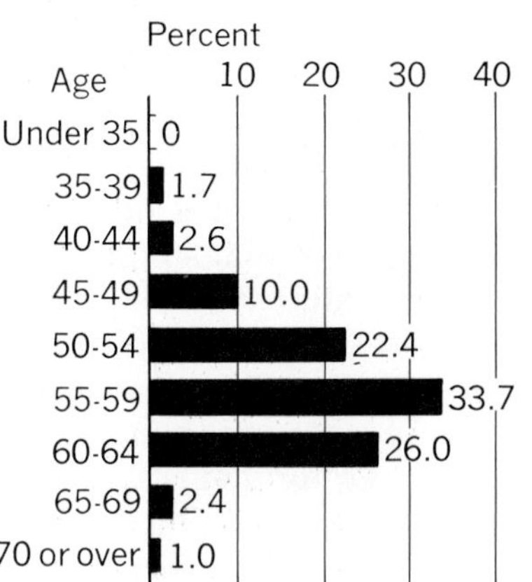

DISSOLUTION OF MONOPOLY

A third approach to the problem of responsibility takes yet another tack. It suggests that the power of big business be curbed by dividing large corporations into several much smaller units. A number of studies have shown that the largest *plant* size needed for industrial efficiency is far smaller (in terms of financial assets) than the giant firms typical of the *Fortune* list of the top 500 industrial corporations (or for that matter of the next 500). Hence a number of economists have suggested that a very strict application of antitrust legislation should be applied, not only to prohibit mergers but to separate a huge enterprise such as General Motors into its natural constituent units: a Buick Company, an Oldsmobile Company, a Chevrolet Company, and so on.

One major problem stands in the way of this frontal attack on corporate power. It is that size leads to good effects as well as bad ones. As John Kenneth Galbraith has wittily remarked, "The showpieces [of the economy] are, with rare exceptions, the industries which are dominated by a handful of large firms. The foreign visitor, brought to the United States . . . visits the same firms as do the attorneys of the Department of Justice in their search for monopoly."

The other side of that coin is that small competitive industry is typically beset by low research and development programs, antilabor practices, and a general absence of the kinds of amenities that we associate with big business. As we shall later see, in some cases more competition might actually do more harm than good.

ANTITRUST

Only a few decades ago, there was virtually unanimous agreement among economists that a strict application of antitrust laws was one of the most effective remedies for the problems of oligopoly. Today this zeal is on the wane, although, as we shall see, it is much too early to write *finis* to antitrust prosecutions designed to break big companies into little ones.

Why has the zeal for antitrust declined? There are a number of reasons. One is that economists have come to recognize that an industry with one or two giant firms and a tail of small firms does not operate very differently—if at all—than does an industry with five or six leading members. Whether concentration ratios give the top four firms 30 percent or 60 percent of an industry does not seem to affect their oligopolistic decision-making. Product differentiation continues. The struggle for market shares goes on. Price leadership persists. Even the breakup of the aluminum industry from a near-monopoly under the domination of Alcoa to an industry in which four firms have big shares of the market does not appear to have changed aluminum prices or aluminum pricing policies.

Economists have also begun to pay more attention to a matter we have stressed several times in our text. This is the fact that industries dominated by big firms have the ability to create technical advances. Competitive firms, as we have seen, may be more efficient at any moment, selling their output at lower prices, but over time, many competitive industries have remained technologically static, whereas the oligopolistic industries—with some exceptions—have been innovators.

A third consideration is the tremendous time lag involved in major antitrust cases. A big antitrust case may go on for twenty or thirty years before it is finally resolved. One may ask whether the eventual savings are worth the huge legal costs.

Moreover, many antitrust actions seem to make little economic sense. For example, antitrust laws prohibit the merger of two firms whose combined assets would be less than those of the industry leader, but the courts do nothing to break up the leader itself. This situation exists because antitrust is against "combination" on principle, but not against bigness, as such. Yet the price policies of one big business often restrain trade as much as if two former competitors were combined.

Thus a great deal of the missionary zeal has ebbed from the antitrust cause. Large cases are still brought. Suits are pending against IBM and A.T.&T., but it is no longer clear what the economic benefits of these suits will be, even if successful.

Defenders of antitrust legislation do not seriously question the above views. It is not really imaginable that General Motors, for example, will ever be broken into a thousand firms each with a capitalization of $40 million, even though GM is big enough to yield that many pieces. In all likelihood, trust busting GM would result in the formation of three or four giant firms, each worth $10 billion or so and each still possessing enormous market power.

But the defenders of antitrust do not want to give up the implicit threat that antitrust prosecution carries. The ghost of Senator Sherman, the sponsor of the original antitrust legislation, sits on the board of directors of all large firms, according to George Stigler, an eminent economist. There the ghost exercises a cautionary influence against actions that might be taken if there were no threat of antitrust action. The ghost thereby serves to prevent the rise of supergiant firms whose political and social power might be considered inimical to our democracy, if not injurious to our economy.

REGULATION

Regulation has been a long-standing American response to the problem of corporate power. Regulation has sought to influence or prohibit corporate actions in many fields: pricing, advertising, designing products, dealing with unions or minority groups, and still other areas. Given the variety of ways in which corporations are regulated, it is hardly surprising that the effectiveness of the regulatory process is very uneven. Yet we can discern two general attributes that affect most regulatory agencies.

First, economic events tend to change faster than the regulations governing them. City building codes that were perfectly appropriate when adopted become obsolete and then retard the use of new techniques and materials that would be more efficient and just as safe. Why are not regulations kept abreast of events? Partly because the political process is simply slower than the economic process, partly because any regulation soon creates its own defenders. Vested interests, formed around existing codes, fight to prevent changes in the regulations. The plumber who installs the copper pipes required by law might not be the plumber who would install the plastic pipes if they were allowed.

Second, regulatory commissions often take on the view of the very industry they are supposed to regulate, because they must turn to that industry for the expertise to staff their own agencies. Thus it is common for a regulatory body to become the captive of its own ward. The Interstate Commerce Commission,

A REGULATION HORROR STORY

An example of how the ICC protects its "clients" against competition was turned up by the Senate Select Committee on Small Business. It concerned a small trucking firm that wished to extend trucking service to two Alabama towns not directly served by any large carrier. After 4½ years of proceedings, the ICC granted the applicant limited approval to serve one of the towns but not the other. In its report, the commission stated that these towns had "only limited transportation needs" and that additional service was therefore not warranted. In effect, the commission *prevented* the second town from enjoying trucking service.

Until very recently, the ICC has limited competition by preventing private truckers from choosing new routes that would greatly shorten trucking hauls, forbidding trucks that carried goods one way to pick up goods for a return load, and limiting the products that certain carriers might legally haul. The commission has ruled that a live chicken is an "agricultural commodity" but a dead chicken is not; that nuts in the shell qualify as agricultural goods but not shelled nuts. These regulations follow from a law that states that motor vehicles carrying agricultural commodities are exempt from ICC regulation. It was therefore in the "interest" of the ICC to define an agricultural commodity as narrowly as possible, to broaden its area of control and minimize the competition that would otherwise arise.

established in 1887 to regulate the railroads, is a prime example of this reversal of roles. When the ICC was established, the railroads were a monopoly that badly needed public supervision. Autos and trucks had not yet come into existence, so that there were few alternative means of bulk transportation in many areas.

By the end of the first quarter of the twentieth century, however, the railway industry was no longer without effective substitutes. Cars, trucks, buses, planes, pipelines—all provided effective competition. At this point, the ICC became interested in protecting the railroads against competition rather than in curbing abuses. One by one, these alternative modes of transport fell under its aegis (or under that of other regulatory agencies), and quasi-monopoly prices were set, as little empires were established for each form of transportation.

As a result, there has been much consideration, recently, of using the mechanism of the marketplace itself to restore a higher level of performance. Where regulation has created fat, comfortable semi-monopolies, *de-regulation may introduce a refreshing change of attitudes and behavior.* This is an approach that has already resulted in the phasing-out of much of the regulation of airline fares and routes, and that may be used to simplify operations in other areas. We will have to see whether the return to stiffer competition brings the results that the deregulators hope for, or merely plunges the industry in a struggle which results in a new call for regulation.

NATIONALIZATION

Then why not nationalize the large firms? The thought comes as rank heresy to a nation that has been accustomed to equating nationalization with socialism. **Yet Germany, France, England, Sweden, Italy, and a host of other capitalist nations have nationalized industries ranging from oil refineries to airlines, from automobile production to the output of coal and electricity.** Hence, Professor

Galbraith has suggested that we should nationalize corporations charged with the public interest, such as the giant armaments producers who are wholly dependent on the Pentagon, in order to bring such firms under public control.

But would nationalization achieve its purpose of assuring social responsibility? In 1971, the Pentagon arranged special contracts and "loans" to save Lockheed Aircraft, one of its "ward" companies, from bankruptcy, the fate of an ordinary inefficient firm. Outright nationalization would only cement this union of political and economic power, by making Lockheed a part of the Pentagon and thus making it even more difficult to put pressure on it to perform efficiently.

Or take the Tennessee Valley Authority, perhaps the most famous American public enterprise. It has been sued for the environmental devastation it has wrought by its strip-mining operations. So, too, the Atomic Energy Commission, which operates "nationalized" plants, has been severely criticized for its careless supervision of radioactive processes.*

The problem is that nationalization not only removes the affected enterprise entirely from the pressures of the market, but almost inevitably brings it under the political shelter of the government, further removing the venture from any effective criticism.

OTHER POSSIBILITIES

All these difficulties make it clear that the problem of social responsibility will not be easy to solve (or for that matter, even to *define*), no matter what step we choose, from Professor Friedman's laissez faire to Galbraith's nationalization. For each of these problems with the corporation, we could easily construct counterparts that have to do with the control over labor unions or over the government itself.

What, then, is to be done? A number of other lines of action suggest themselves. **One is the widening of the legal responsibility of the corporation to include areas of activity for which it now has little or no accountability.** Environmental damage is one of these. Consumer protection is another.

A second step would be a widening of public accountability through disclosure, the so-called fishbowl method of regulation. Corporations could be required to report to public agencies to make known corporate expenditures for pollution control, political lobbying, and so on. Corporate tax returns could be opened to public scrutiny. Unions and corporations both could be required to make public disclosure of their race practices, with regard to hiring or admission, advancement, and rates of pay.

Still another course of action would be to appoint public members to boards of directors of large companies or to executive organs of large unions and to charge these members with protecting the consumers' interest and with reporting behavior that seemed contrary to the public interest. Worker-members of boards of directors might also serve such a useful purpose (there are such members in Germany and a movement toward "workers' co-determination" in a number of other European nations).

*It should be noted that both agencies have recently had a new lease on life and are much more concerned with their public responsibilities. Public bureaucracies, like inefficient private managements, *can* be shaken up.

Finally, there is the corrective action of dedicated private individuals such as Ralph Nader, who rose to fame on his exposé of the safety practices of the auto industry, and who has since turned his guns on pollution, other irresponsibilities of big business, and on poor performance in the federal bureaucracy. Such public pressure is necessarily sporadic and usually short-lived, but it has been a powerful source of social change.

POWER: THE UNRESOLVED PROBLEM

It would be a mistake to conclude this recital with the implication that corporate (or union or government) power can be easily brought under control through a few legal remedies or by the power of public opinion. Certainly many abuses can be curbed, and much better levels of social performance achieved.

Yet mass organizations seem an inescapable concomitant of our age of high technology and increasing social interdependence. Here we should note that, depending on our interests, we stress different aspects of this universal phenomenon. **To some, who fear the continued growth of very large-scale business, the most significant aspect is that we have not managed to control business power. To others, concerned over the emergence of large labor unions, it is labor power that most dangerously eludes effective control. And to still others who are most worried by the growth of big government, it is the growth of public power that is the main problem.**

Thus the question of economic power remains, at best, only partially resolved. As A. A. Berle has written: "Some of these corporations can be thought of only in somewhat the same way we have heretofore thought of nations." Unlike nations, however, their power has not been rationalized in law, fully tested in practice, or well defined in philosophy. Unquestionably, the political and social influence and the economic power of the great centers of production pose problems with which capitalism—indeed, all industrialized societies—will have to cope for many years to come.

LOOKING BACK

KEY CONCEPTS

Consumer sovereignty allows consumers to determine allocation, and produces goods as cheaply as possible

1. Consumer sovereignty has been an important rationale for a market system. Under such a system the consumer enjoys two advantages: (1) The consumer, not the producer, determines the allocation of resources; and (2) the consumer is offered goods that are produced as cheaply and in as large a quantity as possible; that is, at the lowest point on the average cost curve.

Pluses and minuses of market imperfection: advertising and product differentiation have good and bad effects

2. Market imperfections lessen consumer sovereignty over allocation, although the loss is offset by some advantages. Advertising, for example, shapes consumers' tastes for the benefit of producers, but also conveys information to consumers. Production differentiation also brings the benefits of variety, but imposes the cost of waste and trivial product variation.

Big business imposes higher than competitive prices but brings technical progress

3. Monopolistic enterprise is also an infringement on consumer sovereignty; it prevents prices from being the lowest possible. But big business is likely to be more technologically progressive.

Business power has met many suggestions: Friedman suggests that profit-seeking is the only legitimate social function of business, but many businessmen prefer to think of themselves as being socially responsible

4. There are many views as to how business power should be dealt with. The view of conservatives who follow Milton Friedman is that big business is best left alone—that its main social function is to strive after profit, not to "do good." (In fact businesses should not be allowed to use their profits for philanthropy.) Many corporate executives find this view too uncomfortable and seek to define their roles as "professional" managers who deliberately follow socially responsible policies.

Dissolution of monopoly and antitrust policies have not proven very successful, mainly because big business is more technologically advanced than small business

5. The dissolution of monopoly is another approach to business power. So are antitrust measures, designed to break "combinations in restraint of trade," which have long been established policy. Yet both approaches have their limitations. Bigness is often the other side of the coin of technical efficiency and may also bring enlightened employee or social practices. And antitrust activity runs up against problems of cost and time, the efficiency of big companies, and the dubious rationale of antitrust policy itself.

Regulation is often out-of-date and protective

6. Regulation is an obvious answer to big business power, but it also presents difficulties. Regulation is often behind the times and regulators are too often "captives" of the industry they are supposed to regulate.

Nationalization often becomes bureaucratization

7. Nationalization is a further remedy, often used in Europe, but not much in favor in this country. Nationalization may do no more than make a big business into a public bureaucracy.

Accountability, public boards, publicity
Power remains unresolved problem

8. Various other policies include public accountability, public boards of directors, and more public exposure. All these policies may be useful. But the problem of power remains very much unresolved.

ECONOMIC VOCABULARY

Consumer sovereignty 426 **Antitrust** 431 **Nationalization** 433

QUESTIONS

1. Make a list of the main institutional changes you can think of that would be needed if we were to institute a system of perfect competition.
2. Go through a magazine and analyze a dozen ads to see (1) how much genuine information they convey, such as price, technical features, availability, etc., and (2) how much they try to influence taste by suggesting the social or other benefits of using the product, without any economic information. Do the same for a newspaper. Why do you think that "informational" ads are more common in newspapers than magazines?
3. How do you feel about Friedman's ideas on business responsibility? Do you think that Mobil has a right to support "Upstairs Downstairs" and other such public TV shows? How about Mobil's right to publish editorials in support of its views on oil? And how about the contributions of small arms manufacturers to the National Rifle Association?

4. Do you think a businessman has any right to decide what the most socially responsible policy for his company should be? Take the case of moving a plant from one region to another. Should business management alone decide this? If not, who?
5. Would you support the nationalization of a big company such as United States Steel if it were threatened with bankruptcy that would impose terrible economic hardship on its workers and communities? How about nationalizing A.T.&T. if it grew to be as big as the previous "Extra Word" suggests it might?
6. By and large, which do you consider to be the most dangerous *economic* problem: big business, big labor, big government? Which is the most dangerous *political* problem? The most dangerous *social* problem? Whatever your own list, can you imagine a rational argument for a different one? For a list in which the three groups were differently rank ordered according to the areas of danger? Do you think there is a "right" way of looking at this problem?

AN EXTRA WORD ABOUT
THE MULTINATIONAL CORPORATION

The problem of big business is one of old standing, dating back to the period just after the Civil War. But recently that problem has been given a new twist by the appearance of enormous corporations whose business empires literally straddle the globe—the multinational corporations. Take PepsiCo, for example. PepsiCo does not ship its famous product around the world from bottling plants in the United States. It *produces* Pepsi Cola in more than 500 plants in over 100 countries. When you buy a Pepsi in Mexico or the Philippines, Israel or Denmark, you are buying an American product that was manufactured in that country.

PepsiCo is a far-flung, but not a particularly large multinational corporation: In 1979 it was the 57th largest company. More impressive by far is the Ford Motor Company, a multinational that consists of a network of 60 subsidiary corporations, 40 of them foreign-based. Of the corporation's total assets of $23 billion, over one-third is invested in 27 foreign nations; and of its 494,000 employees (as of 1979) more than 175,000 were employed outside the U.S. And if we studied the corporate structures of GM or IBM or the great oil companies, we would find that they, too, are multinational companies with substantial portions of their total wealth invested in productive facilities outside the United States.

Multinational corporations differ from international corporations in that they produce goods and services in more than one country, while international corporations produce most of their goods and services in one country, even though they sell them in many. Volkswagen is a large international corporation, since it sells Volkswagens all over the world; but it is not much of a multinational corporation, since most of its actual production is concentrated in Germany.

If we broaden our view to include the top 100 American firms, we find that two-thirds have such production facilities in at least six nations. Moreover, the value of output that is produced overseas by the largest corporations by far exceeds the value of the goods they still export from the United States. In 1974, sales of foreign affiliates of U.S. multinational firms (which means their wholly or partially owned overseas branches) came to over $115 billion. In the same year, our total exports of manufactures amounted to $47 billion, only 41 percent as much as American firms produced abroad.

INTERNATIONAL DIRECT INVESTMENT

Another way of establishing the spectacular rise of international production is to trace the increase in the value of U.S. foreign direct investment; that is, the value of foreign-located, U.S.-owned plant and equipment (*not* U.S.-owned foreign bonds and stocks). In 1950 the value of U.S. foreign direct investment was $11 billion. In 1978 it was over $168 billion. Moreover, this figure, too, needs an upward adjustment, because it includes only the value of American dollars invested abroad and not the additional value of foreign capital that may be controlled by those dollars. For example, if a U.S. company has invested $10 million in a foreign enterprise whose total net worth is $20 million, the U.S. official figures for our foreign investment take note only of the $10 million of American equity (ownership) and not of the $20 million wealth that our equity actually controls. If we include the capital controlled by our foreign direct investment as a whole, the value of American overseas productive assets may be as large as $300 billion. **In general, something between a quarter and a half of the real assets of our biggest corporations are abroad.**

THE INTERNATIONAL CHALLENGE

The movement toward the internationalization of production is not a strictly American phenomenon. If the American multinationals are today the most imposing (of the world's biggest 500 corporations, over 300 are American), they are closely challenged by non-American multinationals (see Table 28.1). Philips Lamp Works, for example, is a huge Dutch multinational company with operations in 68 countries. Of its 225,000 employees, 167,000 work in nations other than the Netherlands. Royal Dutch/Shell is another vast multinational, whose home is somewhere between the Netherlands and the United Kingdom (it is jointly owned by nationals of both countries): Shell *in the United States* ranks among "our" top 20 biggest companies. Another is Nestlé Chocolate, a Swiss firm, 97 percent of whose $2 billion revenues originate outside Switzerland.

Indeed, if we take the 10 leading capital-exporting nations together (including the United States), we find that in 1967 their combined exports came to over $130 billion, but their combined overseas production amounted to well over $240 billion. In 1970, an economist for the International Chamber of Commerce estimated that total international production—U.S. production abroad, foreign production here, and foreign production in other foreign countries—accounted for as much as *one-sixth* of the total value of all world output, and a much higher fraction of the world output of industrial commodities. It is greater than that today, although we do not know exactly how large international production is.

MOTIVES FOR OVERSEAS PRODUCTION

What drives a firm to *produce* overseas rather than just sell overseas? One possible answer is straightforward. A firm is successful at home. Its technology and organizational skills give it an edge on foreign competition. It begins to export its product. The foreign market grows. At some point, the firm begins to

Company	*Total sales (billions of dollars)*	*Foreign sales as percentage of total*	*Number of countries in which subsidiaries are located*
General Motors	$28.3	19%	21
Exxon	18.7	50	25
Ford	16.4	26	30
Royal Dutch/Shell*	12.7	79	43
General Electric	9.4	16	32
IBM	8.3	39	80
Mobil Oil	8.2	45	62
Chrysler	8.0	24	26
Texaco	7.5	40	30
Unilever*	7.5	80	31
ITT	7.3	42	40
Gulf Oil	5.9	45	61
British Petroleum*	5.2	88	52
Philips Gloeilampenfabrieken*	5.2	NA	29
Standard Oil of California	5.1	45	26

*Not a U.S. firm.

TABLE 28.1 THE TOP 15 MULTINATIONALS, 1971 (latest available data)

calculate whether it would be more profitable to organize an overseas production operation. By doing so, it would save transportation costs. It may be able to evade a tariff by producing goods behind a tariff wall. It may be able to take advantage of lower wage rates. Finally, it ceases shipping goods abroad and instead exports capital, technology, and management—and becomes a multinational.

Calculations may be more complex. By degrees, a successful company may change its point of view. First it thinks of itself as a domestic company, perhaps with a small export market. Then it builds up its exports and thinks of itself as an international company with a substantial interest in exports. Finally its perspective changes to that of a multinational, considering the world (or substantial portions of it) to be its market. In that case, it may locate plants abroad *before* the market is fully developed, in order to be firmly established abroad ahead of its competition.*

ECONOMICS OF MULTINATIONAL PRODUCTION

Whether or not the multinational boom continues at its past rate, the startling rise of multinationals has already changed the face of international economic relationships. **One major effect has been a dramatic shift in the *geographic location* and the *technological character* of international economic activity.**

The shift away from exports to international production has introduced two changes into the international economic scene. One change is a movement of foreign investment away from its original concentration in the underdeveloped areas of the world toward the richer markets of the developed areas. Fifty years ago, in the era of high imperialism, most of the capital leaving one country for another flowed from rich to poor lands. Thus foreign investment in the late nineteenth and early twentieth centuries was largely associated with the creation of vast plantations, the building of railways through jungles, and the development of mineral resources.

But the growth of the multinational enterprise has coincided with a decisive shift away from investment in the underdeveloped world to investment in the industrial world. In 1897, 59 percent of American foreign direct investment was in agriculture, mining, or railways, mainly in the underdeveloped world. By the end of the 1970s, our investment in agriculture, mining, and railways, as a proportion of our total overseas assets, had fallen to about 20 percent; and its geographical location in the backward world came to only 36 percent of all our overseas direct investments. More striking, almost three-quarters of our huge rise in direct investment during the decades of the 1960s and 1970s were in the developed world; and the vast bulk of it was in manufacturing (and oil) rather than in plantations, railroads, or ores. **Thus the multinational companies are investing in each others' territories rather than invading the territories of the underdeveloped world.** This is not to say that they do not wield great power in the backward regions, as we shall see, but their thrust of expansion has been in other industrial lands, not in the unindustrialized ones.

The second economic change is really implicit in the first. **It is a shift away from heavy technology to high technology industries—away from enterprises in which vast sums of capital were associated with large, unskilled labor forces as in the building of railways or plantations—toward industries in which capital is perhaps less strategic than research and development, skilled technical manpower, and sophisticated**

*The internal dynamics that send some firms overseas, but not others, are by no means wholly understood. The internationalization of production is much more widely spread in some industries, such as glass, than in others, such as steel. Drugs are widely produced on an international basis; machine tools are not.

TABLE 28.2
SIZE AND DISTRIBUTION OF U.S. FOREIGN DIRECT INVESTMENT

	1929	*1950*	*1975*
Total (millions)	**$7,528**	**$11,788**	**$133,168**
		Distribution by market (%)	
Canada	27	30	23
Europe	18	14	37
Latin America	47	41	12
Asia, Africa, other	8	15	28
		Distribution by industrial sector (%)	
Manufacturing	24	31	42
Petroleum	15	29	26
Transport and utilities	21	12	n.a.
Mining	15	9	8
Trade	5	7	n.a.
Agriculture	12	5	n.a.
Other	8	6	n.a.

management techniques typical of the computer, petrochemical, and other new industries. Table 28.2 sums up the overall shift.

Note the dramatic shift away from Latin America and away from transport, mining, and agriculture into Europe and manufacturing, a shift that would be even more accentuated if we were not still dependent on oil as a major source of the world's energy. If nuclear power or the fuel cell displace oil within the next two decades, we can expect a still more rapid decline in investment in the backward areas (especially in the Near East), and a proportionately still larger concentration of foreign direct investment in manufacturing.

PROBLEMS FOR POLICY MAKERS

Multinationals have not only changed the face of international economic activity, but also have added considerably to the problem of controlling domestic economies. Assume that a country wants to slow down its economy through monetary policies designed to reduce plant and equipment spending. A restrictive monetary policy at home may be vitiated by the ability of a multinational to borrow *abroad* in order to finance investment at home. Conversely, a monetary policy designed to stimulate the home economy may end up in loans that increase production in someone else's economy. *Thus the effectiveness of national economic policy making is weakened.* Moreover, it is not easy to suggest that monetary policies should be coordinated among countries, since the economic needs of different countries may not be the same: what is right for one country at a given time may be wrong for another.

HOST AND HOSTAGE

The jealous claims of nation-states who seek to retain national control over productive activity within their own borders and the powerful thrust of pan-national corporations for new markets in foreign territories introduces profound tensions into the political economics of multinational production. **On the one hand, the multinational is in a position to win hard bargains from the host country into which it seeks to enter because the corporation is the main bearer of new technologies and management techniques that every nation seeks.** Therefore, if one country—say France—refuses to give a would-be entrant the right to come in (and possibly to cause financial losses to its established firms), the multinational may well place its plants, with their precious economic cargo of productivity, in another country, leaving the recalcitrant nation the loser in the race for international growth.

On the other hand, the power is by no means entirely one-sided; for once a multinational *has* entered a foreign nation, it becomes a *hostage* of the host country. It is now bound by the laws of that country and may find itself forced to undertake activities that are "foreign." In Japan, for example, it is an unwritten law that workers engaged by giant corporations are *never* fired, but become permanent employees. Japan has been extremely reluctant to allow foreign capital to establish manufacturing operations on Japanese soil, to the great annoyance of foreign companies. But if, as now seems likely, Japan is opened to American and European capital, we can be sure that American or European corporations will be expected to behave in the Japanese way with their employees. This will not be an easy course to follow, since these corporations are not likely to receive the special support that the Japanese government gives to its own big firms.

Or take the problem of a multinational that is forced by a fall in demand to cut back the volume of its output. A decision made along strictly economic lines would lead it to close its least profitable plant. But this may bring very serious economic repercussions in the particular nation in which that plant is located—so serious that the government will threaten to take action if the plant is closed. What dictates shall the multinational then follow: those of standard business accounting or those of political accounting?

Or consider the multinational seeking to expand or to alter its operations in an underdeveloped country. This, too, may lead to friction, for as former Under Secretary of State George Ball has candidly asked: "How can a national government make an economic plan with any confidence if a board of directors meeting 5,000 miles away can, by altering its pattern of purchasing and production, affect in a major way the country's economic life?"

AN UNWRITTEN ENDING

There are no answers to these questions as yet. In all likelihood the tension between the pull of economic and of political life will go on, unsatisfactorily resolved, for a long time. The big corporations are certain to continue their multinational thrust. As global producers, they will be the main international carriers of efficiency and development, especially in the high technology areas for which they seem to be the most effective form of organization. But if the power of the nation-state will be challenged by these international production units, it is not likely to be humbled by them. There are many things a nation can do that a corporation cannot, including, above all, the creation of the spirit of sacrifice necessary both for good purposes such as development and for evil ones such as war.

Perhaps all we can say at this stage of human development is that both nation-states and huge corporations are necessary, in that they seem to be the only ways in which we can organize mankind to perform the arduous and sustained labor without which humanity itself would rapidly perish. Perhaps after the long age of capital accumulation has finally come to an end and sufficient capital is available to all peoples, we may be able to think seriously about dismantling the giant enterprise *and* the nation-state, both of which overpower the individual with their massive organized strength. However desirable that ultimate goal may be, in our time both state and corporation promise to be with us, and the tension between them will be part of the evolutionary drama of our period of history.

SECTION 3: Income Distribution in Theory and in Fact

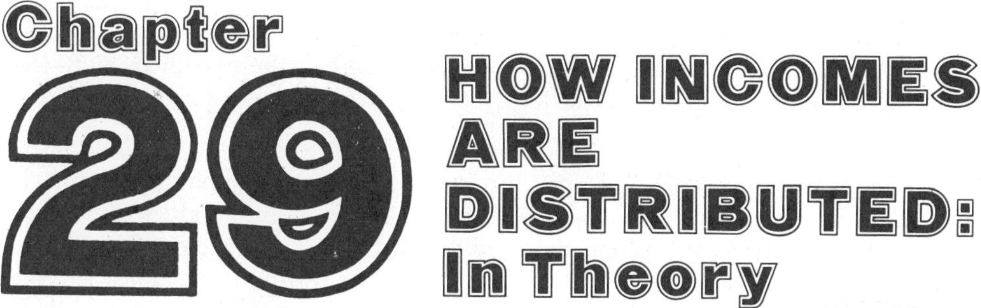

Chapter 29 HOW INCOMES ARE DISTRIBUTED: In Theory

A LOOK AHEAD

With this chapter we enter a new area of microeconomics—income distribution. Chapter 29 presents a discussion of how wages, rents, and interest are determined in the marketplace—in theory. Chapter 30 will look at the real world and discuss why and where the theory doesn't work as well as we should like it to.

One by one we will consider each factor of production, deriving the forces of supply and demand that establish its level of remuneration. Actually, however, there is a central theme that you will soon catch sight of: the marginal productivity theory of income distribution. This theory claims that each factor in a competitive market earns as much as the net revenue that it brings into the firm. Marginal productivity theory thereby becomes the main idea for you to bear in mind—and note especially the surprising conclusion to which it points: There is no such thing, in a competitive world, as exploitation.

Although we have explored in some detail the demand for goods and the calculations of firms in the provision of those goods, we have left unexamined a crucial area of the economy. This is the market for factors, where wages, rent, and interest are determined.

This area is crucial for two reasons. First, it allows us to complete the analysis of the circular flow that has provided the basic pattern of our analysis. When we have understood the factor market we will have knit together the household and the firm in their second major interaction—this time with the household acting as supplier rather than demander, and with the firm providing demand rather than supply.

Second, our analysis is crucial because it leads us to the consideration of a problem of major political and social importance: the *distribution of income*, the main theme in this and the next chapter. In this chapter we shall look into the matter in theory—that is, as incomes would be determined in a perfectly competitive world. In our next chapter, we shall look at the matter in fact—that is, as incomes are set in the imperfectly competitive world of our economy.

FACTORS AND FACTOR SERVICES

We must begin with a simple but distinguishing fact that separates the market for factors from that for goods. When we buy or sell goods, we take possession of, or deliver, an actual commodity. **But when we speak of buying or selling factors, we mean only that we are buying or selling a stream of services that a factor produces.** When we buy or sell "labor," we do not buy or sell the human being who produces that labor—only the value of his work efforts. So, too, when we buy or sell "capital," we are not purchasing or selling a sum of money or a capital asset. We are hiring or offering the use of that money or equipment. Land, too, enters the market for factors as an agency of production whose services we rent but need not actually purchase as so much real estate.

Obviously we can buy land as real estate, and we can buy capital goods and various forms of capital, such as stocks and bonds. (We cannot buy human labor as an entity because slavery is illegal. In former times though, one *could* buy labor outright.) It stands to reason, then, that there should be a relationship between the price of factors, considered as assets (actual capital goods or real estate) and the price of the stream of services that factors produce: the *interest* earned on capital, the *rent* of land. There is such a relationship which we will study later under the heading of "capitalization." Here we must recognize that the market for factors is not a market in which the assets are sold, but in which the productive services—the earnings—of these assets are priced.

As in every market, these prices will be determined by the interplay of supply and demand. Therefore to study the factor market we must first look into the forces that determine the demand for factors, and then into the forces that determine their supply.

DIRECT DEMAND FOR FACTORS

Who buys factor services? Part of the answer is very simple. **A portion of the services of labor, land, and capital is demanded directly by consumers for their own personal enjoyment, exactly as with any good or service.** This kind of demand for factors of production takes the guise of the demand for lawyers and barbers and servants or the demand for plots of land for personal dwellings

The derived demand curve (or the marginal revenue product curve) slopes downward because each factor adds less and less to output as we add that factor. Multiply the falling marginal contribution of the factor times the selling price and you get the curves shown here.

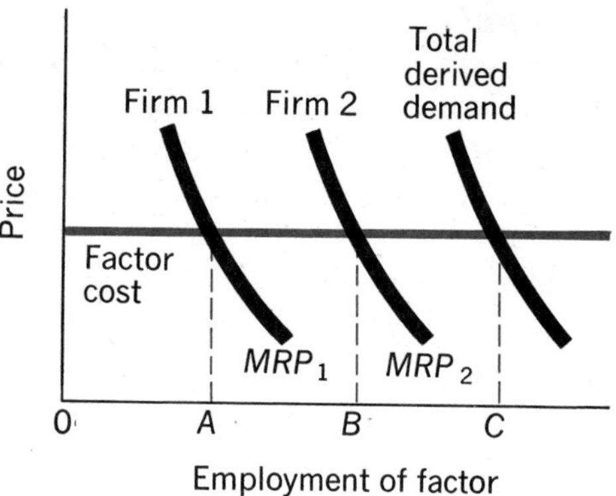

FIGURE 29.1 DERIVED DEMAND FOR FACTORS

or the demand for cars and washing machines or other personal capital goods or the demand for loans for consumption purposes. To the extent that factors are demanded directly for these utility-yielding purposes, there is nothing in analyzing the demand for them that differs from the demand curves we have previously studied.

DERIVED DEMAND

Most factors of production do not earn their incomes by selling their services directly to final consumers. They sell them, instead, to firms. In turn, firms want the services of these factors not for the firm's personal enjoyment, but to put them to profitable use.

Thus we speak of the firm's demand for factors as derived demand. Its demand is derived from the consumers' demand for the output the firm makes. We recall that each firm will hire labor (or any other factor) until the marginal revenue from that factor just equals the marginal costs of hiring that factor.

The marginal output that a factor produces multiplied by the selling price of the product is called its **marginal revenue product.** If a factor produces three extra units of output that are sold for $10 per unit, its marginal revenue product is $30. If the number of units of output falls as more and more of a factor is added to the production process, these diminishing returns cause the marginal revenue product curve or the derived demand curve to slope downward.

We see this in Figure 29.1, where the derived demand for a factor leads Firm 1 to employ quantity *OA*. Derived demand of Firm 2 results in the hire of *OB*, and the summed demand of both firms gives us a market demand of *OC*.

This however leaves us with the question of factor price only half explained. We understand the elements that enter into the demand curve for the factor. But we cannot understand how the price of the factor is established until we know something about the supply curves in the factor market. That is the missing element we need to complete the full chain of the circular flow.

THE SUPPLY CURVE OF FACTORS

What do we know about the willingness and ability of the owners of labor, capital, and land to offer their services in the marketplace at varying prices for these services?

LABOR

By far the most important supply curve in the factor market is that of labor—meaning, let us remember, labor of all grades, from the least skilled workman to the most highly trained scientist or the most effective entrepreneur.

As Figure 29.2 shows, the supply curve for the labor of most individuals has a curious shape. Up to wage level *OA*, we have no trouble explaining things. Economists assume that labor involves *disutility*. Moreover, just as we assume that increasing amounts of a utility-yielding good give us diminishing marginal utility, so we assume that increasing amounts of labor involve *increasing marginal disutility*. Therefore the curve rises up to level *OA* because we will not be willing to work longer hours (i.e., to offer a larger quantity of labor services within a given time period), unless we are paid more per hour.

The backward-bending curve. How then do we explain the backward-bending portion of the rising curve above wage level *OA*? The answer lies in adding to the rising marginal disutility of labor the falling marginal utility of *income* itself, on the assumption that an extra dollar of income to a person who is making $10,000 is worth less than the utility of an additional dollar when that person is making only $5,000. **Above a certain income level, leisure is preferable to more income.**

Together, these two forces explain very clearly why the supply curve of labor bends backward above a certain level. Take a designer who has been tempted to work 70 hours a week by wage raises that have finally reached $20 an hour. Now suppose that wages go up another 10 percent. It is possible of course, that the marginal utility of the additional income may outweigh the marginal disutility of these long hours, so that the designer stays on the job or works even longer hours. If, however, his or her marginal utility of income has reached a low enough point and his or her marginal disutility of work a high enough point, the raise may bring a new possibility: the designer may work *fewer* hours and enjoy the same (or a somewhat higher) income as well as additional leisure. For example, as pay goes up 10 percent the designer may reduce his or her workweek by 5 percent.

Backward-bending supply curves help explain the long trend toward reducing the workweek. Over the last century, weekly hours have decreased by about 40 percent. Although many factors have converged to bring about this result, one of them is certainly the desire of individual men and women to give up the marginal utility of potential income for that of increased leisure.

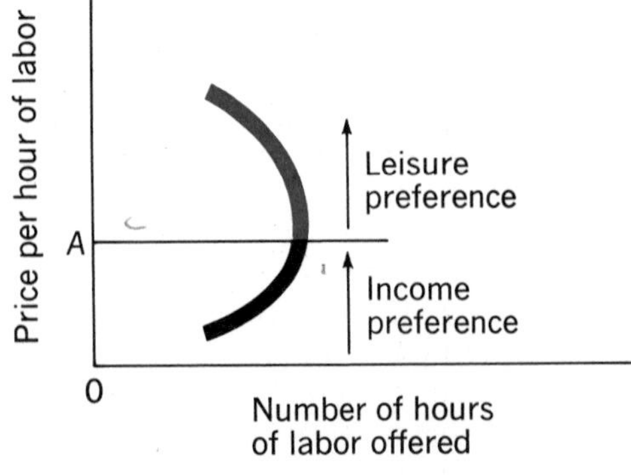

FIGURE 29.2 BACKWARD-BENDING SUPPLY CURVE OF LABOR

A typical labor supply curve bends backward because the balance between the utility of additional income and the disutility of earning it changes from "pro-work" to "pro-leisure."

Individual vs. collective supply. A cautionary note is useful here. We can speak with some degree of confidence about the backward-bending supply curve of individual labor, especially when labor is paid by the hour or by the piece. But we must distinguish the supply curve of the individual from that of the labor force as a whole. As the price of labor rises, some persons will be tempted to enter the labor market because the opportunity cost of remaining "leisured" is now too great. This accounts for the entrance of many housewives into the market as the price for part-time office work goes up. This is the problem of the "participation rates" of the population that enters into the macroeconomic problem of employment. **Here it is useful to understand that the collective supply curve of labor is probably upward sloping rather than backward bending.** (It would be backward bending if wages rose so high that married women, for example, dropped out of the labor force as their husbands' earnings rose, but that does not seem to be the case.)

Psychic income. The supply curve of labor is further complicated because work brings not only disutilities but positive enjoyments. Jobs bring friendships, relieve boredom, may lead to power or prestige. Many people derive deep satisfactions from their work and would not change jobs even if they could improve their incomes by doing so. Indeed, it is very likely that most individuals seek to maximize their "psychic incomes" rather than their money incomes, combining the utilities derived from their earnings and the quite separate utilities from their work, and balancing these gains against the disutilities that work also involves.

The difficulty in speaking about psychic income is that it involves us in an unmeasurable concept—a tautology. Therefore when we speak about the supply curve of labor, we generally make the assumption that individuals behave roughly as money maximizers, an assumption that has prima facie evidence in the long-run exodus from low-paying to higher-paying occupations and from low-wage regions to high-wage regions.

Mobility of labor. More than a million American families change addresses in a typical year, so that over a decade the normal mobility of the labor force may transport 20 million to 30 million people (including wives and children) from one part of the country to another. Without this potential influx of labor, we would expect wages to shoot up steeply whenever an industry in a particular locality expanded, with the result that further profitable expansion might then become impossible.

We also speak of mobility of labor in a vertical sense, referring to the movement from occupation to occupation. Here the barriers to mobility are not usually geographical but institutional (for instance, trade union restrictions on membership) or social (discrimination against the upward mobility of blacks) or economic (the lack of sufficient income to gain a needed amount of education). Despite these obstacles, occupational mobility is also very impressive from generation to generation, as the astounding changes in the structure of the U.S. labor force have demonstrated (see box p. 451).

This is a force tending to reduce the differences between income extremes, since the mobility of labor will not only shift the supply curve to the right in the favored occupations (thereby exerting a downward pressure on incomes), but

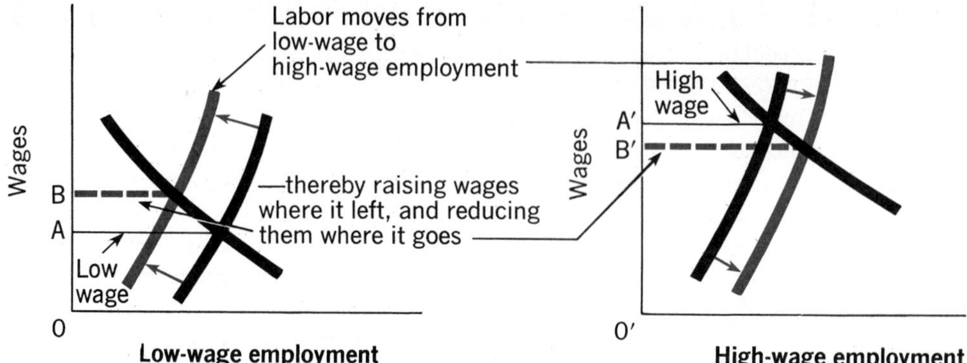

FIGURE 29.3 EFFECT OF LABOR MOBILITY ON RELATIVE WAGES

The diagram shows a low-wage employment paying *OA* wages, and a high one *O′A′*. The movement of labor out of the disfavored occupation or industry and into the favored one raises *OA* to *OB*, and reduces *O′A′* to *O′B′*. Note: The labor that goes into the high-wage employment is not necessarily the same labor that leaves the low-wage area. But as long as supply curves shift, the wage differential will change as shown.

will move the supply curve to the left in those industries it leaves, bringing an upward impetus to incomes. Figure 29.3 shows how this process works.

CAPITAL

What does the supply curve of capital look like? When we say "capital," we are not much interested in the supply of actual machines or equipment. We concern ourselves with the supply of new savings onto the market, the source of the machines of the future. How about the supply curve of savings? Economists have learned that savers change their habits of thrift much less in response to changes in the price of savings (interest) than in response to changes in the level of income. We can see this in Figure 29.4.

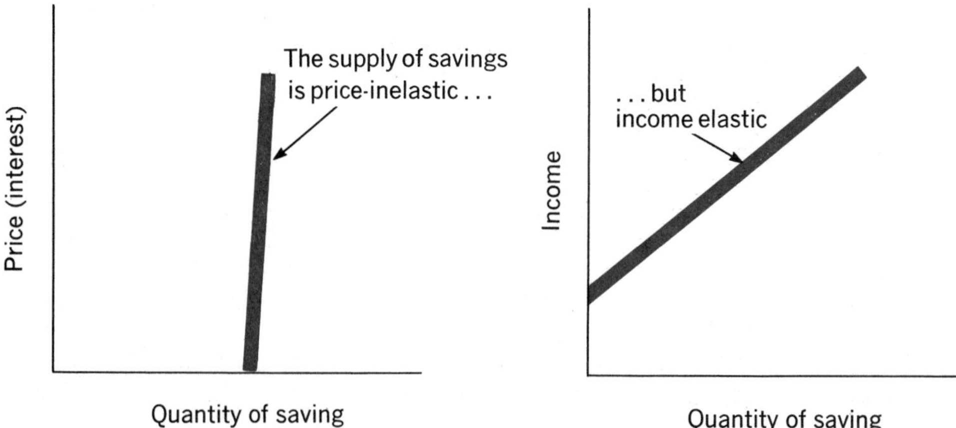

FIGURE 29.4 THE SUPPLY CURVE OF SAVINGS

We do not greatly change our saving habits if interest changes, but we *do* greatly change our saving propensity as income changes. This last is a macroeconomic relationship of great importance.

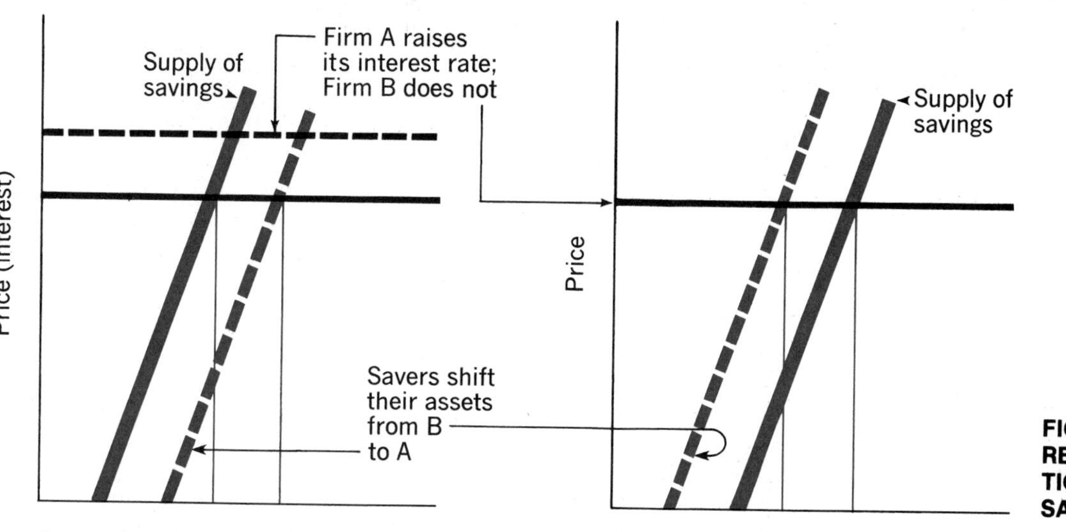

FIGURE 29.5 REALLOCATION OF SAVINGS

The diagram shows us that capital moves, just as labor does, leaving low-remuneration employment for high-remuneration employment.

Allocating Savings. Even though the price of savings may not greatly affect our thriftiness, it has a very important effect on what we do with our savings. As savers, we often reallocate the way we dispose of our savings, shifting our "portfolios" among checking accounts, savings accounts, insurance, or stocks and bonds, as the various returns offered by these assets change (or as our assessment of their risk changes). For example, the rise in interest rates in the 1970s resulted in a tremendous movement from noninterest-bearing checking accounts into interest-bearing savings accounts. Financial institutions also shift real investment funds in response to different rates of return.

Thus, when we picture the supply curve for saving, we should also bear in mind what this curve looks like to any particular demander. From the point of view of an enterprise in the market for capital, savings are highly price elastic; that is, a firm can attract savings by offering a higher return than a competitive enterprise offers. As a result, savers will shift their capital from one enterprise to the other, as in Figure 29.5. This bears an obvious relation to the mobility of labor, and we can indeed speak of it as the *mobility of capital.*

LAND

Finally, let us consider the supply curve of land. At any moment, the total supply of land, like capital, is fixed. To a limited extent, there is a counterpart to saving which adds to capital. By applying capital and labor we can slowly add to land by dredging, clearing forests, reclaiming swamps and deserts. Therefore the long-run supply curve for land is slightly price elastic, as Figure 29.6 shows.

As with capital, however, it is possible to speak of the *mobility of land.* This seems strange since land is obviously not moveable. Land can, however,

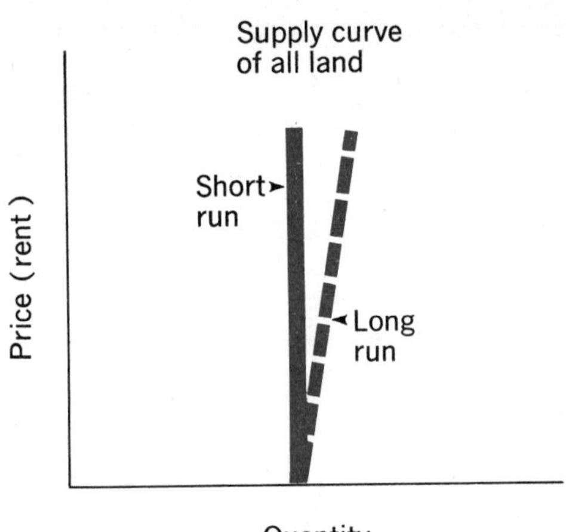

FIGURE 29.6 SUPPLY CURVE FOR LAND

As Figure 29.6 shows, we can add only small amounts to usable land as its price rises. But as Figure 29.7 makes plain, we can add large amounts to usable space. What do you suppose the ratio of space to land is in New York City compared to a Great Plains town? Why is it worth building skyscrapers in New York but not in the Midwest?

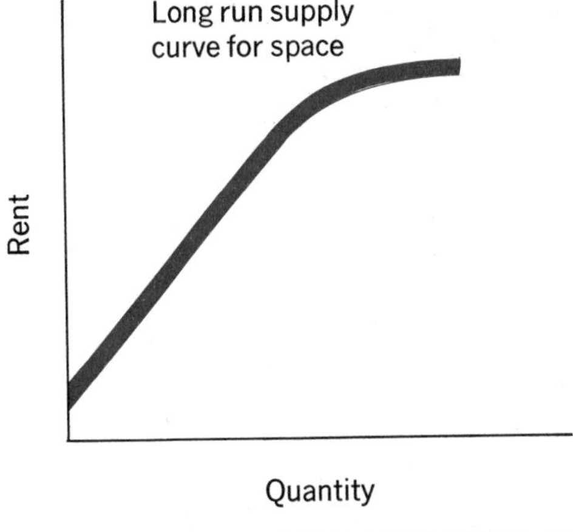

FIGURE 29.7 SUPPLY CURVE FOR SPACE

---

be used for very different purposes, depending on the returns to be had from them. If we picture the supply curve of land for, say, shopping centers or orange groves or industrial sites, we can picture an upward sloping curve, just like the supply curve of capital for any one use. Land can be—and constantly is—moved from use to use, as various enterprises bid for it. Thus the supply curve may be very elastic to any one user, even though the overall supply curve to society is very inelastic.

Land vs. space. In addition, we must differentiate land from space. We can create space much more easily than we can create land. Space is essentially a function of the availability of capital and labor, not of land. Every time we put up a high-rise building where there was previously a low one, we have created

UNITED STATES' WORK PROFILE

What kinds of work do people do in the United States? The table below gives us a picture of the shifting occupational profile of the nation's work force over the last eighty odd years.

Note particularly the striking growth in professional and managerial work, together with the drift from blue- to white-collar jobs. This lies behind most discussion of "postindustrial" society as the direction in which we may be headed.

	Percent of labor force 1900	Percent of labor force 1980
Managerial and professional		
Professional and technical workers	4.1	15.5
Managers, officials, and proprietors (nonfarm)	5.9	11.0
White-collar		
Clerical workers	3.1	18.2
Sales workers	4.8	6.3
Blue-collar		
Skilled workers and foremen	10.3	13.2
Semiskilled workers	12.8	14.9
Unskilled workers	12.4	4.8
Household and other service workers	8.9	13.1
Farm		
Farmers and farm managers	20.0	2.7
Farm laborers	17.6	

more space on the same amount of land. As a result, the supply curve for space will be very price-elastic—a higher price for space (rent) bringing more onto the market, as Figure 29.7 shows. In the long run, space is available in indefinite amounts.

RENTS AND INCOMES

We are almost ready to tie together all our different supply curves, and to describe the over-all working of the factor market. But the importance of time in bringing about increases in land or space alerts us to a very important reason for the existence of very large incomes (and very large disparities of incomes) in the short run. This is the phenomenon of *quasi rent* (also called *economic* rent).

We have already discussed this term on p. 400, where we identified the incomes of intramarginal firms in a competitive industry as consisting of quasi rents. Now we want to examine these rents more carefully, for they will help us in analyzing the distribution of income.

LAND RENT

First let us get rid of some confusing terminology, by distinguishing quasi rents from the earnings of land as a factor of production, which is also called rent. The distinction is clear in thought. It is muddied only because usage has chosen similar words for dissimilar things.

The rent earned by land as a factor of production is the payment we make to its owner for its services to the market. If we cease to pay land rent or pay less rent, the amount of land offered on the market will fall. If we pay more, it will rise. This rent is both a payment made to a factor of production to compensate its owner for its services and an element of cost that must enter into the calculation of selling prices. If a farmer must pay $100 rent to get an additional field, that $100 will clearly be part of the cost of producing a new crop.

QUASI OR ECONOMIC RENT

Quasi rents differ in important ways from true land rent.

1. Quasi rent is not a return earned by the factor, in that the payment has nothing to do with inducing the factor to enter the market.

2. Quasi rents are not a cost that helps to determine selling price. They are earnings determined by selling price.

3. Quasi rents apply to all factors, not just to land.

An illustration may clarify the problem. Figure 29.8 shows the supply curve for "first class" office space in New York City. Notice that over a considerable range there is an unchanging price for space. Up to amount *OX*, you can get all the space you want at rent *OA* (per square foot). This is real land rent, in the sense of being a necessary payment for a factor service. If there were no rent paid, no space would be forthcoming.

Next, look at the situation after we have used up *OX* amount of space. We can rent additional space up to *OY*, but only at rising prices (rents). Perhaps expenditures are needed to induce landlords to upgrade "second-class" space. Each new area that is tempted onto the market at a higher price earns real rent, in that it would not appear unless a higher price were paid. But notice that all the offices previously offered at lower prices are now in a position to ask higher rentals because the price of the marginal unit has increased. Thus we have here a mixture of real rents and economic or quasi rents. **The marginal landlord is receiving real rent. All the other (intramarginal) landlords who can now get higher rentals**

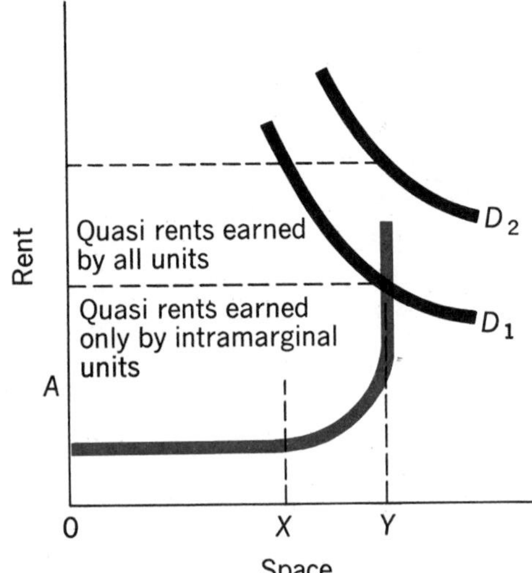

FIGURE 29.8 RENTS AND QUASI RENTS

Are quasi rents scarcity returns? The diagram makes it clear they are. Are they monopoly returns? No, because they can be enjoyed by large numbers of intramarginal firms or individuals.

are the beneficiaries of a scarcity price that gives them a bonus over the real rent they originally received. This bonus is economic or quasi rent.

Finally we reach the point *OY*, at which there is no more space to be had at any price. Suppose the demand for space continues to rise from D_1 to D_2. The price of office space will rise as well, and *all* landlords will be receiving quasi rents on top of their real rents.

RENTS AND PRICES

Here is where we make a clear distinction. True rent is a cost that must be paid to bring land into production. Quasi rent is not such a cost. It is wholly the result of scarcity and plays no role in determining the real cost to society of producing goods or services. If demand fell from D_2 to D_1, a great deal of quasi rent would disappear, although not a foot of office space would be withdrawn.

Thus true rent helps determine price whereas economic or quasi rent is determined by price. We can see that rent must be paid if office space *OX* is to appear, but that quasi rent is not a necessary cost of production for space thereafter.

This conclusion, however, applies only to our analysis of costs from a social point of view. From the point of view of the individual producer, the distinction disappears. A renter must pay the landlord whatever it costs to rent space, be it rent or quasi rent. Thus quasi rents enter into the renter's costs and help determine the price that must be asked for his or her goods.

ECONOMIC RENTS AND ALLOCATION

From the social point of view, economic rent is a waste. If we could eliminate it, say by taxing it away, it would not diminish production at all, only the incomes of the owners of scarce resources.

Quasi rents are therefore wholly "unearned" incomes. Nonetheless, they serve a useful function for society. They allocate a scarce commodity, in this case office space, among various claimants for that commodity.

The fact that quasi rents are a monopoly return is neither here nor there, so far as their rationing function is concerned. If there were no quasi rents, office space would be leased at prices that failed to equate quantities demanded and supplied. There would be a "shortage" of space and rationing would take place on some other basis—first come, first served or political influence or having an "in" with the landlord, instead of through the price mechanism.

ECONOMIC RENTS AND INCOMES

Finally, we must make careful note of the fact that economic rents are not returns limited to land. Take car rentals. Suppose we can rent all the car transportation we need at the going price. Suddenly there is a jump in demand, and the rentable fleet is too small. Rentals will rise. Until additional cars come onto the market, the fleet owners will simply enjoy economic rents (quasi rents) on their cars.

In the same way, the earnings of actors or authors or of anyone possessing scarce talent or skills are likely to be partly economic rents. An actress might be perfectly happy to offer her services for a good movie role at $50,000, but she may be able to get $100,000 because of her name. The first $50,000, without which she would not work, is her wage. The rest is a quasi or economic rent. So, too, a plumber who would be willing to work for standard wages, but who gets double because he is the only plumber in town, earns economic rents. And as we have already seen, these rents explain a part of business profits, as returns going to intramarginal firms.

CAPITALIZATION

Economic rents lead us to the process called *capitalization.* As we have mentioned, buyers of land and capital often have the option of buying the actual real estate or machinery they use, instead of just paying for its services. Capitalization is the means by which we place a value on a factor as an asset.

Suppose that an office building makes $100,000 a year in rentals and that we decide to buy the building. How much would it be worth? The answer depends, of course, on the riskiness of the investment. Some buildings, like some machines or bonds or businesses, are safer buys than others. For each class of risk there is a rate of return established by other buyers and sellers of similar assets. Suppose that the rate of return applicable to our building is 10 percent. Then we will capitalize it at $1 million. This is because $1 million at 10 percent gives us a return of $100,000.

We can capitalize any factor (or any business) by dividing its current earnings by the appropriate interest rate. The appropriate interest rate tells us the opportunity cost of our money: how much we could get for it if we bought some other factor or asset of similar risk. Notice that as the interest rate falls, so does the opportunity cost. We have to be content with a smaller return on our money. Thus if we are buying land that rents for $1,000, and the appropriate interest rate is 5 percent, the land will sell for $20,000 ($20,000 × .05 = $1,000). If the interest rate *falls* to 4 percent, the value of the land will *rise* to $25,000.

CAPITALIZATION AND ECONOMIC RENTS

Capitalization is important in determining the asset prices of factors. It is also important because it gets rid of economic rents! **Suppose the $100,000 rental income were virtually all quasi rent and that the building were sold for $1 million. The new owners of the building will still be making $100,000 a year, *but it will no longer be an economic rent.* It will be a normal market return on the capital they expended. They will have paid for their quasi rents in the opportunity cost of their capital.**

The gainer in the transaction will be the original owner of the building. Perhaps the building cost him very little and the $1 million sale price came as a great capital gain. He will have capitalized his quasi rents into a large sum of capital; but on the sum, in the future, he can expect to make no more than the normal rate of interest.

MARKET PRICE FOR FACTORS

We are finally in a position to assemble the pieces of the puzzle. We have traced the forces that give rise to the supply curves of the different factors, and we understand the explanation for the demand curves as well. Hence we understand

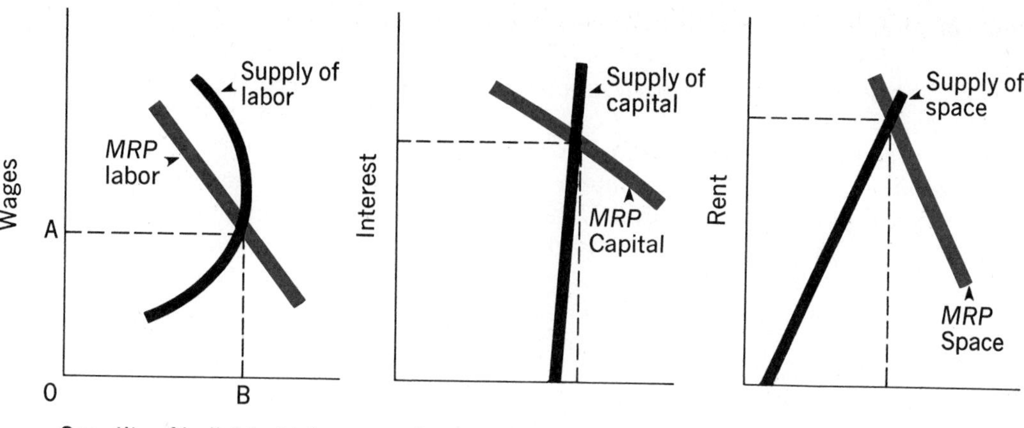

FIGURE 29.9 MARGINAL REVENUE PRODUCTS AND EARNINGS

Despite their different shapes and locations, the various supply curves of the factors always determine the quantity of the factor that will be hired and the remuneration it will receive. In each case, the demand curve is the marginal revenue product curve—the amount of income that the entrepreneur will gain from hiring the factor in question. As our graph shows, these derived demand curves may also have differing shapes or locations, but in all cases the intersection of the two curves gives us the information we want. Notice the important fact that the earnings of each factor will be equal to the marginal revenue it earns for its employer. At quantity *OB* of labor, labor's *MRP* is *OA*. This is its wage. The equality of earnings and *MRP*s is the basis for the claim that in a market of perfect competition there can be no exploitation.

---

how factors are priced in the market, which is to say we understand the mechanism for determining *factor incomes.*

Can we generalize about the result? One would think, in the light of the variety of supply curves we have discussed, that this would be impossible. If we think about the nature of the demand curve for factors, however, we see that this is not so. The shape and position of the supply curve for any factor will determine how much of it appears on the market at any given price. **But whatever the amount of the factor, it will be paid a return equal to the marginal revenue product of that factor.** Remember that the entrepreneur will go on hiring all factors as long as their marginal revenue products are greater than their marginal costs. Thus, whatever the shape or position of the supply curve, the earnings of the factor will always be equal to the marginal revenue it brings to the buyer, as Figure 29.9 shows.

We could draw other curves showing the collective supply of labor, the supply of savings to a given user, or the total quantity of land, but the conclusion would be the same. In each case, the market rate of wages, interest, and rent would be equal to the marginal revenue product of that factor.

THE MARGINAL PRODUCTIVITY THEORY OF DISTRIBUTION

We call this generalization about factor prices the *marginal productivity theory of distribution.* **What it tells us is very simple. The income of any factor will be determined by the contribution each factor makes to the revenue of the** enterprise. Its income will be higher or lower, depending on the willingness and ability of suppliers of factor services to enter the market at different prices; but at all prices, factors will earn amounts equal to the marginal revenue they produce.

Two conclusions follow from this theory. The first is that there can be no exploitation of any factor. Each factor will receive an amount exactly equal to the revenue it produces for the firm.* There can be no unpaid labor or unrewarded land or capital. A worker or capitalist or landlord may not be willing to offer his services at going rates of pay, but none can claim that his earnings are less than the revenues he brings into the firm: For as we have seen, every profit-maximizing entrepreneur must keep on hiring factors until their marginal revenue products equal their marginal cost.

Moreover, no factor can claim that some other factor is paid too much. To be sure, some factors will earn quasi rents, a waste from society's point of view, as we have seen. We have also seen that quasi rents are a temporary phenomenon, slowly eliminated by mobility of factors into an area of scarcity. In the long run, the return to land, capital, and labor will reflect the actual contribution that each makes to output.

PRICE AND PRODUCTIVITY

The second conclusion follows from the first. **It is that all factors will be paid in proportion to their productivity.**

Suppose that an entrepreneur can hire a unit of Factor A, say an acre of land which will produce a marginal revenue product of $20, or an extra worker whose marginal revenue product will be $40. We know that the entrepreneur will have to pay $20 to hire the acre of land and cannot pay more than that, and that he or she will have to pay $40 for the worker and cannot pay less than that.

What accounts for the difference between the earnings of a unit of land and a unit of labor? Their marginal revenue products. But these marginal revenue products, we recall, are only the *physical* marginal products of the factors multiplied by the market value of the output to which they contribute. The value of the output must be the same, since land and labor will both be adding to the output of the same commodity. The difference in their marginal *revenue* products is therefore solely the result of the fact that a unit of land creates fewer units of output than a unit of labor.

It follows, therefore, that factor prices must be proportional to their physical productivities, or that:

$$\frac{\text{Price of Factor A}}{\begin{array}{c}\text{Marginal Productivity}\\ \text{of Factor A}\end{array}} = \frac{\text{Price of Factor B}}{\begin{array}{c}\text{Marginal Productivity}\\ \text{of Factor B}\end{array}}$$

MARGINAL PRODUCTIVITY AND "JUSTICE"

This is a very remarkable solution to the problem of distribution. What it says is that **in competitive systems, all factors will be rewarded in proportion to**

*When a factor is bought directly by a consumer, the factor will receive the money value of the marginal utility it produces for the consumer.

their contribution to output. If an acre of land is only half as productive as a unit of labor, it will be paid only half as much. If it is twice as productive, it will be paid double. If skilled labor produces three times as much as unskilled, its wage rate will be three times that of unskilled, and so on. The resulting pattern of income distribution thus seems both just and efficient. It seems just because everyone is getting all the income he or she produces, and because no one is getting any income he or she has not produced. It seems efficient because entrepreneurs will use factors in a way that maximizes their contribution to output, thereby not only giving the factors their largest possible reward but giving society the greatest overall output to be had from them.

Is this conclusion valid? Do the earnings of land, labor, and capital reflect their contributions to output? The question takes us from a consideration of how the factor market works in theory—that is, under conditions of perfect competition—to a consideration of how it works in fact. It brings us also to look carefully into the question of whether or not marginal productivity establishes a pattern of rewards that can rest its case on some definition of justice. We shall look into these extremely important questions in our next chapters.

LOOKING BACK

KEY CONCEPTS

Factor services

1. The income of the factors of production is derived from the sale of their services—the energy and intelligence of labor, the use of land and capital.

Direct and derived demand; derived demand is the marginal revenue product of the factor

2. The demand for these services sometimes arises directly from their purchaser as in the case of land bought for a home, but generally it is derived demand—the demand of a firm for the revenues the services will bring. These revenues are called the marginal revenue products of the factor. They are the marginal physical increment to production the factor will create, times the selling price of that output.

Supply curve of individual labor is backward bending

3. The supply side of the factor market varies with each factor. Typically, the willingness of individuals to offer their labor increases as earnings rise, and then decreases giving us a backward-bending supply curve of labor. This is because above a certain income level individuals prefer to sacrifice some potential money income for leisure.

Supply curve of savings is price inelastic, except for allocation

4. The supply curve of capital that most interests us is the supply of savings. The flow of savings is very responsive to income changes, much less so to price changes. But the allocation of savings among users is highly price elastic.

Supply curve of land vs. space

5. The supply curve of land is highly price inelastic; but the supply curve for space is very price elastic.

Quasi rents, or economic rents, are scarcity returns. They are price-determined, not price-determining

6. Quasi rent, or economic rent, is the name for scarcity returns that accrue to factors (land, labor, or capital) by virtue of their scarcity. Unlike true rent, a quasi rent does not tempt additional factors onto the market. A quasi rent is therefore price-determined, not price-determining; it results from a high price for the factor at the margin, and does not constitute an explanation of why the marginal factor is high priced. (From the viewpoint of the person who pays a quasi rent, it is, of course, a cost and enters into his costs.)

Quasi rents are socially wasteful, but useful in allocation

7. Quasi rents are a social waste because they do not induce additional production. But they play a useful role in the allocation of scarce resources.

Capitalization determines factor values by dividing their earnings by the appropriate interest rate. Capitalization removes quasi rents

8. Capitalization is the process by which we use factor earnings (including their quasi rents) to determine the value of the factors themselves. We capitalize a factor by dividing its earnings by the appropriate interest rate for its class of risk. Thus as interest rates decline, capitalized values rise. After a capitalized factor is sold; it no longer earns a quasi rent for its purchaser, but simply a normal return for its degree of risk.

Ideally, all factors earn their MRPs

This marginal productivity theory of distribution implies no exploitation

9. We can generalize about factor incomes as ideally determined by the interplay of their supply curves with their respective demand curves. The demand curves are their marginal revenue product curves or the curve of the marginal revenues they will earn for their buyer. This is called the marginal productivity theory of distribution. Under marginal productivity theory each factor receives its full contribution to revenues as its reward. There is no possible exploitation.

$$\frac{P_x}{MP_x} = \frac{P_y}{MP_y}$$

10. All factors will also be paid proportionally to their contributions to revenues. Therefore we can write:

$$\frac{\text{Price of factor X}}{\text{Marginal product of factor X}} = \frac{\text{Price of factor Y}}{\text{Marginal product of factor Y}}$$

ECONOMIC VOCABULARY

Direct vs. derived demand 444
Marginal revenue product 445
Backward-bending supply curve 446
Psychic income 447
Quasi rent 452
Economic rent 452
Capitalization 454
Marginal productivity theory of distribution 455
Exploitation 456

QUESTIONS

1. When suburban homeowners buy real estate, what services are they actually buying? When they hire domestic help, what services are they buying? When they borrow money from a bank?
2. What is meant by the *derived* demand for labor? What is its relationship to the marginal revenue product of labor? To clarify your understanding, do the following: (1) Run over in your mind the law of diminishing returns; (2) be sure you understand how this law affects marginal *physical* productivity; (3) explain how we go from marginal physical product to marginal *revenue* product; and (4) explain how marginal revenue product influences the willingness of the employer to hire a factor.
3. If the rent of a piece of land is $500 and the rate of interest is 5 percent, what is the value of the land? Suppose the rate falls to 2 1/2 percent; does the value of the land rise or fall? If the rental increases to $1,000 and interest is unchanged, what happens to the value of the land?

4. What do you think the supply curve of executive labor looks like? Is it backward bending? Would you expect it to be more or less backward bending than the supply curve of common labor? Why?
5. Exactly what is rent? How does it differ from quasi rent? Is there any similarity between rent and interest, or rent and wages? What is the role of ownership in rent, profits, *and wages?*
6. What is meant by saying that rent is price-determining? What does it mean to say that economic rent is price-determined? Show on a diagram.
7. Explain carefully how factor returns are proportional to their marginal productivities. What conditions would be necessary to make this theoretical conclusion true in the real world?

AN EXTRA WORD ABOUT
THE PROBLEM OF EQUITY

Most Americans—indeed, most people in the modern world—would admit to an underlying bias in favor of equality in their social values. We hear of policies in every nation that seek to diminish the differences between rich and poor. We hear of very few policies that openly advocate greater inequality. Even policies that support greater inequality—for example tax loopholes for millionaires—are justified in terms of their ultimate effect in raising the incomes of *all,* presumably lessening poverty.

Starting with this bias in favor of equality, we need some understanding of the kind of exceptions we may make to the general rule. That is, we need to know and to look carefully into the arguments in favor of inequality. There are four of them.

1. *We agree that inequality is justified if everyone has a fair chance to get ahead.*

Most of us do not object to inequality of outcome—in fact, we generally favor it—if we are convinced that the race was run under fair conditions with no one handicapped at the start.

What are fair conditions? That is where the argument becomes complex. Are large inheritances fair? Most Americans agree that *some* inheritance is fair but that taxes should prevent the full passage of wealth from generation to generation. What about inheritances of talent? No one is much concerned about this. Inheritances of culture? For some time we have been getting exercised over the handicaps that are inherited by persons born in the slum or to nonwhite parents.

2. *We agree to inequality when it is the outcome of individual preferences.*

If the outcome of the economic game results in unequal incomes, we justify these inequalities when they accord with different personal desires. One man works harder than another, so he deserves a larger income. One chooses to enter the law and makes a fortune; the other chooses to enter the ministry and make do with a small income. We acquiesce in these inequalities to the degree that they appear to mirror individual preferences.

3. *We abide by inequality when it reflects merit.*

Merit is not quite the same as fairness or personal preference. It has to do with our belief in the propriety of higher rewards when they are justified by a larger contribution to output. Here is the belief that underpins the idea that factors should be paid their marginal revenue product. We do not object to factors receiving different remunerations in the market, because we can show that each factor contributes a different amount to total output.

This is, of course, only a value judgment. Suppose there are two workers, side by side, on the assembly line. One is young, strong, unmarried, and very productive. The other is older, married, has a large family and many expenses—and is less productive. Should the first be compensated more highly than the second? We find ourselves in a conflict of values here. Our bias toward equality tells us no. Our exception for merit tells us yes. There is no correct solution for this or any other problem involving value judgments. Once again, social values prevail, sometimes paying the younger person more than the older, sometimes both the same, sometimes the older more.

4. *Finally, we agree in violating the spirit of equality when we are convinced that inequality is for the common good.*

The common good is often translated into practical terms of gross national product. Thus we may agree to allow unequal rewards because we are convinced (or persuaded) that this inequality will ultimately benefit us all by raising all incomes as well as the incomes of those who are favored.

The difficult question here is to define the common good. There are many conceptions of what such an objective should be. All incorporate value judgments. Even the common good of survival, which might justify giving a larger reward to those who must be entrusted with survival, is a value judgment. Do all societies deserve to survive? Was Nazi Germany justified in seeking survival at all costs?

EQUITY AND ECONOMICS

These general principles do not describe the way we *should* think about inequality. They are an attempt to describe the way we *do* think about it—the arguments that we commonly hear or raise ourselves to defend an unequal distribution of goods and services or of wealth.

Each of these arguments, as we can see, poses its own tangled problems. And there is every reason that they should be tangled, for the distribution of incomes poses the most perplexing of all economic problems to any society. At one extreme, it criticizes all the privileges and inequalities that every society displays, forcing us to explain to ourselves why one person should enjoy an income larger than he or she can spend, while another suffers from an income too small to permit him a decent livelihood. At the other extreme, it forces us to examine the complications and contradictions of a society of absolutely equal incomes, where each individual (or family?) received the same amount as every other, regardless of differences in physical capacity, life situation, potential contribution to society.

Usually we have to compromise, to find reasons to support income distributions that are neither completely equal or completely unequal. Here is where we lean partly on our actual knowledge of the effects of income distribution on work and output, and partly on our value systems that define allowable exceptions to our basic rule that societies should seek equality as their goal. As our values change—and we are now living in a period when values seem to be changing rapidly—we accord different weights to the various arguments by which we traditionally justify unequal incomes.

THE UNAVOIDABLE PROBLEM

Economic equity is complex, confusing, and often disconcerting. It makes us uneasy, not only because it confronts us with the often shaky presumptions we make about equity, but because we recognize that no solution will ever be found that can be demonstrated to be superior to all others.

Yet there is no escape from trying to specify what is meant by equity. If we fail to make such an effort, we only end up with a hodgepodge of feelings about equity, many of them contradictory or unsatisfying. This does not mean that we can work out a scheme of economic equity free of contradictions or uncertainties. But at least we will have understood why certain contradictions are inherent in the problem of equity, and will be in a position to act with both intelligence and purpose when forced—as are we all—to decide which economic policies are better and which are worse.

Chapter 30 HOW INCOMES ARE DISTRIBUTED: In Fact

A LOOK AHEAD

Here is a chapter in which we examine two matters of great importance:

(1) the way in which income is actually distributed among individuals or families; and

(2) the various ways in which we have tried to achieve a fairer income distribution than the existing one.

Once again, it is important not to get bogged down in facts, although the basic realities are important to know. The question to think about is *why* income distribution does not seem to bear much relation to marginal productivity theory, and *why* various efforts to change income distribution have had very different impacts. Thus we are still interested in theory, even though we zero in on the distribution of income in fact.

At the end of the last chapter we reached the conclusion that the prices of factors could be explained by their marginal productivities. Does this mean that we now have the key to understanding the actual distribution of income in our society? Can we explain riches and poverty, high-paid professions and low-paid ones, in terms of marginal productivity?

The quick answer to that question is "No." Marginal productivity does not explain the basic facts of income distribution as we find it in the United States. Nonetheless, there is a valuable use for the theory. At the end of our chapter we will come back to the question of how we can use marginal productivity. First, however, let us discuss why it fails to explain income distribution as we find it in reality.

RICH AND POOR

Chapter 4 made us familiar with the contours of income distribution. Perhaps you recall our discussion of classes in pages 52–55 or the income parade in the box on p. 55. How much of this panorama can marginal productivity help us understand?

By and large we can eliminate two ends of the income parade. Marginal productivity theory does not explain the existence or persistence of most poverty, and it does not adequately account for the presence of most very high incomes. Let us begin by seeing why this is the case.

POVERTY

Quickly let us review a few major characteristics of American families who are in poverty in 1980.

- About a third of them are black.
- About a half are families headed by a female.
- A seventh of them are over 65 years of age.
- Almost half are juveniles.
- A tenth of the family heads are unemployed.

These are not, of course, the only "reasons" for being poor but they are causative factors that figure to some extent in many cases of poverty. Note, however, these characteristics of poverty have very little to do with productivity. There is no reason to believe that the potential productivity of blacks or women condemns so many of them to low income status. (We shall discuss that question later.) Persons over 65 need not have low marginal productivity. Some of our most prominent artists, statesmen, lawyers, and executives are older than 65. And of course, the marginal productivity of an unemployed person is zero—not because he or she is not productive, but because he or she has no job.

LOW WAGES

Marginal productivity theory therefore gives us very little insight into the reasons for the low income of the bottom fifth of the nation. It sheds light on this bottom bracket only to the extent that its members are employed in very low-wage (presumably low-productivity) jobs. A considerable number of those in poverty do hold low-wage jobs: 40 percent of the poor work. But we shall see that their low pay is better explained by market imperfections than by attributing a kind of innate low productivity to the person who holds the job.

Thus poverty is a question that we must examine from perspectives other than that of marginal productivity. Why does the economy not produce full employment? Why does it have regional differences in productivity? Why does discrimination exist? Why is there a culture of poverty in the slums, from which it is difficult to break away?

Some of these questions are dealt with in this text. Others go beyond the scope or knowledge of economists. Clearly, when we want to explain most poverty, marginal productivity theory will serve us poorly.

RICHES

What about the upper end of the income scale, the top 5 percent of families enjoying incomes over $45,000 or the topmost echelon of millionaires? Can marginal productivity help us explain high incomes?

To some extent perhaps it can. The marginal revenue product—that is, the saleable output—of many skilled professions helps to explain why airplane pilots, surgeons, lawyers, skilled artisans, and TV newscasters have high incomes; but even here there is a problem. Some of these high incomes are quasi rents. Pay is high partly because there are many hurdles placed in the way of learning some

PERPETUATION OF INCOME DIFFERENCES

Possession of wealth has the added advantage of making it easier for the wealthy, or their children, to go to college or professional school. Recall our anecdote on how poverty causes poverty in the box on page 70. Conversely, high incomes cause high incomes.

The accompanying table shows the advantage accruing to children of upper-income families in acquiring the college education that is a stepping stone toward higher incomes for themselves.

Family income (1965)	*% 1966 high-school graduates starting college in 1967*
Under $3,000	19.8%
$3,000–$4,000	32.3
$4,000–$6,000	36.9
$6,000–$7,500	41.1
$7,500–$10,000	51.0
$10,000–$15,000	61.3
Over $15,000	86.7

Another example of the tendency of different income and social levels to reproduce their respective economic levels can be seen in the second table,

Father's occupation when son was 16	*Son's occupation in March 1962*		
	White-collar	*Blue-collar*	*Farm*
White-collar	71.0%	27.6%	1.5%
Blue-collar	36.9	61.5	1.6
Farm	23.3	55.2	21.6

which compares the occupations of sons with those of their fathers, for 1962.

Although the table shows considerable movement out of one's parent's group into other groups, it also shows that the great majority of white-collar families produce white-collar sons. The preponderance of blue-collar families produce blue-collar sons, and most young farmers come from farming families.

highly paid skills. Thus, just as in the case of low wage earners, market imperfections must be taken into account in explaining these extremes of income.

PROPERTY

More important, the topmost echelons of income reflect the unequal ownership of property. As we have seen in Chapter 2, wealth is very unevenly distributed. Almost half of all property income is channeled into the hands of the top 2 percent of households. In 1979, this provided $175 billion for the 1.1 million families at the apex of the pyramid.

Can marginal productivity explain this concentration of property incomes? Not very well. Conventional economic theory explains the accumulation of wealth by saving. Undoubtedly some persons do accumulate modest sums by refraining from consumption, but they do not accumulate fortunes. If you start with $100,000—a sum possessed only by a very small fraction of all families—and if you invest the sum at 10 percent, paying a 50 percent tax on your interest, it would take a lifetime (actually 47 years) to pile up $1 million.

Very few millions are put together this way. The goal of riches seems to have two approaches. One is via the road of inheritance, the source of approximately half of today's fortunes. The other is via the road of instant riches, the main source of new fortunes and in most cases the original source of the old fortunes as well.

INSTANT WEALTH

How does someone become rich overnight? Luck is helpful—once, anyway. People who make a fortune in one endeavor rarely go on to make as great a gain in another. Financial institutions, who employ the best expertise available, actually do not fare any better with their investments than the average performance of the stock market.

If luck seems to play a crucial role in selecting the winner, another element establishes the size of the winnings. Suppose that an inventor figures it will cost $1 million to build and equip a plant to make a newly patented product. The product should sell at a price that will bring a profit of $300,000. A bank puts up the money.

The plant is built and the expected $300,000 profit is realized. Now comes the instant fortune. To the nation's capital markets, the actual cost of the plant is of no consequence. *What counts is its return and the going rate of return on similar kinds of investments.* If that rate is 10 percent, the inventor's plant is suddenly worth $3 million, for this is the sum that will yield $300,000 at a 10 percent return. The inventor is now worth $2 million, over and above what he owes to the bank. He will have risen to the status of an instant millionaire because the financial markets will have capitalized his earnings into capital gains and not because his marginal productivity—or his saving—has made him rich.

THE MIDDLE STRATA

Thus we do not look to marginal productivity theory—although we may use other elements of economic analysis—when we seek to explain the presence of very high incomes. Then what about the middle strata, the 85 percent of families who are above the status of low income and below that of the top 5 percent? Can marginal productivity help us here?

SOME BASIC PROBLEMS

Consider Table 30.1. Can we say, on the basis of marginal productivity theory, that a salaried engineer who earns $20,000 is twice as productive as a laborer who earns $10,000? Or should we say that the engineer is *only* twice as productive as a laborer because the former makes only twice as much? It is hard to make sense of the question, because it is very difficult to figure the marginal revenue products of engineers or laborers. Even if we knew their productivities, it would be difficult to state that earnings in different occupations reflected productivities because of the many barriers to mobility. We will soon discuss this further.

TABLE 30.1 MEDIAN EARNINGS OF MALES, 1978*

Professionals	19,729
Sales workers	16,839
Managers	19,633
Clerical workers	15,289
Manufacturing operatives	13,470
Service workers	11,057
Laborers, nonfarm	12,031

*Full-time, year-round.

Meanwhile consider a second problem. If we examine the earnings of supposedly homogeneous groups such as female secretaries or male laborers or doctors or professors, we find that some members of the occupation may earn four or five times as much as other members. Few people would claim that a highly paid secretary is as productive as *five* low-paid secretaries or that similar productivity differences could be found in other occupations. Results such as these would be far-fetched in the world of pure competition that marginal productivity theory describes.

MARKET IMPERFECTIONS

This last sentence gives us a clue, for it brings us to problems that prevent the market from bringing about the results that theory predicts. **Marginal productivity theory only applies under conditions of pure competition. Market imperfections play the same role in the factor market that noncompetitive market structures play in the market for goods and services. They result in prices higher or lower than the long-run equilibrium prices that a competitive supply and demand setting would produce.** Let us look into some of these imperfections.

IGNORANCE AND LUCK

Markets often fail to bring about a level of earnings corresponding to relative marginal productivities, because marketers do not have all the relevant information. A skilled mason in Connecticut may not know that there is a brisk demand for masons in Arizona—or even Rhode Island. A high-school graduate looking for her first job may not know that the possibilities for high wages are much greater in printing than in retailing. This is one reason why earnings depart from levels that can be explained by a theory based on rational, informed behavior. Luck and chance play roles in determining the spread of ordinary earnings, just as in the attainment of wealth.

MONOPOLIES

Ignorance and luck are involuntary market imperfections. More striking are market imperfections introduced by institutions that *deliberately seek to set factor prices above or below equilibrium prices.* This is the case whenever there is an element of monopolization in the factor market; for instance, in a small town where one landowner controls virtually all the real estate or where a single bank controls the availability of local capital. In these cases we would expect the level of rents or interest to be higher than the equilibrium level. In the same way, if one company dominates the labor market, we may find that wages are *below* their equilibrium levels—that labor is paid less than its marginal revenue product because it has nowhere else to look for work.

One of the most important institutions creating factor monopolies is the labor union. Essentially, a union tries to establish a floor for wages above the equilibrium rate that the market would establish. In this way, the economic effect of a union is exactly like that of a minimum wage law.

In dealing with monopolies of all kinds in the factor market, we have to distinguish between two questions. The first has to do with the earnings of the factors. No one doubts that factor earnings can be depressed below their competitive equilibrium levels in a one-company town or can be raised above their competitive levels by a powerful union. The more interesting question is the effect of such changes on the total earnings of the factor. Can a union, by raising wages, increase total payrolls, or will the effect of higher wages be to shrink payrolls? Look for this question in "An Extra Word" at the end of the chapter.

RENTS AND DISCRIMINATION

Anything that inhibits the mobility of factors—anything that impedes their movement from lower paid to higher paid occupations—creates or perpetuates economic or quasi rents and enters into the explanation of income differences. Barriers of race and wealth, of patents and initiation fees, of geography and social custom—all give rise to shelters behind which such rents flourish. If blacks, for instance, are systematically excluded from managerial positions, the supply of managers will be smaller than otherwise. Existing (white) managers will therefore enjoy economic rents.

The other side of this story is that barriers can constitute sources of *discrimination that lower the earnings of those who are discriminated against.*

DISCRIMINATION AGAINST BLACKS

To what extent does discrimination enter into income distribution in the United States? The most obvious instance has to do with blacks. The average black family has an income well below that of the average white family. In virtually every field, black earnings are less than white earnings in the same jobs. In itself, of course, such facts do not prove that wage discrimination exists. An apologist for the differentials in wages could claim that there is a real difference

TABLE 30.2 MEAN EARNINGS OF BLACKS AS A % OF MEAN EARNINGS OF WHITES, 1978

	BLACK WORKERS Female	Male
18–24	87	79
25–34	105	75
35–44	110	66
45–54	98	57
55–64	72	60
65 and over	52	47
Total	98	65

in the marginal productivity of whites and blacks. In that case the question is whether there has been discrimination at a more basic level; for instance, in the access to human capital.

Only a few years ago, it would have been simple to demonstrate that blacks were systematically prevented from acquiring equal skills or gaining access to jobs on equal terms. Their marginal productivity was lower because they were forced into the bottom jobs of society, unable to gain admission into many colleges, kept out of high-wage trades, and simply condemned by their own past poverty from accumulating the money needed to buy an education that would allow them to compete.

This picture is now changing in some important respects as Table 30.2 shows. Mean earnings of blacks are closer to those of whites than in the past, especially among younger workers. Among black women aged 25–44 they are even higher. This change is the result of a substantial lowering of barriers against blacks entering many professions and occupations.

DISCRIMINATION AGAINST WOMEN

A second major area of discrimination militates against women. Table 30.3 compares women's pay (on a full-time, year-round basis) to that of men. As the table shows, women typically earn substantially less than men in all occupations. A portion of this differential may stem from women withdrawing from the labor force to have children and to nurture them in their early years, but there is no doubt that these "economic" reasons for pay differentials do not begin to account for the full differences we observe.

TABLE 30.3 MALE AND FEMALE EARNING DIFFERENTIALS, 1978, FULL-TIME, FULL-YEAR WORKERS

Occupation	Women	Men
Professional, management	12,647	19,729
Engineers, salaried	10,689	19,633
Sales workers	7,644	16,839
Craft	9,584	15,776
Clerical	9,158	15,289
Operatives	8,005	13,660
Service workers	6,832	11,057
Nonfarm laborers	7,452	12,031
Laborers, farm	n.a.	7,948

There is a striking male-female pay differential. Do you think this reflects differences in marginal productivity?

ECONOMIC RENT IN HIGH PLACES

Much of the very high incomes of corporate managers is also probably economic rent. In 1962, according to Robert Averitt (*The Dual Economy*, Norton, p. 178) the salaries and bonuses paid to the 56 officers and directors of General Motors exceeded the combined remuneration received by the President of the United States, the Vice-President, 100 senators and 435 representatives, 9 Supreme Court Justices, 10 cabinet members, and the governors of 50 states.

How could we ascertain whether the incomes of the General Motors executives (or for that matter, of the officials of government) contained economic rent? The answer is simple: we would have to reduce their incomes and observe whether they reduced their output of work. Presumably that is what the income tax tries to do, and studies indicate that the payment of a portion of income to the government does not seem to affect the supply curve of labor for executive skill. The presumption, then, is that a good part of their income is an economic rent, which the income tax siphons off in part.

Statistics comparing men and women at age 35 show that the average *single* woman will be on her job another 31 years—longer than her male counterpart will work—and the average *married* woman will work another 24 years. Second, the facts show that married women are *less* likely to leave one employer for another than men are (only 8.6 percent of employed women changed employers in a year compared with 11 percent of men). Finally, U.S. Public Health data reveal that on the average, women are absent from work only 5.3 days per year, a fractionally *better* record than men's.

In recent years we have seen a good deal of stirring for equal rights for women, and we get the impression that discrimination against women is disappearing. The statistics do not support this. The proportional gap between male and female earnings of full-time workers has not changed since the 1930s!

PUERTO RICANS, CHICANOS, INDIANS, OTHERS

Blacks are by no means the only racial group that suffers from discrimination. The table below shows the family income of Hispanics relative to white families.

	Income, as % of white family income	
	1969	*1978*
Hispanic	54%	68%

There is a shocking absence of data on the poorest and smallest group of all, the American Indians. Based on reports from about half of U.S. reservations, the median income of American Indians is on the order of *one-third* that of white families.

Now, a more cheerful word. If we look at income data of all ethnic groups, we find only three major groups with incomes below the national average: blacks, those of Spanish heritage, and Indians. Of 100 million Americans who claim ethnic backgrounds, 80 million have incomes *higher* than those of Americans who consider themselves to be ethnically native. In 1972 the ethnic groups with the highest average family income were Russians, then Poles, then Italians.

Will it change? The Women's Liberation movement has won court battles to establish the right of equal pay for equal work, as well as equal rights to jobs, regardless of sex. Perhaps this will begin to alter our prevailing sexist patterns.

The United States has been very slow to admit women to a full range of professional and occupational opportunities. Only about 10 percent of our doctors are women, for example, whereas in West Germany 20 percent and in the U.S.S.R., 70 percent, are women. Perhaps even more surprising, in Sweden 70 percent of overhead crane operators are women, an occupation virtually unknown to women in the U.S.* These surprising percentages at both ends of the social scale leave little doubt that women *could* earn a great deal more than they do, if the barriers of discrimination were removed.

REFERENCE GROUPS

Another distributional problem arises because people have strong feelings about how much they are entitled to. In our competitive model, each person is a rational income maximizer, out for himself. At no time does any supplier of labor look at the wages of *other* laborers, except to determine whether or not he is being paid the competitive rate of return.

Yet real people do not focus narrowly on their own wages but look around them at the entire wage structure. A policeman looks at firemen's wages, at truckers', perhaps even at schoolteachers' incomes. This interest in other incomes has different labels. Sociologists would call it an interest in *reference groups.*

Reference groups seem to be both stable and restricted—people look at groups that are economically close to themselves. This helps explain why very large inequalities in the distribution of economic rewards seem to cause relatively little dissatisfaction, whereas small inequalities can raise a great commotion. A policeman does not expect to make as much as a movie actor—Hollywood is not his reference point. He does expect to make as much as, or more than, a sanitation worker, perhaps as much as a teacher. Changes in the pay of his reference groups therefore bring immediate changes in his estimation of the fairness of his own pay.

As a result of these comparisons, groups strongly resist changes in relative wage rates. Even the person benefitting from a change in relative wages may feel that it is unfair that he or she receive more than someone else. Consequently, labor economists have discovered that wage rates among many groups move together, almost independently of movements in the supply and demand curves in each occupation.

USES OF MARGINAL PRODUCTIVITY THEORY

All these and still other difficulties explain why the distribution of income, even in the middle range, cannot be fully explained by marginal productivity theory, and why we must be very careful in assuming that the theory adequately accounts for variations in earnings—riches and poverty aside.

Should we then forget about the theory? Not quite. For just as the pure theory of competition helped to explain movements and tendencies in the real market, even if not real market prices, so marginal productivity can enlighten us

*The Conference Board, *Record,* Feb. 1971, p. 10.

with respect to economic reality. **It tells us how entrepreneurs behave in hiring factors. It explains the simple but crucial fact that entrepreneurs will not knowingly hire a factor (or a team of factors) that does not "pay its way." Thus the theory of marginal productivity serves as a first approximation to a theory of employment for the firm, even if it does not explain very much about factor incomes.** However incomes are determined—by law, power, custom, or the marketplace—entrepreneurs will be guided in hiring factors by their relative profitability, which is to say, by comparing their cost with the marginal revenue product he can hope to obtain from them. As its marginal productivities rise, more of a factor will be hired. As they fall, less of it will be used.

Thus the theory helps elucidate one aspect of economic life. We simply must be careful not to claim that it explains income distribution or that different levels of earnings are justified by marginal productivity.

CHANGING INCOME DISTRIBUTION

Can we change the distribution of income? Of course we can. Should we? That is a more difficult question. When we speak of deliberately trying to change the distribution of income, our purpose is usually to make it fairer. By *fairer,* we generally mean more equal, although not always. Sometimes we say it is not fair that certain groups, such as schoolteachers, do not get higher incomes, even though they are already receiving incomes that are above the median for the society. In the discussion that follows, we will largely be concerned with ways of making income distribution fairer by making it more equal.*

If you want to change income distribution, you must choose among four basic ways of going about your task. You may try to change the marginal productivities of individuals and then let them fend for themselves on the market. Or you may try to limit the workings of the market, so that certain people will receive larger or smaller incomes even if their marginal productivities remain the same. Or you may let marginal productivities and markets alone and intervene by the mechanism of taxes and transfers, rearranging the rewards of society according to some principle of equity. Finally, you can introduce some system of rewards wholly different from market-determined rewards. This last is the boldest and most far-reaching method, but it is one about which economists have very little to say. Accordingly, we will confine ourselves to the first three methods.

1. CHANGING PRODUCTIVITIES

Assuming that low marginal productivity is a basic reason—if not the only reason—for low incomes, someone who wants to change income distribution would do well to begin by boosting the marginal productivity of the least skilled and trained. How can **human capital** be improved? By and large, by giving *education,* a generalized skill, or *training,* a specialized skill, to those who lack them.

Education and income. A glance at Table 30.4 makes it clear that there is a strong functional relationship between education and lifetime earnings.

We must be careful not to jump to the conclusion that education is the

*See "An Extra Word" on equity at the end of the previous chapter.

TABLE 30.4 MALE EDUCATION AND AVERAGE LIFETIME EARNINGS

	Lifetime earnings (1978)
Elementary school	
0–7 years	$316,000
8 years	388,000
High school	
1–3 years	511,000
4 years	588,000
College	
1–3 years	696,000
4 years or more	826,000

Education and incomes are obviously correlated. This does not mean that education causes the whole difference. The payoff on educational investment is about 7 to 10 percent.

direct cause of these earnings, however. For example, 30 percent of white high-school graduates will end up making more money than the average college graduate, and 20 percent of college graduates will make less than the average high-school graduate. Clearly there is no guarantee that education will pay off for everyone.

There is also a problem of scale. The table shows us that college graduates as a group have higher incomes. This may be because there are fewer of them and they earn scarcity rents. If everyone went to college, the supply and demand situation would be radically different, and the extra earnings of the college group much smaller.

Last there is the problem of circular causation that we have encountered before (see the box, "Perpetuation of Income Differences," in the preceding chapter p. 464). Education may indeed be a factor in increasing lifetime earnings. It is also true that someone coming from a high-income family will receive more education and will probably earn a high income *because of his social station in life.* When we correct for the starting point on the income scale, education still yields a return, but a much smaller one than the figures in Table 30.4 indicate. **Probably the cost of a college education gives its recipient a lifetime return of about 7 to 10 percent on that investment, hardly a bonanza.**

Investment in human capital. Even if the advantages of education are frequently exaggerated in terms of their strictly economic results, there is no doubt that education is a help toward higher income. For one thing, it teaches general skills such as reading, writing, and math. Equally valuable is its teaching of behavior expected in high-level occupations: how to speak politely, how to be punctual, how to relate to authority, and other often overlooked attributes of classroom discipline that prepare us for jobs, especially managerial jobs.

2. INTERVENING ON THE DEMAND SIDE OF THE MARKET

A quite different way of going about the task of changing the income distribution is to intervene on the demand side of the market. The most widespread current intervention is that of minimum wages—whether imposed by law or unions. As we shall see in "An Extra Word" at the end of the chapter, minimum wages have two impacts. They raise earnings for those who are employed, but may cause some other people to lose their jobs. The size of these two groups depends upon the elasticity of demand for labor.

In the last decade there have been two other broad attempts to intervene on the demand side of the labor market. Governments have attempted to alter the demand for workers by antidiscrimination or affirmative action laws and regulations and by subsidizing private on-the-job training.

Antidiscrimination laws apply to every employer. No one can legally deny a person a job or a promotion based upon age, sex, race, or national origin. Affirmative action regulations apply only to firms that do business with government or receive payments from government, but many companies are in this category. Here government requires that the firm, public agency, or university have some plan for altering its distribution of employment in favor of groups that are underemployed relative to their proportion of the population. Usually blacks, Hispanics, and women are designated as the groups requiring affirmative action.

Unfortunately, the intended effects of the legislation have not been realized. **Affirmative action has undoubtedly helped some members of disadvantaged groups, especially well-trained or educated persons, such as black or female teachers, lawyers, or administrators, but there has been very little effect on relative pay differences for average earners in either group.**

3. TAXES AND TRANSFERS

A third means of altering income distribution is to tax high incomes and to subsidize low ones. Taxes and subsidies (or *transfers*, as they are called) are used by all governments to redistribute incomes.

In Chapter 33 we will look into our tax system with some care. Here we are interested only in its effect on income shares. **And by and large, there seems little doubt that the overall effect of this system leaves income shares much as they were before taxes, especially for income receivers above the poverty line and below the top 5 percent.** As we will see later in some detail (p. 524), the impact of federal, state, and local taxes on incomes above $5,000 and below $50,000 is virtually the same. In all brackets, income receivers pay about 20 to 25 percent of their incomes to the government.

If we look at inheritance taxes, which hit wealth, not income, we see a system that appears to be "progressive," i.e., to tax high incomes proportionately more than low ones. Maximum tax rates on estates reach as high as 77 percent. But the loopholes to avoid these very high taxes are so numerous that almost no one pays them. Inheritance tax collections amount to an annual wealth tax of less than 0.2 percent. Obviously, these taxes cannot have much impact on the distribution of wealth.

EFFECTIVENESS OF TRANSFERS

Although taxes do not have much impact on the distribution of income, transfer payments do. If we look at the families in the bottom 20 percent of the population, we find that over 60 percent of their income comes in the form of transfer payments. Without such payments, their share of total income would be less than half of what it is now.

At the same time, existing income transfer programs are not well coor-

AFFIRMATIVE ACTION PROGRAMS

No government program to alter the distribution of earnings has been more controversial than the affirmative action requirements, for affirmative action offends people in a way that anti-discrimination laws do not. People may object violently to the results of anti-discrimination laws or to techniques of compliance, such as busing; but almost no one is willing to argue that an unequal start is a good thing. People may call training programs for the poor inefficient, but no one calls them un-American.

Affirmative action laws make people angry because they seem to be unfair. In order to find qualified members of minority groups, firms or agencies or universities have to pass over fully qualified members of majority groups. Is it fair not to hire a qualified white electrician because affirmative action gives a preference to a black one, or not to hire a young male graduate student as a teacher because a college is short of women instructors?

The fairness issue really comes down to the obligations of one generation to redress the grievances of another. Suppose that discrimination disappeared magically tomorrow. Blacks would still be holding the jobs that were open to them in the discrimination-filled past. If nothing further were done, it would take about 45 years—the time it takes for a generation to pass through the labor market—for the effects of past discrimination to be eliminated. Affirmative action can thus be viewed as an attempt to offset the impact of past injustice.

Does it also create present injustice? Is the white electrician, the male graduate student fairly treated? Most people say no. At the same time, we must try to see the problem from the viewpoint of the whole society as well as from that of the offended person. Is it not possible that a society is becoming more fair, even though some individuals are being treated less fairly? Those persons who suffer from affirmative action today are the victims of our efforts to overcome the unfairness of the past. The problem is therefore whether we can remedy the failures of past generations without inflicting injuries on some members of the present generation.

Ideally there is no reason why not. To raise up a previously disprivileged person does not require that someone else be put down. But the ideal solution requires an expansive economy where the demand for talent outstrips the supply. In a sluggish environment, the fight for advancement becomes a zero sum game, and my gain becomes possible only at the expense of your loss. This has been the situation during the past ten years of inadequate growth. In such a situation there are bound to be losers. The question is: who will they be?

dinated. Some poor people receive a lot of benefits; other poor people receive none. Some programs provide benefits for people who, on a lifetime basis, will not be poor. Programs are often locally administered, leading to benefit levels that differ greatly from state to state.

NEGATIVE INCOME TAX

To overcome these problems, presidents or presidential candidates in both parties have recommended the establishment of a Negative Income Tax. In 1978 the Department of Labor Statistics defined as "poor" an urban family of four having less than $6,600 annual income. Under a Negative Income Tax, we would transfer income to all families having less than that amount. This would have cost about $20 billion, roughly one percent of GNP.

This seems like a simple method of eliminating poverty. It has problems, however. Suppose that we also decided *not* to help people as they rose above the officially defined poverty level, so that we reduced the amount of aid by the amount of any income a poor family earned. Thus, if a family earned $3,000, it would then get $3,600 in assistance. If it earned $4,000, it would get $2,600. If it earned $6,600, it would get nothing.

This seems equitable, at first look. *Actually, it is the same as a 100 percent tax on all earnings under $6,600.* Why should any family bother to earn any sum less then $6,600 if its welfare is immediately reduced by that amount? Would it not be sensible—rational—to stay on relief, rather than take a low-paying and probably unpleasant job?

WORK INCENTIVES

Unfortunately, this is the way many welfare programs have been administered in the past. Not surprisingly, they have resulted in strong disincentives to work. **Accordingly, economists now propose that assistance programs should have work incentives built into them.**

This means we must tax below-poverty earnings at less than 100 percent. To make the arithmetic simple, let's tax at 50 percent—actually a very high tax rate, since it is the top rate currently paid on the highest salaries earned in the United States. If a family earns $1,000, it must then pay $500 in taxes. This now leaves it with an income of $7,100 after taxes ($6,600 in assistance plus $1,000 in earnings, less $500 in taxes).

Note, however, that we are now making transfer payments to people whose pre-tax income is $7,600—*above* our poverty line of $6,600. If we are to avoid taxing away all increases in earned incomes, we shall have to continue to make transfer payments until family earnings reach $13,200. At this point, a family's budget would look like this:

Transfer income	$6,600
Earned income	$13,200
Tax on earnings	– $6,600
Net income	$13,200

THE PROBLEM OF COSTS

This presents us with two problems. The first is economic. Under the plan we have just examined, a "poor" family earning $13,200 would have an advantage over a family that was not deemed "poor" and that earned the same amount, because the second family would owe taxes on all its $13,200 income and would therefore end up less well off than the income-supported family. To remove this inequity, we would have to pay support allowances to *all* families and remove all taxes on nonpoor families' earnings up to $13,200. Costs would rise from the approximately $20 billion needed to eliminate poverty if we impose a 100 percent tax, to a level between $40 and $50 billion. A sharp increase in income tax rates above $13,200 would be necessary to finance this.

THE POLITICAL ISSUE

The second problem is political. Could we persuade the more fortunate to bear the entire income tax burden? With incomes above $13,200, these families

TOWARD AN OPERATIONAL DEFINITION OF FAIRNESS

Can we specify with certainty what a fair income distribution would look like? Of course not. Can we specify a distribution of income that would accord with what most people think is fair? Here we put the question in such a way that we could test the results, for example by an opinion poll.

If we took such a poll, most persons in the United States would probably agree that existing income is not fairly distributed. They consider it unfair that some people are as poor as they are and others are as rich as they are.

Suppose we ask whether the public would approve of an income distribution that had the same shape as that for one group in which the more obvious advantages and disadvantages of the real world were minimized. *That group consists of the white adult males who work full-time and full-year.* It ranges from surgeons to street sweepers. In general, these workers suffer minimally or not at all from the handicaps of race, sex, age, personal deficiencies, or bad economic policies. By examining their earnings rather than their incomes we can eliminate the effects of inherited wealth. Might not such a standard appeal to many people as constituting an operational definition of a just income distribution?

Since the poll has never been taken, we cannot answer the question. But we can examine what income distribution would look like under such a dispensation. The results are shown in the table. It is interesting to note that this standard of fairness, if applied, would reduce the dispersion of income by 40 percent.

Annual earnings ($000s)	*Distribution of income in accordance with "fairness" standard*	*Actual distribution of income, 1970*
$ 0–1	1.7%	10.4%
1–2	1.3	8.3
2–3	1.5	6.9
3–4	3.0	6.8
4–5	4.4	6.2
5–6	6.8	6.7
6–7	8.6	7.0
7–8	10.5	7.8
8–10	19.7	13.2
10–15	27.9	17.7
15–20	11.2	6.8
25 & over	3.3	2.3

would be neither "in" nor "near" poverty. They would have to recognize the unfairness of programs that lock others into low-income brackets with a 100 percent tax on earnings.

There is no economic answer to this question. What is at stake is essentially a political choice between two patterns of income distribution. That choice will be exercised through political programs that will favor one group or another—those at the bottom of the scale or those who are sufficiently affluent to be in the higher taxpaying brackets.

IN REVIEW

Can we change income distributions? Yes, of course. But not all ways of doing so are equally effective. Efforts to change marginal productivities have not yet shown marked results, although this does not detract from their worthwhileness on other criteria. Interventions through minimum wages, unions, or government requirements have undoubtedly benefited some groups but cannot be judged to have made a large-scale difference in our national distribution of income. The impact of taxes (as we shall see in more detail in Chapter 33) has not affected the overall shares. **Only income transfers seem to have made a substantial difference to a large group of the population. In all likelihood, this will be the means by which we can work the quickest changes in income shares, although a determined attack on discriminatory barriers might work the largest and longest lasting effect.**

KEY CONCEPTS

LOOKING BACK

Poverty and riches are not explained by marginal productivity theory

1. Marginal productivity theory does not explain the two ends of the spectrum of income distribution. Most poverty arises from reasons other than low productivity or from reasons that lie behind low productivity. Very high incomes stem from property, rents, capitalization, and luck rather than from measurable high *MRPs.*

Middle strata display large intra-occupational variations

2. The middle strata of income are those most nearly explicable by marginal productivity. But here too there are inexplicable differences, such as the very large variations we find in a given occupation.

Market imperfections lessen the applicability of marginal productivity theory

3. The disturbing elements of the real world are many. One is the presence of monopoly elements in income determination. A second is the influence of discrimination. A third is the role of reference groups. All these and other elements lessen the applicability of marginal productivity theory, which assumes a world of pure competition.

The theory is a useful way of explaining how factor employment is determined

4. Nonetheless, marginal productivity theory is useful as a means of explaining how employment is determined. Given the income of factors, however determined, employers will be guided by *MRPs* when they consider how much of a factor to hire.

Three strategies for income redistribution: productivity, demand, taxes and transfers

5. There are three basic strategies for changing income distribution: changing the productivity of factors, changing the demand for factors, and directly changing incomes by taxes or transfers.

It is difficult to assess the effect of education on income

6. Efforts to change factor productivity by education—building up human capital—are difficult to measure with precision. Undoubtedly education helps individuals toward higher incomes, but the effect is not clear-cut and may not obtain if everyone is equally educated.

Intervening on the demand side to offset discrimination has only limited effectiveness

7. Intervening on the demand side by affirmative action and other programs to remedy discrimination has helped professional blacks and women, but not much affected general earnings of disadvantaged groups.

Taxes do not redistribute incomes in the main strata of recipients. Transfers are very important ways of channeling income to low-income receivers

8. Taxes and transfers have different impacts. The effect of taxes is small in changing the shares of income enjoyed by most groups, with the possible exception of the bottom and very top. The most effective method of transferring income seems to be transfer payments, which amount to 60 percent of the income of the lowest fifth of income receivers.

To be effective, a negative income tax program would be costly

9. Negative income taxes would be a useful way of systematizing this redistributive program, but they present problems of cost and of political impact.

ECONOMIC VOCABULARY

Rents and discrimination 467
Reference groups 470
Human capital 471
Affirmative action 473, 474
Negative income tax 474

QUESTIONS

1. How much of the differences in occupational earnings shown in Table 30.1 do you think can be ascribed to marginal productivity? Can you devise a research program that would enable you to study this with allowance for all market imperfections?
2. Which of the following do you consider to be market imperfections that result in earnings higher than those that would be produced by a free market: (1) certification by state boards before anyone can practice medicine; (2) limiting admission to medical school by aptitude examinations; (3) the costs of education, if these can be covered by a long-term loan.
3. Suppose it could be shown that the marginal productivity of blacks in a given occupation was less than that of whites. Would that explain their lower rates of pay? Justify them?
4. A woman patents a gadget that brings her an annual net income of $100,000. The market return for her category of risky products is 20 percent. What is her patent worth? Can you show that the higher the degree of risk, the *less* will be her capitalized gain?
5. Suppose that we instituted a family allowance program that insured an annual income of $6,000 per family and that we taxed all earned income at one third. How high a total income could a family earn before its tax payments to the government exceeded the government's payments to it?
6. Do you think the present educational system works to reduce or to maintain the structure of inequality in rewards? How would you suggest changing it if you wanted less inequality? If you wanted more?

AN EXTRA WORD ABOUT
UNION RATES AND MINIMUM WAGES

Can unions raise wages? Can the government raise the wages of the poor by imposed minimum wages? Few questions in economics generate such heat. We'll try to throw a little economic light on them, too.

Minimum wages enforced by law and minimum wages enforced by union contract have very similar attributes. Both are equivalent to price supports for agricultural products, in that they establish a price higher than that which the market would establish by itself. If they did not, they would not serve any purpose. Thus in Figure 30.1 we can view the wage line *AB* as established by union or government, for in both cases its effect is to establish a wage floor above that set by the intersection of supply and demand.

Three effects follow. Some workers will lose their jobs because the new higher minimum wage is above their marginal revenue product (or above what the employer estimates their *MRP* to be). In the diagram, this amount of lost employment is represented by Q_1–Q_3. Here are the delivery boys who are let go when the minimum wage is raised to $2.50 an hour and small grocery stores decide to cut down their help. Here are the elevator operators who are replaced by automatic elevators when a union wage contract finally tips the balance in favor of automation.

Second, some workers—those between *O* and Q_3—will find their incomes raised. Here are the grocery boys who are kept on at higher pay; the elevator operators who are not fired but have fatter pay envelopes.

Third, there will be a larger number of workers than formerly—those between Q_1 and Q_2—looking for work. Their condition will be neither better nor worse than before the union floor or the minimum wage, for at the previous wage rate these people were not seeking work, nor did they have any income. Nonetheless, their presence in the labor market will be noted in the statistics of unemployment, and it may have social and political consequences.

Is there a net gain or loss in the situation? As you can see, the increase in earnings of the group that is retained can be compared with the loss in income of the group that is fired. There are, however, problems in such a comparison. It is much easier to calculate gains

The volume of employment would be Q_1 if there were no union or minimum wage. This is also the amount of labor that workers would offer at that wage. At the new higher wage level *AB* employers want to hire only Q_3 worth of labor, while workers are interested in supplying Q_2 worth. As we can see, there must be a labor surplus, just as there is an agricultural surplus when farm prices are set above the market equilibrium.

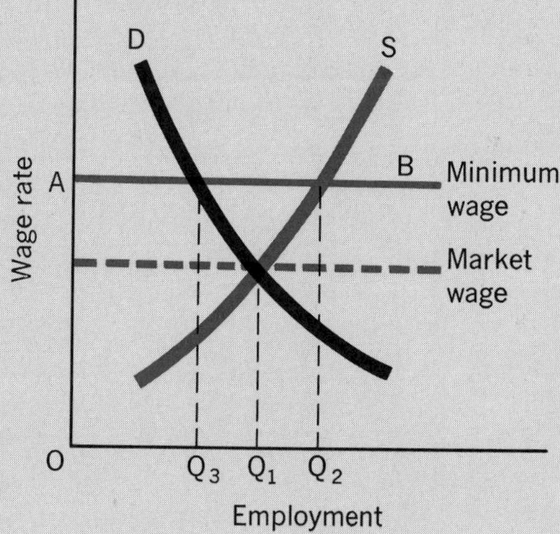

**FIGURE 30.1
EFFECT OF MINIMUM WAGE LAWS**

and losses on a diagram than to compute them in real life. This is because everything hinges on the slopes of the two curves. Suppose, for example, that we think that the demand for labor is extremely inelastic. Then even though unemployment rises, no one will lose his or her job. All will remain employed with higher earnings. To make the point clear, we show this case in Figure 30.2, with a totally inelastic demand curve.

On the other hand, suppose that the demand for labor is highly price elastic. Then many workers could lose their jobs, as you can easily see if you draw a diagram with an elastic curve.

What is the shape of the actual demand curve for labor? Studies indicate that it is probably quite inelastic, so that minimum wage laws do not have a severe adverse effect on total employment. Rather, their effect is likely to be heavily concentrated on certain groups, such as teen-agers. The illustration of delivery boys is not an idle one. A high minimum wage may well result in substantial teen-age unemployment in menial jobs. This has led to suggestions that there should be lower minimum wages for adolescents than for adults, a scheme that has been used in Europe but that has so far been opposed by labor unions in this country.

Union wage settlements also have their gains and losses exactly as do minimum wage laws. Once again the critical factor is the elasticity of the demand for labor. But there is a difference with respect to the impact of union settlements. Minimum wage laws affect only the fringe of workers whose pay is below the minimum. Union settlements typically affect all workers in the industry. The incentive to substitute machines for people or simply to economize on labor is therefore much greater. The economic consequences of a union wage settlement are, accordingly, likely to be more substantial than those of a boost in minimum wages.

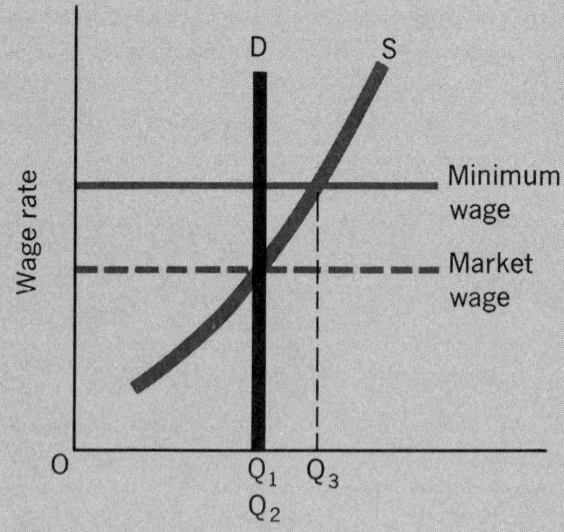

FIGURE 30.2

Part 5 The Major Economic Challenges

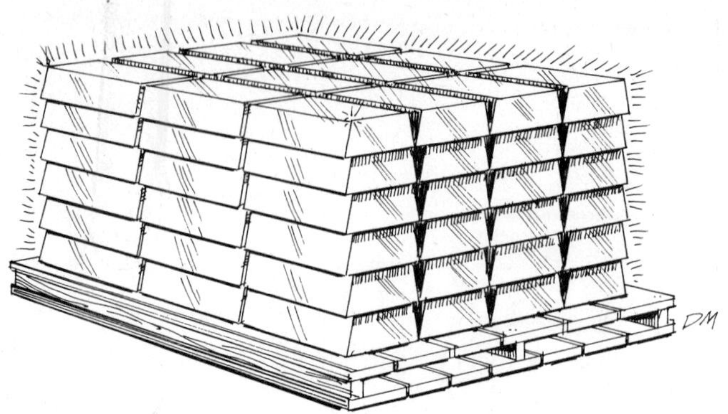

Chapter 31 INFLATION

A LOOK AHEAD

This chapter brings us to the very frontiers of economic knowledge—and ignorance. Inflation is not a problem that is fully understood, therefore it is our own view that is presented here rather than one that is generally accepted, for no such consensus exists.

Three aspects of the inflationary problem will be dealt with here.

(1) Costs. Some costs of inflation are imaginary. Some are threats. Some are real.

(2) Explanations. We shall try to present a cogent argument as to why inflation exists and how it perpetuates itself.

(3) Remedies. There is no sure way of turning off inflation, but we shall examine a number of policies representing a wide spectrum of opinion.

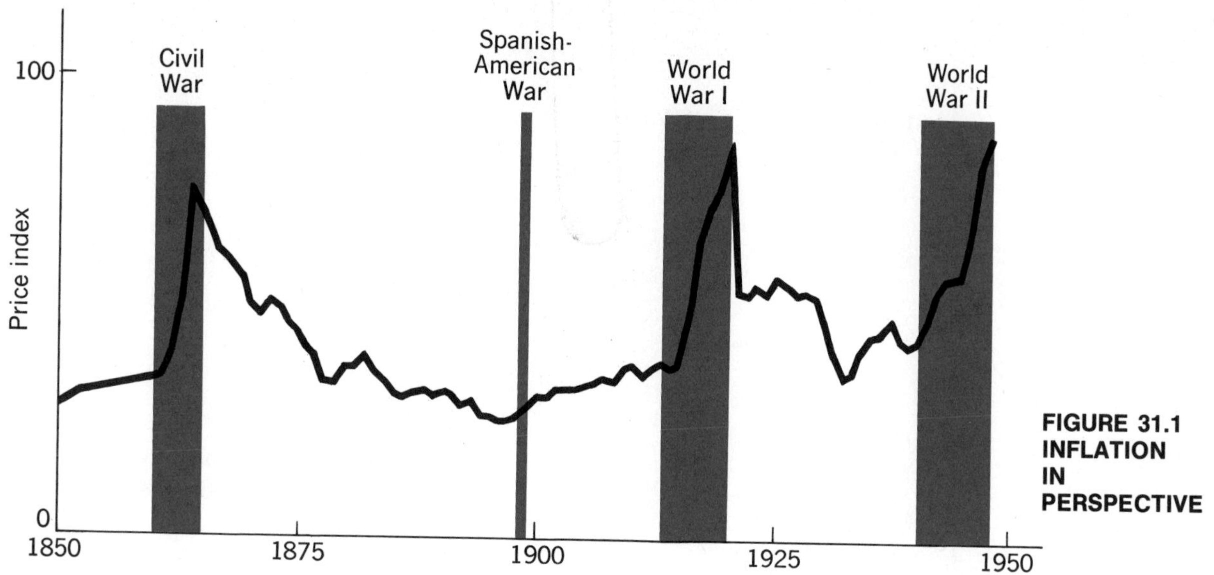

FIGURE 31.1 INFLATION IN PERSPECTIVE

Looking back in history, inflation is a chronic consequence of war. But in the past it was always short-lived.

INFLATION IN RETROSPECT

Inflation is both a very old problem and a very new one. If we look back over history, we discover many inflationary periods. Diocletian tried (in vain) to curb a Roman inflation in the fourth century A.D. Between 1150 and 1325, the cost of living in medieval Europe rose fourfold. Between 1520 and 1650, prices doubled and quadrupled, largely as a result of gold pouring into Europe from the newly opened mines of the New World. In the years following the Civil War, the South experienced a ferocious inflation. And during World War I, prices in the United States rose 100 percent.

Let us focus more closely on the U.S. experience up to 1950 (Figure 31.1). Two things should be noted about this chart. **First, major wars are regularly accompanied by inflation.** The reasons are obvious enough. War greatly increases the volume of public expenditure, but governments do not curb private spending by an equal amount through taxation. Invariably, wars are financed largely by borrowing; and the total amount of spending, public and private, rises rapidly. Meanwhile, the amount of goods available to households is cut back to make room for war production. The result fits the classic description of inflation: Too much money chasing too few goods.

Second, U.S. inflations have always been relatively short-lived in the past. Notice that prices fell during the long period 1866 to 1900, and again from 1925 to 1933. The hundred-year trend, although generally tilted upward, is marked with long valleys as well as sharp peaks.

RECENT INFLATIONARY EXPERIENCE: STAGFLATION

Now examine Figure 31.2, which shows the record of U.S. price changes since 1950. Once again we notice that the outbreak of war has brought price

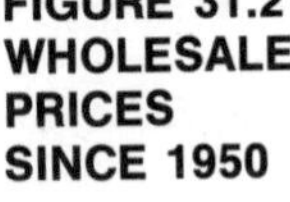

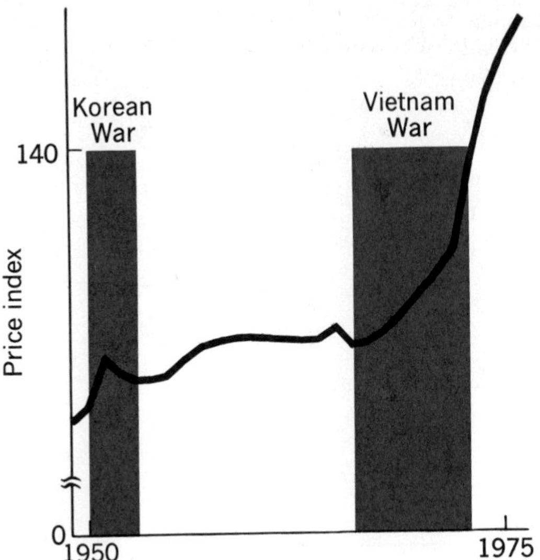

FIGURE 31.2 WHOLESALE PRICES SINCE 1950

After World War II, the pattern changed. Inflation has become chronic and persistent.

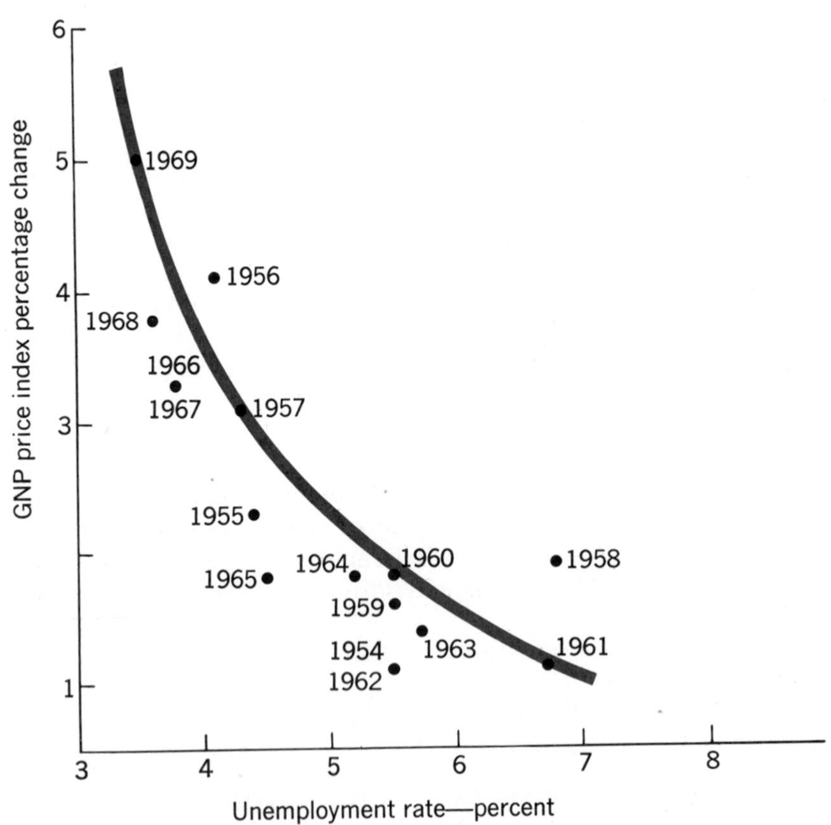

FIGURE 31.3 UNEMPLOYMENT INFLATION RELATION

Until 1969 the Phillips curve looked very clear.

rises, albeit relatively small ones. But in a vital way, contemporary experience differs from that of the past. Peaks of inflationary rises have not been followed by long, gradual declines. Instead, inflation seems to have become a chronic element in the economic situation.

Moreover, the inflation has not only been chronic and persistent, but it has been accompanied by considerable levels of unemployment. We will be looking into unemployment more carefully in our next chapter, but we should note that our rising level of inflation has been accompanied by a rising level of unemployment. In the period 1960–1965, for instance, the rate of inflation averaged 1.6 percent and the average level of unemployment, 5.5 percent. In the years 1975–1979, inflation has jumped to 7.5 percent, and unemployment has also risen, to an average of 7.0 percent.

The presence, side by side, of inflation and unemployment has come as a new puzzle for economists. Economists have always known that inflation was almost inevitable for a system that was bumping up against the boundaries of its production possibilities curve. **But it was widely believed that inflation would go away if we retreated from those boundaries and accepted even a modest amount of unemployment. Now we know that that is not the case. Recession and inflation can exist together in a condition that has become known as *stagflation*—stagnation plus inflation.** Explaining stagflation is the central challenge to economic theory today. Remedying it is the central challenge to economic policy.

THE DISAPPEARING PHILLIPS CURVE

A good way to understand the problem of modern stagflation is to examine what has happened to the most widely accepted recent explanation of inflation, known as the Phillips Curve. Back in 1958 the British economist A. W. Phillips called attention to what then seemed like a very clear-cut and important relationship. This was the correlation between the rate of inflation and the rate of unemployment. The Phillips Curve displaying that relationship for the years through 1969 is shown in Figure 31.3. As you can see, there seems to be a strong correlation—the lower unemployment was, the higher was inflation.

The trouble began as we entered the 1970s. For it became apparent that the relation between unemployment and inflation at least within normal ranges of unemployment was not what we thought. In Figure 31.4 we see the relationship plotted through 1980. There is no longer a predictable association between a given rate of unemployment and its accompanying rate of inflation. Look particularly at the shaded rectangle that covers an unemployment range from about 4.5 percent to 8.5 percent. Inflation rates since 1970 have varied from barely more than 3 percent to over 10 percent—in the early part of 1980 (not shown on the chart) they reached almost 20 percent!

THE COSTS OF STAGFLATION

We will want to look carefully into the reasons behind, and the mechanisms of, this urgent challenge. But first we must take a careful measure of the problem itself. How serious is inflation? What costs does it impose? How costly is the "stag" part of stagflation?

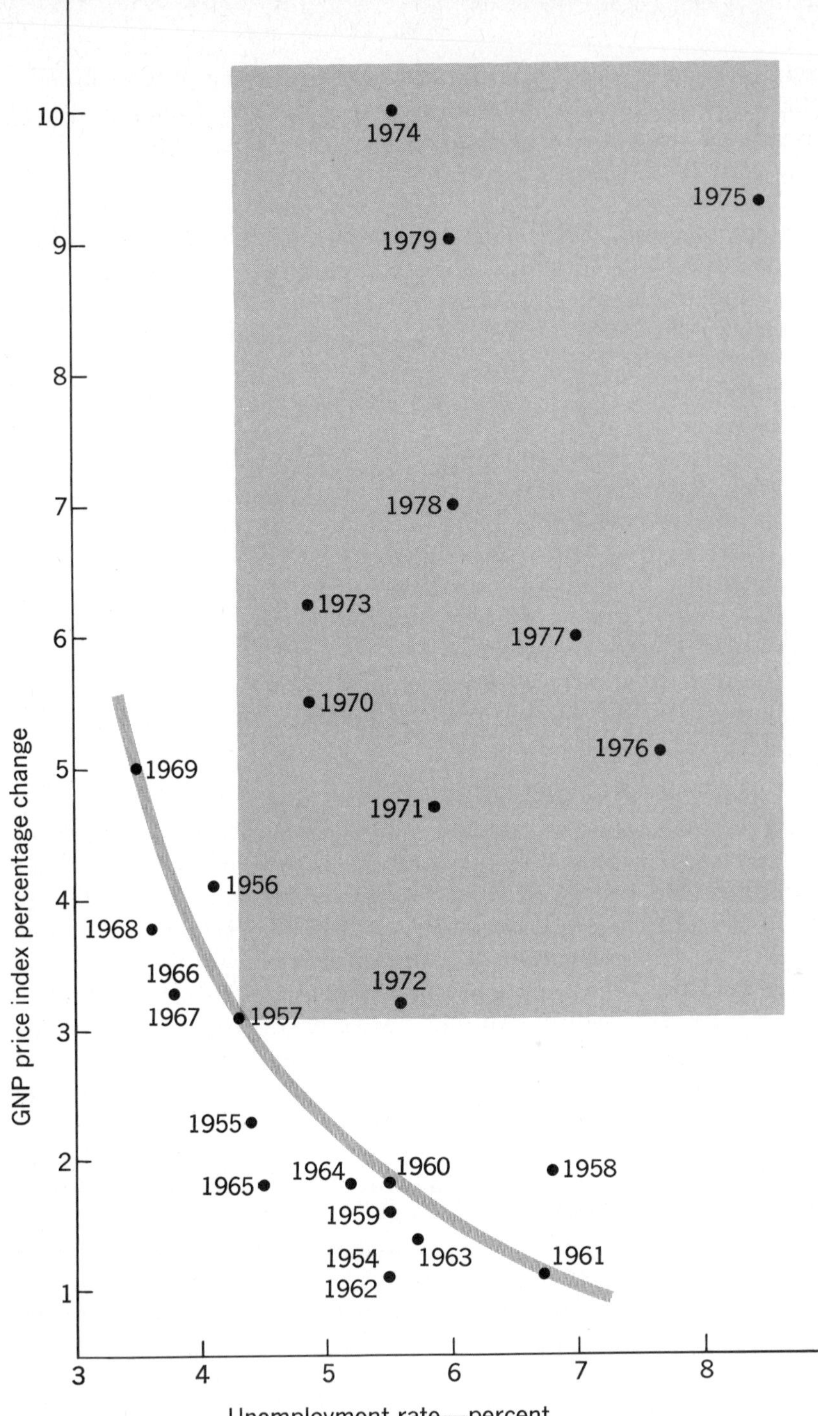

FIGURE 31.4 UNEMPLOYMENT-INFLATION RELATION REEXAMINED

Recent experience makes it clear that there is no reliable unemployment-inflation relation within the "normal" range of unemployment.

SOME IMAGINARY COSTS OF INFLATION

There are real dangers imposed by inflation and certainly there are real costs in stagflation. But there are also imaginary consequences, and we had better clear our heads of those so that we can pay attention to the real problems.

Inflation and Money Illusion. One of the imaginary costs of inflation is that it has been eating away at our real standard of living. This is simply untrue. From 1969 to 1979, real per capita disposable income—income after inflation and taxes and population growth—was up by about 28 percent, as Table 31.1 shows.

TABLE 31.1 PER CAPITA DISPOSABLE PERSONAL INCOME

	Current Dollars	*1972 Dollars*
1969	3,111	3,515
1970	3,348	3,619
1971	3,588	3,714
1972	3,837	3,837
1973	4,285	4,062
1974	4,646	3,973
1975	5,088	4,025
1976	5,504	4,144
1977	6,009	4,285
1978	6,672	4,449
1979	7,279	4,515

Despite inflation, real incomes per capita have risen. The rate of real growth has been about 1.3 percent per year.

Thus the average American is better off, not worse off, than he or she was 8 to 10 years ago—and much better off than he or she was 20 years ago.

Then why the widespread belief that our living standards are declining? Probably the answer is a phenomenon that economists call **the money illusion. This is our tendency to measure our real well-being by the number of dollars we get—not by their purchasing power.** Money illusion brings very sharp psychological costs in a period of inflation because our real incomes lag far behind our money incomes. Take the period 1969–1979 again. Over those years our money incomes rose by over 134 percent. That is, the number of dollars in the average pay envelope in 1979 was easily double the number in 1969. But the increase in purchasing power of those 1979 dollars was only about 28 percent, much less than the increase in their number. Thus we had the illusion that our real incomes had doubled, whereas in fact they had only risen by about a quarter.

Imagine that someone agreed to give you a present of $134 tomorrow morning along with the morning papers. When you opened the envelope, there was only $28 in it. Actually, you are $28 better off than before; but you had expected to be $134 better off. Are you glad or mad? Do you feel lifted up or let down? It is the same in the economic world. If we had experienced a real gain of $100 over the past decade, we would all be very content. But that would have been far, far beyond the limits of our production possibility frontier.

Inflation and Social Perceptions. Another reason for our general feeling of a falling income standard is that inflation turns many personal problems into social problems. In a market system some individuals are always winners and others are losers, either absolutely or by comparison. When there is no inflation, people take these changing positions as part of the economic game, as part of "life." In an inflationary period, however, everyone has a rising *money* income. Those who are losers are those whose income rises less rapidly than the rate of inflation. In a world without inflation, such persons would blame their economic plight on bad luck or on bad judgment or on any number of other factors. Except during a great depression, they would not blame their misfortune on "the system."

During inflation, however, because losers are still receiving money increases —although perhaps not enough to stay abreast of the cost of living—they tend to blame inflation for a condition that may not be the consequence of inflation at all. College professors may blame inflation for their falling real incomes when the real trouble lies in the oversupply of Ph.D.s. Factory workers blame inflation for their very real pinch when the problem is that the rise in female workers and in part-time employment has been cutting into the work week, and thereby lowering weekly wages, even though hourly rates go up.

Inflation as a Zero Sum Game. The confused perceptions that arise during an inflationary period tend to blind us to a very important difference between recessions and inflations. In recessionary times, incomes fall. Unemployed individuals above all suffer real losses in purchasing power. Moreover there is no social gain to be offset against their loss. The purchasing power given up by an unemployed family does not appear in anyone else's pocket.

Not so during inflation. Here, the decline in purchasing power of one unlucky individual or group of individuals is *always* offset by a rise in the purchasing power of some other person or group. *That is because every rise in prices always creates a rise in incomes.* Perhaps the gainer is a strategically placed group of workers whose higher wages are the other side of higher prices. Perhaps it is a group of businessmen for whom higher prices will mean higher profits. But higher prices always mean higher incomes for someone in the system.

Thus inflation is a zero sum game—a game of redistribution in which you win what I lose, or vice versa. Recessions, on the other hand, are not zero sum, but negative sum: Losses incurred by some individuals will not be transferred to others as income.

In analyzing the costs of inflation, therefore, we always have to look for winners and losers. From 1970 to 1980, our real GNP grew by $324 billion in 1972 dollars. Someone had to be receiving that larger real income. Who was it? Just the very rich? The oil companies? The municipal workers? The answer is: All of us. We can see this if we look at the distribution of income by our definitions of poor, working class, middle class, and upper class in Chapter 4. If any one of those groups had gained a major share of our growth in GNP, income distribution would have changed. But a look at Table 31.2 shows that it has not.

TABLE 31.2 SHARES OF INCOME BY FAMILY, 1970 AND 1978

	1970	*1978*
The poor (bottom 20 percent)	5.4	5.2
Working class (next 40 percent)	29.8	29.1
Middle class (next 35 percent)	49.2	50.0
Upper class (top 5 percent)	15.6	15.6

Despite inflation, income shares are almost unchanged.

Hidden Winners and Losers. Of course, there have been some social groups whose well-being has changed over the last years, but those changes have not always accorded with our expectations about inflation. It has always been held, for example, that the worst losers in any inflation would be fixed income receivers. But the single most important class of fixed income receivers in the United States—the recipients of Social Security—have been winners, not losers. This is because Congress has periodically hiked up Social Security benefits ahead of living costs and has now tied those benefits to the cost of living index. From 1970 to 1980, the average elderly family slightly improved its position relative to that of the average family in the nation as a whole!

Striking losers in the last ten years have been stockholders, most of whom are to be found in the upper class. Just as conventional wisdom led us to expect that all pensioners would suffer during an inflation, so it was commonly believed that stockholders would benefit from, or would at least stay abreast of, inflation. Because stocks represented shares of companies whose assets would be rising in value as a result of inflation, they were thought to be a "hedge" against inflation.

That is not how things have turned out. Over the last ten years prices have roughly doubled. The stock market has remained essentially unchanged. This means that the purchasing power of a portfolio made up of average stocks has had its value cut in half! That is about as bad as the fall experienced during the Great Depression!*

It is possible, further, that inflation has exerted its impact painfully on lower- and working-class families even though the distribution of income is roughly unchanged. This is because inflation has been particularly marked in four categories of goods: food, energy, shelter, and medical care. The price of these four necessities has been rising almost 50 percent faster than the price of non-necessities, and the proportion of household budgets going for necessities is markedly greater among the poor and working classes than among the middle and upper classes.[1]

Thus there are certainly real impacts of inflation both on the poor and on the rich. Our analysis shows, however, that we must be very careful in assessing its impact. There has not been an overall deterioration of well-being, even though it *feels* that way. Certain groups have been more severely hit than others; some groups are actually worse off than they were in 1975. For most of us, however, two decades of inflation have brought real, although largely unnoticed, improvements in real living standards.

THE REAL THREATS OF INFLATION

Does this mean we have been worrying needlessly about inflation? That is certainly not our opinion. Even if Americans judged the problem wrongly

*Why have stocks not been a hedge against inflation? There seem to be two reasons. First, interest rates are much higher than dividend rates, so that many investors prefer to put their wealth into short-term bonds rather than stocks. Second, investors are simply gloomy about the future, mainly because of inflation. Rightly or wrongly, many think that a share of IBM is a less solid store of value than a bar of gold.

[1]Leslie Ellen Nulty, *Understanding the New Inflation: The Importance of the Basic Necessities,* Exploratory Project for Economic Alternatives, Washington, 1977; also Nulty, *Challenge* Jan.—Feb., 1979.

because of money illusion or the deceptive impact of inflation, there are ample reasons to place it at the top of the nation's agenda of problems. Specifically, there are four reasons to worry about inflation: the first three are threats and the fourth is an actual cost.

1. Inflation holds out the threat of running away

One of the most disturbing aspects of inflation has been its tendency to accelerate. From 1950 to 1965, for example, the average rate of inflation in the United States was 2 percent per year. During the last half of the 1960s, that rate had picked up to 4 percent. In the first five years of the decade of the 1970s it reached 6 percent. From 1976 to 1980 the rate first declined and then (in 1979) reached 9 percent. In early 1980 it zoomed further, and for a time threatened to reach 20 percent.

This pattern of irregularly accelerating inflation can be discovered in most parts of the world. In the 10 leading industrial nations the price level rose by about 2.5 percent a year during the 1950s; by not quite 3.5 percent a year in the 1960s; by over 9 percent in the 1970s. We can see this irregularly upward-tending pattern in Figure 31.5.

The reason for this acceleration will become clearer shortly when we study the mechanisms of inflation. **Undoubtedly, however, inflation holds the *threat* of "running away"—of quickening its pace until finally the value of money drops to zero and we have a complete social and economic collapse. Even though actual runaway inflations (or hyperinflations) have been very rare, and in all cases the consequence of previous military or social disasters, the spectre of such a possibility is profoundly unsettling.** This is probably the main reason we perceive inflation to be a danger: It is not so much for what it is, but for what it might become.

2. Inflation threatens the value of monetary assets

Closely associated with the threat of a runaway economy is the threat of eroding assets. Inflation eats away at the value of monetary assets such as savings accounts, insurance policies, government bonds, and the like. Moreover, as we have seen, it has also badly eroded the value of stocks, although this may change if the stock market begins to take a brighter view of the future.

The threat of inflation is that it could wipe out the money assets of the middle and upper classes, as runaway inflations in the past have done. To date, however, most families with monetary assets seem to have stayed even with inflation, using their higher money incomes to add to their savings accounts or insurance policies. For example, during the years 1970–1980, the value of savings accounts has risen from $194 to $670 billion, more than enough to allow for inflation. Insurance policies in force have risen from $1,400 to $3,300 billion. Nevertheless, the fear of losing all their monetary assets is acutely experienced by families who hold them, and it is not a threat to be dismissed.

The value of some assets typically rises during inflations. Land is one of these; works of art; antiques—whatever is scarce and deemed to be of lasting value. Some of these investments work out very well, others do not: The land you buy may turn out to be in the wrong place; the picture may be by an artist whose reputation fails. Most significant of all the hedges against inflation is gold, the magical metal. Economists have always pointed out that the value of gold is only magical, and that it is not intrinsically a source of value and true hedge against inflation. So far, economists have been wrong and gold has soared during the inflationary era. How high can it go? The answer lies with your estimate as to how stubborn or persistent are people's beliefs; if the past is any guide, they are very stubborn and very persistent indeed.

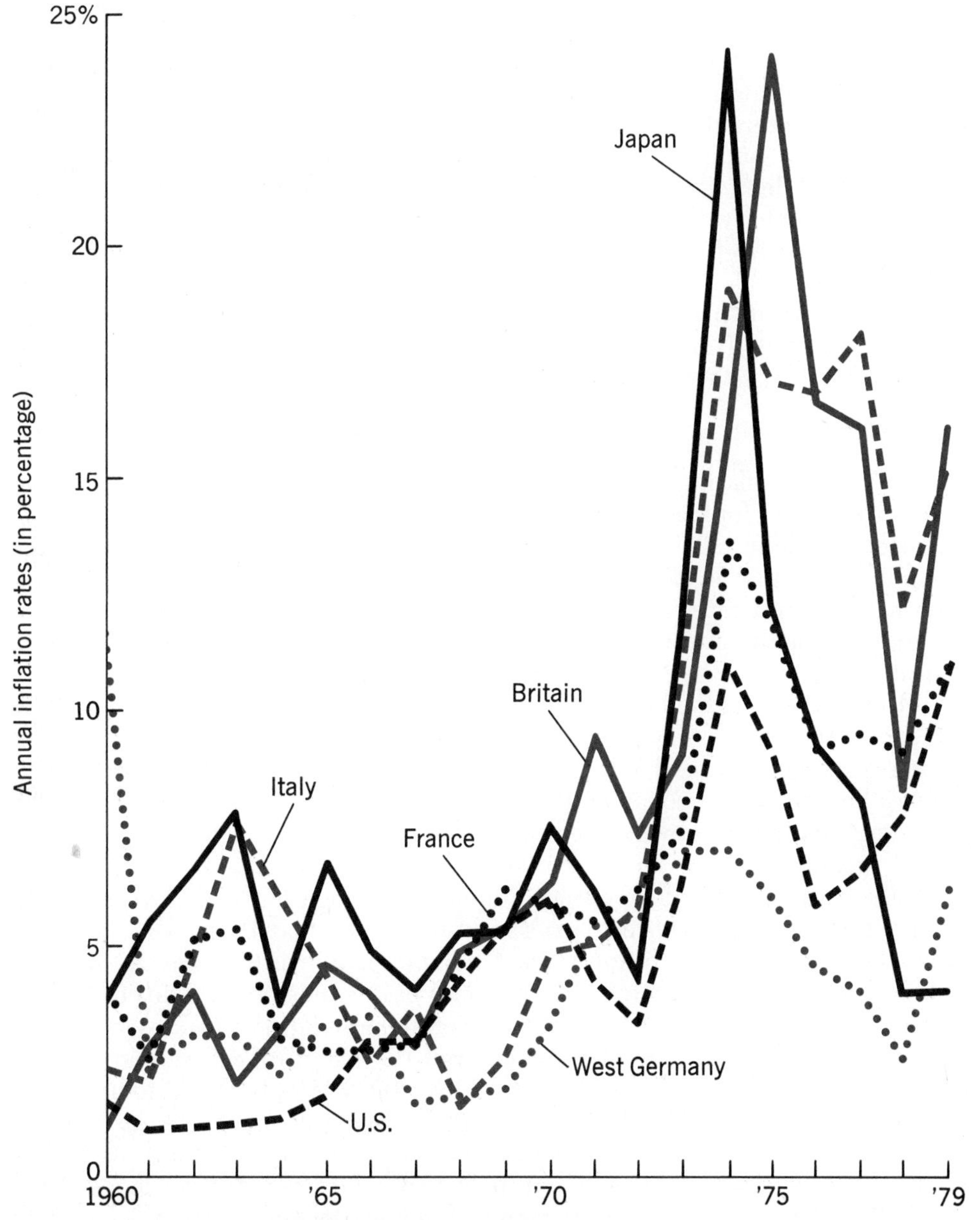

FIGURE 31.5
WORLDWIDE
INFLATION:
SELECTED
COUNTRIES

Inflation has been a worldwide accelerating phenomenon in which U.S. experience was rather favorable until the end of the 70s.

3. Inflation threatens financial instability

Inflation brings serious distortions into the nation's credit structure. One of the most troublesome consequences of inflation is the way it affects the relationship between businesses and banks. In inflationary times it is always advantageous to borrow money, because dollars will be cheaper and more plentiful when it comes time to repay the loan. Therefore businesses seek to borrow funds—but banks are loath to lend, for exactly the same reasons.

Two results follow. **First, interest rates go ever higher to compensate banks for the falling value of the dollars they will receive. This puts a serious crimp in many kinds of investment spending, such as construction. Second, banks refuse to lend for more than short periods of time. The result is that business has to take on short-term loans at high interest rates. As short-term debt piles up, the system becomes vulnerable to any untoward event that will prevent the regular refinancing of debt.** If a bank or a municipality encounters trouble, the whole financial community becomes endangered. Thus New York City's threatened bankruptcy in 1976 brought fears of a general credit collapse. The liquidity of the banking system—its ability to absorb a loss without resorting to panicky measures to raise cash—becomes a matter of general concern, rather than a matter taken for granted. Thus the threat of large-scale financial instability is another very good reason to worry about inflation.

4. Inflation inhibits us from trying to reach potential growth

The real cost of inflation is very clear: It prevents us from trying to use all of our productive power for fear that we may tip an acceptable degree of inflation into an unacceptable or outright dangerous one. **Thus the real cost of inflation is the unemployment that it thrusts upon us—not only the unemployment that stems from high interest rates and lessened investment, but the unemployment that governments deliberately tolerate or encourage in order to prevent inflation from getting worse, or in the hope of making it better.**

Unlike the imagined cost of inflation—the feeling that our living standards are declining—there is nothing imaginary about the cost of unemployment. A person who is without work suffers a real fall in income and a great deal of damage to his or her sense of personal worth. The production that is foregone because of a recession is foregone forever. There is no way ever of enjoying the goods that we do not produce.

The costs of unemployment are important enough for us to devote our entire next chapter to them. But we should recognize that these costs, however large, do not seem as significant to the American people as the costs or threats of inflation, however exaggerated. The reason is easily understood. The costs of unemployment are borne by a small minority of the population and, as we shall see, a minority without much political voice. But the effects of inflation are felt by everyone. Thus it is not surprising that all over the world, the need to hold back inflation has been regarded by governments as being of much greater urgency than the need to remedy unemployment. Governments and electorates alike are ready to accept more unemployment in exchange for less inflation; they are not ready to accept more inflation in exchange for less unemployment.

At the end of this chapter we will discuss various means of trying to hold back inflation. Let us conclude this discussion by emphasizing that stagnation, directly caused by inflation itself or brought about by efforts to stem inflation, is by far the most serious of the actual costs that inflation brings. Indeed, in our opinion, stagnation can be justified only if there is no other way of preventing inflation from running away or from giving rise to the kind of political panic that a chronic inflation threatens to introduce.

EXPLAINING INFLATION

Certainly, then, we want to curb inflation; but in order to do so we must first understand what causes it. Here we encounter a difficulty. There is no general consensus among economists as to the causes or even the mechanisms of inflation comparable to the consensus that exists about many other kinds of problems. What follows, therefore, we loudly and clearly state, is *our* diagnosis of the nature of the inflationary phenomenon. It is to be thought about, and perhaps argued with. We hope that it will shed light; we cannot promise total illumination.

BASIC MARKET INSTABILITY

Our argument begins with a simple but essential fact. It is that market systems are easily disturbed. Wars, changes in political regimes, resource changes, new technologies, shifts in demand, all disturb the equilibrium of the market system as stones cast ripples in a pond.

These unsettling events have caused different kinds of disturbances at different periods in capitalism's political and economic development. For economists, the most important of these disturbances has been the tendency of the market system to develop instabilities in production and prices and employment. We have already encountered these instabilities in the form of business cycles, or tendencies to recession, or in the inflationary propensities of recent years.

It may not seem important to begin from a stress on this deepseated and long visible characteristic of the market system. But once we place instability at stage center, we can see that a pressing question must be answered: **Why does instability in our times result in rising prices rather than in mass unemployment?** To take a specific instance, why did the shock of higher oil prices in 1973 touch off a new wave of inflation? A comparable shock a hundred years earlier—say a sudden fourfold increase in coal prices—would almost certainly have caused a massive depression. What has happened between that day and this to alter the way in which the market system responds to shocks?

PUBLIC BARRIERS AGAINST DEPRESSION

It is not difficult to answer the question. Profound changes have occurred within the social and economic structure of capitalism throughout the world. Of these changes, the most significant for our purposes is the emergence of large and powerful public sectors. In all Western capitalisms these sectors pump out from 30 to 50 percent of all expenditures, providing a floor of economic stability that did not exist before.

This floor does not prevent the arrival of recessions. The market system continues to be vulnerable to shocks and changes as always before. The difference

is that a market system with a core of public spending does not move from recession into depression. The downward effect on production or employment is limited. Cumulative, bottomless depressions are changed to limited, although persisting, recessions.

In addition, the emplacement of the new public sector has greatly increased the political responsibility of governments for the overall macro performance of their economies. That is why central banks cannot carry out the restrictive monetary policies that might bring inflation to a halt. Central banks can and do pull on the string to tighten money. But when they pull too hard, the economy begins to choke. No government can afford to carry out so severe an economic program. The string is therefore quickly relaxed—and inflation goes on its way.

INCREASED PRIVATE RIGIDITY

Related to, but nonetheless distinct from, the rise of the public sector, we can see another vast change when we compare capitalism today and yesterday. This is the much greater rigidity we find in its private sector—that is, the much greater degree of organization and control that marks the structure of business power and labor power.

We have already noted that one of the most striking differences between modern inflations and those of the past is that in former days, inflationary peaks were followed by long deflationary periods when prices fell. Why did they fall? One reason is that it was not unusual, in the nineteenth and early twentieth centuries, for large companies to announce across-the-board wage cuts when times were bad. In addition, prices declined as a result of technological advances and as the consequence of sporadic price wars that would break out among industrial competitors.

Most of that seems a part of the past beyond recall. Technology continues to lower costs, but this has been offset by a "ratchet tendency" shown by wages and prices since World War II. **A ratchet tendency means that prices and wages go up, but they rarely or never come down. This characteristic is due to the increasing presence of concentrated big industry, to stronger trade unions, and to a business climate in which wage cuts and price wars are no longer regarded as legitimate economic policies.** These rigidities have also added to our inflationary propensities.

OTHER BACKGROUND REASONS

There are still other changes that have made today's system more inflation-prone than the system of a hundred, or even fifty, years ago. We are a more service-oriented, less goods-oriented, economy and productivity rises less rapidly in services than in goods. We are more affluent and much less willing to abide meekly by traditional pecking orders in society. These changes tilt the system toward inflation.

Our inflationary experience can also be traced to specific shocks and blows. It received its first impetus from the boost to spending that resulted from the Vietnam War. A powerful stimulus to inflation in other countries resulted from the manner in which the United States used its strategic position during the 1960s to "export" inflation to other nations through its international economic policies. And by no means least has been the effect of "oil shock," first in 1973 when the

Organization of Petroleum Exporting Countries (OPEC) raised petroleum prices from $3 to $11, and then again in 1979 when oil prices jumped from $13 to $28 in the wake of Iran's revolution. In contrast to the inflation-inducing effects of spending, called **demand-pull**, boosts to inflation from wage increases or increases in oil prices are called **cost-push.**

TRANSMITTING INFLATION BY INDEXING

Here we must again pause to reflect. We have suggested that a jump in coal prices in 1870, comparable to oil shock in our time, would probably have had a different effect: Many industries would have had to shut down; steel production would have been dealt a tremendous blow; in all likelihood a great depression would have begun.

Why did the cost-push of higher oil prices result in inflation and not in depression? We have already pointed to background reasons in the presence of a firm government sector and in the more rigid wage and price structure of industry. Now we must pay heed to an equally important transmission mechanism that has made inflation contagious. This is the presence of automatic price-boosters in the economy in the form of arrangements to change various kinds of payment to stay even with the cost of living. Such arrangements are called *indexing.* A few pages back we saw that Congress has indexed Social Security payments so that the checks sent to retired people automatically rise as the cost of living rises. The same kind of indexing arrangements now affect wages and salaries in much of the private sector, or protect industrial purchasers of many commodities. Most people who work expect to get cost-of-living increases whether or not they have worked harder or better.

Indexing changes the way the economy works in profound ways. Higher prices do not serve as a deterrent in an indexed economy as they would in a nonindexed one. Inflation would be self-limiting if prices rose and incomes stayed constant, but indexing means that incomes stay more or less even with prices, as we have already seen. While this may prevent much social hardship, it also tends to make inflation a self-perpetuating process.

Thus when oil shock came, the cost of living was pushed sharply upward and for a moment everyone felt the pinch. Personal savings dropped in 1974 as prices jumped. Then, after a little time, cost of living allowances (COLAs) began to take effect and soon incomes had been given a compensatory boost.

EXPECTATIONS

Along with the boost in incomes came another inflation-transmitting change. Our expectations changed. We began to expect a worsening, not an easing, of prices in the future. Unlike the old days when the prevailing belief was that "What goes up must come down," in an indexed economy we tend to believe that "What goes up will continue to go up."

Expectations are a major transmission mechanism for inflation because inflations, like depressions, have psychological as well as actual causes and self-perpetuating mechanisms. The trigger for depressions in the past has usually been a failure of private investment, whether because of credit shortages, or overbuilding, or threats of war and the like. Once a depression began, however, it continued largely because a psychological factor was lacking—"confidence," it was called during the Great Depression. In the absence of confidence, the rate of investment spending remained depressed.

Whether cost-pushed or demand-pulled, an inflationary boost has a psychological perpetuating mechanism, similar to the lack of confidence that weighs on investment spending during depressions. The mechanism is that of expectations. **Inflation leads individuals to expect more inflation, in part because of indexing. They build those expectations into wage demands, into pricing policies, into household spending behavior. Expectations thus feed on, and justify, themselves. Inflations cannot be stopped until inflationary expectations end.**

CONTROLLING INFLATION

Can we stop inflation? Of course we can. The problem is to stop it with measures that are politically acceptable. Here is a roster of anti-inflationary measures, beginning with very mild ones that probably won't work (but might!) and ending with very severe ones that almost surely would work (but at great cost).

1. Balancing the Federal Budget

One of the most commonly heard quick-cure measures for inflation is that we should balance the federal budget, if necessary by a Constitutional Amendment. Would that stop inflation?

The answer depends very much on how we would balance the budget. For example, if expenditures had been maintained at existing levels, and individual income taxes had been raised by about 5 percent, the federal deficit for 1979 ($11 billion) would have been eliminated. The effect of higher taxes would have served as a downward shock. Inflation might have moderated or even stopped. The question is: Who would have voted for the higher taxes?

Alternatively, tax levels could have been maintained or even cut and federal spending might have been slashed. But where would it have been slashed? About a quarter of all federal expenditures in 1979 went for defense. Few politicians wish to cut defense spending. Roughly half of all spending went for health and income security. There was perhaps room for trimming here, but Social Security and Medicare payments together accounted for over 75 percent of this outlay. Cutting these outlays would not have been politically popular. Another 10 percent of spending went to pay interest on the federal debt: Legally that could not be cut.

That left about $100 billion—a fifth of all federal spending. Of that $100 billion, $75 billion went to states and localities as grants-in-aid. If that item had been eliminated from the budget, the federal government would have shown a substantial surplus in 1979. But state and local governments would have gone deeply into deficit.

Thus when we consider trying to stop inflation by cutting back on federal expenditures, we must look into total public expenditures—federal, state, and local—not just federal spending. In 1979, total public spending was in surplus to the amount of $14 billion, or 0.6 percent of GNP. There was no deficit to eliminate.

To review: We could use cuts in federal spending to give a sharp downward impetus to the economy. The difficulty is finding the areas in which to do it. As

far as the federal deficit is concerned, remember that its deficit may be offset by surpluses in state and local governments.

2. Using tight money to slow inflation down

Tight money is probably the most widely used anti-inflationary policy in capitalist economies today. Does it work? Partly. Tight money has succeeded in reducing the rate of growth, and *perhaps* this has mitigated the rate of inflation. In addition, tight money may hold down inflationary expectations—although some critics claim that very high interest rates, which result from tight money, serve to spur on inflationary expectations!

The problem with tight money is that it leads to on-again, off-again economic policies, often called "stop-go." When prices begin to rise too fast, the money supply is tightened to curb spending. Governments may also trim their budgets. Wage and price guidelines are often announced.

For a time, these stop measures succeed. But then pressures mount in the opposite direction. High interest rates cut into home building. A slowdown in investment causes unemployment to rise. Tight government budgets mean that programs with important constituencies have to be cut back; army bases are closed; social assistance programs abandoned. Business and labor chafe under guidelines. Hence pressures mount for a relaxation. The red light changes to green. The money supply goes up again; investment is encouraged; public spending resumes its former upward trend; guidelines are quietly abandoned. Before long the expected happens: Prices begin to move ahead too rapidly once more, and the pendulum starts its swing in the opposite direction.

3. Downward price shocks

A third approach is to try to break the inflation chain by deliberately causing downward price shocks to offset upward shocks such as oil hikes or very rapid wage increases. How could this be done? One method is to deregulate certain industries and to allow the forces of competition to reduce prices there: The airline industry is a recent example of such a program. Another method is to cut back on taxes that have direct impact on costs: Instead of raising Social Security taxes (which affect employers' costs) or cutting income taxes (which doesn't reduce the cost of living index), the government could concentrate on cutting taxes that bear directly on the cost of living, such as excise and sales taxes.

In addition, government programs that boost prices could be abandoned. The postal service could be opened up to private competition. Agricultural subsidies could be junked. The subsidy paid the merchant marine could go, along with protectionist measures that hold up prices in steel, textiles, shoes, and other commodities. Efforts could be made to break bottlenecks in certain industries such as health care and to eliminate the payment of medical costs by "third parties" (insurance companies).

Such programs could have a very substantial impact on the cost of living. But the problems they present are apparent. Opposing most such cuts is an interest group—the farmers, the companies and labor unions in exposed industries, the comfortably regulated industries that do not want more competition.

4. A major recession

No one doubts that we could stop inflation dead in its tracks by taking really serious measures, such as bringing money expansion to a halt. If we were to stop the growth in the money supply completely, inflation would come to an end, probably fairly rapidly.

The difficulty is that such a monetary strait-jacket would impose very large economic costs. Here we have the example of West Germany and Switzerland to go by. Both these countries have deliberately introduced the kind of major recession that is sometimes advocated. In 1978, for example, industrial employment in West Germany was 12 percent lower than in 1972. In Switzerland it was 10 percent lower. As a result inflation rates in these countries were among the lowest in the world.

Why do we not follow their example? The reason is that the unemployment in Switzerland and West Germany was almost entirely imposed on their foreign workers, who were simply sent back to their native countries—mainly Italy and Yugoslavia, Turkey and Spain. **Scaled up to an economy of our size, the Swiss alone rounded up 10 million workers and sent them home. Which 10 million American workers would we send where? In fact, equivalent cut-backs in the United States would create unemployment rates approaching 30 percent.**

Such a policy would very likely stop inflation dead in its tracks. But the economy would also come to a full stop. What social and political consequences would follow from such a return to conditions of the 1930s cannot be foreseen; few are willing to find out.

5. Voluntary Controls

Another approach is to impose voluntary controls on wages and prices, often in the form of guidelines that suggest limits for acceptable wage and price increases, especially for major industries.

The idea behind guidelines is clear and correct. If everyone would agree to limit his or her increase in income to 5 percent, instead of 8 or 10 percent, the inflation rate would promptly drop and *no one would be any worse off!* Unfortunately, unless everyone cooperates the scheme will not work, and the temptations to cheat are enormous. Think about the situation at a football game. It helps everyone to see the game if all remain seated, and no one sees better if all stand up. But if everyone does stay seated, the few individuals who stand get the best views; whereas if everyone stands, the few who agree to sit down get the worst views!

For exactly the same reasons, voluntary controls have not worked well. Therefore a number of proposals have been devised to make adherence to a voluntary program profitable as well as patriotic. Among these are the TIP (Tax Incentive Plan) plans that call for tax penalties against big companies that agree to wage settlements in excess of guideline rates. The tax penalties are intended to provide incentives for employers to resist such wage increases at the bargaining table; and if all companies agree to hold the line, then no labor union will be disadvantaged.

TIP plans might work. The difficulty they present is administrative, not economic. They call for a degree of supervision and intervention on the part of government that is certain to create bureaucracy and to generate friction. That difficulty may well be worth the price, however, if milder measures fail to arrest the inflationary trend.

6. Mandatory Controls

Last on the list are compulsory controls, possibly of a permanent or stand-by kind, that would be imposed over prices and wages, at least in the big business sector. Such controls are similar to those that would be instantly imposed if war broke out and we faced the prospect of an astronomical inflation.

The difference is that wartime controls work fairly well for two reasons. First, a spirit of patriotism helps enfore them. Second, the overriding necessity of mounting an effective war effort removes all the usual hesitations about the limits of intervention. If controls result in insufficient investment, the government itself builds (or subsidizes) the necessary new plant and equipment. If wage controls reduce labor supplies, government can draft citizens or "freeze" them in their jobs. In peacetime these advantages are not likely to be present. No warlike patriotic spirit exists; indeed the prevailing attitude may well be to find ways of evading controls. And public opinion inhibits the government intervention that might be needed to overcome the problem to which controls would give rise. In addition, controls are onerous. Detailed norms must be written and enforced. In the Korean War we needed 18,000 price and wage inspectors to make the system work. Perhaps the computer can replace some of these inspectors, but not all of them. There is no such thing as wage and price control without a large bureaucracy.

Thus the objection to mandatory controls is two-fold. They are certain to cause a great deal of public irritation. And they will pose an endless series of difficult questions in deciding how prices should be adjusted as our economy changes, grows, and faces new challenges. On the other hand, controls have one major benefit. More surely than any other measure, they will stop the inflationary spiral. If other measures fail, therefore, and if inflation accelerates and public concern mounts, we may yet be forced to resort to this last and most painful policy.

A LAST LOOK

Is there a hope of stopping inflation without controls? The basic problem is that we cannot stop inflation unless we lower some individuals' money incomes. That is simply a matter of definitions, not of economics. Which individuals should they be? Can we devise a method of sharing the cut-back? If we really share it alike, there would be no costs, and we would be rid of the frightening experience of an economy running out of control—or under full controls.

That is about all that an economist can venture to say. The cure for inflation is persuading and educating people to adopt sharing policies that will bring inflation to a painless halt. Failing that, it is to devise policies that will impose the cost of stopping inflation on one group or another in a manner acceptable to the country at large. The difficulty, then, is that the challenge of inflation is not essentially economic. It is political. It involves the distribution and redistribution of gains and losses, the selection of winners and losers. The challenge of inflation is ultimately a challenge to our ability to solve that political problem.

KEY CONCEPTS

LOOKING BACK

Stagflation is a new economic phenomenon

1. Unlike inflations in the past, contemporary inflation has persisted beyond the end of war and despite the presence of unemployment. Hence it is called stagflation—stagnation combined with inflation.

Inflation and unemployment are no longer clear trade-offs

2. Stagflation is reflected in the disappearing Phillips curve. It used to be thought that inflation and unemployment were trade-offs—that an increase in unemployment was accompanied by a decrease in inflation rates. During the 1970s that relation largely disappeared.

An imaginary cost of inflation is that we have suffered a general fall in real income. This is a money illusion

3. Inflation has imaginary as well as real costs. One imaginary cost is that it has undermined our standard of living. This is largely the result of money illusion—the disappointment of not enjoying anything like the full value of our increased money incomes. Another cause is that we tend to blame inflation for economic difficulties that may not be based in inflation at all.

Inflation is a zero sum game. Actual income distribution has not changed much as a result of inflation

4. Inflation is a redistributive process, a zero sum game. Actually, it has not significantly redistributed money incomes among the main classes of income receivers. There have, however, been some winners and losers. Social Security recipients have gained. Owners of stocks have lost. Families in the lower brackets whose expenditures are concentrated on necessities—food, shelter, energy, health—may have been more painfully hit because necessities have risen more than non-necessities.

Inflation poses serious threats of running away, reducing the value of monetary assets, and of financial instability

5. Inflation poses very serious threats. One of these is the threat that it will accelerate faster and faster into a runaway inflation. A second is the associated threat that the value of money assets will be reduced to zero. A third is the threat of widespread financial instability.

The real cost of inflation is the loss it imposes on output and employment—stagnation

6. In addition to threats, inflation has a real cost. Through the effect of inflated interest rates on investment and through its effect on government policies, it retards growth and creates stagnation. The costs of stagnation are real, but borne by a minority. The costs and threats of inflation are diffuse and felt by all. Therefore inflation is felt to be more serious than unemployment.

Inflations, in our view, stem from market instability which is blocked in a downward direction by government and rigidities. Indexing transmits inflationary expectations through the economy

7. Inflation, in our belief, stems from the instability of capitalist economic systems. This instability no longer creates cumulative depressions, due to the intervention of the government sector. Increased institutional rigidity also limits downward price adjustments. In this new situation shocks to the economy create only mild recessions; and upward tendencies in costs, transmitted by indexing, result in inflationary expectations.

Anti-inflation measures include:
- **balanced budgets**
- **tight money**
- **downward shocks**
- **major recessions**
- **voluntary controls**
- **mandatory controls**

8. There is a spectrum of measures to control inflation, none guaranteed to succeed. Balancing the budget imposes the need for stiff taxes or slashed spending, both hard to achieve. Also the total government budget, not just the federal budget, must be balanced. Tight money is largely ineffectual, leading to stop-go policies. Downward price shocks would be hard to implement. A major recession carries huge political and social repercussions. Voluntary controls do not

work well, although TIP policies might help them work. Mandatory permanent controls are a last fall-back, if needed to break the inflationary spiral.

The political challenge

9. Ultimately, inflation poses a political challenge—either to find a means of sharing the diminution in money income that must accompany any slowdown in inflation, or to select winners and losers from the public.

ECONOMIC VOCABULARY

Stagflation 483
Phillips curve 485
Money illusion 487
Zero sum game 488
Ratchet effect 494
Indexing 495
Cost-push 495
Demand-pull 495
Stop-go policies 497
TIP plans 498

QUESTIONS

1. Do you believe that some inflationary costs are only imaginary? Everyone knows that meat prices have soared. Here are data on beef consumption per capita for 1960, 1965, 1970, and 1975:

	1960	*1965*	*1970*	*1975*
Beef (lbs. per capita)	85.1	99.5	113.7	120.1

   Does this make a conclusive case, one way or the other? How about other foods? How would you decide whether there had really been a falling-off in living standards since 1960?
2. Can you give an instance of money illusion from your own experience? How about your parents harping on how much less things cost in their day? Did they necessarily cost less as a percentage of their incomes in those days?
3. Which among many kinds of assets do you consider the most inflation proof? Depression proof? Why? If you had to hold your total fortune in gold or in a collection of industrial stocks for the next 25 years, which would you choose?
4. What kind of event might give rise to a hyperinflation in the U.S.? If such a catastrophe occurred, what policies would you advocate?
5. Is war always inflationary, even if financed by taxes? Is government spending always inflationary? Never inflationary? If the federal government balanced its budget, but the states incurred deficits by selling bonds, would that necessarily be inflationary?
6. How would you try to reckon the costs of inflation versus those of unemployment?
7. Would you be willing to be unemployed, if you were assured that that would keep down the cost of living by some small amount? Would you be willing to designate some one else to lose his or her job, if it could be shown that this would reduce inflation by a perceptible amount?
8. How do you think people should decide whether severe measures, such as a major recession or mandatory controls, are worth their cost?

Chapter

Chapter 32 UNEMPLOYMENT

A LOOK AHEAD

The other side of the coin of inflation, these days, is unemployment; this chapter is designed to tell us something about its causes, its nature, and its cures.

Three main lessons stand out in the pages ahead.

(1) There is an extreme variation in unemployment rates. If the unemployed are our "inflation fighters," they are chosen, as we shall see, in a highly biased fashion.

(2) Unemployment is not just the difference between the labor force and those at work. The idea of participation rates and an elastic labor force gives new meaning to the idea of joblessness.

(3) There are cures for unemployment. They are essentially two: more demand, and a better fit between demand and supply.

At the very end, a hard question: Is unemployment an integral part of capitalism? Perhaps it is, but certainly not to the extent that we have experienced it in recent years.

Ask American citizens what is their *second* most worrisome economic problem and you will likely get agreement that it is unemployment. Unlike inflation, however, unemployment has not been high on the public's complaints for ten years. This is because large-scale unemployment is a fairly recent problem, the consequence of the economic recession of 1973–1975 and the downturn starting in 1980.

RECESSIONS AND UNEMPLOYMENT

Because unemployment and recession are so closely linked, we had better begin by asking: What is a recession? The answer is very simple. **A recession is a drop in the gross national product that lasts for at least 6 months.** The word *depression* is used to refer to a severe drop in GNP, but there is no generally accepted definition of when a recession becomes a depression. People generally call a downturn a recession if their neighbor is unemployed, but a depression if they are unemployed.

Although recessions always bring unemployment, we can suffer from unemployment even without recession if our growth is too slow. Until recently our productivity has increased by about 3 percent and our labor force by about 1 percent (on the average). This means that each year we have the ability to turn out about 4 percent more goods. **Unless our GNP grows by at least that rate, we will not be able to keep up with our rising productivity capacity. The consequence is that there will be unsold goods and workers who are let go or not rehired.**

Let us trace exactly what happens when GNP falls or lags. The pace of business activity slows down. There is less demand for consumer goods and services, less demand for plant and equipment and other business items. Some businesses fire people, other businesses hire fewer new workers. Because our labor force is steadily growing as our population swells, even a small decrease in the willingness to take on new workers spells a sharp rise in unemployment for certain groups, such as young people. When a recession really deepens, as in 1980, it is not just the young who cannot find work, but experienced workers find themselves thrown out of work, as Figure 32.1 shows.

THE UNEMPLOYED AS INFLATION FIGHTERS

Unemployment is a problem that has to be judged differently from the way we judge inflation. Rising prices affect everyone, although some kinds of wage earners or profit-receivers gain while others lose. Unemployment, however, is a sharply focused economic ill.

When we state that 8 percent of the labor force is unemployed, this does not mean that every worker is laid off for 8 percent of the year. It means that some workers are unemployed for long periods of time. Over 50 percent of the total number of weeks of unemployment is typically borne by individuals who are unemployed for more than half a year. Almost half of those who suffer long spells of unemployment end up not with a job, but by withdrawing from the labor force.

The point is that unemployment is a capricious, as well as an uncertain means of fighting inflation. We draft our "inflation fighters" mainly from the age group 16–24, where unemployment rates are three times those of adults. Females are 38 percent more likely to be subject to the anti-inflation draft than males;

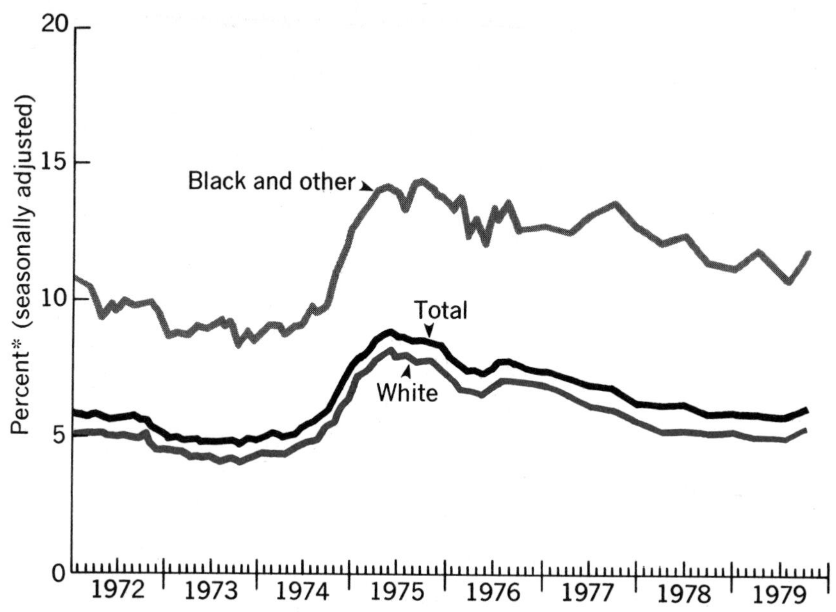

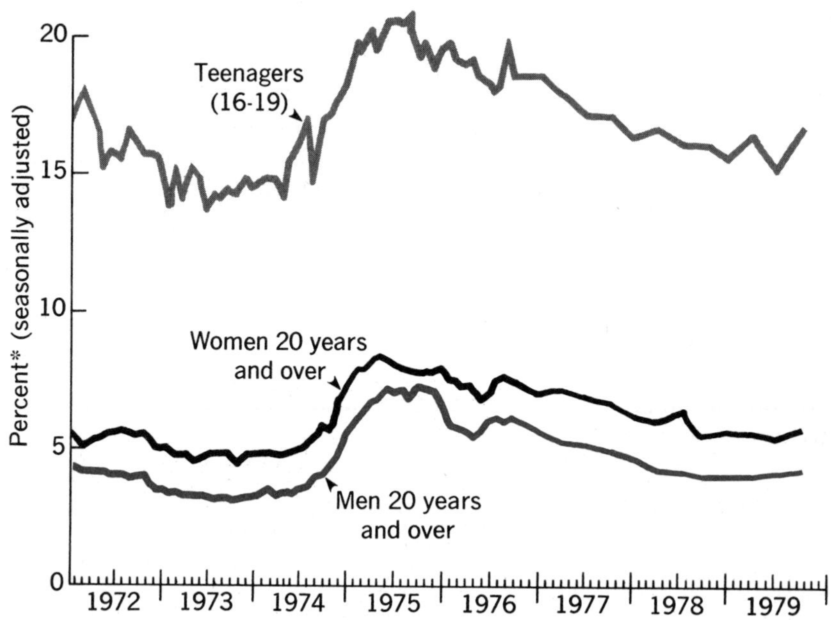

**Unemployment as percent of civilian labor force in group specified.*
Source: Department of Labor

FIGURE 32.1 IMPACT OF RECESSION ON EMPLOYMENT

This table shows two things: (1) racial minorities, women (mostly part-time workers), and teenagers always experience higher unemployment rates than white older males, and (2) when recession hits, all groups suffer, including the core of white experienced workers.

Year	Unemployed (thousands)	Percent of civilian labor force
1929	1,550	3.2
1933	12,830	24.9
1940	8,120	14.6
1944	670	1.2
1960–65 av.	4,100	5.5
1965–70 av.	3,117	3.9
1971	4,993	5.9
1972	4,840	5.6
1973	4,304	4.9
1974	5,076	5.6
1975	7,530	8.5
1976	7,288	7.7
1977	6,855	7.0
1978	6,047	6.0
1979	5,944	5.8

TABLE 32.1 UNEMPLOYMENT IN THE U.S.

Unemployment reached its worst level in 1933. But it was still very severe up to World War II. The record throughout the 1970s has been poor.

Hispanics are 75 percent more likely to be called up than whites. These groups share two characteristics: They tend to be relatively unskilled, and they tend to lack political clout.

As we would expect, the group with the lowest unemployment rate is the group of prime-age white males. There are both economic and political reasons why these are the last to be fired in a recession. Yet, if we want our inflation fighters to come from groups whose wage rates are most significant in setting the national pattern, this is the very group from whom we should be recruiting our soldier. **Our point, of course, is not to urge higher unemployment rates for anyone. It is only to emphasize that unemployment, as an anti-inflation measure, is neither efficient nor equitable. Worse, as we have already seen, it may not be effective.**

SEVERITY OF UNEMPLOYMENT

How serious is unemployment as a national economic problem? Table 32.1 shows us the record of the past few years and gives us the data for earlier, benchmark years to serve as a point of comparison.

The terrible percentages of the Depression years speak for themselves. At the very depth of the Depression, a quarter of the work force was jobless at a time when unemployment insurance and welfare was largely nonexistent. Note, too, that massive unemployment persisted until 1940. Only the advent of World War II finally brought unemployment below 1929 levels.

The record of the 1960s and 1970s is mixed. During the early 1960s, unemployment was at a level considered to be uncomfortably high—roughly between 5 and 6 percent of the labor force. This percentage dropped in the second half of the decade, partly as a consequence of higher spending on armaments.

It is the record of the 1970s that is disturbing. First we watched the number of unemployed soar to over 8 million in May 1975. Then we saw unemployment rates approach 9 percent of the labor force, a rate more serious than any recession in this century, barring only the 1933–40 collapse.

	1978		1978		1978
Males	5.2%	Females	7.2%	Hispanics	9.1%
White Males	4.5	White Females	6.2	16–19	20.6
16–19	13.5	16–19	14.4	Males 20+	6.3
20–24	7.6	20–24	8.3	Females 20+	9.8
25–54	3.0	25–54	4.9		
55–64	2.6	55–64	3.0		
65 & up	3.9	65 & up	3.7		
Black Males	10.9	Black Females	13.1	Total:	6.0
16–19	34.4	16–19	38.4		
20–24	20.0	20–24	21.3		
25–54	6.6	25–54	8.7		
55–64	4.4	55–64	5.1		
65 & up	7.1	65 & up	5.0		

TABLE 32.2 STRUCTURE OF UNEMPLOYMENT

In 1978, the national unemployment rate was 6 percent. This table shows how that average figure conceals very much higher rates among certain groups.

THE DIFFERENTIAL IMPACT OF UNEMPLOYMENT

By the end of the 1970s, the unemployment rate was down to around 6 percent, and some economists argued that this was close to "full" employment for the nation. Their argument was based on the fact that unemployment among the prime-age white group had dropped to under 3.5 percent. By mid 1980, however, unemployment rates were once again moving up towards 1975 levels.

There is no reason to hold that unemployment rates cannot be reduced well below that, as we shall see at the end of this chapter. But if we were to accept 6 percent as full employment, we would be accepting a much higher rate of unemployment for some groups in the population. We have already looked at the unequal odds facing our inflation-fighters. Perhaps we should add that unemployment rates for black teenagers, corrected for those who have dropped out of the system—who are not at school, not at work, and not trying to get work—reveal unemployment rates of up to *90 percent* in central city slums!

Table 32.2 shows us the tremendous spread in the incidence of unemployment, disregarding the pathology of the slum. Notice that black males bear twice the impact of unemployment that white males do, black females double the impact of white females; and all females 50 percent more impact than all males. The table bears study and thought.

MEASURING UNEMPLOYMENT

Before we proceed to policies designed to remedy unemployment we ought to look more carefully into the manner in which we measure it. The statistics of unemployment are gathered by a household-to-household survey conducted each month by the Bureau of the Census among a carefully selected sample. An unemployed person is thereupon defined not merely as a person without a job—for perhaps such a person does not *want* a job—but as someone who is actively seek-

THE GHETTO SKILL MIX

A sad example of the lack of fit between the skills demanded by employers and those possessed by the labor force is to be found in the ghetto, where typically the labor force is badly undertrained. A study by the First National City Bank explored this situation in New York City.

As we can see, in only one category—unskilled service—was the prospective demand for labor roughly in line with the skills available. This meant a reasonable employment prospect for maids, restaurant workers, bellhops, and the like—among the lowest-paid occupations in the nation. As for the common laborer, who comprised over half the "skill pool" of the New York ghetto, his outlook was bleak indeed—less than one percent of new jobs would open in that area. Conversely, for the widest job market in the city—the white-collar trades that offer two-thirds of the new jobs—the ghetto could offer only one-seventh of its residents as adequately trained. These extreme disproportions still apply to the situation in New York and many other slum-ridden cities. If these figures have any meaning, it is that ghetto poverty is here to stay, short of a herculean effort to rescue the trapped ghetto resident.

	Occupational distribution of ghetto unemployed, 1968	*Estimated job openings, 1965–1975*
White collar	13.6%	65.7%
Craftsmen	2.8	7.4
Operatives	14.7	7.7
Unskilled personal service	16.6	18.6
Laborers	52.3	0.6

ing work but is unable to find it. Since, however, the number of people who will be seeking work will rise in good times and fall in bad times, figures for any given period must be viewed with caution.

As employment opportunities drop, unemployment will not rise by an equivalent amount. Some of those looking for work when job opportunities are plentiful will withdraw from the labor force and become part of *hidden unemployment.* When job opportunities expand, these hidden unemployed will reenter the labor force, so that unemployment will not fall as fast as employment rises. Thus the ups and downs in the measured unemployment rate reflect the state of the economy, but the swings are not as large as they would be if the term "unemployment" measured the hidden unemployed.

THE ELASTIC LABOR FORCE

This gives rise to a curious and important result. Measured unemployment is not simply the difference between the number of people working and a fixed labor force. It is the difference between the number working and an elastic, changeable labor force.

The result of measuring unemployment is seemingly paradoxical. It is that employment and unemployment can both rise and fall at the same time, as workers (mainly youths and women) enter the labor market in good times, or as they withdraw in discouragement in bad times. Table 32.3 shows us this parallel rise in both the number working and the number without work. Look at the change between 1973 and 1974.

TABLE 32.3 SHORT-RUN CHANGES IN THE LABOR FORCE (MILLIONS)

	1973	*1974*	*1975*	*1976*	*1977*	*1978*	*1979*
Number in civilian labor force	88.7	91.0	92.6	94.8	97.4	100.4	102.9
Civilian employment	84.4	85.9	84.8	87.5	90.5	94.4	106.9
Unemployment	4.3	5.1	7.8	7.3	7.0	6.0	5.8

Notice that employment and unemployment can *both* rise, as in the period 1973–1974. This is because the labor force is not a fixed, but a variable, reservoir.

PARTICIPATION RATES

We call this elasticity of the labor force its *short-run participation rate.* In Chapter 4 we learned something about long-run participation rates, marked by historical changes in the ratios of men and women in the labor force, or in the proportions of the young and the old at work. Now we see that short-run changes play a significant role in determining the meaning of the phenomenon we call unemployment. The average number of hours worked per week also varies with good and bad times because employees can or cannot get overtime work or can or cannot "moonlight" (take on a second job).

These considerations mean that economists do not judge the severity of a given unemployment rate just by the percentage of the jobless. They also look to participation rates and hours of work. Relatively low participation rates and a fall in average hours worked per week indicate that the impact of a given unemployment rate is more serious than it appears to be.

CAUSES AND CURES

What causes unemployment and what will cure it? We have already more than once studied the principal reason for joblessness—a lack of sufficient aggregate demand. For reasons that we understand very well, when total spending declines, employers let workers go. Thus the first cause of unemployment lies in too little demand, and the first cure lies in restoring demand to a full employment level.

LEVEL OF DEMAND

This is only the first step in our analysis, however, for we must recognize that a level of demand adequate to produce full or high employment in one year will not be adequate the next. First, there is a normal growth of the labor force as a consequence of population growth. This growth may accelerate if an unusually large number of young people, products of an earlier baby boom, are leaving school. In the 1960s there was a flood of such young entrants; now, fortunately, the flood has ebbed (see box on p. 510).

Second, even if there were no increase in the labor force, we experience a normal growth in productivity as the consequence of adding capital equipment, of improving our techniques of production, and of increasing our stock of skill and knowledge. This year-to-year increase in per capita productivity averages 3 percent. Therefore, unless GNP grows by at least that amount, there will not be enough demand to absorb the output of the given labor force. **Thus we need a growth of GNP equal to the increase in the labor force, plus the increase in productivity, to insure a constant rate of employment.**

But suppose that we have too much unemployment and want to grow fast enough to absorb it? Now comes an important twist that results from the elasticity of the labor force. As employment grows, more people enter the labor force, and hours lengthen. This means that we have to increase the level of GNP enough to absorb the original unemployed, plus the addition to the labor force that results from higher participation rates and more hours worked.

The difficulty with revving up GNP to eliminate unemployment is that we rapidly run into inflationary bottlenecks, once unemployment reaches the 5 to 6 percent level. This brings us to familiar terrain, where we must fight out the battle between unemployment and inflation. **We know how to reduce unemployment by raising aggregate demand, but we do not know how to do so without creating unacceptable levels of inflation.**

AUTOMATION UNEMPLOYMENT

Aggregate demand—or rather the lack of it—is the prime cause of unemployment. A subsidiary cause is automation, which may create unemployment or make difficult its cure even if the level of national spending is high.

Automation joblessness, caused by the introduction of machines, is a problem that vexes and worries us, partly because it is real, partly because we do not understand it very well. Technology can be a source of job creation, especially when it brings whole new industries into being. But machines can also displace people from established jobs—and may not create new industries to absorb them.

Looking back over the history of the United States, it seems as if machines steadily pushed people out of the agricultural sector, through the factory, and into the office. Fifty years ago it took almost 40 percent of the work force to feed us; today it takes only 3 percent. The proportion of the labor force that works in manufacturing has been falling very slowly over the last 50 years. It is the service employments that have burgeoned, employing 65 percent of our labor force today compared with 25 percent in 1900.

Modern technology is more and more oriented to service work, the computer being the prime example. Will computer technology displace people from service jobs, or will it expand the role of services and make new jobs? We do not yet know.

STRUCTURAL UNEMPLOYMENT

If automation did bring about unemployment, could we not take care of it through demand management? The question opens up an aspect of the unemployment problem that we have not yet studied. **Unemployment is not solely a matter of people losing jobs, but of people not being able to find new jobs. We can have unemployment that results from a lack of skills or from a mismatch between existing skills and required skills or because workers looking for jobs do not have the characteristics (such as literacy, or ethnic backgrounds, or education) that employers want.**

This kind of unemployment is called *structural unemployment.* Because it is lodged so strongly in specific attributes of the individual, it resists the "easy" cure of higher aggregate demand. Business may be better for an employer, but he may prefer to pay his existing work force overtime, rather than take on a new labor force that does not meet his specifications.

THE IMPORTANCE OF BEING THE RIGHT AGE

A special kind of unemployment arises because the age composition of the labor force changes, sometimes flooding the market with young untrained workers, sometimes with older workers. Take the group aged 14 to 24. This includes those who are finishing their educations as well as those who have finished and are entering the work force. The "cohort" as a whole increased in numbers by roughly 8 to 10 percent from decade to decade in the period 1890 to 1960.

Then in the 1960s an explosion occurred. The so-called baby boom in the years immediately following World War II began to enter these age ranks. In the decade of the 1960s, the 14-to-24-year-old group increased by 52 *percent.* In the 1970s it increased by a customary 11 percent; in the 1980s it will *decline* by 8 percent. We can confidently predict these changes, because the members of this age group are already born.

Beginning in mid 1980s, however, the rate of growth of the labor force will be very slow, except for women. Job prospects should then be very bright.

The remedy for structural unemployment is more difficult than for general lack-of-demand unemployment. New skills or new attributes (such as punctuality) are needed by the "structurally" unemployed, and these are expensive to impart. The Job Corps program of the 1960s, for example, found that it cost about $10,000 to $12,000 to make an unemployed person—often a member of a ghetto group—acceptable to employers. Society was not willing to pay so large a fee, and employers also resisted (or asked large subsidies for) programs to hire and train "unemployables."

The high cost of retraining or of imparting desired work characteristics is one reason why structural unemployment is a difficult problem. Perhaps even more difficult is the question: For what jobs shall the unemployed be trained? Unless we very clearly know the shape of future demand, the risk is that a retraining program will prepare workers for jobs that may no longer exist when the workers are ready for them. And unless the *level* of future demand is high, even a foresighted program will not effectively solve the unemployment problem.

One solution to this problem would be to create a program aimed at creating permanent jobs in specific areas of the public sector, such as the repair, maintenance, and beautification of our inner cities, or the care of the aged. Once again, however, we encounter public resistance. The use of the government as the "employer of last resort" is a potentially powerful weapon for the alleviation of unemployment, but it is a departure that does not yet have the wholehearted endorsement of the public.

UNEMPLOYMENT AND SOCIAL INSURANCE

Next we must glance at a new problem, one that is not yet well researched or understood. This is the possibility that the existence of easily available, relatively high unemployment insurance benefits helps to generate unemployment, especially among low-paid workers.

Unemployment compensation in the United States differs widely among the states. In general, it provides for payment of one-half of an unemployed person's income, up to some maximum weekly benefit. Actual weekly benefits range from $99 in Washington, D.C. to $48 in Mississippi. There is also a limit on how many weeks' unemployment compensation can be claimed. Usually 20 weeks can be collected, although that was temporarily upped to 65 weeks by federal legislation during the 1975–1976 recession.

However, many individuals, such as new entrants into the labor force or employees of government and nonprofit institutions are not eligible for any benefits at all. If a person is not eligible or has exhausted his or her benefits, there is welfare, which also varies from state to state in terms of benefits and eligibility.

Unemployment compensation has been one of the most important social changes of the last 50 years. For what was so frightening about the Great Depression was not merely its terrific rate of joblessness; it was that this economic failure had no social remedy. An unemployed family was literally without any recourse, except its own savings or whatever charity or relief a municipality might provide. The unemployed in the 1930s did not receive unemployment insurance checks. They waited in line at soup kitchens.

Nevertheless, there may well be a cost for the social floor that unemployment insurance has placed under our feet. The cost is that unemployment insurance, because it is not taxable, greatly reduces the incentive to stick to a job. Professor Martin Feldstein has pointed out that the opportunity cost of unemployment is not the comparison of a worker's earnings and his or her unemployment compensation check; it is a comparison of the *after-tax* earnings with that check. The difference may be small. Feldstein believes that our present system encourages unemployment by making it "profitable" to get fired—at least for young or part-time workers. He suggests that we can alleviate the situation by making unemployment benefits taxable.

It is possible that Feldstein is correct in his analysis. Improvements in the equity and the cost of unemployment insurance may be useful reforms. They will not, however, cure the major causes of unemployment itself.

FRICTIONAL UNEMPLOYMENT

We should not leave this discussion of the causes of unemployment without mentioning the normal unemployment that occurs when workers voluntarily leave one job in search of a better one. This kind of unemployment is actually a source of benefit for the economy, because it is one of the ways in which productivity is enhanced, as workers move from declining industries to growing ones.

Nonetheless, we can increase the efficiency of this productivity-promoting flow of labor by reducing the period of "frictional" unemployment as much as possible. The most frequently suggested means of doing so is to provide a nationwide employment service that would make job information available to job searchers, so that a carpenter, wishing to leave an area where work was slow, would know what areas were booming; or a secretary who felt there was no room for promotion in a sluggish business would have available a roster of many other possibilities.

Want ads are a partial, but incomplete, kind of employment service. A full-scale national information service would provide much more complete information; and a full national commitment to minimizing frictional unemployment would even help defray the costs of relocating. Sweden and some other European countries run such labor exchanges, but we have yet to establish one in the United States.

This is by no means a full discussion of all the causes of, or cures for, unemployment. We have, for example, ignored the problem of wage policy, although it must be obvious that unemployment can be generated if unions succeed in pushing up wage rates for certain jobs above the jobs' marginal productivity. And we have paid no heed to the long-run remedy for unemployment played by lengthening the years of schooling, lowering the age of retirement, liberalizing vacation policies, and other changes in social institutions.

But we have covered enough to enable us to draw up a preliminary report on the performance of the economy as a generator of employment. As we saw, when we first examined the data for the 1960s and 1970s, that report is not good. Unemployment has ranged from 3.5 percent in the war-boom years to nearly 9 percent in the 1975 recession. Some of this was frictional unemployment—perhaps 2 to 3 percent of the labor force. All the rest was structural unemployment or the unemployment that resulted from inadequate levels of aggregate demand.

"RESERVE ARMY OF THE UNEMPLOYED"

Is this a consequence of the inherent sluggishness of a capitalist system incapable of attaining high levels of employment except under armaments spending?

Marxists have argued that this is the case and have pointed to the very large workless bottom layer of the American economy. First there are the officially acknowledged unemployed—6 million in 1979. Then there are the underemployed, those who want full-time work but can get only part-time. These are another 4 million. Then there are 1 million who are not looking for work because they think they cannot find it. This gives us a very large "reserve army of the unemployed," to use Karl Marx's term for the jobless whose presence, he argued, served to keep down the wages of those who were employed. Really full employment, a Marxist would claim, would raise wages so high that profits—and capitalism—would disappear.

This is not an analysis to be lightly brushed aside. In Europe, for example, a similar "reserve army" has been created by importing cheap labor from Greece, Spain, Yugoslavia, and Turkey to man the great factories of the continent. When times are bad, many of these "guest workers" are forced to return to their countries of origin; so that the European nations, in fact, export some of their unemployed, as we saw in our last chapter.

U.S. VS. EUROPEAN PERFORMANCE

It may well be, in other words, that some unemployment above the frictional level is needed to prevent wages from squeezing out profits or sending prices skyhigh. Leaders in many countries speak candidly of the need to keep labor "in line," and unemployment is openly acknowledged to be a disciplinary force toward that end. Some degree of unemployment may indeed be inseparable from the operation of a capitalist system.

But what degree? It is also clear that the levels of unemployment that have been generated and tolerated in the United States are not necessary. In Western Europe until very recently, the levels of unemployment have for long periods

Country	Highest	Lowest	Average
United States	6.7%	3.5%	*4.9%*
Canada	7.1	3.9	*5.4*
Japan	1.7	1.1	*1.3*
France	3.0	1.6	*2.3*
West Germany	2.1	0.3	*0.8*
Italy	4.3	2.7	*3.6*
United Kingdom	5.3	1.2	*3.2*
Sweden	2.7	1.2	*1.9*

Source: *The Nordic Economic Outlook*, June 1975.

TABLE 32.4 UNEMPLOYMENT RATES 1960–1974

been far below that of the United States, as Table 32.4 shows—a record of years in which European nations were not "exporting" unemployment but were enjoying a strong boom.

European nations have generally gone much further than we have in providing labor exchanges or in seeking to remedy structural unemployment, and they have been willing to accept a higher level of inflation as a lesser evil than a high level of unemployment.

What is lacking in our nation, to date, is a willingness to place employment at the very head of all the benefits that we expect from an economy, a willingness to bend every effort to achieve the right to work for all. We may still not wholly eliminate structural or aggregate demand employment, but then at least we could not be faulted for having failed to try.

KEY CONCEPTS

LOOKING BACK

The main cause of unemployment is recession

1. The primary causes of unemployment are recessions or depressions.

Unemployment "fighters" are mainly recruited from youth, women, and nonwhites

2. Unemployment has a different impact than has inflation. The effect of inflation is diffused; the effect of unemployment is concentrated. If the unemployed are our "inflation fighters," they are drafted very unevenly, mainly from young workers, women, and nonwhites. These are the groups whose wage rates have least effect on the national wage pattern.

Unemployment has ranged from 5 to 9 percent during the 1970s

3. The severity of unemployment during the 1970s has ranged from 5 to nearly 9 percent. This is a poor showing. Moreover, the differential impact is very high among certain groups.

Participation rates vary, so that employment and unemployment may rise and fall together

4. Unemployment is measured by the inability of a person who is searching for work to find a job. Therefore the question of searching is important in determining who is, and is not, "participating" in the labor force. Because participation rates drop in recessions as discouraged workers withdraw, it is often the case that unemployment and employment both rise or both fall, rather than moving in opposite directions.

We need a 3½ percent increase in GNP to lower unemployment by 1 point

5. The main remedy for unemployment is increasing the level of aggregate demand. The main problem is the risk of accelerating inflation. Because of population growth and normal increases in

productivity, we must increase GNP by about 2½ percent a year just to maintain an even level of employment, and we must increase GNP by 3½ percent to lower the unemployment rate by 1 percent.

Technological unemployment and structural unemployment are different causes for joblessness. They may be combatted by public employment

6. Technology can also create unemployment, displacing labor by machinery as in agriculture. We do not know if the recent burst of computer technology (automation) will have a net labor displacing effect or not. Similar to technological unemployment is structural unemployment, resulting from a mismatch of skills and employers' needs. One remedy for this general kind of unemployment may be public sector employment, using the government as employer of last resort.

Unemployment insurance may magnify unemployment

7. Unemployment insurance is a very important cushion for the unemployed. It is possible, however, that unemployment benefits, because they are tax free, serve to encourage unemployment.

Unemployment may serve a purpose in keeping capitalism going, but European experience shows that unemployment can be reduced far below American levels

8. Unemployment was regarded by Karl Marx as the "reserve army" of capitalism, necessary to keep its wage level down. Recent experience using unemployment to fight inflation bears some resemblance to this. Nonetheless, European experience shows that capitalism can run for long periods with much lower unemployment rates than we have suffered.

ECONOMIC VOCABULARY

Participation rates 508
Structural unemployment 509
Frictional unemployment 511
Reserve army of the unemployed 512

QUESTIONS

rethink training education skills

1. Unemployment rates among the black population in many cities today are worse than during the Great Depression years. What steps do you think should be taken?
2. Do you believe there exists general support for large public employment programs? Why or why not?
3. Do you think the computer on net balance has created jobs? How would you go about researching this question?
4. How much inflation would you yourself accept to lower unemployment by one half? How much inflation do you think the public would accept?
5. Why is frictional unemployment useful but not structural unemployment? If frictional unemployment is useful, why try to reduce it?
6. Explain why we need a rising GNP to maintain a constant level of employment. Would this be true if we had zero population growth but rising productivity? Zero productivity growth but rising population? If we have both, will the target be constant employment or constant unemployment? Or constant unemployment rates?

Chapter 33 TAXING AND SPENDING

A LOOK AHEAD

This is a chapter devoted to the crucial issue of taxes and expenditures—or, more precisely, to the questions: Are taxes fair, and is government spending wasteful? There are, of course, a lot of facts. But the main analytical issues are perhaps more significant than the facts. These are:

(1) Who pays taxes—what is the incidence of taxation? This complicated question is important when we try to gauge the equity of our tax system.

(2) What criteria can we apply to government spending to determine whether or not it is wasteful?

PROPOSITION 13

Few issues have so captured the attention of the public in the last few years as Proposition 13—the famous item on a California ballot in 1978 that called for a drastic reduction in property taxes. A wave of "Proposition 13 thinking" has swept the country. The cry for economy in government was never stronger, nor more popular.

There are two larger questions raised by the Proposition 13 movement. One has to do with the role that the federal government can properly play in influencing the nation's macroeconomic course. This is a question that we have already investigated in our macroeconomic studies and that we have taken up again in the special chapter devoted to inflation.

But there is a second, equally important, side to the question. We shall look into it here. It concerns the microeconomics of taxing and spending. Here the issue is not how big our government spending programs should grow, but rather how equitable are our taxes and how economical our public spending. For at least part of the Proposition 13 outcry reflects a feeling that taxes are not only too high, but unfair; and that our expenditures are not only too large, but too wasteful. In this chapter we shall try to shed some light on this controversy.

REVENUE

All governments need revenue. What is at stake is how much they need and how they get it. A good place to begin is to compare the level of taxation in the United States with that in other capitalist countries.

U.S. VS. FOREIGN TAXES

Table 33.1 gives us the answer. As we can see, the share of total GNP that comes to government as tax revenue is low, not high in the United States.

TABLE 33.1 PERCENTAGE OF GNP RAISED IN TAXES

U.S.	28.0
U.K.	32.8
West Germany	37.3
Sweden	43.5
France	36.9
Canada	33.9
Japan	22.6
Norway	45.9

THE AMERICAN MOOD

In the light of these figures, we might wonder why Americans seem so incensed over the relatively low taxes they pay. This is a question that is closer to sociology than to economics, but it is important enough to warrant a few speculative suggestions:

1. **Americans have always been disposed to regard government as an interloper, not as an integral part of a society.** It therefore follows that the threshold of discontent with government activity is lower in the United States than else-

where. A story to the point is related by the sociologist Seymour Martin Lipset:[1] Like the United States, Canada is a country with a frontier mentality. But look at the difference in the figures chosen by the two countries to symbolize this shared social experience. For the United States, it is the cowboy, symbol of individualism and disregard for government. For Canada, it is the scarlet-clad Mountie, the very personification of law and order.

2. **Americans seem to feel that, relatively speaking, there is a lot of waste and extravagance in their government.** Wastefulness cannot easily be compared among countries, but casual observation leads one to believe that the perceived level of public efficiency and performance may be higher abroad than in the United States. Even conservative politicians in England or Sweden profess their admiration for the health and welfare systems there, although they wish to cut down on "frills." In the United States one often encounters the view that all public spending is a "rip off," and that waste is intolerably high. This may be related to the size and complexity of the United States compared with European nations, to the diversity of our population, and to the peculiar administrative problems of our federal-state-local government. Or it may reflect a level of public honesty that is actually higher in "old-fashioned" Europe than in the United States.

TAX LEVELS VS. TAX INCIDENCE

There is really no objective way of determining the proper level of taxation for any nation. Nearly everyone would agree that it is possible to have too low a level of taxation so that the country was starved for public services, and it is certainly possible to have too high a level. Whether our existing level is a good one depends on our social objectives—a matter about which the public holds conflicting opinions. This is not a question that we can resolve here.

But Proposition 13 is not just a protest against the amount of taxes we pay. There is also a strong feeling that the tax system is unfair. The California voters who threw out Proposition 13 were specifically voicing their concern about property taxes; other tax critics feel that our income taxes are too high, or our corporate taxes, or our sales taxes.

REGRESSIVE, PROGRESSIVE, AND PROPORTIONAL

What is a fair tax? As with so many questions that affect public policy, there is no economic criterion for fair or unfair. But there are some objective measures that enable us to talk about the question more intelligently.

We start by recognizing that all taxes can be classified into three different kinds by their incidence—that is, by analyzing who pays them. Regressive taxes bear more heavily, in percentage terms, on low incomes than high ones: a highway toll, for example, is regressive because 25¢ is a bigger part of a poor driver's income than of a rich driver's. Proportional taxes bear equally on all income groups. Any tax that takes a fixed percent of all incomes—say 25 percent—would be a proportional tax. And a progressive tax is a tax that takes a larger bite—a larger percentage as well as a larger amount—as income rises.

[1] S. M. Lipset, *The First New Nation* (New York: Basic Books, Inc., 1963), p. 251.

There are no economic or even moral rules that enable us to say that one category of taxes is fairer than another. Yet there is no doubt that most economists, politicians, and members of the public do not openly admire regressive taxes. Sometimes we favor regressive revenue measures, such as lotteries, which tend to bear more heavily on the poor than the rich, but then we find ways of rationalizing our decision, such as the popularity of such measures, or their convenience. On the whole, everyone favors proportional taxes or mildly progressive ones. But when progressivity goes "too far"—when very successful entrepreneurs are "penalized" by taxes that virtually wipe out all their incomes—we tend to call that unfair.

TAX INCIDENCE

By these criteria, are our taxes fair or unfair? The answer depends, of course, on their incidence; and as we shall see, it is surprisingly difficult to determine what that incidence is.

To take the most simple-looking case, suppose that the state levies a 5 percent sales tax on all commodities sold at retail. Who pays such a tax?

The question seems nonsensical. Doesn't the consumer pay the tax? Not all of it. When the state levies a sales tax, the cost of commodities rises. This is the same thing as an upward shift in the supply curve, as we see in Figure 33.1. As a result, price rises from P_1 to P_2.

Now, who has paid the tax? The consumer has paid some, but not all. He pays the rise in price P_2–P_1, and he also loses the utilities of the goods he can no longer buy, Q_1–Q_2. But the producer has also paid some of the tax—the amount P_1–P_3, and he has also suffered a loss in revenues because his sales have dropped.

And even this is not an end to the matter. Because the producer's income has fallen, his demand for factors has dropped from D_1 to D_2 (see Figure 33.2). Hence the prices of the factors and the quantities employed will fall. So *factors, too, bear part of the tax.* In Figure 33.2 factors of production suffer a cut-back in

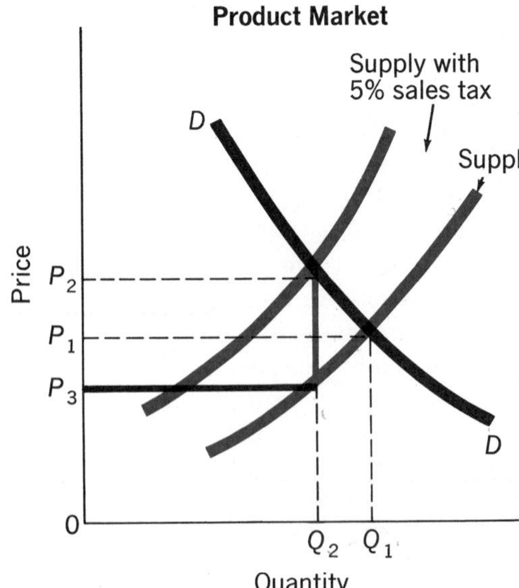

FIGURE 33.1 INCIDENCE OF SALES TAXES

Sales tax per unit is $P_2 - P_3$. The consumer pays part, $P_2 - P_1$, and the producer part, $P_1 - P_3$. The consumer also suffers a fall in consumption from Q_1 to Q_2, and the producer a fall in sales of like amount. Both consumer and producer bear some of the tax.

Factors also bear some of the tax because a fall in producer's revenues shifts his demand curve leftward. Factor income falls from *OX* times *OL* to *OY* times *OM*.

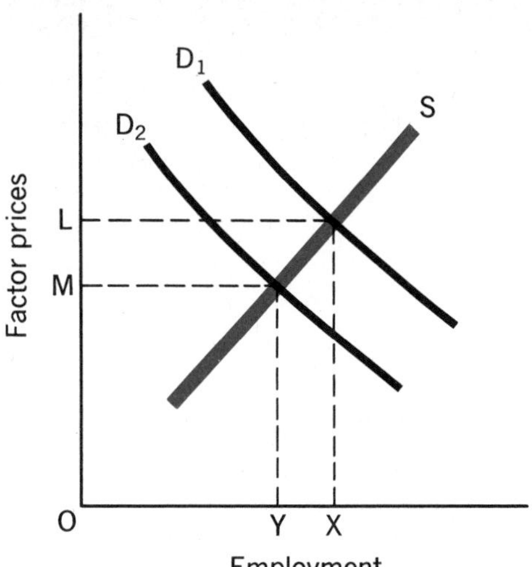

FIGURE 33.2 IMPACT OF SALES TAX ON FACTORS

price from *L* to *M* and a reduction in quantities employed from *X* to *Y*. Hence their incomes will fall from $OL \times OX$ to $OM \times OY$.

As a result, the sales tax will actually be shared by consumers, producers, and factors of production. The point is that the retail storekeeper, who actually makes out the check to the government, or the consumer who pays his pennies of sales tax is very likely not the sole bearer of the tax.

EFFECTS OF ELASTICITY

How much of the tax will the consumer bear? That depends on the elasticity of demand for the product. If demand is very inelastic the storekeeper will mark up items by the amount of the sales tax and will sell as many items as before. In that case, the consumer will pay it all, and the retailer or seller will simply act as the collection agency for the government, as Figure 33.3 shows.

More likely, when a sales tax is imposed, sellers will shave profit margins, to avoid a serious loss of volume. They will make up price by less than the tax and make up the difference out of profits. Sellers and consumers both will then bear the tax.

COMPLEXITY OF INCIDENCE

Are sales taxes fair or unfair? Perhaps we can now see how difficult it is to answer the question. Even in what seems to be a clear case we have to know two things:

1. How much of the tax is shifted "forward" to the consumer, how much is absorbed by the seller or producer, and how much is shifted backward to the factors of production? That requires a knowledge of elasticities of demand and supply that we often do not possess.

2. To determine how much of a sales tax is paid by any one person, we also have to know the extent to which that individual is a consumer, a producer, or a factor. Think about the impact of a 5¢ tax per pack of cigarettes on a tobacconist who does not smoke but who owns 10 shares of American Tobacco. Such are the difficulties of coming to clear-cut pronouncements about tax incidence.

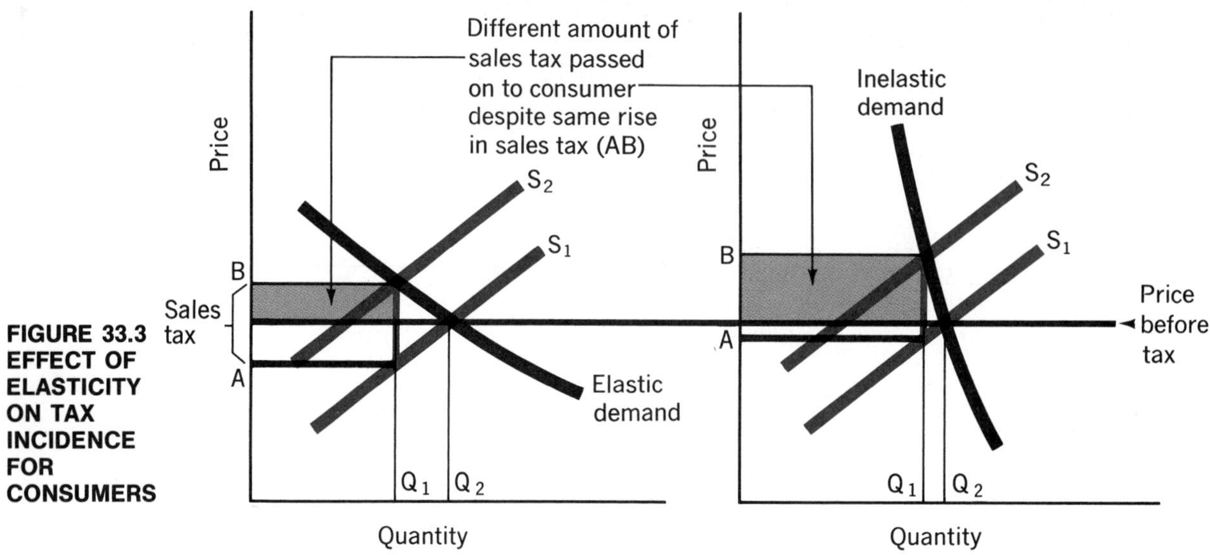

FIGURE 33.3 EFFECT OF ELASTICITY ON TAX INCIDENCE FOR CONSUMERS

Elasticity again makes all the difference. Compare the amount of tax that can be passed along to the consumer in the two cases above. Both goods bear the same sales tax. In the case on the left, demand is elastic, and therefore consumers find substitutes. Quantity sold falls markedly, and the actual rise in price—the amount of the sales tax passed on to the consumer—is only about half the sales tax. Observe how the inelastic demand curve on the right allows a much larger proportion of the tax to be shifted forward.

REGRESSIVITY OF SALES TAXES

Nonetheless, we can venture one generalization. A sales tax on necessities is sure to be passed on to the consumer to a much greater extent than one on luxuries. This is because the demand curve for necessities is, by definition, less elastic than the demand curve for luxuries. Most necessities, such as food, bulk larger in the budgets of low-income families than of high-income families. On the average, food costs absorb about 30 percent of an $8,000 family budget, in contrast with just over 20 percent of an $18,000 budget. Therefore sales taxes on necessities are regressive. **By way of contrast, sales taxes on luxuries may be progressive, if they are levied only on goods bought by upper-class families.** A sales tax on yachts will have a very different incidence on rich and poor than a sales tax on gasoline or on retail items in general.

PERSONAL INCOME TAXES

What about the incidence of a personal income tax? At one level, this is the simplest tax to discuss in terms of its incidence. **If we are taxed on our net incomes, we have only one way of "shifting" the tax. This is to work less, thereby lowering our incomes.** In theory, high income tax rates might deter people from working. Income taxes lessen the marginal utility of additional work, because they take away some of the money income we derive from it. Therefore they may increase our preference for nonwork—leisure.

Actually, studies indicate that very few highly paid persons curtail their efforts significantly because of income taxes. Neither the number of hours we work nor the intensity of our work efforts seems to change if taxes increase or decrease. Economists therefore go on the assumption that income taxes are borne directly by the individuals who pay them, and that they do not significantly alter work habits.

Income taxes may, however, change income tax payment habits. When taxes are felt to be high, people find means of avoiding them. In Sweden, for example, where marginal tax rates go above the 80 percent range, there is a widespread resort to nonmonetary forms of income, or to payments that escape the tax collector's gaze. A lawyer will offer advice free to a carpenter in exchange for a weekend's work on the lawyer's garage. A house painter, asked to submit an estimate, gives two figures: a very high one, if the transaction will be reported to the government, and a much lower one if the job will be paid in cash.

Even in the United States, where marginal tax rates are far below Swedish levels, unreported income may be very large. Guesses on its size run into the tens of billions. And then there is the search for loopholes—legal ways of avoiding income. We will come to those shortly.

PROGRESSIVITY OF INCOME TAXES

Income taxes, levied by federal, state, or local (usually municipal) authorities are all progessive in their structure. Without exception, the rate of taxes rises as income rises: The federal income tax, for example, begins at 14 percent and increases to 50 percent at a taxable income level of $44,000 for a married couple. (It goes to 70 percent on property income.)

However, there is a great deal of difference between rates on paper and actual income taxes paid by families. This is because we do not pay taxes on our total or gross income, but on our taxable incomes. Taxable incomes are our gross incomes less various exemptions and deductions permitted by law. For example, we are allowed to deduct $1,000 for each dependent (including ourselves) in figuring our income tax. We can deduct interest that we pay, which is usually interest on mortgages on our houses. We can deduct all state and local taxes from our federal income tax. We can take off charitable contributions, legitimate business expenses, and a long list of other items.

EFFECT OF DEDUCTIONS

Deductions affect the incidence of the income tax structure in two ways. In the first place, they often create "horizontal" inequities. Two families or individuals with identical incomes may pay very different taxes because one can use a deduction and another cannot. For years, owners of oil properties enjoyed a deduction known as a depletion allowance. It enabled them to reduce their taxable income from oil by as much as a third below the actual oil income. Owners of state and local bonds have for years enjoyed the privilege of not paying any federal tax on the interest from these bonds. Thus, two households, side by side in identical houses, enjoying identical incomes, may pay hugely different taxes. Because of deduction loopholes, many wealthy people escape taxation entirely. In 1969, there were 761 persons with incomes over $100,000 who paid no federal income taxes at all; 56 with incomes over $1 million also paid not a cent of tax.

TABLE 33.2 REAL AND NOMINAL TAX RATES

Adjusted family income ($000)	Scheduled marginal federal income tax rates	Actual average federal income tax rates
0–3	15%	1%
3–5	18	5
5–10	20	7
10–15	24	10
15–20	28	12
20–25	32	14
25–50	39	17
50–75	48	24
75–100	53	27
100–500	61	30
500–1,000	68	33
1,000 +	69	34

Actual taxes paid in different income brackets are much less progressive than marginal tax rates would suggest.

LOSS OF PROGRESSIVITY

In the second place, deductions greatly lessen the progressivity of taxes, as Table 33.2 shows. Deductions have this antiprogressive effect because a deduction is worth much more to a high-income family than to a low-income one. Example: charitable donations. A rich family, whose marginal tax bracket is 50 percent, gives away $100. As a result, its pretax income is reduced by $100, but its tax is reduced by $50. The net cost of the $100 gift is therefore $50 in reduced after-tax spendable income. A poorer family, whose marginal tax bracket is 25 percent, also gives away $100. It thereby saves a tax of $25. Its spendable, after-tax income is reduced by $75. Not only is this loss of spendable income larger in *absolute* terms than for the richer family, but it is certainly larger as a percentage of its total income.

CORPORATE INCOME TAXES

Let us next take a look at the corporate income tax, the source of very substantial sums for federal government.

Who pays a corporation's income tax? Few questions are more uncertain. Some economists think the corporate income tax is essentially a sales tax, borne partly by consumers, partly by the business (in the form of reduced income), partly by the factors of production who suffer a loss in earnings. Others think it is a tax on capital, serving to reduce the flow of capital into the corporate sector. Still others believe that its impact cannot be clearly depicted because most corporate income taxes are paid by big oligopolistic companies, who may use tax increases as an excuse to raise prices in their industry, laying the blame for this on "the government." Some economists even go so far as to say that one of the virtues of the corporate tax is that no one can state with certainty who pays it; therefore, it serves as an excellent way for the government to raise money without clearly imposing a tax on anyone!

DOUBLE TAXATION

Many critics claim that corporate taxes are unfair because they tax the owners of corporations twice on the income their companies have earned. They are taxed once when the corporation pays half of its income to the government—income that would otherwise belong to the shareowner. And they are taxed again when dividends are paid and the owners receive their income.

Many persons who favor progressive taxes would protest that abolition of the corporate income tax would aid the rich. Actually, if corporate income taxes were abolished and all corporate earnings were distributed to shareowners, the bite on wealthy stockholders would be greater, not smaller, than today!

SOCIAL SECURITY TAXES

Social Security taxes pose another problem. There is no question who pays them. They reduce the income of the wage earner and the employer, who may or may not be able to pass forward his share of the tax. The more interesting question is whether this tax is regressive.

At first glance there is no doubt in the matter. Social Security taxes today take 11.7 percent of all wages, half paid by a reduction in the salary check, the other half by the employer. This percentage is the same on all taxed wages, so that the tax seems quite proportional. But there is no tax levied above an established level ($25,900 in 1980), so that high wage earners pay smaller proportions of their earnings. In addition, although Social Security taxes are taken from even the lowest earned income, property income of any kind—interest, rent, dividends, or royalties—is exempt from Social Security. Thus, measured against total income, the Social Security levy is regressive.

Yet in the end, matters are not quite that simple. The payout formula for Social Security is set to give low-income earners more dollars of benefit, per dollar paid in, than high earners. **Therefore, if we offset the regressive tax with the progressive payment schedule, the net impact of Social Security becomes progressive.**

The difficulty is that Social Security taxes are paid at one stage in an individual's life cycle, and the benefits are received at another, later stage. It is not easy to compare costs and benefits when they are separated by long periods of time. This problem is worsened because the ratio between the number of persons working (and paying tax) and those not working (and receiving benefits) is changing in favor of the retired population. An ever larger proportion of our population is living on Social Security, at much higher benefit levels than formerly; and these trends will certainly continue.

This means that it will soon become impossible to finance Social Security by the conventional Social Security taxes unless they are very greatly increased. Because workers are already grumbling at the cut that Social Security takes, it is likely that part of Social Security costs—perhaps the portion that finances Medicare—will be met from general tax revenues, and that Social Security taxes will be lifted much higher. All these changes would further improve the overall progressivity of the Social Security system.

PROPERTY TAXES

Property taxes are very important sources of revenue for states and localities. They are also very hot political items since Proposition 13 put a ceiling on them in California.

One difficulty with property taxes is that inflation can raise the assessed value of real estate much more rapidly than it increases the income of homeowners. What happened in California was that owners found themselves unable to meet taxes that were mounting steadily higher. To be sure, homeowners could sell their houses at a profit. But to buy a new house cost just as much, and did not get around the problem of rising real estate taxes.

Are property taxes always paid by homeowners? Not when they are levied on an owner who rents his property. Then the taxes are usually passed along as higher rents. Because rent payments are a more important budget item for low-income families than for high-income families, these tax-induced rent raises are regressive in their impact. For slum dwellers, who cannot afford to move, they may be terribly high.

Even in the case of a landlord, however, sometimes property taxes are progressive, not regressive. Suppose that property taxes are $250,000 per year on a building whose rentals yield $1 million a year. Net earnings are therefore $750,000. As we know, the building is worth a capital sum that will yield $750,000 at the going rate of return for similar properties. At 10 percent, it will be worth $7,500,000. If property taxes are now raised, the capitalized value of the building will fall. Even though the taxes may be passed forward to renters, the heaviest cost will fall on the owner of the building whose capital has been diminished.

So it is not altogether clear that property taxes are as regressive as they are thought to be. They are regressive only if we estimate their incidence on incomes. If we include their impact of wealth, they can be a very progressive form of taxation!

TOTAL INCIDENCE

Can we sum up the total incidence of the tax system? It must be clear that it is difficult to do so for two reasons. First, the horizontal variances are so great

TABLE 33.3 EFFECTIVE RATES OF FEDERAL, STATE, AND LOCAL TAXES UNDER TWO INCIDENCE ASSUMPTIONS, 1966

Adjusted family income ($000s)	*VARIANT 1*			*VARIANT 2*		
	Federal	*State and local*	*Total*	*Federal*	*State and local*	*Total*
$0–3	8.8%	9.8%	18.7%	14.1%	14.0%	28.1%
3–5	11.9	8.5	20.4	14.6	10.6	25.3
5–10	15.4	7.2	22.6	17.0	8.9	25.9
10–15	16.3	6.5	22.8	17.5	8.0	25.5
15–20	16.7	6.5	23.2	17.7	7.6	25.3
20–25	17.1	6.9	24.0	17.8	7.4	25.1
25–30	17.4	7.7	25.1	17.2	7.1	24.3
30–50	18.2	8.2	26.4	17.7	6.7	24.4
50–100	21.8	9.7	31.5	20.1	6.3	26.4
100–500	30.0	11.9	41.8	24.4	6.0	30.3
500–1,000	34.6	13.3	48.0	25.2	5.1	30.3
1,000 and over	35.5	13.8	49.3	24.8	4.2	29.0
Total	17.6	7.6	25.2	17.9	8.0	25.9

Pechman's study reveals two different tax bites, depending on various assumptions. We do not know which is true.

that average figures are often very little guide to reality. Second, incidence depends on elasticities of supply and demand that are often unknown to us.

In Table 33.3 we see the most recent and sophisticated effort to discover total tax incidence, carried out by Joseph Pechman and Benjamin Okner, both of the Brookings Institution.

Notice the tremendous difference between Variant 1 and Variant 2. In Variant 1, millionaires pay 49 percent of their incomes in taxes. In Variant 2, they pay less than 30 percent. In Variant 1, a very poor family pays less than 20 percent of its income in taxes. In Variant 2, it pays 28 percent.

The difference between the variants lies in the assumptions that are made about the elasticity of supply and demand curves. In Variant 1, where total taxation seems quite progressive, it is assumed that property taxes are borne mainly by landlords and that corporate income taxes ultimately descend on shareholders. In Variant 2, which is roughly proportional and regressive at the lowest and uppermost ends, it is assumed that property taxes are passed forward to the renter, and that corporate income taxes lower consumers' incomes through higher prices, not stockholders' incomes through lower dividends.

A PROPORTIONAL SYSTEM

Which of these variants is more likely to be true? *We do not know*. The actual incidence of taxation remains a matter for conjecture. We should note, however, that the uncertainties relate to the very lowest and highest incomes. Under both sets of assumptions, the tax burden for the groups that we have called the working class, the middle class, and the top 5 percent (although not the top 2 percent) are the same. Under both sets of assumptions, state and local taxes are regressive, and federal taxes are progressive—the two balancing each other out to produce an overall system that is roughly proportional.

Is this overall system fair? If by fairness we mean that our tax incidence should be mildly progressive, the answer is mixed. Some elements of the system, such as Social Security, are not fair. Other elements, such as the federal income tax, are fair. Still others, such as the property tax, are sometimes fair and sometimes not.

To make things even more complicated, we must remember that the taxes a person pays depend very much on where he or she lives. There are some 38,000 taxing authorities in the United States, not counting the federal government. States, municipalities, water districts, school districts, transportation authorities and a host of other agencies can impose public charges, fees, and taxes. The fairness of our personal tax situation is very much determined by our geographic situation.

HORIZONTAL EQUITY AGAIN

It's very difficult, in other words, to pass any kind of overall judgment about the United States tax system(s). On one issue, however, everyone feels alike. Whatever the values that incline us toward progressive or proportional taxation, few people would go on record as favoring preferential or discriminatory taxation. Yet that is, in fact, the kind of tax system that we have.

Tax reform, in fact, is no longer basically focused on the question of progressivity or regressivity in general. The battle rages over the hundreds or thousands of loopholes that benefit small numbers of persons. Because the closing of any particular loophole would bring a tax saving of only a few dollars for most taxpayers, they cannot work up much enthusiasm in mounting an attack on any one provision. The beneficiaries of that provision, on the other hand, stand to gain enormously by it, and they mount an all-out campaign in its favor. Thus lobbying for individual tax breaks is intense. Lobbying against any one loophole is weak.

There have been sporadic efforts to simplify and make more equitable the tax system of our 38,000 tax-levying governments. By and large they have been failures. Only wars, with their overriding imperatives, have proved capable of moving the vested interests and inertias that defend our complex system. Even advisers at the Internal Revenue services are often unable to specify which law applies to a taxpayer.

PUBLIC SPENDING

Taxing is, of course, only half the government's fiscal activity. The other half is spending. It may help if we begin by looking again at the major purposes of federal, state, and local spending in a recent year. Table 33.4 shows us the figures.

TABLE 33.4 GOVERNMENT SPENDING 1978 (BILLIONS)

Purpose	*Federal*	*State and Local*	
National Defense	109	1	
Education	13	116	
Health and Hospitals	9	28	
Social Security and Welfare	157	42	
Police and Fire	1	23	
Transportation	16	24	
TOTAL	383	304	(includes items not shown separately)

THE CRITERION OF WASTE

Now we want to ask a question that relates to our present concern: Is this spending wasteful? How can we answer such a question? One way, of course, is to reflect on how we would decide if private expenditure were wasteful. We have learned by now that there are clear-cut criteria in microeconomics that define waste. For a firm to operate efficiently, for example, it should hire factors until their marginal revenue products equal their marginal costs.

Notice that we do not judge whether a firm's output is wasteful. If there is a demand for its product, that is presumed to be sufficient justification for its existence. Economists recognize that some outputs may be illegal because they are forbidden by government, but there are no "wasteful" outputs as long as there is a market for them!

The public sector is intrinsically different from the private sector. With minor exceptions it does not sell its output and therefore cannot justify it by pointing to market demand. Moreover, as we have seen, much public output consists of public goods such as defense, from which no individual can be excluded, even if he or she did not contribute to its cost. For such goods, there is no conceivable market test to determine whether the "right" level of output has been attained.

When we speak of public waste therefore, we have two problems. The first is to find a way of justifying the particular kinds of outputs, or the levels of outputs, we find in the public sector. How do we justify a defense program or a welfare program of a given size? How do we decide whether or not to spend money on a federal research project that some will call "wasteful" and others will call "indispensable"?

Second, to what extent can we use the criteria of efficiency that we have discovered in microeconomics to analyze the operation of government agencies? Can we speak of marginal revenues and costs, for instance, in the public sphere?

VOTING

Let us start with the first question: **How do we determine, in the absence of a market, whether a program should be undertaken in the first place?**

The answer, as we know, is through voting. Where there is no economic mechanism applicable, we turn to the political mechanism. We vote for or against the general economic programs of candidates or parties. Within Congress or the state legislatures, our representatives vote again. The voting process is the subject of intense efforts to influence its outcome: lobbying, pressure from constituents, log-rolling deals of many sorts. From this pulling and hauling emerges the national economic budget with its appropriations for different public purposes, a process duplicated again at state and local levels.

The process of voting leads to many difficulties in establishing an intelligent level of government spending. One of these difficulties is that, paradoxically, both increasing and reducing government expenditures are popular, vote-getting policies.

As income maximizers, most citizens will vote for government programs that increase *their* incomes. They will vote to lower those expenditures that increase the incomes of others. Thus if each of us were to scrutinize the government's budget we could easily find areas to cut. The problem is, of course, that another citizen may gain from the very activity that we would eliminate. The objective, then, is to find cuts in expenditures that will win voting majorities. As with tax reform, expenditure reform runs into difficulties because particular cuts in spending help most voters only marginally while hurting some voters severely. Thus the beneficiaries of some expenditures form intense lobbying or pressure groups just as tax beneficiaries do.

THE ASYMMETRY OF SPENDING AND TAXING

For this reason there is an interesting difference between appeals for increasing government expenditures and for decreasing them. Expenditure increases are always discussed in terms of the specific programs to be expanded. This rallies a group of intense supporters and arouses only mild opposition from those who are not among the favored, because taxes will be only slightly raised. Conversely, when expenditure reductions are discussed, the emphasis is always placed on the general relief to all taxpayers, and the particular hurt to a few previously favored beneficiaries is passed over in silence.

The presence of staunch supporters and the absence of strong objectors demanding *specific* reductions tips the scale in favor of raising, not lowering, total expenditure. Obviously, this encourages waste in the same sense of high expenditure. On the other hand, the bias in favor of raising expenditures does not mean that the public sector is therefore too large relative to the private sector. Many other biases exist in the system to reduce the valuation that we place on public spending and to inflate the value that we ascribe to private spending. **Economic analysis alone can give us no ultimately correct division between public and private expenditure.**

RATIONAL GOVERNMENT EXPENDITURE

COST-BENEFIT

Now what about the expenditure side? How does a legislator assess the worthwhileness of a proposed expenditure? **Because a public expenditure is rarely planned to make money, a legislator must try to estimate the public benefits that will flow from the expenditure as an offset against its cost.** These benefits may be fairly easy to calculate, as when a government agency plans to build a hospital and estimates what a comparable private hospital might earn. Even if the public hospital provides its services free, these services are surely worth that much to the public simply because it has been relieved of expenditures it would otherwise have made at a private facility.

But often the benefits of a project are exceedingly difficult to calculate. How can we estimate the benefits of a new road? By the tolls that might be collected? But what about the indirect benefits gained by townspeople who are now served more rapidly and efficiently? What about the businesses that spring up alongside the new road? What about improvements in the landscape if billboards are banned?

In point of fact, there is no accurate way of adding up all the benefits of a public project. We can make more or less sophisticated guesses and estimates, but these estimates always contain a large element of uncertainty. We can easily overestimate—or underestimate—the benefit of a project.

Once a project is decided on for better or worse—a road, a school, a training program—considerations of cost effectiveness are exactly the same as they are in a factory, a private house, or any other private venture.

The principle is the use of the most economic combination of inputs to achieve a given output. Here "wastefulness" has the same definition in the public and private sector. It is certainly not easy to translate the principles of efficiency, as an economist describes them, into the complex specifications of a construction job. But the aim is in no way different between the public and private sectors.

OPPORTUNITY COSTS

A second consideration that economists can offer to legislators is the concept of opportunity cost. **The true cost of any public project (like that of any private one) is not the dollars it takes but the alternative projects that cannot be undertaken because resources are committed to the first.**

Opportunity costs are difficult to apply to public projects because the returns from these projects, as we have emphasized, include so many nonmonetary gains. Hence, in practice, most legislators consider each year's appropriations in terms of marginal increases or decreases to existing commitments. Suppose, for example, that you are considering the federal budgetary appropriation for development, a $7 billion commitment in the previous year. In all likelihood, most of your discussion would be concentrated on whether the appropriation should be increased or diminished by, say, $0.5 billion. Your review of the opportunity costs of the project would focus on whether or not that $0.5 billion would be a useful addition to the nation, compared with other uses to which those funds might be put (including their use by taxpayers if you decided to lower taxes by $0.5 billion).

THE IRRELEVANCE OF SUNK COSTS

The concept of opportunity cost brings us to quite another guide to efficient budeting. This is the idea of *sunk costs,* expenditures that have been made in the past and that can no longer be undone.

Here, too, is a distinct similarity between private and public efficiencies. Suppose that you have a dam or a factory half built. A decision must be made whether to continue with the project or abandon it. At this point neither the public legislator nor the private entrepreneur should go back and review whether or not the project should have been started in the first place. The money that has been spent on it is irretrievably lost, both to the public and the private enterprise. The question that is relevant is whether the remaining costs will be justified by the benefits or revenues that are expected ultimately to accrue.

Although a private firm may regret having decided to start up a new branch, an intelligent decision on going through with the project will measure only the remaining costs against the expected revenues. A legislator may rue having voted for a public project, but he will intelligently vote to complete it if the remaining costs will be justified by the total ensuing benefits.

In other words, all sunk costs are irrelevant in making decisions about future actions. Rather, they should be irrelevant. In fact, it is very difficult for decision makers, private or public, to understand that costs incurred in the past are now beyond recall and can be recouped, in part if not in full, only by continuing with a project even though the total undertaking is now deemed to be a losing proposition. The impulse is to stop a project once it has been decided that the initial decision was in error. The common phrases are "not to throw good money after bad" or "to cut our losses."

Curiously, the same failure to evaluate the remaining costs against the total benefits of a project can also lead to waste. Both entrepreneurs and legislators are easily tempted to complete projects that ought to be dropped. A half-built dam or a half-completed factory is testimony to a wrong decision that was made in the past. An honest computation of remaining costs measured against total benefits may show that the project should remain half complete. Since that would be an admission that the initial decision was in error, many projects are completed with hope that unexpected benefits will rescue the decision maker.

THE MARKET IN A FINAL RETROSPECT

This seems a good place to make a final assessment of the wastefulness with which resources are allocated through votes and through spending. Many people look askance at how the public sector allocates its resources. No one needs to be reminded of innumerable scandals having to do with influence peddling or abuse of the public trust by members of federal or state legislatures.

What we should remember, however, is that the voting process is a substitute rationing mechanism. Where one-dollar-one-vote does not work, or is deemed an improper rationing mechanism, a democratic society must choose one-person-one-vote.

The abuses of the voting mechanism may be many and its problems are assuredly difficult. Nonetheless, voting is the way a democracy rations its public output, just as spending is the way a market system rations its private output. Before we wax too indignant about the shortcomings of the voting process, pointing to the waste that accompanies government programs, etc., etc., we should remind ourselves of the inequities that accompany private rationing decisions.

The market mechanism has enormous strengths, but it is certainly not perfect. In fact, we know that it must be imperfect. There are problems the market cannot cope with at all. Moreover, those it does handle reveal the pervasive bias of a voting system in which individuals are measured by their incomes, not by any other gauge of their human value.

Thus all market systems must have public counterparts and complements. It is impossible to have an economic system in which government would play no role whatsover. The exercise of the political will that is so much (and so properly) distrusted is also essential for social survival. In this struggle between the authority of politics and that of the market lies a central issue, not merely of microeconomics but of modern economic society itself.

KEY CONCEPTS

LOOKING BACK

Proposition 13 mentality and its roots

1. In this chapter we try to analyze some of the issues behind the growth of Proposition 13 thinking—a strong sentiment against taxes and spending. We begin by comparing total U.S. taxes, as a percent of GNP, with those abroad, and discover that U.S. levels are lower, not higher than almost all other nations. Why the furor over taxes? Perhaps the reasons are (1) long-standing American attitudes about government, (2) dissatisfaction with the value of services received.

Incidence of taxation is important for equity. Incidence depends heavily on elasticity but is hard to determine

2. The key question, from the point of view of fairness or equity, concerns the incidence of taxation—who actually pays a given tax. Most Americans favor proportional or mildly progressive taxes. But most taxes are shifted forward or backward—to the consumer or to the factors of production. The amount of shifting depends very considerably on the elasticity of the demand curve or supply curves in the product or factor markets. Actual incidence is often very difficult to determine.

Regressive taxes hit low income hardest. Sales taxes are such a tax. Graduated income taxes are progressive, hitting upper income groups proportionately harder than lower, but loopholes greatly lessen this effect

3. Sales taxes tend to be regressive—to bear more heavily on lower incomes than higher ones. Individual income taxes tend to be progressive, although deductions and loopholes greatly lower the actual (as opposed to the scheduled) degree of progressivity. Corporate income taxes are so complex in their incidence that we do not know whether they are passed forward or backward, or are progressive or regressive. Social security taxes are very regressive, because they reach a ceiling on high incomes, but the payout formula makes up for this regressivity. Property taxes can be regressive when they are passed

along as higher rentals, but they can also be progressive when they result in lower capitalized values.

The total tax system has large horizontal inequities

4. The overall incidence of the total tax system is unclear. This is especially true because there is such a multiplicity of tax systems in the United States. There is no doubt that substantial horizontal inequities exist and that it is very hard to get rid of them.

Waste as an economic concept involves efficiency, not the justification of output

5. Waste is an important economic idea. In microeconomics it describes the criteria for efficiency, but it does not refer to the justification for output. In the public sphere it often describes our judgment about the worthwhileness of public efforts, as well as their efficiency.

Allocation problems of voting: asymmetry of spending and taxing

6. We allocate public funds among various purposes by voting, not by market decisions. Voting has many problems as an allocation mechanism. One is that we tend to vote for programs that increase our incomes, but not for programs that increase others' incomes. This leads to an asymmetry between spending and taxing. It is easier to raise budgets by stressing particular advantages which rally strong supporters, than to cut them which spreads benefits diffusely and wins no strong support.

Cost-benefit considerations should include opportunity costs and ignore sunk costs

7. Expenditures should be justified by weighing benefits against costs. This is often difficult to do, because opportunity costs may include nonmonetary elements. In addition, sunk costs are irrelevant to a rational decision, but they are politically difficult to ignore.

Public and private sectors both necessary

8. It is impossible to have an economy without a public sector—that is, without taxation and government expenditure. The public sector has many problems—but it must not be forgotten that the private sector also has its allocational difficulties. This is an inescapable problem of modern society.

ECONOMIC VOCABULARY

Incidence of taxes 518
Regressive, proportional, and progressive taxes 517
Horizontal equity 521, 525
Double taxation 522
Waste 526
Asymmetry of spending and taxing 527
Cost-benefit 528
Opportunity cost 528
Sunk cost 529

QUESTIONS

1. Can you think of arguments that would incline you in favor of a regressive tax system? How about encouraging the rate of saving? Or the idea that those who are richer deserve to be given preference because they have made a larger contribution to society?
2. Assume a payroll tax is levied in all firms. Using supply and demand curves, show who might bear such a tax if the demand for factors was very price-elastic.
3. Suppose that Family A has $1 million in stocks and bonds and an income of $35,000. Family B has no property but an earned income of the same amount. How would

you decide which tax system would yield horizontal equity for the two families? For example, would corporate income taxes affect each alike? Straight income taxes? Capital gains taxes? Is horizontal equity possible when the source of income differs, even though the amount is the same?

4. How would you go about determining whether a business's expenses were a legitimate deduction from its gross income? Assume that no entertainment expenses were allowed for any business. Would this result in horizontal inequities in different businesses? Would this be sufficient argument not to press for this tax change?
5. A congressional committee is considering the construction of a moving sidewalk in Washington, D.C. It is estimated to cost $1 billion, and will give benefits of an estimated $1.5 billion. After six months of work, $1 billion has been spent and the remaining costs are still $300 million. Should you throw "good money after bad" or discontinue the project? What are the project's opportunity costs and sunk costs?
6. Is the process of voting for expenditure democratic because each representative (or each voter) has one vote only? If so, can we call the "voting" of the marketplace democratic? If we think the marketplace is more efficient, why not use it in the voting process, giving each voter as many votes as he or she has dollars?

AN EXTRA WORD ABOUT
THE MILITARY SUBSECTOR

The problem of spending really comes home to roost with the issue of defense. Here is a brief description of the actual size of the defense establishment, followed by some analysis of why it is difficult to escape from this expensive commitment.

THE DOD

The Department of Defense (DOD) is the largest planned economy outside the Soviet Union. Its property—plant and equipment, land, inventories of war and other commodities—amounts to about 7 percent of the assets of the entire American economy. It owns 39 million acres of land, roughly an area the size of Hawaii. It rules over a population of more than 3 million—direct employees or soldiers—and spends an "official" budget of over $100 billion, a budget 40% as large as the entire gross national product of Great Britain.

This makes the DOD richer than any small nation in the world and, of course, incomparably more powerful. That part of its assets represented by nuclear explosives alone gives it the equivalent of 6 tons of TNT for every living inhabitant of the globe, to which must be added the awesome military power of its conventional weapons. The conventional explosives dropped in Indochina *before* the extension of the war to Laos amounted to well over 3 million tons, or 50 percent *more* than the total bomb tonnage dropped on all nations in both European and Pacific theaters during World War II.

The DOD system embraces both people and industry. In the late 1970s the people included, first, some 2 million soldiers deployed in more than 5,000 bases or locations abroad and at home, plus another 900,000 civilian employees located within the United States and abroad. No less important are about 2 million civilian workers who are directly employed on war production, in addition to a much larger number employed in the secondary echelon of defense-related output. This does not include still further millions who owe their livelihood to the civilian services they render to the military.

THE WEB OF MILITARY SPENDING

The web of DOD expenditures extends to more areas of the economy than one might think. All in all, some twenty-odd thousand firms are prime contractors with the DOD, although the widespread practice of subcontracting means that a much larger number of enterprises look to defense spending for a portion of their income. Within the main constituency, however, a very few firms are the bastion of the DOD economy. The hundred largest defense contractors supply about two-thirds of the $40-odd billion of manufactured deliveries; and within this group, an inner group of 10 firms by themselves account for one third of the total.

Meanwhile, the establishment has a powerful political arm as well. In the early 1970s the DOD employed more than 300 lobbyists on Capitol Hill and (a conservative estimate) some 2,700 public relations men in the U.S. and abroad. This close political relationship undoubtedly has some bearing on the Pentagon's requests for funds being given, until recently, only the most cursory congressional inspection, leading among other things to the discovery in 1973 of cost overruns of $24 billion on 38 weapons systems.

This is not to say, of course, that the United States does not need a strong defense capability today. But there is no question that the Pentagon subeconomy has become a major element in, and a major problem for, American capitalism. Indeed, the questions it raises are central: How important is this subeconomy to our economic vitality? How difficult would it be to reduce? Could our economy get along without a military subsector?

MILITARY DEPENDENCY

Let us begin by reviewing a few important facts. At the height of the Vietnam War in 1968, more than 10 percent of our labor force was employed in defense-related work. As the Vietnam War gradually decelerated, this percentage has fallen to about 5.5 percent. Defense expenditures, however, rose to $108 billion in 1979 and are slated to rise more over the next few years.

These global figures do not, however, give a clear picture of the strategic position of defense spending within the economy. The problem is that war-related spending and employment are not distributed evenly across the system but are bunched in special areas and industries. In a survey made in 1967, the Defense Department found that 72 employment areas depended on war output for 12 percent or more of their employment and that four-fifths of these areas were communities with labor forces of less than 50,000. This concentration of defense activity is still a fact of economic life in 1980. The impact of a cutback on these middle-sized communities can be devastating.

In addition, defense-employment is concentrated among special skills as well as in a nucleus of defense-oriented companies. In the late 1960s, about one scientist or engineer out of every five in private industry was employed on a defense-related job. Thirty-eight percent of all physicists depended on war-work. Twenty-five percent of all sheet-metal workers, the same proportion of patternmakers, and fifty-four percent of all airplane mechanics worked on defense projects. These proportions have declined, but defense is still a major employer of these skills. And as we have already remarked, there is a core of companies dependent on military spending for their very existence. These are not usually the largest companies in the economy (for whom, on the average, defense receipts amount to about 10 percent of total revenues) but the second echelon of corporations: Of 30 companies with assets in the $250 million to $1 billion range, 6 depended on war spending for half their incomes, and 7 depended on it for a quarter of theirs.

Thus a cutback in defense spending is always felt very sharply in particular areas, where there may be no other jobs available, or among occupational groups who have no alternative employment at equivalent pay, or in companies that are "captives" of the DOD. Such companies and areas naturally lobby hard for the defense expenditure on which their livelihood depends. So do their representatives in Congress. It is this interweaving of economic and political interests that makes the problem of defense cutbacks so difficult.

CONVERSION POSSIBILITIES

Yet a cutback is not economically impossible. *What is crucial, economically, is that the decline in war-related spending be offset by increases in peace-related spending, to be sure that the overall level of demand would remain high enough to act as a magnet, attracting the displaced workers to other jobs.* Unless we were willing to undertake an ambitious program of public spending or tax cuts, the conversion would certainly generate severe unemployment—and consequent political pressures to maintain military spending.

Meanwhile, it is clear that the armaments economy is not only costing us a vast sum of money, but is also weighing heavily on the Russians. The annual military expenditure of the U.S. and the U.S.S.R. together amounts to about two-thirds of the entire output of the billion people of Latin America, Southeast Asia, and the Near East. Not only is this an opportunity cost of tragically large dimensions, if we consider the uses to which those resources might otherwise be applied, but even in terms of a strictly military calculus, much of it is *total waste, since neither side has been able to gain a decisive advantage despite its enormous expenditures.*

PRISONERS' DILEMMA

How does such a senseless course commend itself to national governments? Needless to say, the answers lie deep in the web of political, economic, and social forces of our times. Analytical reasoning can nonetheless throw some light on the matter by unraveling the peculiar situation involving two prisoners, each of whom knows something about the other and who are being interrogated separately. If *both* prisoners remain silent, both will get very light terms since the evidence against each is not conclusive. If one prisoner squeals on the other, he will get off scot-free as a reward for turning state's evidence, while the other prisoner will get a heavy term. If both prisoners squeal, both will get severe terms, convicted by each other's testimony.

Now, if the two prisoners could confer—and if they trusted each other absolutely—they would obviously agree that the strategy of shared silence was the best for each. But if the prisoners are separated or unsure of each other's trustworthiness, each will be powerfully tempted to rat on the other in order to reduce his own sentence. As a result, since the two are equally tempted, the outcome is likely to end in *both* sides ratting—and in *both* sides getting heavy punishment. Thus the pursuit of individual self-interest lures the two prisoners into a strategy that penalizes them both.

Something very like the prisoners' dilemma afflicts the nations of the world, especially the two superpowers, America and Russia. Although a policy of limited arms spending would clearly be to their mutual best advantage, their distrust of each other leads each to try to get ahead of the other. This state of mutual suspicion is then worsened when special interest groups in each nation deliberately play on the fears of the public. The end result is that both spend vast sums on armaments that yield them no advantage, while the world (including themselves) suffers an opportunity cost on an enormous scale. Only with a frank and candid exploration of shared gains and losses can both prisoners hope to get out of their dilemma. Prospects for a massive conversion of the U.S. arms economy may hinge on our understanding of this central military and political reality of our time.

Chapter 34 DEFENDING THE DOLLAR

A LOOK AHEAD

Our focus shifts from problems at home to problems in the international arena. For several years we have heard about the falling dollar and the need to defend it. This chapter

(1) clarifies what we mean when we say that the dollar is falling, and explains how a nation can "defend" its currency;

(2) teaches us the basic elements of international exchange (treatment in depth must wait until Chapter 37);

(3) gives us a view of the impact on our domestic well-being of international economic trends and our efforts to cope with them.

Foreign trade and international finance used to be subjects that Americans could afford to be ignorant about. In nearly all economic textbooks, including our own, they were reserved for a special section at the end, and it was generally understood that if an instructor had to sacrifice any part of the course because of insufficient time, international economics was the part to go.

That has changed, and changed dramatically, within a very few years. The former invulnerability of the American economy from foreign goings-on has come to an end. The American dollar, once the Rock of Gibraltar in a stormy world, has taken a terrible battering. Millions of American citizens are now directly affected by America's international economic position; all of us are indirectly affected by it. In a word, international economics has become a part of economics with which every student should be familiar.

THE FALLING DOLLAR

The new situation has come home to most of us through headlines that have announced for some years that the dollar is "falling." Sometimes the headlines tell us that gold is soaring, or that the yen or the mark or the Swiss franc have hit new highs. All these phrases mean the same thing—but what is that thing?

THE FOREIGN VALUE OF THE DOLLAR

When the dollar falls in the international money markets, it does not mean that a dollar will buy fewer American goods. That is a very important point to bear in mind. Our dollars fall in domestic value as inflation raises prices, but it is entirely possible for inflation to cheapen the dollar at home—at least for a time—but not cause it to fall on the foreign money markets. Vice versa, it is possible for the dollar to fall abroad but to remain unchanged in its buying power at home.

When we speak of the dollar falling in foreign trade, it means only one thing: A dollar will buy less foreign money—German marks, French or Swiss francs, Swedish krona, or whatever. As a result, it becomes more expensive to buy foreign goods and services.

THE RATE OF EXCHANGE

Suppose, for example, that you enjoy French wine. French wine is sold by its producers for francs, the currency in which French producers pay their bills and want their receipts. Let us suppose that they price their wine at 20 francs the bottle.

How much would 20 franc wine cost in America? The answer depends on the rate at which we can exchange dollars for francs—that is, it depends on the price of francs. We discover this price by going to banks, who are the main dealers in foreign currencies of all kinds, and inquiring what the dollar-franc *exchange rate* is. Let us say we are told it is five francs to the dollar. To buy a bottle of French wine, then, (ignoring transportation, insurance, and other costs) will cost us $4.00 (20 francs ÷ 5 = $4.00).

Now suppose that the dollar "falls." This means that the dollar becomes cheaper on the market for foreign money. It follows, of course, that francs will become dearer in terms of dollars. Instead of getting five francs for a dollar, we now get only four. Meanwhile, the price of wine hasn't changed—it still costs

20 francs. But it now costs us $5.00, not $4.00, to purchase 20 francs. **A falling dollar therefore raises the price of foreign goods in terms of American money.**

Conversely, a rising exchange rate would cheapen them. Let us imagine that we were contemplating a trip to Germany. We inquire into the prices of German hotels, German meals, and the like, and we are told that we can do it comfortably for (let us say) 100 marks per day. "How much is that in American money?" we ask. The answer depends, of course, on the exchange rate. Suppose the rate is three marks to the dollar. Then 100 marks would be the equivalent of $33 a day. But if the dollar happened to be rising, we could be in for a pleasant surprise. Perhaps by the time we were ready to leave, it would have risen to four marks to the dollar. It still costs 100 marks a day to travel in Germany, but we can now buy 100 marks for only $25 dollars.

We must remember, however, that international economics must always be viewed from both sides of the ocean. When the dollar rises, foreign goods or services become less expensive for us. But for a German, just the opposite is true. A German tourist coming to America might be told that he should allow $50 a day for expenses. "How much will that cost me in marks?" he asks his bank. The answer, again, hangs on the exchange rate. If it costs only three marks to buy a dollar, it will obviously be cheaper for the German tourist than if it costs four marks. Notice that this is exactly the opposite of the American tourist's position.

THE DOLLAR CRISIS

International economics has entered our consciousness because we have been reading about the falling dollar. We know now that this means that the price of dollars, on the market for foreign currencies, must have been dropping. Therefore the price of other currencies must have been rising. It does not, however, mean that the price of *all* foreign currencies is higher than a few years ago. Table 34.1 shows the exchange rate of six foreign currencies against the dollar in 1975 and in early 1980.

TABLE 34.1 PRICE OF FOREIGN CURRENCY IN U.S. $

	1975	*1980 (March)*	*% Change*
German mark	$ .41	.57	+39
Japanese yen	.034	.042	+23
Swiss franc	.39	.62	+59
U.K. pound	2.22	2.25	+1
Canadian dollar	.98	.85	−13
Italian lira	.015	.012	−20

Changes in the exchange rate 1975–1980 took the form of higher prices for most, but not all, currencies.

As the table shows, a German mark cost 39 percent more over the period. But notice that an Italian lira cost 20 percent less! Why, then, do we say that the dollar has fallen, when it has actually risen against some currencies? The answer is that it fell against those currencies for which we had the greatest need. We do very little business in Paraguay, for example, so that it matters little how many Paraguayan guaranis we get for a dollar. We do a great deal of business with Germany and Japan, both as buyers and sellers, and so it matters a great deal what happens to those currencies.

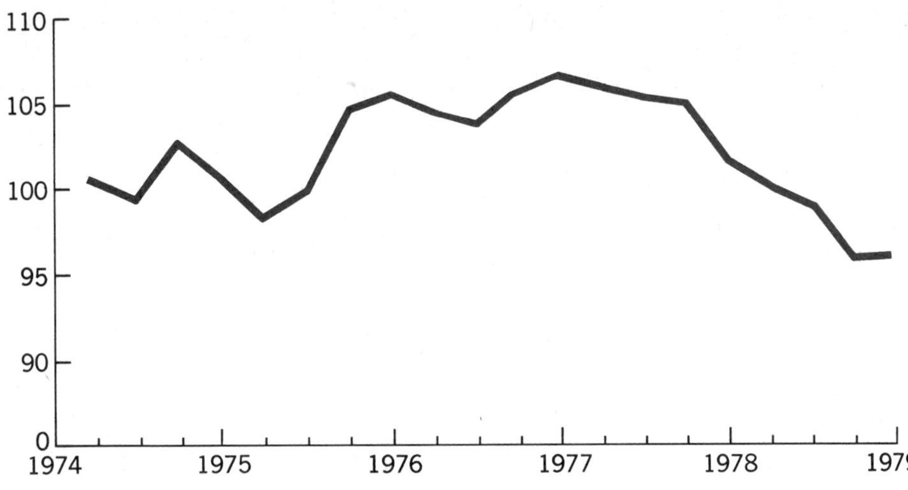

FIGURE 34.1 THE TRADE-WEIGHTED DOLLAR

The value of the trade-weighted dollar has dropped.

When we say that the dollar has fallen, we measure it against a "basket" of foreign currencies, in which different currencies are included according to their degree of commercial use. We call this *a trade-weighted dollar.* Over the last five years, the trade-weighted dollar has fallen by about 14 percent. Most of the fall took place rather precipitously during the early part of 1979, as Figure 34.1 shows.

THE MARKET FOR DOLLARS

Why did the dollar fall? As with all price changes, our first task is to look at the supply and demand situation. And that requires us to investigate the nature of the market for dollars and other currencies.

Here we can best begin by mentally grouping all the kinds of dealings in which dollars and other currencies change hands into two basic markets. **One is the market for currencies to carry on current transactions. The other is the market for currencies to carry on capital transactions.** For a fuller explanation, you can turn to Chapter 37. But you will have no trouble following the story if you bear these two markets in mind.

1. Current Transactions

The first market in which currencies are bought and sold is that in which the current transactions between firms, individuals, or governments are carried out. Here *the demand for dollars* comes from such groups as foreigners who want to import U.S. goods and services, and who must acquire dollars to purchase them; or from foreign tourists who need dollars to travel in the U.S.; or from foreign governments who must buy dollars to maintain embassies or consulates in America; or from firms abroad (American or foreign) that want to send dividends or profits to the United States in dollars. All these kinds of transactions require that holders of marks or francs or yen offer their currencies on the foreign exchange market in order to buy U.S. dollars.

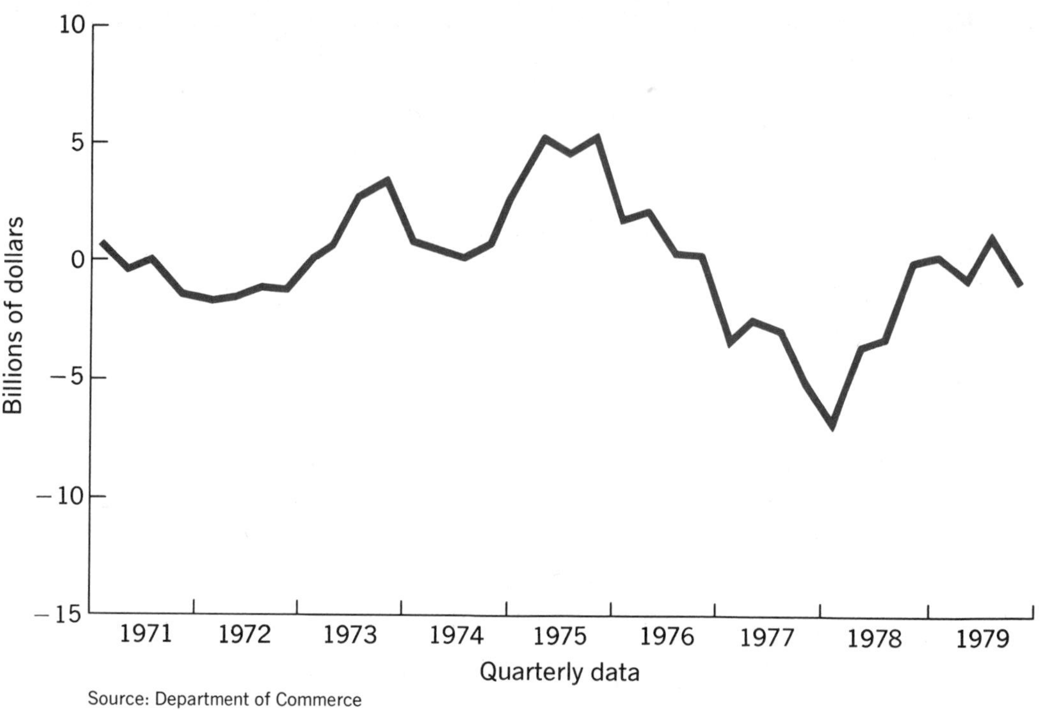

Source: Department of Commerce

FIGURE 34.2 BALANCE ON CURRENT ACCOUNT 1971–1979

The balance on current account sums up all the supplies and demands for dollars needed for trade, travel, remittances of profits, government expenses, and the like. Until roughly 1968, the market for current account always showed a favorable balance. This is no longer the case.

And, of course, there are similar groups of Americans who *supply dollars* to the foreign exchange market for exactly the opposite reasons. Here we find American importers who want to bring in Japanese cameras and must offer dollars in order to acquire the yen to make their purchases; American or foreign firms that are sending dividends or profits earned in the U.S. to a foreign branch or headquarters; Americans or foreign residents who sell dollars in order to buy lire or drachmas or krona to send money to friends or relatives abroad; or the American government which uses dollars to buy foreign currencies to pay diplomatic living expenses or to make military expenditures abroad.

Balance on Current Account. **Taken all together, these supplies and demands for dollars establish what we call our balance on current account.** As Figure 34.2 shows, this balance took a substantial fall after 1970, followed by a sharp rise and then another fall. That is, the graph shows that up to 1968 foreigners were buying more dollars for all the various purposes of current transactions than Americans were selling dollars for those purposes; whereas since the 1970s, the balance has largely gone the other way.

What was the reason for this sharp adverse change in our current balance of payments? Figure 34.3 shows that it was mainly the result of a dramatic fall in our *merchandise balance of trade.* This is a submarket within the larger flow of all current transactions in which we pay heed only to those dollars supplied and demanded to finance imports and exports of merchandise.

Notice that until 1971 the United States had a small positive balance on merchandise account. This meant that we were selling more goods and services abroad, measured in dollars, than the dollar value of the goods and services we were buying there.

What has happened since then to turn the balance from black to red? The answer in part is the OPEC oil crisis which resulted in a sharp rise in the number of dollars we had to supply to buy oil abroad. In 1972 our oil bill was $5 billion. In 1974 it was $27 billion. By 1979 it had grown to $90 billion.

But oil shock was not the only reason for the falling merchandise balance. The United States has experienced a long gradual decline in its competitive position vis-à-vis the other industrial nations of the West, a decline attributable in considerable part to laggard American productivity. In addition, a number of other developments have tilted the merchandise balance away from America—the international agricultural situation, the respective inflation rates of the U.S. and its main competitors, and still other factors.

FIGURE 34.3 MERCHANDISE TRADE BALANCE

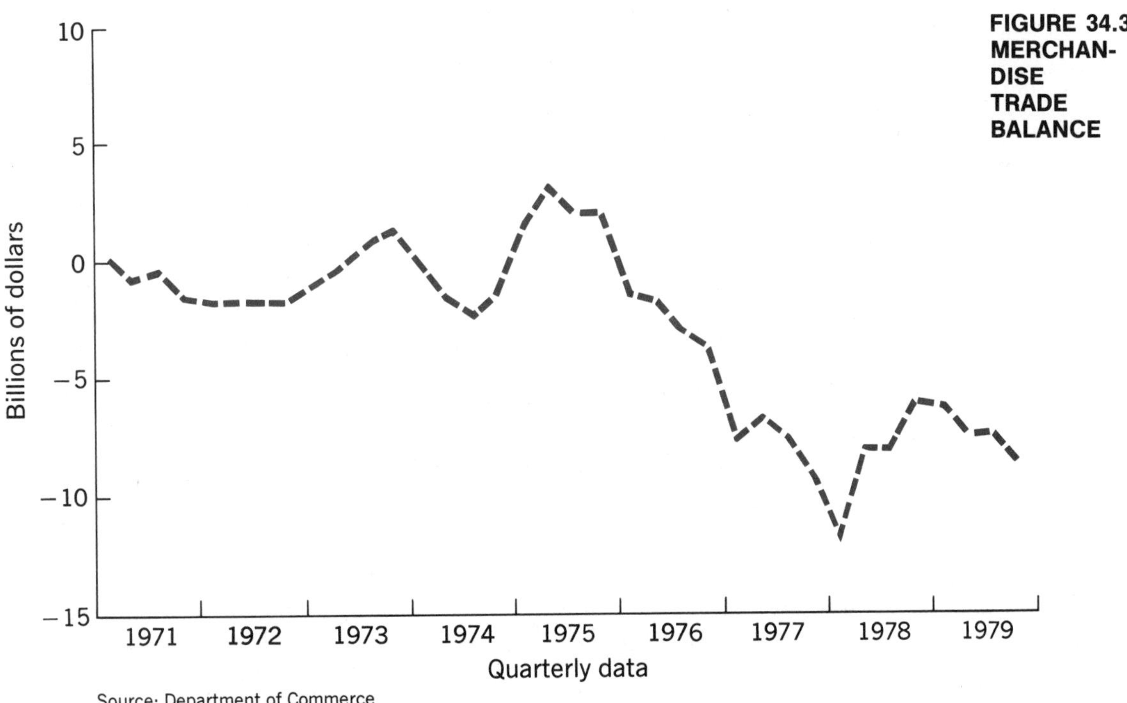

Until 1971, we always sold more merchandise abroad than we bought. Many factors have since eroded that comfortable position: laggard productivity, inflation, oil.

We cannot here analyze all the reasons for the decline of the American merchandise balance. It is enough to see that this is one major reason why the supply of dollars, needed for imports, came to exceed the demand for dollars, needed by foreigners to purchase American exports. When the quantity of any commodity supplied exceeds the quantity demanded, its price drops. The dollar was no exception. It fell.

2. The market for capital

But the market for current transactions is not the only arena in which the supply and demand for dollars establish a price for dollars against other currencies. A second, quite separate market, arises to accommodate the need for dollars and other currencies to finance capital transactions, not current ones. Here are such items as building or buying plant and equipment in another country, or buying the bonds or stocks issued within another nation.

The first of these capital flows is called *direct investment.* It arises from the efforts of American firms (mainly multinationals) to expand their ownership of plants and equipment abroad, and from the corresponding efforts of foreign companies to do the same thing here. In 1978, U.S. firms invested over $17 billion in foreign production facilities, ranging from oil refineries to supermarkets, while foreign companies bought or built direct investments worth $6 billion here. Subsequently in 1979 the supply and demand for direct investment funds also pushed down the price of dollars.

The second part of the capital market is made up of American or foreign individuals or firms who want to add to their overseas portfolio investments of stocks and bonds. Here we have Americans who buy stock in a Swedish firm or who buy German government bonds, and foreign investors who buy General Motors stock or U.S. Treasury bonds. In 1979, the balance on **portfolio account** was also against the U.S.

Balance on Capital Account. Adding direct and portfolio investment together, we have a total of $30 billion more dollars being supplied in 1979 than were demanded. This too pushed the supply curve of dollars to the right and contributed to its drop in price.

Why have we had such large capital outflows? Part of the answer is that American multinational corporations have grown faster than their counterparts here. We have heard much in recent years about an "invasion" of Arab money into American markets, but it has clearly not been nearly as large as the continuing "invasion" of American money abroad. Between 1970 and 1978, U.S. direct investment abroad climbed from $76 billion to $168 billion, while foreign direct investment here only rose from $13 to $40 billion.

The negative flow on portfolio account arises from two main stimuli. One of them is that until recently European interest rates have been higher than American rates. Holders of large liquid balances, such as the treasurers of multinationals or wealthy private investors, "park" their money where the return is greatest. Thus short-term money has sought out the highest return—and the dollar has weakened as a consequence. Second, many private investors invest in the stock markets of different countries. The U.S. stock market has made an indifferent showing over the last decade compared with some of Europe's or Japan's stock exchanges. This too has led to a larger supply of dollars than demand for them.

Speculative Demand. One more very important influence bears on the capital markets for foreign exchange. This is the price of foreign exchange that investors expect to receive in the future. If you think that the German mark will rise against the dollar, you can make money by buying German currency before it appreciates. Thus there is a constant flow of "hot" money from country to country as private investors or multinationals move their funds around, hoping to buy cheap and sell dear. A great deal of this speculative ebb and flow has also gone against the United States, because investors have felt that the United States was irresolute in the "defense" of the dollar, and that therefore the dollar would weaken. Of course, by selling dollars, and buying marks or yen or whatever, speculators have helped that very expectation to come true.

PROBLEMS OF A FALLING DOLLAR

We have just mentioned the defense of the falling dollar and we must soon turn our full attention to that subject which is the theme of our chapter. But before we consider means, we had better think about ends. What are we defending the dollar against? What difference does it make to Americans whether one dollar is worth two marks or three? What difference does it make if the dollar—whatever its exchange rate—is declining to a lower rate?

ARE CHEAP OR DEAR DOLLARS BETTER?

Let us consider the first part of the question. Does it matter how many yen, francs, or pounds a dollar exchanges for?

Like so many economic questions, this has a complicated answer. For the exchange value of a currency affects different individuals or groups or regions in different ways. Suppose that the dollar is cheap. Obviously this is good for anyone who wants to buy a U.S. good or service, using foreign money. It makes travel in the U.S. inexpensive for foreigners. It makes American exports attractive. It makes American stocks or physical plant tempting to foreign investors. All this redounds to the benefit of U.S. exporters or hotel keepers or stockbrokers or owners who want to sell to foreigners.

On the other hand, a cheap dollar penalizes other groups. An American traveling abroad finds prices terribly high. An American importer finds that foreign wines, cameras, cars, sweaters are expensive—and so do his customers. American firms, thinking of investing abroad, are deterred by the high price of foreign exchange. All this is bad for American tourists, consumers, and multinationals.

Is there any reason for giving preference to those groups who benefit from the cheap dollar over other groups who benefit from expensive dollars? From the point of view of our national well-being, there is no particular reason to favor one over another. Is it better for a million consumers to buy cameras cheaper, or for 100,000 steel workers to have higher incomes? There is no cut and dried answer.

FINDING A BALANCING RATE

How, then, does a nation determine the right rate for its exchange, when cheap rates help some groups and expensive rates help others? **The answer is that a nation tries to discover the rate that will roughly balance out all the supplies and all the demands for its currency, so that it has a stable, "equilibrium" relationship between its own currency and those of other nations.**

Consider what happens if country A does not have such an equilibrium relationship. If the rate is too high, there will be a stimulus for country A to buy imports and a deterrent to its exports. The result will be unemployment in its export industries and as a consequence of the multiplier, unemployment elsewhere. Perhaps the most famous case of an overvalued currency was that of England following World War I, when Winston Churchill, then Chancellor of the Exchequer, tried to establish an exchange rate of £1 = $5. At that rate the demand for pounds was far less than the supply, and English exports went into a tailspin, dragging the economy down with them. England suffered a severe depression until its exchange rate was finally reduced to about $4.00.

An undervalued exchange rate also brings problems. Now there is an incentive for foreigners to buy the cheap exports or assets of country A. Foreign money will flow into A's banks, raising the money supply. (Foreign deposits increase M because the new deposits do not come from another domestic bank.) As the money supply increases, inflationary pressures also increase. Country A will suffer from rising prices.

Thus we can present the problem of exchange rates that are too high or too low in this fashion:

Undervalued (too low) exchange rates lead to inflation.
Overvalued (too high) exchange rates lead to unemployment.

EFFECTS OF A FALLING DOLLAR

Defending the dollar, then, means finding an exchange rate that will roughly balance our total supplies and demands for foreign exchange for transactions purposes and capital flows. The fact that the dollar has been falling means that we have not yet found such a rate. The verdict of the marketplace is that the dollar is too high. We know this is the verdict because the demand for dollars vis-à-vis marks and francs and other strong currency has been steadily less than its supplies.

What happens when the dollar falls? Clearly we move from the dangers of an overvalued currency toward those of an undervalued one. That is, a falling dollar spurs our exports and helps employment. It also makes imports more expensive. Alas, in our inflation-prone economy, this results not just in fewer imports, but in another fillip to the price level. Oil prices go up because of the falling exchange rate, along with the price of Hondas and TV sets, coffee and tea.

The net effect of a falling dollar is therefore measured, in part, by the benefit we ascribe to expanding employment minus the cost we assign to higher inflation. As we have seen so often, most people place a higher priority on inflation than on unemployment. We welcome the boost to exports but put more emphasis on the boost to the cost of living.

THE THREAT OF A FALLING DOLLAR

Unfortunately that is not an end to the problems caused by a falling dollar. For in addition to its real costs and benefits, a falling dollar imposes a large overhanging threat. In the end it is this threat, more than the actual effect on employment or prices, that makes the problem of defending the dollar so important and so difficult.

The threat is that the falling dollar will induce a serious crisis in the economy. To many people, especially in business and finance, the news of a falling dollar conveys ominous implications about the state of the U.S. economy. Bankers worry lest international depositors switch funds from U.S. banks to foreign banks, straining the liquidity of the American financial system. Americans who own stocks and bonds worry that the dollar is weak, and begin to sell. A falling stock market and a slumping dollar can cause some corporations to rein in their capital expenditures. These actions in themselves may be sufficient to bring about a genuine financial panic and a fall in GNP.

There is still another repercussion. The government watches these developments with distress and seeks to prevent such a panic. It tries to defend the dollar in various ways including raising interest rates to attract foreign funds and cutting spending to show its determination to stop inflation. **And so the fear of a crisis induces government policy that will bring on a recession. A falling dollar can thereby lead to a falling economy.**

WAYS OF DEFENDING THE DOLLAR

Can we prevent the dollar from falling? Of course we can. Do we want to? That is not so easy to answer, for we shall see that defending the dollar is a difficult course whose benefits may not outweigh costs.

TARIFFS, QUOTAS, AND THE LIKE

One way of defending the dollar is simplicity itself: Take measures to prevent the flow of imports from rising. Anything that will turn the balance of merchandise payments in our favor will unquestionably alter the supply/demand situation and strengthen the dollar.

Is this a sound policy? The answer is not simple. There are certain kinds of imports that we would like to diminish not merely to defend the dollar, but to strengthen the nation. For instance, if we can substitute domestic energy (such as solar or coal) for imported oil, or if we can cut down on oil imports by conservation measures, the United States will gain a much needed measure of strategic independence as well as helping the dollar.

If, however, we cut down imports by blocking cheap shoes, textiles, or steel from abroad, we are simply protecting inefficient industries at home, penalizing Americans by depriving them of the right to buy shoes, textiles, or steel as cheaply as they otherwise might. We can sharpen the point by imagining that our tariff wall was sky high. Then no goods would come into the United States. Would that be good for America?

On the other hand, imports cost jobs. Even if we compensate the workers in threatened industries, or help relocate them, or retrain them, some will not make the transition and will remain unemployed. There is a real human cost to competition—from abroad or home—that should not be lost to sight. This is a matter we look into more fully in Chapter 36.

In sum, defending the dollar by choking off imports is probably a short-sighted policy, with the signal exception of seeking to reduce our dependence on foreign oil. What about helping our exports? Many countries have tried to help *their* exports by giving subsidies of various kinds to their producers, so that they could sell their wares abroad cheaply. We have subsidized some exports by underwriting our merchant marine, by arranging for special deals on U.S. arms sales to foreign nations, and by foreign aid policies that have permitted us to sell large amounts of farm products abroad.

As with imports, it is not possible to give black and white answers about the wisdom of defending the dollar by export assistance. It may be in the national interest to sell $8 billion of arms on easy terms, or to export $1 billion of foodstuffs to the underdeveloped nations under Public Law 480, but these policies should be judged on their own merits. The fact that they help defend the dollar is not, and should not be, a controlling consideration.

RESTRICTIONS ON INVESTMENT

Policies to help exports or to hinder imports affect the balance of payments on current account. But there is also the market for foreign exchange for capital purposes. Can we defend the dollar by intervening in that market?

We recall that there are two basic kinds of transaction in the capital market, direct investment (purchasing plant, equipment, and other assets abroad), and portfolio investment (buying stocks or bonds). We can, of course, defend the dollar by simply passing a law preventing United States companies from acquiring foreign assets. The difficulties here are twofold. The first is that any interference with the free movement of capital tends to lower the efficiency of the market system. We have been reluctant to abridge the right of corporations to invest their funds wherever they can yield the highest return, whether at home or abroad.

Second, the stream of profits from our overseas investments constitutes one of the strongest supports for the dollar. In 1979, for example, there was a demand for $66 billion as the earnings of our foreign-located plants were sent back to the U.S. Against that flow was $34 billion leaving the country as the earnings of foreign companies sent to their various home nations. In this international flow of repatriated earnings, the U.S. is clearly a big gainer. Any restriction on the outflow of direct investment will sooner or later diminish this source of dollar earnings.

INTEREST RATES

A second way of defending the dollar in the capital markets is to seek to attract portfolio investment or short-run capital into the United States. This can be done by raising interest rates to bid for the pool of funds that "shops" in the world's money markets.

We have already seen the problem with this method of defending the dollar. Raising interest rates in order to increase the flow of money into the United States exerts the same effect on the economy as raising interest rates for any other reason. Investment is discouraged. Spending slackens. The economy slows down. The price of defending the dollar is therefore to expose the economy to further unemployment.

THE DOLLAR AND INFLATION

We begin to see that there is a connection between the falling dollar on the international exchange and the falling dollar in terms of purchasing power. Policies to defend the dollar abroad are closely linked to policies to defend it at home. That is, the measures needed to bring about a stable supply-demand situation with respect to the international value of the dollar are closely related to measures needed to bring about a stable supply-demand for dollars and goods at home. Fighting the fall in the dollar is therefore much like fighting inflation, with all its familiar difficulties. If we clamped down on all growth in the United States, for example, and allowed a really large rise in unemployment, we would stop or greatly slow down inflation and simultaneously rescue the dollar. The recession at home would cut deeply into imports and that would redress the balance on current account. The fall in profits would discourage U.S. investment abroad. And a sharp rise in interest rates would tempt speculative and short-term funds into American banks and bonds.

All this, however, comes with a very substantial price tag. We have seen that political realities make it very difficult to consider an all-out recession as a cure for inflation. Even more surely, the American public would not tolerate a deep depression as a cure for the falling dollar, an ailment that mystifies most people. Instead, the cry would likely go up for stiff import quotas or for restrictions on the foreign investments of American companies—policies that also impose costs on our economy, but not such visible costs as a recession.

CENTRAL BANKS

There is still another way of arresting the fall of the dollar. It is to use the resources of our Federal Reserve System to support the dollar.

How can the Federal Reserve support the dollar? It does so by buying dollars. But it would do no good for the Federal Reserve to buy dollars at home, using its deposit-creating powers. This would just increase the money supply. Rather, the Fed must support the dollar by buying dollars with foreign currencies!

The Federal Reserve can do this because it holds supplies of foreign currency—yen, marks, francs, and pounds, as well as gold certificates and other international assets. Thus when the Fed defends the dollar it does so by entering the exchange market as if it were a Swiss, a German, or a Frenchman. It simply offers the currencies of these nations, asking dollars in return.

DIRTY FLOATING

All central banks in all nations including the Federal Reserve, operate in the foreign exchange markets, supporting or depressing the price of their currency against foreign currencies. In using their buying and selling powers, the central banks are not permitting the price of their currencies to be set just by the forces of supply and demand, but by "dirty floating"—free market price plus or minus the demand of the central banks.

This means that the ability of the Federal Reserve—or any other central bank—to intervene in the market is limited by the supplies of foreign currencies or gold or other international assets it has on hand. Take gold. In mid-1979, U.S. gold reserves totaled about 267 million ounces, worth (at over $400 per ounce) well over $100 billion. The Federal Reserve could, if the government so directed, use all of that gold to support the dollar. If it did, undoubtedly the price of the dollar would rise substantially; but would it stay at its new higher price when the gold had been used up? Not unless the basic forces of supply and demand had been permanently affected by the rescue operation—a doubtful assumption.

Curiously enough, a government is always able to lower the price of its currency because it can easily sell unlimited quantities of dollars on the foreign exchange market. But its power to buy its own currency is inherently limited. It can step in to stem a speculative rout, but it is unlikely that it can much affect a falling price trend that emerges from the current and capital flows of the world.

THE VIEW FROM ABROAD

Actually it is not only Americans who are eager to stop the dollar from falling; foreigners are also eager to have stable exchange rates. Consider how the situation looks to them as the dollar weakens. The price of American-make goods keeps steadily declining. Conversely, the price of their own goods becomes ever more expensive in America. Thus, just as there is an outcry in America against the falling dollar, so there is an outcry abroad. Therefore, just as the Federal Reserve may step in to defend the dollar by selling its supplies of foreign currency, foreign banks may also find it in their interest to defend the dollar by selling their own currencies and buying dollars. Much time at international financial conferences is devoted to efforts to work out a coordinated defense of the dollar (and sometimes other currencies) by the joint action of several key central banks. What is always the bone of contention at such conferences is the proper exchange relation. Countries that depend on exports want their currency to be cheap in the world markets; countries that depend on imports want their own money to be dear, so that it will buy a larger amount of other currencies.

THE DOLLAR AS A WORLD CURRENCY

We can see that defending a currency is not only a difficult policy to devise, but a difficult policy to define. But we have left out of consideration a matter of much importance for the United States. It is that the dollar is not merely the currency of this country; the dollar has become a world currency. It is the currency in which many central banks hold much of their own international reserves. Japan, for example, holds billions of U.S. dollars as part of its foreign exchange wealth, along with gold and other major currencies. In addition, there are at least $300 billion U.S. dollars (some estimates run much higher) in European bank deposits. These foreign-located dollars, some owned by European individuals and companies, some by American, are called **Eurodollars.** They are one of the means by which the world carries on its vast international business.

The presence of these enormous quantities of dollars held as the reserves of other countries, or as the monetary medium of the world, adds further importance to the need for a stable dollar. When the dollar falls, it imperils the international value of foreign reserves and foreign deposits, and there is always the risk that central banks or corporations will rush to dump their dollars before a further fall occurs. Once again we have the danger of a self-fulfilling speculative disaster. So the dollar has to be defended to secure international economic stability even more urgently than to secure purely American interests.

NEW INTERNATIONAL CURRENCIES

How can the dollar be defended against a worldwide assault—or simply against worldwide nervousness? One possible way is for the dollar to be replaced by other monetary units as the world's reserve currency. To some extent this is slowly happening as other strong currencies, such as German marks and Swiss francs, are gaining the place formerly occupied by U.S. dollars. Alongside the $300 billion American Eurodollars, there are perhaps as much as $100 billion worth of Euromarks, and there are other smaller international reserves denominated in Swiss francs, in yen, and in other currencies.

A second means of taking the strain off the dollar is the rise in the price of gold. In 1979, the supply of gold in the official reserves of various nations was down slightly in physical quantity from 1971—from 1 billion ounces to 931 million ounces. (The difference, plus the gold production of the intervening years, was now owned by private individuals). But the value of the 931 million ounces, with gold selling at over $400 an ounce, was far larger than formerly. The value of the world's official gold reserves in late 1979 had soared to over $500 billion. Thus gold was worth, in value, more than half the total reserves of all the world's central banks. Without ever having decided to do so, say the champions of gold, the world is returning to a gold standard. If it does, the role of the dollar will be much less critical.

SDRs

No one can foretell what will happen to the future price of gold. Therefore let us consider one final way of relieving the dollar of its international burden. This is the gradual adoption of a wholly new money standard invented by the International Monetary Fund (IMF), a part of the World Bank set up under the auspices of the United Nations. This new monetary unit is called an SDR, Special Drawing Right. It is a kind of "paper gold"—an internationally recognized currency available only to central banks, and linked by the International Monetary Fund authorities to gold and to other main currencies.

SDRs are now held by all the major countries of the world in addition to gold and to supplies of each other's currencies. But SDRs have the special advantage of being issued under international control. There is no way that the world can deliberately bring about an increase in the quantity or value of gold. There is no way that the world can change the value or the amounts of dollars or marks or francs available as international reserves. But the nations of the world can agree to augment the value of SDRs, and by using these to settle international payments in place of dollars, they can gradually relieve the dollar of the task of being the world's principal currency, with all the risks attached thereto.

A LAST LOOK

This is nothing like a full survey of the complicated field of international finance. Just as a beginning for further study, you should read Chapters 36 and 37 where we look into the gains from international trade and the mechanisms of foreign exchange. But the main outlines of the problem are perhaps clear by now. **Defending the dollar really means locating the American economy in the world economy in such a way that its flows of trade and investment roughly balance out.** When they do not balance out, this means that one or both of the main foreign exchange markets is out of kilter. Putting it back into balance ultimately means bringing American production into better adjustment with world production. In turn that means changing the fortunes of American working people and managers—for better and worse—to accord with the economic realities of distant countries and strange peoples. That has long been one of the most difficult problems humanity has faced, as the sad history of international jealousy and war testifies. Defending the dollar successfully means taking steps to make the American economy a partner, not an enemy, in the world economy.

LOOKING BACK

KEY CONCEPTS

A falling dollar in international trade means that dollars buy less foreign currency, not less domestic goods. When the dollar falls, the exchange rate falls for Americans, rises for foreigners

1. A falling dollar has a different meaning in international trade than in a domestic economy. Domestically, a falling dollar means that dollars buy less because of inflation. Abroad, falling dollars means that each dollar buys less foreign currency. The dollar can fall abroad even if we do not have inflation at home, and vice versa. A falling dollar means that the exchange rate falls. From a foreigner's view, when the dollar falls, his own currency rises.

The fall in the dollar means that the demand for dollars is less than their supply in two markets—current account and capital transactions

2. The fall in the American dollar means that its exchange rate with major trading partners has declined. We can analyze this decline in terms of supply and demand in two markets—current account and capital transactions.

Lagging exports and booming oil imports have created an adverse balance on current account

3. The supply/demand situation has moved against America in the current account market because our exports have lagged for various reasons, while our imports, especially oil, have soared. Therefore the balance on current account has shown an excess of supply over demand, pushing down the price of dollars.

The balance on capital account has also been unfavorable due to heavy foreign investment and speculation

4. The market for capital is dominated by money seeking long-term investment in foreign plant, or looking for long- or short-term foreign financial investments. Heavy American investing abroad has also weakened the dollar exchange rate. In addition, pressure on the dollar has come from speculators who sold dollars expecting to buy them back cheaply after they fell.

Cheap dollars boost exports and aid producers; expensive dollars boost imports and aid consumers. The best rate equilibrates supplies and demands for exchange

5. Cheap dollars promote exports but make imports expensive; a high exchange rate has just the opposite effect. Thus cheap dollars benefit producers, and expensive ones help consumers. There is no "best" exchange rate except the one that balances all supplies and demand—an equilibrium rate.

Exchange rates below equilibrium create export surpluses with inflationary repercussions. Rates below equilibrium give import surpluses and unemployment

6. An exchange rate that is below equilibrium and is prevented from rising will produce a surplus in foreign exchange as the value of exports exceeds imports. This may have inflationary results from the rise in money supply. A rate that is above equilibrium will result in an import surplus and may bring unemployment.

The falling dollar has brought a stimulus to inflation and a threat of financial crisis

7. The falling dollar has made imports more expensive and thereby spurred inflation, especially through the impact of higher oil prices. It has also led to severe speculation and the threat of a financial crisis.

This has prompted the Federal Reserve to raise interest rates, with adverse effects on employment.

Defending the dollar by helping exports or hindering imports is a generally poor policy

8. We can try to defend the dollar by measures to help the balance on current account. These include tariffs, import quotas, or steps to promote U.S. exports. There may be valid arguments for each of these policies, but there are also considerable costs associated with them. They are not policies to be lightly adopted just to strengthen the dollar.

Defending the dollar on capital markets threatens our investment income and risks recession

9. Defending the dollar on the capital markets is also difficult. Choking off the flow of American dollars into foreign investment sooner or later costs us the dividend income we would get from these investments. And defending the dollar by higher interest rates means fighting the foreign imbalance by domestic recession.

Central banks try to keep exchange rates stable by intervening—"dirty floating"

10. The reason that supply and demand do not automatically yield equilibrium rates is that central banks intervene to prevent unwanted currency fluctuations. This is called "dirty floating".

The dollar has suffered as a world currency. Higher gold prices and SDRs may reduce world pressure

11. The dollar has been a target for selling because it has become a world currency. The rise in gold prices and the increasing use of SDRs may take some of the pressure off the dollar.

ECONOMIC VOCABULARY

Exchange rate 537
Balance on current account 540
Balance on capital account 542
Portfolio account 542
Undervalued exchange rates 544
Overvalued rates 544
Dirty floating 547
Eurodollars 548
SDRs 549

QUESTIONS

1. If the rate of exchange falls, does this make traveling abroad cheaper or dearer? Does it make imports more or less attractive to a U.S. buyer? Is an American investor more or less liable to buy a German bond if the price of a German mark is 30¢ or 50¢?
2. Explain how a fall in the exchange rate of the dollar against francs must be exactly the same as a rise in the exchange rate of the franc against dollars.
3. If the dollar were absolutely free to rise and fall in price, the way prices do on a freely competitive market, would there ever be a balance of payments problem? Show how there is an exact analogy between "shortages" and "surpluses" and positive or negative balances of payment. What is the factor that prevents the dollar from floating freely to an equilibrium price?
4. What is better for a nation's real standard of living—low-priced foreign goods, or identical high-priced domestic goods? Suppose that the imported goods mean that domestic workers lose jobs. Does that change your conclusion? Is there a conflict between the interest of producers and consumers? How can it best be resolved?
5. How would you try to estimate the relative costs and benefits of defending the dollar or letting it fall? Can these be figured in hard and fast terms? How important are political, as compared to economic, considerations?

Chapter 35 THE ECONOMICS OF ENERGY

A LOOK AHEAD

Energy is one of the most important and difficult problems facing our country—indeed, facing the entire world. Much of the material in this chapter consists of the basic facts needed to make rational decisions about our energy situation and our options for energy policy. The central theme of the chapter is learning how to think about the alternatives for national action from an economic point of view.

It is a commonplace that we are living through an energy crisis—a crisis that becomes visible every time there is a sudden gas shortage, and lines of cars with fuming drivers besiege the harried owners of neighborhood gas stations. Less well understood is the fact that we face more than a crisis. Together with all other industrial nations, we are living through a transition period in which we are being forced to change our energy-using habits, to look for new energy sources, to redesign our energy-generating and energy-consuming technologies. If we handle this transition poorly, we could be severely penalized by a substantial fall in our living standards. If we handle it intelligently, the fall will be less severe, perhaps hardly noticeable at all. Many of the choices before us hinge on engineering and scientific considerations about which economists have nothing to say. But there are important aspects of the future that depend directly on economic decisions and economic reasoning; these are the aspects of the era of transition to which we will address ourselves.

THE GAS SHORTAGE OF 1979

The energy problem, as we shall soon see, goes far beyond oil. Nevertheless, a good place to start unraveling the problem is the gas shortage of 1979. Suddenly—more or less out of the blue—there wasn't enough gasoline to go around. Drivers filled their cars on alternate days of the week, sometimes waiting for hours as long lines inched to the pumps. Violence flared up; cars were burned; a few persons were actually killed. What lay behind that mysterious shortage?

The basic reason was simple enough. A revolution in Iran had severely disrupted oil production in that country, which was then supplying 10 percent of the world's production. Five million barrels of oil per day were cut off from the world's supply. As a consequence, within a few months a relationship of supply to demand that had been in slight surplus turned into shortage. There was simply not enough crude oil to allow the refineries to keep retailers' tanks full.

Then why didn't the price of gas shoot up to whatever prices supply and demand indicated, automatically eliminating the shortage? The answer is that the government regulated the price of gasoline and would not allow the market to clear. Why not? Because the Administration and Congress were both fearful of the political outcry that would have attended $3 or $4 gas. A shortage, with all its hang-ups, seemed preferable to rationing by price.*

To analyze the immediate supply and demand situation of 1979 is, however, to view only the tip of the iceberg. For the question that comes immediately to mind is why the United States, for many years the world's largest oil producer, was so dependent on foreign oil? The question turns our attention away from the crisis of 1979 to the historic trends leading up to that dramatic year.

U.S. OIL SUPPLIES

Actually, the United States had been dependent on oil imports for a long time before 1979. Already in 1960 we were importing a fifth of our domestic consumption. By 1970 imports had grown to a quarter of national use. And by 1979, when the gas shortage occurred, the fraction had risen to almost 50 percent.

*The situation is shown graphically in Figure 22.2.

The reason for the increase was simple. Shortly after World War II, the oil fields of the Middle East, especially in Saudi Arabia, became the object of intensive exploration and development. Soon it became evident that the Middle East contained vast reservoirs of oil, dwarfing American fields in size, and far cheaper in cost. A Chase Manhattan study in 1960 declared that the average cost of production in the Middle East was 16 cents per barrel, compared with $1.73 in the United States.[1]

Therefore the growing availability of Middle Eastern oil posed a serious competitive threat to U.S. oil producers. As a result of their lobbying efforts, import quotas were introduced in 1957, limiting the amount of foreign oil that could be brought into the country. This protectionist policy was justified—as nearly all protectionist measures are—in the name of national security. Ironically, the best way to have protected our nation against a possible emergency would have been to import as *much* foreign oil as possible, conserving our own supplies against a future crisis. Had we done so, we would not today be quite so critically dependent on foreign supplies.

RUNNING OUT OF DOMESTIC OIL

Our quota policy assured a market for U.S. producers, as well as enormous profits for the major oil companies who bought oil at Middle East prices and sold it at U.S. prices. Meanwhile, however, the volume of United States consumption was growing by leaps and bounds. In 1960, total domestic consumption of oil—domestic plus imported—was still under 10 million barrels a day. But each year consumption increased as the American automobile fleet expanded and as oil displaced coal as a prime source of energy for utilities. In 1960, coal provided two-thirds of the fuel used by utilities. Within ten years, it was barely more than half. Oil and natural gas made up the difference. By 1979, domestic consumption had almost reached the 20 million barrels of oil per day level.

While demand for oil was dramatically growing, domestic supplies of oil showed an alarming tendency toward leveling off. Already by 1950, the curve of new oil discoveries had begun to turn down like a curve of diminishing returns. As geophysicist Owen Phillips has written:

> The first billion feet of drilling in the United States yielded discoveries of ninety-five billion barrels of oil; the next, twenty-four billion; the next only seventeen billion, a dramatic indication of the diminishing return as the search for new oil becomes . . . increasingly expensive.[2]

Today there is no doubt that the discovery curve has peaked, bringing with it an inevitable peaking in production. Even the confirmation of the vast Alaskan oil fields in 1970 was no more than a spike on a trend that was decisively headed downward after 1950, as Figure 35.1 shows.

IMPORT DEPENDENCY

The gas shortage therefore pointed to a profound problem for the United States. Our energy requirements were much greater than we could possibly fill with our domestic resources. By the end of the 1970s our domestic energy re-

[1]George W. Stocking, *Middle East Oil* (1970), pp. 423–4.

[2]Owen Phillips, *The Last Chance Energy Book* (Baltimore: Johns Hopkins Press, 1979), p. 43.

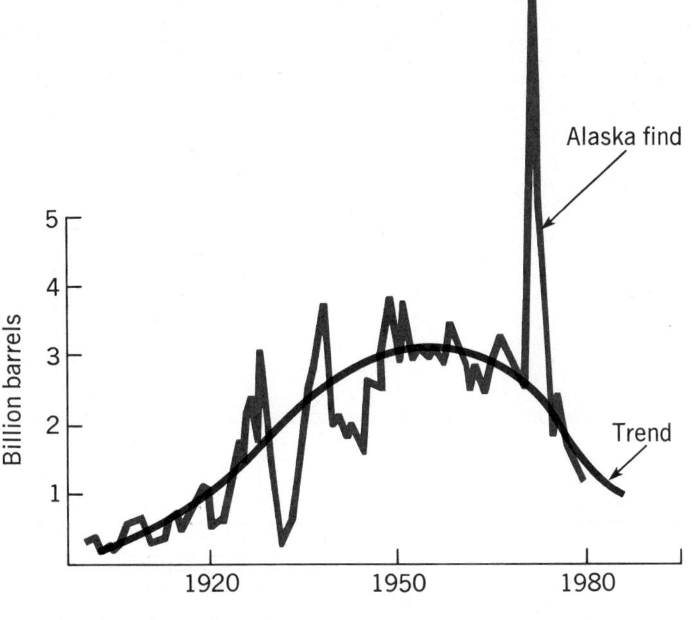

FIGURE 35.1 RATE OF U.S. DISCOVERY

The trend line for oil discoveries has been headed downward since 1950.

Source: Philips, op. cit., p. 39.

---

quirements for all purposes came to the equivalent of about 40 million barrels of oil per day. As Table 35.1 shows, oil and natural gas supplies about three-quarters of our energy, with other sources supplying the rest.

The extent of our dependency on foreign energy is now clear. Let us put that dependency into focus by taking a quick overview in Table 35.2 of the main uses to which we put our total energy.

TABLE 35.1 ENERGY SOURCES, 1977

	Percent
Petroleum	45
(domestic 23)	
(imported 22)	
Natural Gas	28
Coal	19
Nuclear	4
Hydro	4

TABLE 35.2 ENERGY USES, 1978

	Percent
Transportation	26
Residential and Commercial Heating	38
Industrial Power	32
Petrochemical	4

ADJUSTING TO AN EMBARGO

Suppose that oil imports just stopped. What would we do? In all likelihood there would be an immediate imposition of rationing to assure that domestic oil would be allocated to industrial and household users on the basis of need rather than price. This would involve us in all the problems of rationing to which we paid heed in Chapter 22.

It is also possible that we would allow the market to be the rationer of at least a portion of products, such as gasoline. The price of gas under emergency conditions might soar to $5 a gallon, perhaps $10 a gallon. At such prices there would be a tremendous incentive to find substitutes—public transportation, bicycles, electric vehicles, walking. To put it differently, at very high prices, the demand curve becomes increasingly elastic, as Figure 35.2 shows. After we reach price P_1, further cutbacks in supply will no longer boost prices, but only diminish usage.

In round numbers, we can see that by the end of the 1970s we were dependent on imported petroleum for almost the equivalent of the energy that powered our entire transportation fleet of cars, trucks, planes, and trains. Alternatively, we can think of our dependency as equal to 60 percent of all the energy we used to heat our homes, office buildings, stores, and factories. Or we can think of it as providing the energy for three-quarters of all the power generated in our utilities and factories.

The 1979 gasoline shortage was therefore only the tip of a very large iceberg. The American economy has become crucially dependent on imports of foreign oil to maintain its normal operation. Any substantial cut-off of oil would virtually bring the system to a halt.

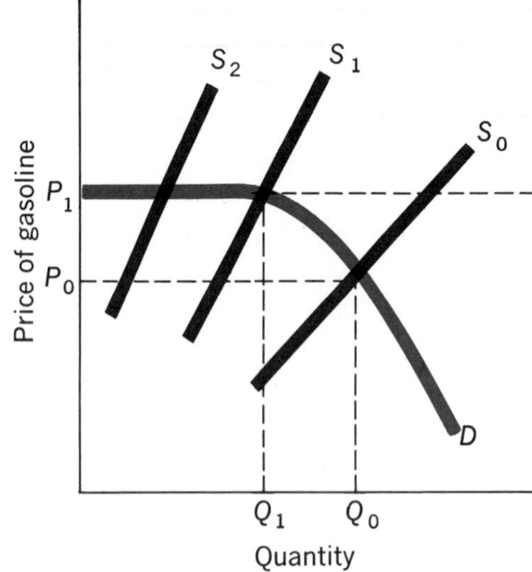

FIGURE 35.2 EFFECT OF VERY HIGH PRICES

At very high prices, demand becomes totally elastic. After price reaches P_1, we just consume less.

THE WORLDWIDE OIL SQUEEZE

The United States is by no means the only nation in an oil squeeze. Indeed, because we still produce half of our own oil, and not least because we are the fortunate possessors of enormous coal fields, we are relatively fortunate in the worldwide energy situation.

The real dimensions of the problem begin to take shape when we widen our lens from our own squeeze to the supply and demand situation of the entire planet. Then we see that the energy crisis is even broader and deeper than at first appears. **Indeed, the crisis is best thought of as the beginning of an era of energy transition—away from oil to coal, perhaps nuclear, and then solar sources, and even more important, away from the careless use of energy to an era of careful economizing of our most important single input.**

WORLD SUPPLY

How much oil is there in the world? We do not know the answer to this with the certainty that enables us to make reasonably firm projections of American supply. For example, new discoveries of oil in Saudi Arabia have exceeded oil production in that country every year so that reserves in that vast oil area are still rising. Then, too, the recent discovery of the Mexican fields, perhaps rivaling those of Saudi Arabia, indicate that important new reservoirs of oil undoubtedly still exist.

The problem is that until very recently world oil demand has been growing faster than supply. For example, between 1960 and 1978 the world automobile fleet tripled, from 98 million vehicles to over 300 million. As a result, by the end of the 1970s, the world's automotive fleet alone consumed one-fifth of all the oil produced in the world.[3] And world demand for oil for electric power production, heating, and petrochemical use has also grown apace, along with western GNPs.

The result is that the situation we saw in the United States is beginning to be reproduced on a world scale. The vast Mexican find is, like the Alaskan find, only a spike on a trend of worldwide oil discovery that now seems to be leveling off or heading downward. By the end of the 1970s, despite the Saudi fields, worldwide proven reserves (including United States reserves) were for the first time shrinking. As a special analyst in *Business Week* put it: "The beginning of the end of the oil age is now in sight."[4]

OIL PRICE SOARS

The cheap oil of the late 1950s and 1960s lasted until the Arab-Israeli War of 1973. During those years, the Organization of Petroleum Exporting Countries (OPEC) was formed to bargain with the oil companies about oil prices and the sharing of oil revenues between the companies and the producing countries. At first very weak, the bargaining position of OPEC was gradually strengthened by the steadily mounting demands for oil. But the balance of power did not really

[3] Lester R. Brown et al., "The Future of the Automobile in an Oil-Short World," *Worldwatch Papers* No. 32, (Washington, D.C.: Worldwatch Institute, 1979), pp. 9, 15.

[4] *Business Week,* July 30, 1979.

shift until the 1973 war. Rallying its members against Israel and her Western supporters, OPEC was able to impose an embargo on shipments of oil to the West. Within a year oil prices had gone through the roof, from $3 to about $12 per barrel.

This was perhaps the boldest, and certainly the most lucrative, exercise of oligopolistic market power ever seen. Within a year the OPEC nations were receiving a flow of $112 billion a year from the world, a flow sufficiently large to worry many Western observers about its effect on worldwide solvency. (The Arab countries avoided that danger by "recycling" their petrodollars to the West through imports from and investments in Western nations.)

Despite cries of outrage from the West, the OPEC price managers were, in all likelihood, only acting as profit-maximizers. OPEC oil prices were not the highest possible prices, but prices that were calculated to maximize revenues after taking into account the effect of those prices on consumption, on the search for substitutes, and (in the case of so strategic a commodity as oil) on political or even military repercussions. As a result, from 1974 to 1979 the price of oil was largely unchanged; in fact, in terms of an inflating world price level, oil actually fell in real terms. Then in 1978, the Iranian Shah was overthrown and oil production in Iran abruptly declined. Other nations, notably Saudi Arabia, increased their production somewhat, but the world market suddenly became tight. The price for "spot" oil—oil sold for immediate delivery rather than on a long-term contract—jumped by as much as $8 above the basic contract price of $13 a barrel. Some emergency deals were made at prices up to $35 per barrel.

OPEC OUTLOOK

The enormous rise in oil prices has encouraged the development of a new view among OPEC producers. Originally eager for a rapid inflow of funds for purposes of economic development or luxury consumption, most OPEC producers today find themselves awash with foreign exchange. They cannot spend their existing revenues without creating further inflation. All of them have therefore lengthened their time horizons. Their rational profit-maximizing course of action, in the light of expected higher oil prices, is to cut back on oil production. This will not only hold down the unwanted inflow of foreign exchange, but will also prolong the life of their physical reserves.

There is no way in which worldwide supply and demand curves for oil can be reliably projected into the future. But all indications point in one direction: Prices are very likely to increase. The reasons are these:

1. As we have just seen, OPEC producers are likely to cut back on oil production to avoid an unwanted inflow of unspendable foreign exchange.

2. Political instabilities, similar to those that have severely cut oil production in Iran, may arise elsewhere in the Arab world. Any political change in Saudi Arabia or Kuwait or the other feudal oil sheikdoms is likely to result in curtailments of deliveries to the West.

3. World oil demand is still rising. After the crisis of 1973, Western nations have economized considerably on oil. The rate of growth for petroleum products has diminished from 7 percent a year to 2 percent. Nonetheless, the demand for oil is still growing, and this too serves as a force for higher prices.

FUTURE OIL SHOCK

These considerations have led virtually every observer to conclude that the probable trend of world oil prices will be up, perhaps very sharply. Estimates by the CIA and other informed agencies have led to predictions that oil will reach a price of over $50 per barrel by 1995 in today's prices.[5] Even optimistic observers expect that oil prices will rise by at least 50 percent within the next few years.[6] Almost certainly we will have to adjust to further oil shocks in the future—and indeed, until we have completed a transition to a less oil-dependent world.

THE AMERICAN PROBLEM

How will the prospective rise in oil prices affect the American economy? One way will be to encourage the development of alternative energy supplies. As the price of oil increases, sources of energy that were formerly ignored because they were too expensive become attractive for investors. We see this, in schematic fashion, in Figure 35.3.

In the late 1950s, the demand for energy was sufficient to render profitable the exploitation of U.S. oil and gas, hydroelectric power, and our more easily accessible coal. (As we know, had it not been for the quota system, oil prices in the United States would have been much lower and we might well have relied almost completely on oil imports.) Today, the higher price of petroleum has made coal in general and even high-cost nuclear energy competitive with oil. Ahead lies the development of synthetic fuels and solar energy, all of which are today still too expensive for commercial use.

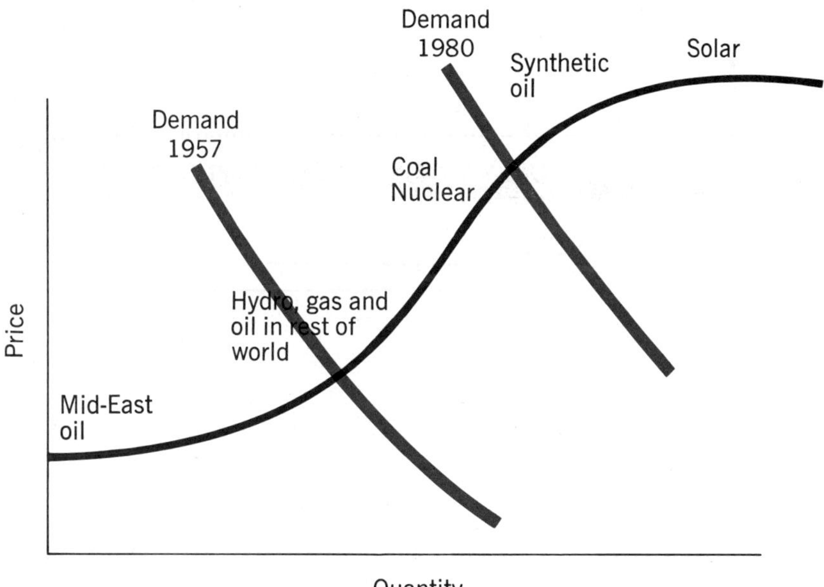

**FIGURE 35.3
THE ENERGY SPECTRUM**

[5]*New York Times,* October 18, 1979, p. D1.

[6]Robert Stobaugh and Daniel Yergin, *Energy Future* (New York: Random House, 1979), p. 39.

THE ENERGY SPECTRUM

It takes a very sophisticated knowledge of engineering to evaluate all the possibilities for expanding and redirecting U.S. energy supplies. But the principal avenues are important enough to warrant a few descriptive words.

1. Conventional oil and gas

According to the latest U.S. Geological Survey (1975), it is highly probable that U.S. reserves of crude oil amount to 220 billion barrels. This is enough to supply our consumption for about 20 years at existing rates of use.

Of course, new reserves will be found. But they will be more expensive and smaller in extent, and will not be enough to arrest the steady shrinkage in our total oil reservoir. This puts into perspective such finds as the much-heralded discovery by Houston Oil and Minerals of 30 to 40 million barrels of oil in a Texas county that was supposedly bone dry, having been picked over and drilled since the 1930s; Houston's discovery is enough to satisfy U.S. consumption for about two days.[7]

There have been about 2 million wells drilled in the United States, so we can be fairly secure that no vast undiscovered resources remain. With one exception. Perhaps as much as two-thirds of the oil in an oil field remains underground, despite drilling, because we lack the means of bringing it to the surface. Higher oil prices will encourage the use of expensive techniques such as injecting steam or chemicals to dissolve that oil. It is hoped that as much as 50 percent of these residues may be directly salvageable by using mining techniques.[8]

2. Shale

Just beyond oil lies oil shale, a form of petroleum-laden rock that has long tantalized energy producers. It is estimated that the Green River formation of Wyoming, Utah, and California contains as much as a trillion barrels of oil locked into its shale.

The problem is again one of cost. The present or prospective methods of extracting or burning shale are still too expensive to justify commercial use at today's prices. In addition, the processing of shale on a scale adequate to supply a substantial portion of national needs would involve enormous indirect costs; a whole landscape would be chewed up, and vast quantities of water (in an already water-short region) required to put the process into operation. Thus shale is still a distant prospect. "A production level equal to about one half of 1 percent of U.S. oil consumption—100,000 barrels a day—would require a billion dollars and a decade for development," write Robert Stobaugh and Daniel Yergin in the much-acclaimed Harvard Business School report in *Energy Future.*[9]

3. Coal

By everyone's agreement, coal is the energy source nearest at hand, at least in the short run. In all likelihood, coal production will rise by 50 percent or more

[7]Phillips, op. cit., p. 48.
[8]*Science,* March 1980, p. 1334.
[9]Stobaugh and Yergin, op. cit., p. 44.

during the next decade. Unlike the case with oil, we have ample supplies from which to draw these expanded outputs. There is enough coal in the United States to last for 300 years, even if we expanded coal output by 500 percent.

But coal has problems. It is a fuel that lends itself poorly or not at all to the biggest demand for energy–the tank of the automobile. Coal is a highly polluting energy source, requiring vast investments in scrubbers and other equipment to prevent utilities or homeowners from inflicting costly damage on the landscape and the people in it. Coal production will almost certainly be expanded by using strip mining, and the social cost of this environmental damage is also very large. Not least, coal has traditionally been a backward industry—low on R & D, poor in labor/management relations and safety. During the last decade, 6,500 lives were lost in coal mining.[10]

Many of these problems can be corrected if coal now becomes the recipient of massive doses of technology and capital; but experts do not see coal as a panacea. The general expectation is that coal output may rise by about 50 percent during the next decade.[11] That will pose enough difficulty in terms of environmental impact and will require the development of new technologies for mining, transporting, and using coal. It will bring some relief to our energy problem, but it will not solve it, at least not within the threatened period ahead.

4. Nuclear Power

Ten years ago, nuclear power seemed the solution to all energy problems. Today it is regarded as one of the biggest and most intractable of the energy problems.

The reasons for the turnabout are three. The first has to do with the growing public awareness of, and anxiety about, the safety of nuclear plants. The accident at Three Mile Island in 1979, the gradual news of a possible major nuclear accident in the Soviet Union in the early 1970s,[12] and the continuing debate among scientists over the problems of storing radioactive wastes, have all generated public alarm and have considerably altered the attitude of the government itself. There is today a general feeling of "wait-and-see" toward the development of nuclear power along the lines of today's technology. As a consequence, each year since 1970 the projections of expected nuclear capacity have been reduced, and a virtual moratorium is now imposed on the industry.

Second, there is a growing awareness that today's technology, even were its problems entirely resolved, is only a short-term solution. This is because the existing technology "burns" uranium, and uranium itself, like oil, is in restricted supply. Here again diminishing return has taken its toll. Geophysicist Phillips writes: "In 1956 the discovery rate in terms of pounds of uranium oxide per foot drilled was 18.6; in 1968, when exploration was much more intense, it had dropped to 6.9, and by 1973 it was only 2.4."[13] According to modern resource estimating techniques, by 1975 we had already extracted 30 percent of all the recoverable uranium in the nation.

[10]Phillips, op. cit., p. 97.

[11]Stobaugh and Yergin, op. cit., pp. 80–81.

[12]See *Science,* October 15, 1979.

[13]Phillips, op. cit., pp. 49–50. For a more optimistic, recent study, see "World Uranium Resources" by K. F. Deffeyes and I. D. MacGregor, *Scientific American,* January 1980.

Third, new technologies that could vastly increase the extent of nuclear power are either dangerous or undeveloped. One of these techniques is the breeder method of creating power, which actually creates more fuel than it uses. The difficulty here is that the fissionable substance is not uranium but plutonium—the metal that is the basis of atomic weaponry. Any large-scale shift to breeder technology would enormously magnify the danger that atomic explosives would fall into the hands of small nations or even terrorist groups. In addition, breeder technology is still in its infancy and no large-scale shift to breeder plants is even imaginable short of several decades. In the distant future beckons the possibility of developing fusion power, a limitless source of energy. But fusion power is still a laboratory experiment and scientists are by no means convinced that it can ever be obtained for more than the milli-fractions of a second during which fusion power has been generated in a few labs.

These uncertainties make it impossible to predict the long-term role that nuclear power will play. Possibly it will one day be entirely safe and in abundant supply; but there is no possibility whatsoever that nuclear power can play more than a marginal role during the period of energy transition immediately before us. Over the next decade or two, nuclear power will remain a long-term hope—not a short-term actuality.[14]

5. Solar

Solar energy presents an attractive long-term alternative source of energy. When we speak of solar energy today, we mean utilizing the energy of the sun directly or through very short-term intermediate processes as when crops, grown by solar input, are then used as fuel (biomass). Direct uses of solar energy include using atmospheric heat or sunlight to warm (or cool) buildings, focusing sunlight on a massive "power tower," using the atmospheric turbulence created by the sun's heat (wind power) or the temperature differentials of sea water (ocean thermal processes), or converting sunlight directly into electricity (photovoltaic cells).

As we would expect, all these uses involve difficulties of one kind or another. Home heating, for instance, is a promising source of energy for certain areas of the country, but has no application to transportation. Wind machines are noisy and irregular. Biomass requires the use of land areas whose growing potential may be required for foodstuffs. Ocean thermal processes require mile-long tunnel-sized tubes suspended in the ocean. Power towers necessitate means of storing power for use when the sun is not shining. Photovoltaics are still in their infancy.

These difficulties in no way detract from the promise of solar power, but they indicate that we cannot expect to move directly into a solar era. Estimates of the proportion of our total energy that could be supplied by solar techniques by the year 2000 vary widely. Long-term projections, involving a radical reshaping of our energy inputs and uses, envisage a very large-scale reliance on solar energy—but only after 50 years of massive technological change.[15] Estimates over a shorter range, up to the year 2000, vary from 7 to 23 percent of total

[14]Stobaugh and Yergin, op. cit., p. 135.

[15]Testimony of Amory Lovins, Select Committee on Small Business and the Committee on Interior and Insular Affairs, U.S. Senate, December 9, 1976.

energy—with, however, the contribution steadily rising.[16] It is certainly possible that late twenty-first century America will be a solar economy, especially if large R & D is soon begun toward that end. But there is no chance that late twentieth century America can look to the sun to replace its dependence on oil.

6. Conservation

There remains one source of energy that we have not discussed—a source that requires no exotic technology, that is safe and clean, and immediately at hand. It is conservation. Another way of describing it is to call it *efficiency*, for conservation means not just using less energy (after all, if our oil supply were to be cut off, we would perforce "conserve" oil) but using energy much more effectively.

We have already begun to utilize this hitherto neglected source of energy. The rise in energy prices has brought about relatively simple energy saving responses but this is only the beginning of a potentially much larger energy input. The cumulative fuel savings from bringing American automobiles up to federally established standards by 1985 will save as much oil, up to the year 2000, as two Alaskan North slopes. That is tantamount to making two such fields (20 billion barrels) available for other uses. By avoiding waste and by using industrial heat to produce local energy (cogeneration techniques), the consumption of industrial energy can be reduced by 25 to 40 percent. Home insulation has been estimated to reduce fuel needs by up to 67 percent. In all, calculations show that for 1973, the standard of living could have been obtained with 40 percent less energy input. This is the equivalent of all the oil—not just the imported oil—used that year.[17]

To be sure, the savings of conservation are "once over" changes, not constantly regenerating changes. A more efficient automobile engine reduces our fuel use per mile in the year it is introduced, but does not drop it further each successive year. If conservation is to provide a continuing source of energy, we must improve our energy efficiency each year, getting ever more productivity from each ton of coal or barrel of oil. It is likely that diminishing returns will be encountered here as elsewhere, so that we can look to conservation for dramatic short-term savings, but not for continuing long-term energy support.

ENERGY INDEPENDENCE

Can we then achieve energy independence without a serious fall in our living standards? It must be clear that the challenge is a formidable one; it is nothing less than converting an economy designed to operate on $2 per barrel oil to one using $40 or $50 per barrel oil. Can we, in short order, change the location of our homes, the design of our transportation systems, the configuration of power networks and industrial plants to reflect the altered requirements of a world where the cost of energy has increased by 2000 percent?

The answer is that we cannot gain this kind of energy independence quickly. For the rest of this century, at the very least, we will have to cope with the problems of running an industrial economy that is no longer economical in terms of its energy inputs. If we are faced with drastic cutoffs of oil imports, this may

[16]See review of forecasts in Stobaugh and Yergin, op. cit., p. 211.

[17]Stobaugh and Yergin, op. cit., pp. 152, 154, 160, 171, 177.

TABLE 35.3

	1977 Actual	Late 1980s Potential
	(millions of barrels/day, oil equivalent)	
Domestic		
Oil	10	10
Natural Gas	9	9
Coal	7	11
Nuclear	1	2
Solar and Hydro	1	4
Imports		
Oil	9	9
Gas	0	1
Conservation	—	8
Total	37	54

Source: Stobaugh and Yergin, *Energy Future*, p. 232

mean making painful adjustments in our economic processes—radical cutbacks in driving, heating, lighting, and perhaps even in producing. If we are fortunate and enjoy only moderate cutbacks in imports, we can work toward a balanced energy supply for the late 1980s, as shown in Table 35.3.

In this scenario, conservation and solar energy provide two-thirds of the growth in energy supplies, and imported oil does not rise at all. *This still leaves us vulnerable to an oil cutoff.* We would not have achieved energy independence in the sense of national self-sufficiency. But we would be on the way toward achieving as much independence as can be hoped for in the short run. Furthermore, we would be pointed in the right direction for achieving an appropriate energy structure for the long run.

PAYING THE BILL

Who has gained, who has lost, in this enormous shift in the energy situation? The winners are relatively easy to identify. The rise in world oil prices has resulted in a tremendous increase in the value of United States oil reserves. After the 1973 oil hike alone, U.S. oil reserves were worth $800 billion more! Their value will rise with every hike in world oil prices. Assuming that existing and improved techniques will allow us to extract 200 billion barrels of oil, a rise in oil prices from $25 to $50 will create instant oil wealth worth $25 × 200 billion or over $5 *trillion* dollars.

WINNERS

Who will share in this bonanza? The immediate winners, if oil prices rise to world levels, will be the owners of U.S. reserves—mainly the big oil companies, and of course, their stockholders. These companies are among the largest in the U.S. economy. In the famed *Fortune* list of the top 500 industrial companies, five of the top ten are oil companies.

Although oil has always been a favored industry in the United States, the government has been unwilling to allow it to reap the huge rents that would accrue from selling domestic oil at world prices. Instead, the government has regulated the price of oil sold in the United States, allowing domestic oil to rise much less than would be the case in a wholly unregulated market, and establishing a series of different prices for "new" oil, "old" oil, and many levels in between. The result has been a maze of regulations that have resulted in some reduction in profits to the oil industry. The transfer of wealth from consumers to producers has been checked but not entirely avoided, and profits of the oil companies have risen substantially. The profits of American oil companies were $8.5 billion in 1970 and $29.5 billion in 1978. A windfall profits tax, passed in 1979, should garner $9 billion per year by 1981.

Other winners will be those industries whose products will be favored by the energy shift. Coal mining should become more profitable. Any company that develops a successful solar energy device is sure to gain. And employees and stockholders connected with winning industries will also be benefited by the energy shift.

LOSERS

Consumers are losers, of course. But not all consumers are equal losers. Much depends on two considerations: where you live and in what income bracket you find yourself.

Take regions first. The Northeast is twice as dependent, per capita, on heating oil than the West. The Southwest is almost a third more dependent on gasoline than the Northeast. A family living in a Florida city spends much less on heating or driving than a family that lives in a Montana farmstead.

Second, income brackets. Energy in its various forms, from heat to gasoline, plays a larger part in the budgets of poor families than well-to-do families. This is because energy is largely used for essentials, and therefore demand curves for heating oil or gasoline tend to be inelastic. For families in the lowest 10 percent of households, energy accounts for a full third of household expenditures, whereas for households in the top 10 percent, it absorbs only 5 percent of household expenses. Therefore, a jump in energy costs will penalize the poor much more severely than the rich.

INFLATION

We have spoken of the consequences of higher energy costs in terms of our capacity to carry on business as usual, or with reference to our wellbeing as consumers of gasoline or heating fuel, or as employees of favored industries. But there is also a general cost imposed on us all by virtue of the diffusion of higher costs throughout the entire economic structure.

About 10 percent of our cost of GNP derives from energy. Thus, to the extent that energy prices rise substantially, they may by themselves constitute one of the main driving forces of inflation. That is a worrisome prospect for the short-term future. If world oil prices rise 50 percent in the next few years, as some observers expect, that would in itself impose a 5 percent hike in the price level. If oil prices double, our domestic prices will go up 10 percent on the average. There is no way of avoiding that inflationary blow altogether. We can only seek to limit its impact by choosing the short-term, high-gain energy path of conservation, while we work as hard as possible toward the long-term route of non-petroleum energy inputs.

ENERGY POLICY

How shall we run our economy to achieve as much energy independence as possible—including independence from oil-induced inflation?

GOVERNMENT INVESTMENT IN R & D

By and large we can distinguish between two kinds of action that must be taken to assure our relatively safe passage through the decades ahead. The first has already been alluded to many times, in our discussion of the energy spectrum. It is the encouragement of massive R & D into new energy sources, from shale and coal through solar.

Much of this initial investment will have to be made by government, directly or through subsidy, along the lines of its successful attack on nuclear energy in the 1940s and on space travel in the 1970s. Indeed, the development of the atom bomb, and of the series of satellites and space vehicles, suggests the scope and extent of the effort that must be made.

The reason this phase of our energy policy must be carried out under government auspices is that the size of the needed research effort, the riskiness of the various alternatives, and the long time span before commercial success is likely all make it impossible for private enterprise to mount an all-out attack. Certainly private R & D will supplement public R & D, but the main thrust of the campaign to bring forth a new technological base must of necessity be placed under government responsibility.

USING THE MARKET

Yet despite massive effort, a switch to new energy sources cannot take place overnight as we have seen. For the next decade or two, we will have to rely heavily on the one source of energy that is instantly available—conservation. And here the choice between market or "planning" is more complex.

If we are faced with a sudden cutoff of imported oil, as might be the case if revolutions continue to disturb the Middle East, it would surely be necessary to resort to warlike measures of allocation, including the rationing of scarce supplies of gasoline and heating oil, in the interests of national security and order. But short of such an emergency, there is reason to think twice about the hasty use of government regulation.

The most efficient rationing mechanism for goods in short supply is still the market. Allowing gasoline and oil to reach their true market values (or using sales taxes to raise them to world market levels) is the only way to indicate the actual opportunity cost that reality has imposed on us. When we allow gasoline, for example, to be sold for less than its true cost, we encourage individuals to consume it as if it were easier to obtain than is the case. Inevitably, that excess consumption creates problems such as long queues at gas stations. We then have to intervene with non-price conservation measures, such as 55 m.p.h. speed limits or regulations about thermostat settings. These regulations may be justified on their own merits of safety or health, but they are not to be recommended as ways of reducing consumption.

In the end, we will probably rely on both market and regulation to achieve conservation. If gasoline becomes very expensive, our democratic ethic will

likely incline us to treat it as a kind of public good to which each person is entitled to a fair share. If gasoline remains affordable, we will probably allow price to play the main allocating role.

POLITICS AND ECONOMICS

These considerations should make it plain that many of the choices forced upon us by the need to shift our patterns of energy production and consumption plunge us into political or moral, as well as economic, dilemmas. Can we find ways of persuading Montanans, for example, to allow their landscape to be defaced in order that Easterners may have enough coal to heat their homes? Or to aircondition their homes? Can we persuade those who oppose nuclear power that a certain level of risk is worthwhile to maintain a steady flow of electricity to light our cities? Or to run our dishwashers? Can we educate a nation accustomed to consuming energy as if it were almost a free good, to give up its snowmobiles, its power boats, its energy-consuming packaging, its two cars in every garage?

All these questions involve profoundly difficult problems of political leadership and compromise, as well as economic calculations of plus and minus.

THE END OF GROWTH?

One last problem should be faced. The energy squeeze can be mitigated, as we have seen. Our standard of living can be maintained, at least for a while. But no one any longer takes for granted that we can continue to race into the future on the path of exponential, self-feeding growth that propelled us in the past. At its roots, the energy situation arises from the barriers that all such systems must sooner or later face: Either they will outpace the ability of their resources to sustain their growth or they will bump into barriers of pollution or ecological danger generated by their mushrooming growth.

The energy squeeze is the first serious brush that our expanding industrial system has encountered with these constraints of nature. Even if enormous new energy sources are discovered, it is unlikely that our growth trajectory could be sustained more than another generation or two. Our industrial processes are already threatening the environment in other ways than that of energy exhaustion. Perhaps the most serious threat is the "greenhouse effect" that results from the continuously growing addition of carbon dioxide to the atmosphere as a byproduct of energy use. Carbon dioxide in the air acts like window glass in a greenhouse, trapping the air that has been heated by the sun. Scientists expect that dangerous consequences could follow from another fifty years of unrestricted increase in combustion. The National Academy of Sciences has warned that we must throttle back on combustion if we are not to disturb the earth's climate. Roger Revelle, Chairman of the Academy Panel on Energy and Climate, has said, "We will have to kick the fossil habit by 2050."[18]

A SPACESHIP ECONOMY

What is certain, then, is that all industrial systems, socialist as well as capitalist, will have to change their attitudes toward growth in the coming decades. In the words of Kenneth Boulding, we will have to give up the idea of our society

[18]*Science News,* July 30, 1977.

as a "cowboy economy" and embrace that of a "spaceship economy"—one in which outputs are not just thrown away, but used as parts of a great process of "throughput" by which mankind recycles its wealth to disturb as little as possible the delicate ecological system on which it depends.

This perspective begins to make us aware of the complexity of the problem of energy and growth. Basically, energy is needed to bring growth to a world that is, in most nations, still desperately poor. Yet growth is already beginning to threaten a world that is running out of "environment." Ahead lies the formidable problem of a world in which growth may encounter ecological barriers on a worldwide scale, bringing the need for new political and economic arrangements for which we have no precedent. The Age of Spaceship Earth is still some distance in the future, but for the first time the passengers on the craft are aware of their spaceship's limitations.

LOOKING BACK

KEY CONCEPTS

The energy crisis is a period of transition

1. The energy crisis really signals the beginning of an era of transition from an oil-based economy to a new technology.

Behind the immediate gas shortage, oil dependency

2. The crisis was first indicated by gasoline shortages that made evident the extent of our dependency on oil imports.

This dependency is permanent and massive

3. Oil production in the United States has peaked and our oil dependency is permanent and massive—about 25 percent of total energy use.

World supply and demand not clearcut, but demand has been rising and supply is likely to be curtailed. Prices will almost surely rise

4. The outlook for world supply and demand is not altogether clear; it depends to a large degree on political considerations governing oil supply as well as on the steady growth of demand. There are today strong reasons to believe that oil production will be curtailed by OPEC. World oil prices are almost certainly headed higher.

Higher oil prices encourage the shift to alternative sources. Many such sources exist, but conservation is the only large short-term energy source

5. As oil prices rise, substitutes become more profitable. There is a long list of alternative energy sources—better oil recovery, shale, coal, nuclear, solar. None can be immediately relied on to replace oil. Our dependency will continue for some decades. Conservation is the only quick new energy source, but it is not cumulative.

New energy patterns create winners and losers: producers vs. consumers. Inflation is also spurred by higher energy costs

6. The shift to a new pattern of energy production and consumption will create winners and losers. Producers are winners though partially checked in their gains by government. Consumers are losers, although different regions bear different burdens and poor families are harder hit than rich ones. In addition, higher energy prices spur inflation.

Energy policy entails heavy public R & D spending for the long run, price-induced conservation in the short run

7. The main policy options are heavy R & D for new energy possibilities, mainly under government auspices, and effective conservation carried out by the price mechanism, supplemented by rationing if need be.

The energy problem is part of the larger problem of the safe limits to growth

8. The energy crisis is part of our encounter with a limited and limiting environment—with the safe limits to growth. It signals our first awareness that we are becoming a spaceship, not a cowboy, economy.

QUESTIONS

1. If an emergency occurs and oil imports are seriously curtailed, what measures would you recommend? Outright rationing? By individual? By family? By car? By licensed driver? By "white market" coupons (see p. 333)?
2. What measures can you think of to allow regional conflicts to be minimized? How would you persuade the residents of Montana to permit large-scale strip or shale mining? Or would you not encourage this? How does a democracy reach such decisions?
3. The major oil companies are today buying substantial reserves of coal against the day when their oil fields will be exhausted. They are thereby beginning to define themselves as energy companies, not oil companies. Do you think this is a good idea? Give some reasons on both sides of the argument.
4. Do you think that the OPEC cartel is justified in acting as a profit maximizer? Is it justified in curtailing oil production even if this brings on a world economic crisis? How would you argue your case before a meeting of OPEC ministers?
5. Can you outline the basic changes that would be imposed on our structure of production if we had to adjust permanently to one-half the energy inputs we now use. How about industry location? Industry processes? End products?

Part 6 The Rest of the World

Chapter 36 THE GAINS FROM TRADE

A LOOK AHEAD

In this chapter we take our first systematic look at the economics of international exchange.* This will introduce us to one of the most useful ideas in all of economics—that exchange can yield gains in productivity. In order to understand this, we will have to master the principle of comparative advantage—the way in which trade can benefit two nations (or regions or individuals), even though one of the two is more productive than the other in everything it does! The answer to this seeming paradox, we shall see, lies in the opportunity cost of not specializing productive effort. After we have learned about the gains from trade, we review the pros and cons of free trade.

*In order fully to understand Chapter 34, "Defending the Dollar," you should know this and the next chapter well!

Until very recently, when the oil crisis changed our conception of our relation to the rest of the world, Americans had always thought that they were more or less self-sufficient. Other nations, we vaguely knew, were heavily dependent on foreign trade—but not the United States.

Even before our oil dependency became clear, was that conception true? It is a fact that throughout the twentieth century the United States imported or exported less than 10 percent of its gross national product. Yet it is worth considering what would have happened to our economy—and what would happen to it still, oil aside—if some mischance severed our connection with the rest of the world.

The first impact would be the loss of certain critical products needed for industrial production. Earlier in our history we were inclined to treat our natural resources as inexhaustible, but the astounding rate of our consumption of industrial raw materials has disabused us of that notion. Today the major fractions of our iron ore, our copper, and our wood pulp come to us from abroad. Ninety percent of the bauxite from which we make aluminum is imported. Ninety-four percent of the manganese needed for high-tempered steels, all our chrome, virtually all our cobalt, the great bulk of our nickel, tin, platinum, asbestos, is foreign-bought. Many of these materials are so strategic that we stockpile them against temporary disruption, but in a few years the stockpiles would be used up and we should be forced to make radical changes in some of our technology.

Then there would be other losses, less statistically impressive but no less irksome to consumer and industry: the loss of Japanese cameras, of British tweeds, of French perfume, of Italian movies, of Rolls Royce engines, Volkswagen cars, Danish silver, Indian jute and madras. Coffee and tea, the very mainstays of civilized existence, would no longer be available! Chocolate, the favorite flavor of a hundred million Americans, would be unobtainable. There would be no bananas in the morning, no pepper at supper, no Scotch whiskey at night. Clearly, shutting down the flow of the imports into America, however relatively self-sufficient we may be, would deal us a considerable blow. Take a look at Figure 36.1. And imagine what it would mean to cut off imports in the case of, say, Holland, where foreign products account for as much as 45 percent of all goods sold in that country.

But we have still not fully investigated the effects of international trade on the United States, for we have failed to consider the impact of a collapse of our exports. The farm country would feel such a collapse immediately of course, for a fifth of our cotton, almost a quarter of our grains, and more than a quarter of our tobacco go overseas. Mining country would feel it because a fifth of our coal and a third of our sulphur are sold abroad. Manufacturing enterprises in cities scattered all over the nation would feel the blow, as a quarter of our metalworking machinery and of our textile machinery, a third of our construction and mining machinery could no longer be sold overseas—not to speak of another thirty to forty industries in which at least a fifth of output is regularly sold to foreign buyers. In all, some three to four million jobs, three-quarters of them in manufacturing or commerce, would cease to exist if our foreign markets should suddenly disappear.

FIGURE 36.1 AMERICANS BUY MANY FOREIGN-MADE GOODS

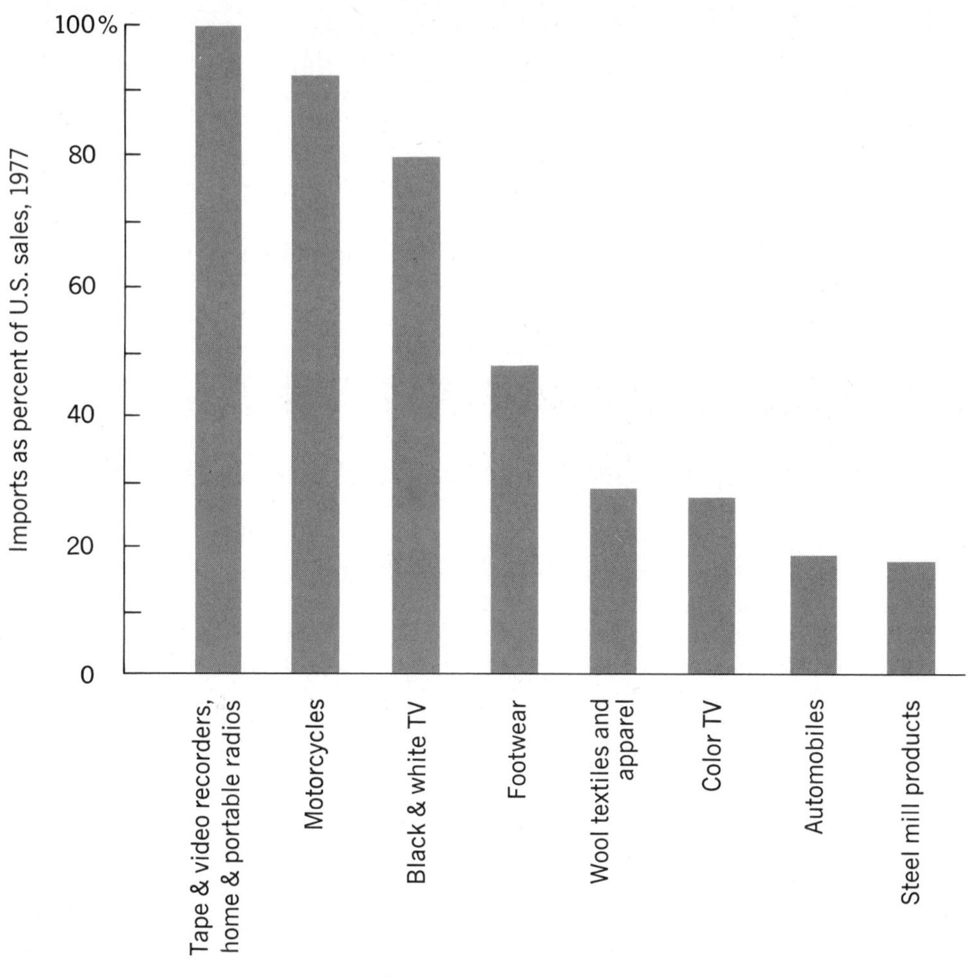

Sources: U.S. Japan Trade Council and American Textile Manufacturers Institute.

Many of those jobs would be replaced by new industries that would be encouraged if our overseas markets and sources of supply vanished. If we could not buy watches or watch parts in Switzerland, we would make more of them here. If we could not sell machine tools to the world, we would no doubt try to use our unemployed skills to make some product or service that could be marketed at home—perhaps one of the items we no longer imported. With considerable effort (especially in the case of strategic materials) we *could* readjust. Hence the question: Why don't we? What is the purpose of international trade? Why do we not seek to improve our relative self-sufficiency by making it complete?

THE BIAS OF NATIONALISM

No sooner do we ask the question of the aims of international trade than we encounter an obstacle that will present the single greatest difficulty in learn-

ing about international economies. This is the bias of nationalism—the curious fact that relationships and propositions that are perfectly self-evident in the context of "ordinary" economics suddenly appear suspect, not to say downright wrong, in the context of international economics.

For example, suppose that the governor of an eastern state—let us say New Jersey—wanted to raise the incomes of his constituents and decided that the best way to do so was to encourage some new industry to move there. Suppose furthermore that his son was very fond of grapefruit and suggested to him one morning that grapefruit would be an excellent addition to New Jersey's products.

The governor might object that grapefruit needed a milder climate than New Jersey had to offer. "That's no problem," his son might answer. "We could protect our grapefruit by growing them in hothouses. That way, in addition to the income from the crop, we would benefit the state from the incomes earned by the glaziers and electricians who would be needed."

The governor might murmur something about hothouse grapefruit costing more than ordinary grapefruit, so that New Jersey could not sell its crop on the competitive market. "Nonsense," his son would reply. "We can subsidize the grapefruit growers out of the proceeds of a general sales tax. Or we could pass a law requiring restaurants in this state to serve state grapefruit only. Or you could bar out-of-state grapefruit from New Jersey entirely."

"Now, my boy," the governor would return, "in the first place, that's unconstitutional. Second, even if it weren't, we would be making people in this state give up part of their incomes through the sales tax to benefit farmers, and that would never be politically acceptable. And third, the whole scheme is so inefficient it's just downright ridiculous."

But if we now shift our attention to a similar scene played between the prime minister of Nova Jersia and his son, we find some interesting differences. Like his counterpart in New Jersey, the son of the prime minister recommends the growing of hothouse grapefruit in Nova Jersia's chilly climate. Admittedly, that would make the crop considerably dearer than that for sale on the international markets. "But that's all right," he tells his father. "We can put a tariff on foreign grapefruit, so none of the cheap fruit from abroad will undersell ours."

"My boy," says the prime minister after carefully considering the matter, "I think you are right. It is true that grapefruit in Nova Jersia will be more expensive as a result of the tariff, but there is no doubt that a tariff looks like a tax on them and not on us, and therefore no one will object to it. It is also true that our hothouse grapefruit may not taste as good as theirs, but we will have the immense satisfaction of eating our *own* grapefruit, which will make it taste better. Finally, there may be a few economists who will tell us that this is not the most efficient use of our resources, but I can tell them that the money we pay for hothouse grapefruit—even if it is a little more than it would be otherwise—stays in our own pockets and doesn't go to enrich foreigners. In addition to which, I would point out in my television appearances that the reason foreign grapefruit are so cheap is that foreign labor is so badly paid. We certainly don't want to drag down the price of our labor by making it compete with the cheap labor of other nations. All in all, hothouse grapefruit seems to me an eminently sensible proposal, and one that is certain to be politically popular."

SOURCE OF THE DIFFICULTY

Is it a sensible proposal? Of course not, although it will take some careful thinking to expose all its fallacies. Will it be politically popular? It may very well be, for economic policies that would be laughed out of court at home get a serious hearing when they crop up in the international arena. Here are some of the things that most of us tend to believe.

Trade between two nations usually harms one side or the other.
Rich countries can't compete with poor countries.
There is always the danger that a country may sell but refuse to buy.

Are these fears true? One way of testing their validity is to see how they ring in our ears when we rid them of our unconscious national bias by recasting them as propositions in ordinary economics.

Is it true that trade between businesses or persons usually harms one side or the other?
Is it true that rich companies can't compete with poor ones?
Is it true that one company might only sell but never buy—not even materials or the services of factors of production?

What is the source of this curious prejudice against international trade? It is not, as we might think, an excess of patriotism that leads us to recommend courses of action that will help our own country, regardless of the effect on others. For, curiously, the policies of the economic superpatriot, if put into practice, would demonstrably injure the economic interests of his own land. The trouble, then, springs from a root deeper than mere national interest. It lies in the peculiarly deceptive problems posed by international trade. What is deceptive about them, however, is not that they involve principles that apply only to relations between nations. All the economic arguments that elucidate international trade apply equally well to domestic trade. The deception arises, rather, for two other reasons:

1. International trade requires an understanding of how two countries, each dealing in its own currency, manage to buy and sell from each other in a world where there is no such thing as international money.

2. International trade requires a very thorough understanding of the advantages of and arguments for, trade itself.

GAINS FROM TRADE

In a general way, of course, we are all aware of the importance of trade, although we have hardly mentioned it since the opening pages of our book. ***It is trade that makes possible the division and specialization of labor on which our productivity is so largely based.*** **If we could not exchange the products of our specialized labor, each of us would have to be wholly self-supporting, and our standard of living would thereupon fall to that of subsistence farmers. Thus trade (international or domestic) is actually a means of *increasing productivity,* quite as much as investment or technological progress.**

The importance of trade in making possible specialization is so great that we should take a moment to make it crystal clear. Let us consider two towns. Each produces two goods: wool and cotton; but Wooltown has good grazing lands and poor growing lands, while Cottontown's grazing is poor, but growing is good. Suppose, moreover, that the two towns had equal populations and that each town employed half its people in cotton and half in wool. The results might look like Table 36.1.

TABLE 36.1 UNSPECIALIZED PRODUCTION: CASE 1

Wooltown and Cottontown each put half their populations to work at wool and cotton, with these results.

Production	*Wooltown*	*Cottontown*
Wool (lbs)	5,000	2,000
Cotton (lbs)	10,000	20,000

As we can see, the same number of grazers in Wooltown turn out two-and-one-half times as much wool as they do in Cottontown, whereas the same number of cotton farmers in Cottontown produce double the amount of cotton that they do in Wooltown. One does not have to be an economist to see that both towns are losing by this arrangement. If Cottontown would shift its woolworkers into cotton, and Wooltown would shift its cotton farmers into wool, the output of the two towns would look like Table 36.2 (assuming constant returns to scale).

TABLE 36.2 SPECIALIZED PRODUCTION

They move all their labor force to the more productive task, with these results.

Output	*Wooltown*	*Cottontown*
Wool	10,000	0
Cotton	0	40,000

Now, if we compare total production of the two towns (see Table 36.3), we can see the gains from specialization.

TABLE 36.3 THE GAIN FROM SPECIALIZATION

Comparing the output of the two towns together, before and after, shows the gains from specialization.

	Combined Towns		*Gain from*
Output	*Mixed*	*Specialized*	*specialization*
Wool	7,000	10,000	3,000
Cotton	30,000	40,000	10,000

In other words, specialization followed by trade makes it possible for both towns to have more of both commodities than they had before. No matter how the gains from trade are distributed—and this will depend on many factors, such as the relative elasticities of demand for the two products—both towns can gain, even if one gains more than the other.

UNEQUAL ADVANTAGES

If all the world were divided into nations, like Wooltown and Cottontown, each producing for trade only a single item in which it has a clear advantage over all others, international trade would be a simple matter to understand. It would still present problems of international payment, and it might still inspire its prime ministers of Nova Jersia to forego the gains from trade for political reasons that we will examine at the end of this chapter. But the essential rationale of trade would be simple to understand.

It is unfortunate for the economics student as well as for the world that this is not the way international resources are distributed. Instead of giving each nation at least one commodity in which it has a clear advantage, many nations do not have such an advantage in a single product. How can trade possibly take place under such inauspicious circumstances?

To unravel the mystery, let us turn again to Cottontown and Wooltown, but this time call them Supraville and Infraville, to designate an important change in their respective abilities. Although both towns still enjoy equal populations, which are again divided equally between cotton and wool production, in this example Supraville is a more efficient producer than Infraville in *both* cotton and wool, as Table 36.4 shows.

TABLE 36.4 UNSPECIALIZED PRODUCTION: CASE II

	Supraville	*Infraville*
Wool output	5,000	3,000
Cotton production	20,000	10,000

In this case, one country is better than the other not just in one activity, but in both.

Is it possible for trade to benefit these two towns when one of them is so manifestly superior to the other in every product? It seems out of the question. But let us nonetheless test the case by supposing that each town began to specialize.

TRADE-OFF RELATIONSHIPS

But how to decide which trade each town should follow? A look at Figure 36.2 may give us a clue. Production-possibility diagrams are familiar to us. Here we put them to use to let us see the results of trade.

What do the diagrams show? First, they establish maximums that each town could produce if it devoted all its efforts to one product. Since we have assumed that the labor force is divided, this means that each town could double the amount

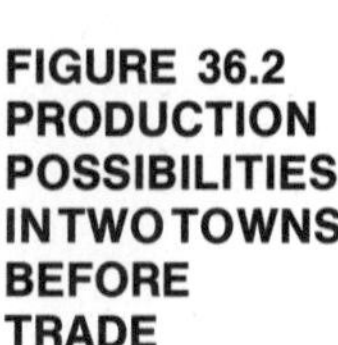
FIGURE 36.2 PRODUCTION POSSIBILITIES IN TWO TOWNS BEFORE TRADE

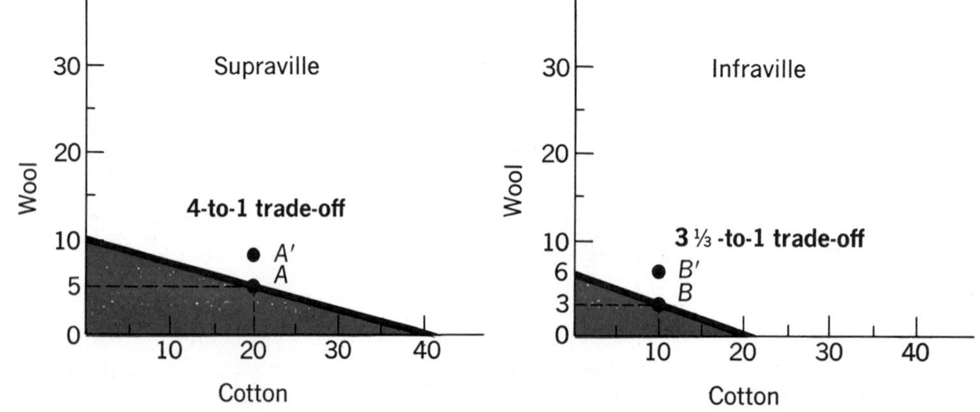

Production-possibility curves are graphic depictions of trade-offs, or (same thing) of opportunity costs. Supraville enjoys a wool/cotton income at point *A*, Infraville at point *B*. Note that points *A'* and *B'* are out of reach for the two towns.

of cotton or wool it enjoys when it divides its workers fifty-fifty. Next, a line between these points shows the production frontier that both towns face.* We see that Supraville is located at point *A* where it has 5,000 lbs of wool and 20,000 lbs of cotton, and that Infraville is at *B*, where it has 3,000 lbs of wool and 10,000 lbs of cotton.

But the diagrams (and the figures in the preceding table, on which they are based) also show us something else. It is that each town has a different "trade-off" relationship between its two branches of production. When either town specializes in one branch, it must, of course, give up the output of the other. *But each town swaps one kind of output for the other in different proportions,* as the differing slopes of the two *p–p* curves show. Supraville, for example, can make only an extra pound of wool by giving up 4 pounds of cotton. That is, it gets its maximum potential output of 10,000 lbs of wool by surrendering 40,000 lbs of cotton. Infraville can reach its production maximum of 6,000 lbs of wool at a loss of 20,000 lbs of cotton. Thus, *rather than having to give up 4 lbs of cotton to get one of wool, it gives up only 3.3 lbs.* Therefore, in terms of opportunity cost—how much cotton has to be given up to get a pound of wool—wool actually costs less in Infraville than in Supraville!

Not so the other way round, of course. As we would expect, cotton costs Supraville less in terms of wool than it costs Infraville. In Supraville, we get 40,000 lbs of cotton by relinquishing only 10,000 lbs of wool—a loss of a quarter of a pound of wool for a pound of the other. In Infraville, we can get the maximum output of 20,000 lbs of cotton only by a surrender of 6,000 lbs of wool—a loss of ⅓ lb of wool rather than ¼ lb of wool for each unit of cotton.†

COMPARATIVE ADVANTAGE

Perhaps the light is beginning to dawn. Despite the fact that Supraville is more productive than Infraville in terms of output per man in both cotton and wool, it is *relatively* more productive in cotton than in wool. And despite the fact that Infraville is absolutely less productive than Supraville, man for man, in both cotton and wool, it is *relatively* more productive in wool. To repeat, it requires a smaller sacrifice of wool to get another pound of cotton in Infraville than in Supraville.

We call this kind of relative superiority *comparative advantage.* It is a concept that is often difficult to grasp at first but that is central to the reason for trade itself. When we speak of *comparative* advantage, we mean, as in the case of Supraville, that among *various* advantages of one producer or locale over another, there is one that is better than any other. *Comparatively* speaking, this is where its optimal returns lie. But just because it must abandon some lesser opportunity, its trading partner can now advantageously devote itself in the direction where *it* has a comparative advantage.

*Why are these lines drawn straight, not bowed as in Chapter 6? As we know, the bowing reflects the law of increasing cost, which makes the gains from a shift in resource allocation less and less favorable as we move from one extreme of allocation to another. Here we ignore this complication for simplicity of exposition. We have also ignored the problem of variable returns when we assumed that each town could double its output of cotton or wool by doubling its labor force.

†It takes long practice to master the arithmetic of gains from trade. It is important, first, to get the idea; then to master the calculations.

This is a relationship of logic, not economics. Take the example of the banker who is also the best carpenter in town. Will it pay him to build his own house? Clearly it will not, for he will make more money by devoting all his hours to banking, even though he then has to employ and pay for a carpenter less skillful than himself. True, he could save that expense by building his own house. But he would then have to give up the much more lucrative hours he could be spending at the bank!

Now let us return to the matter of trade. We have seen that wool is *relatively* cheaper in Infraville, where each additional pound costs only 3.3 lbs of cotton, rather than 4 lbs as in Supraville; and that cotton is *relatively* cheaper in Supraville, where an additional pound costs but ¼ lb of wool, instead of ⅓ lb across the way in Infraville. Now let us suppose that each side begins to specialize in the trade in which it has the comparative advantage. Suppose that Supraville took half its labor force now in wool and put it into cotton. Its output would change as in Table 36.5.

TABLE 36.5
SUPRAVILLE

	Before the shift	*After the shift*
Wool production	5,000	2,500
Cotton production	20,000	30,000

Supraville uses specialization to boost wool production at the expense of cotton.

Supraville has lost 2,500 lbs of wool but gained 10,000 lbs of cotton. Now let us see if it can trade its cotton for Infraville's wool. In Infraville, where productivity is so much less, the entire labor force has shifted to wool output, where its greatly inferior productivity can be put to best use. Hence its production pattern now looks like Table 36.6.

TABLE 36.6
INFRAVILLE

	Before the shift	*After the shift*
Wool	3,000	6,000
Cotton	10,000	—

Specialization is concentrated in wool in Infraville's case.

Infraville finds itself lacking 10,000 lbs of cotton, but it has 3,000 *additional* lbs of wool. Clearly, it can acquire the 10,000 lbs of cotton it needs from Supraville by giving Supraville *more* than the 2,500 lbs of wool it seeks. As a result, both Infraville and Supraville will have the same cotton consumption as before, but there will be a surplus of 500 lbs of wool to be shared between them. As Figure 36.3 shows, *both towns will have gained by the exchange, for both will have moved beyond their former production frontiers* (from A to A' and from B to B').

This last point is the crucial one. If we remember the nature of production-possibility curves from our discussion of them in Chapter 10, any point lying outside the production frontier is simply unattainable by that society. In Figure 36.3, points A' and B' lie beyond the pre-trade P–P curves of the two towns, but trade has made it possible for both communities to enjoy what was formerly impossible.

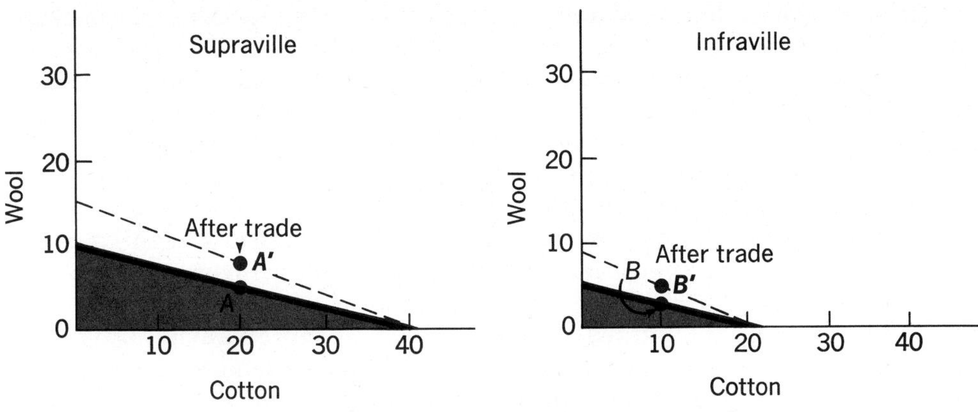

FIGURE 36.3 PRODUCTION POSSIBILITIES IN TWO TOWNS AFTER TRADE

Specialization has made more wool available. This is like moving the *PP* curve outward along the wool axis. Points *A'* and *B'*, formerly out of reach, are now accessible to the two towns. (For clarity's sake, the graph shows a gain much larger than the 500 lbs described in the text.)

OPPORTUNITY COST

Comparative advantage gives us an important insight into all exchange relationships, for it reveals again a fundamental economic truth that we have mentioned more than once before. It is that *cost, in economics, means opportunities that must be foregone.* The real cost of wool in Supraville is the cotton that cannot be grown, because workers are engaged in wool production, just as the real cost of cotton is the wool that must be gone without. In fact, we can see that the basic reason for comparative advantage lies in the fact that opportunity costs vary, so that it "pays" (it costs less) for different parties to engage in different activities.

If opportunity costs for two producers are the same, then it follows that there cannot be any comparative advantage for either; and if there is no comparative advantage, there is nothing to be gained by specializing or trading. Suppose Supraville has a two-to-one edge over Infraville in *both* cotton and wool. Then, if either town specializes, neither will gain. Supraville may still gain 10,000 lbs of cotton for 2,500 lbs of wool, as before, but Infraville will gain only 2,500 lbs of wool (not 3,000) from its shift away from cotton. Thus, the key to trade lies in the existence of *different* opportunity costs.

Are opportunity costs usually different from country to country or from region to region? For most commodities they are. As we move from one part of the world to another—sometimes even short distances—climate, resources, skills, transportation costs, capital scarcity, or abundance all change; and as they change, so do opportunity costs. There is every possibility for rich countries to trade with poor ones, precisely because their opportunity costs are certain to differ.

EXCHANGE RATIOS

But we have not yet fully understood one last important aspect of trade—the *prices* at which goods will exchange. Suppose that Supraville and Infraville do specialize, each in the product in which it enjoys a comparative advantage. Does that mean they can swap their goods at any price?

A quick series of calculations reveals otherwise. We remember that Supraville needed at least 2,500 lbs of wool for which it was going to offer some of its extra production of cotton in exchange. But how much? What price should it offer for its needed wool, in terms of cotton?

Suppose it offered 7,500 lbs of cotton. Would Infraville sell the wool? No, it would not. At home it can grow its own 7,500 lbs of cotton at a "cost" of only 2,273 lbs of wool, for we recall that Infraville traded off one pound of wool for 3.3 lbs of cotton (7,500 ÷ 3.3 = 2,273).

Suppose, then, that Infraville counteroffered to sell Supraville 2,500 lbs of wool for a price of 12,000 lbs of cotton. Would Supraville accept? Of course not. This would mean the equivalent of 4.8 lbs of cotton for a pound of wool. Supraville can do better than that by growing her own wool at her own trade-off ratio of only 4 lbs to one.

We begin to see, in other words, that the price of wool must lie between the trade-off ratios of Infraville and Supraville. Infraville wants to import cotton. If it did not trade with Supraville, it could grow its own cotton at the cost of one pound of wool for every 3.3 lbs of cotton. Hence, for trade to be advantageous, Infraville seeks to get *more* cotton than that, per pound of wool.

Supraville is in the opposite situation. It seeks to export cotton and to import wool. It could make its own wool at the sacrifice of 4 lbs of cotton per pound of wool. Thus it seeks to gain wool for a *lower* price than that, in terms of cotton. Clearly, any ratio between 3.3 and 4.0 lbs of cotton per pound of wool will profit both sides.

THE ROLE OF PRICES

Let us put this into ordinary price terms. Suppose that cotton sells for 30¢ per pound. Then wool would have to sell between 99¢ and $1.20 (30¢ × 3.3 and × 4) to make trade worthwhile.* Let us say that supply and demand established a price of $1.10 for wool. Supraville can then sell its 10,000 lbs of extra cotton production at 30¢, which will net it $3,000. How much wool can it buy for this sum? At the going price of $1.10 per lb, 2,727 lbs. Therefore Supraville will end up with the same amount of cotton (20,000 lbs) as it had before specialization and trade, and with 227 *more* lbs of wool than before (2,500 lbs produced at home plus 2,727 lbs imported from Infraville—a total of 5,227 lbs). It has gained by trade an amount equal to the price of this extra wool, or $249.70.

How has Infraville fared? It has 3,273 lbs of wool left after exporting 2,727 lbs to Supraville from its production of 6,000 lbs, and it also has 10,000 lbs of cotton imported from Supraville in exchange for its wool exports. Thus it, too, has a gain from trade—the 273 lbs of wool (worth $300.30) over the amount of 3,000 lbs that it would have produced without specialization and trade. In brief, *both* sides have profited from the exchange. To be sure, gains need not be distributed so evenly between the trading partners. If the price of wool had been $1.00, trade

*Obviously, these prices are used for illustrative purposes only. And once again, let us reassure you: These calculations are easy to follow but not easy to do by yourself. Familiarity will come only with practice.

still would have been worthwhile, but Supraville would have gained almost all of it. Had the price of wool been $1.19, both sides again would have come out ahead, but now Infraville would have been the larger beneficiary by far. The actual price at which wool would sell would be determined by the supply and demand schedules for it in both communities.

THE CASE FOR FREE TRADE

Would the prime minister of Nova Jersia be convinced by these arguments? Would his son? They might be weakened in their support for hothouse grapefruit, but some arguments would still linger in their minds. Let us consider them.

1. "Our workers cannot compete with low-wage workers overseas."

This is an argument one hears not only in Nova Jersia, but in every nation in the world, save only those with the very lowest wage rates. Swedish workers complain about "cheap" American labor; American workers complain about sweatshop labor in Hong Kong. And indeed it is true that American labor is paid less than Swedish and that Hong Kong labor is paid a great deal less than American. Does that not mean that American labor will be seriously injured if we import goods made under "sweatshop" conditions, or that Swedish labor is right in complaining that its standard of living is undermined by importing goods from "exploited" American workers?

Like the answers to so many questions in economics, this one is not a simple yes or no. The American textile worker who loses his job because of low-priced textile imports *is* hurt; and so is the Swedish worker in an electronics company who loses his job because of American competition. We will come back to their legitimate grievances later. But we must note that both workers would also be injured if they lost their jobs as a result of domestic competition. Why do we feel so threatened when the competition comes from abroad?

Because, the answer goes, foreign competition isn't based on American efficiency. It is based on exploited labor. Hence it pulls down the standards of American labor to its own low level.

There is an easy reply to this argument. The reason Hong Kong textile labor is paid so much less than American textile labor is that *average* productivity in Hong Kong is so much lower than *average* productivity in America. **To put it differently, the reason that American wages are high is that we use our workers in industries where their productivity is very high. If Hong Kong, with its very low productivity, can undersell us in textiles, then this is a clear signal that we must move our factors of production out of textiles into other areas where their contribution will be greater; for example, in the production of machinery.** It is no coincidence that machinery—one of the highest wage industries in America—is one of our leading exports, or that more than 75 percent of our manufactured exports are produced by industries paying hourly wage rates above the national average for all manufacturing industries. In fact, all nations tend to export the goods that are produced at the highest, not lowest, local wages! Why? Because those industries employ their labor most effectively.

This fact opens our eyes to another. Why is it that the American garment industry is worried about competition from Hong Kong, but not the American computer manufacturers or the electrical machinery industry or the farm equipment industry? After all, the manufacturers of those products could also avail themselves of low wages in Hong Kong.

The answer is that American manufacturers can make these products at much lower cost in America. Why? Because the technical skills necessary to produce them are available in the U.S., not in Hong Kong. Thus, if Hong Kong has a comparative advantage over us in the garment trade, we have a comparative advantage over her in many other areas.

But suppose Hong Kong accumulated large amounts of capital and became a center for the manufacture of heavy equipment, so that it sold *both* garments and electrical generators more cheaply than we sold them. We are back to Supraville and Infraville. There would still be a *comparative* advantage in one or more of these products in which we would be wise to specialize, afterward trading with Hong Kong for our supplies of the other good.*

2. **"Tariffs are painless taxes because they are borne by foreigners."**

This is a convincing-sounding argument advanced by the prime minister of Nova Jersia (and by some other prime ministers in their time). But is it true? Let us take the case of hothouse grapefruit, which can be produced in Nova Jersia only at a cost of 50 cents each, whereas foreign grapefruit (no doubt produced by sweated labor) can be unloaded at its ports at 25 cents. To prevent his home industry from being destroyed, the prime minister imposes a tariff of 25 cents on foreign grapefruit—which, he tells the newspapers, will be entirely paid by foreigners.

This is not, however, the way his political opponent (who has had a course in economics) sees it. "Without the tariff," she tells her constituency, "you could buy grapefruit for 25 cents. Now you have to pay 50 cents for it. Who is paying the extra 25 cents—the foreign grower or you? Even if not a single grapefruit entered the country, you would still be paying 25 cents more than you have to. **In fact, you are being asked to subsidize an inefficient domestic industry.** Not only that, but the tariff wall means they won't ever become efficient because there is no pressure of competition on them."

Whether or not our economic candidate will win the electoral battle, she surely has the better of the argument. Or does she? For the prime minister, stung by these unkind remarks, replies:

3. **"But at least the tariff keeps spending power at home. Our own grapefruit growers, not foreigners, have our money."**

There are two answers to this argument. First, the purchasing power acquired by foreigners can be used to buy goods from efficient Nova Jersia producers and will thus return to Nova Jersia's economy. Second, if productive resources are

*Newspapers in Southeast Asia carry editorials seeking protection from American imports because, they say, we do not use labor in our production, and it is unfair to ask its citizens to compete with our machines that do not have to be paid wages.

HIGH WAGES?

How do you tell whether a country is a high-wage country or a low-wage country? If German workers are paid 8 marks per hour, are their wages high or low compared to ours? Clearly, you cannot tell without knowing the exchange rate. If 8 marks can be traded for $1 then German workers are paid the equivalent of $1 per hour. We can then compare the German rates relative to the American. Given the average American wage of $4 per hour, we would conclude that German wages are low. If, however, 1 mark can be traded for 1 dollar, then German workers earn the equivalent of $8 per hour. In this case, German workers are highly paid *relative* to American workers. As a result we cannot really tell whether a country is high-wage or low-wage until we understand exchange rates and what determines them. More on this in the next chapter.

used in inefficient, low-productivity industries, then the resources available for use in efficient, high-productivity industries are less than they otherwise would be, and the total output of the country falls. To keep out foreign grapefruit is to lower the country's real standard of living. The people of Nova Jersia waste time and resources doing something they do not do very well.

4. **"But tariffs are necessary to keep the work force of Nova Jersia employed."**

This is the time to remember our investigation of macroeconomic policies. As we learned in macroeconomics, the governments of Nova Jersia and every other country can use fiscal and monetary policies to keep their resources fully employed. If textile workers become unemployed, governments can expand aggregate demand and generate domestic job opportunities in other areas.

CLASSICAL ARGUMENT FOR FREE TRADE

Are there no arguments at all for tariffs? As we shall see, there are some rational arguments for restricting free trade. **But all of these arguments accept the fact that restrictions depress world incomes below what they would be otherwise. If world production is to be maximized, free trade is an essential ingredient. Free trade must therefore be considered a means of increasing GNP, a means not essentially different from technological improvement in its effect on output and growth. We may not want to maximize GNP, but we need to understand that to advocate restrictions on trade is to advocate lower real incomes.**

These arguments apply cogently to developed countries. They are less persuasive when applied to underdeveloped countries, as we shall see when we discuss imperialism in Chapter 38.

THE CASE FOR TARIFFS

Are *all* arguments against tariffs? Not quite. But it is essential to recognize that these arguments take full cognizance of the inescapable costs of restricting trade. They do not contest the validity of the theory of free trade, but the difficulties of its application. Let us familiarize ourselves with them.

MOBILITY

The first difficulty concerns the problem of mobility. When Hong Kong textiles press hard against the garment worker in New York, higher wages in the auto plants in Detroit are scant comfort. She has a lifetime of skills and a home in New York, and she does not want to move to another city where she will be a stranger and to a new trade in which she would be only an unskilled beginner. She certainly does not want to move to Hong Kong! Hence, the impact of foreign trade often brings serious dislocations that result in persistent local unemployment, rather than in a flow of resources from a relatively disadvantaged to a relatively advantaged industry.

TRANSITION COSTS

Second, even if free trade increases the incomes and real living standards of each country participating in trade, **this does not mean that it increases the income and real living standards of each individual in each country.** Our New York textile worker may find herself with a substantial reduction in income for the rest of her life. She is being economically rational when she resists "cheap" foreign imports and attempts to get her congressman to impose tariffs or quotas.

There is, it should be noted, an answer to this argument—an answer, at any rate, that applies to industrial nations. Since the gains from trade are generally spread across the nation, the real transition costs of moving from one industry, skill, or region to another should also be generally spread across the nation. This means that government (the taxpayers), rather than the worker or businessman, should bear the costs of relocation and retraining. In this way we spread the costs in such a manner that a few need not suffer disproportionately to win the benefits of international trade that are shared by many.

We should also be aware of the possibility that transition costs may actually exceed the short-term benefits to be derived from international trade. Transition costs thus place a new element in the system, since the standard analysis of competitive systems—national or international—ignores them. A country may be wise to limit its international trade, if it calculates that the cost of reallocating its own factors is greater than the gains to be had in higher real income. Remember, however, that transition costs tend to be short-lived and that the gains from trade tend to last. Thus it is easy to exaggerate the costs of transition and to balk at making changes that would ultimately improve conditions.

FULL EMPLOYMENT

Third, the argument for free trade rests on the very important assumption that there will be substantially full employment.

In the days of the mid-nineteenth century when the free trade argument was first fully formulated, the idea of an underemployment equilibrium would have been considered absurd. In an economy of large enterprises and "sticky" wages and prices, we know that unemployment is a real and continuous object of concern for national policy.

Thus, it makes little sense to advocate policies to expand production via trade unless we are certain that the level of aggregate demand will be large enough to absorb that production. Full employment policy therefore becomes an indispensable arm of trade policy. Trade gives us the potential for maximizing production, but there is no point in laying the groundwork for the highest possible output unless fiscal and monetary policy are also geared to bringing about a level of aggregate demand large enough to support that output.

NATIONAL SELF-SUFFICIENCY

Fourth, there is the argument of nationalism pure and simple. This argument does not impute spurious economic gains to tariffs. Rather, it says that free trade undoubtedly encourages production, but it does so at a certain cost. This is the cost of the vulnerability that comes from extensive and extreme specialization. This vulnerability is all very well within a nation where we assume that law and order will prevail, but it cannot be so easily justified among nations where the realistic assumption is just the other way. Tariffs, in other words, are defensible because they enable nations to attain a certain *self-sufficiency*—admittedly at some economic cost. Project Independence, the United States' effort to gain self-sufficiency in energy, is exactly such an undertaking.

In a world always threatened by war, self-sufficiency has a value that may properly override considerations of ideal economic efficiency. The problem is to hold the arguments for national defense down to proper proportions. When tariffs are periodically adjusted in international conferences, an astonishing variety of industries (in all countries) find it possible to claim protection from foreign competition in the name of national "indispensability."

INFANT INDUSTRIES

Equally interesting is the nationalist argument for tariffs advanced by so-called infant industries, particularly in developing nations. These newly formed or prospective enterprises claim that they cannot possibly compete with the giants in developed countries while they are small; but that if they are protected by a tariff, they will in time become large and efficient enough no longer to need a tariff. In addition, they claim, they will provide a more diversified spectrum of employments for their own people, as well as aiding in the national transition toward a more modern economy.

The argument is a valid one if it is applied to industries that have a fair chance of achieving a comparative advantage once grown up (otherwise one will be supporting them in infancy, maturity, and senility). Certainly it is an argu-

TRANSPORTATION COSTS

If every industry must have a comparative advantage in one country or another, how can there be steel industries (or any other) in more than one country? The answer, quite aside from considerations of nationalism, lies in *transportation costs,* which compensate for lower production costs in many products and thereby allow a relatively inefficient industry to supply a home market.

Transportation costs also explain why some industries, such as brickmaking, are spread out in many localities, whereas others, such as diamond cutting, are concentrated in one place. If diamonds were very bulky or bricks very light, the first industry would become more dispersed, and the second less so.

ment that was propounded by the youthful industries of the United States in the early nineteenth century and was sufficiently persuasive to bring them a moderate degree of protection (although it is inconclusive as to how much their growth was ultimately dependent on tariff help). And it is being listened to today by the underdeveloped nations who feel that their only chance of escaping from poverty is to develop a nucleus of industrial employment at almost any cost in the short run.

PRODUCERS' VS. CONSUMERS' WELFARE

We have already reviewed some of these pros and cons in Chapter 34 when we looked into the price of defending the dollar. **Now we can see, however, that the policy of free trade versus the policy of protectionism ultimately resolves into a choice between the well-being of two groups. Free trade favors the welfare of consumers. Protectionism favors the welfare of producers.**

To be sure, consumers are producers and producers are consumers, so that in a frictionless perfect world there would be little to choose between the two. But in a world where frictions are an important part of economic life, it matters very greatly whether we favor policies that benefit almost everyone to some degree, or policies that help or hurt a few people to a considerable degree. That is, in fact, the trade-off when we weigh the gains from trade that accrue as lower prices for textiles or shoes or cars, versus the impact of protectionism on the jobs of textile workers or shoemakers or auto workers.

In a way the difficult choice that we face reminds us of the cost of inflation, felt by all, versus the cost of unemployment, borne by a few. The difference is that the political voice aroused by inflation drowns out the voice aroused by unemployment, whereas the injuries of those affected by foreign competition tend to override the murmur of consumers who would benefit from lower prices.

TRADE AND WELFARE

We pose this dilemma because it is very easy to shrug aside the pains from trade in favor of the gains from trade, forgetting how traumatic it is to have one's livelihood undermined and how little noticed are the compensating benefits of lower prices for imports. Nonetheless, it is vital that we do not allow an appreciation of the harsh realities of adjusting to imports to blind us to the potential benefits of competition as a means of pushing our economy toward its most efficient use of resources.

For the competitive pains of importing goods are not different from the competitive pains of domestic competition—*except for the bias of nationalism.* If the workers in leather shoes are displaced by the rise of a new plastic shoe industry at home, we would not look with favor on a policy of protectionism that prevented a more efficient industry from edging out a less efficient one. Generous policies of assistance for displaced workers can alleviate at least some of the difficulties of adjustment, and this is of course as true for the adjustments of international trade as it is for those of domestic trade.

Therefore it is well to conclude this chapter by recalling that the gains from trade are still those of efficiency. Trade is an indirect means of increasing production, and in a world that is still poor, production is still very much welcome.

LOOKING BACK

KEY CONCEPTS

Bias of nationalism

1. The bias of nationalism is deep and pervasive. It leads us to assume that gains from trade, which we take for granted within a country, do not apply between countries.

Gains from trade stem from the specialization of labor

2. The gains from trade essentially stem from the improvement in productivity that results from specialization or a better division of labor. Trade is an indirect means of enhancing productivity.

Principle of comparative advantage gives gains to trading partners even when one is more productive in all activities

3. The principle of comparative advantage shows that trade is profitable even when one trading partner is more productive in all lines of endeavor than another. This is because it is possible for the superior partner to increase production in the activity that is comparatively best for itself, thus more than making up any loss from shifting resources out of the activity that is comparatively less advantageous.

Specialization always yields more output when opportunity costs differ. Both countries can thereby go beyond their former P–P curves

4. By specializing production, the two trading partners gain a combined output that is larger than they could get by producing without specialization and trade. This is true as long as opportunity costs are not the same in both countries, which is almost always the case. Then specialization allows both countries to go beyond their former P-P curves.

Prices, or exchange ratios, must lie within the ratios of trade-off

5. Exchange ratios, or prices, must lie within the trade-off ratios of actual output. Otherwise the comparative advantages of the two nations would be lost.

The case for free trade is a case for maximizing productivity and consumer well-being

6. The case for free trade stresses the gains for the entire society that come from maximizing production. By allowing "cheap" imports to come in without tariffs, we force labor to move away from low-productivity to high-productivity industry, and we benefit consumers.

The case for protection stresses the benefits to producers—including workers

7. The case for tariffs emphasizes the cost to producers of adjusting to international competition. Workers must relocate. Skills may be obsolete. Local unemployment may result that cannot easily be absorbed. And national self-sufficiency may be impaired.

The arguments for trade are essentially arguments for efficiency and production

8. Essentially the argument comes to a choice between consumer's well-being and producer's well-being. There is no simple way of making this choice. But arguments against foreign competition are also arguments against domestic competition. In the end, we look to competition as a means of increasing efficiency and we look to trade as a means of increasing wealth.

ECONOMIC VOCABULARY

Trade-off relationships 578
Comparative advantage 579
Opportunity cost 581
Mobility 586
Transition costs 586
Self-sufficiency 587
Infant industries 587
Consumers' vs. producers' welfare 588

QUESTIONS

1. What do we mean when we say that trade is "indirect production"?
2. Suppose that two towns, Coaltown and Irontown, have equal populations but differing resources. If Coaltown applies its whole population to coal production, it will produce 10,000 tons of coal; if it applies them to iron production, it will produce 5,000 tons of iron. If Irontown concentrates on iron, it will turn out 18,000 tons of iron; if it shifts to coal, it will produce 12,000 tons of coal. Is trade possible between these towns? Would it be possible if Irontown could produce 24,000 tons of iron? Why is there a comparative advantage in one case and not in the other?
3. In which product does Coaltown have a comparative advantage? How many tons of iron does a ton of coal cost her? How many does it cost Irontown? What is the cost of iron in Coaltown and Irontown? Draw a production-possibility diagram for each town. Show where the frontier lies before and after trade.
4. If iron sells for $10 a ton, what must be the price range of coal? Show that trade cannot be profitable if coal sells on either side of this range. What is the opportunity cost of coal to Irontown? Of iron to Irontown?
5. Is it possible that American watchmakers face unfair competition from Swiss watchmakers because wages are lower in Switzerland? If American watch workers are rendered unemployed by the low-paid Swiss, what might be done to help them—impose a tariff?
6. Is it possible that mass-produced, low-cost American watches are a source of unfair competition for Switzerland? If Swiss watchmakers are unemployed as a result, what could be done to help them—impose a tariff? Is it possible that a mutually profitable trade in watches might take place between the two countries? What kinds of watches would each probably produce?
7. Are the duties on French wines borne by foreigners or by domestic consumers? Both? What, if any, is the rationale for these duties? How would you go about estimating the transition costs if we were to abolish the tariff on all wines and spirits? Who would be affected? What alternative employment would you suggest for the displaced labor? The displaced land?

Chapter 37

INTERNATIONAL TRANSACTIONS

A LOOK AHEAD

We had a glimpse of international exchange when we looked into defending the dollar. Now we must pursue the problem in greater detail.

(1) We are going to examine the mechanics of foreign exchange much as we looked into the mechanics of domestic money creation.

(2) We shall discover how foreign exchange actually works, and how the supplies and demands for foreign exchange create various balances of international exchange.

(3) This will lead us to a study of the role of central banks in international exchange, and the difficulties of finding and "defending" a stable exchange rate.

In our last chapter we learned about one of the sources of confusion that surrounds international trade—the curiously concealed gains from trade itself. Yet our examples of trade have thus far not touched on another source of confusion—the fact that international trade is conducted in two (or sometimes more) currencies. After all, remember that Infraville and Supraville both trade in dollars. But suppose Infraville were Japan and Supraville America. Then how would things work out? We have covered this problem in a very general way in Chapter 34, "Defending the Dollar." Now we are going to study it carefully, step by step.

FOREIGN MONEY

The first thing is to price the various items in Japan and America (assuming that Japan produces both wool and cotton, which she does not). Suppose the result looked like Table 37.1 (these are not real prices, of course).

TABLE 37.1

	United States	*Japan*
Price of wool (lb)	$1.10	¥300
Price of cotton (lb)	.30	¥100

Without exchange rates, quotations in foreign currencies do not tell us whether foreign goods are dear or cheap.

What would this tell us about the cheapness or dearness of Japanese products compared with those of the U.S.? Nothing, unless we knew one further fact: *the rate at which we could exchange dollars and yen.*

Suppose you could buy 400 yen for a dollar. Then a pound of Japanese wool imported into America (forgetting about shipping costs) would cost 75¢ (¥300 ÷ 400), and a pound of Japanese cotton in America would cost $0.25 (¥100 ÷ 400). Assuming that these are the only products that either country makes for export, here we have a case in which Japan can seemingly undersell America in everything.

But now suppose the rate of exchange were not 400 to one but 250 to one. In that event a pound of Japanese wool landed in America would cost $1.20 (¥300 ÷ 250); and a pound of cotton, $0.40. At this rate of exchange everything in Japan is more expensive than the same products produced in the United States.

The point is clear. We cannot decide whether foreign products are cheaper or dearer than our own until we know the rate of exchange, the number of units of their currency we get for ours.

MECHANISM OF EXCHANGE: IMPORTS

How does international exchange work? The simplest way to understand it is to follow through a single act of international exchange from start to finish. Suppose, for example, that we decide to buy a Japanese camera directly from a Tokyo manufacturer. The price of the camera as advertised in the catalog is ¥20,000, and to buy the camera we must therefore arrange for the Japanese manufacturer to get that many yen. Obviously we can't write him a check in that currency, since our own money is in dollars; and equally obviously we can't send him a check for dollars, since he can't use dollars in Tokyo any more than we can use a check from him in yen.

Therefore, we go to our bank and ask if it can arrange to sell us yen to be delivered to the Tokyo manufacturer. Yes, our bank would be delighted to oblige. How can it do so? The answer is that our bank (or if not ours, another bank with whom it does business) keeps a regular checking account in its own name in a so-called correspondent bank in Tokyo. As we might expect, the bank in Tokyo also keeps a checking account in dollars in *its* own name at our bank. If our banker has enough yen in his Tokyo account, he can sell them to us himself. If not, be can buy yen (which he will then have available in Japan) from his correspondent bank in exchange for dollars which he will put into their account here.

Notice that two currencies change hands—not just one. Notice also that our American banker will not be able to buy yen unless the Japanese banker is willing to acquire dollars. And above all, note that banks are the intermediaries of the foreign exchange mechanism because they hold deposits in foreign banks.

When we go to our bank to buy ¥20,000 the bank officer looks up the current exchange rate on yen. Suppose it is 385. He then tells us that it will cost us $51.95 (20,000 ÷ 385) to purchase the yen, plus a bank commission for his services. We write the check, which is deducted from our bank balance and added to the balance of the Tokyo bank's account in this country. Meanwhile, the manufacturer has been notified that if he goes to the Tokyo bank in which our bank keeps its deposits of yen, he will receive a check for ¥20,000. In other words, the Tokyo bank, having received dollars in the United States, will now pay out yen in Japan.

EXPORTS

Exactly the opposite is true in the case of exports. Suppose that we were manufacturers of chemicals and that we sold a $1,000 order to Tokyo. In Japan, the importer of chemicals would go to his bank to find out how many yen that would cost. If the rate were 385, it would cost him ¥385,000 which he would then pay to the Japanese bank. The bank would charge his account and credit the yen to the Tokyo account of an American bank with which it did business, meantime advising the bank here that the transaction had taken place. When the appropriate notice arrived from Japan, our U.S. bank would then take note of its increased holdings of yen and pay the equivalent amount in dollars into our account.

FOREIGN EXCHANGE

Thus the mechanism of foreign exchange involves the more or less simultaneous (or anyway, closely linked) operations of two banks in different countries. One bank accepts money in one national denomination, the other pays out money in another denomination. Both are able to do so because each needs the other's currency, and each maintains accounts in the other country. **Note that when payments are made in international trade, money does not physically leave the country.** It travels back or forth between American-owned and foreign-owned bank accounts *in America.* The same is true in foreign nations, where their money will travel between an American-owned account there and the account of one of their nationals. *Taken collectively, these foreign-owned accounts (including our own overseas) are called "foreign exchange." They constitute the main pool of moneys available to finance foreign trade.*

EXCHANGE RATES

Thus the mechanism of foreign exchange works through the cooperation of banks. But we must go beyond an understanding of the mechanism to see the actual forces of supply and demand at work. And this is confusing because we have to think in two money units at the same time.

BUYING AND SELLING MONEY

We are used to thinking of the price of shoes in terms of dollars. We don't turn around and ask what is the price of dollars in terms of shoes, because consumers don't use shoes to buy dollars.

When we buy pounds or francs or yen, however, we are buying a commodity that is indeed usable as money to buy a different kind of money. Dollars buy francs and marks and yen; and marks, francs, and yen buy dollars. We will have to bear this in mind when we seek to understand the supply and demand curves for international exchange.

Now let us consider an exchange market, say the market for yen (Figure 37.1). The demand curve for yen is easy to understand. It shows us that we will want to acquire larger amounts of yen as they get cheaper. Why? Because cheap yen means relatively cheaper Japanese goods and services. **Really our demand curve for foreign exchange is a picture of our changing demand for foreign goods and services as these goods get cheaper or dearer because the money we use to buy them gets cheaper or dearer.**

Now the supply curve. We can most easily picture it as the changing willingness and ability of Japanese banks to offer yen as we pay high or low prices for yen. (There is a better way of explaining the supply curve, but it takes some hard thought. Those who want to penetrate the mysteries of foreign exchange should look at the box, p. 596.)

EQUILIBRIUM PRICES

What is important is that our diagram shows that there is an equilibrium price for yen that just clears the market. At that price, the amounts of yen that Americans want are exactly equal to the amounts of yen that Japanese want to

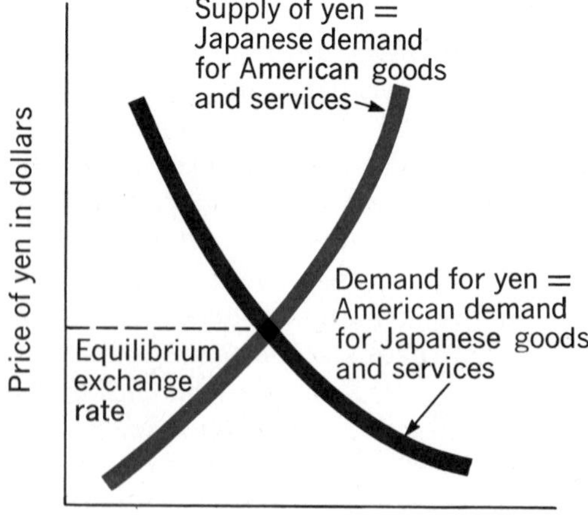

FIGURE 37.1 THE MARKET FOR EXCHANGE

Supply and demand for currencies establish an equilibrium price for them, just as if currencies were shoes or hats.

supply. If we look through the veil of money, we can see that at this price the value of all Japanese goods and services that we will buy must also be equal to the value of all American goods and services that they will buy!

APPRECIATION AND DEPRECIATION OF EXCHANGE RATES

From this, a very important result follows. Suppose that you are a U.S. importer who is eager to buy Japanese automobiles priced at ¥2 million per car. You go to the bank to finance the deal. Here you have an unpleasant surprise. Your banker tells you that exchange is very tight at the moment, meaning that the banker's own yen balances in Japan are very small. As a result, the American banker can no longer offer yen at the old price of, say, 350 to the dollar. The Japanese banks with whom he does business are insisting on a better price for yen—offering only 325 or perhaps even 300 yen for a dollar. Because of supply and demand, the yen has risen in price, or *appreciated;* and the dollar has fallen in price, or *depreciated.*

You now make a quick calculation. At 350 yen to the dollar, a Japanese car that costs ¥2 million will cost $5,714 (¥2,000,000 ÷ 350). At an exchange rate of 300, it would now cost $6,666 (¥2,000,000 ÷ 300). The new higher price is too steep for the American market. You decide not to place the order. Exactly the opposite situation faces the Japanese importer. Suppose he wants to buy a $50,000 IBM computer. How much will it cost *in yen* if he has to pay 350 yen for a dollar? 300 yen?

The principle is very clear. **Movements in exchange rates change relative prices among countries.** At different relative prices, imports will rise or fall, as will exports. If the price of the dollar falls, American exports will be increased and its imports diminished. If the price of the yen rises, Japanese exports will fall and its imports will rise.

Thus a moving exchange rate will automatically bring about an equilibrium between the demand for, and the supply of, foreign exchange, exactly as a moving price for shoes will bring about an equality between the value of the dollars offered for shoes and the value of the shoes offered for dollars! In one case as in the other, there may be time lags. **But the effect of a moving price in both cases is to eliminate shortages and surpluses; that is, to bring about a price at which quantity demanded (of a particular currency or any other commodity) equals quantity supplied.**

BALANCE OF PAYMENTS

What does all this have to do with the U.S. balance of payments? To understand the answer, we first have to understand what we mean by the "balance" of payments. We don't speak of a balance of payments in, say, a market for shoes. Why, then, is there one in the market of foreign exchange?

DISAGGREGATING THE BALANCE OF PAYMENTS

The first part of the answer lies in an important attribute of this market. In a shoe market, all buyers want shoes, presumably to wear. In an exchange market, there are many kinds of buyers (or sellers) who want to buy or sell exchange for different purposes. That is, the so-called balance of payments represents sup-

ANOTHER LOOK AT THE EXCHANGE PROBLEM

Let us trace the exchange process once more, very carefully. The chart of the New York market shows the demand for English pounds in dollars. When it costs $3 to buy £1, our demand is for one million pounds (we can think of them as commodities, like one million shoes). This is point *A*. When the price falls to $2 for £1, our demand rises to 2 million pounds, point *B*. The broken line *AB* is our demand curve for pounds.

Now we move to the London market on the right. We are going to show that the New York demand curve *AB* becomes a London supply curve *A′B′*. To do so, remember that when it costs $3 to buy £1, from the London point of view the price of $1 is 33 pence (one-third of a pound). What is the supply of dollars at this price? It is equal to the number of dollars spent for pounds in New York. At the $3 price, we bought one million pounds. Our supply of dollars is therefore $3 million. This gives us point *A′* in the London market.

It is now simple to get point *B′*.

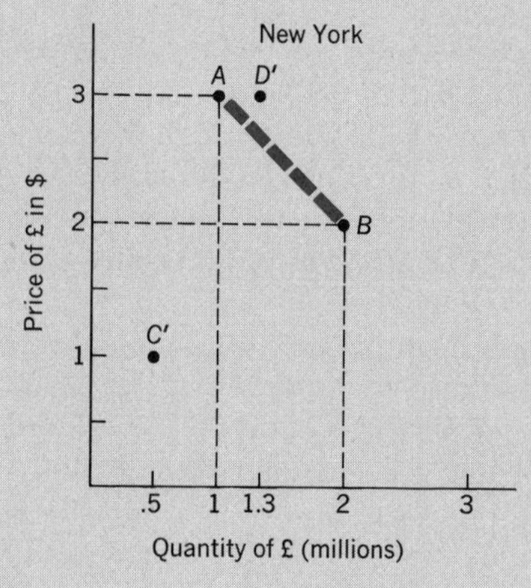

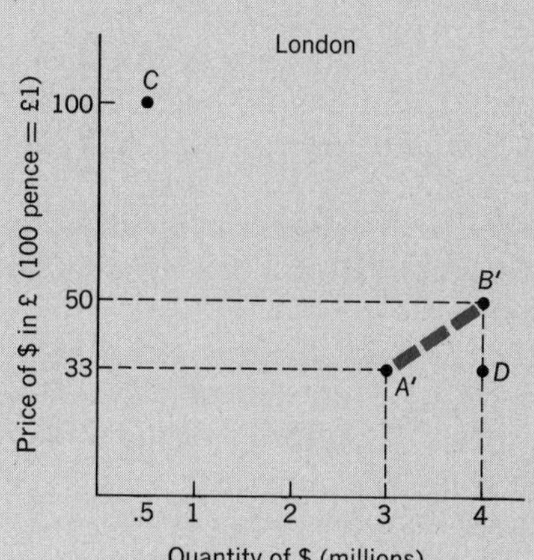

ply and demand for foreign exchange by *different groups* in each economy. When all supplies and all demands are added together, the two totals must balance because we then have an identity: Purchases ≡ Sales (i.e., the purchases of any currency, such as dollars, must equal the sales of that currency). But they need not balance for any particular group in the economy. As a result, deficits and surpluses refer to groups that are demanding more foreign exchange than they supply, or supplying more than they demand.

ITEMS IN THE U.S. BALANCE OF PAYMENTS

We know a little about these groups from Chapter 34. Now let us study them in much greater detail by examining the actual balance of payments for the United States for 1978 (Table 37.2). We begin with some obvious and self-explanatory figures—the exports and imports of *merchandise*. As we can see, in 1979 exporters sold $182.1 billion, earning that many dollars (foreign buyers had to supply us with dollars to that amount). U.S. importers bought $211.5 billion worth of foreign goods, supplying that many dollars to the foreign exchange mar-

When £1 falls to \$2 in New York, \$1 rises to 50 pence (one-half pound) in London. How many dollars are supplied at this price? We can see in the New York diagram that we bought £2 million at \$2 each, spending \$4 million. Hence in the London market, we locate point *B'* at a price of 50 pence and a quantity of dollars equal to 4 million.

Now we have a demand curve in New York and a supply curve in London. We need a supply curve in New York and a demand curve in London. We'll start in London, with a high price for dollars. Point *C* shows us that when it costs £1 to buy \$1, the demand for dollars is small—only \$.5 million are demanded. But this point on the demand curve also gives us a supply of pounds: .5 million "units" of dollars at £1 each, or a total of £.5 million. Back in New York this shows up as point *C'*. (Remember: \$1 = £1.)

Now back to London. The price of dollars falls to 33 pence or ⅓ of a pound. At that price, suppose Britishers demand \$4 million, point *D*. To buy \$4 million at 33 pence each, Britishers will have to spend 132 million pence, or £1.32 million. This gives us the supply of pounds in the New York market at the price that corresponds to \$1 = 33 pence. This price is \$3 = 100 pence (one pound). Point *D'* locates the supply curve at that price. We suggest you draw the two new curves: *CD,* the demand for dollars, and *C'D'*, the supply of dollars.

Each panel now has an equilibrium price. In London it is a little over 33 pence, say 37 pence. *But the New York price must be the very same price, expressed in dollars instead of pounds.* If 37 pence = \$1 in London, then in New York £1 must equal \$2.70 (\$1.00 ÷ .37). And if we look at the equilibrium price in New York, so it does.

This is not really surprising. The price of pounds in dollars is the same thing as the price of dollars in pounds "upside down." It is as if pounds were shoes and we were saying that a pair of shoes that cost \$10 is the same thing as 10 dollars costing 1 pair of shoes. But it takes a while to get used to the idea of two markets in which supply and demand are linked, as in the case of international exchange. With a little practice, the mystery begins to evaporate.

ket. On net balance, the merchandise trade showed a balance of −\$29.4 billion—a deficit arising from an excess of imports over exports. This creates a net supply for dollars on the foreign exchange market.

The second group of items consists of supplies and demands for exchange to pay for *services* rather than goods. In our table we note a few of these major transactions. Note that *military transactions* gave rise to a small loss of foreign exchange to pay for expenses at U.S. bases abroad. *Travel and transportation* mainly shows us that American tourists were demanding more foreign currencies to voyage abroad than foreigners were demanding dollars to travel here. It also shows the net balance between U.S. payments for foreign carriers (or example, a flight on Lufthansa or the charter of a Greek freighter) and foreign payments for U.S. transportation (flights on PanAm or cargo on a U.S.-owned ship).

More interesting is the item for *investment income.* This reflects the flow of profits from U.S. companies in foreign nations to their home offices in the United States, minus the flow from foreign companies in the United States to their home offices abroad. When IBM in Italy sends profits back to its U.S. headquarters, it

TABLE 37.2 THE UNITED STATES BALANCE OF PAYMENTS, 1978 (BILLIONS OF DOLLARS)

1. *Merchandise*		
Exports	+182.1	
Imports	−211.5	
Balance on merchandise	−29.4	
2. *Services*		
Military transactions	−1.2	
Travel & transportation	−2.9	
Net investment income	+32.4	
Other	+6.3	
Balance on services	+34.6	
Balance on mdse and services		+5.2
3. *Unilateral transfers*		
Remittances	−.9	
Government transfers	−5.5	
Balance on current account		−1.2
4. *Capital outflow*		
Private	−58.5	
Government	−4.9	
5. *Capital inflow*		
Private	+49.1	
Government	−14.1	
Balance on capital	−28.4	
6. *Statistical discrepancy*	+28.7	

What we call "the" balance of payments is actually a summation of a number of smaller balances of payments for particular purposes such as trade, service items, or other areas shown above.

buys dollars with its local bank balances of lire, creating a demand for dollars. When Nestlé sends profits back to *its* headquarters, it uses its dollar balances to buy Swiss francs. From this large inflow of earnings we must subtract a small outflow of government interest payments going abroad. When we net out these flows, we can see that investment income was a strong source of dollars for the United States in 1979, amounting to $32.4 billion.

TWO PARTIAL BALANCES

If we now sum up all items on the merchandise account and all items on service account we get the so-called balance of goods and services. In 1979 this came to $5.2 billion that we earned, net, on these items.

Next we move to a further item, under the category of *unilateral transfers.* Here we find remittances, or the sums that persons residing in America send to private individuals abroad, less any sums coming the other way from Americans residing abroad and sending their pay home. The pay that an American working abroad might send home would be a remittance that would earn us dollars; the sums sent home by a Britisher working in the United States would require the purchase of pounds.

This is augmented by *government unilateral transfers*—sums sent abroad by the government for foreign aid, emergency relief, and so on. Of course, these sums are not actually sent abroad; rather, the U.S. government opens a dollar account for the recipient nation, which then uses these dollars. But in using them, the recipient country again sells dollars for other currencies. Together, these unilateral transfers, public and private, amounted to $6.4 billion that we spent on foreign exchange.

Summing up again, we now reach a new partial balance—**the balance on current account,** which showed a deficit of $0.3 billion in 1979. In other words, the sum of all our supplies and demands for foreign exchange on current account in 1979 cost us $0.3 billion.

ITEMS ON CAPITAL ACCOUNT

The next items reflect supplies and demands for foreign exchange associated with capital investments (not *income* from these investments, which we have already counted). This may include investment by U.S. companies in plant and equipment abroad, less investment by foreign companies in plant and equipment here; or purchases of foreign long-term securities by Americans less American stocks or bonds bought by foreigners. These *private capital* flows cost us a net $9.4 billion in 1979 (an outflow of $58.5 billion less an inflow of $49.1 billion). That outflow was augmented by *government capital transactions*—the purchases of foreign government securities by the U.S. government, less any purchases of U.S. bonds by foreign governments. The net balance on *both* private and public capital account gave rise to a net outflow on capital account of $28.4 billion.

Capital inflows and outflows can also be divided into short-term and long-term capital inflows and outflows (not shown in Table 37.2). In 1979 there was a short-term capital inflow of $5 billion. The most important of these consists of the transfer from one country to another of private balances, belonging to individuals or companies, that are moved about in response to interest rates or for speculative reasons. The treasurer of a multinational company may "park" his extra cash in Sweden one year and in the United States the next, depending on where he can earn more interest in short-term securities or special bank accounts. Some individuals and even some small governments move their bank balances from country to country in search of the best return or in anticipation of a move in exchange rates that will benefit them. This movement of short-term capital tends to be volatile and can on occasion give rise to speculative "flights" from one nation to another.

SUMMING UP THE ACCOUNTS

As we have seen, very different motivations apply to these different actors on the foreign exchange market. Exports and imports reflect the relative price levels and growth of output of trading countries. Tourism is also affected by prices abroad, as well as by the relative affluence of different countries. Flows of corporate earnings arise from investments made in the past. Long-term private capital items reflect estimates of the *future* earning power of investments home or abroad. Short-term capital is guided by interest rates and speculative moods. Government flows hinge largely on foreign policy decisions.

Whatever the different motives affecting these flows, each gives rise to supplies of, or demands for, dollars. Thus we can sum up the net outcome of all these varied groups to discover the overall demand and supply for dollars. As must always be the case, they are in balance. The balance on current account plus the statistical discrepancy are exactly equal to the deficit on the capital account.

THE "BALANCE"

What we have traced thus far are the various groups whose economic (or political) interests caused them to supply dollars to or demand dollars on the exchange market. But we have arrived at a curious stopping point.

Our description has shown that it is entirely possible that the quantity of foreign exchange demanded by one country will be larger (or smaller) than the quantity of foreign exchange supplied to it. In fact, only by chance would the total requirements of foreign exchange of importers and exporters of goods and services and capital balance out. But the existence of a difference between the total quantities supplied and demanded should present no problem. **Just as in a market for shoes, the price of foreign exchange should change, exactly as we describe it beginning on p. 101, altering the quantities that different groups would want to buy or sell.** An equilibrium price for foreign exchange should clear the exchange market just as an equilibrium price for shoes clears the shoe market. No "balance" of exchange would remain, any more than there is a "balance" of shoes.

FIXED VS. FLEXIBLE EXCHANGE RATES

Does a balance remain? Until recently there *was* always a balance. This was because the price of foreign exchange was not free to rise and fall to whatever price cleared the total supply and demand for exchange. Instead, the price was set by international arrangment: exchange rates were "fixed," just as a government might fix the prices of shoes. And in one case as in the other, the existence of a fixed price gave rise to shortages or surpluses—not of shoes, but of foreign exchange itself.

Today we do not have fixed exchange rates, and theoretically there should be no balance, just as there are no shortages or surpluses in a free-price market for goods. In fact, as we have already noted in Chapter 34, the exchange rate is not entirely free, so that some shortages or surpluses develop.

CENTRAL BANKS

In order to understand better how these balances arise and what we can do about them, we must back up and examine the role played by a crucial institution in the world of international finance—the central bank. Central banks are the national banks we find in all countries. One of their functions, as we know, is to play a role in the determination of the appropriate quantity of money for domestic purposes. But a second role is equally important. **Central banks are agencies of their governments, who buy or sell foreign exchange, making their own currencies available to foreigners when they buy foreign exchange and absorbing their own currency from foreigners when they sell foreign exchange. By buying at a price established by agreement, they "peg" the exchange of their currencies.**

From our earlier study of international exchange we know how central banks acquire the capacity for these transactions in foreign exchange. Private banks in all countries have the option of transferring their own supplies of foreign exchange to their central bank, receiving payment in their own currency. For example, let us suppose that the Chase Manhattan Bank finds itself with large and unwanted supplies of francs. It can exchange these francs for dollars with the Federal Reserve. The Chase Manhattan Bank will then get a dollar credit at the Federal Reserve, and the Federal Reserve will be the owner of the francs formerly belonging to Chase. In the same way in their home countries, the Bank of Yokohama or Barclay's Bank or the Swiss Bank can exchange their holdings of dollars for yen or pounds or Swiss francs, in each case receiving a credit at their central bank in their own currencies and transferring their holdings of foreign currencies to their government bank.

HOW CENTRAL BANKS WORK

Thus central banks are the holders of large amounts of foreign exchange, which they acquire indirectly from the activities of various groups in their own nations. The central banks are therefore the last group whose own actions must balance out the unbalanced flows that arise under "fixed" or imperfectly free rates. There are two ways in which this can be done.

1. Gold flows

For many years, while all exchange prices were fixed, any balances left over were settled by the shipment of gold from one central bank to another. For example, all through the early 1960s, the United States balanced its accounts partly by selling gold to cover any deficit in its Official Reserve Transactions Balance. The sale of gold was exactly like an export. Foreign central banks paid us in dollars from their holdings of dollar exchange, and this dollar inflow offset any deficit of dollars arising from other transactions.

Since 1971, gold shipments have been abandoned as a means of settling up foreign balances. Instead central banks use their reserves of foreign currencies or of SDRs as ways of making good their international obligations (p. 549).

2. "Dirty Floating"

Today we have a system that is nominally free, but not entirely free—a system called "dirty floating." The major central banks have agreed not to intervene in the exchange market, except to stabilize it against speculative raids. They are supposed to offset short-run fluctuations that would make business difficult, but not to alter long-run trends.

In fact, however, all central banks have intervened considerably beyond this point. The Japanese have frequently been accused of buying foreign currencies, thereby keeping down the price of the yen to encourage Japanese exports. Other countries have also intervened at crucial moments. The result is that exchange rates float, but they do not float all the way to the equilibrium price that a wholly free market would yield.

As a result, shortages and surpluses still appear in international accounts, evidenced by changes in the amounts of liquid liabilities (foreign-held bank accounts) held by most governments. In fact the intervention of central banks into the exchange market has been *greater* under dirty floating than under fixed exchange rates. No nation has been willing to watch its rates rise and fall freely. All have sought hard to "defend" their currencies from unwanted movement up or down. For example, in the United States in 1978, foreign liquid balances rose by $34 billion. If the liquid liabilities of any government are persistently large and positive, we can be sure that its central bank is intervening to buy foreign exchange in order to hold the price of its own currency down. If the balances are large and negative, we can be certain the bank is selling foreign exchange, in order to hold the value of its currency above the price that the free market would enforce.

CURING A BALANCE OF PAYMENTS PROBLEM

What happens if an adverse balance of payments remains, whether because exchange rates are fixed in ratios that do not allow the market to clear, or because dirty floating keeps draining reserves of exchange from a central bank?

There are numerous policies that nations can follow to try to improve their balance of payments position. But two of them are so important that they warrant discussion.

DEVALUATION

The first major policy is one that is no longer a live option because rates are not officially fixed, but until the advent of floating, it was the key policy maneuver. The policy was to change the value of one's currency in terms of gold or of the dollar, then in terms of the central world monetary unit. By lowering the price of one's currency in terms of gold, the currency was made cheaper on the world market.

Devaluation had two effects. It instantly increased the demand for the devalued currency by importers in other lands who could now buy that country's product less expensively. When the British pound was officially devalued from $2.80 to $2.40 in the last half of the 1960s, it meant that the buying power of an American dollar in England was raised 14 percent. This stimulated British exports, brought tourists by droves, and tempted short-term funds into England to buy a "cheap" currency.

There was, however, a second effect—the mirror image of the first. Devaluation instantly raised the price in England of foreign currencies. After devaluation, foreign exchange was 14 percent higher in England. This served to cut back on some imports, but it was also the cause of higher prices for those imports that could not be cut back.

Thus the consequence of devaluation was to lower the standard of living for the devaluing country. This is one reason why the regime of fixed rates never worked very well. Countries struggled against devaluation—or else, when a general world depression struck, vied with each other in currency wars to become the lowest priced exporter. For the United States, whose currency had become the linchpin of the international monetary system after World War II, the fixed exchange system was particularly onerous because we felt that we could not devalue the dollar without harming the many countries we had persuaded to hold dollars as their reserves, rather than exercise their right to convert those dollars into gold.

DEFENDING CURRENCIES

When the fixed exchange rate system broke down in early 1971 a new era began, marked by the instability we studied in our chapter "Defending the Dollar." There we saw the array of policies that a nation can use to raise or lower, or simply stabilize, its exchange rate.

All these policies, from protectionism to high interest rates to using the reserves of central banks, have the same purpose. They seek to insulate an economy and its currency from the forces impinging on it from the rest of the world —forces that are creating a pressure on the price of its currency through the mechanism of the balance of current transactions or the balance of capital flows.

More and more, the lesson of the last decades has been that the currents of world trade and capital flow are very difficult to resist. Even so strong an economic entity as the United States can be seriously affected by the forces of the world market. For in fact these forces reflect basic realities of the world economy such as relative rates of productivity growth or of inflation, so a nation that falls behind in productivity or that rushes ahead in inflation must expect to suffer in the international struggle to sell goods and to attract capital.

BACK TO FIXED RATES?

Because the forces of international production and finance do indeed manage to penetrate even the strongest defenses, and because the threat of large-scale crisis implicit in a falling dollar (or any other major currency), there is growing talk of the need to return to a system of fixed rates, or even to the old-fashioned gold standard.

The problem with fixed rates, however, is that they establish international monetary stability only at the expense of domestic instability. A fixed ratio of foreign exchange, to be successful, means that a nation must trim its domestic economic life to fit into the pattern of supply and demand for its currency that the larger world has established. This is all very well if the resulting level of employment is high; but what if it is not? What if the rate of exchange that balances out the supply and demand for a nation's currency also creates large-scale unemployment and distress? Will any nation in today's world of high nationalistic sentiment allow its domestic economy to be ruled by the impersonal dictates of gold or established exchange rates? If not—if there would be a constant struggle to renegotiate better rates—are we not back to the problem of a floating rate, the very problem we have been dealing with for the last difficult years?

A DIFFICULT PROSPECT

The challenge of international economic life today is therefore to find a viable course lying between policies that subordinate national economic independence to the cause of international stability, and policies that seek national stability at the risk of international turmoil. The difficulty with the first course is the opposition it arouses from electorates who do not want their livelihoods and well-being injured for the benefit of something as abstract as "international

monetary equilibrium"; and the difficulty with the second course is that the threats of international instability can be extremely grave, as we know from looking into "Defending the Dollar."

There is no easy resolution of this problem, itself the expression of a world in which nations are half united and half disunited, partially bound together in a cooperative endeavor and partially locked in a competitive struggle for power and wealth. At bottom, the difficulties and dangers of the international economic situation are only a reflection of the graver and darker political risks inherent in our world today. We have no choice but to grapple with them as best we can.

LOOKING BACK

KEY CONCEPTS

Exchange rates establish international prices

1. Exchange rates constitute the link that makes mutual trade between nations feasible or not. Exchange rates determine whether a country's wares are cheap or dear to a foreigner.

In foreign exchange transactions, money does not travel overseas but from domestic to foreign accounts in the same nation

2. In the determination of exchange rates two currencies change hands, not one. Importers or exporters buy or sell currencies to banks in their own lands. Correspondent banks credit or debit accounts of the exporter or importer in the partner country. Money does not travel between the countries. It only travels between domestic and foreign-owned accounts in both countries. The term "foreign exchange" means the sum of the foreign currency owned by banks, such as the Japanese-owned deposits in U.S. banks and the American-owned deposits in Japanese banks.

The demand and supply curves for foreign exchange reflect the demand and supply for goods and assets of another country as its exchange rises or falls

3. Our demand curve for foreign exchange consists of the varying amount of foreign exchange we need as the prices of foreign goods are raised or lowered because of changes in the exchange rate. Our supply curve of foreign exchange is the amount of our currency that we relinquish to foreign buyers as the price of imports changes.

An equilibrium price clears an exchange market as it does any other market

4. In a perfect exchange market there will be an equilibrium price that will clear the market. There will be no unsold dollars, just as there will be no unsold shoes.

The balance of payments aggregates numerous submarkets of which the two main divisions are current and capital account transactions

5. The balance of payments consists of an aggregate of many sub-balances. The two overall principal sub-balances are the market for transactions on current account (merchandise, services, and public and private transfers) and the market for transactions on capital account (direct and portfolio investment, and short-term funds).

There can always be positive or negative balances in different subaccounts, but not in the overall total account—unless exchange rates are fixed or do not float freely

6. In a wholly free market, where each currency was priced by the forces of supply and demand, there would be no balance of all accounts, although there could be positive balances in some accounts, offset by negative balances in others. In the actual world, fixed exchange rates or semi-free (dirty floating) rates establish balances, just as price floors or ceilings create shortages or surpluses.

Central banks are buyers of last resort who settle up accounts. They no longer do so by shipping gold but mainly by holding other currencies as a reserve

7. To the extent that balances exist, central banks become the buyers of last resort. Formerly, they settled up the shortages or surpluses by shipping gold. Today, imbalances are settled by shipping SDRs or balances of other currencies, or by allowing balances to remain in another country's currency.

Neither fixed nor floating rates have worked very well. There may be no adequate solution to this problem in a world of competitive nationalism

8. The world has moved from fixed to floating rates. Imbalances can no longer be dealt with by devaluation—changing the official (fixed) rates of exchange. Instead, the complex mass of policies called "defending" currencies results in efforts to alter the supply-demand balance. These defenses have not been very successful and currency instability persists with considerable risks. Whether we can return to a policy of fixed rates is doubtful, for that requires subordination of domestic economic policy to international economic rules and regulations. In a world of competitive nationalism there may be no escape from this dilemma.

ECONOMIC VOCABULARY

Foreign exchange 593
Appreciation and depreciation 595
Balance of payments on current and capital account 599
Fixed and flexible exchange rates 600
Dirty floating 601
Devaluation 602

QUESTIONS

1. If you wanted to buy a Swiss watch and discovered that it cost 500 francs, what would you need to know to discover if it were cheaper or more expensive than an American watch that cost $200?
2. If you bought the watch, how would you pay for it? What would happen to your bank check? How would the Swiss exporter be paid?
3. Suppose that a Swiss importer decides to buy an American computer. He finds that the rate of exchange is 2 Swiss francs to the dollar. The computer costs $140,000. How does he make payment?
4. Suppose that the Swiss franc/dollar rate changes from 2 to 1 to 3 to 1. What does the watch now cost? The computer?
5. Is a deficit in a balance of payments market the same thing as a surplus in a commodity market?
6. Can dirty floating persist in one direction? What are the limits to a central bank's ability to influence exchange rates?

Chapter 38 THE UNDER-DEVELOPED WORLD

A LOOK AHEAD

The great majority of mankind lives under economic conditions very different from those of modern industrial capitalism. This chapter examines the conditions of underdevelopment—the economic situation of nations exposed to the pressures and pulls of the modern world, but very far removed from it in terms of their way of life. Two problems will command our attention in this chapter.

(1) We will gain some understanding of the economic causes for underdevelopment and the economic steps that may be taken to overcome it.

(2) We must learn about the social and political aspects of underdevelopment, for economics by itself is inadequate to give us an appreciation of this major problem in world politics and history.

Why are the underdeveloped nations so pitiably poor?* Only a half-century ago it was common to attribute their backwardness to geographic or climatic causes. The underdeveloped nations were poor, it was thought, either because the climate was too debilitating or because natural resources were lacking. Sometimes it was just said that the natives were too childlike or racially too inferior to improve their lot.

Bad climates may have had adverse effects. Yet, many hot areas have shown a capacity for sustained economic growth (for example, the Queensland areas of Australia), and we have come to recognize that a number of underdeveloped areas, such as Argentina and Korea, have completely temperate climates. So, too, we now regard the lack of resources in many areas more as a *symptom* of underdevelopment than a cause—which is to say that in many underdeveloped areas, resources have not yet been *looked for.* Libya, for instance, which used to be written off as a totally barren nation, has been discovered to be a huge reservoir of oil. Finally, little is heard today about native childishness or inherent inferiority. (Perhaps we remember how the wealthy classes in Europe similarly characterized the poor not too many centuries ago.) Climate and geography and cultural unpreparedness unquestionably constitute obstacles to rapid economic growth—and in some areas of the globe, very serious obstacles—but there are few economists who would look to these disadvantages as the main causes of economic backwardness.

Why then are these societies so poor?

The answer is that these are poor societies because they are *traditional* societies—that is, societies which have developed neither the mechanisms of effective command nor of the market by which they might launch into a sustained process of economic growth. Indeed, as we examine them further we shall have the feeling that we are encountering in the present the anachronistic counterparts of the static societies of antiquity.

Why did they remain traditional societies? Why, for instance, did Byzantium, which was economically so advanced in contrast with the Crusaders' Europe, fall into decline? Why did China, with so many natural advantages, not develop into a dynamic economic society? There are no fully satisfactory answers. Perhaps the absence of economic progress elsewhere on the globe forces us to look upon our Western experience not as the paradigm and standard for historic development, but as a very special case in which various activating factors met in an environment peculiarly favorable for the emergence of a new economic style in history. The problem is one into which we cannot go more deeply in this book. At any rate, it is today an academic question. The dominant reality of our times is that the backward areas are now striving desperately to enter the mainstream of economic progress with the West. Let us examine further their chances for doing so.

CONDITIONS OF BACKWARDNESS

Every people, to exist, must first feed itself; there is a rough sequence to the order of demands in human society. But to go beyond existence, it must achieve a certain level of efficiency in agriculture, so that its efforts can be turned in

*For a graphic view of this poverty, see "An Extra Word" at the conclusion of this chapter.

SNAPSHOTS OF UNDERDEVELOPMENT

DAMASCUS: In famine years the children of the poor examine the droppings of horses to extract morsels of undigested oats.

CALCUTTA: 250,000 people have no home whatsoever; they live, eat, defecate, mate, and die in the streets.

HONG KONG: Large numbers of families live in floating villages that tourists like to photograph. A family of six, eight, or ten occupies a home approximately the size of a rowboat.

CALI, COLOMBIA: When the rains come, the river rises and the sewers run through the homes of the poor.

HYDERABAD: Child labor employed in sealing the ends of cheap bracelets is paid eight cents per *gross* of bracelets.

KATMANDU, NEPAL: Life expectancy is between 35 and 40 years. Tuberculosis is chronic. One hears people coughing themselves to death at night.

NEW DELHI: "Oh, sir! Someone has dropped ice cream on your shoes! I will clean them." The tourist finds himself propped against a building, with two boys, each shining one shoe. "Oh, sir! Your laces are frayed. See, they break! I will sell you a new pair." The tourist buys the new pair. As he leaves, an Old India Hand says to him: "Have to watch those little beggars. Fling mud on your shoes." These are the tactics which poverty generates.

other directions. What is tragically characteristic of the underdeveloped areas is that this first corner of economic progress has not yet been turned.

Consider the situation of that all-important crop of the East, rice. Table 38.1 shows the difference between the productivity of rice fields in the main Asiatic countries and those of the United States, Australia, and Japan.

What is true of rice can be duplicated in most other crops.* It is a disconcerting fact that the backward peasant nations that depend desperately on their capacity to grow food cannot even compete in these main products with the advanced countries: Louisiana rice undersells Philippine rice, California oranges are not only better but cheaper than Indonesian oranges.

TABLE 38.1 RICE PRODUCTION 1975

	(100 kilograms per hectare)
U.S.	51.0
Australia	51.2
Japan	61.9
India	18.3
Indonesia	26.9
Thailand	17.1
Philippines	17.6
China	32.4

A vivid example of what "low productivity" means.

*Table 38.1 shows only the productive differentials of equal *areas* of land. When we consider that a single American farmer tends up to a hundred times as large an acreage as a peasant in an underdeveloped area, the difference of output *per man* would be much more striking. The "Green Revolution" (discussed near the end of the chapter) has improved the situation, but we do not yet have the data we need to determine outputs for the new rice strains. Despite the improvement, a vast gulf still separates U.S. agricultural productivity from that of the underdeveloped nations.

Why is agriculture so unproductive? One apparent reason is that the typical unit of agricultural production in the underdeveloped lands is far too small to permit efficient farming. "Postage stamp cultivation" marks the pattern of farming throughout most of Asia and a good deal of Africa and South America. John Gunther, reporting the situation in India over a generation ago, described it vividly. It has not changed materially since that time.

> There is no primogeniture in India as a rule, and when the peasant dies his land is subdivided among all his sons with the result that most holdings are infinitesimally small. In one district in the Punjab, following fragmentation through generations, 584 owners cultivate no less than 16,000 fields; in another, 12,800 acres are split into actually 63,000 holdings. Three-quarters of the holdings in India as a whole are under ten acres. In many parts of India the average holding is less than an acre.[1]

In part, this terrible situation is the result of divisive inheritance practices which Gunther mentions. In part, it is due to landlord systems which drain away the surplus from peasants' land; in part, to the pressure of too many people on too little soil. There are many causes, with one result: Agriculture suffers from a devastatingly low productivity brought about by grotesque man/land ratios.

These are, however, only the first links in a chain of causes for low agricultural productivity. Another consequence of these tiny plots is an inability to apply sufficient capital to the land. Mechanical binders and reapers, tractors and trucks are not only impossible to use efficiently in such tiny spaces, but they are costly beyond the reach of the subsistence farmer. Even fertilizer is too expensive: In much of Asia, animal dung is used to provide free fuel rather than returned to the soil to enrich it.

This paralyzing lack of capital is by no means confined to agriculture. It pervades the entire range of an underdeveloped economy. The whole industrial landscape of a Western economy is missing: No factories, no power lines, no machines, no paved roads meet the eye for mile upon mile as one travels through an underdeveloped continent. Indeed, to a pitiable extent, an underdeveloped land is one in which human and animal muscle power provide the energy with which production is carried on. In India in 1953, for instance, 65 percent of the total amount of productive energy in the nation was the product of straining man and beast. The amount of usable electrical power generated in *all of India* would not have sufficed to light up New York City. Of course, progress has been made since. But in 1975, energy consumption in India averaged 221 kg per capita (coal equivalent). By way of contrast, in Ireland it averaged 3,097 kg; in Canada, 9,880.

SOCIAL INERTIA

A lack of agricultural and industrial capital is not the only reason for low productivity. As we would expect in traditional societies, an endemic cause of low per capita output lies in prevailing social attitudes. Typically, the people of an underdeveloped economy have not *learned* the "economic" attitudes that foster rapid industrialization. Instead of technology-conscious farmers, they are tradition-bound peasants. Instead of disciplined workers, they are reluctant and

[1] *Inside Asia* (New York: Harper, 1939), p. 385.

untrained laborers. Instead of production-minded business people, they are trading-oriented merchants.

For example, in the 1960s Alvin Hansen reported from his observations in India:

> Agricultural practices are controlled by custom and tradition. A villager is fearful of science. For many villagers, insecticide is taboo because all life is sacred. A new and improved seed is suspect. To try it is a gamble. Fertilizers, for example, are indeed a risk. . . . To adopt these untried methods might be to risk failure. And failure could mean starvation.

In similar vein, a UNESCO report told us:

> In the least developed areas, the worker's attitude toward labour may entirely lack time perspective, let alone the concept of productive investment. For example, the day labourer in a rural area on his way to work, who finds a fish in the net he placed in the river the night before, is observed to return home, his needs being met. . . .

An equally crippling attitude is evinced by the upper classes, who look with scorn or disdain upon business or production-oriented careers, or who see in economic change a threat to their station in society. More than a decade ago, UNESCO reported that of the many students from the underdeveloped lands studying in the United States—the majority of whom come from the more privileged classes—only 4 percent were studying a problem fundamental to all their nations: agriculture. This has not changed over time.

All these attitudes give rise to a *social inertia* that poses a tremendous hurdle to economic development. A suspicious peasantry, fearful of change that might jeopardize the slim margin yielding them life, a work force unused to the rhythms of industrial production, a privileged class not interested in social change, all these are part of the obdurate handicaps to be overcome by an underdeveloped nation.

FURTHER PROBLEMS: POPULATION GROWTH

In these problem areas, the underdeveloped economy resembles the premarket economies of antiquity. But in addition to this, the underdeveloped lands often face an obstacle with which the economies of antiquity did *not* have to cope; a crushing rate of population increase that threatens to nullify their efforts to emerge from backward conditions.

Only a few figures are needed to make the point. Let us begin with our southern neighbor, Mexico. If Mexican population continues to grow at current rates, Mexico's population will rise from 67 million in 1979 to 600 million in only 70 years. If birth rates fall in accordance with the most optimistic estimates, Mexican population will still be a staggering 300 million in 70 years. Or take the Caribbean and Central American area. In some thirty years, at present growth rates, that small part of the globe will outnumber the entire population of the United States. South America, now 5 percent less populous than we, will be 200 percent larger than our present population. India could then number a billion souls.

We have already seen one result of the relentless proliferation of people in the fragmentation of landholdings. But the problem goes beyond mere fragmentation. Eugene Black, formerly president of the International Bank for Reconstruction and Development (the World Bank) has written that in India a population equivalent to that of all Great Britain has been squeezed out of any landholding whatsoever—even though it still dwells in rural areas. Consequently, population pressure generates massive and widespread rural poverty, pushing inhabitants from the countryside into the already overcrowded cities. Five hundred families a day move into Jakarta from the surrounding Javanese countryside, where population has reached the fantastic figure of 1,100 per square mile.

Even these tragic repercussions of population growth are but side effects. The main problem is that population growth adds more mouths almost as fast as the underdeveloped nations manage to add more food. They cancel out much economic progress by literally eating up the small surpluses that might serve as a springboard for faster future growth.

Ironically, this population explosion in the underdeveloped countries is a fairly recent phenomenon, attributable largely to the incursion of Western medicine and public health into the low-income areas. Prior to World War II, the poorer countries held their population growth in check because death rates were nearly as high as birth rates. With insecticides and antibiotics, death rates have plunged dramatically. In Ceylon, for example, death rates dropped 40 percent in one year following the adoption of malaria control and other health measures. As death rates dropped in the underdeveloped areas, birth rates, for many reasons, continued high, despite efforts to introduce birth control. In the backward lands, children are not only a source of prestige and of household labor for the peasant family, but also the only possible source of "social security" for old age. The childless older couple could very well starve. As parents or grandparents, they are at least assured of a roof over their heads.

THE POPULATION OUTLOOK

Is there a solution to this problem? The mood of demographers has swung between despair and cautious hope over the past decades. New birth control methods have, from time to time, offered the chance for dramatic breakthroughs. Poor birth control programs have repeatedly dashed these hopes.

Today a mood of cautious optimism is to be found among most demographers. This is because the most recent figures show a truly significant drop in the birthrates of the underdeveloped world—the first large scale drop on record. Although their populations are still rising, because births outnumber deaths, it is now imaginable that within another generation the population flood will have been tamed. **Demographers hope that population in the underdeveloped world will stabilize by the middle of the next century. It has already stabilized in the developed world.**

An important warning has to be sounded along with the optimism. For many poor nations, the population problem will not be solved just because birth control is now a worldwide reality. A peasant family that has only four children is still adding to population growth, even if not as seriously as when it had ten children; many poor nations will be pushed to the very brink of survival during the next two or three decades because of an inability to match mouths with food. Thus as a long-term problem, population is less of a concern than it was. As a short-term problem it continues high on the list of the world's ills.

NINETEENTH-CENTURY IMPERIALISM

This gives us a brief introduction to underdevelopment as it exists today. Before we turn to the problem of how this condition can be remedied, we must inquire into one more question. Why did not the market society, with all its economic dynamism, spread into the backward areas?

The answer is that the active economies of the European and American worlds *did* make contact with the underdeveloped regions, beginning with the great exploratory and commercial voyages of the fifteenth and sixteenth centuries. Until the nineteenth century, unfortunately, that contact was little more than mere adventure and plunder. And then, starting in the first half of that century and gaining momentum until World War I, came that scramble for territory we call the Age of Imperialism.

What was this imperialism? It was, in retrospect, a compound of many things: militarism, jingoism, a search for markets and for sources of cheap raw materials to feed growing industrial enterprises. Insofar as the colonial areas were concerned, however, the first impact of imperialism was not solely that of exploitation. On the contrary, the incursion of Western empires into the backward areas brought some advantages. It injected the heavy doses of industrial capital: rail lines, mines, plantation equipment. It brought law and order, often into areas in which the most despotic personal rule had previously been the order of the day. It introduced the ideas of the West, including, most importantly, the idea of freedom, which was eventually to rouse the backward nations against the invading West itself.

Yet if imperialism brought these positive and stimulating influences, it also exerted a peculiarly deforming impulse on the underdeveloped—indeed, then, totally undeveloped—economies of the East and South. In the eyes of the imperialist nations, the colonies were not areas to be brought along in balanced development, but essentially immense supply dumps to be attached to the mother country's industrial economy. Malaya became a vast tin mine; Indonesia, a huge tea and rubber plantation; Arabia, an oil field. In other words, economic development was steadily pushed in a direction that most benefited the imperial nations, not the underdeveloped countries themselves.

The result today is that the typical underdeveloped nation has a badly lopsided economy, unable to supply itself with a wide variety of goods. It is thereby thrust into the international market with its one basic commodity. For instance, in South America we find that Columbia is dependent on coffee for three-quarters of its exports; Chile, on copper for two-thirds of its foreign earnings; Honduras, on bananas for half of its foreign earnings. On the surface, this looks like a healthy specialization of trade. We shall shortly see why it may not be.

Economic lopsidedness was one unhappy consequence of imperialism. No less important for the future course of development in the colonial areas is a second decisive influence of the West: its failure to achieve political and psychological relationships of mutual respect with its colonial peoples. In part, this was no doubt traceable to an often frankly exploitative economic attitude, in which the colonials were relegated to second-class jobs with third-class pay, while a handful of Western whites formed an insulated and highly paid managerial clique. But it ran deeper than that. A terrible color line, a callous indifference to colonial aspirations, a patronizing and sometimes contemptuous view of "the natives" runs all through the history of imperialism. It has left as a bitter heritage not only an identification of capitalism with its worst practices, but a political and social wariness toward the West, a wariness that deeply affects the general orientation of the developing areas.

IMPERIALISM TODAY

What about imperialism today? Certainly it has changed. The naked land grabs are in the past, when imperialism often meant only the acquisition of territory that would look good on a map. In the past, also, are the seizures of raw materials on the unfair terms characteristic of mineral empires built in the late nineteenth century. Less prominent are attitudes of racial superiority, so infuriating to peoples whose culture was often of far greater delicacy and discrimination than that of the West.

Thus, the nature of this imperialism is now changing, partly under the pressures exerted by a restive Third World, partly as a result of developments within the advanced nations themselves. Imperialism today refers, as much as anything else, to the exposure of traditional societies to the full blast of the powerful market forces emanating from the capitalist core of industrial societies—a blast that often violently upsets traditional societies as they are pulled, willy nilly, into the world market.

Curiously enough, this raises questions that reverse to some extent the older problems of imperialism. For example, the rise of the multinational corporation puts the relationship of advanced and backward countries in a new light. The fear of being drawn into the world market on disadvantageous terms, and of being subordinated to the dictates of foreign enterprises, continues to mobilize sentiment against imperialism in the underdeveloped world. At the same time, the backward nations also want some of the things the multinationals offer. Big multinationals pay higher wages, keep more honest books, provide better working conditions and fancier career opportunities, and bring in more technological expertise than do the domestic enterprises of the host nation.

The result is that the problem of imperialism in our day has taken an unexpected turn. On the economic side of the question, the danger now is as much that the big companies will bypass the backward nations as that they will dominate them.

Meanwhile, the political element of imperialism seems to be diminishing. The erstwhile capitalist empires of Germany, Belgium, Netherlands, England, Portugal, have disappeared. What is left is a strong effort on the part of the United States to preserve its ideological and political influence, particularly in Latin America and Southeast Asia, but the debacle of the American Vietnam policy indicates that the prospects for a successful policy of this kind are limited, at best.

THE ENGINEERING OF DEVELOPMENT

Up to this point we have concentrated our attention mainly on the background of underdevelopment. Now we must ask a more forward-looking, more technically "economic" question: How can an underdeveloped nation emerge from its poverty?

From what we have learned, we know the basic answer to this question. To grow, an underdeveloped economy must build capital.

But how is a starving country able to build capital? When 80 percent of a country is scrabbling on the land for a bare subsistence, how can it divert its energies to building dams and roads, ditches and houses, railroad embankments and factories that, however indispensable for progress tomorrow, cannot be eaten today? If our postage-stamp farmers were to halt work on their tiny unproductive plots and go to work on a great project like, say, the Aswan Dam, who would feed them? Whence would come the necessary food to sustain these capital workers?

BUILDING CAPITAL FROM SAVED LABOR

At first glance the situation seems hopeless. Still, when we look again at the underdeveloped lands, the prospect is not entirely bleak. In the first place, these economies have unemployed factors. In the second place, we find that a large number of the peasants who till the fields are not feeding themselves. They are also, in a sense, taking food from one another's mouths.

As we have seen, the crowding of peasants on the land in these areas has resulted in a diminution of agricultural productivity far below that of the advanced countries. Hence the abundance of peasants working in the fields obscures the fact that *a smaller number of peasants, with little more equipment—perhaps even with no more equipment—could raise a total output just as large.* **By raising the productivity of the tillers of the soil, a work force can be made available for the building of roads and dams, while this transfer to capital building need not result in a diminution of agricultural output.**

SAVING OUTPUT

This rationalization of agriculture is not the only requirement for growth. **When agricultural productivity is enhanced by the creation of larger farms** (or **by improved techniques on existing farms), part of the ensuing larger output per person must be saved.** In other words, peasants who remain on the soil cannot enjoy their enhanced productivity by raising their standard of living and eating up all their larger crops. Instead, the gain in output per cultivator must be siphoned off the farm. It must be saved by the peasant cultivators and shared with their formerly unproductive cousins, nephews, sons, and daughters who are now at work on capital-building projects. We do not expect hungry peasants to do this voluntarily. Rather, by taxation or exaction, the government of an underdeveloped land must arrange for this indispensable transfer. Thus in the early stages of a *successful* development program there is apt to be no visible rise in the individual peasants' food *consumption,* although there must be a rise in their food *production.* What is apt to be visible is a more or less efficient—and sometimes harsh—mechanism for assuring that some portion of this newly added productivity is not consumed on the farm but is made available to support the capital-building worker. This is a problem that caused the Russian planners much trouble in the early days of Soviet industrialization.

What we have just outlined is not, let us emphasize, a formula for immediate action. In many underdeveloped lands, as we have seen, the countryside already crawls with unemployment, and to create, overnight, a large and efficient farming operation would create an intolerable social situation. We should think of the process we have just outlined as a long-term blueprint which covers the course of development over many years. It shows us that the process of development takes the form of a huge internal migration from agricultural pursuits, where labor is wasted, to industrial and other pursuits, where it can yield a net contribution to the nation's progress.

PROBLEM OF EQUIPMENT

Capital building is not just a matter of freeing hands and providing them with food. Peasant labor may construct roads, but it cannot, with its bare hands, build the trucks to run over the roads. It may throw up dams, but it cannot fashion the generators and power lines through which a dam can produce energy. In other words, what is needed to engineer the great ascent is not just a pool of labor. It is also a vast array of industrial equipment.

How is this equipment obtained? In an industrialized economy, by expanding the machine-tool (the capital equipment building) subsector. But an underdeveloped economy does not have a capital-equipment building sector and cannot take the time to create one. Consequently, **in the first stages of industrialization, before the nucleus of a self-contained industrial sector has been laid down, a backward nation must obtain its equipment from abroad.**

This it can do in one of three ways. (1) It can buy the equipment from an industrialized nation by the normal process of *foreign trade.* Libya, for example, can sell its oil and use the foreign currency it receives to purchase abroad the tractors, lathes, and industrial equipment it needs. (2) It can receive the equipment by *foreign investment* when a corporation in an advanced nation chooses to build in a backward area. This is the route by which the United States got much of its capital from Britain during the nineteenth century, and it is the means by which the underdeveloped nations themselves received capital during their colonial days. (3) It may receive the foreign exchange needed to buy industrial equipment as a result of a grant or a loan from another nation or from a United Nations agency such as the World Bank. That is, it can buy industrial equipment with *foreign aid.*

(1) FOREIGN TRADE

Of these three avenues of industrialization, the most important is foreign trade. In 1974 the underdeveloped nations earned just over $100 billion from exports. By no means all of this was available for new capital goods, however. About $60 billion was needed for food and vital raw materials. Some $10 billion was needed to pay interest on foreign debts. This left $30 billion for *all* manufactures, from pharmaceuticals and Mercedes Benzes to lathes, tractors, and jet aircraft.

A problem that has plagued the underdeveloped world in seeking to increase its trade earnings is that their lopsided economies have typically made them sellers of raw materials on the world market.

As sellers of raw commodities—usually only one raw commodity—they face a highly inelastic demand for their goods. Like the American farmer, when they produce a bumper crop, prices tend to fall precipitously and demand does not rise proportionately. At the same time, the industrial materials they buy in exchange tend to be firm or to rise in price over the years.

Terms of trade. Thus the terms of trade—the actual *quid pro quo* of goods received against goods offered—have usually moved against the poorer nations, who have given more and more coffee for the same amount of machinery. In 1957 and 1958, when commodity prices took a particularly bad tumble, the poor nations actually lost more in purchasing power than the total amount of all foreign aid they received. In effect, they subsidized the advanced nations! As another example, it has been estimated that falling prices cost the African nations more, in the first two decades since World War II, than all foreign funds given, loaned, or invested there.

It is possible—we do not yet know—that tightening markets in resources may now reverse this trend. The last few years have seen enormous sums flowing into the coffers of Middle Eastern governments, many of whom may become lenders, not borrowers, on the international capital markets. If the world resource picture worsens, the underdeveloped countries may find themselves the beneficiaries of inelastic demand curves, and the developed nations may be the ones complaining about the terms of world trade.

Third and fourth worlds. In fact, the example of OPEC (the Organization of Petroleum Exporting Countries) has raised the possibility that the underdeveloped world must now be considered as consisting of at least two subworlds. One consists of those nations with low per capita GNPs that possess the raw material resources, or in some cases the organizational skills, to give promise of a potential fairly rapid rise in per capita incomes. Mexico, with its huge oil deposits is such a country; Brazil, another; Venezuela, a third.

Contrasting with this third world is a fourth, made up of those nations that seem at present to offer little or no hope for rapid growth. Bangladesh, Burma,

HUMAN CAPITAL AGAIN

An allied problem of no less importance arises from the lack of technical training on which industrialization critically depends. At the lowest level, this is evidenced by appalling rates of illiteracy (up to 80 or 90 percent) which makes it impossible, for instance, to print instructions on a machine or a product and expect them to be followed. And at a more advanced level, the lack of expert training becomes an even more pinching bottleneck. Before Nigeria's destructive civil war, United Nations economists figured that Nigeria alone would need some 20,000 top-level administrators, executives, technicians, etc., and twice as many subordinates over the next 10 years. On a world-wide scale, this implies a need for at least 700,000 top-level personnel and 1,400,000 second-level assistants. Not 1 percent of these skilled personnel exists today in the poor countries, and to "produce" them will be a task of staggering difficulty. Yet, without them it is often impossible to translate development plans into actuality.

Egypt, Ethiopia, India, and Pakistan are among these least hopeful nations whose aggregate population is well over one billion.

Even among many third world nations (except for the oil producers), foreign exchange reserves are still very scarce, and the effort to increase them by exports is intense. One way that has commanded more and more attention is through the development of *commodity stabilization agreements,* not dissimilar to the programs that have long supported American farm prices. Recently, the Western nations have recognized the need for some such device if the underdeveloped countries are to be able to plan ahead with any assurance of stability.

Another possibility lies in the prospect of encouraging diversified exports from the underdeveloped nations—handicrafts, light manufactures, and others. The difficulty here is that these exports may compete with the domestic industry of the advanced nations: witness the problems of the American textile industry in the face of textile shipments from Hong Kong. No doubt a large source of potential earnings lies along this path, and it is likely to rise as the advanced nations gradually allow the backward countries more equal access to their own markets.

(2) FOREIGN INVESTMENT

A second main avenue of capital accumulation for the backward nations is foreign investment. Indeed, before World War II, this was *the* source of their industrial wealth. Today, however, it is a much diminished avenue of assistance. The former capital-exporting nations are no longer eager to invest private funds in areas over which they have lost control and in which they fear to lose any new investments thay might make. For reasons that we have discussed, many of the poorer nations view Western capitalism with ambivalence. They need capital, technology, and expertise; but the arrival of a branch of a powerful corporation run by faraway headquarters looks to them like another form of the domination they have just escaped. As a result, foreign investment is often hampered by restrictive legislation in the underdeveloped nations, even though it is badly needed.

In 1975, $21 billion of private capital was invested in the developing countries, but nearly all of it went to the higher income nations. Probably not much more than $3 billion went overseas as foreign investment into the poorest fourth world nations.

Another difficulty is that Western corporations partially offset the growth-producing effects of their investments by draining profits out of the country. In the period 1950–1965, for example, the flow of income remitted from Latin America to the United States was $11.3 billion, three times larger than the flow of new capital into Latin America. In 1978, income of $4.5 billion was transmitted to the United States, and only $3.7 billion was sent back to Latin America. This pattern of economic flow should not be misinterpreted as implying that foreign investment is a negative influence: The plant and equipment that the West has sent abroad remains in the underdeveloped world, where it continues to enhance the productivity of labor, or perhaps to generate exports. But the *earnings* on this capital are not typically plowed back into still more capital goods, so that their potential growth-producing effect is far from realized.

THE GREEN REVOLUTION

In the critical life-and-death race between mushrooming populations and recalcitrant nature, hopes have been buoyed by the Green Revolution, the name given to efforts to discover high-yielding strains of rice and wheat. Working in field laboratories in Mexico and elsewhere, scientists of the Rockefeller Institute have developed a number of promising new varieties, including the famous IR-8 rice. Some of these new varieties allow two and even three crops to be grown where formerly only one was harvested.

The Green Revolution has been a considerable scientific triumph, but its impact on development has been less spectacular. For one thing, the new strains require vast amounts of fertilizer and water, both in short supply in those areas of the world where present yields are lowest. Second, because the seeds require complementary inputs of fertilizers or tube-well irrigation ditches, the new grains are mainly introduced by the richer peasants. In lands where transportation facilities are lacking, their bumper crops may not find a ready market, and local prices may fall, to the despair of the poor peasant whose output has not risen. Thus the Green Revolution may actually contribute to the poverty of the lowest classes.

These social repercussions, coupled with the vast costs needed to introduce the new seeds on a wide basis, have tempered the first rosy expectations of the food scientists. Nonetheless, the Green Revolution is vital in enabling the world to buy a little precious time while birth control efforts and new production and distribution techniques are worked out.

(3) FOREIGN AID

These considerations enable us to understand the special importance that attaches to the third channel of capital accumulation: foreign aid. Surprisingly, perhaps, in the light of the attention it attracts, foreign aid is not a very large figure. International assistance, from *all* individual nations and from the UN and its agencies, ran at a rate of about $6 billion per year throughout the 1960s and rose to $14 billion only after the OPEC nations devoted considerable sums from their oil earnings for development purposes.

Even $14 billion is an insignificant figure compared with the total GNP of the underdeveloped world. But it is a sizeable fraction—perhaps as much as 15 percent—of the gross investment of South Asia, and more than that in poorest Africa.

In addition, foreign aid plays a number of subsidiary roles not performed by private investment. It is the source of much technical assistance, which allows the underdeveloped countries to overcome handicaps imposed by their lack of skilled personnel. Aid also provides food, often desperately needed in times of crop failure—the United States food program has been a major source of famine relief to Asia and Africa. In addition, foreign aid is sometimes given in "soft" loans repayable in the currency of the developing nation rather than in scarce hard currencies. Such loans are unobtainable from private lenders.

All these forms of international assistance make possible the accumulation of industrial capital much faster than could be accomplished solely as a result of the backward lands' export efforts or their ability to attract foreign private capital.* To be sure, an increase in foreign earnings or in private capital imports would have equally powerful effects on growth. But we have seen the difficulties in the way of rapidly increasing the receipts from these sources. For the near future, foreign aid represents the most effective channel for *quickly* raising the amount of industrial capital which the underdeveloped nations must obtain.

ECONOMIC POSSIBILITIES FOR GROWTH

Against these handicaps, can the underdeveloped nations grow? Can the terrible conditions of poverty be relegated to the past? Economic analysis allows us to ask these questions systematically, for growth depends on the interplay of three variables.

1. The rate of investment that an underdeveloped nation can generate

As we know, this depends on the proportion of current effort that it can devote to capital-creating activity. In turn, the rate of saving, the success in attracting foreign capital, the volume of foreign aid—all add to this critical fraction of effort on which growth hinges. **The *rate of investment* is the driving force of growth.**

2. Productivity of the new capital

The saving that goes into new capital eventually results in higher output. But not all capital boosts output by an equal amount. A million-dollar steel mill, for example, will have an impact on GNP very different from that of a million-dollar investment in schools. In the short run, the mill may yield a higher return of output per unit of capital investment; in the long run, the school may have the edge. But in any event, the effect on output will depend not merely on the amount of investment, but on the **marginal capital/output ratio** of the particular form of investment chosen.

3. Population growth

Here as we know, is the negative factor. If growth is to be achieved, **output must rise faster than population.** Otherwise, per capita output will be falling or static, despite seemingly large rates of overall growth.

CAPITAL/OUTPUT RATIO

With these basic variables, is growth a possibility for the backward lands? We can see that if investment were 10 percent of GNP and if each dollar of new investment gave rise to a third of a dollar of additional output, a 10 percent rate of capital formation would yield a 3.3 percent rate of growth of output (10 percent × one-third). This is about equal to population growth rates in the nations with the highest rates of population increase.

The trouble is that most of the backward nations, especially in the fourth world, have investment rates that are closer to 5 than to 10 percent of GNP. In that case, even with a marginal capital/output ratio of one-half, growth rates

*Note "make possible." There is some disturbing evidence that foreign aid may displace domestic saving, so that an underdeveloped country receiving aid may relax its own efforts to generate capital. Much depends on the political will of the recipient country.

would not be enough to begin a sustained climb against a population growth of 2.5 percent (5 percent × ½ = 2.5 percent). And this gloomy calculation is made gloomier still when we confront the fact that the labor force is rising faster than the population as a whole, as vast numbers of children become vast numbers of workers. In the 1970s in Latin America it was estimated that at least 25 *percent* of the working-age population was unemployed. In the decade since then, unemployment as a percent of the labor force seems to have increased in virtually every underdeveloped country.

THE RANGE OF PERFORMANCE

No one can confront these realities and fail to be impressed with the harshness of the outlook for the underdeveloped world. Overall, the 140 third and fourth world countries have barely made perceptible progress during the last fifteen years of unprecedented developmental effort. Indeed, the World Bank, looking back recently on the period 1960–1974, discovered to its dismay that 40 percent of the populations of these countries, despite statistics that seemed to indicate growth, remained in a condition of "absolute poverty."[2]

To be sure, there are important exceptions to this generally disappointing performance. The OPEC nations, as we have noted, are forging ahead on their oil revenues, and some of them now have very high growth rates. So, too, a number of non-OPEC nations have succeeded in mobilizing foreign and domestic capital and national and international entrepreneurship to create extremely impressive growth records, as Table 38.2 shows.

TABLE 38.2 SELECTED GROWTH RATES, GNP PER CAPITA, 1960–1974

	Percent
Singapore	7.6
Republic of Korea	7.3
Hong Kong	6.6
Taiwan	6.5
Puerto Rico	5.3
Brazil	6.3

Source: Jameson and Wilbur, op. cit.

Some underdeveloped countries have shown an impressive growth rate.

SOCIAL STRESSES

Unfortunately, that is not an end to the story. Even the most successful economic development imposes enormous strains on society. This is because the process of dynamic change, especially under the aegis of a market system, does not lift all sectors or classes equally. On the contrary, it favors some and disfavors others, sometimes actually depressing their standard of well-being, at other times merely exposing them to the sense of being unfairly left behind. The skyscrapers that symbolize development in so many surging nations are often within the sight of persons who must still live in mud huts, and the new factories are just around the corner from artisans' stalls. In fact, the artisans may now be exposed

[2]Gerald Meier, ed., *Leading Issues in Economic Development* (N.Y.: Oxford University Press, 1979) pp. 1, 5, 395. See also Kenneth Jameson and Charles K. Wilbur, *Economic Directions in Development* (Notre Dame: Univ. of Notre Dame Press, 1979), pp. 188, 189.

to the blast of competition from goods made in those factories, and the dwellers in those mud huts are exposed to the unsettling influence of a way of life that they never knew existed.

Thus economic development typically brings discontent. The gulf between rich and poor widens; resentments and fears sharpen. The revolution in Iran, once thought to be a paragon of successful development, reveals how unstable can be the social situation in an economically prosperous society—an instability that is very likely present in many booming Middle Eastern nations, as well as in some of the fast-growing Asian and Latin American success stories.

THE POLITICAL SIDE

These considerations enable us to understand how social tensions and economic standards can rise at the same time. And this prospect, in turn, enables us to appreciate the fearful demands on political leadership, which must provide impetus, inspiration, and, if necessary, discipline to keep the great ascent in motion. The stresses of the early industrial revolution in England, with its widening chasm between proletariat and capitalist, are not to be forgotten when we project the likely course of affairs in the developing nations.

In the politically immature and labile areas of the underdeveloped world, this exercise of leadership typically assumes the form of "strong-man" government. In large part, this is only the perpetuation of age-old tendencies in these areas; but in the special environment of development, a new source of encouragement for dictatorial government arises from the exigencies of the economic process itself. Powerful, even ruthless government may be needed, not only to begin the development process, but to cope with the strains of a *successful* development program.

It is not surprising, then, that the political map reveals the presence of authoritarian governments in many developing nations today. The communist areas aside, we find more or less authoritarian rule in Egypt, Pakistan, Burma, South Korea, Indonesia, and a succession of South American juntas. From country to country, the severity and ideological coloring of these governments varies. Yet in all of them we find that the problems of economic development provide a significant rationale for the tightening of political control. At least in the arduous early stages of growth, some form of political command seems as integral to economic development as the accumulation of capital itself. What this portends for the political future of the world is the question to which our last chapter is addressed.

KEY CONCEPTS

The conditions of underdevelopment are a complex amalgam of tradition, low productivity, social inertia, and population pressure

LOOKING BACK

1. Underdeveloped nations are traditional societies. Typically they evidence extremely low rates of growth, poor productivity, and considerable social inertia. In addition, their problems are often compounded by high rates of population growth. This last problem is now less threatening for the long run, but it is still a major short-run hurdle.

Imperialism has been a common shaping experience of the underdeveloped countries. Imperialism today still exposes traditional societies to world market forces

2. The underdeveloped countries have all had experience with imperialism. In the nineteenth century this was a combination of economic exploitation, military conquest, and socio-political intolerance. In our own time, it is mainly evidenced in the exposure of the backward lands to the ruthless forces of the world market. This is a two-sided process, for the multinationals also bring benefits of technology and efficiency.

Development is a capital-building process

3. The development process hinges on building capital. This can be done by economizing on the labor used for agriculture and directing it to capital projects. But the rise in agricultural productivity must be used to support those working on capital projects, not for the higher consumption of agricultural workers.

Capital equipment cannot be generated by shifting labor from agriculture. The main source is foreign trade

4. Not all capital can be accumulated by saving agricultural labor and redirecting it to capital-building projects. Equipment of various sorts must also be acquired. The main avenue of acquisition is foreign trade. Until recently the terms of trade have been adverse for most underdeveloped lands; the rise of OPEC has changed that, at least for the oil-producing countries.

Private foreign investment, mainly through multinationals, brings productivity but imposes a drain in foreign exchange

5. Private foreign investment is a second source of capital and technology. Here we encounter the complex problems posed by the relations of the underdeveloped lands and the multinationals. The repatriation of profits means that foreign investment creates a foreign exchange problem for the backward countries although foreign investment enhances productivity.

The UN remains an important source of aid

6. International aid, both bilateral and through the United Nations, remains a very important source of capital, technology, and relief.

Development is a function of investment and its productivity—divided by population growth

7. The rate of economic growth depends on the amount of investment, its productivity (the capital/output ratio), and on population growth, a negative factor.

Social and political strains are inseparable from development

8. Social and political stress is inseparable from economic change. Development is likely to give rise to strong-man governments to cope with those stresses.

ECONOMIC VOCABULARY

Imperialism 612 **Terms of trade** 616 **Capital/output ratio** 619

QUESTIONS

1. In what ways do you think underdeveloped countries are different from the American Colonies in the mid-1600s? Think of literacy, attitudes toward work and thrift, and other such factors. What about the relationship to more advanced nations in each case?
2. Why do you think it is so difficult to change social attitudes at the lowest levels of society? At the upper levels? Are there different reasons for social inertia at different stations in society?

3. Many economists have suggested that all advanced nations should give about 1 percent of their GNP for foreign aid. In the U.S., that would mean a foreign aid appropriation of $25 billion. We now appropriate about $3 billion. Do you think it would be practicable to suggest a 1 percent levy? How would the country feel about such a program?
4. What are the main variables in determining whether or not growth will be self-sustaining? If net investment were 8 percent of GNP and the capital/output ratio were ¼, could a nation grow if its rate of population increase were 2¼ percent? What changes could initiate growth?
5. What do you think is the likelihood of the appearance of strong-arm governments in the underdeveloped world? For the emergence of capitalist economies? Socialist ones? Is it possible to make predictions or judgments in these matters that do not accord with your personal preferences?

AN EXTRA WORD ABOUT
UNDERDEVELOPMENT

It is difficult to compress the problem of underdevelopment into one chapter; it deserves book-length treatment. But here is a small array of charts and tables* that will give you more perspective on underdevelopment. We have presented them without comment, because they speak for themselves. They will repay a few minutes of your time now by giving you food for many hours of reflection afterward.

TABLE 38.3 POPULATIONS HAVING INSUFFICIENT PROTEIN/ENERGY SUPPLY, 1970

	Total population (millions)	*Population with insufficient protein/energy supply*	
		Millions	*Percent*
Developed countries*	**1,072**	28	3
Developing countries†	**1,755**	434	25
Latin America	**284**	36	13
Africa	**279**	67	24
Near East	**171**	30	18
Far East	**1,021**	301	30
World†	**2,827**	462	16

Note: The table is based on the daily per capita supply of grams of protein and kilocalories contained in the food locally available.
*Europe, North America, U.S.S.R., and Japan.
†Excluding Asian centrally planned economies.

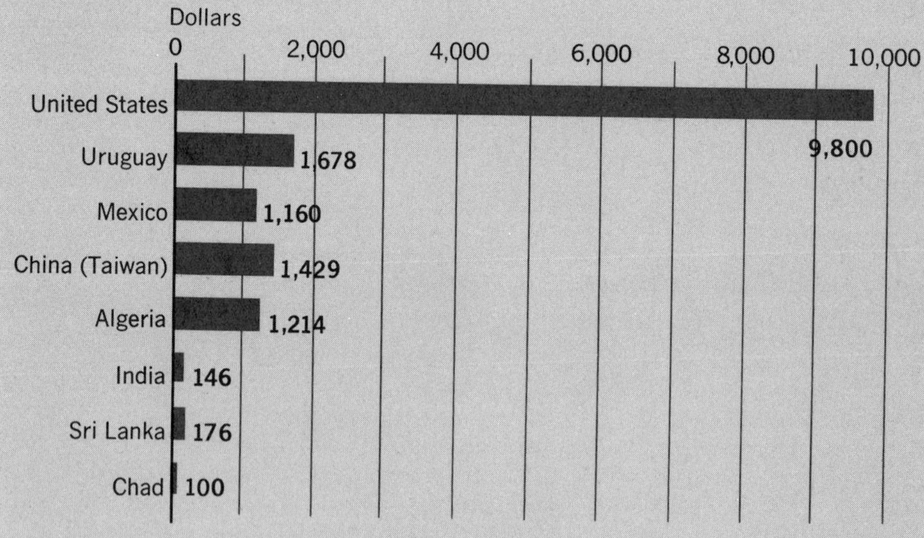

FIGURE 38.1 PER CAPITA GNPs, 1973

*From Overseas Development Council, *The U.S. and World Development* (New York: Praeger, 1976).

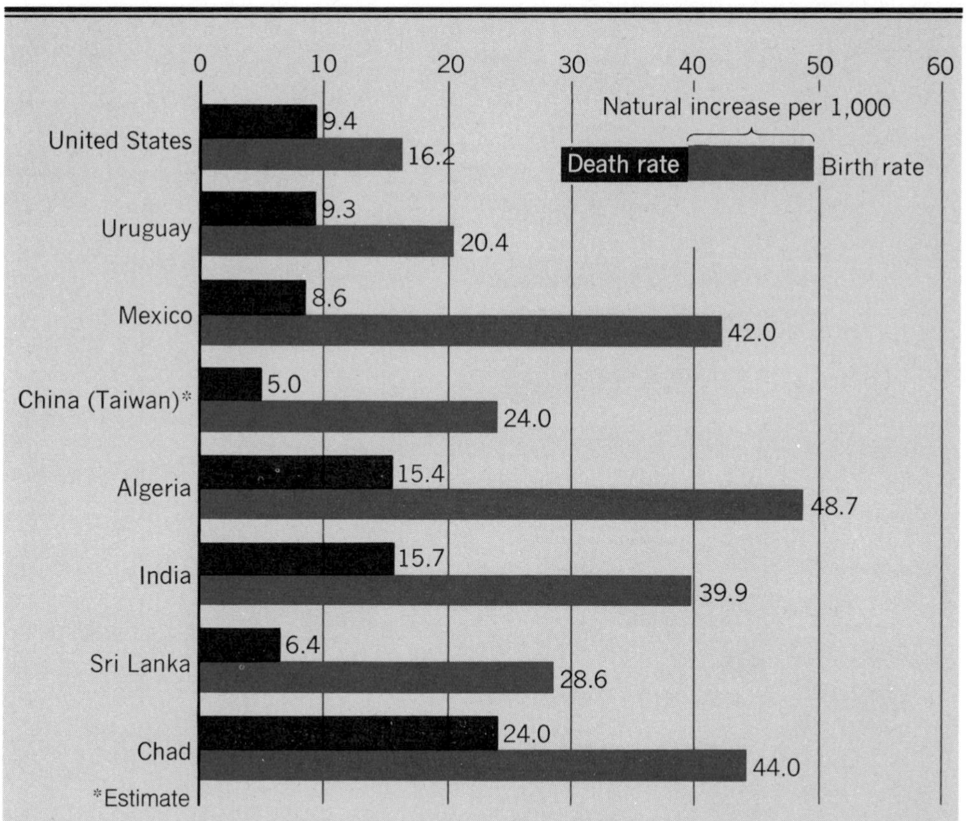

FIGURE 38.2

Death and birth rates per 1,000 (1970–1975 average).

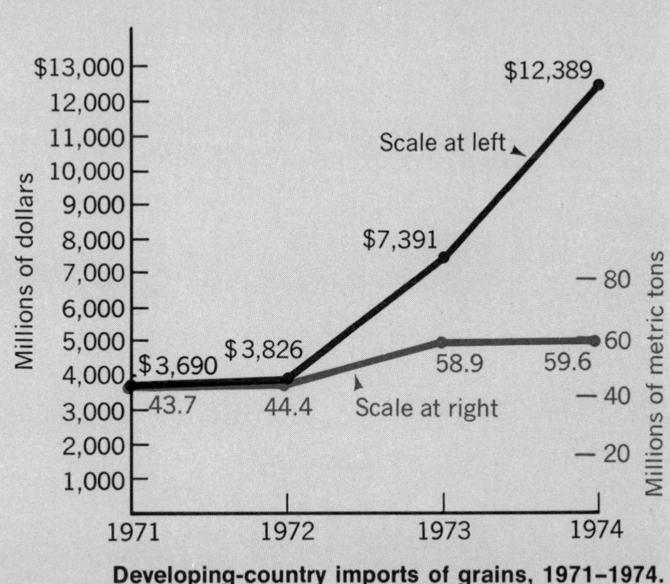

FIGURE 38.3

Developing-country imports of grains, 1971–1974.

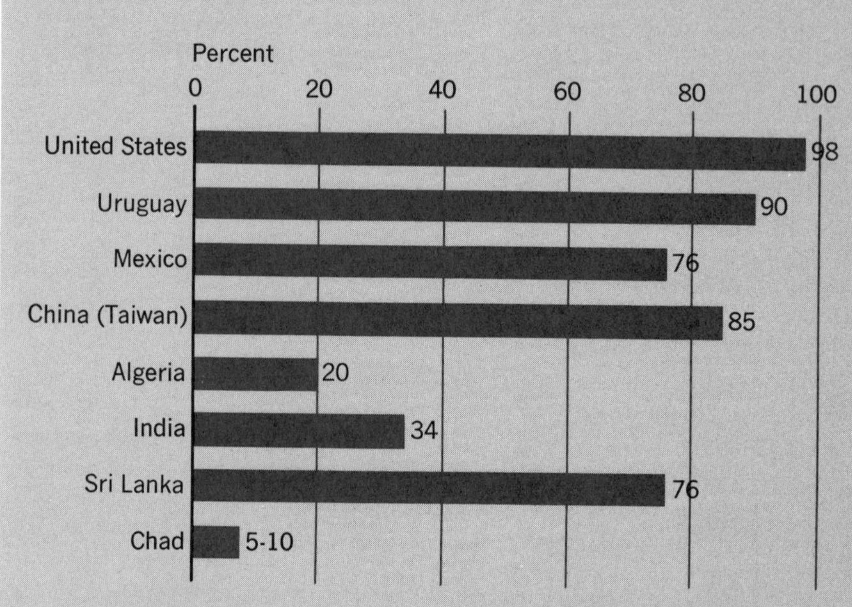

FIGURE 38.4 LITERACY (PERCENTAGES) 1974

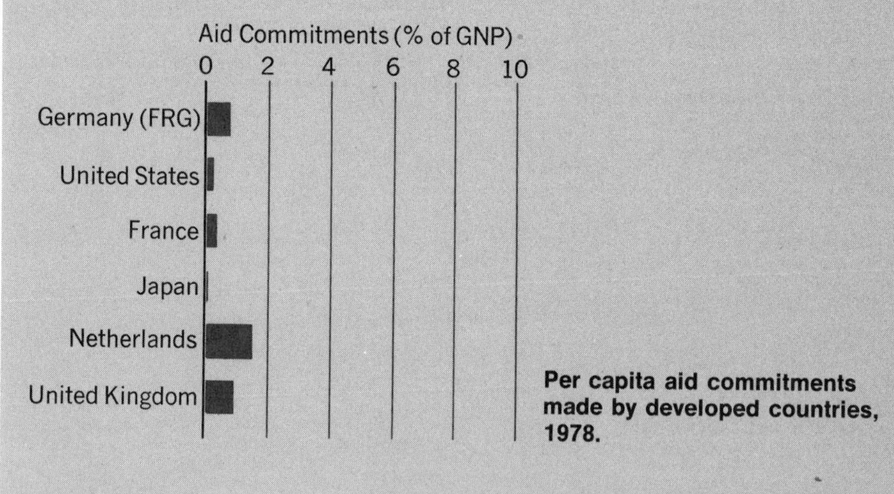

Per capita aid commitments made by developed countries, 1978.

FIGURE 38.5

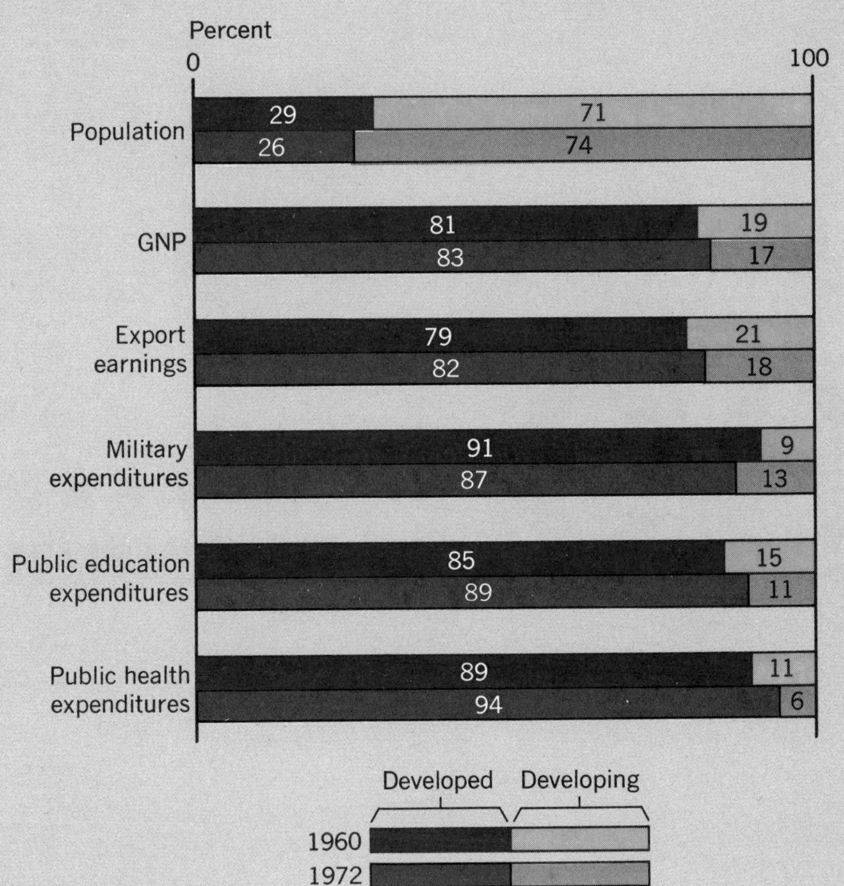

FIGURE 38.6

Relative shares of selected resources and expenditures of developed and developing countries, 1972 (percentages).

Chapter 39 FROM MARKET TO PLANNING

A LOOK AHEAD

At the end of our book, we step back for a long historic overview.

(1) This leads us to consider the relationship of the market system to societies in different stages of historic evolution.

(2) From here we look to the development of the system of planning—first in a centrally planned system such as the USSR, then as a direction in which market societies themselves seem to be slowly moving.

(3) Last, we try to take the measure of the strengths and weaknesses of market and planned economic societies, and to identify the problems shared by both.

The beginning of worldwide economic development is a genuine watershed in human history. An active and dynamic form of economic life, until recently the distinctive characteristic of the industrial West, is about to be generalized over the face of the globe. The process of diffusion will take generations, but it marks a profound, irreversible, and truly historic alteration in the economic condition of humankind.

Yet, if the process of economic growth is henceforth to be carried out on a global scale, it is also clear that there will be significant change in the auspices under which this process is likely to unfold. It is command rather than the market system which is in the ascendant as the driving force in the underdeveloped regions. And when we combine the geographic extent of these regions with those where communism has become firmly entrenched, it seems that command now bids fair to become *the* dominant means of organizing economic activity on this planet, as tradition was, not very long ago.

But again there is a difference. During the centuries when tradition held sway over most of the world, the economies run by the market system were the locus of progress and motion. Today one cannot with assurance say the same; nor will we be able to, in the future, for a preeminent motive of the rising economies of command is to *displace* the market societies as the source of the world's economic vitality.

Does this mean that economic history now writes finis to the market system? Does it mean that the market, as a means of solving the economic problem, is about to be relegated to the museum of economic antiquities or at best limited to the confines of North America, Western Europe, and Japan? The question brings to a focus our continuing concern with the market system. Let us attempt in these last pages to appraise its prospects.

STAGES OF ECONOMIC DEVELOPMENT

We might well begin an appraisal by taking a last survey of the array of economic systems that mark our times. It is, at first glance, an extraordinary assortment: We find, in this fourth quarter of the twentieth century, a spectrum of economic organization that represents virtually every stage in economic history, from the earliest and most primitive. But at second look, a significant pattern can be seen within this seemingly disordered assemblage. The few remaining wholly traditional economies, such as those of the South Seas or tribal Africa, have not yet begun to move into the mainstream of economic development. A much larger group of underdeveloped nations, in which institutions of economic command are now rising amid a still traditional environment, have just commenced their development efforts and are now coping with the initial problems preparatory to eventual all-out industrialization. Going yet further along we find the economies of full command, such as China and Russia. Here we find national communities that are (or recently were) wrestling with the gigantic task of rapid massive modernization. Finally, we pass to the market economies of the West, to encounter societies with their developmental days behind them, now concerned with the operation of high-consumption economic systems.

The categorization suggests a very important general conclusion. The eco-

nomic structures of nations today bear an integral relation with their stage of economic development. Acts of foreign intervention aside, the choice of command or market systems is not just the outcome of political considerations or ideologies and preferences. It is also, and perhaps primarily, the result of functional requirements that are very different at different levels of economic achievement.

INCEPTION OF GROWTH

We have already noted this connection in our discussion of the underdeveloped areas. Now, however, we can place what we have learned into a wider frame of reference. For if we compare the trend of events in the underdeveloped economies with the equivalent stage of development in Western history, we see a significant point of resemblance between the two. The emergence of command in the development-minded countries today has a parallel in the mercantile era, when the Western nations also received a powerful impetus toward industrialization under the organizing influence of the "industry-minded" governments of the seventeenth and early eighteenth centuries.

Thereafter, to be sure, the resemblance ceases. In the West, following the first push of mercantilism, it was the market mechanism that provided the main directive force for growth; in the underdeveloped lands, as we have seen, this influence is likely to be preempted to a much larger extent by political and economic command.

PRESENT VS. PAST

Three main reasons lie behind this divergence of paths. **First, the underdeveloped areas today start from a lower level of preparedness than did the West in the seventeenth and eighteenth centuries.** Not only have the actual institutions of the market not yet appeared in many backward lands, but the whole process of acculturation has failed to duplicate that of the West. In many ways—not all of them economic—the West was ready for economic development. A similar readiness is not in evidence in the majority of the backward lands today, with the result that development, far from evincing itself as a spontaneous process, comes about as the result of enforced and imposed change.

Second, the West was able to mount its development effort in leisurely tempo. This is not to say that its rate of growth was slow or that strong pressures did not weigh upon many Western countries, arousing within them feelings of dissatisfaction with their progress. Yet the situation was unlike that of the backward areas today. Here immense pressures, both of population growth and of political impatience, create an overwhelming need and desire for speed. As a result, the process of growth is not allowed to mature quietly in the background of history, as it did for much of the West, but has been placed at the very center of political and social attention.

Finally, in a manner denied to the West, underdeveloped countries can see ahead of them the goal they seek to reach. Suffering from so many handicaps, they enjoy one not inconsiderable advantage. Because they are the rear-guard rather than the vanguard, they know where they are going. They do not wish to reach this goal, however, by retreading the painful and laborious path marked out by the West. Rather, they intend to shortcut it, to move directly to their chosen destination by utilizing the mechanisms of command to bring about the great alterations that must be made.

IS COMMAND SUCCESSFUL?

Can economic command significantly compress and accelerate the growth process? The remarkable performance of the Soviet Union suggests that it can. In 1920 Russia was but a minor figure in the economic councils of the world. Today it is a country whose economic achievements bear comparison with those of the United States. Russia has many economic problems that we will examine shortly. But no one can deny that it has made tremendous economic progress.

The case of China is less clear-cut. Until the famine disaster of 1959–1960, Chinese economic growth was double or triple that of India; since then, perhaps because of the convulsions of the Cultural Revolution, its record is less easy to appraise. We are not sure if it has grown more rapidly than India in *quantitative terms;* but by the reports of all observers, its *qualitative* improvements in health, education, and welfare are strikingly better than those of India.

But it is wise not to exaggerate the advantages of a command system. If it holds the potential for an all-out attack on backwardness, it also contains the possibilities of substantial failure, as in the disappointments of the planned Cuban economy. The mere existence of a will to plan is no guarantee that the plans will be well drawn or well carried out or reasonably well obeyed.

In addition, the striking economic success demonstrated by some market-run systems, such as those in Table 38.2 make it impossible to assert categorically that only a command system can move a traditional society off dead center. Thus there may be more Taiwans and Singapores in the future, as well as more Soviet Unions and Chinas. But looking at the very low level of development in much of the fourth world and the antipathy of many African, Asian, and Latin American countries for Western capitalist nations, it seems likely that command systems of one kind or another will play the major role in bringing development to the still lagging areas of the world.

PLANNING AND ITS PROBLEMS

What are the advantages, what are the problems of planning? The subject is large enough to fill many books, and this short chapter will not attempt to discuss the full economics of planning. But a few general remarks may serve as an introduction to the subject.

How is planning carried out? This question goes to the heart of the matter, for all planned economies have found their central difficulty in going from the vision of a general objective to the actual attainment of that objective in fact. It is one thing to plan for 6 percent growth, another to issue the directives to bring forth just the right amounts of (quite literally) hundreds of thousands of items, so that 6 percent growth will result.

SOVIET PLANNING

In the Soviet Union this complicated planning mechanism is carried out in successive stages. The overall objectives are originally formulated by the Gosplan,

SOCIALISM AND COMMUNISM

What is the difference between *socialism* and *communism?* In the West, *socialism* implies an adherence to democratic political mechanisms, whereas *communism* does not. But within the socialist bloc there is another interesting difference of definition. Socialism there represents a stage of development in which it is still necessary to use "bourgeois" incentives in order to make the economy function; that is, people must be paid in proportion to the "value" of their work. Under communism, a new form of human society will presumably have been achieved in which these selfish incentives will no longer be needed. Then will come the time when society will be able to put into effect Karl Marx's famous description of communism: "From each according to his ability; to each according to his need."

In a true communist economy—the final terminus of economic evolution according to Marx—there were hints that the necessary but humdrum tasks of production and distribution would take place by the voluntary cooperation of all citizens, and society would turn its serious attention to matters of cultural and humanistic importance. Indeed, in a famous passage in *State and Revolution,* Lenin described the activities of administering a socialist state as having been simplified by the previous stage of capitalism "to the utmost, till they have become the extraordinarily simple operations of watching, recording, and issuing receipts, within the reach of anybody who can read and who knows the first four rules of arithmetic."

the State Planning Agency. The long-term overall plan is then broken down into shorter one-year plans. These one-year plans, specifying the output of major sectors of industry, are then transmitted to various government ministries concerned with, for example, steel production, transportation, lumbering, and so forth. In turn, the ministries refer the one-year plans further down the line to the heads of large industrial plants, to experts and advisers, and so on. At each stage, the overall plan is thus unraveled into its subsidiary components, until finally the threads have been traced as far back as is feasible along the productive process—typically, to the officials in charge of actual factory operations. The factory manager of, for instance, a coking operation is given a planned objective for the next year, specifying the output needed from his plant. He confers with his production engineers, considers the condition of his machinery, the availability of his labor force, and then transmits his requirements for meeting the objective back upward along the hierarchy. In this way, just as "demand" is transmitted downward along the chain of command, the exigencies of "supply" flow back upward, finally reaching the top command of the planning authority, the Gosplan itself.

SUCCESS INDICATORS

The coordination and integration of these plans is a tremendously complicated task. Recently the Soviets adopted techniques of computer analysis which have considerably simplified the problem. Even with sophisticated planning techniques, however, the process is bureaucratic, cumbersome, slow, and mistake-prone. A Russian factory manager has very little leeway in what he produces or in the combination of factors that he uses for production. Both inputs and outputs are carefully specified for him in his plan. What the manager *is* supposed to do is to beat the plan, by overproducing the items that have been assigned to his plant. Indeed, from 30 to 50 percent of a manager's pay will depend on bonuses tied directly to his overfulfillment of the plan, so that he has a very great personal incentive to exceed the output "success indicators" set for him.

All this seems sensible enough. Trouble comes, however, because the manager's drive to exceed his factory's quota tends to distort the productive effort from the receivers' point of view. For example, if the target for a textile factory is set in terms of yards of cloth, there is every temptation to weave the cloth as loosely as possible, to get the maximum yardage out of a given amount of thread. Or if the plan merely calls for tonnages of output, there is every incentive to skimp on design or finish or quality, in order to concentrate on sheer weight. A cartoon in the Russian satirical magazine *Krokodil* shows a nail factory proudly displaying its record output: one gigantic nail suspended from an immense gantry crane. On the other hand, if a nail factory has its output specified in terms of the *numbers* of nails it produces, its incentive to overfulfill this "success indicator" is apt to result in the production of very small or thin nails.

PROFIT AS A "SUCCESS INDICATOR"

What is the way out of this kind of dilemma? A few years ago, a widely held opinion among the Russian planners was that more detailed and better integrated planning performed on a battery of computers would solve the problem. Few still cling to this belief. The demands of planning have grown far faster than the ability to meet them: Indeed, one Soviet mathematician has predicted that at the current rate of growth of the planning bureaucracy, planning alone would require the services of the entire Russian population by 1980. Even with the most complete computerization, it seems a hopeless task to attempt to beat the problem of efficiency by increasing the fineness of the planning mechanism.

For a time, the wind for reform in the Soviet Union blew from quite another quarter. **Led by economist E. G. Liberman, there was a growing demand that the misleading plan directives of weight, length, etc., be subordinated to a new "success indicator" independently capable of guiding the manager to results that will make sense from the overall point of view. And what is that overriding indicator? It was the *profit* that a factory manager could make for the enterprise!**

We should note several things about this profit. To begin with, it was not supposed to arise from price manipulations. Factory managers were to continue to operate with the prices established by planners; but they were to *sell* their output and *buy* their input, rather than merely deliver or accept them. This meant that each factory was to be responsive to the particular needs of its customers if it wished to dispose of its output. In the same way, of course, its own suppliers would have to be responsive to the factory's needs if the suppliers were to get the factory's business.

Second, the profit would belong not to the factory or its managers, but to the State. A portion of the profit would indeed be allocated for bonuses and other rewards, so that there would be a direct incentive to run the plant efficiently, but the bulk of the earnings would be transferred to the State.

PLANNING UNDER LENIN AND STALIN

Official literature of the Communist movement gives little guidance for running a socialist society. Marx's *Das Kapital,* the seminal work of communism, was entirely devoted to a study of capitalism; and in those few essays in which Marx looked to the future, his gaze rarely traveled beyond the watershed of the revolutionary act itself. With the achievement of the revolution, Marx thought, a temporary regime known as "the dictatorship of the proletariat" would take over the transition from capitalism to socialism, and thereafter a "planned socialist economy" would emerge as the first step toward a still less specified "communism."

Many of the problems of early Soviet history sprang from the total absence, on the part of its rulers, of any comprehension of the staggering difficulties of planning in fact rather than in thought. The initial Soviet attempt to run the economy was a disastrous failure. Under inept management (and often cavalier disregard of "bourgeois" concerns with factory management), industrial output declined precipitously; by 1920 it had fallen to *14 percent* of prewar levels. As goods available to the peasants became scarcer, the peasants themselves were less and less willing to acquiesce in giving up food to the cities. The result was a wild inflation followed by a degeneration into an economy of semibarter. For a while, toward the end of 1920, the system threatened to break down completely.

To forestall the impending collapse, in 1921 Lenin instituted a New Economic Policy, the so-called NEP. This was a return toward a market system and a partial reconstitution of actual capitalism. Retail trade, for instance, was opened again to private ownership and operation. Small-scale industry also reverted to private direction. Most important, the farms were no longer requisitioned but operated as profit-making units. Only the "commanding heights" of industry and finance were retained in government hands.

There ensued for several years a bitter debate about the course of action to follow next. While the basic aim of the Soviet government was still to industrialize and to socialize (i.e., to replace the private ownership of the means of production by state ownership), the question was how fast to move ahead—and, indeed, *how* to move ahead. The pace of industrialization hinged critically on one highly uncertain factor: the willingness of the large, pri-

THE MARKET AS A PLANNING TOOL

Thus, profits were to be used as an efficiency-maximizing indicator, just as we saw them used in our study of microeconomics.

Indeed, to view the change even more broadly, we can see that the reintroduction of the use of profits implied a deliberate return to the use of the *market mechanism* as a means of achieving economic efficiency. Not only profits but also interest charges—a capitalist term it would have been heresy to mention in the days of Stalin—were to be introduced into the planning mechanism to allow factory managers to determine for themselves what was the most efficient thing to do, both for their enterprises and for the economy as a whole.

This drift toward a market mechanism is still largely untried in the Soviet Union, and we do not know how far it will ultimately progress. The objectives of the most recent plans have called for a much greater emphasis on consumer goods, and speak of "an extensive use of economic-mathematical methods," which implies a continuing reliance on the computer rather than a rapid movevate peasant sector to deliver food for sustaining city workers. To what extent, therefore, should the need for additional capital goods be sacrificed in order to turn out the consumption goods that could be used as an inducement for peasant cooperation?

The argument was never truly resolved. In 1927 Stalin moved into command and the difficult question of how much to appease the unwilling peasant disappeared. Stalin simply made the ruthless decision to appease him not at all, but to *coerce* him by collectivizing his holdings.

The collectivization process solved in one swoop the problem of securing the essential transfer of food from the farm to the city, but it did so at a frightful social (and economic) cost. Many peasants slaughtered their livestock rather than hand it over to the new collective farms; others waged outright war or practiced sabotage. In reprisal, the authorities acted with brutal force. An estimated five million "kulaks" (rich peasants) were executed or put in labor camps, while in the cities an equally relentless policy showed itself vis-à-vis labor. Workers were summarily ordered to the tasks required by the central authorities. The right to strike was forbidden, and the trade unions were reduced to impotence. Speedups were widely applied, and living conditions were allowed to deteriorate to very low levels.

The history of this period of forced industrialization has left abiding scars on Russian society. It is well for us, nonetheless, to attempt to view it with some objectivity. If the extremes to which the Stalinist authorities went were extraordinary, often unpardonable, and perhaps self-defeating, we must bear in mind that industrialization on the grand scale has always been wrenching, always accompanied by economic sacrifice, and always carried out by the more or less authoritarian use of power.

We might note in passing that universal male suffrage was not gained in England until the late 1860s and 1870s; Aneurin Bevan has written: "It is highly doubtful whether the achievements of the Industrial Revolution would have been permitted if the franchise had been universal. It is very doubtful because a great deal of the capital aggregations that we are at present enjoying are the results of the wages that our fathers went without." (From Gunnar Myrdal, *Rich Lands and Poor.* New York: Harper, 1957, p. 46.)

ment in the direction of freer trade. Nonetheless, economists talk of *torgovat* (trading) instead of *snabzhat* (allocating). Gradually, market mechanisms seem to be insinuating themselves into the Soviet economic system. It is still not a market society—far from it—but that is the direction of change.

MARKET SOCIALISM

Meanwhile, the trend toward the market has proceeded much further in a large part of Eastern Europe; above all in Yugoslavia. There, the market rules very nearly as supreme as it does in Western capitalist countries. Yet the Yugoslavs certainly consider themselves a socialist economy. As in the U.S.S.R., enterprise profits do not go to the "owners" of the business but are distributed as incentive bonuses or used for investment or other purposes under the overall guidance of the State. And again as in the U.S.S.R., the market is used as a deliberate instrument of social control, rather than as an institution that is above question. **Thus, the main determination of investment, the direction of develop-**

ment of consumer goods, the basic distribution of income—all continue to be matters established at the center as part of a planned economy. More and more, however, this central plan is allowed to realize itself through the profit-seeking operations of highly autonomous firms, rather than through being imposed in full detail upon the economy.*

MARKET VS. PLAN

The drift of planning toward markets raises a question of fundamental importance. Why plan at all? Why not let the market take over the task of coordination that has proved such a formidable hurdle for industrial planners, for is not the market itself a planning mechanism?

After all, in the market the signal of profitability serves as the guide for allocation of resources and labor. Entrepreneurs, anticipating or following demand, risk private funds in the construction of the facilities that they hope the future will require. Meanwhile, as these industrial salients grow, smaller satellite industries grow along with them to cater to their needs.

The flow of materials is thus regulated in every sector by the forces of private demand making themselves known by the signal of rising or falling prices. At every moment there emanates from the growing industries a magnetic pull of demand on secondary industries, while in turn, the growth salients themselves are guided, spurred or slowed down by the pressure of demand from the ultimate buying public. And all the while, counterposed to these pulls of demand, are the obduracies of supply—the cost schedules of the producers themselves. In the cross fire of demand and supply exists a marvelously sensitive social instrument for the integration of the overall economic effort of expansion.

ECONOMIES IN MID-DEVELOPMENT

This extraordinary integrative capacity of market systems returns us to the consideration of the suitability of various economic control mechanisms to different stages of development. We have seen that central planning is likely to be necessary to move stagnant, traditional economies off dead center. Once the development process is well under way, however, the relative functional merits of the market and the command mechanisms begin to change. After planning had done its massive tasks—enforcing economic and social change, creating an industrial sector, rationalizing agriculture—another problem begins to assume ever more importance. This is *the problem of efficiency*, of dovetailing the innumerable productive efforts of society into a single coherent and smoothly functioning whole.

In the flush period of mid-development the market mechanism easily outperforms the command apparatus as a means of carrying out this complex coordinating task. Every profit-seeking entrepreneur, every industrial salesman, every cost-conscious purchasing agent becomes in effect part of a gigantic and continuously alert planning system within the market economy. Command systems

*One of the important, truly socialist aspects of the Yugoslav economy is that factory managers are hired and fired and supervised by workers' councils elected from within the factory. To what degree these councils represent a true democratization of factory life, or to what extent they are only vehicles for political control, we do not yet know.

do not easily duplicate their efforts. Bottlenecks, unusable output, shortages, waste, and a cumbersome hierarchy of bureaucratic forms and officials typically interfere with the maximum efficiency of the planned economy in mid-growth.

What we see here is not just a passing problem, easily ironed out. One of the critical lessons of the twentieth century is that the word *planning* is exceedingly easy to pronounce and exceedingly difficult to spell out. When targets are still relatively simple, and the priorities of action beyond dispute—as in the case of a nation wrenching itself from the stagnation of an ineffective regime—planning can produce miracles. **But when the economy reaches a certain degree of complexity, in which the coordination of ten activities gives way to the coordination of ten thousand, innumerable problems arise, because planned economies enjoy no natural congruence between private action and public necessity.**

Here is where the market comes into its own. As we know from our study of micro theory, each firm must combine its factors of production with one eye on their relative costs and the other on their respective productivities, finally bringing about a mix in which each factor is used as effectively as possible, given its cost. Thus in seeking only to maximize their own profits, the units in a market system inadvertently tend also to maximize the efficiency of the system as a whole.

PRIVATE AIMS, PUBLIC GOALS

Even more remarkable: One operating rule alone suffices to bring about this extraordinary conjunction of private aims and public goals. *That single rule is to maximize profits.* By concentrating on that one criterion of success and not by trying to maximize output in physical terms or by trying to live by a complicated book of regulations, entrepreneurs in a competitive environment do in fact bring the system toward efficiency. In other words, **profits are not only a source of privileged income, but also an enormously versatile and useful "success indicator" for a system that is trying to squeeze as much output as possible from its given inputs.**

Futhermore, the market mechanism solves the economic problem with a minimum of social and political controls. Impelled by the drives inherent in a market society, the individual marketer fulfills his public economic function without constant attention from the authorities. In contradistinction to his counter part in a centralized command society, who is often prodded, cajoled, or even threatened to act in ways that do not appeal to his self-interest, the classical marketer obeys the peremptory demands of the market as a voluntary exercise of his own economic "freedom."

Thus it is not surprising that we find many of the motivating principles of the market being introduced into command societies. For as these societies settle into more or less established routines, they too can utilize the pressure of want and the pull of pecuniary desire to facilitate the fulfillment of their basic plans.

Economic freedom, as we know it in the West, is not yet a reality or even an official objective in any of these countries. The right to strike, for example, is not recognized, and nothing like the fluid consumer-responsive market system is allowed to exert its unimpeded influence on the general direction of economic development. But the introduction of more and more discretion at the factory level argues strongly that the principles of the market society are apt to find their place in planned societies at an appropriate stage of economic development.

HIGH CONSUMPTION ECONOMIES

Thus our survey of successive stages of development brings us to a consideration of Western economic society; that is, to the advanced economies that have progressed beyond the need for forced industrialization and now enter the stage of high consumption.

From our foregoing discussion, it is clear that the market mechanism finds its most natural application in this fortunate period of economic evolution. Insofar as the advanced Western societies have reached a stage in which the consumer is not only permitted but encouraged to impose personal wants on the direction of economic activity, there is little doubt that the market mechanism fulfills the prevailing social purpose more effectively than any other.

1. Public goods

Nonetheless, as we noted in Chapter 24 the market is not without its own grave problems, even in this regard. **Firstly, the market is an inefficient instrument for provisioning societies—even rich societies—with those goods and services for which no price tag exists, such as education or local government services or public health facilities.**

A market society buys such public goods by allocating a certain amount of taxes for these purposes. Its citizens, however, tend to feel these taxes as an exaction in contrast with the items they voluntarily buy. Typically, therefore, a market society underallocates resources to education, city government, public health or recreation, since it has no means of bidding funds into these areas, in competition with the powerful means of bidding them into autos or clothes or personal insurance.

2. Income distribution

A second and perhaps even deeper-seated failing of the market system is its application of a strictly economic calculus to the satisfaction of human wants and needs. As we said before, the market is an assiduous servant of the wealthy, but an indifferent servant of the poor. Thus it presents us with the anomaly of a surplus of luxury housing existing side-by-side with a shortage of inexpensive housing, although the social need for the latter is incontestably greater than the former. Or it pours energy and resources into the multiplication of luxuries for which the wealthier classes offer a market, while allowing more basic needs of the poor to go unheeded and unmet.

3. Externalities

These shortcomings are aggravated by the tendency of market systems to ignore externalities. **We have seen in Chapter 24 how the failure to capture social costs within the calculus of private benefits leads to patterns of production that are often freighted with serious consequences.** These externalities can be corrected within the market framework, but only by the imposition of an element of command—of political decision—over the workings of the market, whether by taxes, subsidies, or outright regulation.

In considering the side effects of market systems, we should not forget that elusive but very important externality we call "the quality of life." We count as gains the increases in GNP that result from the market system, but we do not give much heed to the commercialism, the trivialization, the psychological frustration and dissatisfaction that also accompany so much market activity.

4. Malfunctions

This recital of the failings of a market system ends with the micro and macro ills that spring up as a consequence of its operations. We know the severity and extent of these maladies, having just finished an examination of micro and macro economics. **But it is well to remember that inflation and unemployment, the urban plight and the threat to the environment are all to some degree the products of the hugely vital, but careless and even dangerous momentum that the market imparts to the social process.** We must beware of linking every social ill with the economic system in which it appears, but it would be equally foolish to absolve the market for all responsibility for the malfunctions that threaten our well-being.

THE RISE OF PLANNING

There is no need to dwell further on the deficiencies of the market system. **In one way or another, all its difficulties are indicative of one central weakness. This is the inability of the market system to formulate stimuli or restraints other than those that arise from the marketplace itself.**

So long as the public need roughly coincides with the sum of the private interests to which the market automatically attends, this failing of the market system is a minor one. But in an advanced economic society, it tends to become ever more important. As primary wants become satisfied, the public aim turns toward stability and security, objectives not attainable without a degree of public control. As technological organization becomes more complex and massive, again a public need arises to contain the new agglomerations of economic power. So, too, as wealth increases, pressure for education, urban improvement, welfare and the like comes to the fore, not only as an indication of the public conscience, but as a functioning requirement of a mature society. And finally, the public stimulus and management of continued growth take on increased political urgency as the ecological problems of industrial societies multiply.

We have already paid much attention to the rise of planning in the advanced market societies as a corrective force to deal with just such problems. Now we can generalize the economic meaning of this trend. **Planning arises in the advanced market societies to offset their inherent goal-setting weaknesses, just as the market mechanism arises in advanced command societies to offset their inherent motivational weaknesses.** In other words, planning and market mechanisms, in those societies which have begun to enter the stage of high consumption, are not mutually incompatible. On the contrary, they powerfully supplement and support one another.

COMMON PROBLEMS

What we see today is *the appearance of similar problems in advanced industrial societies.*

When we examine capitalism and socialism, we usually pay special attention to the problems that separate and distinguish these two kinds of societies. Here it is important to realize that they are also bound together by certain common difficulties.

What is the nature of these overarching problems? As we would expect, they stem from the very technical capability and social organization that bring similar economic mechanisms into being. Three problems in particular seem of major importance.

1. Control over technology

One of the most important attributes of modern history is lodged in a striking difference between two kinds of knowledge: the knowledge we acquire in physics, chemistry, engineering, and other sciences, and that which we gain in the sphere of social or political or moral activity. The difference is that knowledge in some sciences is cumulative and builds on itself, whereas knowledge in the social sphere does not. The merest beginner in biology soon knows more than the greatest biologist of a century ago. By way of contrast, the veteran student (or practitioner) of government, of social relations, of moral philosophy is aware of his modest stature in comparison with the great social and moral philosophers of the past.

The result is that all modern societies tend to find that their technological capabilities are constantly increasing, while the social, political, and moral institutions by which those capabilities are controlled cannot match the challenges with which they are faced. Television, for example, is an immense force for cultural homogenization; medical technology changes the composition of society by altering its age groups and life expectancy; rapid transportation vastly increases mobility and social horizons; and the obliterative power of nuclear arms casts a pervasive anxiety over all of life. All these technologically rooted developments fundamentally alter the conditions and problems of life, but we do not know what social, political, and moral responses are appropriate to them. As a result, all modern societies—socialist and capitalist—experience the feeling of being at the mercy of a technological and scientific impetus that shapes the lives of their citizens in ways that cannot be accurately foreseen nor adequately controlled.

2. The problem of participation

The second problem derives from the first. Because advanced societies are characterized by high levels of technology, they are necessarily marked by a high degree of organization. The technology of our era depends on the cooperation of vast masses of men, some at the levels of production, some at the levels of administration. The common undergirding of all advanced industrial societies lies not alone in their gigantic instrumentalities of production, but in their equally essential and vast instrumentalities of administration, whether these be called corporations, production ministries, or government agencies.

CONSERVATIVE PLANNING

All through Europe we see a reliance on planning that is both greater and more outspoken than anything we have encountered in the United States. In our own country, we have arrived at a consensus as to fiscal and monetary policy as the proper implements for achieving a stable and satisfactory rate of growth. But in most European nations, there is visible a further commitment to planning as a means of achieving publicly determined patterns of resource allocation as well as adequate rates of growth.

In France, for example, a central planning agency, working in consultation with Parliament and with representatives of industry, agriculture, labor, and other groups, sets a general plan for French growth—a plan that not only establishes a desired rate of expansion but determines whether or not, for example, the provincial cities should expand faster or slower than the nation as a whole, or where the bulk of new housing is to be located, or to what degree social services are to be increased. Once decided, the plan is then divided into the various production targets needed for its fulfillment, and their practicality is discussed with management and labor groups in each industry concerned.

From these discussions arise two results. First, the plan is often amended to conform with the wishes or advice of those who must carry it out. Second, the general targets of the plan become part of the business expectations of the industries that have helped to formulate them. To be sure, the government has substantial investment powers that can nudge the economy along whatever path has been finally determined. But in the main, French "indicative" planning works as a *self-fulfilling prophecy*—the very act of establishing its objectives sets into motion the behavior needed to realize them.

In England, Germany, the Netherlands, Italy, and Scandinavia, we see other forms of government planning, none so elaborately worked out as the French system, but all injecting a powerful element of public guidance into the growth and disposition of their resources.

The plans have not been wholly successful. Inflation has been the curse of Europe to an even greater degree than it has here; and nothing like a successful "incomes policy" has been worked out in any nation. But considerable success has been attained in the allocation of resources for public purposes through planning, and in the shaping of the general contours of national development.

What is beyond dispute is that a basic commitment to planning seems to have become an integral part of modern European capitalism. *Note, however, that all these planning systems utilize the mechanism of the market as a means for achieving their ends.* The act of planning itself is not, of course, a market activity; but the realization of the various desired production tasks for industry is entrusted largely to the pull of demand acting on independent enterprises. Thus the market has been utilized as an instrument of social policy.*

*Anyone who wishes to learn more about the important subject of European planning should read Andrew Shonfield, *Modern Capitalism: The Changing Balance of Public and Private Power* (New York: Oxford University Press, 1969). See also *Industrial Policy and the International Economy,* The Trilateral Commission, 1979.

The problem is then how the citizen is to find a place for his individuality in the midst of so much organization; how he is to express his voice in the direction of affairs, when so much bureaucratic management is inescapable; how he is to participate in a world whose technological structure calls for ever more order and coordination. This is a matter which, like the sweeping imperative of technology, affects both capitalism and socialism. In both kinds of societies, individuals feel overwhelmed by the impersonality of the work process, impotent before the power of huge enterprises—above all, the state itself—and frustrated at an inability to participate in decisions that seem more and more beyond any possibility of personal influence.

No doubt much can be done to increase the feeling of individual participation in the making of the future, especially in those nations that still deny elementary political freedoms. But there remains a recalcitrant problem of how the quest for increased individual decision-making and participation can be reconciled with the organizational demands imposed by the technology on which all advanced societies depend. This is a problem that is likely to trouble societies—capitalist or socialist—as long as technology itself rests on integrated processes of production and requires centralized organs of administration and control.

3. The problem of the environment

All industrial nations face an era in which exponential growth is beginning to absorb resources at rates faster than we may be able to provide them with new technologies; **and all industrialized societies—indeed, the whole world—may soon be entering an era in which environmental limitations will impose a slowdown on rates of growth.**

Moreover, we stand at a period in history when underdeveloped nations are belatedly making their own bid for a share in the rising output per capita that has until now mainly been confined to advanced nation-states.

In this period of long-run economic stringency, industrial socialist and capitalist nations again seem likely to share common problems—not only in bringing about a controlled slowdown in output, but in achieving social harmony under conditions that no longer allow their citizens to look forward to ever-higher standards of material consumption. Here, too, similar social and political problems may override differences in economic institutions and ideologies.

ENVOI

In a larger sense, then, we go beyond economics to the common human adventure in which economic systems are only alternate routes conducting humanity toward a common destination. Perhaps it is well that we end our survey of economics with the recognition that the long history of the market system does not project us onto a final stage in social history. Rather we arrive at a state in which some kinds of problems—the pitifully simple problems of producing and distributing goods—find resolution only to reveal vastly larger problems springing from the very technology and organization that supplied the earlier answers.

LOOKING BACK

KEY CONCEPTS

The stages of economic development in the West have used command to change traditional structures into market systems

1. The economic structures of nations, especially with respect to market, tradition, and command, seem to bear a relation to their stages of economic development. In the West, we have begun with traditional societies, used command to mobilize ourselves for growth, and then developed full market mechanisms.

Underdeveloped countries will probably rely less on the market

2. We do not know if the underdeveloped nations will follow this pattern, but their late start, their extreme needs, and their ability to "foresee" the future suggest that the market will play a lesser role.

The problem of planning is the coordination of the economy. This is difficult to achieve without the "success indicator" of profit

3. Planning is a complex and difficult means of running an industrial society. The main task is to coordinate the myriad activities of society into a consistent whole. This is the task that the market performs easily through the "success indicator" of profit. The challenge for centrally planned systems has been to devise other success indicators. So far this has not been very successful, and centrally planned systems have been extremely inefficient, once their initial days of easy growth are over.

Many socialist economies are experimenting with limited market mechanisms where profit provides the "success indicator"

4. As a result many socialist economists are cautiously introducing aspects of the market to remedy the frictions and inefficiencies of planning. Profit maximization provides a self-enforcing "success indicator" that works to direct private action into the channels directed by market preference.

Market systems have their own failures. Hence high consumption market systems display a drift toward more policy and planning

5. Nevertheless, market systems develop their own problems. They do not provide for public goods. They distribute income in ways that fail to satisfy moral criteria. They cannot reflect externalities. And they have their particular malfunctions, such as instability. All these difficulties lie at the heart of the global drift of high-consumption market systems toward a greater degree of policy and planning.

Certain problems seem to transcend the market/planning division: controlling technology, assuring economic and political participation, and safeguarding the environment

6. Looking beyond the present we can discern three problems that high-consumption economies seem to share, whether market or planned. They are: controlling their technologies; arranging for the participation of workers and citizens in the administration of economic as well as political affairs; and maintaining satisfactory economic performance within an increasingly fragile and restrictive ecological environment.

ECONOMIC VOCABULARY

Success indicator 632 **Market socialism 635**

QUESTIONS

1. How do you account for the presence in the world today of such radically different forms of economic organization as Switzerland and Saudi Arabia, Canada and China?

2. What is meant by the congruence between self-interest and public requirement in a market economy? Is this the same as the Invisible Hand? Does it mean that whatever is good for General Motors is good for America? That General Motors will automatically do whatever is good for America?
3. Do you think that a capitalist system is essential for economic freedom? If so, how do you explain the fact that many people think that Yugoslavia is "freer" than South Africa? Is it possible to make precise statements about this issue? General statements?
4. What technological process seems to you to require control? Arms? Urbanization? Genetic experimentation?
5. Take a moment to think about how you think modern society ought to be organized. If you were president, what three things would you put at the top of your economic agenda?

GLOSSARY

Acceleration principle See accelerator effect

Accelerator effect The effect—sometimes stimulating, sometimes depressing—exerted on investment by changes in consumption expenditure.

Allocation The act of apportioning or distributing resources or incomes.

Anti-trust legislation Legislation designed to minimize or prevent monopolistic behavior or monopolistic market structures.

Appreciation of exchange A rise in the ability of one nation's currency to buy the currency of another nation.

Average productivity The contribution to output of the average unit of any input. This is obtained by dividing total output by the number of units of the input. It is not the same as the contribution of the last, or marginal unit.

Average propensity to consume The relation between consumption and income, C/Y. It differs from the marginal propensity $\Delta C/\Delta Y$ because the latter is concerned only with spending out of marginal incomes.

Average propensity to save The relation between saving and income S/Y. It differs from the marginal propensity $\Delta S/\Delta Y$ because the latter is concerned only with saving out of marginal income.

Automatic stabilizers Institutional provisions that result in automatic stimulation of the economy in recession times and dampening of it in boom times. The counter-cyclical flows of unemployment insurance or farm subsidies, and the effect on consumption of the graduated income tax are key elements in these stabilizers.

Backward bending supply curve A supply curve of labor services that displays a preference for fewer hours of labor (more leisure) when the price of labor rises above a certain level.

Balance of payments A set of accounts that records transactions between two countries. See balance on current and capital accounts.

Balance on capital account The net sum of demands and supplies for foreign exchange for all items on capital account, mainly direct and portfolio investment.

Balance on current account The net sum of demands for and supplies of foreign exchange for all items on current account, mainly merchandise exports and imports and similar transactions.

Bonds Obligations issued by private or public institutions with fixed dates of repayment and stated interest rates or coupons. See yields.

"Bottom" The level of GNP when income is entirely used for consumption, and investment is therefore zero.

Budget The amount of spending power possessed by an economic actor.

Business cycles The more or less regular recurrence of recession and prosperity. Some cycles (usually in inventories) may be of 2–3 years' duration; others (in GNP) typically of 7–11 years' length.

Capital All means of production that have been produced by man. Also often used to refer to a financial sum of wealth.

Capital goods Final output used for production, not consumption. See investment.

Capitalism An economic system in which the means of production—land, labor, and capital—are privately owned and coordinated mainly by a market system.

Capitalization Calculation of a sum of wealth by dividing a flow of income by a rate of interest. A piece of land that yields an income of $100 is capitalized at $1,000 if interest rates are 10 percent ($1,000 ÷ 0.10 = $100) or at $500 if interest rates are 20 percent.

Capital/output ratio Relationship between the values of the capital stock and the flow of output of a firm, industry, or nation. Marginal capital/output ratios relate increases in output to increases in the capital stock.

Ceteris paribus Latin phrase meaning "other things being equal." The phrase refers to the need to allow for variations in the conditions that affect an experiment or an observation. For example, *ceteris paribus* requires us to make allowance for changes in income or taste when we are seeking to establish the relation of quantity demanded and price.

Circular flow The continuous circuit of spending, from households to firms and from firms back to households.

Claims Legal rights on income or wealth.

Clearing markets A market condition in which quantities demanded just balance quantities supplied.

Cobwebs Erratic jumps in prices that characterize markets that do not constantly adjust over time. Cobwebs may describe a sequence of prices that "explode" or oscillate or gradually converge to equilibrium.

Comparative advantage The relative edge enjoyed by one nation (or region or economic actor) in producing one commodity compared to another. A country can have a comparative advantage in producing a commodity even if its absolute productivity in that commodity is less than that of its trading partner.

Competition The vying of buyers and sellers in a marketplace. Competition has two aspects: (1) the contest of buyers against sellers, (2) the mutual rivalry of sellers against sellers and buyers against buyers.

Complement The technical linkage of commodities, such as cars and gasoline. Increases in the demand for a commodity automatically raises the demand for its complement.

Concentration The degree of market control enjoyed by the largest firms in an industry. Concentration ratios often measure the percentage of industry sales enjoyed by the largest four or eight firms.

Conglomerates Large corporations, usually formed by merger, that operate in widely different markets.

Constraints Barriers or boundaries to desired behavior.

Consumer sovereignty The power exerted by consumer demand over the allocation of resources.

Consumption Use of output for purposes of private enjoyment.

Cost Cost in everyday speech refers to the expenses incurred in production. In economics it refers to missed opportunities—opportunities foregone because resources are committed to a given use. This is called opportunity cost. (See also *Sunk cost.*)

Cost-benefit analysis The attempt to calculate the direct and indirect costs and benefits, whether paid or not, of any economic action.

Cost push An explanation of inflation that stresses increases in factor prices such as higher real wages, or the increase in cost of resources or other inputs. (See *Demand pull.*)

Credit crunch A severe restriction of bank credit, forcing the drastic curtailment of bank lending to businesses or consumers.

Crowding out The effect of government borrowing on the ability of the private sector to obtain funds on the loan markets.

Deepening capital Increasing the value of capital per worker.

Deficit spending Spending that is financed not by current tax receipts but by borrowing, or by drawing on past reserves.

Demand Willingness and ability to buy. Demand is a schedule that relates the quantities demanded with differing prices. (See also *Quantity demanded.*)

Demand gap The shortfall in demand that arises when the spending of the combined sectors is not enough to maintain a given level of GNP, or a necessary rate of growth of GNP.

Demand pull An explanation of inflation that stresses the effect of spending on the price level. Demand pull is usually focused on the effects of government or business spending. (See *Cost push.*)

Dependent variables Quantities whose value is determined by the value of another "independent" variable, contained in the equation.

Depreciation The decline in the value of capital goods over time. The term is also used to designate the funds set aside to replace the worn-out capital.

Depreciation of exchange A fall in the ability of one nation's currency to buy the currency of a foreign nation.

Derived demand Demand for factors of production that results from the demand for goods and services.

Devaluation A policy deliberately intended to cheapen the exchange value of a currency in order to encourage exports. (Technically, devaluation means cheapening one's currency in terms of gold.)

Diminishing returns The eventual tendency of outputs to rise more slowly than input as more and more of one factor is added to fixed amounts of other factors. Also known as the *law of variable proportions.*

Direct investment	Investment in plant and equipment, as contrasted with financial investment.
Direct taxes	Taxes levied by local, state or federal governments on incomes.
Dirty floating	Intervention by central banks in foreign exchange markets to raise or lower the exchange rate of their own currencies.
Discounting	Application of an interest rate to calculate the present value of a sum of money expected to be received or held in the future. At a rate of discount of 10 percent, $100 due a year hence is worth $90 today.
Discount rate	The term applied to the interest rate charged by the Federal Reserve banks or loans made to their member banks.
Diseconomies of scale	Increases in unit cost resulting from inefficiencies of technology or organization at rising levels (scales) of output.
Disinvestment	A failure to create investment equal to the wear and tear on existing capital. Disinvestment means a diminution of capital wealth.
Disposable personal income	Factor earnings plus transfers less direct taxes. Disposable personal income therefore defines aggregate household spending power.
Dissaving	Expenditure that exceeds income. Dissaving requires that a dissaver use past savings, or borrowing, to finance the additional expenditure.
Distribution	The process of allocating output or income among the population. Also used to refer to the results of this process, for example when we say that "income distribution is very unequal."
Ecology	Relationship of life processes to the natural and social environment.
Economic profit	Profit after the deduction of interest on capital. Profit is any residual after all factors have been paid their full values.
Economic rent	See *Quasi rent.*
Economies of scale	Reductions of cost resulting from improved technology or organization at rising levels (scales) of output.
Efficiency	Relation of output to input.
Elasticity	A measure of the relation between price and quantity, or between income and quantity. If the percentage change in quantity demanded is greater than the percent change in price or income, we speak of elastic demand; if it is less, of inelastic demand.
Endogenous	Influences internal to a system. The rise in income that results from the multiplier effect is endogenous to the determination of GNP.
Entrepreneur	The person whose economic task is to direct the enterprise. His or her main task is to choose the proper scale, to make the best combination of factors, and to establish the best level of output. The entrepreneur may or may not own the enterprise, and therefore may or may not receive profits.
Entry	The ability to move into a market or line of production.
Equations	Mathematical statements usually involving dependent and independent variables in a functional relationship.
Equilibrium	A self-correcting and self-perpetuating level of prices or economic activity. Equilibrium prices equate quantities demanded and supplied, and

thereby "clear" markets. Equilibrium flows of output, such as GNP, balance opposing tendencies of savings and investment to create a self-perpetuating flow.

Equimarginal rule The general guide to optimization through equalizing the marginal returns of all factors.

Equity Ownership, usually stock ownership.

Eurodollars Supplies of dollars held by foreign or American banks in Europe.

Ex ante The view looking forward. Ex ante refers to economic activity that has not yet taken place. Ex ante quantities or values may therefore differ from ex post figures, after the event.

Excess capacity A market situation in which the capacity to produce is larger than the output desired by the market. Excess capacity is typical of oligopolistic industries.

Excess reserves Bank reserves (cash or deposits at the Federal Reserve) over the required amount.

Exchange rate The price of foreign currencies in terms of one's own currency.

Exogenous Influences originating outside the system. An exogenous influence on GNP would be a change in the weather, or a war.

Exploitation Payment to a factor of less than the value of the output it produces.

Ex post The view looking backwards. Ex post refers to economic activity that has already happened. (See *Ex ante.*)

External debts Debts owed by members of one community, usually a nation, to another community or nation. (See *Internal debts.*)

Externalities Effects (good or bad) imposed by the act of production, or consumption, for which no price is charged. A typical bad or negative externality is the pollution imposed on the public by smoke from a factory.

Factor market The market in which the services of labor, land or capital are sold. Factor markets regulate wages, rents, and interest rates.

Factor of production The name given to the main kinds of inputs, land, labor, and capital, in a market society.

Federal Reserve Banks One of the 12 federally created central banks. Commercial banks may become members of the Federal Reserve System, but are not themselves Federal Reserve Banks.

Federal Reserve System The formal institution of central banking in the United States, structured around 12 Reserve Banks and governed by a Board of Governors.

Feudalism The economic and political organization of Europe subsequent to the fall of the Roman Empire. Its central aspect was the presence of relatively self-sufficient manors or estates, ruled by lords for whom peasants or serfs worked as "vassals" or legally tied dependents.

Final goods Goods that have reached the end of the production process. Typically these are of four kinds: consumption goods, investment or capital goods, government or public goods, and exports.

Fiscal policy Government efforts to control the level of employment or prices by spending and taxing, rather than by monetary policy.

Fixed costs — Costs that do not change with the level of output. These are usually contractual costs such as rent, depreciation, etc.

Fixed exchange rates — Exchange relationships between currencies fixed by government agreement and maintained by the action of central banks.

Foreign exchange — Supplies of foreign currencies held by the banks or government of any nation.

Fractional reserves — The legal permission to hold reserves equal to less than 100 percent of bank deposits. Fractional reserves multiply the effect of new deposits on the money supply.

Free riding — The ability of economic actors to enjoy the utilities of certain outputs without paying for them.

Full employment budgets — Calculation of the impact on GNP of government receipts and expenditure flows assuming that receipts and expenditures are at the levels corresponding to full employment.

Functional relationships — Relationships in which the value of one variable is determined by another.

GNP (gross national product) — The dollar value of the final output of the economy for a fixed period, usually a year. GNP is the sum of consumption, gross domestic investment, government purchases, and net exports.

Graphs — Visual representations of functional relationships or of the movements of variables through time.

Gross investment — The use of resources to create capital, whether as an addition to existing wealth or as a replacement for worn-out capital.

Gross national income — The sum of factor incomes, tax receipts, and depreciation accruals. GNI is always identical with GNP.

Growth — Increase in output. See nominal growth and real growth.

High powered money — Excess reserves in commercial banks that can increase the money supply. (See *Fractional reserves.*)

Horizontal equity — A pattern of tax incidence that results in equal payments of tax among all members of the same income level.

Human capital — The money value of skills or education.

Identities — Mathematical statements of definition.

Imperialism — Domination by a highly developed, powerful nation. Specifically used to describe the penetration of capitalist nations into the underdeveloped world.

Incidence of taxation — The pattern of impact of taxation. The incidence of taxation attempts to discover where the burden of a tax ultimately falls.

Increasing cost — The tendency of cost per unit to rise as the volume of output exceeds the point of greatest efficiency. (See *Law of increasing cost.*)

Increasing returns — The initial tendency of output to rise faster than input, as one factor is added to fixed amounts of other factors.

Independent variables — Quantities whose value is determined independently—that is, outside the equation.

Indexing — Adjustment of nominal payments in accordance with a price index.

Indirect taxes — Taxes levied by local, state, or federal government on the value of output. Cigarette or gas taxes are instances of indirect taxes.

Infant industries — Newly founded industries, especially in developing nations, that require tariff protection in order to achieve competitive scale.

Inflation — A process in which prices in nearly all markets display a chronic upward tendency.

Injections — Any expenditures that raise the flow of income. The main injections are net investment, deficit spending, an excess of exports over imports, or a consumer spending wave, financed by drawing on past saving or on credit.

Interest — The price of the factor capital.

Intermediate goods — Goods or services that enter into final goods. For example, wheat is an intermediate good entering into bread.

Internal debts — Debts owed by members of a community, usually a nation, to one another.

Intersectoral offsets — Spending by one sector, usually business or government, used to offset the insufficient spending of another sector.

Inventories — Goods on raw materials that have been produced but not yet sold to final purchasers. All increases in inventories are counted in the national accounts as net investment.

Investment — The act of building capital. (See *Real vs. financial investment.*)

Invisible Hand — A famous phrase used by Adam Smith to indicate that individuals who followed their private self-interest would in fact fulfill a larger purpose, as if "led by an Invisible Hand."

Law of increasing cost — Eventual tendency of costs of a given output to rise as additional inputs of all factors (not just one) are used to produce it.

Law of variable proportions — The tendency of output first to rise more rapidly than input, then more slowly, as one factor is added to fixed amounts of other factors.

Leakages — Channels through which additional income is diverted from respending by households. The four main leakages are: private saving, business profits, taxes, and imports.

Liquidity — Condition of having immediately spendable resources, such as cash or very easily saleable securities, such as very short-term government notes.

Liquidity preference — The differing proportions of one's wealth that one seeks to hold in liquid form at differing interest rates. High interest rates impose high opportunity costs on holding cash. Therefore, usually we prefer to be less liquid when we can use our cash to earn high interest. Conversely, we seek more liquidity when the opportunity cost is low. Risk also plays an important part in determining our willingness to be liquid or illiquid.

$M1_A$ — See *Money supply.*

Macroeconomics — That portion of economics concerned with large scale movements of the economy, such as growth or decline, inflation or deflation.

Marginal — Additional, incremental, (plus or minus).

Marginal cost — The change in the cost of a firm resulting from a change in its output.

Marginal efficiency of investment — The value of the expected returns of new investment discounted to the present.

Marginal productivity — The change in output that can be ascribed to the addition or subtraction of any factor.

Marginal propensity to consume — The relation between additional income and additional spending: $\Delta C/\Delta Y$. (See *Average propensity to consume.*)

Marginal propensity to save — The relation between additional income and additional saving: $\Delta S/\Delta Y$. (See *Average propensity to save.*)

Marginal revenue — The change in the revenue of a firm resulting from a change in its output.

Market share — Proportion of an industry's sales enjoyed by a firm.

Market socialism — Socialist economies that continue to use markets as allocation mechanisms or as incentive systems, in addition to central planning of major elements such as investment.

Market system — The structure of exchange relations of buying and selling that sustains the economic process of capitalism.

Maximizing — The driving force of economic activity described as the pursuit of the largest possible amount of pleasurable wealth.

Mercantilism — The prevailing mode of economic organization in the period between late feudalism and early capitalism, characterized by a highly regulated domestic economy and an effort to achieve a surplus of exports over imports.

Microeconomics — That portion of economics concerned with the activity of individuals and firms, mainly with regard to the allocation of resources.

Mixed economies — Economies that combine attributes of capitalism, such as private property and market mechanisms with elements of socialism, in particular welfare structures and some degree of government control over economic activity.

Mobility — The capacity to change economic location or function.

Monetarism — The body of theory that stresses the importance of the quantity of money in determining the rate of inflation and the level of activity.

Money illusion — The tendency to base economic behavior on nominal rather than real prices.

Money stock — See *Money supply.*

Money supply — There are many ways of calculating the money supply. Perhaps the most common is cash held by the public, plus demand deposits at commercial banks. This is designated $M1_A$. (We have called this M in our text.) Various other definitions ($M1_B$, M2, M3) expand the basic definition by adding various other liquid assets.

Monopolistic competition — Market structures in which there are large numbers of sellers of differentiated products.

Monopoly — A single seller who supplies the entire output of a given market.

Multinational corporations — Corporations that derive a substantial proportion of their income or sales from overseas production, as contrasted with exports.

Multiplier-accelerator — The joint interaction of the multiplier effect, which creates additional income from an injection, and the accelerator effect which creates additional investment from a rise in consumption.

Multiplier effect — The tendency of injections to create increases in income larger than the original injections. The multiplier effect results from the marginal propensity to consume.

National income — The total amount of factor incomes earned over a period of time. National income does not include transfer payments.

Nationalization — Purchase or seizure by the government of a privately owned firm.

Negative income tax — Transfer payments made to households that earn less than a designated amount of income.

Net investment — The use of resources to create additional capital goods.

Net national product — Gross national product minus depreciation. Net national product is also national income (factor earnings) plus the value of indirect taxes.

Nominal growth — Increase in output measured in current dollars, without allowance for changes in the purchasing power of dollars. If we compare the GNPs of two years, without deflating the dollar amounts, we are comparing nominal growth.

Nominal values — The values or prices of objects in current terms with no adjustment for changes in the value of the monetary unit.

Oligopoly — A market structure in which output is provided by a small enough number of sellers, so that one seller can anticipate that others will react to changes in his strategy. In a competitive market there are so many participants that no firm can expect its own actions to disturb the workings of the market.

Open market operations — The buying or selling of government bonds by the Federal Reserve, as a means of expanding or contracting the reserves of commercial banks.

Opportunity cost — The wealth or enjoyments that cannot be obtained because resources or inputs are already committed to a given purpose. All economic activities entail opportunity cost. Every act of consumption or production rules out the possibility of some alternative action.

Overhead costs — Costs associated with administration or sales, rather than with direct factory-floor production.

Optimization — The search for the most efficient allocation of wealth or resources.

Participation rate — The proportion of the population of working age that is actively seeking work.

Per capita GNP — Gross national product divided by the population.

Phillips curve — The presumed statistical correlation between unemployment and inflation first pointed out by A. W. Phillips.

Physiocracy — A school of economic thought developed by Francois Quesnay (1694–1774) that stressed the productive power of the land.

Portfolio investment — Financial investment, as opposed to real investment in plant and equipment.

Price index — A statistical measure of price levels in which one year is chosen as a base, and the other years expressed as a percentage of that base.

Price leadership	Role played by an industry leader who is the first to change prices in an oligopolistic market.
Production	The use of labor and resources to create wealth.
Production-possibility curve	A graphic depiction of the total outputs available to a society. Production-possibility curves are usually bowed outward because of the law of increasing cost.
Production-possibility frontier	The outer limit of production possibilities as we move resources from one use to another. (See *Production-possibility curves.*)
Productivity	A measure of output per unit of input over a given period of time, such as yearly or hourly output per worker or per machine.
Progressive incidence	A pattern of taxation that imposes proportionally heavier burdens on high income groups than on low income groups.
Propensity to consume	The relation between consumption and income: C/Y. (See also *Marginal propensity to consume.*)
Propensity to save	The relation between saving and income: S/Y. (See also *Marginal propensity to consume.*)
Proportional incidence	A pattern of taxation that imposes equal percentage burdens on all income levels.
Psychic income	The value of non-monetary income in terms of utilities.
Public goods	Outputs provided by the public sector and not allocated by the price mechanism.
Purchasing power	The ability to buy.
Pure competition	A market structure characterized by large numbers of actors, easy entry and exit, undifferentiated products, and widespread information about market conditions.
Quantity demanded	The amount of a commodity or service that we are willing and able to buy at a given price. (See also *Demand.*)
Quantity equation	$MV = PT$. (See *Quantity theory.*)
Quasi rent	Returns to a factor that derive solely from its scarcity, above the returns needed to induce the factor into production. Also called economic rent.
Quantity supplied	The amount of a commodity or service that we are willing and able to supply at a given price. (See also *Supply.*)
Quantity theory	The theory that relates the level of prices solely to the quantity of money.
R & D	Research and development. Research can be "basic"—inquiry that has no immediate commercial or economic orientation, or "applied"—inquiry directed at shaping knowledge for a given purpose. Development refers to commercial readying of goods or processes.
Rational expectations	The tendency of markets to foresee and anticipate actions intended to alter market outcomes.
Rationality	The assumption that men can intelligently adapt their actions (means) to their purposes (ends).

Rationing — The distribution of resources according to some allocation mechanism. The mechanism may be the price system, or it may be a nonmarket system, such as coupons.

Real growth — Increases in output corrected for changes in the purchasing power of the currency.

Real vs. financial investment — Real investment is the act of devoting resources to capital formation. Financial investment denotes the purchase of equities, claims or other instruments that channel personal savings into banks or businesses.

Regressive incidence — A pattern of taxation that imposes proportionally larger burdens on low income groups than on high ones.

Rent — Rent is the return paid to the owner of land or any resource for the use of his property. It is a payment necessary to bring that resource into production, and therefore differs from a quasi rent which is a payment that results only from scarcity and is larger than that needed to bring the factor into use.

Replacement investment — Investment that is designed to renew worn-out capital. Replacement investment plus net investment equals gross investment.

Reserve requirement — The proportion of deposits that must be kept in vault cash or at a Federal Reserve Bank. Reserve requirements are set by the Board of Governors of the Federal Reserve System.

Reserves — Deposits that may not be loaned or invested. Reserves must be held in cash or at a Federal Reserve Bank.

Saving — The act of not using income for consumption. Saving is a financial act when we put money in a bank, but its real meaning is to relinquish a claim on resources.

Scale — The size of operations, mainly of a plant. Scale is usually determined by the physical characteristics of the capital equipment used, although land or labor may be the determining elements.

Scatter diagram — Graphic representation of two variables showing their associated pairs.

Schedule — A list of different values of a variable, such as quantities or prices.

SDRs — Special Drawing Rights, an international reserve currency unit created by the International Monetary Fund (IMF), an agency of the United Nations.

Sector — A division of the economy with common characteristics. Usually we speak of the public and the private sector; of the consumption, investment, and government sectors; or of the agricultural, industrial, and service sectors.

Shortage — The failure of a market to clear when the price is below equilibrium levels and there are unsatisfied buyers at the going price.

Stagflation — An economic condition of simultaneous inflation and stagnation—that is, rising prices and inadequate growth.

Sticky prices — The tendency of many prices to remain unchanged despite changes in demand and supply. This may be the consequence of contracts (a wage or rent contract) or of institutional inertia.

Stocks — Legal instruments of ownership in corporations.

Stop-go policies Alternations of restrictive and stimulative fiscal and monetary measures.

Substitution The capacity of one commodity to provide the utilities of another. Increases in the price of a commodity result in increases in the demand for its substitutes.

Sunk cost The cost, either in money or in foregone opportunities, that has been incurred up to the present with respect to any economic act of production.

Supply Willingness and ability to sell. Supply is a schedule that relates the quantities offered with differing prices. (See also *Quantity supplied*.)

Surplus The failure of a market to clear when the price is above equilibrium levels and there are unsatisfied sellers at the going price.

Terms of trade A comparison of the quantities of goods that are required to gain a given amount of goods in return. For example, the Brazilian terms of trade could measure the number of sacks of coffee needed to "buy" a computer.

Tight money A condition, associated with restrictive monetary policy, that makes it difficult for borrowers to obtain bank loans.

Trade-off An exchange relationship denoting how much of A is needed to obtain a unit of B.

Transactions demand The amount of cash we need to carry on normal economic transactions. At higher levels of economic activity there is normally a higher demand for transactions balances, for such purposes as meeting payrolls, or financing ordinary expenditures.

Transfers Any payment from one person or institution to another made for purposes other than to remunerate work. Social security is a transfer payment; so is the payment of an allowance to a minor, or a charity payment.

Unemployment Inability to find acceptable work at the going wage level.

Utility Pleasure or wellbeing.

Variable costs Costs that change directly with output, such as wages, or materials costs.

Variable proportions See *Law of variable proportions.*

Velocity of circulation The number of times a unit of currency is used during a period of time, usually a year. The velocity of circulation is calculated by dividing output (GNP) by the money supply.

Wealth Production that yields utilities.

Widening capital Matching additional workers with amounts of capital equal to those used by previously employed workers.

Yields The income paid by a bond compared with its market value. A bond issued at a price of $1,000 with a "coupon" of $100 (interest payable annually) will have a yield of 20 percent if the bond can be bought on the market at $500. It will have a 10 percent yield if its price is the original issue price. Its yield will fall to 5 percent if the market price of the bond rises to $2,000.

Zero sum game A contest in which every gain is matched by an exactly equivalent loss.

INDEX

A

B

C

D

F

G

H

I

N

O

P

Q

R

S

T

Z